MOTIVES FOR WRITING

maty mom ∅s
mathias

30968 3

MOTIVES FOR WRITING

FOURTH EDITION

ROBERT KEITH MILLER

University of St. Thomas

Boston   Burr Ridge, IL   Dubuque, IA   Madison, WI   New York
San Francisco   St. Louis   Bangkok   Bogotá   Caracas   Kuala Lumpur
Lisbon   London   Madrid   Mexico City   Milan   Montreal   New Delhi
Santiago   Seoul   Singapore   Sydney   Taipei   Toronto

McGraw-Hill Higher Education 🎗

A Division of The McGraw-Hill Companies

Motives for Writing

Published by McGraw-Hill, an imprint of The McGraw-Hill Companies, Inc., 1221 Avenue of the Americas, New York, NY 10020. Copyright © 2003, 1999, 1995, 1992, by The McGraw-Hill Companies, Inc. All rights reserved. No part of this publication may be reproduced or distributed in any form or by any means, or stored in a database or retrieval system, without the prior written consent of The McGraw-Hill Companies, Inc., including, but not limited to, in any network or other electronic storage or transmission, or broadcast for distance learning.

This book is printed on acid-free paper.

4 5 6 7 8 9 0 DOC/DOC 0 9 8 7 6 5 4

ISBN 0-7674-1683-X

Vice president and Editor-in-chief: *Thalia Dorwick*
Senior developmental editor: *Renée Deljon*
Senior marketing manager: *David S. Patterson*
Senior production editor: *David M. Staloch*
Senior production supervisor: *Richard DeVitto*
Design manager: *Violeta Díaz*
Interior designer: *Susan Breitbard*
Cover designer: *Cassandra Chu*
Photo researcher: *Alexandra Ambrose*
Art editor: *Emma Ghiselli*
Compositor: *Thompson Type*
Typeface: *11/12 Bembo*
Paper: *45# New Era Matte*
Printer and binder: *RR Donnelley & Sons*

Cover image: *Tree Through Four Seasons* © Matheisl/Getty Images/FPG.

Text and photo credits appear on pages 750–755, which constitute an extension of the copyright page.

LIBRARY OF CONGRESS CATALOGING-IN-PUBLICATION DATA

Motives for writing / [compiled by] Robert Keith Miller.-4th ed.
  p. cm.
  Includes index.
  ISBN 0-7674-1683-X
  1. College readers. 2. Report writing-Problems, exercises, etc. 3. English language—rhetoric—Problems, exercises, etc. I. Miller, Robert Keith, 1949–

PE1471.M65 2002
808'.0427-dc21   2002020858

www.mhhe.com

Preface

The fourth edition of this book continues to reflect the belief that helping students to discover and fulfill their motives for writing will help them to write well. As its title suggests, *Motives for Writing* emphasizes the importance of the writer's purpose—the reason for composing and the ends the writer seeks to achieve. In focusing upon purpose, I have been influenced by the work of such theorists as James Britton, James Kinneavy, and James Moffett, all of whom have shown that understanding the aims of discourse can contribute to better communication. I believe that an emphasis on these aims can help students to develop the active minds that are essential for making sense of the world and conveying that sense to others. I also believe that students familiar with the aims of writing are well prepared for writing in their courses across the curriculum. Each of these aims—or motives, as they are called here—is the subject of one of the introductions provided for Chapters 1–10. The introduction for the book as a whole, "Writing for Your Life," places the aims with other elements of the rhetorical situation, such as audience and context, and discusses strategies for invention, arrangement, and revision so that students will be better prepared to accomplish their aims. It also introduces students to how to conduct research and how to honor the conventions of academic discourse—new material requested by users of the third edition.

All of the introductions are designed to provide both teachers and students with flexibility. There are frequent reminders that the aims of discourse can be pursued by different means, and the discussion of planning and drafting encourages writers to choose the methods that work best for them. The entire book reflects the conviction that different writers work well in different ways—and the same writer may work well by using different approaches at different times. I have seen in my classrooms that providing students with choices can enable them to overcome the difficulties that writers encounter. Mindful of these difficulties, I have tried to keep the book's rhetoric as simple and direct as possible and to choose readings that speak to a diverse range of students.

The reading selections illustrate the various motives for writing and provide examples of different writing styles and patterns of arrangement. Although the readings vary in length—with the longer, more challenging selections concentrated toward the end of most chapters—they all address issues that are likely to inspire good class discussion. Of the 77 selections, 34 are new in the fourth edition. The choices have resulted in a collection that is both culturally and rhetorically diverse: The writers included in this edition discuss diversity in terms of race, class, gender, geography, religion, and sexual orientation; and their works include personal essays, feature articles, documented arguments, critical assessments, short fiction, and poems. I have nevertheless retained a number of familiar pieces both because they have proven records as classroom favorites and because I wanted to spare instructors the necessity of undertaking an entirely new class preparation. Gloria Naylor, Annie Dillard, Martin Luther King, Jr., George Orwell, Alice Walker, and Jonathan Swift are a few of the authors represented by well-known works.

An alternative table of contents groups selections on related topics for users interested in pursuing a particular subject or theme. Moreover, the apparatus for each selection includes links making connections with other selections within the book, as well as directing students to additional resources in print and online. Headnotes provide information about authors and the context in which their work originally appeared. Although some "Questions for Discussion" are designed simply to gauge reading comprehension, most raise concerns that invite readers to think about what they have read and to formulate their own responses. Every reading is also followed by three "Suggestions for Writing." Individual readers may well identify other questions and suggestions; I did not attempt to exhaust the possibilities of any piece. My goal was simply to encourage thoughtful responses to reading, and I believe that such responses, when encouraged, can take any number of directions.

Instructors familiar with the third edition will find that I have made changes in the book's structure. In response to reviewers who recommended less emphasis on expressive discourse and more emphasis on academic discourse, I condensed two chapters in the third edition ("Writing to Record a Memory" and "Writing to Explore Experience") into one: "Writing to Understand Experience." In addition to incorporating examples of academic discourse into Chapters 2, 3, and 7, I also incorporate them into a chapter new to this edition, Chapter 5: "Writing to Analyze Images." The design of this new chapter responds to research on the extent to which students learn visually as well as to rising interest in visual rhetoric. It also provides another way for instructors to give writing assignments that call for both creative and critical thinking.

Instructors new to *Motives for Writing* will find that this book also includes chapters designed to elicit other kinds of writing that are rarely included in standard textbooks. While Chapters 1 through 5 prompt students to consider what they want an audience to learn or to think, Chapter 6 ("Writing to Move Others") and Chapter 8 ("Writing to Amuse Others") encourage students to focus on changing how an audience feels. Chapter 9, "Writing to Experiment with Form," emphasizes how an essay can be as "creative" as a story or a poem. And Chapter 10, "Writing to Understand Reading," extends the discussion of literary discourse by inviting students to think about stories, poems, and a short play.

Most chapters begin with short, readily accessible readings and conclude with more demanding pieces. And the motives themselves have been arranged according to the degree of difficulty inexperienced writers are likely to have with them. The sequence of chapters begins with a writer-centered motive in "Writing to Understand Experience," then turns to subject-centered motives such as "Writing to Report Information" and "Writing to Interpret Information," followed by such audience-centered motives as "Writing to Move Others" and "Writing to Persuade Others." But because every chapter is self-contained, the various motives can be studied in any sequence that seems appropriate for a specific class—just as the readings within any chapter can be read in a sequence determined by individual interests or needs.

A word here about the rhetorical modes: This book takes the position that writing seldom involves conforming to a fixed pattern, that a single piece usually involves several modes, and that no mode is limited to any one motive. In other words, I present the modes as means for generating ideas when pursuing different aims—not as models to which writers should make their thoughts conform. I believe that instruction based on fixed patterns of arrangement can turn writing into an academic exercise that bears little relation to the way writers write in the world beyond the classroom. Patterns such as definition, classification, and comparison are more likely to grow out of the act of writing than to be imposed at the outset as a framework to which invention must be subordinate. Because the modes can be useful for instructors and students who wish to focus on organization, I include discussion of them in the introduction to Chapters 3, 4, 5, and 7. The book also includes an Index to the Readings by Rhetorical Strategy (Mode); however, the text as a whole presents arrangement as one of the writer's tools, not an end in itself.

In completing this edition of *Motives for Writing,* I have accumulated many debts. Leslie Adrienne Miller helped me to select new poems for the book, and, in the process of doing so, introduced me to works by many poets whom I want to keep reading. My friends Mary Rose O'Reilley, Lon Otto, John O'Brien, and Erika Scheurer offered good counsel whenever I turned to them. In addition, Erika somehow found time in a demanding schedule to read the manuscript with care and to write the Instructor's Manual—work for which I am deeply grateful. Andrew J. Leet provided timely assistance with photocopying manuscript and helping me to review page proof. I also want to thank the following instructors for sharing their experience with the first three editions of the book: Funwi F. Ayuninjam, Kentucky State University; Roy Baggett, North Central Texas College; T. M. Barnhill, B.A., M.A. English, Gadsden State Community College; Stephen Bonin, North Central Texas College; Carol Ann Britt, San Antonio College; Amanda Crowell, University of Missouri-St. Louis; Mary Dell Heathington, North Central Texas College; Bill Franklin, North Central Texas College; Janet Goddard, University of Missouri-St. Louis; Bernie Hall, Lee College; Linda Hasley, Redlands Community College; Megan L. Knight, University of Iowa; Kaye Kolkmann, Modesto Junior College; Janet Kraft, Long Beach City College; Kim Long, Shippensburg University; Ian Marshall, Penn State Altoona; Nellie McCrory, Ph.D., Gaston College; Katherine P. McFarland, Ph.D., Shippensburg University; Delma Mcleod-Porter, McNeese State University; Tracy Michaels, Shoreline Community College; Eleanor Montero, Ph.D., Daytona Beach Community College; Douglas L. Okey, Spoon River College; Marilyn Ortmann, Westchester Community College; Erica F.

Riley, Des Moines Area Community College; Dorothy S. Ryan, University of Massachusetts-Dartmouth; Roberta Silverman, California State University-Dominguez Hills; David Sims, Pennsylvania College of Technology; Thomas Staudter, Westchester Community College; Ian C. Storey, Central Michigan University; Jeffrey S. Tormala, Central Michigan University; and Dave Waddell, California State University, Chico, Butte College, Shasta College. April Wells-Hayes, copyeditor, was consistently helpful when preparing the final manuscript for production. We had worked together on the first edition of this book, and it was a pleasure to be reunited on the fourth. Barbara Armentrout provided timely and much appreciated assistance with locating biographical information about authors and resolving issues in documentation style. Brian Gore located numerous web sites from which students could benefit. At McGraw-Hill, Alex Ambrose, photo researcher, and designers Susan Breitbard and Violeta Díaz all provided expert help. Marty Granahan was a model of efficiency and good humor when negotiating permissions agreements. Carole R. Crouse read page proof with careful attention. During the long and complicated process of getting the manuscript into print, David Staloch, my production editor, was inventive and steadfast in honoring with grace and wit numerous requests from me. Finally, I am glad to acknowledge the generous and thoughtful support of Renée Deljon, the acquisitions editor who convinced me to create this edition and proved endlessly resourceful as the work developed.

A Summary of What's New in the Fourth Edition

The changes to this edition of *Motives for Writing* are explained in detail above; the following list shows, at a glance, what's new:

Over 40% of the Readings.   34 of the 77 selections in the text are new to this edition, offering timely selections on topics such as cell phones, racial profiling, and terrorism.

Expanded "Links."   A new "Links" box now appears after each selection to refer students to related readings in the text, related readings elsewhere in print, and relevant resources on the World Wide Web.

Writing to Analyze Images.   Chapter 5 includes essays on topics from classical art to print advertising, Web pages, and product packaging. It also includes a wealth of images as well as a guide to writing about visuals.

Expanded Introduction.   The book's introduction, "Writing for Your Life," now includes an expanded discussion of peer review and a new section focused on how to write academic papers, as well as a discussion of how to do research and use documentation.

Streamlined Organization. The previous edition's first two chapters were combined to create the new Chapter 1, "Writing to Understand Experience." Academic motives for writing are focused early on in Chapter 2, "Writing to Report Information," and Chapter 3, "Writing to Interpret Information."

Increased Emphasis on Academic Writing and Research. In addition to the new coverage in the book's general introduction and the emphasis on academic motives for writing beginning with Chapter 2, examples of academic writing, including documented works, appear throughout the book. Both MLA and APA styles are now illustrated (see pages 38–48, 257–273, and 563–577). MLA style is also used for the "Elsewhere in Print" lists that follow every selection.

Web Site to Accompany *Motives for Writing*, Fourth Edition. The book's new Web site, located at <mhhe.com/motives>, provides links to information related to the readings' topics, themes, and authors.

Additional Resources Available

More Digital Solutions. McGraw-Hill also offers other technology products for composition classes. Three of those products are briefly described below. For information about the following, and additional electronic resources, please visit the McGraw-Hill Higher Education Web site's English pages at <www.mhhe.com/catalogs/hss/english> and its "Digital Solutions" pages at <www.mhhe.com/catalogs/solutions>.

> **PageOut.** McGraw-Hill's widely used click-and-build Web site program offers a series of templates and many design options, requires no knowledge of HTML, and is intuitive and easy-to-use. With PageOut, anyone can produce a professionally designed course Web site in very little time.

> **AllWrite!** Available online or on CD-ROM, AllWrite! offers over 3,000 exercises for practice in basic grammar, usage, punctuation, context spelling, and techniques for effective writing. The popular program is richly illustrated with graphics, animation, video, and Help screens.

> **Webwrite.** This online product, available through our partner company MetaText, makes it possible for writing teachers and students to, among other things, comment on and share papers online.

Brief Contents

Contents

1   WRITING TO UNDERSTAND EXPERIENCE   51

4 WRITING TO EVALUATE SOMETHING   275

5 WRITING TO ANALYZE IMAGES   341

6 WRITING TO MOVE OTHERS 443

8 WRITING TO AMUSE OTHERS 579

9 WRITING TO EXPERIMENT WITH FORM 619

10 WRITING TO UNDERSTAND READING   671

Readings Arranged by Subject and Theme

Education

Environment

Ethics and Morality

Family

Gender Issues

Health and Wellness

Identity

Language and Learning

Sports

MOTIVES FOR WRITING

Introduction
Writing for Your Life

Writing can change your life. It can help you deepen your understanding of yourself as well as achieve the goals you set for yourself. It can help you make sense of the information that assaults you every day and present ideas so that others will take you seriously. And it can broaden your world by enabling you to communicate effectively with people you have never met.

Despite the tremendous advantages of writing well, many people persuade themselves that they can never learn to write, because they believe that writing is a talent they were denied at birth. People who think in these terms are unlikely to write well, because they lack the motivation to take their writing seriously. It is true that some people learn to write more easily than others because they have a certain aptitude for it or because they have been encouraged by parents, friends, or good teachers. But to a large extent writing is a skill that can be learned by anyone willing to take the trouble. Believe that you will fail, and you are likely to fail. Believe that you can succeed, and you will have begun to succeed. It will certainly take time and effort to write successfully, for writing involves hard work; but you will find that this investment will pay rich dividends.

You probably know more about writing than you realize, but you may not know how to use that knowledge to accomplish the full range of writing you need to do. You may have been discouraged by assignments that seemed silly and pointless. If so, you probably wondered, "Why?" and, when you finished, "So what?" What you sensed was that real writing is done for a real purpose: Someone has a motive for writing—a motive stronger than simply wanting to complete an assignment. There are, as you will see, many motives for writing. Whatever the specific motive may be, however, writers write because they understand that writing is a way to satisfy a purpose that is important to them.

This book takes the position that successful writing begins with having a motive for writing and understanding how that motive can be fulfilled. The ten chapters that follow this introduction discuss a number of these motives and show how various writers have realized them: to understand experience, to report information, to interpret information, to evaluate something, to analyze images, to move others, to persuade others, to amuse others, and to experiment with form. The final chapter emphasizes writing to understand reading, but the entire book assumes that reading is intimately connected to writing. Recognizing, through reading, the motives of other writers can help you discover your own sense of what you hope to accomplish when you write and so understand the principles likely to help you succeed.

■■■■ UNDERSTANDING YOUR RHETORICAL SITUATION

Any act of writing involves five elements that together form what is called the rhetorical situation:

- author
- audience
- purpose
- topic
- context

As writers pursue different motives, they emphasize certain elements of the rhetorical situation over others. Writing about personal experience focuses mainly on satisfying the needs of the writer. Moving, persuading, and amusing others focus mainly on eliciting appropriate responses from the audience. Although reporting and interpreting information, evaluating something, analyzing images, and writing about literature certainly satisfy the writer's needs and require the writer to think about the reader's needs, they all focus to varying degrees on the subject matter or topic. Whatever your emphasis, though, you can seldom lose sight of any of these elements of the rhetorical situation for long.

Author

Some writers do their best work in the early morning, others at night. Some need a quiet place, and others write happily with music playing and friends wandering around the room. In short, different writers write best in different environments. To the extent that your time and circumstances permit, you should choose the environment that allows you to be most productive.

Although writers have different habits and write in different ways, all good writers have at least one common characteristic: They are active readers. As readers, they are constantly acquiring new information, much of which they may never use, although some of it will help them write. To put it simply: The more you know, the more you have to say, and the easier it is to discover ideas for writing.

But good writers are also readers in another sense: They are critical readers of their own work. When they write—and especially when they revise—they consider their work not only from their own point of view (by asking, for example, "Have I said what I wanted to say?") but also from the point of view of readers (by asking, for example, "Is this point clear?"). Such writers understand that writing is a form of communication.

One way of thinking about the variety of possible transactions between writers and readers is to envision them on a scale ranging from the personal and private at one end to the impersonal and public at the other, with additional motives brought into play as you move from the private toward the public. This is not to say that any one type of writing is necessarily better than another, just different. Successful writing calls on the writer's ability to analyze the rhetorical situation and make appropriate adjustments.

Audience

A good sense of audience is one of the most important factors in writing well. Inexperienced writers often write as if they did not really expect anyone else to read what they have written. There are, without question, times when writers write solely for their own benefit, putting on paper words they have no intention of sharing with others; but most writing involves communicating with other people. The "others" with whom we communicate can range from a single individual, whom we may or may not know, to a large group that includes people we have never even met. When addressing an unfamiliar audience, beware of being ethnocentric—of assuming that your nation or cultural group is at the center of human affairs. Realize that readers from other regions may not be receptive to your ideas. And don't make the mistake of thinking that all your readers are exactly like you. In a large audience they may come from different socioeconomic groups, from different ethnic groups, and from different geographic regions. At least half of them may be of a different gender. Your readers may also differ in ways that are not readily apparent. A large audience, or even a small one, can include readers who differ in religious faith, political affiliation, and sexual orientation. As a general rule, your writing will benefit if you are aware of how readers differ, for this awareness can help you avoid questionable generalizations and language that have the potential to exclude or offend.

You can see how audiences differ if you think about a time when you wrote an essay explaining something to your fellow students but also had to turn it in to a college professor. Had you not had to turn it in, you might have used different language or different examples. Your peers and your teacher could need to know different things; or your peers could need their information more urgently than your teacher does. You must decide carefully how much information to give each audience, what order to put it in, and what to leave out.

Whoever these "others" may be, however, they are your readers; you must engage their attention and help them understand what you have to say. One strategy for reaching these readers is to identify with them as much as possible—to become as much like them as you can, to put yourself in their shoes, to see through their eyes. Identifying with readers in this way requires imagination. To some extent, of course, you always construct your audience imaginatively, even when you write for a particular person you believe you know well—your English teacher, for instance. Because there is much about that audience you do not know, you must create to some extent an imaginary image of it. If you present yourself as a credible, well-intentioned writer, your readers are likely to be willing to join this imaginative creation and play whatever role is required of them.

In most rhetorical situations, you can appeal to your audience by honoring the following principles:

- When planning and drafting, try to imagine more than one type of audience. Imagining different audiences can help you choose appropriate topics—topics that would interest both you and your readers. If you are writing for a particular audience, especially one with power and expertise, you may benefit from constructing another audience in your mind, one with which you feel comfortable. Doing so can help you draft the first (and often most difficult) version of the work at hand because you won't feel intimidated.

- When revising early drafts of your work, keep your real audience clearly in mind. Ask yourself if you have failed to provide any information your readers will need to understand the truth you are trying to convey. Similarly, ask yourself if you have dwelt too long on any point, providing information you can safely assume your readers already know.

- Whoever your readers may be, recognize their values and needs, and do not rely too much on their patience and cooperation. If readers find that they have to work unnecessarily hard, or if they feel that a writer is underestimating their knowledge or intelligence, they will often stop reading, even if the material is important.

Purpose

A writer's *purpose* is essentially the same as a writer's *motive;* both terms are used to describe what a writer hopes to accomplish. The benefit of having a clear sense of purpose is obvious: You are much more likely to accomplish your objective if you know what it is. When you are reading other people's writing, a good way to understand purpose is to ask yourself why the writer chose to approach a topic one way rather than another. For example, when reading a humorous essay, you might immediately recognize that the writer's motive was to amuse, but you might enrich your understanding of the essay by considering why someone would want to be amusing on the topic this writer chose.

This book identifies a number of motives for writing, each of which will be discussed individually in the chapters that follow this general introduction. Keep in mind, however, that writing often reveals an interplay among various motives. For example, although the primary purpose of an argument may be to persuade readers to accept some belief or undertake some action, an argument might easily include paragraphs devoted to informing, amusing, or moving readers. Having more than one purpose is fine as long as one purpose does not conflict with another in the same work. As a general rule, however, you should try to make one purpose prevail within any one work, for this will help make the work unified and coherent.

Topic

Although the terms *subject* and *topic* often are used interchangeably, a distinction can be made between them. *Subject* often is used to describe the general area that a writer has considered; *topic* identifies the specific part of that subject that the writer has discussed. Writers often begin with a subject and then narrow it down to a topic suitable for the work (and audience) they have in mind. If you are interested in writing about the Second World War, for example, you could not hope to discuss more than a small part of this subject in a four- or five-page essay. The subject contains many possible topics, and you might decide to write about the attack on Pearl Harbor or the firebombing of Tokyo—both of which topics might be narrowed even further. Decisions about how much to include depend on for whom you are writing (and why) as well as on the length appropriate for the context.

By narrowing a subject to a specific topic, you focus attention on something you want your readers to see in detail. To use an analogy: If you are watching a football game from a seat high up in a large stadium, you have a very large field of view, much of which is totally irrelevant to the game—thousands of spectators, the curve of the bleachers, the pitch of the ramps, and so on. Unless you find some way to narrow that field of view, you will be distracted by these irrelevancies, and you will not be able to get a clear view of exactly what is happening on the field. Binoculars will help immensely, for you can train them on the players, and the binoculars will magnify the images of the players so you can see more details of each play. However, to see the players clearly, you have to adjust the focus of the binoculars. Just as you have too large a field of view from the top of the stadium, you may at first target too large an area to write about; and as you proceed, you may discover that you are most interested in a much smaller part of it. Thus, just as you would at the ball game, you must shut out some details and focus on others.

Finally, a good topic will lead to your saying something worth saying. Some topics have been written about so extensively that you may find it difficult to communicate something that your readers do not already know. A writer with an original topic, or a topic about which something new can be said, has a head start on maintaining readers' interest. Because choosing a topic is such an important part of writing well, additional advice on how to do it is included later in this introduction.

Context

Writing is also influenced by the particular event or circumstance that prompted it—what is called the *context* for writing. Writing an essay in class, for example, may be very different from writing an essay out of class to be turned in next week—even though the author, audience, purpose, and topic have remained the same. Or suppose you want to write a letter to a friend. If you are a thoughtful writer, your tone will reflect what you know of your friend's state of mind, even though the basic elements of the rhetorical situation have remained the same: A light letter full of jokes might not be appropriate if you know that your friend has just sustained a serious loss. A sense of context helps writers satisfy these conventions.

When considering the context for a specific work, you can benefit from thinking about *time*. A college professor, for example, may expect more from an essay written near the end of her course than she did from an essay written early in the term. You can also benefit from considering what writing specialists sometimes call *climate*—whatever is happening in the world of the writer and the audience when the writing takes place. Just as both readers and writers may be influenced by temperature (as when working in a room that is either too hot or too cold) and weather (especially when weather is unusually severe, as would be the case, for example, when reading or writing in a community suffering from drought or flood), they may also be influenced by the political, economic, and social events taking place at the time. A recent crime wave or an international political crisis, for instance, may be on many people's minds. Experienced writers often consider such events when choosing a topic and deciding how to present it. On some occasions, readers might be glad to be distracted from an oppressive climate; on others, they may question the wisdom of a writer who seems altogether oblivious of current events.

In summary, any document that you compose for others to read should be informed by your purpose, your audience, and your context. Even when you are confident about your purpose, remember to think clearly about your audience, imagining what this audience expects from you and considering the context in which the transaction between writing and reading will take place. Moreover, you must have a clearly focused topic that is suitable for your purpose, audience, and context. Remember that you are the author of any text with your name on it. Draw upon your strengths, and think critically about all aspects of your work.

■ ■ ■ ■ PREPARING TO WRITE

How do writers go about meeting the demands we have just discussed? The answer is that there are about as many ways as there are writers; everyone has his or her own process. Generally speaking, however, every successful writing process includes *planning, drafting, revising,* and *editing,* even though the writer may sometimes be engaged in all of these activities at once. That is, there is no predetermined order in which these activities must occur, no obligation to complete one activity before beginning another. When we write, we loop back and forth over our own mental tracks time and again, rethinking, rearranging, restating, researching. We may not complete one loop before we're off in another direction with another loop. And we don't necessarily begin at the beginning; sometimes, we finish at the beginning. Writing, in short, is a fairly chaotic process. Still, we do know something about it.

Finding a Topic

Writers need something to write about, and finding a topic is often the most difficult part of the process. Writing often goes best when we can write about something we are vitally interested in and know a good deal about; sometimes, however, we are required to write on a topic dictated by someone else or by circumstances. In that case, the preliminary work becomes deciding what to say about that topic. Regardless of whether we have chosen the topic or have had it imposed on us, however, we must decide what to include and what to leave out. We must also settle on the order in which to present our material. Some of this work may go on informally while we are actually doing other things, but some of it is more deliberately structured, as in the lists we may make to ensure that we don't forget important points.

So how do we know what we want to write about? Conventional wisdom tells new writers, "Write what you know," "Write about what you enjoy." This can be sound advice but unhelpful if you're not sure what you know or why what you enjoy would interest other readers. Moreover, there will be many occasions when you will be expected to demonstrate that you have learned about a topic through research—even if you initially feel uncertain about that topic.

For most of us, a choice of subject is seldom entirely free, and for everyone the subject for writing derives directly from the rhetorical situation. In this way, college writing is not really very different from writing on the job. In college writing, the choice of a topic is conditioned by the courses in which the writer is enrolled—by the academic discipline as well as the dictates of the professor. In the working world, the topic depends on the constraints of employment—the employer's attitudes and requirements, as well as the needs of clients and customers. Insofar as we have choices, we are well advised to follow our interests, keeping in mind that our topic should be appropriate for our audience, our purpose, and our context.

Consider the full rhetorical situation in which you are writing: Precisely what do you hope to accomplish, and what information do you need to do it? Ask yourself who will read your writing, bearing in mind that your audience may be larger than it seems: You might write a memo to your boss, but your boss may decide to distribute it to other people in the company. Remember also the context for writing: You may have a topic you want to bring to the attention of your boss, but the time isn't right. You may have to wait for a more opportune occasion. In the meantime, you have to find something else to say.

CHAOTIC PROCESSES Ways of exploring a subject fall rather naturally into two groups: chaotic processes and structured processes. Among the chaotic processes for exploring subjects are those that rely on the subconscious knowledge we all have. They are time-tested techniques for encouraging that kind of knowledge to surface so that we can impose order on it. Depending on your inclination and your topic, two of these techniques— *brainstorming* and *freewriting*—may be interchangeable; the other technique, *mapping,* places ideas in spatial relationships to each other. You may already be familiar with these methods; if they have worked for you in the past, by all means continue to use them. If you've never tried them, you may find them useful. But if they don't work for you, try something else, perhaps some of the structured processes described on pages 11–16.

Brainstorming A time-honored way to increase creativity and productivity is to get a small group of people together for unstructured discussion—a process called *brainstorming;* but it can also be used successfully by one person looking for ideas about a subject. It involves listing everything that occurs to you (or that others say) about the idea as fast as possible in a limited period of time. You can do it over and over, checking your list at the end of each spurt of intensive thinking.

To try it out, get a pen or pencil and a sheet of paper. Set a clock or timer for fifteen minutes. Concentrate on your subject. Ask yourself what you know about it, and jot down your answers. As ideas come to the surface, jot them down as fast as you can. Don't worry about spelling or sequence or anything except putting ideas on paper. And don't worry about whether your answers seem worthwhile; you can evaluate them later. The point is to get as many thoughts as you can on paper. If you keep your mind working, a good idea may come only after a dozen that you'll reject later. Stop when the alarm goes off, and take a few minutes to look over your jottings. Mark ideas you find useful or interesting. (Colored markers ease the task of grouping those that seem to go together.) If you think you still don't have enough to go on, you can brainstorm again, perhaps focusing on one of the ideas you wrote down or taking a new direction; but do give yourself a rest between sessions.

❧ *Freewriting*   Like brainstorming, *freewriting* is done nonstop, occurs intensely for a short period of time, and is done without worrying about audience. Although freewriting will produce much that is unusable, it can also produce much that will be surprisingly important, attesting to the notion that our subconscious minds contain enormous amounts of valuable information. Freewriting is a way to get some use out of this information, and it may very well give us a focus for the rest of our work on the subject. Sometimes, when we find a topic through brainstorming, freewriting unlocks a wealth of ideas about that topic.

Some writers like to think informally about an idea before they put pen to paper; others simply like to begin and see what comes out. Both approaches are okay. When you begin writing, don't worry if you can't think of something to write. Just write anything; it doesn't matter what it is or whether it makes sense. Don't stop for any reason—to figure out how to spell a word, to choose between two terms, or for any other reason. Don't worry if you find yourself straying from your guide sentence at the top of the page. The new direction may be useful. When the time you set for this exercise has passed, stop writing and look at what you have. If you find a good idea, you may be able to develop it as you draft and revise.

❧ *Journaling*   Keeping a journal allows you to record in detail, for your own benefit, whatever you have in mind. Unlike a diary, which is used simply to record meetings and events, a journal is more personal and reflective, focusing on how a writer reacts to experience. A journal is less likely to note what the writer ate for breakfast than it is to discuss how the writer responded to a novel, a sunset, or a quarrel. Many writers find this kind of writing highly satisfying.

Journals can be designed in different ways with different motives in mind. The two most common types are the *personal journal* and the *reading journal*. In a personal journal, you write primarily about yourself and your world. Personal journals can be a useful resource when you are preparing to write essays that focus on your own experience—as in Chapter 1, "Writing to Understand Experience." In a reading journal, you focus on responses to what you are reading—including summaries of difficult assignments that you may want to review when preparing for an exam, as well as reactions to what you have read: what you liked, disliked, or wanted to learn more about. Reading journals are an excellent resource when you are preparing to undertake college writing assignments, such as "Writing to Report Information" (Chapter 2), "Writing to Interpret Information" (Chapter 3), "Writing to Persuade Others" (Chapter 7), and "Writing to Understand Literature" (Chapter 10). An additional advantage of a reading journal is that writing about what you read increases the likelihood of retaining what you learned. If you are interested in experimenting with a reading journal, you could begin by keeping one devoted to your reading this quarter or semester.

No matter how much experience a writer may have, it is not unusual to feel, at times, that "there's nothing to write about." Most people know more than they realize, and reviewing the entries in either a personal journal or a reading journal can often help writers recall events and ideas that they had somehow lost sight of—thus generating topics for further writing.

Because we write journals for ourselves, we can write quickly without worrying about grammar, style, or what someone else might think of us. So unless you are keeping a journal that you wish to share with someone or that you are required to submit for evaluation, do not allow concerns about audience to interfere with the free flow of ideas in your journal. You are writing for the audience you know best of all: yourself.

By keeping a journal in which you write daily, you can protect yourself from the anxiety some people feel when they are forced to write. The more writing you do, the more natural it becomes to write. Another advantage is that you can explore responses to what has happened or what you have read—personal responses that you would be reluctant to discuss with anyone, believing them too trivial, too personal, or too confusing to share with others. Journal writing can be a form of freewriting, with one sentence leading to another that you had not anticipated when you began to write. When you are writing for yourself in this way, some entries will be stronger than others. But it would be a mistake to try to edit yourself as you write, attempting to write a consistent series of well-crafted passages, each of the same length. Do not worry about grammar or punctuation or spelling. And do not worry about wandering off the point. Although you will not want your journal writing to be point*less,* the point can be anything you want it to be, when you are your own audience.

Mapping   Mapping (sometimes called *clustering* or *webbing*) is a way of visually analyzing the parts of a subject. Write the subject in the middle of your paper and circle it. From the edges of the circle, draw lines radiating outward to nodes labeled to represent the main parts of the subject. Repeat this process for each of those nodes until you have exhausted all the information you have. You will notice that some parts generate several levels, whereas others do not, and that the interrelationships between parts of the idea are easy to see in this kind of graphic. Consider Figure 1, but note that it is only an example and that no two maps look alike.

Brainstorming, freewriting, and mapping can be used together to bring some order to the chaotic information that surfaces from the unconscious. Try pulling some of the related ideas that surfaced during a brief brainstorming session into a single statement; jot the statement down at the top of a sheet of paper you can use for freewriting. When you are through freewriting, look at what you have produced and try to map related ideas. This activity will focus your efforts to find the vein of gold in a pile of earth.

STRUCTURED PROCESSES Structured processes are conscious ways to encourage thinking along specific lines. People have been using these techniques successfully for centuries. In classical times, Aristotle provided numerous ways to get below the surface of a subject. They are called *topoi,* from which our

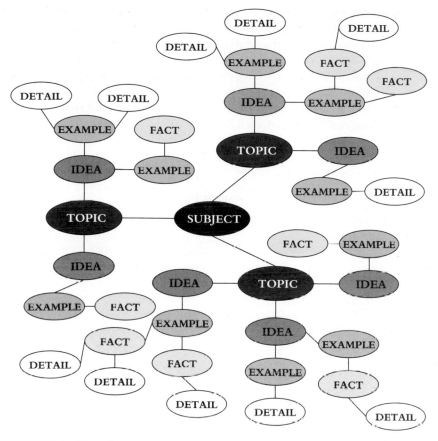

FIGURE 1. Mapping

word *topic* has been derived. In the twentieth century the philosopher Kenneth Burke offered an alternative way to explore a subject by using five elements he called the *pentad*. A related method, *journalists' questions,* lists six aspects of a subject; and *varying perspectives* offers at least nine ways to view a subject.

♦ *Classical Topics*   It is often useful to look at a subject from the perspectives originally developed by Aristotle to help generate ideas. Aristotle proposed asking certain questions to define what something is and others to compare and contrast it with other things. Still other questions help writers examine possible relationships: cause, antecedent, contraries, contradictions. Questions about circumstances explore matters of possibility and factuality. And questions about testimony—authority, statistics, maxims, law, examples—can help writers support their points.

Originally designed as ways to discover proofs in persuasive writing, Aristotle's topics provided a foundation for the work of many other rhetoricians and have played an important role in education for more than two thousand years. One advantage of these topics is that they remind us to consider both the general qualities and the particular features of any given subject. At least one of Aristotle's questions should always be appropriate, whatever we want to write about. The answers we give help us decide what we want or need to say.

Aristotle identified thirty-two topics, and few people are able to keep them all in mind. But without memorizing a long list of topics, you can still benefit from classical rhetoric by asking yourself a series of questions when you prepare to write. These questions can help you not only to generate ideas when you feel stymied but also to narrow and focus a subject so that you can choose an appropriate topic:

- Should I provide an *example* of what I mean?
- Should I *divide* this subject into parts, discuss each separately, or focus on a single part?
- Can I *classify* this subject by putting it within categories?
- Would it be useful to *narrate,* or provide a brief story?
- Would it be appropriate to see this subject as a *process* and explain how it takes place?
- Should I explain what *caused* this subject or what its *effects* will be?
- Should I *define* what I mean?
- Should I *describe* the features of my subject?
- Should I *compare* my subject with something similar or *contrast* it with something with which it might be confused?

Providing the answers to these questions has led some people to think that writing needs to be organized along the lines that the topics suggest. You may have already studied a book that taught you how to write a "description" or a "definition." Such assignments have a certain value, but it is much like the value that practicing scales has for a musician. Outside of classes in composition, a writer is unlikely to wake up some morning and decide, "Today, I am going to write an essay of comparison and contrast." Writers are much more likely to begin with a motive or subject and then decide on a plan that best suits what they want to say. When you use classical topics or questions derived from them, think of them as a way to get started rather than as a pattern of organization that you are bound to follow.

The Pentad Kenneth Burke believed that neither reading nor writing can be passive. Burke's pentad explains how this active response takes place and provides a useful means for generating ideas for writing. Burke defines five elements that are always present to some degree in a piece of writing:

- scene
- purpose

- act

- agent

- agency

For instance, a writer may concentrate attention on a particular locale in a particular moment in time; these are a part of what Burke calls *scene.*

Similarly, a writer may choose to emphasize a *purpose,* that is, a motive, rationale, or reason; a goal, aim, or objective; an intention or design; a mission or cause. And, of course, the writer may choose to focus on an event, an *act,* which may involve examining something that happens but may also include delving into the meaning of the event. Sometimes a writer chooses to spotlight an *agent,* which may be a person but may also be a force or a power or a catalyst for producing an event. The other element the writer may examine is *agency,* an instrument that causes something, the mechanism or vehicle by which something is accomplished.

But even if a writer has emphasized one element of the pentad, you should be able to find the others if you look for them. Burke's own analogy may help you understand how these various elements are related to one another. He compared them to the five fingers on a hand—separate but ultimately joined. Tracing down one finger will help you make a path to another. We can, of course, cross our fingers or clench them together. Similarly, we can consider any element of the pentad in combination with any other to establish a relationship (what Burke called a *ratio*) among the elements. And these relationships expand meaning. For instance, an act can be examined in its relationship to the scene, the agent, the agency, and the purpose, just as the scene can be examined in relationship to act, agent, agency, and purpose; and so on. These expanded perspectives from which to view the subject matter are useful to writers as well as to readers. They help us understand more fully and more clearly what we mean to say as well as what some other writer meant us to know. Two examples illustrate how this method works. The first shows that the method is especially useful when we apply it to drama (hence the method is called *dramatistic*), and the second shows how suggestive it can be when we think about any subject.

This book includes a play called *Trifles,* in which the scene is a farmhouse, the act is a murder, and the agency is a piece of rope. When we consider the act in terms of the scene, we learn the agent and the agent's purpose—who killed the victim and why. An examination of the scene alone tells us that the farmhouse is old, cold, messy, and deserted. Examining the scene in light of the act reveals much about the killer's motivation—what kind of a husband the victim was, the fact that the couple had no children, and a number of other things that lead us to decide who committed the murder.

For the second example, suppose the subject is hot weather. We can examine what people do and how they feel in hot weather, when and where hot weather occurs and what the world looks like when it is hot, what causes hot weather, how hot weather develops, and what purpose it serves. And as Burke argued, we will discover the most if we view each of these parts of the pentad in relation to every other part (the ratios). This dramatistic method has been used to analyze all kinds of subjects and to reveal how the elements of which a subject is composed relate to each other. For example, what happens when we see the act in relation to the scene? In our example about hot weather, we can look at what people do (act) in certain cultures (scene) when it is hot. Or we can examine how people respond to hot weather in the South and in the North or how we lived with hot weather before air conditioning.

If you think about the pentad in this way, your understanding of an event changes as you combine and recombine the elements. This leads to Burke's idea that the pentad is enriched and expanded by considering the combinations in the context of social concerns and economic processes. When we do that, we gain a new perspective on what we see. For instance, keeping the effects of rural isolation in mind when reading *Trifles* reveals that economic forces created a brutal, insensitive husband who emotionally abused his wife for years—an understanding that can lead us to see that neither agent nor agency in this play is as simple as it first appears.

How, then, can the pentad help you as a writer? If you use it as a tool to analyze what others have written, you will discover that you have much to say about that piece. But you can also use it as a means of writing something entirely on your own. Burke himself described dramatism as "a generating principle." Suppose that you have been asked to write about a significant personal experience. Once you have identified that experience (or act, in Burke's terms), you have to decide where to begin your essay, how much to include, and what points to emphasize. In one case, the pentad might lead you to discover the importance of scene, and much of the essay you write will then focus on how the scene contributed to the act. In another instance, you may realize that you want to emphasize the means by which an act was done or the agents who committed it.

⚠ *Journalists' Questions* Journalists' questions are similar to Burke's pentad, but they do not incorporate the relationships to the same extent. They look only at *who* did *what* to whom, *when* and *where,* and *why* and *how.* Journalists often try to convey much of this information early in a news story so their audience can grasp the heart of the story immediately. Here, for example, is the opening paragraph of a front-page story in the *New York Times* on August 18, 2001:

> Detroit, Aug. 17—The Ford Motor Company said today that it was eliminating 5,000 salaried jobs in North America and planned to reduce production this fall, the latest sign that the auto industry may no longer be able to prop up the stumbling American economy.

Notice how much information the reader is given in these few words:

- *Who?* Ford Motor Company. Most American readers are familiar with the name of this company and what it manufactures. The "who" in this case is a major U.S. corporation.

- *What?* "Said today that it was eliminating 5,000 salaried positions and planned to reduce production this fall [. . .]." The "what" is a significant job cut and a reduction in the number of vehicles produced.

- *When?* "Today" refers to August 17, the date the story was filed. Readers on the eighteenth, when the story was published, would understand that "when" was "yesterday."

- *Where?* Most American readers know that the major U.S. automobile companies are headquartered in Detroit. But the "where" is also established by the name of the city in which the story was filed, which is indicated immediately before the date. And the jobs being cut are in North America.

- *Why?* Ford's announcement is "The latest sign that the auto industry may no longer be able to prop up the stumbling American economy." Now we understand why the story is news. Although the loss of 5,000 jobs at Ford is significant in itself, this information indicates that the auto industry as a whole is in trouble and that the American economy is at risk.

- *How?* "Salaried workers" establishes that white-collar jobs will be eliminated and that the jobs of workers in manufacturing and assembly are not immediately at risk. Additional jobs are likely to be lost, however, once production is reduced.

Readers of the story that followed could expect to learn more answers to all of these questions. *How* will Ford decide which jobs to eliminate? To *what* extent will production be reduced? *Why* did the company get into financial trouble? *Where* are the plants that are most likely to be affected?

Journalists' questions work well for exploring almost any kind of subject, and by answering each of them, you can discover interesting material for writing. Although not all the questions will be suitable for every subject, this method almost always gives you something to say.

Varying Perspectives   Another way to explore a subject is based on the particle-wave-field theory of physics. Scientists and other people who are most comfortable with empirical information often find this technique more helpful than the less structured ones. *Varying perspectives* involves thinking of a subject as something in a stable state (static), as something that changes through time and space (dynamic), and as something that exists in relationship to other things (relational). Within each of these contexts, this method also involves seeing a subject as a single entity, as a member of a group or class, and as part of a larger system. Thus, a single rose (static, single entity), say, is part of a class of objects called plants (static, class). Plants are part of a larger system of biology (static, system). That single rose might change over time from a bud (static, single) to a full-blown blossom, to a husk, and finally to a berrylike object (single, dynamic) containing seeds. Those seeds are part of the seasonal cycle of renewal (single, relational). We can thus construct a matrix that gives us several different perspectives from which to examine a rose.

Dealing with Writer's Block

It is easy to get sidetracked in your writing at this point. You may even talk yourself into a case of writer's block. You know what you are going to write about, and you know what the main points are, but you just can't seem to begin writing. There's that empty computer screen or piece of blank paper staring back at you. How do you overcome writer's block? Many of the techniques useful for exploring ideas are also useful for getting over this snag, but you should consider, too, whether you are trying to write in a setting conducive to doing good work. You may be tensing up simply because you are trying to work in the wrong place or in the wrong clothes.

Make yourself as comfortable as you can, but don't get so comfortable that you will fall asleep. Fish out your favorite sweatshirt, loosen your belt, clear your desk, sharpen your pencils or start your computer, provide yourself with a stack of paper or some fresh disks, arrange the lighting, set a snack nearby, and sit down. Take up a pencil, or place your fingers on the keys, and begin to freewrite. At this point it doesn't matter what you write. You are just breaking through your block. As soon as your ideas are flowing freely, you can begin to be more conscious of what you are saying and how the pieces are going together. Perhaps the section you are working on isn't very congenial just at the moment. So change it; start on something else. You don't have to begin at the beginning. You can begin with something that will flow easily for you and fit it into the whole later on. This method has been called *chunking*. Writers begin with a piece of writing they feel comfortable working on and develop that piece as far as it needs to go. Then they set it aside and take up another piece, sometimes at the same sitting, sometimes not. When all the pieces are done, writers fit them into a whole, linking them with appropriate transitional material and providing introductions and conclusions.

If you are particularly susceptible to writer's block, it may be a good idea to do what Ernest Hemingway used to do by ending each writing session at a point where you feel sure you know what will come next. That way you can pick up quickly where you left off. Other things you can do to stave off writer's block include talking into a cassette recorder and then transcribing what you have dictated, rereading material you have already written, writing on the backs of old drafts so that you don't really have a blank sheet of paper, writing on small pieces of paper so as not to be intimidated by a large one, writing e-mail to friends to exercise your writing muscles, writing in a journal, or using a special pen or pencil—one that has already written a number of completed compositions or feels especially good in your hand. If none of these techniques helps, try anything you think will help. Exercise, ride your bicycle, go for a walk, wash dishes, shovel snow, or do some other physical task that requires little concentration but during which a good idea may come to you if you keep your mind receptive. You will come back to writing refreshed. If that doesn't seem fruitful, put the idea of writing aside for the time being; go to a movie, watch television for an hour, read a couple of chapters of a novel. But be alert for ways you may be fooling yourself out of, rather than into, writing. If you find a way to overcome a block, remember it and use it whenever you need it, much as baseball players wear lucky socks or eat certain meals before games.

As you write more and more, you will acquire a variety of techniques that will help you get over future writing blocks. Some writers keep files of interesting material they find while reading for leisure, just as they do when they are actually researching. Others keep a journal in which they record ideas and perceptions that may be useful in the future. When you feel like writing, you can go to this material to find a subject to explore, and you can consult it for help when you are stuck.

Arranging Ideas

How can you arrange your ideas in an effective sequence? Some writers find it helpful to make an outline or to list the order in which they will present their main points. Others prefer going wherever the writing takes them. Even when they prepare an outline, they end up not following it. There is nothing intrinsically wrong with that; writing is, after all, one of the best ways to learn, and you will generally wind up with something that can be reworked into a worthwhile piece of prose. Writing often takes its own shape as you do it, and plans developed beforehand often need to be reconsidered. That's all right, too. Planning and drafting can occur over and over until you feel that you have said exactly what you intended. The point is that some kind of organization needs to be evident in the writing when it is completed, whether or not the plan for it was there from the beginning.

Some writers work one way on one project and a different way on the next. The important thing to understand about planning is that your plans are not contracts. They can easily be changed during drafting and revision. So there's no single, correct way to plan that will work every time you write. Any plan that works for you—and produces an arrangement that works for your audience—is the correct plan for that particular writing activity. With that in mind, let's look at a number of different methods.

OUTLINES   There are several kinds of outlines, each of which might suit a different kind of project or a different kind of writer. Some outlines are exceedingly detailed, presenting almost as much information as the completed project will. Others are very sketchy, offering only a general indication of where to go next. The kind you need depends on a combination of your discipline, your comfort, and your project. But if you find that your readers frequently comment that they can't follow what you're writing about, you probably need to make your outline a little more detailed. Or when you finish drafting, you may need to outline your draft meticulously and compare the "before" outline with the "after" one. At the least you will see where you need to revise heavily, and you may even be able to chart where the revision should go. Conversely, if your readers tell you that your writing seems mechanical and predictable, you need to loosen up a little. Making your outline less formal may be one way to go about it.

LISTS AND JOTTINGS The most informal kind of outline is a list you jot down on a scrap of paper or keep in your head. It may be as informal as listing two or three points you don't want to forget. Such a list for a paper on, say, hunting elephants for ivory, may look like this:

> health hazards
> economic consequences
> poaching
> U.S. trade policy
> popularity of ivory in Asia
> endangered species
> effects on other animals

Nothing is indicated about other points you may plan to include, nor is anything noted about the order in which the points will appear, although you can easily add numbers once you decide on the sequence you think will be best. Furthermore, as your plan evolves, you may find that some items on your list are not appropriate; if so, just ignore them. This kind of outline is for you alone, and you don't need to worry about making it more comprehensive if it does the job for you. Many students find this kind of outline helpful in taking essay examinations because it is brief enough to occupy a very small space and doesn't take much time to produce. But it can be suitable for other occasions as well.

Here is a somewhat more detailed list for the same writing project:

1. Place in endangered species lists
    Reasons, locations
2. Place in environmental chain
    Above and below in food chain
    Relationship to other animals
    Meaning for humans
3. Who hunts ivory
    Licensed hunters
    Poachers
4. Human impact
    Physical dangers of elephant hunting:
        From elephants
        From authorities
    Health hazards:
        Food-related—rotting meat, malnutrition
        Ivory-related—elephant anthrax

⁎FORMAL OUTLINES   A formal outline for the same paper would indicate the relationships between main points and details more clearly than a list:

> Thesis: Hunting elephants for ivory has two negative effects: It causes environmental damage, and it is dangerous to humans.

I. Environmental effects
    A. Endangered species
        1. Reasons
        2. Locations
    B. Place in environmental chain
        1. Relationship of elephant to other animals
            a. Effect on food chain
            b. Maintenance of grasslands
        2. Importance of elephant for humans
II. Human impact
    A. Physical dangers of elephant hunting
        1. Unpredictability of elephants
        2. Crackdown by governments on poachers
    B. Health hazards
        1. Carcasses left to rot
        2. Elephant anthrax
            a. Conditions for infecting humans
            b. Locations of the disease

Notice that the formal outline is a graphic representation of the paper and that it shows balance and completeness. For this reason, some people insist that if there is an item 1, there must be an item 2, or if there is an item A, an item B must follow. Actually, there is no hard-and-fast rule, but common sense suggests that if there is, say, no item 2 to accompany item 1, either the writer has not pursued the subject far enough, or the main heading and subheading can be combined. For example, if there were only a human disease issue and no consideration of geography in point 2 under "Health hazards," the idea should be expressed as "2. Elephant anthrax dangerous to humans." Beginning with uppercase roman numerals, a formal topic outline relies on indented uppercase letters of the alphabet, Arabic numbers, lowercase letters, Arabic numbers in parentheses, and so on to reflect various levels of relationships. Each topic should be grammatically parallel with other topics on the same level.

Any topic outline can easily be turned into a sentence outline by stating all points as sentences. A sentence outline has the advantage of helping writers be specific. For instance, "B. Health hazards" could become "B. Elephant hunting poses health hazards."

Formal outlines can be developed as plans for writing, as tools for revision, or as guides for readers. Most writers need flexibility in the plans they make to guide their writing, because the human mind often develops new insights during drafting. If you do make a formal outline before you write, review it when drafting to see whether you have lost sight of any points you intended to make and if you need to incorporate new points that have occurred to you. You may find that you are satisfied with the direction your writing has taken. But you could see ways to improve your organization.

NUTSHELLS, ABSTRACTS, AND CAPSULES   Another way to bring some order to writing is to use a summary paragraph (sometimes called a nutshell, abstract, or capsule). Consider this paragraph, for example:

> Under the microscope we can see that blood is composed of a watery fluid called plasma, in which certain formed elements are suspended. The formed elements are different types of cells—red blood cells, white blood cells and platelets. —Louis Faugeres Bishop

It is easy to imagine how we could use this paragraph as a nutshell for organizing a paper that would follow. The first group of paragraphs following this one could describe red blood cells, what they look like, how they are made, what their parts are; the next group of paragraphs might offer the same kind of information about white blood cells; and the final paragraphs could describe platelets. That is, indeed, how Bishop developed this piece of writing, and the technique works well for many situations.

CLASSIC ORATION   The classic pattern for presenting information was in full use at least two thousand years ago, and that pattern continues to be useful today, especially in writing to persuade. People who gathered to listen to the great orators of classical times generally knew that, right after they had been exhorted to pay attention, they would get background information on the subject, which would be followed by a clear statement of what issues would be addressed and what position the speaker would take. Then they could expect information that would confirm the speaker's point and refute the opposing viewpoint. And finally, they usually expected a summary of what had been said and sometimes even a call to act on it. (A variation in the sequence could draw attention to a particular part of the oration and thereby divert attention from another part.) In other words, a classic oration had the following outline:

- *Introduction:* Gain the attention and confidence of your audience, and indicate what problem you will address.
- *Statement of issues, facts, or circumstances:* Give the relevant background information, and describe present conditions.
- *Proof of the case:* Establish your own position and why you believe it.
- *Refutation of opposing viewpoints:* State the objections and any complications; then show why these points should not trouble the audience.
- *Conclusion:* Sum up, highlight important points, point out future directions, and call for action.

Originally developed for oral presentations, this sequence became well established because nearly everyone used the same pattern or some variation of it—thus making it easy for listeners to follow the speech. And if the sequence varied, the listeners could depend on their experience to know which part they were listening to. Even today, we often expect presentations to follow a familiar pattern.

■■■■ DRAFTING, REVISING, AND EDITING

Once we have an idea of what we want to write about and how we want to arrange our ideas, we may begin *drafting,* writing ideas down in a sequence that allows for their development. Here is where the "looping back" (or recursive) nature of the writing process is most readily apparent. We may draft several pages to discover what we want to say and then throw out all but two or three sentences. Or if we are more confident of what we mean to say, we may draft several pages before we are interrupted; then when we come back to the writing, we may start out by revising what we have written, or we may find ourselves starting over—but we'll save the writing we're not using because it may be useful later. We may also draft a part of the writing we feel most comfortable about first to warm up our brains in an effort to hit our intellectual stride for the more difficult parts. It doesn't matter if the piece of writing we do first will go near the end. We'll put it where it belongs when we have a clearer vision of the shape of what we're saying.

When we've developed these pieces of writing, we can weave them together—a process we may have begun earlier. If we begin to see gaps that we have to fill with new writing, we're doing part of our job as writers. And if we haven't already done so, we have to find a way to begin and a way to conclude. We may have been *revising* all along, reshaping sentences that disappoint us as soon as we see them and rearranging paragraphs when we are only midway through our initial draft. But when we can see the whole composition, we can move into a different kind of revising, testing everything we say against what we have already said and what comes later to seek the greatest possible clarity and coherence.

Unlike revising, which often generates new writing, *editing* is primarily devoted to polishing what we have already written. When editing, we look for ways to tighten our prose, eliminating wordy constructions or unnecessary repetition. We also check our grammar, punctuation, and spelling. Many writers treat editing as the final stage in their writing process; they recognize that there is no point in perfecting material they may eliminate during a revision. Others find comfort in fixing errors when they are briefly stymied at an earlier point in the process (instead of stopping work altogether), but there work is also likely to benefit from additional editing when they reach the end of their writing process.

Although there's no real order to the parts of the writing process, we obviously can't revise what was never written; and we've stopped all the other parts of the process when we do final proofreading. It is therefore within the boundaries defined by finding a topic and proofreading the final copy that the writing process occurs.

Drafting

Drafting means writing a preliminary version of a work that you will later revise. That is, it means getting your ideas on paper (or screen) so that you can work with them. If you think of drafting as "writing the paper," you put yourself at risk. Thinking in these terms can lead to writer's block by making drafting seem excessively important. And if you think *drafting* means "writing," you may be less likely to appraise your work critically before preparing another version of it. Drafting is simply one of the stages of the writing process, and experienced writers usually compose more than one draft of what they write.

Unlike planning and revision—both of which can be undertaken at various times throughout a busy day—drafting usually requires a block of uninterrupted time. If you have twenty minutes free between classes, you can brainstorm or refine a paragraph or two that are already drafted. But when you are ready to write the first draft of a paper, you should set aside at least two or three hours when you can give your undivided attention to this work. You may finish your draft much sooner, but knowing that you have a few hours at this point in the writing process will help you avoid feeling tense. Providing yourself with adequate time for drafting can also protect you from being forced to stop prematurely just as your ideas have started to flow.

You may be thinking by now, "Doesn't this guy know how busy I am? Where can I ever find two or three hours to draft a paper?" The answer is that busy people can usually find time to do the things they genuinely want or need to do—even if it means getting up earlier, staying up later, or putting another activity aside. But no one expects you to invest an afternoon in everything you draft. You will probably spend more time on some projects than on others because some are more important to you. And as you become a more experienced writer, you may find that you need less time for drafting. Because experienced writers expect to revise their work, they often draft quickly, aware that they are composing only a preliminary version of their work.

Recognizing that writing a good introduction can be difficult, some writers draft by beginning in the middle and compose an introduction only after they have drafted several pages. But other writers draft most comfortably after they have composed an introduction that pleases them, and there are even some writers who need to write a good title before they can draft with any ease. Such writers like the sense of direction they obtain from a title or an introduction, for a good title or introduction often reveals a writer's thesis. Follow the procedure that seems best suited to you.

DISCOVERY DRAFTS   Alert and energetic, you are generating lots of ideas. It's all right to go ahead and let them flow; write them down as fast as you can. Writers frequently begin with only a general idea of what they want to discuss, and they simply let the ideas flow naturally until they have figured out what point or points they really want to make. If you write without any kind of formal plan, letting your ideas on a specific topic flow and take shape as you set them down, you are producing a *discovery draft,* an extended piece of freewriting in which you try to stick to a topic. For this kind of draft, the end is usually signaled by the discovery of the point you want your essay to make or of unexpected material to support that point.

The important thing to remember is that the discovery draft is only a beginning, a way to let ideas find their own shape; ultimately you will have to identify the most effective plan inherent in the draft and reshape it with this plan in mind. In other words, a discovery draft can help you define the main point of the paper you are planning and generate related material, making it easier for you to then write a more focused, orderly draft or to arrange your ideas into a plan that will guide your next draft.

Your Main Point or Thesis

Drafting should normally lead to identifying a main point or thesis. A thesis is usually stated early in a piece of writing, probably in the first paragraph or two (or the first chapter of a book), and is repeated at some point later. However, because writers continue to think about ideas as they write, the thesis with which a writer begins may not be the thesis that governs the completed work. In other words, writers often begin drafting with a main point in mind, only to find that the thesis has changed as the essay unfolded. Don't be alarmed if you think your thesis is changing or if you cannot identify a clear thesis in your draft; clarifying your thesis is something you can take care of later.

Neither writing nor reading would be much fun if all writers had to work the same way. Although classical rhetoric emphasized the need to follow pre-determined patterns, modern rhetorical theory has given writers much more freedom. Thus, writers may state the main point early in an essay and restate it in the conclusion, or they may engage the attention of the reader by experi-menting with introductions that at first seem unrelated to the topic. Moreover, writers are not always bound to a single main point. Sometimes, particularly in a long piece, a writer will develop two or more main points. And when pursu-ing some motives, a writer may not have a thesis as that concept is usually understood. When writing to understand experience, for example, a writer may unify the work by a search for meaning rather than by a central idea that can be stated in a sentence or two.

You should recognize, however, that writing without either a thesis or a clearly defined goal can leave readers feeling confused. When you read a piece that seems pointless, you may feel that you missed something. As a reader, you may be willing to go back and reread; but as a writer, you should recognize that some readers are not going to take the time. So if you are writing without a thesis, be sure to consider the expectations of your audience. You should also consider your motive for writing: Writing to understand experience or to experiment with form may not need a thesis, but writing for other motives, such as writing to evaluate or to persuade, will. In short, ask yourself whether you are following a strategy suitable for your rhetorical situation.

Developing Your Ideas

By itself, even a well-crafted thesis statement will not suffice to make your readers understand what you have to say. Readers resist taking in new information unless you can support your thesis with details and examples, provide support for any other claims you make, and link new ideas to information already familiar to your audience.

Details help readers to picture what you have in mind. Consider the following paragraph from Edward Abbey's "Death Valley." He has just stopped at a gas station in the middle of the valley on a morning when the temperature is already 114 degrees:

> Sipping cold drinks, we watch through the window a number of desert sparrows crawl out of the grills of the parked automobiles. The birds are eating tourists—bugs and butterflies encountered elsewhere and smashed, baked, annealed to the car radiators. Like the bears of Yellowstone, the Indians of Arizona, and roadside businessmen everywhere, these birds have learned to make a good thing off passing trade. Certainly they provide a useful service; it's a long, hot climb out of here in any direction, and a clean radiator is essential.

Where an inexperienced writer might have settled for writing, "We were glad to get something cold to drink when we were in Death Valley, because we felt like we were in the middle of nowhere," Abbey efficiently describes a scene that helps readers to imagine that they are there with him—conveying a relationship between the natural world and the people who drive through it. We learn that there are birds in Death Valley, what kind of birds they are, how difficult it must be for them to survive, and how nature seems to be able to accommodate at least some of the incursions of humans. As readers, we can be pleased that Abbey was a trained observer of the natural world who paid close attention to what he saw and heard. In many cases, your own observations will provide the details you need to develop your ideas; in others, however, you will need to find the supporting details through research and close reading.

This brief excerpt from Abbey also contains elements of Kenneth Burke's pentad, one of the strategies discussed earlier in this chapter for generating ideas (see pages 12–14). The *scene* is a gas station/store in Death Valley in the morning; the *act* is the eating of bugs and butterflies; the *agents* are the birds; the *agency* is the cars that have brought the insects into the Valley; and the *purpose* is survival. But if we can see all this, it is because of Abbey's descriptive detail. The bugs aren't simply somewhere outside the window; they are "smashed, baked, annealed to the car radiators." The birds must be small if they can crawl in and out of the grills to reach the radiators, and, as already noted, they must be hungry if they are willing to go to the trouble. There are only two additional details that we might ask for in terms of additional development: What kind of cold drink was Abbey sipping? (Was it a beer or a Diet Pepsi?) And whom does that "we" include?

Note also that Abbey attempts to link his material to what readers may already be able to visualize by comparing the birds to "the bears of Yellowstone, the Indians of Arizona, and roadside businessmen everywhere." Even readers who have never visited the American West should be able to grasp the comparison to "roadside businessmen everywhere." Annie Dillard, in an essay that appears in Chapter 9, "Writing to Experiment with Form" (pages 633–636), uses a similar strategy when describing a meal she ate on a trip through the Amazon watershed:

> Lunch, which was the second and better lunch we had that day, was hot and fried. There was a big fish called doncélla, a kind of catfish, dipped whole in corn flour and beaten egg, then deep fried. With our fingers we pulled off soft fragments of it from its sides to our plates, and ate; it was delicate fish-flesh, fresh and mild. Someone found the roe, and I ate of that too—it was fat and stronger, like egg yolk, naturally enough, and warm.

In this short paragraph, we learn not only what Dillard had for lunch but also how it was prepared, how it was eaten, and how it tasted. Moreover, references to "catfish" and "egg yolk" help readers who have never eaten a meal like this to get a sense of how it tasted.

In addition to using details about a specific scene or experience to develop their ideas, writers also use *examples.* Consider the following example from "Levi's," an essay by Marilyn Schiel that appears in Chapter 1, "Writing to Understand Experience" (pages 57–59).

> Mothers stayed home. Unlike dads, mothers didn't work. Mothers made the beds, cooked the meals, cleaned the house, baked the cookies, tended the garden, squeezed the clothes through the wringer-washer, hung washed clothes to dry on lines strung through the basement, ironed everything—including sheets and towels—scrubbed the floors while kneeling on pink rubber pads, walked seven blocks pulling an empty Red-flyer wagon to buy groceries, struggled seven blocks home with a week's worth of carefully budgeted supplies, and picked out clothes for their children to wear. —Marilyn Schiel, "Levi's"

In this case, Schiel has listed a series of examples illustrating the responsibilities of a stay-at-home mother with young children in the 1950s (as well as using some details, such as the references to "pink rubber pads" and "an empty Red-flyer wagon"). And by listing all these examples in a single sentence, she demonstrates that the claim that "mothers didn't work" was ironic. The examples make it clear that mothers worked very hard, even if they were not earning a paycheck.

Use details and examples to develop your own ideas as you draft.

✦ Revising

Revising distinguishes writing from speaking: Revision affords the writer a second (or third, or tenth) chance to get the meaning right. Donald Murray, a professional writer and writing teacher, explains that he always produces a "zero draft," a draft that is even rougher than a first draft. Then he feels he can get down to the business of writing as he reshapes those rough ideas into the first of many drafts. Many writers feel, as Murray does, that they aren't writing when they're drafting; they're writing only when they're revising.

Good writers can often be distinguished from poor writers by their attitude toward revision. Good writers don't expect to get it right the first time. Poor writers assume that they have. As we have seen, writing is a dynamic, unpredictable process: It doesn't begin with planning and then proceed systematically through drafting, revising, editing, and proofreading. Each of these activities can occur or recur at any moment during the production of a finished piece of prose. You may even get an idea you want to include in your paper just as you are typing the final word of the final draft. If that happens, don't be discouraged; and above all, don't throw that good idea away. Just work it into your paper and produce another final copy. Conversely, you may know from the very first moment you set pencil to paper what the final words of your piece will be. Go ahead and write them down. Let them stay there throughout your whole effort as a beacon to aim for. There's no right or wrong way to go about the process of writing, but revision should be part of whatever process works best for you..

Revising involves considerably more than fixing up the spelling and punctuation before you pass your writing on to a reader. It is easier to understand what revising is if we break the word into its parts: *re,* meaning "again," and *vis-ing,* meaning "seeing." Revising is seeing again, taking another look. Even though writers often do some revising as they draft, revision is most productive when something written days or weeks ago can be viewed with "new" eyes, almost as another person would see it. (Days and weeks are desirable incubation periods for writing, but writers do not always have that luxury. It is often possible, however, to let writing incubate overnight.) When you revise in this way, if you are alert and keep your audience in mind, you will notice parts that are unclear, inaccurately phrased, poorly organized, or inadequately explained.

Think of revision as reentering the writing on at least three different levels to see what works and what might need changing: appraising the content, checking the organization, and refining the style.

APPRAISING CONTENT   On the first or deepest level, you can look at whether you have conveyed the proper meaning, done what you promised the reader you would do, provided enough support, and focused clearly enough on your main point. You can use several techniques to reenter and review your writing at this level. One good way to see whether you have said what you intended to say is to read your manuscript aloud and pretend to be your audience. If it helps, try to read your writing as if you were the person you most admire. You may immediately see where you have gone astray. You can also do the same exercise pretending that you have just received the manuscript in the mail.

Another technique is to try to answer the following questions:

- Have I stressed the important issues?
- Have I made sure my point is clear?
- Have I backed all claims with evidence?
- Is my evidence credible?
- Have I dealt fairly with my audience?
- Did I promise anything that I could not deliver?
- Have I accounted for any objections that might be raised?
- Has my attitude been appropriate? Have I been honest and direct, or do I seem glib or apologetic?

Revision at this level is not merely a way to fix problems that you can see on the page. It is also a way to identify where you need to say more. Play the audience role again, this time looking for what is not said. Are there any points that have not been made that should have been? Would an example make a point clearer? Are there any unexplored consequences or loose ends? Is anything that readers may not understand taken for granted?

CHECKING ORGANIZATION   When you have answered these questions as well as you can, you are ready to move on to a closer examination of structure, considering the sequence in which you have arranged your ideas. You may already have cut some sentences that didn't seem to fit and decided to move others to different paragraphs. But since your first level of revision may have led to major changes, including the addition of new material, you should now focus on your essay's structure.

Did you follow your outline or depart from it? If you departed from your outline, is it because drafting generated unexpected ideas that you believe are important and wish to retain somehow? Or did you simply get off track? Do you need to delete any paragraphs? Combine any? Split others up? Shift them around? Do you still need to develop your ideas with new paragraphs? If so, where would they go? Have you provided transitions so that each paragraph seems to follow from the one that precedes it?

Pay particular attention to the first and last paragraphs, which receive extra emphasis. Readers have certain expectations for these paragraphs. A good introductory paragraph will capture the attention of readers and provide them with a sense of where the work is going. A good concluding paragraph will draw the work together.

Although writers sometimes begin by drafting a strong introduction or conclusion, they may find that these paragraphs no longer fit the essay they have written. You can't be altogether sure what you are introducing until you have written what you want to introduce. And revision could also lead you to decide that you have begun before the beginning or ended after the ending. For instance, you may get off to a slow start and write a paragraph or two that add little to the paper; in this case you may find that the second or third paragraph provides the best beginning. Similarly, you may sometimes ramble on a bit after you have said what you needed to say; in this case, the conclusion of your paper may be buried somewhere before the point where you stopped writing.

If you discover that you need to write a new introduction, you could try starting with a nutshell paragraph that states the major points the following paragraphs will discuss. But for variety, try beginning with an anecdote, example, quotation, unusual detail, or statement of the problem you hope to resolve. If you find that you need a conclusion, you can restate or summarize your major points. But this strategy often works best for long papers during which readers might lose sight of an idea. Repeating key points may be unnecessary in a short work, and it may leave some readers feeling as if you doubt their intelligence. When trying to write an effective conclusion, you can often benefit from asking yourself, "Why have I told you all this?" or, as a reader might put it, "So what?" Thinking along these lines may lead you to take one last step that will make the significance of your paper clear. Another effective strategy is to repeat an element found in the introduction, thus framing the work with two paragraphs that seem related to each other. You can also try rephrasing your thesis or asking your readers to undertake an action that seems appropriate.

IMPROVING UNITY AND COHERENCE   Even if an essay is well organized in term of the sequence in which you have arranged your paragraphs, there may be other gaps in your organization. If you were thinking and writing quickly when drafting, you may have made leaps in thought that are clear to you but will not be clear to readers. Look closely at the arrangement of sentences in each paragraph and determine if each sentence leads logically to the sentence that follows. You may discover sentences that do not belong in the paragraphs in which they appear because they are unrelated to the main idea of these paragraphs. In a *unified* paragraph, every sentence in that paragraph relates to its main idea. Similarly, you may find a paragraph in which every sentence relates to the main idea of the paragraph, but the sentences are not arranged in a meaningful pattern. In a *coherent* paragraph, each sentence leads logically to the next. In other words, a paragraph can be unified without being coherent. To improve the coherence of a paragraph, you may need to rearrange the sentences it already contains, add new sentences that help link the existing sentences together, or add transitional expressions (such as "for example" or "on the other hand") to clarify how a sentence relates to what has immediately preceded it.

You can also improve coherence through repetition—focusing on one idea and going back to it repeatedly—and by association—linking new information to a previously established idea.

The following paragraph by Mark Doty, from a work included in Chapter 1, "Writing to Understand Experience," illustrates both repetition and association:

> Desire I think has less to do with possession than with participation, the will to involve oneself in the body of the world, in the principle of things expressing itself in splendid specificity, a handful of images: a lover's irreplaceable body, the roil and shimmer of sea overshot with sunlight, a handful of cherries, the texture and weight of a word. The word that seems most apt is *partake;* it comes from Middle English, literally from the notion of being a part-taker, one who participates. We can say we take part *of* something but we may just as accurately say we take part *in* something; we are implicated in another being, which is always the beginning of wisdom, isn't it—that involvement which enlarges us, which engages the heart, which takes us out of the routine limitations of self?

Doty uses repetition by repeating *participation, body,* and *word.* He uses association by linking *desire* with *participation* and linking *participation* to related terms such as *partake* and *part.* He also associates *participation* with terms such as *implicated, involvement,* and *engages* in addition to associating *body* with *being.* Moreover, when you read this passage in context, you will find that Doty is using repetition and association to link this paragraph with those preceding it—paragraphs that include references to language, cherries, desire, and a specific lover.

REFINING STYLE   After studying the structure of your work as a whole as well as the unity and coherence of your paragraphs, check to see whether individual sentences can be improved. Here are a few basic points to bear in mind:

- Vary the length of your sentences. If too many sentences are short, your writing will seem choppy. If too many sentences are long, your readers may grow tired and impatient. A mixture of lengths usually works best; but note that short sentences are more emphatic than long ones, so use short sentences to make key points.
- Vary the structure of your sentences. If too many sentences follow a subject-verb-object pattern, your writing may seem monotonous. Try beginning with an adverb, a phrase, or a subordinate clause.

Check the rhythm of your sentences by reading them aloud and listening carefully to how they sound.

■ If your sentences are often described as "too long," your problem may be wordiness, which refers to redundancy, padding, and clutter. Look for unnecessary repetition. See also whether you can reduce wordiness by eliminating qualifiers and intensifiers such as *rather, very,* and *quite.* Look for phrases such as *in the event that, on the part of, it seems to me that, as a matter of fact, in view of, the point that I am trying to make* and see whether you can phrase them more precisely or delete them.

■ Use the active voice, which means making the grammatical subject of a sentence the same as the doer of the action: I *broke your bowl* (active), as opposed to *Your bowl was broken by me* (passive). Note that the passive voice is wordier and also allows a writer to duck responsibility, thus reducing clarity: *Your bowl was broken.* As a general rule, use the passive voice only if the receiver of an action is more important than the doer or if the doer is unknown.

■ Rework your sentences so that the verb reflects an action rather than a state of existence. For instance, write *Eating rich desserts makes you fat* instead of *Getting fat is often the result of eating rich desserts.* In general, avoid using an abstract subject with a linking verb and an abstract complement. Instead of saying *Overeating is a leading cause of weight gain,* say *Overeating makes you fat.*

■ Make sure that elements that should be parallel are parallel. That is, use the same pattern and the same grammatical forms to express words, phrases, and clauses that have the same function and importance. For example: I have learned how much water I am using when I *wash my car, water the lawn,* or *take a shower.*

■ Check your sentences for clichés and jargon. *Clichés* are those tired expressions that show up in your paper without your having thought about them, such as *in today's society, at the crack of dawn,* or *hitting the books. Jargon* is language specific to a particular group or field. If you find yourself writing about *font managers* and *scalable outlines,* for example, you had better be sure that your audience consists of only computer experts; other readers would be grateful for simpler language.

Editing

When you believe that you have said what you want to say the way you want to say it, you are ready to edit your paper. Check your grammar. Make sure that each sentence is complete. Check each subject–verb pair to make sure that they agree. Correct dangling modifiers (words or phrases that do not logically modify the sentence elements with which they are placed) and shifts in tense, person, or tone. Look for instances of mixed metaphors (a combination of metaphors that cannot be easily pictured) and faulty predication (the use of a predicate that does not fit the subject with which it is used). Make sure that all your pronouns clearly refer to their antecedents.

Pay attention to spelling, mechanics, and punctuation. If you are using a computer, this is the time to run your spelling checker. But don't expect a computer program to identify every problem. If you used *there* when you needed *their,* or mistyped *fro* (as in *to and fro*) instead of *for,* your spelling checker is unlikely to notice. Honor standard conventions for such issues as when to use a comma or whether to italicize a title.

Be careful about the final appearance of your paper. First impressions are just as important in writing as they are in social relationships. But don't confuse good typing with good writing. A beautifully printed essay on thick, expensive paper may be a pleasure to see and hold, but what ultimately matters is what you have written and how well you have written it. Consider the presentation of your final draft as a symbol rather than a disguise. It should look good because it is good.

Peer Review

Soliciting help from well-disposed, thoughtful readers can help you gain a new perspective on what you have written. You can begin to recognize your own developing maturity as a writer when you are able not only to accept and profit from constructive criticism but also to seek it out. Professional writers seldom rely on their own judgment alone. They test what they have written by having others read it—family, friends, colleagues, professional editors—to determine whether the writing communicates what the writer intended or needed to say. And very often, these early readers make suggestions that help the writer produce a more effective text.

Whenever possible, move beyond your circle of family and friends by sharing drafts with students who are working on the same assignment. When peer review is undertaken by a group of people in the same writing situation, the advice given is especially likely to be helpful. For example, if you are writing a paper about a book that you have studied in class, other readers of this book will be well equipped to respond to what you have written. Peer review by friends who have not read the book in question may alert you to problems in organization and sentence structure but not to a misunderstanding of the text you are discussing. Moreover, members of an in-class writing group will be familiar with the assignment sheet and the instructor's evaluation criteria. If peer review is not a scheduled part of a course you are taking, see if you can meet outside of class with two or three other students. And if this is not possible, make sure that readers outside the class—such as a friend or a writing center tutor—understand the assignment behind the draft you are asking them to review.

Peer review can be beneficial at almost any point in the writing process. Some writers like to share early drafts to see how their topic and purpose appeal to readers. Others like to make all the improvements they can on their own before soliciting responses from peers. One advantage to using peer review early in the writing process is that you get a sense of how readers are likely to respond to your material before you invest a lot of time and energy in it; another is that you may get helpful advice about how to develop and organize your ideas. An advantage to using peer review late in the writing process is that your readers are less likely to identify problems of which you are already aware and which you are capable of fixing. Moreover, readers can see that you have taken your project seriously. On the other hand, if you have taken a work through several drafts and edited it with care, you may be reluctant to make substantial changes recommended by your reviewers even if these changes would be beneficial. And if you submit a very rough draft for peer review, readers could think that you are wasting their time. When to use peer review should be determined by your own needs as a writer as well as by the expectations and resourcefulness of your peers. The manner with which you present your work to them will influence how helpful they will be to you. And you may find that you want to benefit from peer review at more than one stage in your writing process.

GETTING USEFUL RESPONSES If you pass a draft to a reader or a group of readers and say nothing more than, "Here it is; let me know what you think," you may be putting an unfair burden on others. Without any guidance or orientation from you, they have to figure out what you are trying to accomplish and what kind of help would be most useful for you. Make your own early readers understand that you are not just looking for praise. Be frank with them about anything that concerns you and direct their attention specifically to those points of concern, but also be open to comment on things you have not considered.

You can significantly increase your chance of getting real help if you introduce your draft to readers with an orientation composed along the following lines:

➢ *Explain Your Purpose* Tell your readers exactly what you are trying to accomplish in this essay. If you have a thesis, tell them what it is and how you have tried to support it. If you are working without a thesis, explain why that is and where you see yourself heading.

✷ *Identify Your Strengths* Tell your readers what parts of your draft you like. Doing so will help them help you build upon what you are already doing well. It will also help readers understand that there are some aspects of your draft that you want to preserve.

✐ *Identify Your Concerns* If you have studied your draft, you are likely to have some concerns about it, such as "I am worried about the unity and coherence of my paragraphs," "I ran out of ideas and worry that I have not developed my paper enough," or "I didn't know how to end this paper. I'd be especially grateful for help with my conclusion." Instead of keeping your concerns to yourself, get them out in the open. Doing so draws attention to the areas that worry you. This strategy focuses the attention of readers and can generate specific advice within a limited amount of time.

An orientation like this one can be given orally when you are working in a writing group. Or it can be written up as a cover letter when you are giving a draft to someone who will read your work elsewhere.

Because writing is so intimately bound up with who we are, we all feel that we put ourselves at risk when we show our writing to others. From its earliest flowering as the private, interior, and highly specific expression of the young child, communication becomes increasingly public until it reaches the impersonal and distant stage most often represented by academic discourse (see pages 25–49). As we learn to risk showing our writing to others, we mature as writers, but we never really lose the fear that someone may think us fools or idiots. Cynthia Ozick refers to this feeling of risk when she says that writing is "an act of courage." And Barbara Mellix says, "Each experience of writing was like standing naked and revealing my imperfection, my 'otherness.'" So it is understandable if a writer feels hurt or defensive when his or her writing has elicited something other than a totally favorable response. Writing is intensely personal. We offer the world a part of ourselves, and we don't want to be rejected. But it is important to overcome undue sensitivity if you want to write well. Be honest with others and encourage others to be honest with you. You may find yourself wincing every now and again when criticism is directed at your work, and you may get some unhappy looks when you offer criticism to others. But pleasure in a job well done ultimately outweighs any aches along the way.

GIVING USEFUL RESPONSES   When you review someone's writing, do not think you are being kind if you ignore problems that you see in it. Tactful, constructive criticism is always appropriate; personal attacks never are. Consider how you felt when you submitted work for peer review. Were you disappointed when no one offered any useful advice? Upset when someone came on too strong? Or grateful when you got clear responses from readers who were taking the trouble to give you some real help?

Respond to the Writer's Concerns   Pay close attention to how a writer presents his or her work, and be sure to offer the kind of help requested. If a writer asks for help with his organization and you respond by discussing his punctuation, you are talking past each other rather than having a real conversation about the work in question. When offering criticism, be specific but kind. That means responding in a friendly voice and framing your comments as personal responses rather than as final verdicts. If you say "I have trouble following the second half of your paper because I don't see how it relates to your thesis," you are offering a personal response. But if you say, "the organization is poor throughout the second half of your essay, and those pages have nothing to do with your thesis," you are offering a final verdict. Because other reviewers may have different responses, you would be wise —and kind—to speak only for yourself. But although it is important to treat others with respect, you are failing to respect the responsibility you have been given if you overlook major problems in order to seem polite.

Praise   Almost every writer welcomes praise, and people who invite you to read their work may feel anxious about how you will respond. Look for parts of the draft that you can praise sincerely. Explain why you like them.

Ask Permission   You may discover problems in the draft that the writer has not identified as concerns. Instead of plunging in and telling the writer more than he or she may be prepared to hear, ask if you could talk about other issues that concern you. Most writers will respond affirmatively when asked, but the asking shows that you are being respectful and helps make subsequent discussion safe for all concerned.

■ ■ ■ ■ WRITING PAPERS IN ACADEMIC DISCIPLINES

Writing for college courses often demands that you honor specific conventions determined by your purpose, audience, and context (see pages 3–7). Scholars use the phrase *academic discourse* to describe the kind of formal writing done for college courses by students who need to sound professional and well informed. Academic discourse is also used by college professors when they present papers at professional conferences and submit articles to scholarly journals. What college professors consider to be successful examples of academic discourse is shaped by the conventions of their own discipline. These conventions vary from one discipline to another.

When writing academic discourse, you will benefit from following the writing process described earlier in this chapter, by planning, drafting, revising, and editing (see pages 7–31) before you submit a final product for evaluation. But as you move through this process, you must pay close attention to your assignment and make sure to satisfy your instructor's expectations. The audience and the context determine your topic and purpose as well as how you need to present yourself. For instance, your political science instructor might expect you to demonstrate an objective attitude rather than a partisan one in a report summing up the results of a recent session of Congress. Your diction and tone will influence how you sound—whether you seem biased or fair-minded, timid or confident, casual or professional. For example, your physics professor might wonder if you knew what you are talking about if you substituted the word *doughnut* for the technical term *torus* in a report on fusion reaction; *doughnut* is the wrong level of language for this context, even though it can mean *torus* and might be used in an informal conversation between physicists.

Moreover, writing a formal paper in the sciences often requires a pattern of organization that is inappropriate for writing in the humanities. Thus, a paper reporting the results of research in psychology might begin with a summary (or abstract) and then move on to separate sections devoted to research methods, results, and implications. (For an example of an abstract, see page 563.) A paper interpreting a work of English literature, on the other hand, is unlikely to open with an abstract or include a section on research methodology.

In addition to including essays written for a nonacademic audience of thoughtful adults—such as those in Chapter 1, "Writing to Understand Experience," and Chapter 9, "Writing to Experiment with Form"—this book also includes examples of academic discourse from several disciplines. You will find these examples included in Chapters 2, 3, 5, and 7. Although the nature of academic discourse changes from one discipline to another, it can also vary within a specific discipline. For example, a paper written for oral presentation at a scholarly conference may be less formal than the revised version of that paper subsequently submitted for publication. And different journals within a field may have different editorial policies; one might publish only articles that are research based, whereas another might welcome a personal narrative describing a classroom practice or an essay reflecting on an issue being debated by scholars in that discipline.

Addressing the full extent to which academic discourse can vary is beyond the scope of this introduction. Nevertheless, you can make appropriate writing decisions if guided by the following advice.

Studying Literature Published in Your Discipline

The textbooks you are assigned in a college course often can give you a sense of the style of writing used in that discipline. And your instructor might distribute examples of successful papers written by other students. But one of the best ways to understand the nature of academic discourse in a specific field is to study periodical literature published in the discipline you are studying.

Because so much information is now available online through the World Wide Web, many students limit themselves to downloading material from it. Excellent sources can be found this way, but they may appear alongside sources that are unreliable. To visit the Web is to visit a world where all sorts of voices try to claim your attention. The democratic nature of the Web is part of its appeal: There is no governing body of scholars or editors determining who gets to have space on the Web. So a search for information on the Web can lead you to a site created by scholars at a major university or to one put together quickly by a ten-year-old. This is good news for the ten-year-old, who gets a chance at being heard. But sorting through all the possibilities available on the Web can be time-consuming—and potentially misleading when you need to make decisions about academic discourse. The Web sources that you downloaded may be shorter than comparable articles published in print, and they are almost certainly going to be arranged differently because of the nature of the medium: A print source can be read from start to finish, with each section leading logically to the next. A Web source is likely to make different kinds of information available through links that can be clicked on at different times, making both the nature of the text and the experience of reading it less sequential. (For a discussion on Web site design, see pages 355–371.) Moreover, material on the Web may be composed for the general public rather than for scholars, so sites you visit may not be composed in academic discourse.

You will, of course, benefit from using the Web on many occasions. But drawing upon electronic databases available through your college or university can lead you to reputable examples of academic discourse. These databases can be accessed through systems such as these:

FirstSearch	Covering more than forty indexes, *FirstSearch* enables researchers to access articles published in thirteen subject areas: Art and Humanities, Business and Economics, Conferences and Proceedings, Consumer Affairs and People, Education, Engineering and Technology, General and Reference, General Science, Life Sciences, Medicine and Health Sciences, News and Current Events, Public Affairs and Law, and Social Sciences. Its "Article 1st" option indexes material from almost 12,500 journals.
ERIC	Indexing articles and conference papers in all areas of education, *ERIC* can be accessed through online service provided by *SilverPlatter,* to which many college libraries subscribe.
PsychLit	Also available through *SilverPlatter, PsychLit* provides abstracts of articles in psychology as well as citations that will identify how you can find the full text of these articles.
Medline	Indexing more than seven thousand journals in medicine and biology, *Medline* is also accessed through *SilverPlatter.*
MLA Bibliography	Essential for research in English and American Literature, the *MLA Bibliography* indexes books as well as articles. It too can be accessed through *SilverPlatter.*

Familiarity with these systems will help you when completing research assignments, and many of the "Suggestions for Writing" that appear at the end of each selection in Chapters 1–10 invite you to do some research. In some cases, you will be able to obtain the entire text of an article when you use an electronic index, an option called "full-text retrieval." Often, however, you will need to consult the periodicals housed in your library, either in bound volumes or on microform, in order to get the text of the articles you have located. (For additional information on research, see pages 102–104.)

Unlike the World Wide Web, which publishes an enormous range of material, much of which is nonacademic, electronic indexes will direct you to examples of academic discourse that have been carefully selected and edited for publication. But if you just want to get a sense of how academic discourse sounds in your field, you can reserve these indexes for occasions when you need to locate material on a specific topic and, instead, undertake a much simpler exercise: Go to the periodical room in your college or university library and browse among the current issues on display. Then choose three or four from your field, and read the first few pages of several articles, paying attention to their tone and diction. You are likely to find that different writers have different voices, even when working within the conventions of academic discourse. But you are also likely to find consistency in diction, documentation, and organization. When you note that an article is divided into subsections, examine what these divisions reveal about the pattern of organization and what issues writers in that discipline are expected to address.

Consulting Handbooks

You may already own—or be able to acquire easily—a writing handbook composed for college students that covers grammar, spelling, punctuation, documentation, and mechanics as well as discussion of the writing process. A handbook of this kind provides a useful resource when you need to get a clear answer to questions about such issues as capitalization, italics, abbreviations, and the correct use of verbs and pronouns. A good handbook is also likely to furnish an introductory guide for formatting papers and documenting source material. Just as you can benefit from keeping a reliable dictionary on or near your desk, you can also benefit from keeping a writing handbook close at hand long after completing the course for which you purchased it.

But if you want to master academic discourse in a specific field, you should also have access to a handbook especially designed for writers in that field. These handbooks include:

American Chemical Society. *The ACS Style Guide: A Manual for Authors and Editors.* 2nd ed. Washington: Amer. Chem. Soc., 1998.

American Institute of Physics. *AIP Style Manual.* 4th ed. New York: Amer. Inst. of Physics, 1990.

American Mathematical Society. *A Manual for Authors of Mathematical Papers.* Rev. ed. Providence: Amer. Mathematical Soc., 1990.

American Medical Association. *American Medical Association Manual of Style.* 9th ed. Baltimore: Williams, 1997.

American Psychological Association. *Publication Manual of the American Psychological Association.* 5th ed. Washington: Amer. Psychological Assn., 2001.

Associated Press. *The Associated Press Stylebook and Libel Manual.* Rev. ed. Reading: Perseus, 1998.

The Chicago Manual of Style. 14th ed. Chicago: U of Chicago P, 1993.

Council of Biology Editors. *Scientific Style and Format: The CBE Manual for Authors, Editors, and Publishers.* 6th ed. New York: Cambridge UP, 1994.

Gilbaldi, Joseph. *MLA Handbook for Writers of Research Papers.* 5th ed. New York: Modern Language Assn., 1999.

Harvard Law Review. *A Uniform System of Citation.* 16th ed. Cambridge: Harvard Law Review, 1996.

Linguistic Society of America, *LSA Bulletin,* Dec. issue, annually.

Turabian, Kate L. *A Manual for Writers of Term Papers, Theses, and Dissertations.* 6th ed. Chicago: U of Chicago P, 1996.

United States Geological Survey. *Suggestions to Authors of the Reports of the United States Geological Survey.* 7th ed. Washington: GPO, 1991.

United States Government Printing Office. *Style Manual.* Washington: GPO, 2000.

Each of these handbooks addresses a number of issues, including information on document design and the documentation of sources. Among the most widely consulted are *The Chicago Manual of Style,* which is used by editors at numerous journals and publishing companies; *The MLA Handbook for Writers of Research Papers,* which sets forth the conventions that students in English courses are expected to follow when citing sources; and the *Publication Manual of the American Psychological Association,* which describes the format, organization, and documentation guidelines for writing in the social sciences.

Documenting Research

Because many of the "Suggestions for Writing" that follow the reading selections in *Motives for Writing* encourage you to do research—and because your instructor will almost certainly expect you to document your research—here is a short introduction to the key components of the two styles that are most widely used in college courses: MLA style and APA style.

MLA-STYLE PARENTHETICAL CITATIONS As an alternative to footnotes or endnotes, the MLA (or Modern Language Association) recommends that writers include parenthetical citations in the text of their work whenever they use a quotation, idea, statistic, or fact that they obtained elsewhere. These citations include the author's (or authors') last name, followed by the page where the material in question can be found. Leave a space between the author's name and the page number, but do not separate them with punctuation or abbreviate the word *page.* If you mention the author's name when introducing the material you obtained from him or her, you should give only the page number, because the author's name would be redundant. Here are five examples showing how the same source can be cited, depending on how it is being introduced or used. In this case, the work being drawn upon is *King Leopold's Ghost,* a book by Adam Hochschild. (See page 40 for the bibliographic form for citing this work.)

Standard Citation

Central African sculpture influenced artists such as Picasso because "the human face and figure are broken apart and formed again in new ways and proportions that had previously lain beyond the sight of traditional European realism" (Hochschild 73).

The period follows the parenthetical citation.

Citation When Author's Name Appears in the Text

> Hochschild argues that in central African sculpture "the human face and figure are broken apart and formed again in new ways that had previously lain beyond the sight of traditional European realism" (73).

Because the author's name appears shortly before the quote, it is not repeated in the parenthetical citation.

Citation When More Than One Work by the Same Author Appears in the Bibliography

> Hochschild argues that in central African sculpture "the human face and figure are broken apart and formed again in new ways that had previously lain beyond the sight of traditional European realism" (<u>Ghost</u> 73).

A key word from the work's title is added if the bibliography includes more than one work by the author in question. In this case, the author's name appears in the text. If the author's name appears in the parenthetical citation, a comma separates the author's name from the shortened title: (Hochschild, <u>Ghost</u> 73).

Long Citation

> Discussing the sculpture that was brought back to Europe from the Congo, Hochschild argues:
>
> > It is easy to see the distinctive brilliance that so entranced Picasso and his colleagues at their first encounter with this art at an exhibit in Paris in 1907. In these central African sculptures some body parts are exaggerated, some shrunken; eyes project, cheeks sink, mouths disappear, torsos become elongated; eye sockets expand to cover almost the entire face; the human face and figure are broken apart and formed again in new ways and proportions that had previously lain beyond the sight of traditional European realism. (73)

When a quotation takes more than four lines of text, it should be set off as a block, indented ten spaces (or one inch) from the left margin. Quotation marks are not used, because they would be redundant: The indention indicates quotation. In this case, the period ends the sentence because the page number is clearly linked to the quotation.

Indirect Quotation

> In a letter about his work to end colonial abuse in the Congo, E. D. Morel confides that his "home life is reduced to microscopic proportions" (qtd. in Hochschild 210).

The abbreviation *qtd.* stands for "quoted." In this case, the reference to E. D. Morel establishes who wrote the words in question. The reference to Hochschild establishes where the quotation was found.

→**MLA WORKS CITED LIST**   At the end of a paper using MLA-style parenthetical citations, you should add a bibliography that provides additional information about the sources you used. This bibliography is called "Works Cited" and should include all sources cited but no sources that you did not cite. The entries in this list are arranged alphabetically according to the authors' last names. When an entry takes more than one line, additional lines should be indented five spaces (or one-half inch).

→*Book with One Author*

> Hochschild, Adam. King Leopold's Ghost: A Story of Greed, Terror, and Heroism in Colonial Africa. Boston: Houghton, 1998.

When a book has a subtitle, include it (preceded by a colon) after the title. MLA-style calls for identifying commercial publishers by choosing a key word from the company's name. In this case, Houghton Mifflin becomes Houghton. Following this principle, Random House becomes Random, and Alfred Knopf becomes Knopf (because words like "House" and "Alfred" are less specific).

→*Book with More Than One Author*

> Pope, Jr., Harrison, Katherine A. Philips, and Roberto Olivarda. The Adonis Complex: The Secret Crisis of Male Body Obsession. New York: Free, 2000.

When a book has more than one author, give the last name first only for the first author because this last name determines where to place the entry in the list of works cited. Follow the order with which the authors are listed on the title page. A title like "Jr." or "III" follows the last name.

→ *Edited Book*

> Busby, Mark, and Dick Heaberlin, eds. From Texas to the World and Back: Essays on the Journeys of Katherine Anne Porter. Fort Worth: Texas Christian UP, 2001.

The editors' names take the place of an author's name, and they are identified as editors by the abbreviation *eds.* For a book with only one editor, use the abbreviation *ed.*

→ *Reprinted Book*

> Cather, Willa. The Professor's House. 1925. New York: Vintage, 1990.

This work was first published in 1925, but the text used was published in 1990. Omitting the date of original publication would give the impression that the book was first published in 1990. The 1925 edition cannot be cited unless that is what was actually used. Citing the date of first publication along with the date of the reprint tells readers that this book was attracting readers sixty-five years after it first appeared; it also establishes exactly which edition was used in case variations appear from one edition to another.

⤳ Translated Book

> Godelier, Maurice. <u>The Enigma of the Gift</u>. Trans. Nora Scott. Chicago: U of
>   Chicago P, 1999.

The translator's name appears immediately after the title. When citing material published by university presses, use the abbreviations U for University and P for Press. The University of Chicago Press becomes U of Chicago P; Oxford University Press would become Oxford UP; the University Press of Virginia becomes UP of Virginia.

→ Article in a Scholarly Journal

> Sicinski, Michael. "Valie Export and Paranoid Counter-Surveillance." <u>Discourse</u>
>   22.2: 71–91.

The volume number follows the journal title and precedes the pages between which the article can be found. In this case, an issue number is included after the volume number, and a period separates the two numbers, indicating that this is issue 2 of volume 22. Issue numbers are not necessary when a journal's pages are numbered consecutively throughout the year (so that each issue begins with the page number that would follow from the last page in the preceding issue).

→ Article in a Magazine

> Hilton, Isabel. "Royal Blood." <u>New Yorker</u> 30 July 2001: 42–57.

Include the issue's date immediately after the magazine's title. In this case, the citation is for a magazine published weekly, so the day of the month is placed before the month. (In the case of a monthly magazine, give only the month and year: Feb. 2002.) Abbreviate the names of months except for those that are only three or four letters long: May, June, and July. The MLA calls for the use of the following abbreviations: Jan., Feb., Mar., Apr., Aug., Sept., Oct., Nov., and Dec.

When a magazine article begins on one page and is continued elsewhere in the magazine (not on the next page of text), give the page where the article begins and add the mathematical symbol for plus: 17+.

⤳ Article in an Anthology

> Yaeger, Patricia. "White Dirt: The Surreal Landscapes of Willa Cather's South."
>   <u>Willa Cather's Southern Connections: New Essays on Cather and the South</u>.
>   Ed. Ann Romines. Charlottesville: UP of Virginia, 2000. 138–55.

In this case, the citation indicates that the article by Yaeger was first published in the anthology edited by Romines. If an article was reprinted in an anthology (after being first published elsewhere), the MLA instructs writers to provide information about the original publication as well as the anthology in which the work was located.

> Cushman, Ellen. "The Rhetorician as an Agent for Social Change." <u>College Composition and Communication</u> 47 (1996): 7–28. Rpt. in <u>On Writing Research: The Braddock Essays 1975–1998</u>. Ed. Lisa Ede. Boston: Bedford, 1999. 372–89.

Note that two sets of pages are given: the pages in the journal issue where the piece originally appeared and the pages between which the piece can be found in the anthology that was consulted. Note also that the abbreviation *Rpt.* stands for "reprinted."

With two exceptions, all of the essays, articles, poems, and stories included in *Motives for Writing* were originally published elsewhere. Information about original publication can be found in the headnotes preceding each selection; additional information can be found in "Acknowledgments" at the end of this book. This information will help you locate additional details about first publication if your instructor requires you to use MLA style when citing material from this textbook.

→ *Web Site*

> <u>Alternatives to Food Irradiation</u>. 8 Aug. 2001. Organic Consumers Assn. 5 Sept. 2001 <http://www.purefood.org/irrad/Alternatives.cfm>.

The MLA recognizes that standards for citing electronic publication are likely to evolve as electronic media continue to evolve. But if you wish to cite a personal or professional Web site, you must include the URL (or address for this site) so that your audience can access it if necessary. The example above begins with the underlined title of the site, followed by the date it was created (or last updated). If a specific organization or institution is associated with the site, its name appears after the site's date. You then add the date on which you accessed the site (since the site may change over time), followed by the URL. Locate the URL with angle brackets < >.

When a site has an author, begin the entry with the author's name (last name first). If a site has neither an author nor a title, begin with a description such as *Home Page,* but do not underline it or put it in quotation marks.

This form can be adopted for citing material from online journals and newspapers, but in these cases you are likely to have both an author and a title, as well as a title for the periodical. The periodical title would follow the article's title and would be followed by the date of posting, followed by the date of access if you are citing a magazine or a newspaper. (If you are citing the online version of a scholarly journal, only the date of posting is necessary.) As in the entry for a Web site, end with the complete URL located within angle brackets.

You will find additional examples of MLA style for bibliographies elsewhere in this textbook. Every selection in the ten chapters following this introduction includes a box entitled "Links," directing you to material related to the selection in question. These boxes include lists titled "Elsewhere in Print," and every item in these lists is in MLA style. "Hitler and the Occult: The Magical Thinking of Adolf Hitler" by Raymond L. Sickinger in Chapter 3 (pages 257–272) shows how a complete work looks when documented in MLA style; in this case you will find examples of both parenthetical citation and an MLA-style "Works Cited" list. Another MLA-style bibliography appears at the end of the selection by Susan Bordo in Chapter 5 (pages 409–410).

An additional aspect of MLA style appears in the introductions to chapters, several of the reading selections, and some of the discussion questions following readings. You are probably accustomed by now to using an ellipsis (. . .) when you wish to omit a few words within a quotation, or an ellipsis with a period (. . . .) when you wish to omit the end of a sentence and resume quoting a new sentence. The MLA expects writers to use brackets [ ] around any ellipses they introduce when editing the words of someone else. Brackets indicate that what appears within them was not part of the original source, and writers may use brackets to add a word or two into a quotation that would help make the quotation clearer—for example, by identifying an unclear pronoun reference. Bracketing an ellipsis follows from the same reasoning: If you add something to a quotation, even an ellipsis indicating that you have left some words out, you should include this addition within brackets. This rule helps readers to distinguish an ellipsis that was added to a source (because it appears in brackets) from one that appeared in the original source (because it appears without brackets). It is not necessary to add an ellipsis at the beginning or end of a quotation when it is clear that the quotation itself begins in the middle of a sentence or ends before the end of a sentence:

> Adam Hochschild praises "the distinctive brilliance" of central African sculpture (73).

Or:

> Recognized for its "distinctive brilliance" (Hochschild 73), central African art can be found in major museums throughout the world.

APA PARENTHETICAL CITATIONS   Like the MLA, the APA (American Psychological Association) encourages writers to use parenthetical citations instead of footnotes or endnotes for documentation. Like the MLA, the APA also expects writers to document quotations, ideas, statistics, and facts that are not common knowledge. The most significant difference between the two styles of parenthetical citation is that, unlike MLA, which calls for the author's last name and the page number, APA calls for the author's last name and the year in which the author's work was published. There are two reasons for this: Social scientists want to see immediately how current is the research being cited, and writers in the social sciences often cite entire studies as opposed to specific passages. But when a specific passage is cited, APA-style parenthetical citation can incorporate a page reference in addition to the author's name and the year of publication.

> Good teaching requires integrity and emotional commitment (Palmer, 1998).

Or:

> Palmer (1998) argues that good teaching requires integrity and emotional commitment.

Or:

> Palmer believes that education is fostered through the creation of a "community of truth" (1998, p. 128).

APA-STYLE REFERENCE LISTS   APA-style bibliographies are titled "References"; they include information about the sources cited in the article or book, and these sources are arranged in alphabetical order by the authors' last names. APA style observes rules for capitalization and punctuation that are quite different from those of the MLA:

- Only the first word of a book or article title (and the first word of the subtitle if there is one) is capitalized. All other words appear in lower case (unless the word would be capitalized when it is not part of a title, in which case the capital is retained).
- Article titles do not appear within quotation marks.
- The main words in a journal title (unlike an article or book title) are all capitalized.
- Books and journal titles are italicized as are some punctuation marks.

Moreover, the APA calls for using different kinds of indentation in bibliographic entries, depending upon whether a writer is submitting "copy manuscript" or "final manuscript." Copy-manuscript indentation should be used when an article or book is submitted to a publisher; final-manuscript style should be followed by students submitting a paper to a college or university professor. The following examples are indented in final-manuscript style.

Book with One Author

> Palmer, P. J. (1998). *The courage to teach: Exploring the inner landscape of a teacher's life.* San Francisco: Jossey-Bass.

First and middle names are indicated only by initials. Only the first word in the title and subtitle is capitalized. A colon separates the title from the subtitle. When the state of publication is unclear, add it after the city: Bakersfield, CA, but not San Francisco, CA.

Book with Two or More Authors

> Belenky, M. F., Clinchy, B. M., Goldberger, N. R., & Tarule, J. M. (1986). *Women's ways of knowing: The development of self, voice, and mind.* New York: Basic.

Place last name first for all authors, and use the ampersand (&) instead of "and."

Translated Book

> Mauss, M. (1990). *The gift: The forms and reason for exchange in archaic societies* (W. D. Halls, Trans.). New York: Norton. (Original work published 1922)

In this case, the English translation was published long after the work was published in its original language.

Article in a Scholarly Journal

> Connors, G. L., & Walitzer, K. S. (2001). Reducing alcohol consumption among heavily drinking women: Evaluating the contributions of life skills training and booster sessions. *Journal of Consulting and Clinical Psychology, 69,* 447–456.

Capitalization of journal titles differs from capitalization of book and article titles. Quotation marks are not used around the article title. Continuous underlining links the volume number to the journal title. If citing from a journal in which each issue begins with page 1, add the issue number within parentheses immediately after the volume number, but do not underline the issue number: 27 (3).

Article in a Magazine

> Denny, M. (2001, May). The rewards of chance. *Natural History, 110,* 75–82.

The month is inserted after the year. In this case, the magazine is published monthly. If citing from a magazine published weekly, add the day listed on the issue: (2002, March 14).

Article in an Anthology

> Delacour, J. (1996). A model of the brain and the memory system. In H. L. Roitblat & J. Meyer (Eds.) *Comparative approaches to cognitive science* (pp. 305–327). Cambridge: MIT.

A period follows the article title but not the book title. In this case, the anthology has two editors. When an anthology has a single editor, use the abbreviation *Ed.* instead of *Eds.*

→ *Web Site*

> *Eating Disorders Awareness and Prevention Home Page* (September 6, 2001). Seattle: Eating Disorders Awareness and Prevention, Inc. Retrieved September 10, 2001 from the World Wide Web: *http://www.edap.org/*

When an author is not identified, begin with the title followed by the date of posting or the most recent update. (In the above example, words after the first are capitalized because they are part of a name that would be capitalized outside a title.) Provide the name of the sponsoring organization even if this repeats information in the title. Provide the date you used this site, and conclude with the URL (which is not followed by a period). When an author is identified, use the following pattern: author/date/title/city of publication/sponsoring organization/date of access/electronic address.

For an example of an APA-style article, see "Privacy, the Workplace, and the Internet" by Seumas Miller and John Weckert (pages 563–577).

In addition to providing examples of MLA and APA style, this book also includes examples of Chicago-style endnotes in Iris Chang's "The Nanking Safety Zone" (pages 167–198) and Barbie Zelizer's "Conveying Atrocity in Image" (pages 428–439). A full discussion of these three styles can be found in the manuals published by the Modern Language Association, the American Psychological Association, and the University of Chicago, all of which are included in the list on pages 37–38.

Commonly Asked Questions

When you are getting ready to submit a college paper for evaluation, one of the following questions may occur to you. The answer may appear on your assignment sheet, or your instructor may answer in class or by e-mail. The responses provided below, however, can help you to make appropriate decisions on your own.

→ **DO I NEED A TITLE PAGE?** Different instructors have different expectations, so you would be wise to learn if the instructor for whom you are writing a paper has a preference. But the Modern Language Association does not require a title page, recommending instead that students place all the information that would appear on such a page on the first page of the paper (see Figure 2). The American Psychological Association does recommend the use of a title page (see Figure 3), which can be modified if you are writing a paper for any course in which the instructor requires a title page. (*The Chicago Manual of Style* advises editors how to design the title page of a book, but it does not address how to submit a college paper).

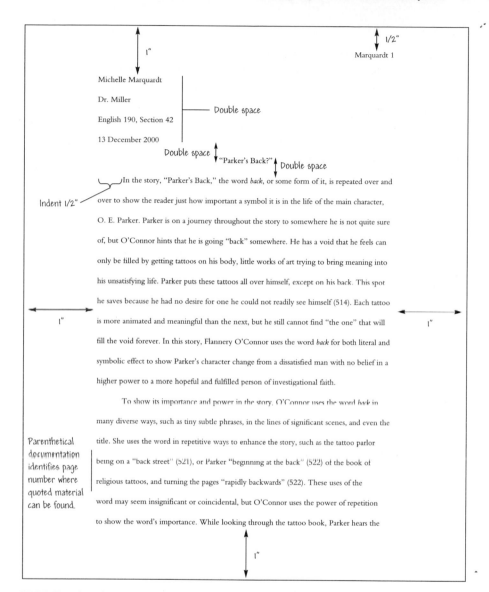

1"

1/2"

Marquardt 1

Michelle Marquardt

Dr. Miller

English 190, Section 42 ———— Double space

13 December 2000

Double space "Parker's Back?" Double space

Indent 1/2" In the story, "Parker's Back," the word *back*, or some form of it, is repeated over and

over to show the reader just how important a symbol it is in the life of the main character,

O. E. Parker. Parker is on a journey throughout the story to somewhere he is not quite sure

of, but O'Connor hints that he is going "back" somewhere. He has a void that he feels can

only be filled by getting tattoos on his body, little works of art trying to bring meaning into

his unsatisfying life. Parker puts these tattoos all over himself, except on his back. This spot

he saves because he had no desire for one he could not readily see himself (514). Each tattoo

1" is more animated and meaningful than the next, but he still cannot find "the one" that will 1"

fill the void forever. In this story, Flannery O'Connor uses the word *back* for both literal and

symbolic effect to show Parker's character change from a dissatisfied man with no belief in a

higher power to a more hopeful and fulfilled person of investigational faith.

To show its importance and power in the story, O'Connor uses the word *back* in

many diverse ways, such as tiny subtle phrases, in the lines of significant scenes, and even the

Parenthetical documentation identifies page number where quoted material can be found. title. She uses the word in repetitive ways to enhance the story, such as the tattoo parlor

being on a "back street" (521), or Parker "beginning at the back" (522) of the book of

religious tattoos, and turning the pages "rapidly backwards" (522). These uses of the

word may seem insignificant or coincidental, but O'Connor uses the power of repetition

to show the word's importance. While looking through the tattoo book, Parker hears the

1"

FIGURE 2. First page of an MLA-style paper

→ **DOES IT MATTER WHAT FONT I USE OR HOW LARGE MY MARGINS ARE?** Academic papers should have a clear, professional appearance. Use a standard font such as Courier or Times New Roman, and avoid unusual fonts like Script or Gothic. Font size should be neither too small to be easily readable nor so large that you end up looking as if you were trying to fill space. An 11- or 12-point font is usually acceptable.

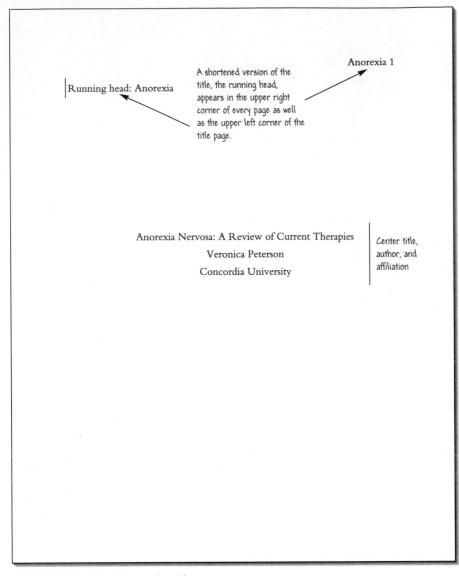

FIGURE 3. An APA-style title page

In both MLA-style and APA-style papers, set your margins for one inch at the top and bottom of each page and on both sides of the text. The page number appears at the right margin, one-half inch from the top.

In addition, be sure to double-space your paper. Double-spacing helps readers follow your text and allows room for writing comments.

↝ **CAN I USE THE FIRST PERSON?** The most likely answer is a clear "probably." Like any other writing decision, choosing whether or not to write in the first person should be informed by your purpose, topic, audience, and context. Doing so is natural when writing to understand experience (Chapter 1). And the first person can also be useful when fulfilling the other motives for writing discussed in this book. For example, you will find that Rebecca Solnit, Eric Schlosser, Elizabeth Kolbert, and Jennifer Eagan all use the first person to some extent when writing to report information (see Chapter 2), because it helps readers see how they obtained the information in question—as when they interviewed people. A restaurant review like Dara Moskowitz's "The Sad Comedy of Really Bad Food" (Chapter 4) also uses the first person appropriately: Readers expect the reviewer to tell them what food she ate and what she thought of the service. And in arguments such as "Letter from Birmingham Jail" (Chapter 7), personal experience is a key source, so once again the use of the first person is appropriate.

As a rule, *I* sounds friendlier and less stuffy than *one*. But it should not be overused. One reason instructors sometimes discourage the use of the first person is that inexperienced writers include phrases such as "I think," "I feel," or "I believe" in dozens of sentences when the information is redundant: If it is your paper, your audience will assume that the ideas in it are your own. Nevertheless, these phrases can play a useful role in helping you to distinguish your own views from the views of others you are including in your work: "Although John Anderson argues that the Electoral College should be abolished, I believe that we should retain it." When you use the first person in drafting, consider, when revising, whether each use is justified and if any can be omitted.

If you find yourself in a writing situation in which you have been told not to use the first person, you can avoid it from the moment you begin the draft. On the other hand, you might find it easier to use the first person when drafting and then delete it when revising. Although this practice may seem like extra work, it could help you to draft quickly and to convey your thoughts in your own voice. That voice may still linger in the paper once you have deleted the first person. If you draft as if you were a faceless member of some impersonal organization, you may end up sounding unnecessarily dry and remote.

■■■■ A FINAL NOTE

Additional advice about writing is provided in the introductions to each of the following ten chapters. Do not be overwhelmed by the advice in these introductions or in the introductory material you have just read. No one expects you to become a perfect writer by the end of the semester. Writing well is a lifelong challenge. The immediate challenge, the one confronting you in the weeks ahead, is to understand the principles that can help you become the best writer you can be. Although these principles can be studied in the abstract, they are best understood through examples and practice. If you want to write well, you must be prepared to write often and to appraise your work critically. You must also be prepared to read often and to think critically about what you read. The essays, articles, stories, and poems collected in this book offer you an opportunity to exercise your reading and thinking skills, and they will introduce you to authors and topics you may want to read more of in the future.

1

Writing to Understand Experience

When you write to understand experience, you do not settle for simply recording what has happened to you. Instead, you draw upon that record to examine the significance of what happened. The writers in this chapter draw upon memories to help them understand who they are, how they became that way, what they like, or what they want. Because they are writing about their own lives, they all use the first person—as you are likely to do when you write about your own experience. But although they are writing about themselves, they are not writing for themselves alone. They are also writing to share their experience with readers. Writing to understand experience thus achieves at least two goals: Writers come to a better understanding of themselves, and readers come to understand experience different from their own.

In addition to generating reflections about the past, writing to understand experience can also prompt writers to reflect on what their present lives are like: what they enjoy, dislike, or fear. In this chapter, essays such as "Levi's" by Marilyn Schiel and "Life with Father" by Itabari Njeri illustrate how writers sometimes seek to understand the past. Others, like "Grub" by Scott Russell Sanders and "Sweet Chariot" by Mark Doty, move back and forth between the past and the present, using the past to understand what is happening in the present. Like these writers, you will usually have a range of options when writing to understand experience.

GAINING PERSPECTIVE

When choosing a topic, recognize that writing to understand experience requires effort. During or immediately after an experience, we seldom know what its implications will be or why we acted in a particular way. Distance, the passage of time, is essential. Distance enables Itabari Njeri, for example, to understand why her father was often angry and sometimes brutal. Writing about a current romance may allow you to vent your feelings, but you could easily find yourself unable to move beyond the expression of these feelings. You might, however, write successfully about a former romance if you have the distance necessary to understand it and the discipline to make the effort. Writing to understand experience relies on thought and reflection more than on emotion and confession. Thinking can be difficult when your heart is full.

Your motive for such thinking and writing is to discover something rather than to report something you knew before you began to write. The act of writing will generate insight. Do not suppose, however, that writing to understand experience means finding a truth that is conveniently stored somewhere in your head, some secret knowledge that, once uncovered, will explain everything you want to understand. Writing often leads to new perceptions. If you write thoughtfully about experience, you will be constructing knowledge as you proceed.

As you prepare to write about experience, remember that you can achieve a unique perspective. No one else can know exactly what you know. What you discover and how much you tell are your choice, though. Take some risks, but do not think that you have to confess all. What ultimately matters is the degree of insight you achieve through writing and the clarity with which you convey that insight to readers—not the degree to which you reveal your personal life. To a large extent, the topic matters less than what you do with it.

As an essay like Marilyn Schiel's "Levi's" suggests, a thoughtful writer can write meaningfully about a topic as apparently simple as a pair of used jeans. Most people would think, "What could be simpler than that?" And inexperienced writers might not even consider writing on such a topic, because they have convinced themselves that writers need extraordinary material in order to be interesting. But interest is something the writer creates. Some writers are capable of making the extraordinary seem boring; others help us see what is wonderful about the ordinary. In Schiel's hands, the memory of a pair of jeans becomes a vehicle for understanding her life. With a good eye for detail, Schiel helps readers to visualize triple-roll cuffs with sidewalk burns, real pockets marked with metal rivets, and a difficult-to-manage button fly. But by the time we finish the essay, we can see what Schiel was like, what her brother was like, and what her mother was like. We also come away understanding something of what it meant to grow up in the 1950s. Another writer could address much more personal material without reaching a better understanding of experience.

GETTING STARTED

Although some people are more reflective than others, most people spend at least some time trying to figure out reasons for the things they have done or felt. For instance, suppose you do not drink alcohol and that this principle normally governs your conduct. But at a party one evening, you decide to take a drink that someone offers you. Then you take another. You lose control of yourself, feel ill the next morning, and wonder why you engaged in behavior you carefully avoided in the past. You may also wonder who saw you when the alcohol had taken effect and what they thought of you. Attempting to answer such questions can motivate writing to understand experience.

The answer to the first question, "Why did I do it?" may lead you to make discoveries about yourself by looking inward and examining your feelings and ideas. Marilyn Schiel illustrates this approach as she writes to express why acquiring a pair of blue jeans was so important to her when she was a little girl. The answer to the second question, "Who saw me do it?" may lead you to understand experience by seeing yourself through the eyes of others. Scott Russell Sanders uses the second approach when, as he is leaving a restaurant, he speculates about another customer:

> She might figure me for a carpenter, noticing my beard, the scraggly hair down over my collar, my banged-up hands, my patched jeans, my flannel shirt the color of the biscuits I just ate, my clodhopper boots. Or maybe she'll guess mechanic, maybe garbageman, electrician, janitor, maybe even farmer.

In addition to trying to see yourself as others see you, you can move beyond yourself by focusing on how something (or someone) has helped make you the person you have become or led you to do something that you might not have done. In this chapter, Gloria Naylor explores how her understanding of language evolved through experience, and Mark Doty explores how his childhood religious experience helps him understand why he feels that he "cannot be queer in church." You might also look for parallels between what you see in the world around you and how you perceive yourself. Annie Dillard engages in this kind of exploration when she reflects on an unexpected encounter with a weasel while she is out for a walk. Similarly, Edward Hoagland draws upon his experience living in a remote part of Vermont to understand why he benefits from living simply and close to nature.

Search through your memories to find experiences that have made you the way you are. Perhaps you can pull them together to show, for instance, the development of an interest in art or how travel made you more tolerant of other people's customs. Or you might explore why you have lost interest in something that once mattered to you, or why have grown away from a person to whom you were once close.

Another possibility is to explore the significance of behavior with which you are content. For example, if you enjoy getting up earlier than most people, you might explore how early rising affects you. This is the approach Edward Hoagland takes when he explores his relationship to the part of Vermont in which he has chosen to live. Alternatively, you might write about a habit you would like to change. Have your friends complained that you always interrupt them? You might want to explore that behavior to see when you began it, why you do it, and what it says about you.

For other ideas, look at the beginnings of the essays in this chapter. For example, Scott Russell Sanders tells us that he was inspired by a newspaper report that "Indiana leads the nation in fat." Perhaps your own reading—of a newspaper, magazine, or novel, or an essay in this chapter—will prompt reflections that inspire you to write to understand experience. Or you may find inspiration in a film, play, or television program that provokes a strong personal response.

Conversations, too, may generate topics for essays about experience. If you've ever said something you later regretted or played a conversation over in your mind, you may have the beginnings of an essay. Gloria Naylor's essay, for example, can be traced back to a kind of conversation—the first time she heard a disturbing term spoken to her with contempt. Similarly, Mark Doty draws upon the memory of sermons he listened to as a child: He hears certain words spoken and then responds to them later in his life. When you talk to a friend about some event that has left you feeling uneasy, you may discover that you have more to say than you realized. The give-and-take of conversation may lead to a clearer understanding of what you are talking about. Consider writing to understand experience as a way to continue such a conversation—or even to initiate it.

FOCUSING AND ARRANGING IDEAS

Essayists usually focus on something specific because they are working on a small canvas. In this chapter, Marilyn Schiel focuses on a pair of blue jeans, Scott Russell Sanders on a meal, Itabari Njeri on her father, Gloria Naylor on a word, and Annie Dillard on an encounter with a wild animal. Mark Doty, in contrast, focuses initially on religious experiences that helped shape his childhood, then on his current attitude towards the church, and then on memories of his recently deceased partner—multiple foci that he draws together at the end of his piece. His work, which he composed as the opening chapter to a book, demonstrates how experienced writers sometimes choose to break with convention.

When writing an essay of your own, however, you will almost always benefit from making your focus specific. You are more likely to write in depth and say something meaningful when you have discussed a specific topic and remained focused on it. Consider, for example, how much Dillard conveys about encountering a weasel while out for a walk one evening. An essay of similar length that tried to address all the animals she has seen would lack the depth and intensity she achieves in "Living Like Weasels."

But having a clear focus does not mean that you must limit yourself to a single memory in an essay about experience. Recording one memory can sometimes lead to another. When this happens, you should feel free to tie one memory to another. Writing to understand experience can become a voyage of self-discovery that takes you far away from where you began. A short essay, however, does not afford room for every memory that occurs to you. If you find yourself wanting to move from one memory to another, ask yourself if they are closely related or if you are being lured away from your original focus by material that might best be saved for another occasion. (If they are not closely related, you might jot the extra one in your journal or notebook to use another time.)

Two of the works in this chapter demonstrate how writers can include more than one memory without losing their focus. In "Life with Father," Itabari Njeri records several closely related memories of her father as she seeks to understand the experience of growing up in the same apartment with him. More ambitiously, Mark Doty links memories of his grandmother and his religious background with memories of the partner who had recently died. Ultimately, these seemingly different memories come together as he focuses on understanding the nature of desire.

In an essay of your own, you might start in the middle of a story—if the middle provides an opening that would attract the readers' attention—and then go back to the beginning before finishing with the conclusion. There is no single method of organization that works all the time. But if you are new to writing or worried about keeping your ideas organized, take your lead from Marilyn Schiel, Annie Dillard, and Mark Doty, all of whom arrange events in chronological order as they try to understand the nature of these events.

Moreover, keep in mind three principles when planning how to share a memory with readers:

- Give readers a clear indication of when your memories are located in time.

- Remember that your own experience is different from the experiences of your audience. References to people or places that seem clear to you may not be clear to readers. When you prepare to revise what you have drafted, read as if you are a member of your audience, and clarify any references that seem unclear.

- Whether you are writing chronologically or moving backward and forward in time for dramatic effect, save a strong scene for the ending so your essay does not trail off after reaching an early climax.

You may already have used writing to understand experience, or you may have convinced yourself long ago that writing about your personal experience is something you want to avoid. If you are uncomfortable writing about yourself, you can write meaningfully about the experiences of other people if you have been paying attention to lives other than your own. For example, you could write to enrich your understanding of someone you know well by writing about that person's character or behavior, as Itabari Njeri does when writing about her father or Mark Doty when writing about his grandmother. Both of these writers also write about themselves, but you could choose to focus exclusively on another person. Consider also how Gloria Naylor focuses on the use of language and how Edward Hoagland focuses on his relationship to the environment. In both cases, we get a sense of the writers' values, yet the focus is not on the writers themselves but on parts of the world in which they live.

Once again, don't assume that an essay about experience must be deeply personal. Some of the best essays examine life from a distance. If you watch television talk shows, you may get the misguided impression that discussion of experience must deal with sexual abuse, dysfunctional families, or chemical dependency. An inexperienced writer who attempts to discuss such intimate material may subsequently regret what she or he has revealed to others. Remember that an evocative essay can be written about nothing more intimate than a pair of Levi's or a walk by a pond. You are the best judge of what is significant to you, and you are ultimately responsible for what you decide to share with others. The challenge is to convey significant experience—be it large or small—without embarrassing yourself or your readers.

LEVI'S

Marilyn Schiel

In "Levi's," Marilyn Schiel paints a picture of the past that focuses on a pair of blue jeans. Think about how the clothes people wear help determine what acts they perform—what they can and cannot do. As you read, ask yourself why the Levi's were so important to Schiel. What would they enable her to do? If you have seen reruns of such TV series as "Leave It to Beaver" or "Father Knows Best," you have some knowledge of American values in the fifties and early sixties. Draw on what you know of that era so that you can locate Schiel's memoir in a context of time and place.

Schiel is a high school English teacher in Stevens Point, Wisconsin. She wrote this essay for a writing course when working for her Masters degree in the late 1980s. It was first published in 1992.

They weren't boot cut, or spiked leg, or 501. They weren't stone washed, or acid bleached, or ice black. They weren't Guess, or Zena, or Jordache. They were just blue jeans—old, worn Levi's.

My ten-year-old brother wore blue jeans. I wore slacks. In summer, cotton pastel pants with embroidered bunnies or ducks. In winter, grey corduroys with girl-pink flannel lining. I wanted to wear blue jeans.

As a five-year-old I didn't understand the difference between cause and coincidence. My brother's jeans meant he could wander his two-wheel bike blocks from home after school; he could, with a crew of blue-jeaned boys, build a tree house in the oak in the vacant lot next door; he could carry a BB gun all the way to the cemetery to shoot at squirrels. I had to be content triking my embroidered bunnies up and down the driveway; I had to settle for building domino houses on the living room floor; I could shoot only caps at imaginary black-hatted cowboys in the basement. I wanted to wear blue jeans.

But little girls in my 1950 world didn't wear blue jeans. Big girls didn't wear them either. Big girls didn't even wear pastel cotton slacks or winter corduroys. At least my mother, the big girl I knew best, didn't. When the family gathered for breakfast, seven days a week sharp at 7:30, Mom was already in uniform, a shirtwaist dress garnished with a colored, beaded necklace that matched clip-on earrings. By the 1960s June Cleaver may have been an anachronism, but in the early 1950s she lived at my house.

Mothers stayed home. Unlike dads, mothers didn't work. Mothers made the beds, cooked the meals, cleaned the house, baked the cookies, tended the garden, canned the vegetables, squeezed the clothes through the wringer-washer, hung washed clothes to dry on lines strung through the basement, ironed everything—including sheets and towels—scrubbed the floors while 5 kneeling on pink rubber pads, walked seven blocks pulling an empty Red-flyer wagon to buy groceries, struggled seven blocks home with a week's worth of carefully budgeted supplies, and picked out the clothes their children would wear. My brother got blue jeans. I got embroidered bunnies.

Then, in 1953, my world changed. Elvis took us all to Heartbreak Hotel; Eisenhower brought us home from Korea; and my mother went to work. The hardware store Dad bought pulled Mom from the home to the business. Her transition from the breadbaker to a breadwinner taught my mother that women, big or little, didn't have to wear embroidered bunnies anymore.

The change was more evolutionary than revolutionary. She still wore the housewife uniform—but now she wore it to work. She still did the laundry, but now with an automatic washing machine and electric dryer. We still ate breakfast together at 7:30, but now cereal and milk replaced eggs and bacon. The ironing went out every Tuesday night to a house on the hill behind the railroad tracks and came back folded every Wednesday evening. And as a businesswoman, my mother discovered that sometimes function was more important than fashion, at least for little girls.

Those old, worn Levi's of my brother's met the expectations of the advertisements. They survived an entire season of his hard wear and, unlike most of his clothes, were outgrown before worn out. And as mother used to say about anything that might be salvaged for use, "These old pants still have a little life left in them."

Not only did they have some life left in them, but they were going to give that life to me. A year earlier they would have been boxed with other we-don't-want-them-anymore clothes for the "naked children" of some foreign country I'd never heard of or, if the postage wasn't too expensive, shipped off to my poor cousins in South Dakota. With her newfound economic acumen and with her slowly evolving awareness of a woman's place, my mother looked at those blue jeans differently than she would have the year before. Maybe she looked at me a little differently, too.

"Marilyn, come here," she called from my brother's room. That in itself 10 tripped anticipation. Now that Bob was approaching adolescence, his room held the mystery earned of secrecy. The door to his room was open; my mother leaned over the bed folding and sorting boy-clothes. Shirts in one stack, pants in another, worn to see-through-thin garments in still a third pile. But smoothed out full length along the edge of Bob's bed were a pair of old, worn Levi's.

"Here, try these on." She held them up against my seven-year-old middle. "I think these will fit you if you roll up the legs."

And fit they did, more like a gunnysack than a glove, but they were blue jeans and they were my brother's—and they were now mine. Cinched tightly with an Indian-beaded belt scrounged from my brother's dresser, the chamois-soft denim bunched in unplanned pleats at my waist. No more sissy elastic for me. Triple-roll cuffs still scuffed the ground by my shoe heels when I walked—my excuse for the swaggering steps those Levi's induced. After a time sidewalk burns frayed the bottom edge, finally denoting my singular ownership. Metal rivets marked the pockets and seam overlaps. Gone were the telltale girl-white overstitching outlines. And those pockets. Real pockets. Not that patch pocket pretend stuff of girl-pants, but deep inside pockets of white, soft, gather-in-my-fist material that could be pulled inside out in search of the disappeared dime.

But those Levi's marked more than my move from little-girl clothes to big-brother clothes. Indeed, they were the only hand-me-downs ever handed down. Instead, those old ratty pants marked my move to freedom, freedom from the conventional girl-stuff my mother had so carefully fostered only one year earlier. Maybe my mother—who was learning the difference between roofing nails and wood screws, who was learning to mix paint in the vise-gripping shake-machine bolted to the floor in the back room of the hardware store, who would later teach me to cut glass, make keys, and clean Surge milk pumpers—wanted me to know what she was learning about women's work and men's work. I don't know. I just know that those Levi's—old, worn, with a difficult-to-manage button fly—meant the world to me, at least the limited world offered by my neighborhood.

The next summer I got my first two-wheeled bike, a full-size, blue, fat-tire Schwinn off the store's showroom floor. It was mother who convinced Dad that I didn't need training wheels. "If you want her to learn to ride, put her on it and let her ride." Oh, I dented the fenders some that summer and suffered some scars from the inescapable tip-overs, but I learned to ride as well as the boys. And by the end of the summer, Mom was packing peanut butter sandwiches for me to take on fishing expeditions down at the Chippewa River below the railroad trestle.

Along with the traditional dolls and play cookware, Christmas Eve brought chemistry kits and carpenter tools. Even my brother acknowledged my newfound worldliness. Better than any gift were the after-school hours spent helping him rebuild an old auto engine in the basement. I didn't do much, but watching him work and occasionally fetching wrenches taught me where pistons went and what they did, and that my big brother didn't mind having me around.

By junior high, I had my own .22. Our family Sundays in the fall found three of us in the woods searching for squirrel. My brother elected to hunt a more dangerous game, senior high school girls. Dad wore that goofy brown billed hat with cold-weather earflaps; I wore wool side-zipping slacks from the juniors department at Daytons, topped by a crew-neck matching sweater—style in a seventh-grade girl mattered even in the woods; Mom wore a turtleneck under one of Dad's wool shirt-jacs pulled out to hang over her blue jeans—old, worn Levi's.

QUESTIONS FOR DISCUSSION

1. How does Schiel characterize her mother in this piece? What causes her mother to change? Does Schiel approve of this change?

2. Why did Schiel want to wear jeans when she was a little girl? What details in this essay help you understand her point of view?
3. The first three sentences in this essay begin with the same two words, and the fourth provides only a minor variation. What is the effect of paragraph 1? Do you note any other examples of repetition in this essay? What does repetition contribute to the essay as a whole?
4. Consider the third sentence in paragraph 5. What is the effect of conveying so much information in a single sentence?
5. In the last glimpse of herself that she provides, Schiel remembers wearing a pair of slacks from a fashionable department store rather than the jeans that once meant so much to her. What is this meant to show?

SUGGESTIONS FOR WRITING

1. Remember a favorite possession that you had when you were young. Write about that item in enough detail for readers to understand why it mattered to you.
2. Write about a time when you were denied the chance to do something because other people considered it unsuitable for your gender.
3. Write about how a difference in gender enriched or complicated your relationship with a sibling, friend, or colleague.

LINKS ■ ■ ■

■ WITHIN THE BOOK

Like Schiel, several other writers in this book challenge gender expectations. If this subject interests you, see "Tough Break" (pages 133–138) and "Women's Brains" (pages 230–235).

■ ELSEWHERE IN PRINT

Dru, Ricki. *The First Blue Jeans.* New York: Contemporary, 1987.
Friedan, Betty. *The Feminine Mystique.* 1963. New York: Dell, 1984.
Goodwin, Doris Kearns. *Wait Till Next Year: A Memoir.* New York: Simon, 1997.
Kaledin, Eugenia. *Daily Life in the United States, 1940–1959: Shifting Worlds.* Westport: Greenwood, 2000.
Layman, Richard, ed. *American Decades, 1950–1959.* Detroit: Gale, 1994.

■ ONLINE

- American Cotton Museum
  <http://www.cottonmuseum.com>

▪ **ONLINE** *(continued)*

- The American 1950s
  <http://www.english.upenn.edu/~afilreis/50s/home.html>
- June Cleaver
  <http://www.leaveittobeaver.org>
- Levi Strauss & Co.
  <http://www.levistrauss.com/index.htm>

GRUB

Scott Russell Sanders

Distinguished Professor of English at Indiana University, where he has taught since 1971, Scott Russell Sanders is also a contributing editor to Audubon. *The author of many books and essays, he has been awarded fellowships from the Guggenheim Foundation, the National Endowment for the Arts, and the Lily Endowment, among many other awards. When describing his writing process, he observes: "Of the sentences that come to me, I wait for the one that utterly convinces me, then I wait for another and another, each building upon all that went before and preparing for all that follows, until, if I am patient and fervent and lucky enough, the lines add up to something durable and whole."*

Sanders often writes about family and community, which are among the issues you will find in the following essay. As you read it, be alert for what Sanders comes to understand as he reflects upon why he is eating an unhealthy breakfast. If you are surprised that a writer could discover something about himself by considering why he eats "slithery eggs and gummy toast," ask yourself if what you eat and where you eat it says anything about who you are.

The morning paper informs me that, once again, Indiana leads the nation in fat. The announcement from the Centers for Disease Control puts it less bluntly, declaring that in 1989 our state had the highest percentage of over-weight residents. But it comes down to the same thing: on a globe where hunger is the rule, surfeit the exception, Indiana is first in fat.

I read this news on Saturday morning at a booth in Ladyman's Cafe, a one-story box of pine and brick wedged between the Christian Science Reading Room and Bloomington Shoe Repair, half a block from the town square. It is a tick after 6 A.M. My fellow breakfasters include a company of polo-shirted Gideons clutching Bibles, a housepainter whose white trousers are speckled with the colors of past jobs, two mechanics in overalls with "Lee" and "Roy" stitched on their breast pockets, three elderly couples exchanging the glazed stares of insomniacs, and a young woman in fringed leather vest and sunglasses who is browsing through a copy of *Cosmopolitan*. Except for the young woman and me, everyone here is a solid contributor to Indiana's lead in fat. And I could easily add my weight to the crowd, needing only to give in for a few weeks to my clamorous appetite.

I check my belt, which is buckled at the fourth notch. Thirty-two inches and holding. But there are signs of wear on the third and second and first notches, tokens of earlier expansions.

The lone waitress bustles to my booth. "Whatcha need, hon?" Her permed hair is a mat of curls the color of pearls. Stout as a stevedore, purple under the eyes, puckered in the mouth, she is that indefinite age my grandmother remained for the last twenty years of her long life.

"What's good today?" I ask her.   5

"It's all good, same as every day." She tugs a pencil from her perm, drums ringed fingers on the order pad. Miles to go before she sleeps. "So what'll it be, sugar?"

I glance at the smudgy list on the chalkboard over the counter. Tempted by the biscuits with sausage gravy, by the triple stack of hotcakes slathered in butter, by the twin pork chops with hash browns, by the coconut cream pie and glazed doughnuts, I content myself with a cheese omelet and toast.

"Back in two shakes," says the waitress. When she charges away, a violet bow swings into view among her curls, the cheeriest thing I have seen so far this morning.

I buy breakfast only when I'm on the road or feeling sorry for myself. Today—abandoned for the weekend by my wife and kids, an inch of water in my basement from last night's rain, the car hitting on three cylinders—I'm feeling sorry for myself. I pick Ladyman's not for the food, which is indifferent, but for the atmosphere, which is tacky in a timeless way. It reminds me of the truck stops and railroad-car diners and jukebox cafés where my father would stop on our fishing trips thirty years ago. The oilcloth that covers the scratched Formica of the table is riddled with burns. The seat of my booth has lost its stuffing, broken down by a succession of hefty eaters. The walls, sheathed in vinyl for easy scrubbing, are hung with fifty-dollar oil paintings of covered bridges, pastures, and tree-lined creeks. The floor's scuffed linoleum reveals the ghostly print of deeper layers, material for some future archaeologist of cafés. Ceiling fans turn overhead, stirring with each lazy spin the odor of tobacco and coffee and grease.

There is nothing on the menu of Ladyman's that was not on the menus I   10
remember from those childhood fishing trips. But I can no longer order from it with a child's obliviousness. What can I eat without pangs of unease, knowing better? Not the eggs, high in cholesterol, not the hash browns, fried in oil, not the fatty sausage or bacon or ham, not the salty pancakes made with white flour or the saltier biscuits and gravy, not the lemon meringue pies in the glass case, not the doughnuts glistering with sugar, not the butter, not the whole milk.

Sipping coffee (another danger) and waiting for my consolatory breakfast, I read the fine print in the article on obesity. I learn that only thirty-two states took part in the study. Why did the other eighteen refuse? Are they embarrassed? Are they afraid their images would suffer, afraid that tourists, knowing the truth, would cross their borders without risking a meal? I learn that Indiana is actually tied for first place with Wisconsin, at 25.7 percent overweight, so we share the honors. For Wisconsin, you think of dairies, arctic winters, hibernation. But Indiana? We're leaders in popcorn. Our hot and humid summers punish even the skinny, and torture the plump. Why us? There's no comment from the Indiana Health Commissioner. This gentleman, Mr. Woodrow Myers, Jr. (who is now on his way to perform the same office in New York City), weighed over three hundred pounds at the time of his appointment. He lost more than a hundred pounds in an effort to set a healthy example, but has since gained most of it back. He doesn't have much room to talk.

My platter arrives, the waitress urging, "Eat up, hon," before she hustles away. The omelet has been made with processed cheese, anemic and slithery. The toast is of white bread that clots on my tongue. The strawberry jelly is the color and consistency of gum erasers. My mother reared me to eat whatever was put in front of me, and so I eat. Dabbing jelly from my beard with a paper napkin as thin as the pages of the Gideons' Bibles, I look around. At six-thirty this Saturday morning, every seat is occupied. Why are we all here? Why are we wolfing down this dull, this dangerous, this terrible grub?

It's not for lack of alternatives. Bloomington is ringed by the usual necklace of fast food shops. Or you could walk from Ladyman's to restaurants that serve breakfast in half a dozen languages. Just five doors away, at the Uptown Cafe, you could dine on croissants and espresso and quiche.

So why are we here in these swaybacked booths eating poorly cooked food that is bad for us? The answer, I suspect, would help to explain why so many of us are so much bigger than we ought to be. I sniff, and the aroma of grease and peppery sausage, frying eggs and boiling coffee jerks me back into the kitchen of my grandparents' farm. I see my grandmother, barefoot and bulky, mixing biscuit dough with her blunt fingers. Then I realize that everything Ladyman's serves she would have served. This is farm food, loaded with enough sugar and fat to power a body through a slogging day of work, food you could fix out of your own garden and chicken coop and pigpen, food prepared without spices or sauces, cooked the quickest way, as a woman with chores to do and a passel of mouths to feed would cook it.

"Hot up that coffee, hon?" the waitress asks.

"Please, ma'am," I say, as though answering my grandmother. On those fishing trips, my father stopped at places like Ladyman's because there he could eat the vittles he knew from childhood, no-nonsense grub he never got at home from his wife, a city woman who had studied nutrition, and who had learned her cuisine from a Bostonian mother and a Middle Eastern father. I stop at places like Ladyman's because I am the grandson of farmers, the son of a farm boy. If I went from booth to booth, interviewing the customers, most likely I would find hay and hogs in each person's background, maybe one generation back, maybe two. My sophisticated friends would not eat here for love or money. They will eat peasant food only if it comes from other countries—hummus and pita, fried rice and prawns, liver pâté, tortellini, tortillas, tortes. Never black-eyed peas, never grits, never short ribs or hush puppies or shoofly pie. This is farm food, and we who sit here and shovel it down are bound to farming by memory or imagination.

With the seasoning of memory, the slithery eggs and gummy toast and rubbery jam taste better. I lick my platter clean.

Barely slowing down as she cruises past, the waitress refills my coffee once more, the oil-slicked brew jostling in the glass pot. "Need anything else, sugar?"

My nostalgic tongue wins out over my judgment, leading me to say, "Could I get some biscuits and honey?"

15

"You sure can."   20

The biscuits arrive steaming hot. I pitch in. When I worked on farms as a boy, loading hay bales onto wagons and forking silage to cows, shoveling manure out of horse barns, digging postholes and pulling barbed wire, I could eat the pork chops and half a dozen eggs my neighbors fed me for breakfast, eat corn bread and sugar in a quart of milk for dessert at lunch, eat ham steaks and mashed potatoes and three kinds of pie for supper, eat a bowl of hand-cranked ice cream topped with maple syrup at bedtime, and stay skinny as a junkyard dog. Not so any longer. Not so for any of us. Eat like a farmer while living like an insurance salesman, an accountant, a beautician, or a truck driver, and you're going to get fat in a hurry. While true farmers have always stored their food in root cellars and silos, in smoke shacks and on canning shelves, we carry our larders with us on haunches and ribs.

The Gideons file out, Bibles under their arms, bellies over their belts.

With the last of my biscuits I mop up the honey, thinking of the path the wheat traveled from Midwestern fields to my plate, thinking of the clover distilled into honey, of grass become butter, the patient industry of cows and bees and the keepers of cows and bees. Few of us still work on the land, even here in Indiana. Few of us raise big families, few of us look after herds of animals, few of us bend our backs all day, few of us build or plow or bake or churn. Secretaries of Agriculture tell us that only four percent of our population feeds the other ninety-six percent. I have known and admired enough farmers to find that a gloomy statistic.

I am stuffed. I rise, stretch, shuffle toward the cash register. The woman in the fringed vest looks up from her *Cosmopolitan* as I pass her booth. She might figure me for a carpenter, noticing my beard, the scraggly hair down over my collar, my banged-up hands, my patched jeans, my flannel shirt the color of the biscuits I just ate, my clodhopper boots. Or maybe she'll guess mechanic, maybe garbageman, electrician, janitor, maybe even farmer.

I pluck a toothpick from a box near the cash register and idly chew on it   25
while the waitress makes change. "You hurry back," she calls after me.

"I will, ma'am," I tell her.

On the sidewalk out front of Ladyman's, I throw my toothpick in a green trash barrel that is stenciled with the motto "Fight Dirty." I start the car, wincing at the sound of three cylinders clapping. I remember yesterday's rainwater shimmering in the basement, remember the house empty of my family, who are away frolicking with relatives. Before letting out the clutch, I let out my belt a notch, to accommodate those biscuits. Thirty-three inches. One inch closer to the ranks of the fat. I decide to split some wood this morning, turn the compost from the right-hand bin to the left, lay up stones along the edge of the wildflower bed, sweat hard enough to work up an appetite for lunch.

QUESTIONS FOR DISCUSSION

1. Why is Sanders eating breakfast in a restaurant? Why has he chosen Ladyman's when he could be dining on "croissants and espresso and quiche"?

2. Why is it that Sanders hesitates to eat food he enjoys? How has his life changed since he was a young man?
3. The essay begins with what turns out to be an exaggeration about Indiana. Why do you think Sanders waits for several paragraphs before reporting more about the study first cited in paragraph 1?
4. What role does the waitress play in this essay? How does she help Sanders enjoy a bad meal?
5. Consider the description of himself that Sanders provides in paragraphs 3 and 24. Why is it misleading? What is the woman reading *Cosmopolitan* unlikely to realize?

SUGGESTIONS FOR WRITING

1. Are there any foods you enjoy even though you know they aren't good for you? Of all the things you eat, is there any food you are most likely to eat when you are alone? Write an essay about eating that will help you to understand something about yourself.
2. Visit a place that reminds you of your past. Write a description of it that will make readers understand what you see and feel when you visit there.
3. Spend some time in a coffee shop or café, recording in a journal what you witness there. Then write an essay exploring how you felt in that place and what factors contributed to that feeling.

LINKS ■ ■ ■

■ WITHIN THE BOOK

In "The Sad Comedy of Really Bad Food" (pages 293–295), Dara Moskowitz shows how a professional food critic writes about a restaurant.

■ ELSEWHERE IN PRINT

Mamet, David. *The Cabin: Reminiscence and Diversion.* New York: Turtle Bay, 1992.
Sanders, Scott Russell. *The Country of Language.* Minneapolis: Milkweed, 1999.
———. *The Force of Spirit.* Boston: Beacon, 2000.
———. *Hunting for Hope: A Father's Journey.* Boston: Beacon, 1998.
———. *The Paradise of Bombs.* Athens: U of Georgia P, 1987.
———. *Secrets of the Universe.* Boston: Beacon, 1991.

■ ONLINE

• Brief Biography
  <http://www.indiana.edu/~mfawrite/sanders.html>

■ **ONLINE** *(continued)*

- Eating in America
  <http://rcswww.urz.tu-dresden.de/~english2/food>
- Eating on the Road
  <http://www.roadfood.com>

LIFE WITH FATHER

Itabari Njeri

A graduate of the Columbia University School of Journalism, Itabari Njeri (born Jill Stacy Moreland) is a contributing editor at the Los Angeles Times Magazine. *In 1990, she won the American Book Award for her memoir* Every Good-Bye Ain't Gone: Family Portraits and Personal Escapades. *Although she has worked as a professional actress and singer as well as a journalist, she is best known for writing memoirs. When discussing the impulse to write about experience, in an interview for* Contemporary Authors, *she said: "To impose order on the chaos of memory is a universal impulse fueling the desire to write autobiography. But first and foremost, I wanted to illuminate the beauty, pain, and complexity of a particular piece of the African diaspora, a piece central to the American experience. I wanted to tell the truth and make it sing."*

Njeri discusses both race and singing in the following selection. The scene is a Harlem apartment during the mid-1960s—a time when African Americans were struggling for civil rights. The scene thus includes not only the apartment but also the era in which the author was growing up. As you read this account of family conflict, think about how racial prejudice in the world beyond the apartment can help account for the personal conflicts that happened within it.

Daddy wore boxer shorts when he worked; that's all. He'd sit for hours reading and writing at a long, rectangular table covered with neat stacks of *I. F. Stone's Weekly, The Nation, The New Republic,* and the handwritten pages of his book in progress, *The Tolono Station and Beyond.* A Mott's applesauce jar filled with Teacher's scotch was a constant, and his own forerunner of today's wine coolers was the ever-present chaser: ginger ale and Manischewitz Concord grape wine in a tall, green iced-tea glass.

As he sat there, his beer belly weighing down the waistband of his shorts, I'd watch. I don't know if he ever saw me. I hid from him at right angles. From the bend of the hallway, at the end of a long, dark, L-shaped corridor in our Harlem apartment, it was at least thirty feet to the living room where my father worked, framed by the doorway. I sat cross-legged on the cold linoleum floor and inspected his seated, six-foot-plus figure through a telescope formed by my forefinger and thumb: bare feet in thonged sandals, long hairy legs that rose toward the notorious shorts (I hated those shorts, wouldn't bring my girlfriends home because of those shorts), breasts that could fill a B cup, and a long neck on which a balding head rested. Viewed in isolation, I thought perhaps I'd see him clearer, know him better.

Daddy was a philosopher, a Marxist historian, an exceptional teacher, and a fine tenor. He had a good enough voice to be as great a concert artist as

John McCormack, one of his favorites. The obstacles to that career couldn't have been much greater than the ones he actually overcame.

The state of Georgia, where my father grew up, established its version of the literacy test in 1908, the year he was born. If you substituted Georgia for Mississippi in the story that Lerone Bennett Jr. relates in *Before the Mayflower: A History of Black America,* the main character could easily have been my father: A black teacher, a graduate of Eton and Harvard, presents himself to a Mississippi registrar. The teacher is told to read the state constitution and several books. He does. The registrar produces a passage in Greek, which the teacher reads. Then another in Latin. Then other passages in French, German, and Spanish, all of which the teacher reads. The registrar finally holds up a page of Chinese characters and asks: "What does this mean?" The teacher replies: "It means you don't want me to vote."

Apocryphal, perhaps, but the tale exemplified enough collective experi-   5
ence that I heard my father tell virtually the same story about a former Morehouse College classmate to a buddy over the phone one afternoon. At the punchline, he fell into a fit of laughter, chuckling hard into a balled fist he held at his mouth. Finally, he said, "Fred, I'll have to call you back," then fell back on the bed, in his boxer shorts, laughing at the ceiling.

He claimed he burst out laughing like this once in a class at Harvard. A law professor, discussing some constitutional issue in class, singled out my father and said, "In this matter, regarding men of your race—".

"Which race is that?" my father boomed, cutting him off, "the 50 yard or the 100?" But it seemed to me he always related that particular tale with a sneer on his lips.

He'd been at Harvard studying law on a postdoctoral scholarship from 1942 to 1943. After receiving his Ph.D. in philosophy from the University of Toronto ten years earlier, he had headed toward the dust bowls others were escaping in the mid-1930s and became the editor of a black newspaper, the *Oklahoma Eagle,* in Tulsa. He eventually returned to academia and by 1949 was the head of the philosophy department at Morgan State University in Baltimore. That's where he met my mother, a nurse many years his junior.

My mother—who commits nothing to paper, speaks of the past cryptically, and believes all unpleasantries are best kept under a rug—once leaked the fact that she and my father took me to a parade in Brooklyn when I was about three. We were standing near the arch at Grand Army Plaza when he suddenly hauled off and punched her in the mouth, with me in her arms. My mother, a very gentle and naive woman, said the whole thing left her in a state of shock. My father had never been violent before.

They separated, and I seldom saw my father again until my parents reunited   10
when I was seven. We moved into my father's six-room apartment on 129th Street, between Convent Avenue and St. Nicholas Terrace. It was certainly far more spacious than the apartment I'd lived in with my mother on St. James Place in Brooklyn. The immediate neighborhood was an attractive, hilly section

of Harlem, just a few blocks from City College. All things considered, I hated it. More precisely, I hated my father, so I hated it all.

Because of his past leftist political affiliations, Daddy had lost his government and university jobs. Now, out of necessity but also desire, he decided to devote his time to teaching younger people. He wanted to reach them at a stage in their lives when he felt he could make a difference. He joined the faculty of a Jersey City high school and began teaching journalism, history, and English. He also taught English at night to foreign-born students at City College. His students, I came to learn, loved him; his daughter found it hard to. I made the mistake of calling him Pop—once. He said, "Don't ever call me that again. If you don't like calling me Daddy, you can call me Dr. Moreland."

Once, my mother deserted me, leaving me alone with him. She went to Atlanta for several weeks with my baby brother to tend my ailing Grandma Hattie, my father's mother. Since I hadn't known this man most of my seven years on the planet, and didn't like him much now that I did, I asked him if I could stay around the corner with a family friend, Aunt Pearl. "If she asks you to stay, fine. But don't ask her," he told me. Naturally I asked her.

When he asked me if I had asked her, I hesitated. But I was not a child inclined to lie. So I said, "I don't want to lie. I asked her." I got a beating for that, a brutal beating with a belt that left welts and bruises on my legs for months.

My father felt children should be hit for any infraction. Further, they should be seen and not heard, speak only when spoken to, etc. From the day he hit me, the latter became my philosophy, too. I never consciously decided to stop speaking to my father, but for the next ten years, I rarely initiated a conversation with him. Later he would tell me, "You were a very strange child."

But if I would not accept him as a father, my curiosity would not let me 15 deny him as a teacher. One day, a question about the nature of truth compelled a thaw in my emotional cold war—nothing less could have. Truth changes, a classmate in the seventh grade had insisted that day. It is constant, I argued, and went to my father for confirmation.

People's perceptions change, I explained. New information debunks the lies of the past, but the truth was always there. And I told my father what I had told my mostly white classmates in a Bronx junior high school at the height of the civil rights movement: Black people were always human beings worthy of the same rights other Americans enjoyed, but it took hundreds of years of a slave system that dehumanized the master as well as the slave and a social revolution before most white Americans would accept that truth.

My father turned from his worktable, took off his glasses, with their broken right temple piece, and released a long and resonant "Yesssss." And then he spoke to me of a rational cosmos and what Lincoln had to do with Plato. When our philosophical discussion ended, we each went to our separate corners.

My father had a beaten, black upright piano in the parlor, badly out of tune. But its bench was a treasure of ancient sheet music: Vincent Youman's "Through the Years," with a picture of Gladys Swarthout on the frayed cover. And I loved the chord changes to "Spring Is Here."

I ventured from the sanctuary of my blue-walled room one summer after-noon, walking down the long hallway toward the kitchen, then stopped abruptly. I heard my father in the kitchen several feet away; he was making an ice-cream soda, something as forbidden to him as alcohol since he was a dia-betic. I heard the clink of a metal spoon against a glass as he sang, "For I lately took a notion for to cross the briny ocean, and I'm off to Philadelphia in the morning." It was an Irish folk song made famous by John McCormack. I backed up. Too late. He danced across the kitchen threshold in his boxer shorts, stopped when he spotted me in the shadows, then shook his head. He smiled, lifted one leg and both arms in a Jackie Gleason "and away we go" motion, then slid off.

Minutes later he called me. "Jill the Pill, you know this song!" I knew all   20
the songs and wrote down the words to "Moon River" for him. Then he asked me to sing it. I was always ready to sing, even for my father.

He sat on the edge of his bed with the lyrics in his hand as I sang. When I finished the phrase "We're after the same rainbow's end, waitin' round the bend, my huckleberry friend," my daddy looked at me and said what others would tell me years later but with far less poetry: "My girl, you have the ce-lestial vibration." And then he asked me to sing it again and told me it was "wonderful." Then I left him.

For days, maybe weeks, a tense calm would reign in the apartment. Then, without warning, the hall would fill with harsh voices. My father stood in the narrow, shadowy space hitting my mother. "Put it down," he yelled. "Put it down or I'll . . ."

My mother had picked up a lamp in a lame effort to ward off his blows. His shouting had awakened me. I'd been sick in bed with the flu and a high fever. When he saw me open my bedroom door he yelled, "Get back in your room." I did, my body overtaken by tremors and the image of my mother branded on my eyeballs. I swore that I would never let anyone do that to me or to anyone else I had the power to help. I had no power to help my mother. It was an oath with terrible consequences, one I'd have to disavow to permit myself the vulnerability of being human.

I know my father's fury was fueled by his sense of insignificance. He felt himself to be an intellectual giant boxed in by mental midgets. Unlike Ralph Ellison, Paul Robeson, or Richard Wright°—all contemporaries and acquain-tances of my father's—he was never acknowledged by the dominant culture whose recognition he sought. He could be found, Ellison once told me, pontif-icating in Harlem barbershops, elucidating the dialogues of Plato for a captive audience of draped men, held prone, each with a straight-edge razor pressed against his cheek.

Ralph Ellison: American novelist (1914–1994) best known for *The Invisible Man* (1952). *Paul Robeson:* American singer, actor, and political activist (1898–1976). *Richard Wright:* American writer (1908–1960), best known for *Native Son* (1940).

My father's unreconciled identities—the classic schizophrenia of being   25
black and an American, the contradictions of internalizing whole the cultural
values of a society that sees you, when it sees you at all, as life in one of its
lower forms—stoked his alcoholism. And since my father at once critiqued
the society that denied him and longed for its approbation, he lived with the
pain-filled consciousness of one who knows he is a joke. I think sometimes
he laughed the hardest, so often did I stumble upon him alone, chuckling into
his balled fist at some silent, invisible comedian.

When his drunken rages ended, he slept for days, spread out on the bed
wearing only his boxer shorts. I watched him on those days, too, daring to
come closer, safe with the knowledge that Morpheus° held him. I examined
his face, wondering who he was and why he was. As I watched, he'd lift his
head off the pillow, then fall back muttering: "Truth and justice will prevail."

QUESTIONS FOR DISCUSSION

1. Njeri opens her essay with a vivid description of her father sitting in his
   underpants and drinking scotch out of an applesauce jar. What do the details
   in this opening reveal, and how do they prepare for the essay that follows?
2. What makes Daddy laugh in paragraphs 4–6? Is the laughter good-humored?
3. Njeri records that she hated Daddy and "would not accept him as a
   father." Does she succeed in making this response understandable to you as
   a reader? What personal factors kept the two in "separate corners"?
4. Consider Njeri's discussion of the family violence she witnessed and experienced as a child. What does she understand now that she is an adult?
5. Does Njeri seem at all reconciled with the past she is recalling? Were you
   led to feel any sympathy for her father?
6. How do you interpret the concluding line, " 'Truth and justice will prevail' "? What does this belief say about Njeri's father? Does it have any additional significance for writers trying to understand experience?

SUGGESTIONS FOR WRITING

1. Njeri's father tells her, "You were a very strange child." Think about times
   when your behavior seemed strange to others, even though it made perfect sense to you. Write about one such time so that readers can understand what the people around you failed to grasp at the time.
2. When she was in junior high school, Njeri believed, "perceptions change
   [. . .]. New information debunks the lies of the past, but the truth was always there." Write about a person toward whom your own perceptions
   have changed as you have grown more mature. Describe that person as
   you initially saw him or her, and then record what you have since come to
   understand.

Morpheus: In Greek mythology, one of the children of Sleep.

3. Write an essay about how you have determined your race and how this racial identity has influenced your life.

LINKS ▪ ▪ ▪

▪ WITHIN THE BOOK

Martin Luther King, Jr.'s "Letter from Birmingham Jail" (pages 534–548) provides background that can help you understand the father's anger in Njeri's essay.

▪ ELSEWHERE IN PRINT

Ellison, Ralph. *Invisible Man.* 1952. New York: Vintage, 1995.
hooks, bell. *Yearning: Race, Gender, and Cultural Politics.* Boston: South End, 1990.
Njeri, Itabari. *Every Good-Bye Ain't Gone: Family Portraits and Personal Escapades.* New York: Times, 1990.
———. *The Last Plantation: Color, Conflict, and Identity: Reflections of a New York Black.* Boston: Houghton, 1997.
———. *Sushi and Grits: The Challenge of Diversity.* New York: Random, 1993.
West, Cornel. *Race Matters.* Boston: Beacon, 1993.
Wright, Richard. *Black Boy: A Record of Childhood and Youth.* 1945. New York: Harper, 1998.

▪ ONLINE

- Brief History of Harlem
  <http://www.adcorp.org/harlem.htm>
- I. F. Stone
  <http://www.spartacus.schoolnet.co.uk/USAstoneW.htm>
- Marxist History
  <http://www.academicinfo.net/poliscimarx.html>

"MOMMY, WHAT DOES 'NIGGER' MEAN?"

Gloria Naylor

Born and raised in New York City and a graduate of Brooklyn College, Gloria Naylor was inspired to write fiction after reading Toni Morrison's The Bluest Eye *in 1971, the first novel that she had read by an African-American woman and a work that she has described as "so painfully eloquent that it becomes a song." Since then, she has done graduate work in African-American studies at Yale University and has taught at the University of Pennsylvania, Princeton University, and Brandeis University, among other schools. Her novels include* The Women of Brewster Place *(1982), which won the American Book Award in 1983. She is also the founder of a multimedia production company, One Way Productions, dedicated to presenting positive images of black cultures.*

Naylor recognizes that terms such as "black" and "white" are problematic and in a lecture at Yale stated, "To be black or white in America is nothing but a political construct." In the following selection, first published by the New York Times Magazine, *Naylor explores how language is constructed and used by focusing on a term that is usually associated with racial prejudice. As she does so, drawing upon childhood memories, she shows how the meaning of a term depends upon the rhetorical situation in which it appears: who is using the word, in what context, for what purpose, and to what audience.*

Language is the subject. It is the written form with which I've managed to keep the wolf away from the door and, in diaries, to keep my sanity. In spite of this, I consider the written word inferior to the spoken, and much of the frustration experienced by novelists is the awareness that whatever we manage to capture in even the most transcendent passages falls far short of the richness of life. Dialogue achieves its power in the dynamics of a fleeting moment of sight, sound, smell and touch.

I'm not going to enter the debate here about whether it is language that shapes reality or vice versa. That battle is doomed to be waged whenever we seek intermittent reprieve from the chicken and egg dispute. I will simply take the position that the spoken word, like the written word, amounts to a nonsensical arrangement of sounds or letters without a consensus that assigns "meaning." And building from the meanings of what we hear, we order reality. Words themselves are innocuous; it is the consensus that gives them true power.

I remember the first time I heard the word "nigger." In my third-grade class, our math tests were being passed down the rows, and as I handed the papers to a little boy in back of me, I remarked that once again he had received a much lower mark than I did. He snatched his test from me and spit out that word. Had he called me a nymphomaniac or a necrophiliac, I couldn't have been more puzzled. I didn't know what a nigger was, but I knew that what-ever it meant, it was something he shouldn't have called me. This was verified when I raised my hand, and in a loud voice repeated what he had said and watched the teacher scold him for using a "bad" word. I was later to go home and ask the inevitable question that every black parent must face—"Mommy, what does 'nigger' mean?" •

And what exactly did it mean? Thinking back, I realize that this could not have been the first time the word was used in my presence. I was part of a large extended family that had migrated from the rural South after World War II and formed a close-knit network that gravitated around my maternal grandparents. Their ground-floor apartment in one of the buildings they owned in Harlem was a weekend mecca for my immediate family, along with countless aunts, uncles, and cousins who brought along assorted friends. It was a bustling and open house with assorted neighbors and tenants popping in and out to exchange bits of gossip, pick up an old quarrel or referee the ongoing checkers game in which my grandmother cheated shamelessly. They were all there to let down their hair and put up their feet after a week of labor in the factories, laundries, and shipyards of New York.

Amid the clamor, which could reach deafening proportions—two or three conversations going on simultaneously, punctuated by the sound of a baby's crying somewhere in the back rooms or out on the street—there was still a rigid set of rules about what was said and how. Older children were sent out of the living room when it was time to get into the juicy details about "you-know-who" up on the third floor who had gone and gotten herself "p-r-e-g-n-a-n-t!" But my parents, knowing that I could spell well beyond my years, always demanded that I follow the others out to play. Beyond sexual misconduct and death, everything else was considered harmless for our young ears. And so among the anecdotes of the triumphs and disappointments in the various workings of their lives, the word "nigger" was used in my presence, but it was set within contexts and inflections that caused it to register in my mind as something else.   5

In the singular, the word was always applied to a man who had distin-guished himself in some situation that brought their approval for his strength, intelligence or drive:

"Did Johnny really do that?"

"I'm telling you, that nigger pulled in $6,000 of overtime last year. Said he got enough for a down payment on a house."

When used with a possessive adjective by a woman—"my nigger"—it became a term of endearment for husband or boyfriend. But it could be more than just a term applied to a man. In their mouths it became the pure essence of manhood—a disembodied force that channeled their past history of struggle and present survival against the odds into a victorious statement of being: "Yeah, that old foreman found out quick enough—you don't mess with a nigger."

In the plural, it became a description of some group within the commu-nity that had overstepped the bounds of decency as my family defined it: 10

Parents who neglected their children, a drunken couple who fought in public, people who simply refused to look for work, those with excessively dirty mouths or unkempt households were all "trifling niggers." This particular circle could forgive hard times, unemployment, the occasional bout of depression—they had gone through all of that themselves—but the unforgivable sin was lack of self-respect.

A woman could never be a "nigger" in the singular, with its connotation of confirming worth. The noun "girl" was its closest equivalent in that sense, but only when used in direct address and regardless of the gender doing the addressing. "Girl" was a token of respect for a woman. The one-syllable word was drawn out to sound like three in recognition of the extra ounce of wit, nerve or daring that the woman had shown in the situation under discussion.

"G-i-r-l, stop. You mean you said that to his face?"

But if the word was used in a third-person reference or shortened so that it almost snapped out of the mouth, it always involved some element of communal disapproval. And age became an important factor in these exchanges. It was only between individuals of the same generation, or from an older person to a younger (but never the other way around), that "girl" would be considered a compliment.

I don't agree with the argument that use of the word "nigger" at this social stratum of the black community was an internalization of racism. The dynamics were the exact opposite: The people in my grandmother's living room took a word that whites used to signify worthlessness or degradation and rendered it impotent. Gathering there together, they transformed "nigger" to signify the varied and complex human beings they knew themselves to be. If the word were to disappear totally from the mouths of even the most liberal of white society, no one in that room was naïve enough to believe it would disappear from white minds. Meeting the word head-on, they proved it had absolutely nothing to do with the way they were determined to live their lives.

So there must have been dozens of times that the word "nigger" was *15* spoken in front of me before I reached the third grade. But I didn't "hear" it until it was said by a small pair of lips that had already learned it could be a way to humiliate me. That was the word I went home and asked my mother about. And since she knew that I had to grow up in America, she took me in her lap and explained.

QUESTIONS FOR DISCUSSION

1. What two motives led Naylor to become a writer?
2. How does Naylor describe her family background? Why is it relevant to the question she is exploring in this essay?
3. How many different meanings of *nigger* does Naylor provide in this essay? Why is it that the word can be understood only in the context in which it is used and the inflection with which it is spoken? What elements of the

situation described in paragraph 3 alerted Naylor to the use of a "bad word" before the teacher confirms that she had been insulted?

4. What does Naylor mean when she writes that some people consider the use of *nigger* by blacks to be "an internalization of racism"? Why does she believe that it shows the opposite?

5. Consider the final paragraph of this essay. What does the last sentence imply?

SUGGESTIONS FOR WRITING

1. Identify another word that can be either insulting or affectionate depending on how it is used. Explore what the varied meanings of your term reveal about the people who use it.

2. According to an expression known to many children, "Sticks and stones can break your bones, but words can never hurt you." Is this true? Write an essay exploring the extent to which words can cause injury.

3. Write an essay focused on a lesson about language you learned as a child and whether or not you have chosen to honor that lesson as an adult.

LINKS ▪ ▪ ▪

▪ WITHIN THE BOOK

Racism is also the focus of selections by Stuart Taylor, Jr. (pages 524–527), Martin Luther King, Jr. (pages 534–548), and Audre Lorde (pages 712–713).

▪ ELSEWHERE IN PRINT

Naylor, Gloria. *Bailey's Café.* New York: Harcourt, 1992.
———. *Linden Hills.* New York: Ticknor, 1985.
———. *Mama Day.* New York: Ticknor, 1988.
——— *The Women of Brewster Place.* New York: Viking, 1982.
Pemberton, Gayle. *The Hottest Water in Chicago: On Family, Race, Time, and American Culture.* Boston: Faber, 1992.

▪ ONLINE

▪ Anti-Defamation League
<http://www.adl.org>

▪ Online *Oxford English Dictionary* Entry for "Nigger"
<http://www.english.uiuc.edu/fontenot/259/nigger.htm>

▪ The Unofficial Gloria Naylor Pages
<http://www.lythastudios.com/gnaylor>

EARTH'S EYE

Edward Hoagland

Born in New York City, educated at Harvard, and a member of the American Academy of Arts and Letters, Edward Hoagland has been writing about nature since, at the age of nine, he composed a poem about a frog. The author of many works about the outdoors, including several volumes of essays, he also edited the twenty-nine–volume Penguin Nature Library. "Nature writing," he notes, "is biology with love." A long-term resident of Vermont, where he teaches at Bennington College, Hoagland often explores the contrast between rural and urban experience.

The following essay was first published in 1999 by Sierra, *a monthly magazine committed to the advancement of policies that preserve the American environment. Its title refers to ponds. As you read "Earth's Eye," note how Hoagland links ponds to other parts of the environment that he wants to honor.*

Water is our birthplace. We need and love it. In a bathtub, or by a lake or at the sea, we go to it for rest, refreshment, and solace. "I'm going to the water," people say when August comes and they crave a break. The sea is a democracy, so big it's free of access, often a bus or subway ride away, a meritocracy, sink or swim, and yet a swallower of grief because of its boundless scale—beyond the horizon, the home of icebergs, islands, whales. Tears alone are a mysterious, magisterial solvent that bring a smile, a softening of hard thoughts, lend us a merciful and inexpensive respite, almost like half an hour at the beach. In any landscape, in fact, a pond or creek catches and centers our attention as magnetically as if it were, in Thoreau's phrase, "earth's eye."

Lying on your back in deep meadow grass facing a bottomless sky is less focusing, but worth a drive of many hours, as weekend traffic will attest. Yet the very dimensions of the sky, which are unfathomable after the early surge of pleasure that they carry, cause most of us to mitigate their power with preoccupations such as golf or sunbathing as soon as we get outdoors. That sense of first principles can be unnerving, whereas the ground against our backs—if we lie gazing up into the starry night or a piebald day—is seething with groping roots and sprouting seeds and feels like home, as the friendliest dappled clouds can't be. Beyond the prettiest azure blue is black, as nightfall will remind us, and when the day ends, cold is the temperature of black.

A pond, though, is a gentle spot (unless you are Ophelia°). Amber- or pewter-colored, it's a drinking fountain for scurrying raccoons and mincing deer, a waterbugs' and minnows' arena for hunting insect larvae, a holding pen

---

Ophelia: A character in *Hamlet* who drowns herself in a pond.

for rain that may coalesce into ocean waves next year. Mine flows into the St. Lawrence River. I live in Vermont and spent a hundred dollars once to bulldoze a tadpole pond next to my little stretch of stream. A silent great blue heron, as tall as a Christmas tree, and a castanet-rattling kingfisher, a faster flier and brighter blue, showed up to forage for amphibians the next year. Garter snakes also benefited from the occasional meal of a frog, and a red-tailed hawk, cruising by, might grab a snake or frog. More exciting, a bull moose began using it as a hot-weather wallow, soaking for half an hour, mouthing algae, munching sedges, and browsing the willows that lean from the bank. A beaver cut down some poplar saplings to gnaw and stitch into a dam for creating a proper flow, but the depth remained insufficient to withstand a New England winter, so he retreated downstream to a wetland in my woods.

I bought this land for eighty-five dollars an acre in 1969, and today a comparable hideaway would probably still cost no more than about the price of a good car. We're not talking luxury: As with so much of life, your priorities are what count, and what you wish to protect and pay attention to. I've been a sinner in other ways, but not in this respect.

Remoteness bestows the amenity of uninterrupted sleep. No telephone or electric line runs by, and the hikers and pickups are gone by sunset. When the season of extravagant daylight shortens so I can't simply sleep from dusk to dawn, I light candles or kerosene, but in balmy weather I can nap with equal ease at any hour in the meadow too, or watch the swallows and dragonflies hawk after midges, as the breezes finger me and a yellowthroat hops in the bushes to eat a daddy long-legs. At dark the bats hawk for bugs instead, or an owl hunts, all wings, slow and mothlike, till it sees a rodent. The trees hang over a swimming hole nearby, with a dovish or a moonlit sky showing beyond the leaves like a kind of vastly enlarged swimming hole, until I feel I was born floating in both the water and the air. It's a hammock all the more beguiling because if you relax too much while swimming and let yourself sink, you might conceivably drown. Similarly, in the meadow, if you lazed too late into the fall, woolgathering, snow could fill your mouth.

Nature is not sentimental. The scenery that recruits our spirits in temperate weather may turn unforgiving in the winter. It doesn't care whether we love it and pay the property taxes to save it from development, having walked over it yard by yard in clement conditions. When the birds flee south and other creatures, from bears to beetles, have crawled underground to wait out the cold, we that remain have got to either fish or cut bait: burn some energy in those summer-lazy muscles cutting wood, or take some money out of the bank.

A mountain can be like that all at once. Summer at the bottom, winter at the top; and you climb through all the climates of the year as you scramble up. In the past half-century I've climbed Mount Jefferson in Oregon (a cousin died there in a fall soon afterward) and Mount Washington in New Hampshire, Mount Katahdin in Maine and Mount Etna in Sicily. I've clambered a bit in Wyoming's Wind Rivers and in the Absaroka Range; also in British Columbia and North Yemen; in the Western Ghats in southern India and the

Alpes Maritimes in the south of France; and have scrambled modestly in the High Sierras, Alaska's Brooks Range, and on the lower slopes of Mount Kinyeti in the Imatong Massif in southern Sudan. More particularly, I climbed all of Vermont's firetower mountains, back when Vermont still used towers to locate fires, instead of planes.

This feast of variety is part of a writer's life, the coin of the realm you inhabit if you sacrifice the security Americans used to think they'd have if they weren't freelance in their working lives. In reality, everybody winds up being freelance, but mountains telescope the experience. During a weekend you climb from flowery summer glades to the tundra above treeline, slipping on patches of ice, trudging through snowdrifts; the rain turns to sleet. The view is rarefied until a bellying, bruise-colored sky turns formidable, not pretty. Like climbing combers° in a strong surf, there's no indemnity if you come to grief. You labor upward not for money but for joy, or to have *been somewhere,* closer to the mysteries, during your life. Finding a hidden alpine col,° a bowl of fragile grassy beauty, you aren't just gleeful; you are linked differently.

Leaving aside specific dangers like riptides, vertigo, or terrific cold, I found I was comfortable on mountainsides or in seawater or in caves or wilderness swatches. In other words, I was fearful of danger but not of nature. I didn't harbor notions of any special dispensation, only that I too was part of it. I'd fought forest fires in the Santa Ana Mountains of Southern California when I was twenty and had discovered that moderate hardship energized yet tempered me, as it does many people, just like the natural sorties for which one puts on hiking shoes and ventures where barefoot peoples used to go. In central Africa I've walked a little with tribesmen like the Acholi and the Didinga, who still tend to be comfortable when nearly naked, and have seen that the gap between us seems not of temperament or of intuitions but only acculturation.

As virtual reality captures our time and obsessive attention, some of the   10
pressures that are killing nature may begin to relent. Not the primary one of overpopulation, which is strangling the tropics; but as people peer more and more into computer screens and at television, the outdoors, in affluent countries, may be left in relative peace. This won't stop the wholesale extinction of species, the mauling of the ocean, or other tragedies, but close to home may give a respite to what's left of nature.

Where I live alone each summer, four families lived year-round eighty years ago. The other new landowners don't choose to occupy their holdings even in warm weather because of the absence of electricity. An unusual case, yet I think indicative, and supported by the recent return of numbers of adaptive sorts of wildlife, like moose and fisher, to New England—though, in contrast, along the lake a few miles downhill, cottages perch atop one another,

---

combers: Long waves.
col: A depression or pass in a mountain range.

motorboats and water-skiers buzz around, and trollers use radar fish-finders to trace the final sanctuaries of the schools that the lake still holds.

Just as habitat is the central factor in whether birds and animals can survive, what *we* are able to do in the woods will be determined by land regulation or taxing policy and public purchases. Maine's private timberlands have remained unpopulated because of America's lavish need for toilet paper—as Vermont's trees too make paper, cotton-mill bobbins, cedar fencing, and yellow-birch or maple dowels that become furniture legs. Any day, I watch truckloads of pulp-wood go by. And in the California Sierras above Lake Tahoe, or on the pristine sea island of Ossabaw, off Savannah, Georgia, I've devoted lovely, utterly timeless hours to exploring refuges that seem quite empty of people but are actually allotted in careful fashion by state or federal agencies for intensive recreational use. The animals hide while the sun is up and feed when it's down. This is the way it will have to work. Levels of life on the same acreage. Or else it won't work at all.

I can be as jubilant indoors, listening to Schubert or Scott Joplin, as when sauntering underneath a mackerel sky on a day striped yellow, red, and green. Indeed, the density of sensations in which we live is such that one can do both—enjoy a virtuoso pianist through a headset outside. We live two lives or more in one nowadays, with our scads of travel, absurd excesses of unread informational material, the barrage of Internet and TV screens, wallpaper music, the serializing of polygamy, and the elongation of youth blurring old age. A sort of mental gridlock sometimes blocks out the amber pond, the mackerel sky, the seething leaves in a fresh breeze up in a canopy of trees, and the Walkman's lavish outpouring of genius too. Even when we just go for a walk, the data jam.

Verisimilitude, on computer screens or in pictorial simulation, is carrying us we don't entirely know where. I need my months each year without electricity and a telephone, living by the sun and looking down the hill a hundred times a day at the little pond. The toads sing passionately when breeding, observing a hiatus only at midmorning when the moose descends from the woods for his therapeutic wallow, or when a heron sails in for a meal. I see these things so clearly I think our ears have possibly changed more than our eyes under the impact of civilization—both the level of noise and subtleties of sound are so different from hunter-gatherer whisperings. I'm a worrier, if not a Luddite.° The gluttonies that are devouring nature are remorseless, and the imbalances within the human family give me vertigo. The lovely old idea that human life is sacred, each soul immortal, is in the throes of a grand mal° seizure; overpopulation is doing it in. I didn't believe that anyway, but did adhere to the transcendental idea that heaven is right here on earth, if we perceive and insist on it. And this faith is also becoming harder to sustain.

Luddite: Someone who destroys machinery, believing that machines take jobs away from people. *grand mal:* French for "great ailment," a form of epilepsy that leads to loss of consciousness and foaming at the mouth.

"Religion is what the individual does with his own solitariness," as A. N.   15
Whitehead° said. ("Thus religion is solitariness; and if you are never solitary,
you are never religious," he added.) I fall back on elemental pleasures like my
love of ponds, or how my first sight of any river invariably leaves me grin-
ning. And the sheen of rainwater on a bare black field in March. The thump
of surf, combed in the wind and foaming, glistening, yet humping up again
like a dinosaur. Yet fish don't touch me as much as animals, perhaps because
they never leave the water. Frogs *do*; and I seem to like frog songs even more
than bird songs, maybe because they're two-legged like us but can't fly either
and were the first vertebrate singers. But I especially respond to them because
they live a good deal more than we do in the water.

Frogs are disappearing worldwide in a drastic fashion, perhaps because of
ultraviolet rays or acid rain; and I may finally cease to believe that heaven is
on earth, if they do. Water without dolphins, frogs, pelicans, cormorants will
not mean much to me. But in the meantime I like to search out springs in
the high woods where brooks begin—a shallow sink in the ground, perpetu-
ally filling. If you carefully lift away the bottom covering of waterlogged
leaves, you'll see the penny-sized or pencil-point sources of the groundwater
welling up, where it all originates—the brook, the pond, the stream, the lake,
the river, and the ocean, till rain brings it back again.

QUESTIONS FOR DISCUSSION

1. According to Hoagland, tears "lend us a merciful and inexpensive respite,
   almost like half an hour at the beach." What do you think he means by this?
2. Why is nature unsentimental, and why might contemporary readers need
   to be reminded of this?
3. Why does Hoagland choose to live in a remote area without electricity or
   telephone? How does he benefit from this choice?
4. To what extent is this essay a critique of contemporary American culture?
   What does it reveal about Hoagland's dislikes?
5. This essay begins and ends with references to water. Why does Hoagland
   emphasize the importance of water?

SUGGESTIONS FOR WRITING

1. Write an essay exploring your own relationship with the outdoors.
2. Consider the quotation from A. N. Whitehead in paragraph 15: "Religion is
   what the individual does with his own solitariness." Write about a way in
   which you use your own "solitariness" to foster inner growth.
3. Write an essay exploring an aspect of your life from which you need "a
   merciful and inexpensive respite."

A. N. Whitehead: Alfred North Whitehead (1861–1947), British philosopher and mathematician
who moved to the United States.

LINKS ■ ■ ■

■ WITHIN THE BOOK

For another essay about how being outdoors can foster inner growth, see "Living Like Weasels" by Annie Dillard (pages 84–87).

■ ELSEWHERE IN PRINT

Hoagland, Edward. *Balancing Acts*. 1992. New York: Lyons, 1999.

---. *Compass Points: How I Lived*. New York: Pantheon, 2001.

---. *The Courage of Turtles: Fifteen Essays about Compassion, Pain, and Love*. New York: Random, 1970.

---. *Walking the Dead Diamond River*. New York: Random, 1973.

Thoreau, Henry David. *The Maine Woods*. 1864. New York: Penguin, 1980.

---. *Walden: Or Life in the Woods*. 1854. New York: Dover, 1995.

Whitehead, Alfred North. *Science and the Modern World*. 1925. New York: Free, 1997.

■ ONLINE

- A. N. Whitehead
  <http://plato.stanford.edu/entries/whitehead>
- Brief Biography
  <http://www.calacademy.org/casnews/feb96/herbst.html>
- Shakespeare's *Ophelia*
  <http://www.shakespeare-online.com/playanalysis/opheliachar.asp>
- *Sierra Club Magazine*, Archived Writings by Edward Hoagland
  <http://www.sierraclub.org/search.asp>
- The Thoreau Reader
  <http://eserver.org/thoreau>

LIVING LIKE WEASELS

Annie Dillard

One of our country's most respected writers and the winner of a Pulitzer Prize for nonfiction, Annie Dillard teaches at Wesleyan University in Connecticut. In many of her works, she seeks to understand how close attention to nature can contribute to the development of a spiritual life. She has also written about the nature of writing. In "Write Till You Drop," she states: "The writer knows her field—what has been done, what could be done, the limits—the way a tennis player knows the court. And like that expert, she, too, plays the edges. That is where the exhilaration is. She hits up the line. In writing she can push the edges. Beyond this limit, here the reader must recoil." As you read the following selection, be alert for ways Dillard "plays the edges," and if you find that she goes beyond your limits as a reader, be prepared to explain why. Be alert also for what she comes to understand about life by looking a wild animal in the eye.

A weasel is wild. Who knows what he thinks? He sleeps in his underground den, his tail draped over his nose. Sometimes he lives in his den for two days without leaving. Outside, he stalks rabbits, mice, muskrats, and birds, killing more bodies than he can eat warm, and often dragging the carcasses home. Obedient to instinct, he bites his prey at the neck, either splitting the jugular vein at the throat or crunching the brain at the base of the skull, and he does not let go. One naturalist refused to kill a weasel who was socketed into his hand deeply as a rattlesnake. The man could in no way pry the tiny weasel off, and he had to walk half a mile to water, the weasel dangling from his palm, and soak him off like a stubborn label.

And once, says Ernest Thompson Seton—once, a man shot an eagle out of the sky. He examined the eagle and found the dry skull of a weasel fixed by the jaws to his throat. The supposition is that the eagle had pounced on the weasel and the weasel swiveled and bit as instinct taught him, tooth to neck, and nearly won. I would like to have seen that eagle from the air a few weeks or months before he was shot: Was the whole weasel still attached to his feathered throat, a fur pendant? Or did the eagle eat what he could reach, gutting the living weasel with his talons before his breast, bending his beak, cleaning the beautiful airborne bones?

I have been reading about weasels because I saw one last week. I startled a weasel who startled me, and we exchanged a long glance.

Twenty minutes from my house, through the woods by the quarry and across the highway, is Hollins Pond, a remarkable piece of shallowness, where I like to go at sunset and sit on a tree trunk. Hollins Pond is also called Murray's Pond; it covers two acres of bottomland near Tinker Creek with six inches of water and six thousand lily pads. In winter, brown-and-white steers stand in the middle of it, merely dampening their hooves; from the distant shore they look like miracle itself, complete with miracle's nonchalance. Now, in summer, the steers are gone. The water lilies have blossomed and spread to a green horizontal plane that is terra firma to plodding blackbirds, and tremulous ceiling to black leeches, crayfish, and carp.

This is, mind you, suburbia. It is a five-minute walk in three directions to   5 rows of houses, though none is visible here. There's a 55-mph highway at one end of the pond, and a nesting pair of wood ducks at the other. Under every bush is a muskrat hole or a beer can. The far end is an alternating series of fields and woods, fields and woods, threaded everywhere with motorcycle tracks—in whose bare clay wild turtles lay eggs.

So. I had crossed the highway, stepped over two low barbed-wire fences, and traced the motorcycle path in all gratitude through the wild rose and poison ivy of the pond's shoreline up into high grassy fields. Then I cut down through the woods to the mossy fallen tree where I sit. This tree is excellent. It makes a dry, upholstered bench at the upper, marshy end of the pond, a plush jetty raised from the thorny shore between a shallow blue body of water and a deep blue body of sky.

The sun had just set. I was relaxed on the tree trunk, ensconced in the lap of lichen, watching the lily pads at my feet tremble and part dreamily over the thrusting path of a carp. A yellow bird appeared to my right and flew behind me. It caught my eye; I swiveled around—and the next instant, inexplicably, I was looking down at a weasel, who was looking up at me.

Weasel! I'd never seen one wild before. He was ten inches long, thin as a curve, a muscled ribbon, brown as fruitwood, soft-furred, alert. His face was fierce, small and pointed as a lizard's; he would have made a good arrowhead. There was just a dot of chin, maybe two brown hairs' worth, and then the pure white fur began that spread down his underside. He had two black eyes I didn't see, any more than you see a window.

The weasel was stunned into stillness as he was emerging from beneath an enormous shaggy wild rose bush four feet away. I was stunned into stillness twisted backward on the tree trunk. Our eyes locked, and someone threw away the key.

Our look was as if two lovers, or deadly enemies, met unexpectedly on   10 an overgrown path when each had been thinking of something else: a clearing blow to the gut. It was also a bright blow to the brain, or a sudden beating of brains, with all the charge and intimate grate of rubbed balloons. It emptied our lungs. It felled the forest, moved the fields, and drained the pond; the world dismantled and tumbled into that black hole of eyes. If you and I looked at each other that way, our skulls would split and drop to our shoulders. But we don't. We keep our skulls. So.

He disappeared. This was only last week, and already I don't remember what shattered the enchantment. I think I blinked, I think I retrieved my brain from the weasel's brain, and tried to memorize what I was seeing, and the weasel felt the yank of separation, the careening splashdown into real life and the urgent current of instinct. He vanished under the wild rose. I waited motionless, my mind suddenly full of data and my spirit with pleadings, but he didn't return.

Please do not tell me about "approach-avoidance conflicts." I tell you I've been in that weasel's brain for sixty seconds, and he was in mine. Brains are private places, muttering through unique and secret tapes—but the weasel and I both plugged into another tape simultaneously, for a sweet and shocking time. Can I help it if it was a blank?

What goes on in his brain the rest of the time? What does a weasel think about? He won't say. His journal is tracks in clay, a spray of feathers, mouse blood and bone: uncollected, unconnected, loose-leaf, and blown.

I would like to learn, or remember, how to live. I come to Hollins Pond not so much to learn how to live as, frankly, to forget about it. That is, I don't think I can learn from a wild animal how to live in particular—shall I suck warm blood, hold my tail high, walk with my footprints precisely over the prints of my hands?—but I might learn something of mindlessness, something of the purity of living in the physical senses and the dignity of living without bias or motive. The weasel lives in necessity and we live in choice, hating necessity and dying at the last ignobly in its talons. I would like to live as I should, as the weasel lives as he should. And I suspect that for me the way is like the weasel's: open to time and death painlessly, noticing everything, remembering nothing, choosing the given with a fierce and pointed will.

I missed my chance. I should have gone for the throat. I should have lunged for that streak of white under the weasel's chin and held on, held on through mud and into the wild rose, held on for a dearer life. We could live under the wild rose wild as weasels, mute and uncomprehending. I could very calmly go wild. I could live two days in the den, curled, leaning on mouse fur, sniffing bird bones, blinking, licking, breathing musk, my hair tangled in the roots of grasses. Down is a good place to go, where the mind is single. Down is out, out of your ever-loving mind and back to your careless senses. I remember muteness as a prolonged and giddy fast, where every moment is a feast of utterance received. Time and events are merely poured, unremarked, and ingested directly, like blood pulsed into my gut through a jugular vein. Could two live that way? Could two live under the wild rose, and explore by the pond, so that the smooth mind of each is as everywhere present to the other, and as received and as unchallenged, as falling snow?

We could, you know. We can live any way we want. People take vows of poverty, chastity, and obedience—even of silence—by choice. The thing is to stalk your calling in a certain skilled and supple way, to locate the most tender and live spot and plug into that pulse. This is yielding, not fighting. A weasel doesn't "attack" anything; a weasel lives as he's meant to, yielding at every moment to the perfect freedom of single necessity.

I think it would be well, and proper, and obedient, and pure, to grasp your one necessity and not let it go, to dangle from it limp wherever it takes you. Then even death, where you're going no matter how you live, cannot you part. Seize it and let it seize you up aloft even, till your eyes burn out and drop; let your musky flesh fall off in shreds, and let your very bones unhinge and scatter, loosened over fields, over fields and woods, lightly, thoughtless, from any height at all, from as high as eagles.

QUESTIONS FOR DISCUSSION

1. What do you think Dillard means when she writes, "A weasel is wild"? What does it mean to be "wild," and what is attractive about "the wild"?
2. Consider the story of the weasel that is borne aloft by an eagle and eaten in the air. What does this example reveal about weasels, and why is Dillard using it?
3. The setting of this essay isn't some remote forest, but rather a small pond in a suburb. "There's a 55-mph highway at one end of the pond, and a nesting pair of wood ducks at the other," writes Dillard. "Under every bush is a muskrat hole or a beer can." Why is this setting significant?
4. What does Dillard hope to learn from nature? Why is she attracted to the weasel that looks her in the eye?
5. According to Dillard, "Down is a good place to go, where the mind is single. Down is out, out of your ever-loving mind and back to your careless senses." In what sense—or senses—is she using "down," "single," and "careless"?
6. In her conclusion, Dillard urges readers "to grasp your one necessity and not let it go." Is this advice you are prepared to follow? How can you tell when it's wise to let something go or essential to hold on "wherever it takes you"?

SUGGESTIONS FOR WRITING

1. Write about an animal that you have observed closely; focus on what draws you to this animal.
2. Write an essay exploring your relationship to nature—whether it be hiking in a wilderness area or stepping over blades of grass springing up between the cracks of a city sidewalk.
3. What is your own "single necessity"—the desire that would be the most difficult for you to abandon? Write an essay that would help other people understand why this desire is so important to you.

LINKS ■ ■ ■

■ WITHIN THE BOOK

For another example of Dillard's work, see "The Deer at Providencia" (pages 633–636).

■ ELSEWHERE IN PRINT

Dillard, Annie. *An American Childhood.* New York: Harper, 1987.

---. *Holy the Firm.* New York: Harper, 1977.

---. *Pilgrim at Tinker Creek.* 1974. New York: Harper 1988.

---. *Teaching a Stone to Talk: Expeditions and Encounters.* New York: Harper, 1982.

King, Carolyn M. *Natural History of Weasels and Stoats.* Ithaca: Comstock, 1989.

Seton, Ernest Thompson. *Trail of an Artist-Naturalist: The Autobiography of Ernest Thompson Seton.* New York: Scribner, 1940.

---. *Wild Animals I Have Known.* 1898. Toronto: McClellan, 1996.

■ ONLINE

- American Museum of Natural History
  <http://www.amnh.org>

- Ernest Thompson Seton Institute
  <http://www.etsetoninstitute.org>

- *New York Times,* Interviews and Articles
  <http://www.nytimes.com/books/99/03/28/specials/dillard.html>

SWEET CHARIOT

Mark Doty

Winner of the National Book Critics Circle Award, the Rome Prize, and many other awards, Mark Doty is the author of several volumes of poetry including My Alexandria *(1993),* Atlantis *(1995), and* Sweet Machine *(1998). In the early nineties, he turned to writing nonfiction as a way of coming to terms with the death of the man he had been partnered with for twelve years.* Heaven's Coast, *the book that emerged from this process, has been described by the* New York Times *as a "terrifying and elegant work." In it, Doty describes what it is like to care for a partner with AIDS, how it feels to grieve, and how nature and writing can help heal a damaged spirit. The following selection is taken from the first chapter of* Heaven's Coast. *As you read it, remember that it is part of a longer work that explores the various topics introduced here: faith, doubt, love, grief, and desire.*

In a 1998 interview for The Cortland Review, *Doty provides a sense of what motivates him to write about his personal experience: "I don't feel that this openness has been a choice, although of course on some less-than-conscious level it must be. Rather it feels to me as if it's simply the course my life has taken, beginning in the early eighties with the process of coming out. I felt then a great thirst for directness, an imperative to find language with which to be direct to myself, which was of course the result of having been, like many young gay men, divided from my self, from the authentic character of my desire. I felt that I had to hide for years! And the result of that for me, once I began to break through the dissembling, was a thirst for the genuine."*

I grew up in two religions.

The first one—comforting, strange, rigorous, in its way—was comprised of an astonishing and lovely set of images. It was a religion given to me primarily by my grandmother, whose East Tennessee faith had the kind of solidity and rock-depth upon which Jesus must have intended to found His church. *She* was Peter's rock, unshakable, holding us all up—or at least holding me up; I was too small to have much of a sense of what she meant to my parents or to her husband, my cantankerous and difficult grandfather who outlived her by twenty years. My memories of her are very particular ones: a day out behind our house when she and I picked dandelion and poke greens, sunlight filtering through the thin flowered rayon dress she wore—this would have been 1957 or '58—and she showed me the right leaves to pick for the greens she'd boil with fatback to serve with the chicken she plucked and set to roast in a black graniteware pan sparked with a whole firmament of stars. In that house, where she and my grandfather lived with us, their room was a secret source of meaning and depth. I didn't like him much but I liked his things: a drawer full of beautiful useless old fountain pens with marbled cases, cigar boxes full of rubber bands, stuff saved for the day it would surely be needed. I loved her with all my heart, and everything that was hers: the green rocking chair, a fruitcake tin filled with swirled peppermint candies, the Bible with the words of Jesus printed in red, like holidays on a calendar. She would set me up on her lap and, rocking all the while, read Bible verses to me. I'm not sure if I remember especially her readings from Revelation or if it simply feels to me now, whenever I hear someone mention a phrase like "last days" or "apocalypse," that the scent of her—lavender, peppermint, and clean old dresses—and the texture of her clothes, the Bible's leatherette cover and onionskin pages, are forever commingled with those words; some essence of her imbues them. It was she who presented me with my first religion, which was the religion of images, and they were given to me in Bible verses and in the songs we sang on the porch swing, summer nights: the sweet chariot coming to carry us home, the moon turning to blood, the angels sounding the trump so that all the dead would clap hands and arise, the thin veil of this world—thin as her sprig-scattered skirt!—parting at last and opening into a world we need not fear, though it would be awesome, a world made true and just and bright and eternally resonant as the songs we sang.

I loved the word *chariot*. I couldn't sing it without thinking of the cherries in my uncle's orchard, which I'd seen once, and where my father had lifted me up into the branches so that I could pick the half-ripe fruit. Sweet chariot, sweet cherries, gold and red and green, a kind of glowing flush like heat on the skin of the little fruit, which was smooth and cleft and satisfying on the tongue as the word: *chariot*. This was the way the images invited us to dream into them.

I don't think I had any awareness of the second religion, the codes of explanation and prohibition, until after her death. I was five. She died of a heart attack, throwing her bedroom window open, in winter, and gasping for air. I remember most vividly being wrapped in a quilt, one she made, I imagine. I watched TV very early in the morning, at an hour when I wasn't usually awake, and saw the minister come in his black jacket and collar, his odd flowery scent. And then gladiolas around her coffin, and again that sweet essence of peppermint and lavender, and little ribbons decorating the flowers on her grave. I dreamed that she came to see me, in the night, and stood beside a cane chair in a circle of lamplight to speak to me—very softly and intimately and comfortingly, though I haven't any memory at all of what she said.

My understanding of a more worldly religion began after that. One Sunday there was a sermon especially for children—I believe this was in a Presbyterian church in Nashville, or perhaps in Memphis—instead of the usual Sunday School Bible stories accompanied by big colored pictures. (What were they? I wanted to say chromolithographs, or engravings, perhaps because the pictures and their sense of the world, an ancient and quaint exoticism they portrayed, seem so firmly of the nineteenth century.) This Sunday, no "Baby Moses in the Bulrushes" or "Joseph in His Coat of Many Colors." Instead, the minister told us a story about the terrible dangers of desire. 5

A little girl's mother had baked a particularly beautiful pie, and set it on the dining table to cool, saying to her daughter, "Make sure that you do not touch this pie." The girl thought about this, and tried not to touch the impossibly attractive thing. But after a time, overcome by her longing, she simply could not resist anymore, and she decided that if she snitched—that was the word he used, *snitched* (a particularly pinched, ratlike little word, it seems to me now, full of disdain and pettiness)—just one little piece it would be all right. So she did, taking the little bit of pie into the closet and eating it in the dark where no one could see her. The morsel eaten, she was still filled with hunger; the pie was so good, she wanted it so badly. So she would snitch just one more piece, and eat it in the dark surrounded by the comforting wool of her parents' coats. But, of course, that didn't satisfy her either; once a contract with appetite had been entered into, there wasn't any turning back. And standing in the dark, her hands and lips covered with the evidence of her need, the little girl felt, suddenly, seen. She was watched and she knew it, and so she turned her face upward into the dark from which that sense of witness came, and there, floating above her, was the eye of God: enormous, missing nothing, utterly implacable.

My parents told me that when we came home after this sermon, I hid under my bed and wouldn't come out. I don't recall that now, but I do remember inventing a new game, which I used to play alone, since my sister was ten years older and I might as well have been an only child. We lived that year in a big old farmhouse on a horse farm we rented. The horses used to wander on their own business—nameless, cared for by others. In my new game I marked off some portion of the yard by the abandoned chicken coop and named it Hell, and I'd play devil, racing about the perimeter with my pitchfork, poking at souls, meting out punishments, keeping them in line. With a girl who lived down our road I'd play a game in which we took turns dying and going to heaven, which I imagined as a kind of garden with a maze, a rose garden, where I would meet a blond and milk-pale Jesus. *I come to the garden alone, while the dew is still on the roses. . . .* But that game, which was soon forbidden to us by a relative who said: "You mustn't play that, it might come true," was a game of images, of peace and stillness. My game of Hell was an enactment of energy and ferocity, of power and defiance. I think I have responded to the religion of prohibition in this way ever since.

Perhaps if my grandmother had lived, and if we'd stayed in Tennessee, my two religions would have merged, and I would have grown away from the images I was originally given, or felt oppressed by them. But because I was split off from that world, the landscape of my childhood and of the songs seems permanent to me, sealed, untouchable, a mythic landscape of hymns, with their rivers and flowers, their cherry trees and blood and moons. We moved away from my parents' families, on to suburbs in Arizona and Southern California and Florida, and into a succession of increasingly polite Protestant churches which finally evaporated into a bland social gesture which was easily set aside. My mother, late in her life, found a religion of imagery again in an Anglican church so high and so influenced by the architecture and pageantry of Mexican Catholicism as to be a kind of spiritual theater. I came, after a while, to seek the images of comfort and challenge and transformation in art. My mother, with her love of painting and music and beauty, had helped me to look there, but I think I understood intuitively that there was no sustenance for me in the religion of explanation and prohibition.

The explanations were never good ones—the world as trial by fire, proving ground to earn God's love or His forgiveness for having been human—and it was apparent to me even at an early age that the notion that anyone around me actually *understood* God's will or could articulate it was patently ridiculous. There's a wonderful line in Charles Finney's quirky book, *The Circus of Dr. Lao,* which I read as a kid, an Americanized version of a speech of Hamlet's: "There are more things in heaven and earth, madam, than even a lifetime of experience in Abalone, Arizona, could avail you of."

The prohibitions were worse than the explanations. They suggested that   10
the divinity had constructed the earth as a kind of spiritual minefield, a Chutes and Ladders game of snares, traps, and seductions, all of them fueled by the engines of our longing; the flames of hell were stoked by human heats. As if desire were our enemy, instead of the ineradicable force that binds us to the world.

I cannot be queer in church, though I've tried, and though I live now in a place where this seems to be perfectly possible for a great many people. Here in Provincetown we have a wonderful Unitarian church, with a congregation largely gay and lesbian, and it pains me a bit to have to admit that when I have gone to services there I have been utterly, hopelessly bored. There's something about the absence of imagery, an oddly flaccid quality of neutrality in the language of worship. I long for a kind of spiritual intensity, a passion, though I can certainly see all the errors and horrors spiritual passions have wrought. I don't know what I want in a church, finally; I think the truth is that I *don't* want a church. My friend Phil has sweetly and politely informed me that it's a spiritual experience for him to be in the company of his fellows, worshiping together at the U.U.,° and that my resistance to it is really a sort of aesthetic snobbery, a resistance to its public language and marriage of spirituality and social life. I don't want to judge anyone's way of finding a soulful commonality, but nothing puts me less in mind of ultimate things than the friendly meetings held within my local church's square-boned New England architecture and flourishes of trompe l'oeil.°

Perhaps my discomfort has to do, still, with issues of desire. Wind, glimmering watery horizon and sun, the watchful seals and shimmered flurries of snow seem to me to have far more to do with the life of my spirit. And there is somehow in the grand scale of dune and marsh and sea room for all of human longing, placed firmly in context by the larger world: small, our flames are, though to us raging, essential. There is something so *polite* about these Sunday

---

U.U.: Unitarian Universalist.
trompe l'oeil: French for "trick of the eye," this phrase describes paintings and murals that convey an illusion of structure or space.

gatherings of tolerant Unitarians that I feel like longing and need must be set aside. Isn't the part of us that desires, that loves, that longs for encounter and connection—physical and psychic and every other way—also the part of us that knows something about God? The divine, in this world, is all dressed up in mortal clothes, and longing and mortality are so profoundly intertwined as to be, finally, entirely inseparable.

My lover of twelve years died just last month. It astonishes me to write that sentence. It astonishes me that I am writing at all; I have not, till now, and I didn't know when the ability to focus might come back to me. I haven't yet been able to read, and there are many other things I haven't even begun to approach, in the face of this still unbelievable absence. I will be sorting out and naming the things I learned from Wally for years to come, probably for the rest of my life, but here is one thing I know now.

All the last year of Wally's life, he didn't stop wanting. He was unable to walk, since some kind of insidious viral infection which his useless doctors didn't seem to know the first thing about gradually took away his ability to control his body. But he wasn't ever one of those people who let go. Oh, he did, in the sense of accepting what was happening to him, in the sense of not grasping onto what he couldn't have, but he lived firmly in his desires. From the bed where he lived all that year he'd look out onto the street at anything in pants walking by and be fully, appreciatively *interested*. I never for a minute felt hurt by this or left out; it wasn't about me. It was about Wally's way of loving the world. I think in his situation I would have been consumed by frustration and a sense of thwarted desire, but he wasn't. Because his desire wasn't about possession, and his inability to fulfill it wasn't an issue; it was to be in a state of wanting, to be still desiring beauty and grace and sexiness and joy. It was the wanting itself that mattered.

A couple of months before Wally died we heard about a couple in the city, one of whom was ill, who needed to give up their little dog, since they felt they couldn't take care of him.   *15*

Wally talked and talked about this until it became clear that what he really wanted was for Dino to come to live with us. We already had a dog, Arden, a calm black retriever with a meditative, scholarly disposition, but Wally had his heart set on a new dog who'd sleep next to him and lick his face.

The day that I went to Manhattan to pick up Dino, Jimi and Tony changed their minds; they weren't ready to let him go. Wally was so disappointed that I went to the animal shelter with the intention of finding a small, cuddly dog who'd fit the bill.

What I found was a young golden retriever with enormous energy, a huge tongue, and a phenomenal spirit of pleasure and enjoyment. He didn't just lick Wally's face, he bathed his head, and Wally would scrunch up his face and then grin as though he'd been given the earth's brightest treasure.

Sometimes late at night he'd tell me about other animals he wanted to adopt: lizards, a talking bird, some fish, a little rat.

I don't know many men who would want a new dog, a new pact with domestic life, with responsibility, with caring for the abandoned, in the final   *20* weeks of their lives. There's a Polaroid I took of Wally with golden Beau curled up and sleeping in our rented hospital bed beside him. He could barely use his hands then—our friend Darren and I would feed him, and give him drinks to sip through a straw—but he's reaching over with his beautiful hardly functional hand to stroke Beau's neck. That is how I will always see my love: reaching toward a world he cannot hold and loving it no less, not a stroke less.

Desire I think has less to do with possession than with participation, the will to involve oneself in the body of the world, in the principle of things expressing itself in splendid specificity, a handful of images: a lover's irreplaceable body, the roil and shimmer of sea overshot with sunlight, a handful of cherries, the texture and weight of a word. The word that seems most apt is *partake*; it comes from Middle English, literally from the notion of being a part-taker, one who participates. We can say we take a part *of* something, but we may just as accurately say we take part *in* something; we are implicated in another being, which is always the beginning of wisdom, isn't it—that involvement which enlarges us, which engages the heart, which takes us out of the routine limitations of self?

The codes and laws fall away, useless, foolish, finally, hollow little husks of vanity.

The images sustain.

The images allow for desire, allow room for us—even require us—to complete them, to dream our way into them. I believe with all my heart that when the chariot came for Wally, green and gold and rose, a band of angels swung wide out over the great flanks of the sea, bearing him up over the path of light the sun makes on the face of the waters.

I believe my love is in the Jordan, which is deep and wide and welcoming, though it scours us oh so deeply. And when he gets to the other side, I know he will be dressed in the robes of comfort and gladness, his forehead anointed with spices, and he will sing—joyful—into the future, and back toward the darkness of this world.   *25*

QUESTIONS FOR DISCUSSION

1. Why are images important to Doty? What images help him to remember his grandmother and his lover?
2. What is the difference between the two religions that shaped Doty's childhood?
3. After discussing the religions of his childhood, Doty moves on to discuss his current thoughts about religion and to link these thoughts to the death of his lover. How successful is he in drawing these topics together?
4. According to Doty, what is the value of desire? How does it differ from possession?
5. In the last sentence of this selection, Doty refers to "the darkness of this world." In what sense is the world of the living a dark place?

SUGGESTIONS FOR WRITING

1. In paragraph 6, Doty retells a story that made him hide under the bed when he was a little boy. Write about a time in your own childhood when you were frightened or upset by a story or conversation with an adult.
2. Write about an image or group of related images that are a comfort to you.
3. Consider Doty's definition of *desire* and how he links it to *partake*. Then write an essay defining a term that is important to you and may not be understood by others.

LINKS ■ ■ ■

■ WITHIN THE BOOK

For an example of Doty's poetry, see "Visitation" (pages 728–730).

■ ELSEWHERE IN PRINT

Brehony, Kathleen A. *After the Darkest Hour: How Suffering Begins the Journey to Wisdom.* New York: Holt, 2000.
Doty, Mark. *Firebird: A Memoir.* New York: Harper, 1999.
———. *Heaven's Coast: A Memoir.* New York: Harper, 1996.
———. *Still Life with Oysters and Lemon: On Objects and Intimacy.* Boston: Beacon, 2001.
———. *Sweet Machine: Poems.* New York: Harper, 1998.
Finney, Charles. *The Circus of Dr. Lao.* New York: Viking, 1935.

■ ONLINE

- Brief Biography
  <http://www.poets.org/poets/poets.cfm?prmID=92&CFID=3714437&CFTOKEN=59232937>
- Gay and Lesbian Rights
  <http://www.hrc.org/issues/index.asp>
- Grief and Bereavement
  <http://www.growthhouse.org/death.html>
- Living with AIDS
  <http://www.nlm.nih.gov/medlineplus/aidslivingwithaids.html>

2

Writing to Report Information

Ask yourself whether, in the course of a single week, you do any of the following: ask directions, consult the telephone directory, look something up in a book, read a newspaper, check gasoline prices, or listen to a weather report. All these efforts to acquire data are things people do routinely to negotiate the pathways of their world. This task is becoming both easier and more challenging as a result of technology. Today, we have almost instant electronic access to vast reserves of data. But to keep from being overwhelmed by the data we acquire and to avoid overwhelming others when we report to them, we need to learn how to sort, select, and arrange data—and thereby turn data into information.

Data in this sense means unorganized, unconstructed bits and pieces. Billions of them. Information is constructed out of data by a particular person or group of people with particular concerns they wish to communicate. So information always involves a rhetorical situation. The challenge is to transform data into information by furnishing a context and a social purpose.

To understand the nature of data, you must be able to distinguish among facts, inferences, and opinions. *Facts* are independently verifiable events, statistics, and statements: The Arkansas River runs southwest from central Colorado into Kansas; Enron filed for bankruptcy protection on December 2, 2001; genetic engineering has produced square tomatoes. *Inferences* are reasonable suppositions drawn from facts. Naperville, Illinois, had a population of 22,600 in 1970, 42,600 in 1980, and 83,000 in 1989. We can combine these facts and infer that by the year 2000 Naperville had a population well in excess of 100,000, because a clear pattern of population growth exists. So data also consist of inferences. Finally, an *opinion* is a belief that may or may not be accurate but that nevertheless exists and must therefore be taken into account by those who report information. You might think that Naperville would be an exciting place to move to, or you might think that it is getting too big. Whether an opinion is reliable matters a great deal in some rhetorical situations—in writing to evaluate, for example, or writing to persuade (which are discussed in other chapters). But right or wrong, an opinion becomes data once it is shared with others. No longer yours alone, it has become one of those random bits and pieces with which others must cope.

Our main concern in this chapter is with the way we draw on data to transfer information from one mind to another. Although this is a very complex process—one that has been studied at length by psychologists, neurologists, and communication specialists—there is agreement that the most powerful way to transfer information from one mind to another is through language. Our concern here is specifically with written language.

GUIDELINES FOR REPORTING INFORMATION

Reading for information is very different from reading to enter imaginatively into another person's life or to reflect at length about ideas. When people read for information, they appreciate having clear signals from the author that will alert them to the most important points and give them the opportunity to skim the rest. They also appreciate having some idea of the scope of the article and why they are expected to read it.

Writing that reports information need not always have a thesis. A newspaper article, after all, rarely has a thesis, but the lack of one does not mean that it consists of random pieces of data. It is still arranged in a pattern so that readers can make sense of it. Business reports, too, frequently consist simply of narratives of what has happened or of text that exists mainly to link numbers in some meaningful way. In this chapter, Peter Stark relies on narrative to report on the nature and treatment of hypothermia. Iris Chang also uses narrative—in this case to convey the horror of the atrocities that followed the Japanese conquest of Nanking in 1937 and to report how a few foreign residents of that city devoted themselves to helping the Chinese. But many reports benefit from having a clear thesis explicitly stated early on. Rebecca Solnit, for example, opens her report on the environmental effects of gold mining by referring to "contaminated groundwater," "mercury-caused madness," and "vanishing wildlife"—claiming "the costs are still rolling in, and if you want to know who's picking up the bill, look in a mirror." Several pages later, she restates her thesis when concluding her report: "In the end, gold mining, like all other environmental dilemmas, shows the consequences of valuing what can be pocketed and possessed over 'the gift of life.'"

Philosopher H. Paul Grice provides four rules to guide the transfer of information so clear communication takes place, and to help writers decide what to tell and how to tell it when reporting information. In Grice's scheme, reporters of information should observe the rules of quantity, quality, relevance, and manner.

To observe the rule of *quantity,* you need to give your readers just enough information—but no more—so they can understand what you want them to know, so there are no gaps to impede their understanding, and so they do not drown in data. An example may help. In "Why McDonald's Fries Taste So Good," Eric Schlosser mentions several chemical plants at which aromas for processed food are created: International Flavors & Fragrances, Givaudan, Haarmann & Reimer, Takasago, Flavor Dynamics, Frutarom, and Elan Chemical. He also notes that there are "dozens" of such companies in New Jersey and indicates that other companies exist elsewhere. He chooses, however, to report about his visit to one of these companies.

The rule of *quality* dictates that you give correct, accurate information. Because those who report information must observe the rule of quantity as well as quality, they should use the best material at their disposal. When determining which material is of the best quality, they should consider whether examples and sources are reliable and representative. They may discover sensational material that could capture the attention of their audience but reject it when they find that they cannot verify its accuracy. Readers, however, are also responsible for appraising the quality of the information they receive. Some reporters are more reliable than others, and most use inferences and opinion as well as facts— which means that readers must distinguish the kind of information they are receiving and decide whether they can trust it. Although Schlosser reports a visit to only one flavor company, International Flavors & Fragrances, he helps his audience to understand that this example is of good quality by noting that IFF is "the world's largest flavor company" and that it has developed the aromas for "famous, widely advertised products ranging from potato chips to antacids."

The rule of *relevance* means that the reader gets the information the writer promises and is not distracted by unrelated material. If you are reading about the fast-food industry, you might expect information on how flavors are manufactured, but you would not expect to read several paragraphs about how to cook with tofu. When reporting about International Flavors & Fragrances, Schlosser establishes the relevance of this example by noting that, while there, he saw "a french fryer identical to those I'd seen at innumerable fast-food restaurants." And he concludes his report with a reference to the artificial aroma of grilled hamburger. The references to french fries and hamburger make his visit to IFF relevant to his discussion of McDonald's.

Finally, the rule of *manner* means that accurate information is presented clearly and plausibly. Eric Schlosser's report is plausible because he includes expert testimony from sources inside the industry he is investigating and recognizes that artificially created flavors can be appealing—demonstrating that he is not one-sided. Moreover, the information he reports is presented clearly and without sarcastic commentary. Thus, the rule of manner requires a credible reporter framing information so that readers can understand it. This is not determined simply by the reporter's being personally self-confident—although that contributes to credibility—but also by the reporter's demonstrating his or her own fair-mindedness and ability to distinguish fact from opinion.

Implicit in Grice's four rules is a point that should be emphasized: Writers transfer information most effectively when they help readers connect it to something they already know. For example, Jennifer Egan helps readers understand self-mutilation by linking it to the popularity of tattooing and piercing. And after reporting that a ton of rock and earth at one of the mines she investigated yielded "a mere hundredth of an ounce per ton," Rebecca Solnit conveys the environmental consequences of this fact by envisioning the effect for a single consumer of gold jewelry: "Ever since, I've pictured a truck driver ringing the doorbell of a home to say, 'Ma'am, about that new wristwatch: Would you like your seventy-nine tons on the front lawn or on the back? You'll want to keep the kids and dog off 'cause of the acid and arsenic.'"

USING APPROPRIATE LANGUAGE

Students are often advised to couch all their information in neutral, precise, objective language, because informing is supposed to be evenhanded; but that does not mean taking all the life out of your prose. Too much scientific and informative writing sounds as if it were produced by a machine. As the clear, direct prose of Peter Stark reveals, you can report information and still let your own personality show through. Presenting information while conveying a human voice helps readers remain interested in the information without damaging any of its value.

If you are to offer the appropriate information, reporting requires you to pay special attention to the interests and abilities of your audience. When you write for general readers, you should not expect them to understand specialized vocabulary and advanced concepts, and it is usually your responsibility to select a topic that will interest your readers and present it in an appealing way. Consider the following excerpt from a college textbook for an introductory course in astronomy:

> Based on his determination that the sun was much larger than the earth, Aristarchus proposed that the sun was at rest and the earth moved around it in a yearly orbit. This *heliocentric* (sun-centered) model was opposed to the prevailing *geocentric* (earth-centered) model. The concept of a heliocentric universe was immediately challenged. If the earth moved in an orbit, the stars would appear to shift relative to one another, depending on the position of the earth in its orbit. This phenomenon, called *parallax,* was not observed. Aristarchus' reply to this objection was that the stars must be extremely far away, making any parallax shifts too small to notice.
> —*Thomas Michael Corwin and Dale C. Wachowiak,* The Universe: From Chaos to Consciousness

The authors have considered their audience. They have not talked down to their readers but have recognized that vocabulary may be a problem. They have described *parallax,* a fairly difficult concept, using simple, clear language.

Compare that passage with one from Gilbert E. Satterthwaite's *Encyclopedia of Astronomy,* which also describes parallax but is directed to more sophisticated readers:

> The angle subtended at a heavenly body by a baseline of known length, usually designated P or π. It is of course directly related to the distance; the word has therefore come to be used by astronomers as synonymous with distance.
>
> The baseline used for nearer objects, such as the members of the solar system, is the equatorial radius of the earth; parallaxes determined on this basis are termed *geocentric parallaxes* [...]. For more distant objects, the baseline used is the semimajor axis of the Earth's orbit; these are termed *heliocentric parallaxes.*

Satterthwaite's discussion goes on in considerable detail to discuss various kinds of parallaxes, but he can assume that his readers are motivated to read his discussion and have the knowledge to understand fine points—a different audience from Corwin and Wachowiak's.

SUMMARIZING AND SYNTHESIZING INFORMATION

As you transform data into information, you need to know how to summarize and synthesize.

To *summarize* is to condense: Summaries report the main points—and only the main points—of something you have heard, read, or witnessed. For example, here are the first three paragraphs of a story that appeared in the *New York Times* on July 26, 1998:

> Murder in the United States has been dropping dramatically for years, to the lowest level since the modern crime wave began in the 1960's. But this encouraging decline has masked a fundamental fact—that there is no such thing as an American murder rate.
>
> In fact, there are sharp regional differences in homicide, with the South having by far the highest murder rate, almost double that of the Northeast, a divergence that has persisted for as long as records have been kept, starting in the 19th century. The former slaveholding states of the old Confederacy all rank in the top 20 states for murder, led by Louisiana, with a rate of 17.5 murders per 100,000 people in 1996. The 10 states with the lowest homicide rates are in New England and the northern Midwest, with South Dakota's the lowest at 1.2 murders per 100,000 people.
>
> Experts note, in addition, that much of the disparity in murder rates between the South and other sections of the country stems from a difference in the character of Southern homicide. In the South,

many murders are of a personal and traditional nature: a barroom brawl, a quarrel between acquaintances or a fight between lovers. Elsewhere, homicides usually begin with another crime, like a robbery gone bad, and typically involve strangers.

Summarizing these paragraphs means understanding what they mean and restating in your own words the points you consider important. Here's a summary of the passage:

> The murder rate in the United States is highest in the South, where almost twice as many murders are committed as in other regions. Southern murders are also more personal than those committed elsewhere.

This summary reduces the passage to approximately one-seventh of its original length. Statistics have been left out, and references to Louisiana, South Dakota, the Midwest, and New England have also been omitted as well as data about the declining murder rate for the nation as a whole and examples of the background behind many Southern murders. The summary is accurate, but its utility would depend on the audience, the context, and the purpose for which it would be used. Some readers might require more detail, such as an explanation of "personal," and a writer with those readers in mind would summarize the passage differently. Remember that your audience, context, and purpose determine what kind of information you report and how much of it you expect readers to need.

To *synthesize* is to put data of different kinds together in meaningful ways. Synthesis means creating information by sorting through data, identifying relationships, and presenting them in a coherent pattern. When you are summarizing, you are usually working with data from a single source. When you are synthesizing, you are reaching out to draw together data from many different sources. When writing about the Japanese conquest of Nanking, for example, Iris Chang draws not only on previously published works on her subject but also upon new material that she discovered through research, including letters and diaries of eyewitnesses and military records in the National Archives. By drawing upon diverse historical sources, Chang synthesizes extensive data on the subject she chose to study. (For another example of synthesis, see pages 257–274.)

OBTAINING DATA

Although writing to report information does not necessarily require you to gather more knowledge than you already have, there may be times when you lack adequate knowledge to finish your paper. Research can provide you with additional data. There is no reason to assume, however, that research must be confined to libraries or to the World Wide Web. If you have ever wondered how food is prepared in a local fast-food restaurant, you might consider doing some field research—touring the facility, asking questions of employees—and then writing an informative, behind-the-scenes report. To obtain data for her essay, Jennifer Egan visited a troubled teenage girl in her home and in the residential facility into which she had been placed; to get a sense of her life, she even attended parties with this girl. Or if you are interested in writing a profile like Tim Rogers's profile of Vivian Villarreal, one of the best pool players in the United States, you might interview that person and perhaps his or her associates.

When interviewing someone, always do some preliminary research so you will be able to ask knowledgeable questions. Schedule the interview in advance, and prepare a list of questions that are specific enough to find out what you need to know but allow the person you are interviewing enough latitude to be comfortable. Try to know your questions by heart so you can talk naturally with this person without stopping to find and read one of the questions you wrote down. And if you want to use a tape recorder, always ask your interviewee's permission to do so.

For many topics, however, you will need to consult material that has already been published. Many guides to research are in print, and you will also find a chapter on how to do research in most composition handbooks. Teaching in detail the research strategies available for writers is beyond the scope of this introduction, but you should be aware of some basic principles:

- Research is not limited to long, formal papers with lengthy bibliographies, such as a ten-page "research paper" due at the end of the semester. Writers often need to consult sources when working on shorter assignments prompted by a number of different motives for writing.

- A good search strategy involves consulting different kinds of sources, including electronic databases, books and articles, and sometimes government documents and personal interviews. Don't get discouraged if you can't find a book on your topic in your local library or if the periodicals you need have been checked out by someone else. You may be able to get the information elsewhere.

- Writers who use sources should be careful to remain in control of their material and not let a paper become a collection of undigested data from which the writer's own voice has disappeared.

- Information that comes from sources should be documented appropriately. (Handbooks published by the Modern Language Association and the American Psychological Association, among other groups, provide guidance. See pages 37–46.)

The fastest, most efficient way to do research today is by electronic searching. Many colleges and universities provide students with free accounts that allow them to electronically "visit" their own libraries and others around the nation, to correspond electronically with like-minded people who share similar interests, and to search online data depositories maintained by government and business. Not only are new information sources such as electronic databases available online; traditional standbys such as *The Readers' Guide to Periodical Literature* are also available electronically, either online or on CD-ROM. *InfoTrac,* a computerized index for periodicals in general circulation, will also direct you to the kind of short, accessible articles covered by *The Readers' Guide.* By using a program like *FirstSearch,* however, you can gain access to approximately 12,500 journals. Available online through OLLC, *FirstSearch* also allows for specialized searches within various academic disciplines. (See page 36.)

For recent information on specific topics, you will often need to consult periodical literature or material, like magazines and newspapers, that is published periodically. Again, whenever possible, take advantage of electronic resources. More and more professional journals are being published electronically, and general-interest magazines such as *Newsweek* are also now online. Thus, you may be able to use electronic means not only to find a citation but also to retrieve the full text of an article. For information in scholarly publications you will need to consult a specialized index. Articles about psychology, for example, can be located by searching the printed volumes of *Psychological Abstracts* or the electronic database of *PsycLIT.*

You can also locate books electronically in your own library and also in other college and university libraries (and some municipal ones). If you do locate a book held in the collection of a library other than your own, you can usually request it to be sent to you through interlibrary loan. Moreover, some books are available in electronic format, so you may be able to download an appropriate text from a personal computer. Consult your reference librarian for more information about what research tools are available in this rapidly changing branch of information science.

Whatever research strategies you use and whatever resources are available to you, remember that obtaining data is only one part of the process of reporting information. Do not allow the quest for data to become an end in itself. As we have seen, data become useful as they are transformed into information. To transform data, you must allow yourself plenty of time for writing and revising.

AS FREEZING PERSONS RECOLLECT THE SNOW—FIRST CHILL, THEN STUPOR, THEN THE LETTING GO

Peter Stark

Peter Stark is a travel writer who specializes in writing about adventures in cold climates. In a review of Stark's Driving to Greenland: Arctic Travel, Nordic Sport, and Other Ventures into the Heart of Winter, *a critic for* Kirkus Reviews *describes Stark as a "daredevil writer" who "brings you to places you never dreamed of going, takes all the lumps, and gets you home safe and sound." You will get a sense of how Stark takes readers on well-guided adventures through the following selection, which was first published in 1997 by* Outside *magazine, to which Stark is a regular contributor. In that publication, the article was subtitled: "The Cold Hard Facts of Freezing to Death." As you read, be alert for any "facts" that Stark reports. But also consider how he uses narration to locate these facts within a story designed to hold the attention of readers.*

When your Jeep spins lazily off the mountain road and slams backward into a snowbank, you don't worry immediately about the cold. Your first thought is that you've just dented your bumper. Your second is that you've failed to bring a shovel. Your third is that you'll be late for dinner. Friends are expecting you at their cabin around eight for a moonlight ski, a late dinner, a sauna. Nothing can keep you from that.

Driving out of town, defroster roaring, you barely noted the bank thermometer on the town square: minus 27 degrees at 6:36. The radio weather report warned of a deep mass of arctic air settling over the region. The man who took your money at the Conoco station shook his head at the register and said he wouldn't be going anywhere tonight if he were you. You smiled. A little chill never hurt anybody with enough fleece and a good four-wheel-drive.

But now you're stuck. Jamming the gearshift into low, you try to muscle out of the drift. The tires whine on ice-slicked snow as headlights dance on the curtain of frosted firs across the road. Shoving the lever back into park, you shoulder open the door and step from your heated capsule. Cold slaps your naked face, squeezes tears from your eyes. You check your watch: 7:18. You consult your map: A thin, switchbacking line snakes up the mountain to the penciled square that marks the cabin.

Breath rolls from you in short frosted puffs. The Jeep lies cocked sideways in the snowbank like an empty turtle shell. You think of firelight and saunas and warm food and wine. You look again at the map. It's maybe five or six miles more to that penciled square. You run that far every day before breakfast. You'll just put on your skis. No problem.

There is no precise core temperature at which the human body perishes *5*
from cold. At Dachau's cold-water immersion baths, Nazi doctors calculated
death to arrive at around 77 degrees Fahrenheit. The lowest recorded core
temperature in a surviving adult is 60.8 degrees. For a child it's lower: In 1994,
a two-year-old girl in Saskatchewan wandered out of her house into a minus-
40 night. She was found near her doorstep the next morning, limbs frozen
solid, her core temperature 57 degrees. She lived.

Others are less fortunate, even in much milder conditions. One of
Europe's worst weather disasters occurred during a 1964 competitive walk on
a windy, rainy English moor; three of the racers died from hypothermia,
though temperatures never fell below freezing and ranged as high as 45.

But for all scientists and statisticians now know of freezing and its physiology, no one can yet predict exactly how quickly and in whom hypothermia
will strike—and whether it will kill when it does. The cold remains a mystery, more prone to fell men than women, more lethal to the thin and well
muscled than to those with avoirdupois,° and least forgiving to the arrogant
and the unaware.

The process begins even before you leave the car, when you remove your
gloves to squeeze a loose bail back into one of your ski bindings. The freezing
metal bites your flesh. Your skin temperature drops.

Within a few seconds, the palms of your hands are a chilly, painful 60
degrees. Instinctively, the web of surface capillaries on your hands constricts,
sending blood coursing away from your skin and deeper into your torso. Your
body is allowing your fingers to chill in order to keep its vital organs warm.

You replace your gloves, noticing only that your fingers have numbed *10*
slightly. Then you kick boots into bindings and start up the road.

Were you a Norwegian fisherman or Inuit hunter, both of whom frequently work gloveless in the cold, your chilled hands would open their surface capillaries periodically to allow surges of warm blood to pass into them
and maintain their flexibility. This phenomenon, known as the hunter's
response, can elevate a 35-degree skin temperature to 50 degrees within seven
or eight minutes.

Other human adaptations to the cold are more mysterious. Tibetan Buddhist monks can raise the skin temperature of their hands and feet by 15
degrees through meditation. Australian aborigines, who once slept on the
ground, unclothed, on near-freezing nights, would slip into a light hypother-
mic state, suppressing shivering until the rising sun rewarmed them.

You have no such defenses, having spent your days at a keyboard in a
climate-controlled office. Only after about ten minutes of hard climbing, as
your body temperature rises, does blood start seeping back into your fingers.
Sweat trickles down your sternum and spine.

---

avoirdupois: French for "excess weight."

By now you've left the road and decided to shortcut up the forested mountainside to the road's next switchback. Treading slowly through deep, soft snow as the full moon hefts over a spiny ridgetop, throwing silvery bands of moonlight and shadow, you think your friends were right: It's a beautiful night for skiing—though you admit, feeling the minus-30 air bite at your face, it's also cold.

After an hour, there's still no sign of the switchback, and you've begun to worry. You pause to check the map. At this moment, your core temperature reaches its high: 100.8. Climbing in deep snow, you've generated nearly ten times as much body heat as you do when you are resting.

As you step around to orient map to forest, you hear a metallic pop. You look down. The loose bail has disappeared from your binding. You lift your foot and your ski falls from your boot.

You twist on your flashlight, and its cold-weakened batteries throw a yellowish circle in the snow. It's right around here somewhere, you think, as you sift the snow through gloved fingers. Focused so intently on finding the bail, you hardly notice the frigid air pressing against your tired body and sweat-soaked clothes.

The exertion that warmed you on the way uphill now works against you: Your exercise-dilated capillaries carry the excess heat of your core to your skin, and your wet clothing dispels it rapidly into the night. The lack of insulating fat over your muscles allows the cold to creep that much closer to your warm blood.

Your temperature begins to plummet. Within 17 minutes it reaches the normal 98.6. Then it slips below.

At 97 degrees, hunched over in your slow search, the muscles along your neck and shoulders tighten in what's known as pre-shivering muscle tone. Sensors have signaled the temperature control center in your hypothalamus, which in turn has ordered the constriction of the entire web of surface capillaries. Your hands and feet begin to ache with cold. Ignoring the pain, you dig carefully through the snow; another ten minutes pass. Without the bail you know you're in deep trouble.

Finally, nearly 45 minutes later, you find the bail. You even manage to pop it back into its socket and clamp your boot into the binding. But the clammy chill that started around your skin has now wrapped deep into your body's core.

At 95, you've entered the zone of mild hypothermia. You're now trembling violently as your body attains its maximum shivering response, an involuntary condition in which your muscles contract rapidly to generate additional body heat.

It was a mistake, you realize, to come out on a night this cold. You should turn back. Fishing into the front pocket of your shell parka, you fumble out the map. You consulted it to get here; it should be able to guide you back to the warm car. It doesn't occur to you in your increasingly clouded and panicky mental state that you could simply follow your tracks down the way you came.

And after this long stop, the skiing itself has become more difficult. By the time you push off downhill, your muscles have cooled and tightened so dramatically that they no longer contract easily, and once contracted, they won't relax. You're locked into an ungainly, spread-armed, weak-kneed snowplow.

Still, you manage to maneuver between stands of fir, swishing down   25
through silvery light and pools of shadow. You're too cold to think of the beautiful night or of the friends you had meant to see. You think only of the warm Jeep that waits for you somewhere at the bottom of the hill. Its gleaming shell is centered in your mind's eye as you come over the crest of a small knoll. You hear the sudden whistle of wind in your ears as you gain speed. Then, before your mind can quite process what the sight means, you notice a lump in the snow ahead.

Recognizing, slowly, the danger that you are in, you try to jam your skis to a stop. But in your panic, your balance and judgment are poor. Moments later, your ski tips plow into the buried log and you sail headfirst through the air and bellyflop into the snow.

You lie still. There's a dead silence in the forest, broken by the pumping of blood in your ears. Your ankle is throbbing with pain and you've hit your head. You've also lost your hat and a glove. Scratchy snow is packed down your shirt. Meltwater trickles down your neck and spine, joined soon by a thin line of blood from a small cut on your head.

This situation, you realize with an immediate sense of panic, is serious. Scrambling to rise, you collapse in pain, your ankle crumpling beneath you.

As you sink back into the snow, shaken, your heat begins to drain away at an alarming rate, your head alone accounting for 50 percent of the loss. The pain of the cold soon pierces your ears so sharply that you root about in the snow until you find your hat and mash it back onto your head.

But even that little activity has been exhausting. You know you should   30
find your glove as well, and yet you're becoming too weary to feel any urgency. You decide to have a short rest before going on.

An hour passes. At one point, a stray thought says you should start being scared, but fear is a concept that floats somewhere beyond your immediate reach, like that numb hand lying naked in the snow. You've slid into the temperature range at which cold renders the enzymes in your brain less efficient. With every one-degree drop in body temperature below 95, your cerebral metabolic rate falls off by 3 to 5 percent. When your core temperature reaches 93, amnesia nibbles at your consciousness. You check your watch: 12:58. Maybe someone will come looking for you soon. Moments later, you check again. You can't keep the numbers in your head. You'll remember little of what happens next.

Your head drops back. The snow crunches softly in your ear. In the minus-35-degree air, your core temperature falls about one degree every 30 to 40 minutes, your body heat leaching out into the soft, enveloping snow. Apathy at 91 degrees. Stupor at 90.

You've now crossed the boundary into profound hypothermia. By the time your core temperature has fallen to 88 degrees, your body has abandoned the urge to warm itself by shivering. Your blood is thickening like crankcase oil in a cold engine. Your oxygen consumption, a measure of your metabolic rate, has fallen by more than a quarter. Your kidneys, however, work overtime to process the fluid overload that occurred when the blood vessels in your extremities constricted and squeezed fluids toward your center. You feel a powerful urge to urinate, the only thing you feel at all.

By 87 degrees you've lost the ability to recognize a familiar face, should one suddenly appear from the woods.

At 86 degrees, your heart, its electrical impulses hampered by chilled nerve tissues, becomes arrhythmic. It now pumps less than two-thirds the normal amount of blood. The lack of oxygen and the slowing metabolism of your brain, meanwhile, begin to trigger visual and auditory hallucinations. 35

You hear jingle bells. Lifting your face from your snow pillow, you realize with a surge of gladness that they're not sleigh bells; they're welcoming bells hanging from the door of your friends' cabin. You knew it had to be close by. The jingling is the sound of the cabin door opening, just through the fir trees.

Attempting to stand, you collapse in a tangle of skis and poles. That's OK. You can crawl. It's so close.

Hours later, or maybe it's minutes, you realize the cabin still sits beyond the grove of trees. You've crawled only a few feet. The light on your wristwatch pulses in the darkness: 5:20. Exhausted, you decide to rest your head for a moment.

When you lift it again, you're inside, lying on the floor before the woodstove. The fire throws off a red glow. First it's warm; then it's hot; then it's searing your flesh. Your clothing has caught fire.

At 85 degrees, those freezing to death, in a strange, anguished paroxysm, often rip off their clothes. This phenomenon, known as paradoxical undressing, is common enough that urban hypothermia victims are sometimes initially diagnosed as victims of sexual assault. Though researchers are uncertain of the cause, the most logical explanation is that shortly before loss of consciousness, the constricted blood vessels near the body's surface suddenly dilate and produce a sensation of extreme heat against the skin. 40

All you know is that you're burning. You claw off your shell and pile sweater and fling them away.

But then, in a final moment of clarity, you realize there's no stove, no cabin, no friends. You're lying alone in the bitter cold, naked from the waist up. You grasp your terrible misunderstanding, a whole series of misunderstandings, like a dream ratcheting into wrongness. You've shed your clothes, your car, your oil-heated house in town. Without this ingenious technology you're simply a delicate, tropical organism whose range is restricted to a narrow sunlit band that girds the earth at the equator.

And you've now ventured way beyond it.

There's an adage about hypothermia: "You aren't dead until you're warm and dead."

At about 6:00 the next morning, his friends, having discovered the stalled Jeep, find him, still huddled inches from the buried log, his gloveless hand 45 shoved into his armpit. The flesh of his limbs is waxy and stiff as old putty, his pulse nonexistent, his pupils unresponsive to light. Dead.

But those who understand cold know that even as it deadens, it offers perverse salvation. Heat is a presence: the rapid vibrating of molecules. Cold is an absence: the damping of the vibrations. At absolute zero, minus 459.67 degrees Fahrenheit, molecular motion ceases altogether. It is this slowing that converts gases to liquids, liquids to solids, and renders solids harder. It slows bacterial growth and chemical reactions. In the human body, cold shuts down metabolism. The lungs take in less oxygen, the heart pumps less blood. Under normal temperatures, this would produce brain damage. But the chilled brain, having slowed its own metabolism, needs far less oxygen-rich blood and can, under the right circumstances, survive intact.

Setting her ear to his chest, one of his rescuers listens intently. Seconds pass. Then, faintly, she hears a tiny sound—a single thump, so slight that it might be the sound of her own blood. She presses her ear harder to the cold flesh. Another faint thump, then another.

The slowing that accompanies freezing is, in its way, so beneficial that it is even induced at times. Cardiologists today often use deep chilling to slow a patient's metabolism in preparation for heart or brain surgery. In this state of near suspension, the patient's blood flows slowly, his heart rarely beats—or in the case of those on heart-lung machines, doesn't beat at all; death seems near. But carefully monitored, a patient can remain in this cold stasis, undamaged, for hours.

The rescuers quickly wrap their friend's naked torso with a spare parka, his hands with mittens, his entire body with a bivy sack. They brush snow from his pasty, frozen face. Then one snakes down through the forest to the nearest cabin. The others, left in the pre-dawn darkness, huddle against him as silence closes around them. For a moment, the woman imagines she can hear the scurrying, breathing, snoring of a world of creatures that have taken cover this frigid night beneath the thick quilt of snow.

With a "one, two, three," the doctor and nurses slide the man's stiff, curled *50* form onto a table fitted with a mattress filled with warm water which will be regularly reheated. They'd been warned that they had a profound hypothermia case coming in. Usually such victims can be straightened from their tortured fetal positions. This one can't.

Technicians scissor with stainless-steel shears at the man's urine-soaked long underwear and shell pants, frozen together like corrugated cardboard. They attach heart-monitor electrodes to his chest and insert a low-temperature electronic thermometer into his rectum. Digital readings flash: 24 beats per minute and a core temperature of 79.2 degrees.

The doctor shakes his head. He can't remember seeing numbers so low. He's not quite sure how to revive this man without killing him.

In fact, many hypothermia victims die each year in the process of being rescued. In "rewarming shock," the constricted capillaries reopen almost all at once, causing a sudden drop in blood pressure. The slightest movement can send a victim's heart muscle into wild spasms of ventricular fibrillation. In 1980, 16 shipwrecked Danish fishermen were hauled to safety after an hour and a half in the frigid North Sea. They then walked across the deck of the rescue ship, stepped below for a hot drink, and dropped dead, all 16 of them.

"78.9," a technician calls out. "That's three-tenths down."

The patient is now experiencing "afterdrop," in which residual cold close to the body's surface continues to cool the core even after the victim is removed from the outdoors. 55

The doctor rapidly issues orders to his staff: intravenous administration of warm saline, the bag first heated in the microwave to 110 degrees. Elevating the core temperature of an average-size male one degree requires adding about 60 kilocalories of heat. A kilocalorie is the amount of heat needed to raise the temperature of one liter of water one degree Celsius. Since a quart of hot soup at 140 degrees offers about 30 kilocalories, the patient curled on the table would need to consume 40 quarts of chicken broth to push his core temperature up to normal. Even the warm saline, infused directly into his blood, will add only 30 kilocalories.

Ideally, the doctor would have access to a cardiopulmonary bypass machine, with which he could pump out the victim's blood, rewarm and oxygenate it, and pump it back in again, safely raising the core temperature as much as one degree every three minutes. But such machines are rarely available outside major urban hospitals. Here, without such equipment, the doctor must rely on other options.

"Let's scrub for surgery," he calls out.

Moments later, he's sliding a large catheter into an incision in the man's abdominal cavity. Warm fluid begins to flow from a suspended bag, washing through his abdomen, and draining out through another catheter placed in another incision. Prosaically, this lavage operates much like a car radiator in reverse: The solution warms the internal organs, and the warm blood in the organs is then pumped by the heart throughout the body.

The patient's stiff limbs begin to relax. His pulse edges up. But even so the jagged line of his heartbeat flashing across the EKG° screen shows the curious dip known as a J wave, common to hypothermia patients. 60

"Be ready to defibrillate," the doctor warns the EMTs.°

For another hour, nurses and EMTs hover around the edges of the table where the patient lies centered in a warm pool of light, as if offered up to the sun god. They check his heart. They check the heat of the mattress beneath him. They whisper to one another about the foolishness of having gone out alone tonight.

And slowly the patient responds. Another liter of saline is added to the IV. The man's blood pressure remains far too low, brought down by the blood

---

EKG: Electrocardiogram.
EMT: Emergency Medical Technician.

flowing out to the fast-opening capillaries of his limbs. Fluid lost through perspiration and urination has reduced his blood volume. But every 15 or 20 minutes, his temperature rises another degree. The immediate danger of cardiac fibrillation lessens, as the heart and thinning blood warm. Frostbite could still cost him fingers or an earlobe. But he appears to have beaten back the worst of the frigidity.

For the next half hour, an EMT quietly calls the readouts of the thermometer, a mantra that marks the progress of this cold-blooded protoorganism toward a state of warmer, higher consciousness.

"90.4 . . ." 65

"92.2 . . ."

From somewhere far away in the immense, cold darkness, you hear a faint, insistent hum. Quickly it mushrooms into a ball of sound, like a planet rushing toward you, and then it becomes a stream of words.

A voice is calling your name.

You don't want to open your eyes. You sense heat and light playing against your eyelids, but beneath their warm dance a chill wells up inside you from the sunless ocean bottoms and the farthest depths of space. You are too tired even to shiver. You want only to sleep.

"Can you hear me?" 70

You force open your eyes. Lights glare overhead. Around the lights faces hover atop uniformed bodies. You try to think: You've been away a very long time, but where have you been?

"You're at the hospital. You got caught in the cold."

You try to nod. Your neck muscles feel rusted shut, unused for years. They respond to your command with only a slight twitch.

"You'll probably have amnesia," the voice says.

You remember the moon rising over the spiky ridgetop and skiing up 75 toward it, toward someplace warm beneath the frozen moon. After that, nothing—only that immense coldness lodged inside you.

"We're trying to get a little warmth back into you," the voice says.

You'd nod if you could. But you can't move. All you can feel is throbbing discomfort everywhere. Glancing down to where the pain is most biting, you notice blisters filled with clear fluid dotting your fingers, once gloveless in the snow. During the long, cold hours the tissue froze and ice crystals formed in the tiny spaces between your cells, sucking water from them, blocking the blood supply. You stare at them absently.

"I think they'll be fine," a voice from overhead says. "The damage looks superficial. We expect that the blisters will break in a week or so, and the tissue should revive after that."

If not, you know that your fingers will eventually turn black, the color of bloodless, dead tissue. And then they will be amputated.

But worry slips from you as another wave of exhaustion sweeps in. Slowly 80 you drift off, dreaming of warmth, of tropical ocean wavelets breaking across your chest, of warm sand beneath you.

Hours later, still logy and numb, you surface, as if from deep under water. A warm tide seems to be flooding your midsection. Focusing your eyes down there with difficulty, you see tubes running into you, their heat mingling with your abdomen's depthless cold like a churned-up river. You follow the tubes to the bag that hangs suspended beneath the electric light.

And with a lurch that would be a sob if you could make a sound, you begin to understand: The bag contains all that you had so nearly lost. These people huddled around you have brought you sunlight and warmth, things you once so cavalierly dismissed as constant, available, yours, summoned by the simple twisting of a knob or tossing on of a layer.

But in the hours since you last believed that, you've traveled to a place where there is no sun. You've seen that in the infinite reaches of the universe, heat is as glorious and ephemeral as the light of the stars. Heat exists only where matter exists, where particles can vibrate and jump. In the infinite winter of space, heat is tiny; it is the cold that is huge.

Someone speaks. Your eyes move from bright lights to shadowy forms in the dim outer reaches of the room. You recognize the voice of one of the friends you set out to visit, so long ago now. She's smiling down at you crookedly.

"It's cold out there," she says. "Isn't it?"

85

QUESTIONS FOR DISCUSSION

1. What assumptions has Stark made about the social class of skiers and the people most likely to be reading this piece when it was first published?
2. What kinds of people are especially at risk of freezing to death?
3. What mistakes are made by the character Stark invented for this article? Could any of them have been avoided?
4. How can hypothermia be treated? Under what circumstances can someone suffering from profound hypothermia have any chance of surviving?
5. Stark reports "the cold hard facts of freezing to death" within a fictional narrative that traces what happens to an imaginary character exposed to severe cold overnight. How effective is this strategy? Did it influence the extent to which you were willing to trust the information he is reporting?

SUGGESTIONS FOR WRITING

1. Write an essay reporting how you were treated for a sports injury. Research medical literature on your injury and indicate whether other methods of treatment could have been used in your case.
2. Consider the risks that people face when engaging in a sport or other activity of interest to you. Write a report in which you alert readers to these risks.
3. Research heat exhaustion and report how people can protect themselves from the effects of prolonged exposure to extreme heat.

LINKS ■ ■ ■

■ **WITHIN THE BOOK**

For other male views of the outdoors, see "Earth's Eye" by Edward Hoagland (pages 78–82) and "Winners" by Lon Otto (pages 684–689).

■ **ELSEWHERE IN PRINT**

Cobb, Norma, and Charles Sasser. *Arctic Homestead: The True Story of One Family's Survival and Courage in the Alaskan Wilds.* New York: St. Martin's, 2000.

Janowsky, Chris, and Gretchen Janowsky. *Survival: A Manual That Could Save Your Life.* Boulder: Paladin, 1986.

Stark, Peter. *Driving to Greenland: Arctic Travel, Nordic Sport, and Other Ventures into the Heart of Winter.* New York: Lyons, 1994.

---. ed. *Ring of Ice: True Tales of Adventure, Exploration, and Arctic Life.* New York: Lyons, 2000.

---. and Steven M. Krauzer. *Winter Adventure: A Complete Guide to Winter Sports.* New York: Norton, 1995.

Weiss, Hal. *Secrets of Warmth: For Comfort and Survival.* Brooklyn: Vibe, 1988.

■ **ONLINE**

- Frostbite
  <http://www.emedicine.com/emerg/topic209.htm>

- Hypothermia
  <http://www.nlm.nih.gov/medlineplus/hypothermia.html>

- Medical Experiments from the Holocaust and Nazi Medicine
  <http://www.remember.org/educate/medexp.html>

THE NEW GOLD RUSH

Rebecca Solnit

A board member of Citizen's Alert—an environmental group in Nevada—and a Guggenheim Fellow, Rebecca Solnit is the author of Savage Dreams: A Journey into the Landscape Wars of the American West. *In "The New Gold Rush," she describes one such "war": the conflict between a major industry and citizens whose lives are being damaged by that industry. It was first published in the July/August 2000 issue of* Sierra, *a magazine devoted to promoting respect for nature and environmentally responsible public policies. Joan Hamilton, the editor-in-chief of* Sierra, *writes that Solnit "has consistently delivered vivid, solid, provocative prose" and "helps environmentalists see the world from a perspective midway between the fields of ecology and art." As you read "The New Gold Rush," be alert for how Solnit locates information about mining within a larger story.*

The museums of California's Gold Country (as the Sierra Nevada foothills are still called) are full of picturesque sepia-toned photographs of those who made a killing in the Gold Rush, and visiting schoolchildren dress up in historic costumes and play at panning for gold. For a more up-to-date education, though, they should play at testing contaminated water, treating mercury-caused madness, or surveying for vanishing wildlife. By 1857, miners had extracted 760 tons of gold from these hills—and left behind more than ten times as much mercury, as well as devastated forests, slopes, and streams. The profits were quickly spent, but the costs are still rolling in, and if you want to know who's picking up the bill, look in a mirror. Until recently, gold was the measure of value for all other things. Gold was money, and money in its material form was gold, the fulcrum between the concrete world of commodities and the abstraction that is their exchange value. Gold anchored national economies, providing the basis for their currencies. Until 1933, higher-denomination U.S. coins were still made of gold; paper money was originally just a receipt that could be exchanged for governmental gold and silver upon demand.

In the 1970s the United States went off the gold standard, though, and now none of the world's major economies are tied to hoards in vaults. (*The Economist* calls these national stockpiles the "spent fuel of an obsolete monetary system.") The scramble by Australia, Britain, and other nations to sell off much of their gold reserves has contributed to the rapid decline in gold prices in recent years, which has had the benefit of curtailing some mining companies' operations and the detriment of bankrupting others before they've cleaned up their messes.

Unlike most other products of extractive industry, gold has little practical use. Of the 2,500 tons produced worldwide each year, 85 percent goes into

115

jewelry. All the gold ever mined—an estimated 125,000 tons—would form only a 60-foot cube. Of that amount, 80 percent is still around, in bank vaults, personal jewelry boxes, and jewelry stores. Ninety percent of the gold ever mined has been mined since 1848.

How do you measure gold against a landscape? How do you weigh 760 tons of cold metal against the splendor of a 400-mile-long mountain range teeming with grizzly, elk, antelope, and spring-run salmon? How do you weigh it against, clear, fast-flowing rivers, an enormous bay full of wetlands, aquatic life, and edible fish? How do you compare it to the dozens of small Indian nations who for thousands of years had woven their local places and creatures into marvelous stories?

When the Gold Rush ended in California, it moved across the Sierra to Nevada, with the usual effects: the indigenous inhabitants displaced and slaughtered, and Native food sources—fish, game, and piñon pines—devastated. To feed the smelters of Eureka in central Nevada, all the piñon and juniper for 50 miles was cut down by 1878.

Today Nevada produces nearly three-quarters of the nation's, and 10 percent of the world's, gold supply. The state's modern gold rush began when geologists located the Carlin Trend—a 50-by-5-mile belt across northeastern Nevada's Humboldt Basin bearing "invisible gold" in particles too small to be seen. The Trend's first open-pit mine came in 1965, but it was the steep rise of gold prices in the 1980s and the introduction of cyanide heap-leaching that made mining such low-grade ore profitable.

The history of gold mining is about technology making it profitable to go after ore of lower and lower grade. High-grade ore is still refined in roasters and mills, but the low-grade stuff goes into leach heaps, huge hills of pulverized ore mounded atop plastic liners. Cyanide solution is poured through the pile, and the gold particles it carries with it are then extracted from the poisonous runoff. This allows gold to be mined from low-grade ore on a scale none of those men in the sepia-tone photographs could have imagined. Modern gold mining follows a law of diminishing returns, displacing earth and water on a gargantuan scale and producing poison on a large scale, all for the sake of the little ring on your finger. For example, the Mary Harrison Mine that opened in 1853 in Coulterville, near Yosemite, yielded from one-third to one-half an ounce of gold per ton. In 1997 the Barrick Corporation's Betze-Post Mine in the center of the Carlin Trend moved 159 million tons of rock and earth to produce 1.6 million ounces of gold—a mere hundredth of an ounce per ton. Its pit is now up to 1,600 feet deep, a mile wide, and a mile and a half long. Ironically, points out Nevada activist Chris Sewall, this so-called invisible gold leads to colossal pits that can be seen from space, with 350-foot-high leach heaps covering as much as 300 acres.

(Carrie Dann, a Western Shoshone leader battling a gold mine in her own backyard, once said that everyone who buys gold jewelry should have to deal with the consequences too. Ever since, I've pictured a truck driver ringing the doorbell of a home to say, "Ma'am, about that new wristwatch: Would

5

you like your seventy-nine tons on the front lawn or the back? You'll want to keep the kids and dog off 'cause of the acid and arsenic.")

Modern mining is intensely toxic: A teaspoon of 2 percent cyanide solution would kill you. In the beginning, cyanide-laced drainage was left to break down in open ponds where waterfowl would sometimes land and die; nowadays, mines are obliged to cover the ponds with nets. Gold ore often contains sulfur, which forms sulfuric acid when exposed to air and water. The acid draws other heavy metals—including arsenic, antimony, lead, and mercury—out of the ore heaps and into the environment. At the Yerington pit in western Nevada, a toxic plume is moving toward the well field that supplies water for the Yerington Paiute Reservation. The mining corporation that created the catastrophe has gone bankrupt, and the Paiutes are trying to get Superfund designation for the site.

Nevada is the driest state in the Union, but profligate with water when it comes to gold mining. Its springs and mountain streams feed large aquifers and the slender Humboldt River, which meanders nearly 400 miles west from its beginnings in the northeast corner of the state. But 18 large mines in the Humboldt region are working below the water table, so they must "dewater" the mine sites by pumping out underground water at stunning rates. The Betze-Post Mine alone has pumped out more than a half a million acre-feet, and the Lone Tree Mine northeast of Winnemucca pumps an amount equal to one-seventh of the Humboldt's annual flow.

Groundwater, remarks water historian Mark Reisner, "is as nonrenewable as oil." A 5 million acre-foot deficit is being created in the Humboldt Basin—1.6 trillion gallons, the equivalent of 25 years of the river's annual flow. Some of this water is pumped into the Humboldt River, where it generates higher stream flow and wetter wetlands before leaving the region. Some irrigates alfalfa fields. Some is used to process the ore and becomes contaminated with cyanide, acids, and heavy metals. Some is "recharged," or put back into the ground, although it's not necessarily the same pure water that was pumped out, nor will it go back from whence it came.

Nevada hydrologist and Great Basin Minewatch director Tom Myers estimates the water table around the mines is being drawn down as much as 1,000 feet, creating deep subterranean "cones of depression." When the pumps stop, water will be drawn back to these areas to fill up the mine pits, creating a string of deep dead lakes, including the two largest man-made lakes in Nevada. Local springs, streams, and parts of the Humboldt River may dry up. The water table will be radically rearranged. Nobody knows exactly what will happen. Myers' models allow for various scenarios, none of them pretty.

Advocates for natural Nevada are unfortunately as rare as rainfall. "Nobody moves to northern Nevada for the scenery," says Myers. "You and I know how beautiful it is, but the public doesn't." Few writers and artists celebrate the Great Basin, which may be one reason why so much of it is still unpopulated and unprotected. It is an austere country, with great seas of fragrant sagebrush and grass sweeping up to juniper and piñon at higher elevations, whose ranges

10

conceal marvelous clefts and canyons where streams make small oases of wild rose, cottonwood, aspen, and willow alive with butterflies, songbirds, and the rare—but unlisted—sage grouse. Another endangered subspecies, the Lahontan cutthroat trout, lives in the Humboldt River. Pronghorn still range in the remoter places, but mining roads are making those places less and less remote. Between 1985 and 1997, new mining and prospecting roads carved up more than 350,000 acres of previously roadless national forest land. The figures for Bureau of Land Management land are probably greater, but no one has calculated them.

Mining is devouring Nevada, but the state gets little in return: 12,000 jobs and a one percent tax on the gross. About 25 percent of the gross is profit, most of which goes out of state or country. In 1994, Toronto-based Barrick Gold, the world's second-largest gold corporation, paid less than $10,000 to the Department of the Interior for land containing an estimated $8.4 billion in gold, thanks to the 1872 Mining Act. That notorious legislation allows anyone to patent a mining claim on public land for nominal fees and then work it as they will. Newer regulations limit how much a mine can contaminate its surroundings and require a minimal cleanup afterward, but the land is still given away to all comers, foreign or domestic.

Yet it's an open question as to whether the land is the government's to give away. Just as the California Gold Rush took place on land that still legally belonged to its resident tribes, in Nevada's gold rush region, the Western Shoshone have never ceded their land or accepted payment for it. The $26 million the United States originally proposed to pay is laughable compared with the quantities of gold taken from the region every year, as were the diminutive payments California Indians received for their land long after the Gold Rush.

At any rate, all the gold in Nevada can't pay for a ruined ecosystem. In southern Crescent Valley, Nevada, a huge new mine has opened up, Cortez Gold's Pipeline Deposit Mine. For thousands of years there had been nothing here but sagebrush through which any creature might move freely, and even a few years back when I worked as a land-rights activist with the Western Shoshone it was open space threatened by nothing worse than a few cows. Now it is dominated by steep slopes of waste-rock piles and fenced-off cyanide leach heaps hundreds of feet high and thousands long, mounds for which a correspondingly large hole exists nearby. To allow it to work under the water table, the mine pumps 25,000 gallons per minute into black pipes that lead to a distant grid of rectangular "recharge" ponds, from which the water is supposed to drain back into the aquifer. But the recharge isn't working the way it's supposed to; much of it is spreading into the valley instead, making it unnaturally green and turning the family cemetery of the Danns, an extended family of Western Shoshones who have lived in the valley for generations, into spongy marsh.

Traditional Western Shoshones like Carrie Dann have been fighting to get their land back throughout most of this century. Her outrage about the mining in Crescent Valley is unblunted by 5 years of living with the Pipeline Mine and 30 years of living with the smaller Cortez Mine nearer her home. "Mining is against our culture, against our spiritual ways," she says. "They're pumping all the life out of the earth. It's not humane, it's not right. It'll be paid for by children not even here yet." Gold mining in California contaminated surface water, she says, but in Nevada the poison is underground. "How do you control that? Are they going to tell me that they're going to control underground water contamination when we can't clean aboveground contamination?

"To me water is a gift of life."

Gold has been prized because it is the most inert metal, changeless and incorruptible. Water is prized for its opposite qualities of fluidity and mobility. To value gold over water is to value economy over ecology, that which can be locked up over that which connects all things.

The oldest story I know about gold is also about water. I thought of the story of King Midas when Chris Sewall, an organizer for the Western Shoshone Defense Project, took me to look at the recharge ponds and acid mine-drainage of the shut-down Buckhorn Mine, just over the mountains behind the Danns' home. (Until a few embankments were bulldozed, acid from the mine ran down the road and into beautiful Willow Creek, leaving it covered with dead earthworms.)   20

When King Midas was first granted the golden touch, says Ovid, he was "delighted with the misfortune which had befallen him." But then even the water he tried to drink turned to gold as it touched his lips. Parched with thirst, he begged the god Bacchus to take back his gift. Bacchus sent him to a sacred spring to "wash away his crime" and recover his ability to drink, to touch, to live. Afterward, Midas hated riches and dwelt in the forest.

Midas is also the name of a tiny town just up the road from the Twin Creeks Mine, which in 1996 had proposed putting a huge tailings pile over the site of the 1911 "Shoshone Mike" massacre, in which the U.S. Cavalry murdered a family of eight traditional Newe people in the last Indian massacre of its career. Twin Creeks assured Western Shoshones that its tailings would "protect the site in perpetuity."

Last year I toured Barrick's Betze-Post Mine—the largest gold mine in North America and third largest in the world—and was amazed how much the pit had grown since 1992 when I saw it last. I was equally amazed when Barrick's young tour guide told me and the leathery, upbeat Texas retirees who made up our group that "the first inhabitants of the Elko area were fur trappers in 1828." Another guide showed us a faint flush of green on one of the steep embankments and told us that it meant that the landscape had been restored to its natural condition. Before the mine, biologists noted that the site was an active "lek," or sage grouse dancing ground, where more than 100 of the imperiled birds used to gather. Now there are none. One day even the creek disappeared: Maggie Creek, which runs past Barrick's mines, vanished into a sinkhole.

Some states are seeking to avoid Nevada's fate. Last year in eastern Washington, the Okanogan Highlands Alliance got the Interior Department to interpret the 1872 Mining Act in the environment's favor for the first time. The law provides for a five-acre mill site per mining claim, but modern mining takes up far more room—so Battle Mountain Gold Corporation's permits for Buckhorn Mountain were denied on the grounds that the mill site was over the allowable size. Interior later reversed its decision, but this year, Washington State denied Battle Mountain water rights, effectively blocking the mine.

(As part of its campaign, the Okanogan Highlands Alliance started bottling   25
Buckhorn water labeled with their slogan—"Pure Water Is More Precious Than Gold." This is literally true: The 2,000 gallons of water it would take to produce an ounce of gold worth about $280 was itself worth $3,540 bottled. Despite its defeat in Washington, Battle Mountain is still at work in Nevada.)

In eastern Montana, Pegasus Gold Corporation's Zortman-Landusky Mine, the world's very first large-scale cyanide heap-leach mine when it opened in 1979, will also be Montana's last. In 1996, the mine was fined $37 million for its acid mine drainage and cyanide contamination, fined again in 1997 for stream contamination, and went bankrupt in 1998. That left the state to pay tens of millions for a cleanup that still won't create pure water or restore Spirit Mountain, now just a pile of poisonous powder. At the Fort Belknap Reservation next to the mine, cyanide flowed from taps. "Our worst nightmares have come true," says Rose Main, a White Clay Assiniboin from Fort Balknap. "Now we're living in them." The mined land had originally been part of the reservation, but when gold was discovered on it in the 1890s, the boundaries were redrawn. Thanks to this disaster and many like it, Montanans recently voted to ban all new or expanded cyanide heap-leach mines.

In the end, gold mining, like all other environmental dilemmas, shows the consequences of valuing what can be pocketed and possessed over "the gift of life." Where will the modern Midases find a stream pure enough to wash away their crimes?

QUESTIONS FOR DISCUSSION

1. What does Solnit achieve by linking her study of contemporary gold mining in Nevada with mining practices in nineteenth-century California?
2. Why is gold still being mined at a time when nations are selling off gold reserves? What creates a market for gold even though it no longer backs major currencies?
3. Consider the series of questions Solnit raises in paragraph 4. How does she expect readers to respond to these questions?
4. Solnit locates all of paragraph 8 within parentheses. What is the rhetorical effect of this punctuation?
5. What does this article reveal about Native American views of the environment?
6. What are the environmental consequences of gold mining in Nevada?
7. Although Solnit is reporting information, not writing an argument, does her report lead you to favor any changes in laws regulating mining?

SUGGESTIONS FOR WRITING

1. Write about the environmental consequences of a major industry in your own community or state.
2. Interview people who like to wear gold jewelry and report how they respond to information about gold-mining practices.
3. Solnit notes that "the Western Shoshone have never ceded their land or accepted payment for it." Research how the federal government has tried to determine what lands belong to the Western Shoshone or other Native Americans, and report your findings.

LINKS ▪ ▪ ▪

▪ WITHIN THE BOOK

See "Earth's Eye" by Edward Hoagland (pages 72–82) for another view about the value of a pristine environment.

▪ ELSEWHERE IN PRINT

Abbey, Edward. *The Journey Home: Some Words in Defense of the American West.* 1977. New York: Dutton, 1991.

Berry, Wendell. *The Gift of Good Land: Further Essays, Cultural and Agricultural.* San Francisco: North Point, 1981.

Lapp, Rudolph M. *Blacks in Gold Rush California.* New Haven: Yale UP, 1977.

Mann, Ralph. *After the Gold Rush: Society in Green Valley and Nevada City, California 1849–1870.* Stanford: Stanford UP, 1982.

Solnit, Rebecca. *Savage Dreams: A Journey into the Hidden Wars of the American West.* San Francisco: Sierra, 1994.

———. *Wanderlust: A History of Walking.* New York: Viking, 2000.

▪ ONLINE

- Brief Biography
  <http://www.banffcentre.ab.ca/press/contributors/solnit_rebecca.htm>

- Environmental Impact of Mining
  <http://directory.google.com/Top/Science/Environment/Mining>

- Environmental Protection Agency
  <http://www.epa.gov>

- Gold Mining Issues
  <http://www.goldminingoutlook.com>

WHY McDONALD'S FRIES TASTE SO GOOD

Eric Schlosser

Eric Schlosser is the author of Fast Food Nation, *which has been described as "a groundbreaking work of investigation and cultural history, likely to transform the way America thinks about the way it eats." Discussing what motivated him to do the research for this book, he told an interviewer, "I'm not a radical vegetarian, although I have a lot of respect for vegetarians and I think a lot of their arguments are very compelling. I came to this project as a person who has eaten enormous amounts of fast food and as a person who has probably eaten more hamburgers than any other type of food." "Why McDonald's Fries Taste So Good" is an excerpt from Schlosser's book. It was published in a 2001 issue of the* Atlantic Monthly, *to which Schlosser is a regular contributor. Read primarily by college-educated men and women, the* Atlantic Monthly *has been published since 1857. Each issue includes well-regarded analyses of social and political concerns, fiction, and poetry, as well as reviews of books and movies.*

The french fry was "almost sacrosanct for me," Ray Kroc, one of the founders of McDonald's, wrote in his autobiography, "its preparation a ritual to be followed religiously." During the chain's early years french fries were made from scratch every day. Russet Burbank potatoes were peeled, cut into shoestrings, and fried in McDonald's kitchens. As the chain expanded nationwide, in the mid-1960s, it sought to cut labor costs, reduce the number of suppliers, and ensure that its fries tasted the same at every restaurant. McDonald's began switching to frozen french fries in 1966—and few customers noticed the difference. Nevertheless, the change had a profound effect on the nation's agriculture and diet. A familiar food had been transformed into a highly processed industrial commodity. McDonald's fries now come from huge manufacturing plants that can peel, slice, cook, and freeze two million pounds of potatoes a day. The rapid expansion of McDonald's and the popularity of its low-cost, mass-produced fries changed the way Americans eat. In 1960 Americans consumed an average of about eighty-one pounds of fresh potatoes and four pounds of frozen french fries. In 2000 they consumed an average of about fifty pounds of fresh potatoes and thirty pounds of frozen fries. Today McDonald's is the largest buyer of potatoes in the United States.

The taste of McDonald's french fries played a crucial role in the chain's success—fries are much more profitable than hamburgers—and was long praised by customers, competitors, and even food critics. James Beard loved McDonald's fries. Their distinctive taste does not stem from the kind of potatoes that McDonald's buys, the technology that processes them, or the restaurant equipment that fries them: other chains use Russet Burbanks, buy their french fries from the same large processing companies, and have similar fryers in their restaurant kitchens. The taste of a french fry is largely determined by the cooking oil. For decades McDonald's cooked its french fries in a mixture of about seven percent cottonseed oil and 93 percent beef tallow. The mixture gave the fries their unique flavor—and more saturated beef fat per ounce than a McDonald's hamburger.

In 1990, amid a barrage of criticism over the amount of cholesterol in its fries, McDonald's switched to pure vegetable oil. This presented the company with a challenge: how to make fries that subtly taste like beef without cooking them in beef tallow. A look at the ingredients in McDonald's french fries suggests how the problem was solved. Toward the end of the list is a seemingly innocuous yet oddly mysterious phrase: "natural flavor." That ingredient helps to explain not only why the fries taste so good but also why most fast food—indeed, most of the food Americans eat today—tastes the way it does.

Open your refrigerator, your freezer, your kitchen cupboards, and look at the labels on your food. You'll find "natural flavor" or "artificial flavor" in just about every list of ingredients. The similarities between these two broad categories are far more significant than the differences. Both are man-made additives that give most processed food most of its taste. People usually buy a food item the first time because of its packaging or appearance. Taste usually determines whether they buy it again. About 90 percent of the money that Americans now spend on food goes to buy processed food. The canning, freezing, and dehydrating techniques used in processing destroy most of food's flavor— and so a vast industry has arisen in the United States to make processed food palatable. Without this flavor industry today's fast food would not exist. The names of the leading American fast-food chains and their best-selling menu items have become embedded in our popular culture and famous worldwide. But few people can name the companies that manufacture fast food's taste.

The flavor industry is highly secretive. Its leading companies will not   5
divulge the precise formulas of flavor compounds or the identities of clients. The secrecy is deemed essential for protecting the reputations of beloved brands. The fast-food chains, understandably, would like the public to believe that the flavors of the food they sell somehow originate in their restaurant kitchens, not in distant factories run by other firms. A McDonald's french fry is one of countless foods whose flavor is just a component in a complex manufacturing process. The look and the taste of what we eat now are frequently deceiving—by design.

THE FLAVOR CORRIDOR

The New Jersey Turnpike runs through the heart of the flavor industry, an industrial corridor dotted with refineries and chemical plants. International Flavors & Fragrances (IFF), the world's largest flavor company, has a manufacturing facility off Exit 8A in Dayton, New Jersey; Givaudan, the world's second-largest flavor company, has a plant in East Hanover. Haarmann & Reimer, the largest German flavor company, has a plant in Teterboro, as does Takasago, the largest Japanese flavor company. Flavor Dynamics has a plant in South Plainfield; Frutarom is in North Bergen; Elan Chemical is in Newark. Dozens of companies manufacture flavors in the corridor between Teaneck and South Brunswick. Altogether the area produces about two thirds of the flavor additives sold in the United States.

The IFF plant in Dayton is a huge pale-blue building with a modern office complex attached to the front. It sits in an industrial park, not far from a BASF plastics factory, a Jolly French Toast factory, and a plant that manufactures Liz Claiborne cosmetics. Dozens of tractor-trailers were parked at the IFF loading dock the afternoon I visited, and a thin cloud of steam floated from a roof vent. Before entering the plant, I signed a nondisclosure form, promising not to reveal the brand names of foods that contain IFF flavors. The place reminded me of Willy Wonka's chocolate factory. Wonderful smells drifted through the hallways, men and women in neat white lab coats cheerfully went about their work, and hundreds of little glass bottles sat on laboratory tables and shelves. The bottles, contained powerful but fragile flavor chemicals, shielded from light by brown glass and round white caps shut tight. The long chemical names on the little white labels were as mystifying to me as medieval Latin. These odd-sounding things would be mixed and poured and turned into new substances, like magic potions.

I was not invited into the manufacturing areas of the IFF plant, where, it was thought, I might discover trade secrets. Instead I toured various laboratories and pilot kitchens, where the flavors of well-established brands are tested or adjusted, and where whole new flavors are created. IFF's snack-and-savory lab is responsible for the flavors of potato chips, corn chips, breads, crackers, breakfast cereals, and pet food. The confectionery lab devises flavors for ice cream, cookies, candies, toothpastes, mouthwashes, and antacids. Everywhere I looked, I saw famous, widely advertised products sitting on laboratory desks and tables. The beverage lab was full of brightly colored liquids in clear bottles. It comes up with flavors for popular soft drinks, sports drinks, bottled teas, and wine coolers, for all-natural juice drinks, organic soy drinks, beers, and malt liquors. In one pilot kitchen I saw a dapper food technologist, a middle-aged man with an elegant tie beneath his crisp lab coat, carefully preparing a batch of cookies with white frosting and pink-and-white sprinkles. In another pilot kitchen I saw a pizza oven, a grill, a milk-shake machine, and a french fryer identical to those I'd seen at innumerable fast-food restaurants.

In addition to being the world's largest flavor company, IFF manufactures the smells of six of the ten best-selling fine perfumes in the United States, including Estée Lauder's Beautiful, Clinique's Happy, Lancôme's Trésor, and Calvin Klein's Eternity. It also makes the smells of household products such as deodorant, dishwashing detergent, bath soap, shampoo, furniture polish, and floor wax. All these aromas are made through essentially the same process: the manipulation of volatile chemicals. The basic science behind the scent of your shaving cream is the same as that governing the flavor of your TV dinner.

"NATURAL" AND "ARTIFICIAL"

Scientists now believe that human beings acquired the sense of taste as a way to avoid being poisoned. Edible plants generally taste sweet, harmful ones bitter. The taste buds on our tongues can detect the presence of half a dozen or so basic tastes, including sweet, sour, bitter, salty, astringent, and umami, a taste discovered by Japanese researchers—a rich and full sense of deliciousness triggered by amino acids in foods such as meat, shellfish, mushrooms, potatoes, and seaweed. Taste buds offer a limited means of detection, however, compared with the human olfactory system, which can perceive thousands of different chemical aromas. Indeed, "flavor" is primarily the smell of gases being released by the chemicals you've just put in your mouth. The aroma of a food can be responsible for as much as 90 percent of its taste.

The act of drinking, sucking, or chewing a substance releases its volatile gases. They flow out of your mouth and up your nostrils, or up the passageway in the back of your mouth, to a thin layer of nerve cells called the olfactory epithelium, located at the base of your nose, right between your eyes. Your brain combines the complex smell signals from your olfactory epithelium with the simple taste signals from your tongue, assigns a flavor to what's in your mouth, and decides if it's something you want to eat.

A person's food preferences, like his or her personality, are formed during the first few years of life, through a process of socialization. Babies innately prefer sweet tastes and reject bitter ones; toddlers can learn to enjoy hot and spicy food, bland health food, or fast food, depending on what the people around them eat. The human sense of smell is still not fully understood. It is greatly affected by psychological factors and expectations. The mind focuses intently one some of the aromas that surround us and filters out the overwhelming majority. People can grow accustomed to bad smells or good smells; they stop noticing what once seemed overpowering. Aroma and memory are somehow inextricably linked. A smell can suddenly evoke a long-forgotten moment. The flavors of childhood foods seem to leave an indelible mark, and adults often return to them, without always knowing why. These "comfort foods" become a source of pleasure and reassurance—a fact that fast-food chains use to their advantage. Childhood memories of Happy Meals, which come with french fries, can translate into frequent adult visits to McDonald's. On average, Americans now eat about four servings of french fries every week.

The human craving for flavor has been a largely unacknowledged and unexamined force in history. For millennia royal empires have been built, unexplored lands traversed, and great religions and philosophies forever changed by

10

the spice trade. In 1492 Christopher Columbus set sail to find seasoning. Today the influence of flavor in the world marketplace is no less decisive. The rise and fall of corporate empires—of soft-drink companies, snack-food companies, and fast-food chains—is often determined by how their products taste.

The flavor industry emerged in the mid–nineteenth century, as processed foods began to be manufactured on a large scale. Recognizing the need for flavor additives, early food processors turned to perfume companies that had long experience working with essential oils and volatile aromas. The great perfume houses of England, France, and the Netherlands produced many of the first flavor compounds. In the early part of the twentieth century Germany took the technological lead in flavor production, owing to its powerful chemical industry. Legend has it that a German scientist discovered methyl anthranilate, one of the first artificial flavors, by accident while mixing chemicals in his laboratory. Suddenly the lab was filled with the sweet smell of grapes. Methyl anthranilate later became the chief flavor compound in grape Kool-Aid. After World War II much of the perfume industry shifted from Europe to the United States, settling in New York City near the garment district and the fashion houses. The flavor industry came with it, later moving to New Jersey for greater plant capacity. Man-made flavor additives were used mostly in baked goods, candies, and sodas until the 1950s, when sales of processed food began to soar. The invention of gas chromatographs and mass spectrometers—machines capable of detecting volatile gases at low levels—vastly increased the number of flavors that could be synthesized. By the mid-1960s flavor companies were churning out compounds to supply the taste of Pop Tarts, Bac-Os, Tab, Tang, Filet-O-Fish sandwiches, and literally thousands of other new foods.

The American flavor industry now has annual revenues of about $1.4 billion. Approximately 10,000 new processed-food products are introduced every year in the United States. Almost all of them require flavor additives. And about nine out of ten of these products fail. The latest flavor innovations and corporate realignments are heralded in publications such as *Chemical Market Reporter, Food Chemical News, Food Engineering,* and *Food Product Design.* The progress of IFF has mirrored that of the flavor industry as a whole. IFF was formed in 1958, through the merger of two small companies. Its annual revenues have grown almost fifteenfold since the early 1970s, and it currently has manufacturing facilities in twenty countries.

15

Today's sophisticated spectrometers, gas chromatographs, and headspace-vapor analyzers provide a detailed map of a food's flavor components, detecting chemical aromas present in amounts as low as one part per billion. The human nose, however, is even more sensitive. A nose can detect aromas present in quantities of a few parts per trillion—an amount equivalent to about 0.000000000003 percent. Complex aromas, such as those of coffee and roasted meat, are composed of volatile gases from nearly a thousand different chemicals. The smell of a strawberry arises from the interaction of about 350 chemicals that are present in minute amounts. The quality that people seek most of all in a food—flavor—is usually present in a quantity too infinitesimal to be measured in traditional culinary terms such as ounces or teaspoons. The chemical that provides the dominant flavor of bell pepper can be tasted in amounts as low as 0.02 parts per billion; one drop is sufficient to add flavor to five average-size swimming pools. The flavor additive usually comes next to last in a processed food's list of ingredients and often costs less than its packaging. Soft drinks contain a larger proportion of flavor additives than most products. The flavor in a twelve-ounce can of Coke costs about half a cent.

The color additives in processed foods are usually present in even smaller amounts than the flavor compounds. Many of New Jersey's flavor companies also manufacture these color additives, which are used to make processed foods look fresh and appealing. Food coloring serves many of the same decorative purposes as lipstick, eye shadow, mascara—and is often made from the same pigments. Titanium dioxide, for example, has proved to be an especially versatile mineral. It gives many processed candies, frostings, and icings their bright white color; it is a common ingredient in women's cosmetics; and it is the pigment used in many white oil paints and house paints. At Burger King, Wendy's, and McDonald's coloring agents have been added to many of the soft drinks, salad dressings, cookies, condiments, chicken dishes, and sandwich buns.

Studies have found that the color of a food can greatly affect how its taste is perceived. Brightly colored foods frequently seem to taste better than bland-looking foods, even when the flavor compounds are identical. Foods that somehow look off-color often seem to have off tastes. For thousands of years human beings have relied on visual cues to help determine what is edible. The color of fruit suggests whether it is ripe, the color of meat whether it is rancid. Flavor researchers sometimes use colored lights to modify the influence of visual cues during taste tests. During one experiment in the early 1970s people were served an oddly tinted meal of steak and french fries that appeared normal beneath colored lights. Everyone thought the meal tasted fine until the lighting was changed. Once it became apparent that the steak was actually blue and the fries were green, some people became ill.

The federal Food and Drug Administration does not require companies to disclose the ingredients of their color or flavor additives so long as all the chemicals in them are considered by the agency to be GRAS ("generally recognized as safe"). This enables companies to maintain the secrecy of their formulas. It also hides the fact that flavor compounds often contain more ingredients than the foods to which they give taste. The phrase "artificial strawberry flavor" gives little hint of the chemical wizardry and manufacturing skill that can make a highly processed food taste like strawberries.

A typical artificial strawberry flavor, like the kind found in a Burger King strawberry milk shake, contains the following ingredients: amyl acetate, amyl butyrate, amyl valerate, anethol, anisyl formate, benzyl acetate, benzyl isobutyrate, butyric acid, cinnamyl isobutyrate, cinnamyl valerate, cognac essential oil, diacetyl, dipropyl ketone, ethyl acetate, ethyl amyl ketone, ethyl butyrate, ethyl cinnamate, ethyl heptanoate, ethyl heptylate, ethyl lactate, ethyl

20

methylphenylglycidate, ethyl nitrate, ethyl propionate, ethyl valerate, heliotropin, hydroxyphenyl-2-butanone (10 percent solution in alcohol), α-ionone, isobutyl anthranilate, isobutyl butyrate, lemon essential oil, maltol, 4-methylacetophenone, methyl anthranilate, methyl benzoate, methyl cinnamate, methyl heptine carbonate, methyl naphthyl ketone, methyl salicylate, mint essential oil, neroli essential oil, nerolin, neryl isobutyrate, orris butter, phenethyl alcohol, rose, rum ether, γ-undecalactone, vanillin, and solvent.

Although flavors usually arise from a mixture of many different volatile chemicals, often a single compound supplies the dominant aroma. Smelled alone, that chemical provides an unmistakable sense of the food. Ethyl-2-methyl butyrate, for example, smells just like an apple. Many of today's highly processed foods offer a blank palette: Whatever chemicals are added to them will give them specific tastes. Adding methyl-2-pyridyl ketone makes something taste like popcorn. Adding ethyl-3-hydroxy butanoate makes it taste like marshmallow. The possibilities are now almost limitless. Without affecting appearance or nutritional value, processed foods could be made with aroma chemicals such as hexanal (the smell of freshly cut grass) or 3-methyl butanoic acid (the smell of body odor).

The 1960s were the heyday of artificial flavors in the United States. The synthetic versions of flavor compounds were not subtle, but they did not have to be, given the nature of most processed food. For the past twenty years food processors have tried hard to use only "natural flavors" in their products. According to the FDA, these must be derived entirely from natural sources— from herbs, spices, fruits, vegetables, beef, chicken, yeast, bark, roots, and so forth. Consumers prefer to see natural flavors on a label, out of a belief that they are more healthful. Distinctions between artificial and natural flavors can be arbitrary and somewhat absurd, based more on how the flavor has been made than on what it actually contains.

"A natural flavor," says Terry Acree, a professor of food science at Cornell University, "is a flavor that's been derived with an out-of-date technology." Natural flavors and artificial flavors sometimes contain exactly the same chemicals, produced through different methods. Amyl acetate, for example, provides the dominant note of banana flavor. When it is distilled from bananas with a solvent, amyl acetate is a natural flavor. When it is produced by mixing vinegar with amyl alcohol and adding sulfuric acid as a catalyst, amyl acetate is an artificial flavor. Either way it smells and tastes the same. "Natural flavor" is now listed among the ingredients of everything from Health Valley Blueberry Granola Bars to Taco Bell Hot Taco Sauce.

A natural flavor is not necessarily more healthful or purer than an artificial one. When almond flavor—benzaldehyde—is derived from natural sources, such as peach and apricot pits, it contains traces of hydrogen cyanide, a deadly poison. Benzaldehyde derived by mixing oil of clove and amyl acetate does not contain any cyanide. Nevertheless, it is legally considered an artificial flavor and sells at a much lower price. Natural and artificial flavors are now manufactured at the same chemical plants, places that few people would associate with Mother Nature.

A TRAINED NOSE AND A POETIC SENSIBILITY

The small and elite group of scientists who create most of the flavor in 25 most of the food now consumed in the United States are called "flavorists." They draw on a number of disciplines in their work: biology, psychology, physiology, and organic chemistry. A flavorist is a chemist with a trained nose and a poetic sensibility. Flavors are created by blending scores of different chemicals in tiny amounts—a process governed by scientific principles but demanding a fair amount of art. In an age when delicate aromas and microwave ovens do not easily co-exist, the job of the flavorist is to conjure illusions about processed food and, in the words of one flavor company's literature, to ensure "consumer likeability." The flavorists with whom I spoke were discreet, in keeping with the dictates of their trade. They were also charming, cosmopolitan, and ironic. They not only enjoyed fine wine but could identify the chemicals that give each grape its unique aroma. One flavorist compared his work to composing music. A well-made flavor compound will have a "top note" that is often followed by a "dry-down" and a "leveling-off," with different chemicals responsible for each stage. The taste of a food can be radically altered by minute changes in the flavoring combination. "A little odor goes a long way," one flavorist told me.

In order to give a processed food a taste that consumers will find appealing, a flavorist must always consider the food's "mouthfeel"—the unique combination of textures and chemical interactions that affect how the flavor is perceived. Mouthfeel can be adjusted through the use of various fats, gums, starches, emulsifiers, and stabilizers. The aroma chemicals in a food can be precisely analyzed, but the elements that make up mouthfeel are much harder to measure. How does one quantify a pretzel's hardness, a french fry's crispness? Food technologists are now conducting basic research in rheology, the branch of physics that examines the flow and deformation of materials. A number of companies sell sophisticated devices that attempt to measure mouthfeel. The TA.XT2i Texture Analyzer, produced by the Texture Technologies Corporation, of Scarsdale, New York, performs calculations based on data derived from as many as 250 separate probes. It is essentially a mechanical mouth. It gauges the most-important rheological properties of a food—bounce, creep, breaking point, density, crunchiness, chewiness, gumminess, lumpiness, rubberiness, springiness, slipperiness, smoothness, softness, wetness, juiciness, spreadability, springback, and tackiness.

Some of the most important advances in flavor manufacturing are now occurring in the field of biotechnology. Complex flavors are being made using enzyme reactions, fermentation, and fungal and tissue cultures. All the flavors created by these methods—including the ones being synthesized by fungi—are considered natural flavors by the FDA. The new enzyme-based processes are responsible for extremely true-to-life dairy flavors. One company now offers not just butter flavor but also fresh creamy butter, cheesy butter, milky butter, savory melted butter, and super-concentrated butter flavor, in liquid or powder form. The development of new fermentation techniques, along with new techniques for heating mixtures of sugar and amino acids, have led to the creation of much more realistic meat flavors.

The McDonald's Corporation most likely drew on these advances when it eliminated beef tallow from its french fries. The company will not reveal the exact origin of the natural flavor added to its fries. In response to inquiries from *Vegetarian Journal,* however, McDonald's did acknowledge that its fries derive some of their characteristic flavor from "an animal source." Beef is the probable source, although other meats cannot be ruled out. In France, for example, fries are sometimes cooked in duck fat or horse tallow.

Other popular fast foods derive their flavor from unexpected ingredients. McDonald's Chicken McNuggets contain beef extracts, as does Wendy's Grilled Chicken Sandwich. Burger King's BK Broiler Chicken Breast Patty contains "natural smoke flavor." A firm called Red Arrow Products specializes in smoke flavor, which is added to barbecue sauces, snack foods, and processed meats. Red Arrow manufactures natural smoke flavor by charring sawdust and capturing the aroma chemicals released into the air. The smoke is captured in water and then bottled, so that other companies can sell food that seems to have been cooked over a fire.

The Vegetarian Legal Action Network recently petitioned the FDA to issue new labeling requirements for foods that contain natural flavors. The group wants food processors to list the basic origins of their flavors on their labels. At the moment vegetarians often have no way of knowing whether a flavor additive contains beef, pork, poultry, or shellfish. One of the most widely used color additives—whose presence is often hidden by the phrase "color added"—violates a number of religious dietary restrictions, may cause allergic reactions in susceptible people, and comes from an unusual source. Cochineal extract (also known as carmine or carminic acid) is made from the desiccated bodies of female *Dactylopius coccus Costa,* a small insect harvested mainly in Peru and the Canary Islands. The bug feeds on red cactus berries, and color from the berries accumulates in the females and their unhatched larvae. The insects are collected, dried, and ground into a pigment. It takes about 70,000 of them to produce a pound of carmine, which is used to make processed foods look pink, red, or purple. Dannon strawberry yogurt gets its color from carmine, and so do many frozen fruit bars, candies, and fruit fillings, and Ocean Spray pink-grapefruit juice drink.

In a meeting room at IFF, Brian Grainger let me sample some of the company's flavors. It was an unusual taste test—there was no food to taste. Grainger is a senior flavorist at IFF, a soft-spoken chemist with graying hair, an English accent, and a fondness for understatement. He could easily be mistaken for a British diplomat or the owner of a West End brasserie° with two Michelin

30

West End brasserie: A small restaurant serving beer and wine; located, in this case, within a fashionable part of London.

stars. Like many in the flavor industry, he has an Old World, old-fashioned sensibility. When I suggested that IFF's policy of secrecy and discretion was out of step with our mass-marketing, brand-conscious, self-promoting age, and that the company should put its own logo on the countless products that bear its flavors, instead of allowing other companies to enjoy the consumer loyalty and affection inspired by those flavors, Grainger politely disagreed, assuring me that such a thing would never be done. In the absence of public credit or acclaim, the small and secretive fraternity of flavor chemists praise one another's work. By analyzing the flavor formula of a product, Grainger can often tell which of his counterparts at a rival firm devised it. Whenever he walks down a supermarket aisle, he takes a quiet pleasure in seeing the well-known foods that contain his flavors.

Grainger had brought a dozen small glass bottles from the lab. After he opened each bottle, I dipped a fragrance-testing filter into it—a long white strip of paper designed to absorb aroma chemicals without producing off notes. Before placing each strip of paper in front of my nose, I closed my eyes. Then I inhaled deeply, and one food after another was conjured from the glass bottles. I smelled fresh cherries, black olives, sautéed onions, and shrimp. Grainger's most remarkable creation took me by surprise. After closing my eyes, I suddenly smelled a grilled hamburger. The aroma was uncanny, almost miraculous—as if someone in the room were flipping burgers on a hot grill. But when I opened my eyes, I saw just a narrow strip of white paper and a flavorist with a grin.

QUESTIONS FOR DISCUSSION

1. Schlosser claims that approximately "90 percent of the money that Americans now spend on food goes to buy processed food." What is "processed food," and why do you think Americans eat so much of it?
2. What factors determine how we taste the food we eat?
3. What is the difference between "natural" and "artificial" flavor?
4. Consider paragraph 20. What is the rhetorical effect of listing so many chemicals in a single paragraph?
5. Why do vegetarians have reason to be concerned about the flavor industry?
6. What effect has this article had upon your appetite? Are you likely to make any changes in your diet?

SUGGESTIONS FOR WRITING

1. Write an essay explaining why you choose to eat the foods you most frequently buy.
2. Research the food plan at your college or university and explain how dieticians select the offerings that are available to you on campus.
3. Find out what preservatives are most commonly used in processed food and explain what effect, if any, they have upon human health.

LINKS ■ ■ ■

■ **WITHIN THE BOOK**

To help you understand why Americans buy certain foods, see "Please, Please, You're Driving Me Wild" by Jean Kilbourne (pages 413–426).

■ **ELSEWHERE IN PRINT**

Brenner, Joël Glenn. *The Emperors of Chocolate: Inside the Secret Worlds of Hershey and Mars.* New York: Random, 1999.

Kroc, Ray, and Robert Anderson. *Grinding It Out: The Making of McDonald's.* 1977. New York: St. Martin's, 1990.

Love, John F. *McDonald's: Behind the Arches.* New York: Bantam, 1986.

Risch, Sara J., and Chi-Tango Ho. *Flavor Chemistry: Industrial and Academic Research.* Washington, DC: American Chemical Soc., 2000.

Schlosser, Eric. *Fast Food Nation.* Boston: Houghton, 2001.

Teranishi, Roy, Emily L. Wick, and Irwin Hornstein, eds. *Flavor Chemistry: Thirty Years of Progress.* New York: Kluwer, 1999.

■ **ONLINE**

- Archived Articles of Eric Schlosser
  http://www.search.atomz.com/search/
  ?sp-q=schlosser&spa=sp09210600>

- A Chat with Eric Schlosser
  <http://www.usnews.com/usnews/chat/schlossertran.htm>

- The Impact of McDonald's
  <http://www.mcdonaldization.com/main.shtml>

- International Flavors and Fragrances
  <http://www.iff.com>

- The Secret History of French Fries
  <http://www.stim.com/Stim-x/9.2/fries/fries-09.2.html>

TOUGH BREAK

Tim Rogers

The following selection illustrates a kind of report frequently undertaken by journalists and freelance writers: the profile of an individual. Profiles usually combine description and narration to convey a sense of what makes someone distinctive or newsworthy. In this case, Tim Rogers focuses on a successful woman—one of the best women billiard players in the country. As you read, be alert for how he attempts to engage the attention of readers and how he combines information with personal impressions. Note how he sounds in this piece, and consider whether his manner might be different if he were writing about a man or a well-known athlete.

Rogers is a Dallas-based writer who first published "Tough Break" in American Way, *the in-flight magazine of American Airlines. After you have read this piece, you might also consider the assumptions it makes about audience—what kind of people are likely to be reading an in-flight magazine and what expectations they would have as they browse through one.*

Vivian has gone to call her mother, which seems an odd thing for a grown woman to do on a date, especially when it's a long-distance call from a bar pay phone. I hope it's not a sign the night is going badly. To be honest, I don't recall if the word *date* actually came up all that often in our phone conversations. Maybe the word I used was closer to *interview*. The dinner we just shared must have gone to my head. Vivian, truth be told, has come to San Francisco for The Connelly National Nine Ball Championship of women's pool. The twenty-nine-year-old is currently ranked the third-best woman player in the world by the Women's Professional Billiard Association. She won the championship last year, and hopes to repeat. I have come for Vivian. While I'm currently not ranked in the world standings, whenever I play my roommate, Joe, I usually win. I only hope Vivian will be my pool partner for the night, that she'll carry me for a few games. That, and I aim to find out what happens when long hair and manicured nails get mixed up with balls and sticks and other implements generally reserved for men.

Just as I begin to think Vivian's been gone too long, she walks into the room. She explains that when she's on the road for a tournament, she always calls home to let the folks in San Antonio know she's safe. She takes a seat next to me, against a wall, in a row of red vinyl chairs—the sort you'd find in a gas station. Then I relax, because I know I've got Vivian Villarreal, arguably the best woman pool player in the world, right where I want her: in a bar, where no one recognizes her, waiting to play a game of pool.

Our names sit below six others on a chalkboard, so I have time to size up this place called Paradise Lounge. A three-piece jazz band is going pretty good in the next room. Hanging lamps cast light over the pool tables; people standing back from them are only lit from the waist down, their faces hidden in the shadow and smoke above. A guy in leather pants has the table Vivian and I are waiting to play on. Between shots, he talks about motorcycles. A woman in black stretch-pants wobbles around telling anyone who will listen, "Someone just spilled my WHOLE DAMN DRINK!"

Leather Pants loses to a guy with a red beard—by the looks of it, he eats well. At some point during Red Beard's game, Vivian becomes impatient. When it ends, and there's a brief pause before the next name on the list steps up, Vivian slides out of her chair and asks the room a rhetorical question: "Who's next?"

She hands me her lipstick, strides up to the table, and has the balls racked   5 before anyone can stop her. As she picks out a stick—before she's even taken her first shot—Red Beard turns to me: "Is she in town for the tournament?"

I quickly pocket the lipstick.

"Tournament?" I ask. "What tournament?" *That walk,* I think. *He could tell just by the way she walked to the table.*

"There's a women's professional nine-ball tournament in town."

"You don't say."

Then Red Beard breaks, doesn't sink anything, and Vivian takes over. She   10 has a fast hard stroke. She's often ready for the next shot before the balls have stopped rolling and recovered from her last shot. She runs the table in maybe two minutes.

Red Beard doesn't look like he's accustomed to women beating him. He preempts the next name on the chalkboard and racks for Vivian, who breaks with an explosion that sends the cue ball leaping off the felt. Heads turn. While she's busy running the table again, Red Beard and I watch.

"Looks like she's ready to bet some money," he tells me over the jazz. "Does she ever bet?"

"Bet?" I ask.

Over dinner, Vivian told me about a night in a San Antonio bar a few years back. She was playing for $1,000 a game. Even after she ran nine racks in a row, the man she was playing didn't know when to give up. Vivian went home with $25,000.

"Um, no," I inform Red Beard. "As a matter of fact, I don't think she   15 does bet."

Vivian also told me that gambling—never hustling, which involves dishonesty, misrepresenting your talent; only simple betting—is part of her past. But I wasn't entirely convinced. Neither is Red Beard—about the betting or the tournament, because he lures Vivian to an empty table, without saying a word, by setting up a diamond-shaped nine-ball rack.

Nine ball, you see, is a *contest;* whereas eight ball, what drunk men in smoky bars play, is merely an *amusement.* In eight ball, or stripes and solids, you smack your balls around in any order. Your opponent smacks his balls around. Then, whoever finishes hacking first goes for the eight.

In nine ball, both players shoot at the same balls, sinking them in numerical order, one through nine. And, so long as you strike the proper ball first, the nine ball may be sunk any time, either by a combination shot or a carom. Which means the game of nine ball requires control, strategy. It's the difference between fishing and fly-fishing, between checkers and chess.

So Red Beard trades nine-ball games with Vivian. It turns out he can handle a stick—at least on a bar table—and Vivian chats him up between shots, learning his name is Ron. She starts to draw attention to herself, the way she has of shooting hard and generally not missing much. Leather Pants and a few others have formed an audience in the shadows.

Meanwhile, I slouch a little lower in my vinyl chair and wonder if I'll ever   *20* get a chance to play pool with Vivian. I'm afraid I've been relegated to the role of lipstick holder.

Just south of the Bay Bridge, a pool hall called The Great Entertainer comes to life around noon. It is here that the best women pool players from around the world have gathered for the National Championships. The place resembles a warehouse with a high ceiling and exposed concrete columns. Jazz plays over the sound system, while regulars shoot pool outside the tournament area. From behind black drapes comes periodic applause.

At the front counter, a man with a cue stick case slung over his shoulder asks for a ticket to the tournament. "You mean to the girlie show?" the cashier behind the counter jokes, demonstrating that at least one employee has yet to get in touch with his inner, nurturing side. His term of endearment also suggests that he hasn't had a look yet behind the black curtains.

Vivian and the rest of the girlie show, sometimes known as the Women's Professional Billiard Association, have gotten two strange notions into their heads: First, physics and linear algebra can't distinguish between the sexes. Friction, inertia—all that stuff seems to work for the women. When they hit a ball, they expect it to roll.

Their second notion (and here their male counterparts really seem to disagree): Pool is just a game. In a sport still dominated by pinkie rings and testosterone, ideas like these are nothing short of radical. Maybe even a little dangerous.

For one thing, they lead to an awful lot of hugging. Before tournament   *25* play begins, Vivian runs into the two women in the world currently ranked above her, Loree Jon Jones and Robin Bell. Vivian knows she'll likely have to beat one or both of these women to take home first place and the $7,500 that goes with it. One expects tension, icy stares, and cold greetings; but instead, they make with the warm fuzzies. The display seems appropriate for one of those *Unsolved Mysteries* long-lost twin-sister reunion episodes, but a little surprising for professional pool players.

"The men would be kneeing each other in the groin," observes a silver-haired gentleman in a double-breasted blazer. Robert Byrne, a trick-shot legend and author of best-selling pool instruction books, says the women go about things a little differently "because the men come up from the hustling background, where it's you against the world, and you're playing for your supper, and it's a vicious world out there when you're on the road. The women don't come from that kind of background. . . . You look at the women, and then you look at the men: The women make the men look like the war in Bosnia. It's ego gone wild. It's territorial aggression. It's power-seeking. It's back-stabbing."

"The men are just interested in gambling and winning money from each other," says Vivian. "We have come together as a . . . [she struggles for the right word] family. We are all friends, and we want the sport to grow. Selfishness will only get you so far. . . . That's why we're not affiliated anymore with the men."

The women decided they'd had enough in 1992. Previously, the men and women marketed their tournaments together, but the guys always insisted on acting like, well, like *guys*. So last year, the WPBA started organizing its own events.

"When we separated from the men," Vivian says, "they never, ever thought that we could make it without them. But we're so successful now. The women never used to be close to the men as far as prize money. But now, there are about four of us who are making *more* money than them."

As recently as 1990, the women had only two events they could call their   30 own, in which only women played. In 1993, that number jumped to fourteen, one more tournament than the men played. Prize money topped $440,000, and of the top five money-winners—men and women—three were women. Excluding endorsements, this means Vivian made about $35,000 last year playing pool. And in 1994, the WPBA landed its first corporate sponsor: Gordon's gin and vodka proclaiming "the fun, refreshing mixability of Gordon's is a perfect fit."

But don't get the wrong idea. Gordon's didn't get involved with women's pool for family values. They know the women can flat-out shoot.

It's almost midnight behind the black curtains at The Great Entertainer, and Vivian is playing her fifth match of the day, tearing through the one-loss bracket. Tomorrow, ESPN shows up to tape the finals, and she wants to be there. But she's already lost one match in a double-elimination tournament. It has played out the way the seedings said it should: Across the table from Vivian, noticeably not looking for hugs, stands Robin Bell.

A guy with a Heineken in his hand watches Vivian from the bleachers. She just ran the first rack in a race to nine games, and he's lost his patience. "I don't even think she's a girl," he mutters. "Even the way she walks is like a man. It's hell on your ego."

Vivian's father taught her how to play pool at Mollie's, her grandmother's San Antonio bar. He also taught her how to walk. He would make her practice walking in heels, back and forth in the living room, while he gave pointers from the couch. "If they had such a thing as a school for walking," he would tell her, "I'd send you."

It's the same walk that Ron must have noticed at the Paradise Lounge   35 before he went to trading nine-ball games with her on that bar table. But the bar table was like a small, wet quilt compared to what Vivian has to work with now. The tournament tables are almost twice as big as most bar tables, and the cloth is so fast that the balls slide like they're on ice. Players describe good tables as "tight"; these are the tightest.

Into the fifth game, Vivian has her stroke going. It's the stroke that the other women all talk about. No matter how difficult the shot—it could be a full-table combination with a match tied at eight—Vivian always takes two practice strokes and shoots. She works so quickly that other women say they can't watch her shoot while they're playing her. It throws them off, takes them out of their own rhythm.

And then there's the break. Going into the fifteenth game, now past midnight, the match is tied at seven games each. Spectators have switched from beer to coffee. Earlier in the match, Vivian was breaking conservatively, holding back so she wouldn't send balls flying off the table. But she won the last two games and looks confident. She chalks up and lets loose.

Most players use one cue stick for breaks and another for play. They don't want to risk shattering their good shooting sticks, which often run thousands of dollars. Vivian isn't most players. She breaks with a $15,000 custom-made Omega, with nice touches like inlaid eighteen-karat gold, silver, and mastodon ivory.

It was at a tournament in Chicago that she fell in love with the stick. A rep from Omega told her she could practice with it before a match, and after she ran a few racks without missing a shot, Vivian said she wanted to finish the tournament with it. Her coach tried to stop her; it usually takes a player anywhere from six months to a year to get used to a new stick. Vivian didn't listen, and won the tournament, becoming the top-ranked woman in the world at the time. That convinced the Omega folks to sign her up for endorsements, with part of the deal being Vivian's custom-made cue.

The stick, the walk, the stroke—Vivian looks as if she's too much for 40 Robin Bell to handle tonight. Vivian plays out the fifteenth game with precision, drawing the cue ball back for a perfect leave on the nine. With this game behind her, she'll need one more to finish the race to nine games, and then it's back to the hotel for some rest. Tomorrow, the lights and ESPN.

And then she does the unthinkable. She misses. She misses the straight-in shot on the nine. It rolls, seems to trip on its own yellow stripe, and rattles around in the mouth of the corner pocket. It just stops and seems to peer over the edge. And Bell finishes it off. And goes on to win the next game after sinking the five ball in a pocket she wasn't even aiming for. But it doesn't matter. Slop counts, and Bell wins the match.

Vivian has got to be kicking herself for the fourth game, much earlier in the match, when her honesty might have cost her the tournament. She fouled on a safe, failing to drive a ball to a rail. She was nice enough to point this out to Bell, who hadn't noticed. Someone in the stands said a man would never have done that, pointed out a mistake to an opponent. With ball in hand, Bell promptly set the cue down for a two-nine combo, lined it up, and knocked it down. Vivian's mistake was Bell's game.

Vivian will return tomorrow for the finals, but she'll watch from the bleachers. For now, she gives Robin Bell a congratulatory hug, signs a few autographs, and takes her father's walk through the black curtains.

I did finally get to play pool with Vivian. We eventually left the Paradise Lounge that night and headed to a place called the Bus Stop. Ron recommended it, told us to "Tell 'em Ron sent ya." And, "Oh, boy, they're going to just looove you."

Vivian, again, got to the table a few names before her turn, and this time   45
we played partners. At some point in our first game, one of our opponents, a guy with his short sleeves rolled up, asked if Vivian was in town for the nine-ball tournament. Vivian ran the table that game and the next.

I got my chance to shoot in game three. We had two balls left on the table, plus the eight, and the other guys had just scratched. I put the cue right where I wanted it. Lining up my shot, though, I discovered my heart literally racing, which got me to feeling a bit foolish, and I think it threw me off. Plus the table—you know, it wasn't real tight.

I sank our two balls and muffed the eight. We lost.

As we got up to leave, Vivian told me I played well. But Short Sleeves wasn't done with us. "What?" he said. "You guys lose *one game,* and you leave?"

"The tournament," I said. "She's got to get up early."

Like Vivian's father, mine taught me to shoot pool, too (obviously, he   50
didn't do as good a job as Vivian's dad). And my father gave me this piece of pool-shooting advice, which I shared with Vivian outside the Bus Stop: "Always leave them wanting more." And I handed her the lipstick.

QUESTIONS FOR DISCUSSION

1. At the beginning of his article, Rogers pretends that he is having a date with Vivian Villarreal and draws attention to her long hair and manicured nails. How would you describe his tone? Do you think it is appropriate?
2. In the world of professional billiards, what is the difference between gambling and hustling?
3. How does Rogers respond to the needs of readers who know little about billiards? Where does he include specific data about the sport?
4. How does the behavior of women professional billiard players differ from that of their male counterparts?
5. Drawing on the information reported in this article, how would you describe Vivian Villarreal?

SUGGESTIONS FOR WRITING

1. Interview a woman athlete in a sport that interests you and report on how she trains, what support she receives, what obstacles she has overcome, and what goals she has for the future.
2. Gather data on athletic programs at your school or in a nearby school district; then report on how well sports for men and women are funded and how those funding decisions are made.
3. Research how women have managed to succeed in a profession dominated by men. Report what you learn.

LINKS ■ ■ ■

■ **WITHIN THE BOOK**

Rogers' article shows a woman succeeding in a game traditionally associated with men. In "The Deer at Providencia" (pages 633–636), Annie Dillard is the only woman in a group of North American travelers to the Amazon watershed.

■ **ELSEWHERE IN PRINT**

Blundell, William E. *The Art and Craft of Feature Writing, Based on the Wall Street Journal Guide.* New York: NAL, 1988.

Cahn, Susan K. *Coming On Strong: Gender and Sexuality in Twentieth-Century Women's Sport.* New York: Free, 1994.

Lee, Jeanette, and Adam Scott Gershenson. *The Black Widow's Guide to Killer Pool: Become the Player to Beat.* New York: Three Rivers, 2000.

McCumber, David. *Playing off the Rail: A Pool Hustler's Journey.* New York: Random, 1996.

Smith, Lissa, ed. *Nike Is a Goddess: The History of Women in Sports.* New York: Atlantic Monthly P, 1988.

■ **ONLINE**

■ Vivian Villarreal
   <http://www.vivianvillarreal.com/start.html>

■ Women Athletes in the Media
   <http://www.feminist.org/research/sports5a.html>

■ Women's Professional Billiard Association
   <http://www.wpba.com>

UNCHARTERED TERRITORY

Elizabeth Kolbert

Elizabeth Kolbert is a staff writer and political correspondent for The New Yorker, *a weekly magazine much respected for the quality of fiction and poetry it publishes as well as for its feature articles on various aspects of contemporary culture.* The New Yorker *published the following selection in 2000. In this piece, Kolbert reports about a charter school she visited in New Jersey—one of close to forty states that are experimenting with charter schools in response to widespread concern about the quality of public education. These schools are publicly funded but usually operate under rules and requirements that differ from those of public schools. Although the laws governing such schools vary from state to state, these semiprivate schools receive "charters" (or contracts to operate) when they set out achievement goals and measurements that are approved by local officials. These charters can be revoked when a school fails to fulfill its goals. Some charter schools have become recognized for excellence; others have been closed because of mismanagement. Traditionally, charter schools have been run by not-for-profit groups. In "Unchartered Territory," Kolbert reports about a company that runs a chain of schools for profit—hence her title.*

Before you read it, think about what you liked and disliked about your own elementary school education. Then, as you read, consider what the school Kolbert describes is trying to accomplish and whether or not your own experience makes you sympathetic to the objectives and methods in question.

Anacostia, in southeastern Washington, D.C., is poor in most of the familiar ways. Much of the housing is decrepit, too many of the storefronts sell liquor or cash checks, and every few blocks there's a mural depicting, in exaggeratedly cheerful colors, happy, purposeful activity. To walk the neighborhood's streets and see any kind of commercial possibility takes a forceful and none too fastidious imagination. To look at its schools and see a promising new business opportunity takes a vision like Steven Wilson's.

Wilson is a lanky forty-one-year-old with prominent cheekbones and close-cropped hair that sticks out in different directions, perhaps as a fashion statement or perhaps just as an accident of physiognomy. His background in education is slight. He has never taught in a school, or administered one, and his formal training is limited to a few courses he took when he was an undergraduate at Harvard. Four years ago, he founded a company called Advantage Schools, and the year after that the company opened its first venture, a charter school on the east side of Phoenix. Like the charter-school movement in general, Advantage has expanded at a dizzying pace. It now has fifteen schools: New ones opened this fall in Detroit; in Benton Harbor, Michigan;

and in Fairburn, Georgia. A sixteenth, which is under development and scheduled to open next summer, will be in Anacostia. Within two years, Wilson hopes to be running thirty schools, almost all of them in inner-city neighborhoods.

I first met Wilson last spring, in the Manhattan offices of U.S. Trust. The bank is one of Advantage's backers, and, along with several major venture-capital firms, including Chase Capital and Kleiner Perkins Caufield & Byers, it has helped finance the company to the tune of more than sixty million dollars. Wilson was late to arrive, having just come from a meeting where he was seeking yet more financing. After we shook hands, we were shown into a conference room, where a plate of exquisite little cookies had been set out. As we drank the bank's coffee from gold-rimmed china cups, Wilson told me he thought that one of the reasons so many urban schools had failed was a misplaced emphasis on equity. A lot of public-school administrators, he said, subscribe to the notion that "the only kind of change that's good is change that affects every child equally"—an idea that he labeled "appalling," since "if you applied that test you'd never do anything."

Wilson argues that fostering competition among schools is a good way to get results—"People like to try different things and get a chance to demonstrate that their way is more effective," he says—and that fostering capitalism is even better. While most charter schools are not aimed at turning a profit, there is nothing to prevent enterprising businessmen from running them with that goal in mind. Wilson's goal is to run his schools in such a way that roughly one out of every five dollars spent on them goes toward operating his company.

Wilson is not the first to try to make money off the failures of the public schools, and he may not, in the end, be the best positioned to succeed at it, but his strategy is, in many ways, the most logical. Advantage's plan is to offer a low-cost education to the poor and, by exploiting the most recent educational reforms, get taxpayers to finance the entire enterprise. When it suits him, Wilson can speak as eloquently as the next guy about society's obligation to needy students; in a recruitment brochure for teachers, for example, Advantage urges them to "join the revolution" and "help save the next generation of urban youth." At the same time, Wilson is quite clear about the core of his ambition. "I'm an entrepreneur," he told me.

Last spring, I spent several days sitting in on classes at Golden Door, an elementary school that Advantage operates in Jersey City. The school is housed in a brand-new faux-Federalist building with arched windows and the simulacrum of a clock tower out front. Jersey City constructed the building, ostensibly as a community center, and now leases it to the company. It sits across the street from a huge parking garage and just a few blocks away from the local elementary school, P.S. 37. Eighty per cent of the children who attend Golden Door are eligible for the federal school-lunch program, meaning that those from a family of three, for example, have a household income of less than twenty-seven thousand dollars.

One morning, I arrived at the school in time for a second-grade reading lesson. The teacher, Brian Stiles, told the students to get out their textbooks; he himself picked up what appeared to be a huge spiral notebook. "Find lesson seventy-eight," Stiles told the class. "Touch column one. Word one is 'seagulls.' What word?" He snapped his fingers.

"Seagulls!" the students answered, in unison.

"Seagulls are birds that are seen around the ocean," Stiles went on. "They are sometimes called gulls. Word two is 'elevator.' What word?" He snapped his fingers again.

"Elevator!" 10

"Read, spell, read 'elevator.' Get ready." He snapped his fingers.

"Elevator. E-l-e-v-a-t-o-r. Elevator."

"Elevator! Beautiful. Everybody, word three is 'surface.' What word?" Another snap of the fingers.

"Surface!"

"Read, spell, read 'surface.' Get ready." He snapped his fingers. 15

"Surface. S-u-r-f-a-c-e. Surface."

After some more spelling and vocabulary words—"pirates," "instant," "handkerchief"—the children turned to a reading-comprehension lesson. Stiles was still working from his notebook. He asked a student to read from the text.

"You're going to read about big storm clouds," the student said. "Here are facts about clouds: Clouds are made up of tiny drops of water."

"Everybody, I want you to look at that fact," Stiles said. "The fact is that clouds are made up of tiny drops of water. Everybody say that fact. Get ready."

He snapped his fingers. 20

"Clouds are made up of tiny drops of water."

Stiles had another student continue to read. "In clouds that are very high, the water drops are frozen."

"Everybody, where are the clouds that have frozen water drops?" He snapped his fingers.

"High!"

Much like a fast-food franchise, an Advantage school comes as a package, 25 and to sign on with the company is, at least in theory, to accept this package in a McMuffin to McFlurry sort of way. Advantage students, whether they live in Kalamazoo or Newark, are required to wear uniforms (maroon on top, khaki on the bottom), to pass through the halls silently, in single file, and to obey the rules posted in every classroom: "Follow directions the first time they are given"; "Get attention the right way"; "Don't work ahead." The company issues a twenty-page Code of Civility, which lists ten Keys to Success, beginning with Responsibility and ending with True Friendship, by way of Perseverance and Truth, and it expects students to pledge, in writing, to adopt them. The curriculum is the same in all the schools and so, almost to the letter, are the teaching methods.

"Teachers have been socialized in schools of education, and taught to apply their own creativity to a problem," Wilson once told me, when I asked how he had arrived at Advantage's pedagogical program. "That's nice up to a point, but the idea that we should have tens of thousands of teachers all around the country trying to stumble upon the best way to teach reading to a first grader is kind of psychotic, right?"

The system that Advantage uses to teach reading is known as Direct Instruction. The system is also used for math, and was developed some thirty-five years ago at the University of Illinois by Siegfried Engelmann, an advertising executive who became interested in education after conducting research on how often kids needed to hear a slogan before they memorized it. A typical reading lesson, like the one about clouds, consists of a series of questions that the teacher poses and the students answer in unison, often repeating what they have just been told. There is rarely any doubt about what constitutes the right answer.

In Stiles's class, every time there was a break in the lesson the kids began chatting and pestering one another and rifling through their desks, stalling for time. To maintain order, Stiles used a system of warnings and punishments recorded on a wall hanging at the back of the class. The hanging had little clear-plastic pockets, each containing a student's name and several squares of construction paper in different colors. At the beginning of each day, Stiles told me, the green square was out front in every pocket. When someone misbehaved, the yellow square came forward—I saw this happen to one girl who refused, several times, to follow directions—and then, after still more infractions, the blue one, and, finally, the red would be moved to the front. Later, I saw the same wall hanging in the other classrooms I visited at Golden Door; it, too, I learned, was mandated by Advantage, as part of what the company calls its Classroom Positive Management Systems.

Stiles, who is thirty-six, has been working at Golden Door since it opened, in trailers, two years ago. Before that, he was a buyer for men's sportswear, a job he quit because he found it unsatisfying. He seemed like a nice enough person, and also probably a competent teacher, but since so much of what he did was scripted it was hard for me to tell. At the end of the reading class, Stiles showed me his notebook, and I saw that the entire lesson had been printed out for him, including the cues for when to snap his fingers.

Over the last eight years, thirty-six states have amended their education *30* laws to make the creation of charter schools possible. This legislation has been supported by groups that favor privatizing government services, like the Heritage Foundation, and, in a more grudging sort of way, by some teachers' unions, like the National Education Association—and by politicians on the right and also by many on the left. Al Gore, who said in his speech at the Democratic Convention that he would never "go along with any plan that would drain taxpayer money away from our public schools and give it to private schools in the form of vouchers," has backed charter-school legislation, and so has George W. Bush.

The sudden rush to embrace charter schools could be described as either the most dramatic development in educational reform since desegregation or as an essentially conservative effort to forestall real change. In contrast to vouchers, charter schools are supposed to expand families' options wholly within the existing public-school framework. A charter school is a public school that, thanks to a special dispensation—or charter—from the state, operates outside the jurisdiction of the local school district. Such a school cannot teach the Gospels, but for the most part it can ignore the local union contracts. It is free to develop its own curriculum and code of conduct.

Already, some two thousand charter schools have opened, enrolling about half a million students. The vast majority of these schools are operated by local nonprofit organizations, and the educational theories that guide them are as various as the communities they serve—which, according to charter-school advocates, is precisely the point. There are charter schools that stress "traditional values," charter schools that emphasize "project-based learning," charter schools that have an Afrocentric curriculum, charter schools that focus on community service, and charter schools for the performing arts. The notion behind the movement as a whole is that parents and teachers should be allowed to innovate (Advantage, of course, operates on the opposite theory), and that from the process of coming together to create a school a heightened sense of purpose will emerge, producing better educational results. Whether this notion is, in any rigorous way, true is impossible to know at this point, and the answer may remain unknowable. Charter schools are, in effect, a series of social-science experiments for which no control groups have been established.

Each student who attends a charter schools brings with him an allotment of public-school aid, which is diverted from the regular public-school system in the area. The sum varies from state to state and, in some states, from district to district, with high expenditure-per-pupil districts, like White Plains, New York, paying as much as $11,609 dollars for each student, and low-expenditure states, like Kansas, paying as little as $3,820. (Jersey City pays $9,251.) The states specify how much money the schools will get, but they don't dictate how the money should be spent, or even whether it needs to be expended on students. Ideally, Wilson hopes to use fifteen per cent of the money he gets to pay for services, like accounting and equipment leasing, that are provided by his company's central staff. He plans to take another seven per cent straight off the top, as a "management fee" for Advantage.

Most states do not allow commercial enterprises to hold charters directly, but Advantage gets around this by finding local groups that will run a school on paper while in practice turning operations over to the company. This arrangement can work out extremely well, as it has in Jersey City, where Advantage has teamed up with the mayor, Bret Schundler, who is an outspoken advocate of school choice. It can, however, also work out disastrously, as it did in Albany, where in 1999 the company opened a school in partnership with a local chapter of the Urban League. An investigation into the chapter suggested that the group's president had misapplied nearly ninety thousand dollars in school aid. Over the summer, the Urban League and Advantage severed their relationship, and the whole fiasco has been widely described as a case study of how not to put together a charter school.

Advantage has its headquarters in Boston, in a suite of spare, loft-like offices near North Station. When I visited recently, the company was in the midst of trying to hire a chief financial officer, and Wilson had gathered his top staff for a search meeting. He sat on one side of a long table, next to the company's president, Geoffrey Swett, who joined Advantage after running a chain of dialysis centers, and across from its vice-president for human resources, Thomas Saltonstall, who worked previously at a rival dialysis company. An executive headhunter was participating in the meeting via speaker-phone.

Six candidates were being considered for the C.F.O. job, and the group at the table went through them one by one, with the goal of narrowing the field. Instead, the meeting seemed to go in reverse, so that the one candidate who, at the start, had been on the verge of being dropped from the list wound up back in the running. There was a lot of discussion about what kind of background made the most sense for Advantage—was it experience in a regulated industry or experience in retail?—but Wilson's overriding concern, it seemed, was drive. "There's only two categories: energy generator or energy absorber," he said at one point. "There's no in-between. It's a binary thing." At another point, he observed. "The last thing we want is someone who brings in this culture of complaining. That is just radioactive." Several of the candidates, according to the headhunter, were a little shaky on Advantage's business plan, and wanted more information about it. No one around the table seemed to find this disconcerting.

Advantage is Wilson's third startup company—an impressive statistic even in the current business climate. He started his first company when he was twenty-one, dropping out of college in order to do so. The company marketed a kind of technology known as data-acquisition systems, which connect computers to instruments that measure things like light or pressure or temperature. A few years later, he sold that company and immediately started a new one, to develop control systems for automated-process plants. This second company, according to Wilson, achieved its goals technically but not financially. "I've experienced very modest success and more substantial failure," he told me. "I probably shouldn't reveal that."

In explaining why he believes it is possible to run schools that are better than the regular public schools but also cost less to operate, Wilson likes to say that a typical large urban district spends at least forty per cent of its budget on administration alone. This purported waste is essential not just to his calculations but to those of the entire for-profit public-school industry, which has received a huge boost from charter-school legislation. In a recent, unrelentingly sunny report on the industry's future, analysts at Merrill Lynch asserted that only about half of what is spent on regular public K–12 education is spent in the classroom. "We can't think of another service industry that exists where fifty percent of the money is spent outside of where the service is rendered," they wrote.

These figures may correspond to what many taxpayers suspect about administrative costs, but the experts in public-school financing I spoke with all described them as far off the mark. They noted that while it was possible to classify costs like counseling and school buses as administrative or, alternatively, as money spent outside the classroom, this does not make them any less essential. "Is there money to be made here?" asked Jim Wyckoff, an associate professor at the State University of New York in Albany who has conducted an extensive study of New York State public-school financing. "There might be. But is a lot of it going to come from what is typically called administration? I doubt it."

At the moment, Advantage is not showing a profit, the funding it's get- 40 ting from Chase and Kleiner Perkins is going toward easing the deficits at its schools. In this lack of profitability Advantage is no different from its rivals; with revenues of two hundred and twenty million dollars, for example, Edison Schools, the largest of the for-profit school companies, lost forty-nine million last year. In Boston, I was told that various economies of scale would allow Advantage to operate in the black when it reached its target of thirty schools; a few weeks later, Wilson told me that on the basis of more recent figures he believed the company *could* begin to see a return much sooner than that, perhaps as early as this year—but because the company will put that money toward opening new schools it will almost immediately go back into the red. One of the great discoveries of contemporary capitalism, of course, is that it is possible to become very rich without ever coming up with a business plan that actually works, and one of the reasons Advantage was looking for a new C.F.O. was to begin the process of preparing for an initial public offering. This, I was told, could happen at any time.

There is no lunchroom at Golden Door; the students take their meals in the classroom, under the supervision of a teacher. The ostensible rationale for this practice is that meals are part of the educational program—students will be learning while they eat. In one class I visited, I watched some third graders grapple with pizza. The food, courtesy of the federal school-lunch program, arrived in large quilted bags of the sort used by Domino's deliverymen. The students picked up trays, collected their slices, along with a cup of juice and an orange, and then went back to their desks. While they were eating, they chatted, held burping contests, and examined Pokémon cards. One student was using a utensil as some sort of catapult. "If I see you doing that again, you will not get a spoon," the teacher, a middle-aged woman, told him. When the kids were done, they dumped their trash in the garbage, stacked their trays, and went off to recess, leaving stray bits of paper on the floor. After they left, I asked the teacher what the educational objective of this particular lunch hour had been. "Supposedly, they're learning to speak quietly," she said, and shrugged.

Whatever its heuristic value, Golden Door's lunch policy obviously makes good financial sense. The school did not have to build a cafeteria, and now it does not have to maintain it, or heat it, or clean it. Instead of hiring aides, it simply asks teachers to give up half of their own lunch hour to keep order.

Other elements of the school's program are similarly equivocal. Advantage places a great deal of emphasis on basic skills; in Brian Stiles's class, for example, I saw a schedule for second graders. It showed them spending three and a half hours a day on Direct Instruction in reading, writing, and spelling, and another hour on Direct Instruction in math, which left just over ninety minutes to be divvied up, according to a complicated weekly rotation, among gym, Spanish, science, art, music, and history. Missing almost entirely from the schedule were the exercises in self-expression and discovery typically associated with elementary school: the illustrated reports that get tacked on the walls, or the scraggly seedlings groping toward the windows. In Stiles's classroom, there were some simple cutouts of hot-air balloons hanging from the ceiling; these were the only student-made decorations in the room, and he told me it had been difficult, given the rigors of the curriculum, to find the time to make them.

Advantage's emphasis could reflect a pedagogical decision about what skills matter most in life or, just as plausibly, an economic calculation. The pledge that Advantage makes when it launches a new school is that, over five years, the standardized-test results of virtually every student will improve, though by how much varies substantially according to how well, or how badly, the student scored initially. (According to figures provided to me by the company, reading scores at Golden Door last year did improve significantly for the youngest children but much less so for older children.) Since it's very difficult to measure progress on intangibles like creativity or independent thinking, in a school that is run as a business it probably doesn't make much sense to devote a whole lot of resources to them.

As for Direct Instruction, Wilson and other Advantage executives told me   45   that the method had been chosen because it was demonstrably the most effective. In its literature, the company asserts that research has "overwhelmingly supported the superiority of DI over all other programs," a claim that, to say the least, exaggerates the supporting data. At the same time, Advantage's reliance on Direct Instruction follows altogether logically from the company's efforts to keep salary costs down. Most of the teachers I met at Golden Door were inexperienced, and a few told me that they had tried to get jobs in public-school systems but, for one reason or another, had been unable to do so. Direct Instruction leaves so little to the teacher's discretion that classroom experience, not to say talent or imagination, seems almost beside the point. "Advantage could train a monkey," one teacher told me.

When I asked Wilson about what I saw as the ambiguity of the company's educational model, he told me that it was "no different, really, from that of any other school, because every school has limited resources, has a budget." In terms of the quality of education, he said he did not believe that Advantage had made any meaningful sacrifices in its efforts to economize. "Frankly, some programs are just much, much more efficient, even though people don't like to hear that word in education."

I talked to dozens of students at Golden Door about their experiences, and when word got around that I was a reporter more kids sought me out, eager to relate their stories. A few of the kids had complaints. One serious-looking fifth grader told me that she missed the regular public school she used to attend. "The other school had more activities and projects and trips," she said, adding that she had once won a prize for a project on a woman she admired. Many more, though, said they were happy. Another fifth grader, with pigtails, told me, "I love this school. I was about to stay back, and this school gave me another chance."

Over and over again, kids talked about violence they had seen, or even participated in, at their previous schools, and how much more secure they felt at Golden Door. "I like this school because they have rules about not touching the other kids," one girl told me. "I feel more protected." Last spring, Golden Door had enough room to admit only one new class of kindergartners. Posted near the main entrance was a roster of children who had been wait-listed; a hundred and eighty-one names were on it.

Wilson doesn't pretend that the program he is providing for students in Jersey City and in Detroit is one that would hold much appeal in wealthier districts like Summit or Bloomfield Hills. "We shouldn't be struggling to find one approach that's right for everybody," he told me. "The needs of our urban students resulting from their backgrounds and their previous educational and social deprivations in some cases are very different from the needs of the son or daughter of an affluent suburban parent."

If one considers the public schools a primary institution of democracy, it 50 is hard not to be discomfited by this separate-but-not-altogether-equal philosophy. Everything that I saw in Advantage's Boston office—the emphasis on drive and risk-taking and innovation—reflected a corporate culture that was fundamentally at odds with the cookie-cutter, don't-work-ahead design of its schools. Answering on command and respecting authority are not entrepreneurial virtues, though they do have a place farther down the economic order. It struck me as not insignificant that, while Advantage schools serve mostly black and Hispanic kids, everyone I met in the corporate headquarters, except for a single receptionist, was white.

Yet dwelling on this discomfort may itself be a luxury: The choice that parents in the inner city are confronting is not one about abstract ideals, or even about the appropriate role of profit in public education; it is a choice for the most part between dysfunctional public schools and some alternative— any alternative. And if these parents choose to send their kids to Advantage, if only because they feel that the kids will be safer there, who, in the end, can blame them?

QUESTIONS FOR DISCUSSION

1. What accounts for the rapid rise of charter schools? What kinds of problems are they meant to address?

2. Consider the references to "exquisite little cookies" and "gold-rimmed china cups" in paragraph 3. What do these details convey to you?
3. Do you agree that fostering competition among schools is a good way to improve the quality of such schools?
4. Consider the reading lesson described in paragraphs 7–24. Would you want your child to be taught by this method?
5. How typical of charter schools are the schools offered by Advantage?
6. In paragraph 36, Kolbert quotes Steven Wilson: "There's only two categories: energy generator or energy absorber [. . .]. There's no in-between." When you read classifications such as "energy generator" and "energy absorber," what kind of people come to mind? Do you agree that all people can be placed in one of these two categories?
7. Based on the information in this article, what is your opinion of Steven Wilson and the schools for which his company is responsible?

SUGGESTIONS FOR WRITING

1. Write a report on classroom practices and homework assignments in a class you have taken within the last two years.
2. Research the state of public education in a major American city and report what you learn about facilities and instruction.
3. Research charter schools and find a school that seems admirable. Write about what that school is doing right.

LINKS ▪ ▪ ▪

▪ WITHIN THE BOOK

For information about how children are treated in another culture, see "In Japan, Nice Guys (and Girls) Finish Together" (pages 207–210).

▪ ELSEWHERE IN PRINT

Finn, Chester E., Jr., Bruno V. Manno, and Gregg Vanourek. *Charter Schools in Action: Renewing Public Education.* Princeto: Princeton UP, 2000.

Freire, Paolo. *Pedagogy of the Oppressed.* Trans. Myra Bergman Ramos. 1970. New York: Continuum, 2000.

Hassel, Bryan C. *The Charter School Challenge: Avoiding the Pitfalls, Fulfilling the Promise.* Washington, DC: Brookings Inst., 1999.

Rose, Mike. *Lives on the Boundary: The Struggles and Achievements of America's Underprepared.* New York: Free, 1989.

Rosenblatt, Louise. *Literature as Exploration.* 1938. New York: MLA, 1996.

(continues)

LINKS ■ ■ ■ *(continued)*

■ **ONLINE**

- Advantage Schools
  <http://www.advantage-schools.com>
- The Case Against Charter Schools
  <http://www.aasa.org/publications/sa/2001_05/2001_manno.htm>
- Charter Schools
  <http://www.uscharterschools.org>

THE THIN RED LINE

Jennifer Egan

Jennifer Egan is a novelist who frequently contributes articles to the New York Times Magazine, *which published the following report in 1997. To determine why adolescents— especially girls—are mutilating their bodies, Egan focused on the case of a specific teenager in Chicago and supplemented this case study by interviewing psychiatrists and other mental health professionals. Although the behavior engaged in by the girl may seem unlike anything you have ever witnessed, be alert, as you read, to details that could help you see how a similar girl might be living somewhere near you.*

One Saturday night in January, Jill McArdle went to a party some distance from her home in West Beverly, a fiercely Irish enclave on Chicago's South Side. She was anxious before setting out; she'd been having a hard time in social situations—parties, especially. At 5 feet 10 inches with long blond hair, green eyes and an underbite that often makes her look as if she's half-smiling, Jill cuts an imposing figure for 16; she is the sort of girl boys notice instantly and are sometimes afraid of. And the fear is mutual, despite her air of confidence.

Jill's troubles begin with her own desire to make everyone happy, a guiding principle that yields mixed results in the flirtatious, beer-swilling atmosphere of teen-age parties. "I feel I have to be all cute and sexy for these boys," she says. "And the next morning when I realize what a fool I looked like, it's the worst feeling ever. . . . 'Oh God, what did I do? Was I flirting with that boy? Is his girlfriend in school tomorrow going to give me a hard time? Are they all going to hate me?'"

Watching Jill in action, you would never guess she was prone to this sort of self-scrutiny. Winner of her cheerleading squad's coveted Spirit Award last year, she is part of a Catholic-school crowd consisting mostly of fellow cheerleaders and the male athletes they cheer for, clean-cut kids who congregate in basement rec rooms of spare, working-class houses where hockey sticks hang on the walls and a fish tank sometimes bubbles in one corner. Jill is a popular, even dominating presence at these parties; once she introduced a series of guys to me with the phrase, "This is my boy," her arm slung across the shoulders of some shy youth in a baseball cap, usually shorter than she, whose name invariably seemed to be Kevin or Patrick.

But in truth, the pressures of adolescence have wreaked extraordinary havoc in Jill's life. "Around my house there's this park, and there used to be like a hundred kids hanging out up there," she says, recalling her first year in high school, two years ago. "And the boys would say stuff to me that was so disgusting . . . perverted stuff, and I'd just be so embarrassed. But the older girls assumed that I was a slut. . . . They'd give me dirty looks in school." Blaming herself for having somehow provoked these reactions, Jill began to feel ashamed and isolated. Her unease spiraled into panic in the spring of that year, when a boy she'd trusted began spreading lies about her. "He goes and tells all of his friends that I did all this sexual stuff with him, and I was just blown away. It made me feel dirty, like I was absolutely nothing."

Jill, then 14, found herself moved to do something she had never done 5 before. "I was in the bathroom going completely crazy, just bawling my eyes out, and I think my mom was wallpapering—there was a wallpaper cutter there. I had so much anxiety, I couldn't concentrate on anything until I somehow let that out, and not being able to let it out in words, I took the razor and started cutting my leg and I got excited about seeing my blood. It felt good to see the blood coming out, like that was my other pain leaving, too. It felt right and it felt good for me to let it out that way."

Jill had made a galvanizing discovery: Cutting herself could temporarily ease her emotional distress. It became a habit. Once, she left school early, sat in an alley and carved "Life Sucks" into her leg with the point of a compass. Eventually, her friends got wind of her behavior and told her parents, who were frightened and mystified. They took Jill to Children's Memorial Hospital, where she was treated for depression and put on Prozac, which she took for a few months until she felt better. By last summer she was cutting again in secret and also burning—mostly her upper thighs, where her mother, who by now was anxiously monitoring Jill's behavior, wouldn't see the cuts if she emerged from the family bathroom in a towel. Last summer, Jill wore boxers over her bathing suit even to swim. By January, her state was so precarious that one bad night would have the power to devastate her.

No one recognized Jill's behavior as self-mutilation, as it is clinically known (other names include self-injury, self-harm, self-abuse and the misnomer delicate self-cutting), a disorder that is not new but, because it is finally being properly identified and better understood, is suddenly getting attention. Princess Diana shocked people by admitting that she cut herself during her unhappy marriage. Johnny Depp has publicly revealed that his arms bear scars from self-inflicted wounds. The plot of "Female Perversions," a recent movie that fictionalized the book of the same name by Louise Kaplan, a psychiatrist, hinges on the discovery of a young girl cutting herself. And Steven Levenkron, a psychotherapist who wrote a best-selling novel in the 1970's about an anorexic, recently published "The Luckiest Girl in the World," about a teen-age self-injurer.

"I'm afraid, here we go again," Levenkron says, likening the prevalence of self-injury to that of anorexia. "Self-injury is probably a bit epidemic." Dr. Armando Favazza, a professor of psychiatry at the University of Missouri–Columbia Medical School, estimates the number of sufferers at 750 per 100,000 Americans, or close to two million, but suggests that the actual figure may be higher.

Long dismissed by the psychiatric community as merely a symptom of other disorders—notably borderline personality disorder—self-mutilation is generating new interest as a subject of study. Dr. Barbara Stanley of the New York State Psychiatric Institute explains: "Some of us said, maybe we shouldn't be focusing so much on diagnostic studies. . . . Maybe this behavior means something unto itself."

Indeed it does. Favazza, whose book *Bodies Under Siege* was the first to com-   10
prehensively explore self-mutilation, defines it as "the direct, deliberate destruction or alteration of one's own body tissue without conscious suicidal intent." His numbers apply to what he calls "moderate/superficial self-mutilation" like Jill's, rather than involuntary acts like the head banging of autistic or retarded people, or "coarse" self-mutilations like the eye enucleations and self-castrations that are occasionally performed by psychotics. Moderate self-mutilation can include cutting, burning, plucking hairs from the head and body (known as trichotillomania), bone breaking, head banging, needle poking, skin scratching or rubbing glass into the skin.

The fact that awareness of self-mutilation is growing at a time when tattooing, piercing, scarification and branding are on the rise has not been lost on researchers. While experts disagree on the relationship between the behaviors, the increasing popularity of body modification among teenagers, coupled with the two million people injuring in secret, begins to make us look like a nation obsessed with cutting. Marilee Strong, who interviewed nearly 100 injurers for her book, *A Bright Red Scream,* to be published in 1998, calls it "the addiction of the nineties."

On that Saturday night in January, despite Jill's anxious resolutions, things at the party ultimately went awry. "It was really late," she says, "and I was supposed to stay at my best friend's house, but she left and I didn't go with her. I was drunk, and it was me down there in the basement with all these boys. . . . I'd walk by and they'd grab my butt or something, so I sat on a chair in the corner. And they tipped the chair over and made me fall off of it."

Realizing she was in a situation she would punish herself for later, Jill went upstairs and tried in vain to get a friend to leave the party with her. She had nowhere to stay—no way to get home without calling her parents—so she ended up at the home of her friend's brother, who was in his 20s and lived near the party. This proved to be another mistake. "I wake up there the next morning, and these guys were basically dirty 20-year-olds," she says, "and they tell me: 'You want a job living here with us? We'll pay you a hundred bucks if you strip for us once a week.' . . . I was just like: 'I have to go home! I have to go home!'"

But by now, a cycle of shame and self-blame was already in motion. On finally arriving at the two-story brick house where she lives with her parents and brothers (one older, one younger), Jill learned that she was being grounded for not having called home the night before. Her bedroom, right off the kitchen, is a small, makeshift room with accordion doors that do not seal off the noise from the rest of the house. "All Sunday I just slept and slept, and I was just so depressed, so disgusted with myself.... I felt like the dirtiest thing ever because of everything that had happened the night before."

For all her popularity, Jill felt too fragile that morning to ask her friends   15
for reassurance. "I feel really inferior to them, like they're so much better at everything than me," she says of the other cheerleaders. "I feel like I have to be the pleaser, and I can never do anything wrong. When I fail to make other people happy, I get so angry with myself."

That Sunday, no one was happy with Jill: her parents, the friend whose house she hadn't slept at and, in her fearful imagination, countless older girls who by now had heard of her sloppy conduct at the party and were waiting to pounce. "Monday morning came and I was scared to death to have to go to school and see people," she says. "I started cutting myself. First I used a knife—I was in the bathroom doing it and then I told my mom because I was scared. She was like, 'Why the hell are you doing this? You're going to give me and your father a heart attack.'... She took the knife away. So then I took a candle holder and went outside and cracked it against the ground and took a piece of glass and started cutting myself with that, and then I took fingernail clippers and was trying to dig at my skin and like pull it off, but it didn't help anymore, it wasn't working.... That night, I was like, 'My mom is so mad at me, she doesn't even care that I was doing this,' so that's when I took all the aspirin."

Jill isn't sure how many aspirin she took, but estimates it was around 30. "That night was like the scariest night in my life," she says. "I was puking and sweating and had ringing in my ears and I couldn't focus on anything." Still, she slept through a second day before telling her parents what was really ailing her. They rushed her to a hospital, where she wound up in intensive care for three days with arrhythmia while IV's flushed out her system, and she was lucky not to have permanently damaged her liver.

"That was very shocking, to think that she was going through so much pain without us being aware of it," says her father, Jim McArdle, a ruddy-faced police lieutenant with a soft voice, who chooses his words carefully. "There's a ton of denial," he admits. "It's like: 'It happened once, it's never going to happen again. It happened twice, it's not going to happen three times.' The third time you're like...." He trails off helplessly.

Self-injury rarely stops after two or three incidents. According to the only large-scale survey ever taken of self-injurers (240 American females), in 1989, the average practitioner begins at 14—as Jill did—and continues injuring, often with increasing severity into her late 20s. Generally white, she is also likely to suffer from other compulsive disorders like bulimia or alcoholism. Dr. Jan Hart, who surveyed 87 high-functioning self-injurers for her 1996 doctoral dissertation at U.C.L.A., found their most common professions to be teacher and nurse, followed by manager.

The notion of teachers, nurses, and high-school students like Jill seeking   20
out ways to hurt themselves in a culture where the avoidance of pain and discomfort is a virtual obsession may seem paradoxical. But it isn't. People harm

themselves because it makes them feel better; they use physical pain to obfuscate a deeper, more intolerable psychic pain associated with feelings of anger, sadness or abandonment. Often, the injury is used to relieve the pressure or hysteria these emotions can cause, as it did for Jill; it can also jolt people out of states of numbness and emptiness—it can make them feel alive.

These mood-regulating effects, along with a certain addictive quality (over time, the injurer usually must hurt herself more frequently and more violently to achieve the same degree of relief), have prompted many clinicians to speculate that cutting, for example, releases the body's own opiates, known as beta-endorphins. According to Lisa Cross, a New Haven psychotherapist who has treated self-injurers, patients have for centuries described the sensation of being bled in the same terms of relief and release as she hears from self-injurers. And people who have been professionally scarred or pierced sometimes describe feeling high from the experience.

Women seeking treatment for self-injury far outnumber men. There are many speculations as to why this might be, the most common of which is that women are more likely to turn their anger inward. Dusty Miller, author of *Women Who Hurt Themselves,* believes that self-injury reflects a culturally sanctioned antagonism between women and their bodies: "Our bodies are always too fat, our breasts are too small. . . . The body becomes the object of our own violence."

But the fact that few men are treated for self-injury doesn't mean they aren't hurting themselves, too. Among adolescent injurers, the ratio of boys to girls is near equal, and cutting is rampant among both male and female prisoners. Self-Mutilators Anonymous, a New York support group, was initiated 11 years ago by two men, one of whom, Sheldon Goldberg, 59, gouged his face with cuticle scissors, "deep digging" to remove ingrown hairs. "I would have so many bandages on my face from cutting that I would sit on the subway all dressed up to go to work," says Goldberg, a former advertising art director, "and people would look at me and I would realize a wound had opened up and I was bleeding all over my shirt." Now, five reconstructive operations later, the lower half of Goldberg's face is solid scar tissue. "But men can get away with it," he says. "When people ask me what happened, I say: 'I was in the war. I was in a fire.' Men can use all the macho stuff."

It's February, and a frigid midwestern wind thumps at the windows of Keepataw Lodge at the Rock Creek Center, a general psychiatric institution in Lemont, Ill. It is the home of the SAFE (Self-Abuse Finally Ends) Alternatives Program, the nation's only in-patient treatment center for self-injurers, started in 1985. Jill, in jeans, hiking boots and a Pucci-style shirt, lounges on an upholstered banquette in the lodge's skylighted atrium. She has been here 10 days, spending her mornings in the hospital's adolescent program completing assignments her school has faxed in, dividing her afternoons between individual and group therapy.

She's ebullient—partly from sheer relief at being surrounded by people with her same problem. "It's really weird how many people in the group have

25

my same kind of thinking," she says, repeatedly removing and replacing a pen cap with hands scarred by cigarette-lighter burns. "How they grew up feeling like they didn't deserve to feel their feelings, like they had to keep people happy. . . . I don't even know who I am anymore, because everything I do depends on what other people want."

Her cheerleading friends have visited, bearing get-well cards and magazines, but Jill finds playing hostess on the grounds of a mental hospital a tall order. "I'd make up things like, 'Oh, I have a group in 10 minutes, so you guys better leave,' because I couldn't take it to have them sitting there and me not knowing how to make them happy in such a weird environment," she says.

Her parents arrive to meet with her doctor and then take Jill home after her group therapy; for insurance reasons, she must continue the 30-day SAFE program from home as an outpatient. (Blue Cross refused to cover her hospitalization costs before SAFE because her problem was "self-inflicted"; the family is appealing.) Jim and Nancy McArdle are warm, open people who seem a little shellshocked by their sudden immersion in the mental-health system. Jim, who in happier times likes to kid and joke, sits tentatively at a table with his hands folded. Jill is the most animated of the three. "I'll just turn it off, like I never even knew what that was," she says of the behavior that landed her in the hospital only three weeks ago. An anxious glance from her mother, an attractive woman with reddish brown hair who works as a respiratory therapist, gives Jill pause. "Last time we thought it was going to be fine too," she reflects. "But then eventually it just all fell back even worse than it was before. It's scary to think about. I don't want to spend my life in hospitals."

This is a reasonable fear. Most of Jill's fellow patients at SAFE are women in their late 20s and early 30s, many of whom have been hospitalized repeatedly since their teen-age years, some of whom have children. (SAFE accepts men, but its clientele is 99 percent female.) In free moments during the program's highly structured day, many of these patients can be found on the outdoor smoking deck, perched on white lawn chairs under an overhead heating lamp beside a thicket of spiky trees. (Unlike many psychiatric wards, SAFE does not lock its doors.) The deck's cynosure is a white plastic bucket clogged with what look to be thousands of cigarette butts; even when the deck is empty of smokers, the air reeks.

"Hi! What's your diagnosis?" Jane C., a Southerner in her early 30s, cheerfully queries a patient who has just arrived. "Bipolar? Me, too! Although that can mean a lot of different things. What're your symptoms?" Jane, who insisted her last name not be used, is one of those people who can't bear to see anyone left out. She has olive skin, an animated, birdlike face and wide, dark eyes like those in Byzantine paintings. She smiles even while she's talking.

The patient bums a cigarette from her, and Jane lights it. "Cheers," she says, and the two women touch cigarettes as if they were wine glasses.   30

Jane once made a list called Reasons for Cutting, and the reasons numbered more than 30. But the word she uses most often is power. Like many self-injurers (65 percent according to the 1989 survey; some believe it is much higher), Jane reports a history of sexual abuse that began when she was 7. Shortly thereafter, she raked a hairbrush across her face. By age 10, she was in her parents' bathroom making her own discovery of the razor blade. "I cut right in the fold of a finger," she says. "It was so sharp and so smooth and so well hidden, and yet there was some sense of empowerment. If somebody else is hurting me or making me bleed, then I take that instrument away and *I* make me bleed. It says: 'You can't hurt me anymore. I'm in charge of that.'"

Sometimes Jane pounds her head repeatedly against a wall. "When my head's spinning, when I'm near hysteria, it's like a slap in the face," she says. "I've had multitudes of concussions—it's amazing I have any sense at all." It is virtually impossible to imagine this polished, friendly young woman doing any of these things. Much like Jill, Jane, herself a former cheerleader, masks her vulnerabilities with an assertive and jovial persona. "She's created this face to the world that's totally in control when there's really chaos going on underneath," says Dr. Wendy Friedman Lader, SAFE's clinical director. "There's something very adaptive about that, but it's a surreal kind of existence." Even Jane's many scars are well hidden, thanks to what she calls her "scar-erasing technique," which sounds something like dermabrasion.

Like many victims of early trauma, Jane is plagued by episodes of dissociation, when she feels numb or dead or separate from her body. Cross, the New Haven psychotherapist, explains the genesis of dissociation this way: "When you are abused, the natural thing to do is to take yourself out of your body. Your body becomes the bad part of you that's being punished, and you, the intact, positive part, are far away." But what begins as a crucial self-protective device can become an inadvertent response to any kind of stress or fear. "There have been times when I don't even feel like I'm alive," Jane says. "I'll do something to feel—anything. And that's usually cutting. Just seeing blood. . . . I don't know why."

At SAFE, Jane C. is often in the company of Jamie Matthews, 20, a quiet, watchful young woman with pale skin and long brown hair who seems to bask in her friend's overabundant energy. Cutting herself, Jamie says, is a way of coping with her rage. "I would get so angry and upset and so tense, so all I could think about was the physical pain, doing it harder and doing it more. And then afterwards it was a relief . . . sometimes I would sleep."

As a student at a small college in upstate New York, Jamie lived in a dormitory, so privacy was a major preoccupation. "I would lie in bed at school— that was the best place for me to do it because if my roommate walked in, she would think I was sleeping—and I would lay on my back with the knife underneath me, and then pull it out the side, across my back." Jamie already completed the SAFE program once, last summer, but relapsed back at school. The last time she injured herself, she says, was when it felt best. "It was actually pleasureful. It gave me chills; it was that kind of feeling. I sat there smiling, watching myself bleed." Descriptions like these, along with the intimate rituals that accompany some people's injuring—candles, incense, special instruments—have led some clinicians to compare self-injury to masturbation.

35

Jamie's self-injury has caused her a multitude of problems, yet there is almost a tenderness in her voice when she speaks of her self-harming acts. "It's all mine," she says. "It's nothing that anybody can experience with me or take from me. I guess it's like my little secret. I've got physical scars. . . . It shows that my life isn't easy. I can look at different scars and think, yeah, I know when that happened, so it tells a story. I'm afraid of them fading."

Self-injury can appear, at first, to be a viable coping mechanism; the wounds are superficial, no one else is getting hurt and the injurer feels in control of her life. But what begins as an occasional shallow cut can progress to sliced veins and repeated visits to the emergency room. As with any compulsion, the struggle to resist one's urges can eclipse all other thoughts and interests, and despair over the inability to control the behavior can even lead to suicide attempts. "It's like a cancer," says Cross. "It just seems to start eating into more and more of your life."

Jane C. managed to hide her problems for many years. She was married and had a successful career as a sales executive at a medical-supply company, whose wares she frequently used to suture and bandage her self-inflicted wounds. Eventually, despite her vigilant secrecy, Jane got caught—her mother appeared at her house unexpectedly and found her in the bathroom, drenched in blood. Weakened by her emotional turmoil and a severe eating disorder, Jane ultimately almost passed out on the highway while driving home from a sales call, and finally left her job three and a half years ago. "I went on disability, which was really hard on my pride," she says. "I've never not worked in my whole life."

Jane C.'s discovery by her mother is a fairly routine step in the life cycle of self-injury—for all the secrecy surrounding it, it is finally a graphic nonverbal message. "I think that there's a wish implicit in the injury that someone else will notice and ask about it," says Christine Sterkel, a psychologist with SAFE. This was clearly true in Jill's case; after burning her hands, she covered the wounds with Band-Aids until Christmas morning, then appeared before her family without them. "In the park, she cracked a bottle and cut both her wrists," a friend of Jill's told me. "Everyone gathered around her, and I think that's what she wanted. She was crying and I'd be hugging her and stuff and then she'd raise her head and be laughing."

Later in the afternoon, Jill, Jane C., Jamie and the other SAFE patients settle on couches and chairs for one of the many focused group therapy sessions they participate in throughout the week. Patients must sign a "no-harm contract" before entering the program; group therapy is a forum for grappling with the flood of feelings they would normally be numbing through self-injury. It is not, as I had envisioned, an occasion for trading gruesome tales of the injuring itself. Karen Conterio, SAFE's founder, has treated thousands of patients and rejects the public confessional that is a staple of 12-step programs. "Self-mutilation is a behavior, it's not an identity," she says, and encourages patients to save their war stories for individual therapy.

Beyond that caveat, Conterio, 39, a lithe, athletic woman with short blond hair, lets her patients set the agenda. Today, Jill and the others discuss their

40

feelings of shame—shame they repressed by injuring, shame over the injuring itself. At emergency rooms, their wounds were often mistaken for suicide attempts, which in most states requires that a patient be locked up in a psychiatric ward, often in physical restraints.

Later, in a small office adorned with mementos given to her by former patients—a knit blanket, a papier-mâché mask—Conterio tells me that she's less concerned with guiding patients toward a specific cause for their self-injury than with helping them learn to tolerate their feelings and express them verbally—in other words, begin functioning as adults. Still, revisiting one's past is a key step in this process. As Maureen Ford, a psychologist at SAFE, puts it: "Self-injury is a kind of violence. So how is it that violence has entered their life in some way previously?"

In Jill McArdle's case, the answer isn't obvious. She is part of an intact, supportive family; as far as she knows, she has never been sexually abused. But there were problems. Jill's brother, a year older than she, was born with health troubles that cost him one kidney and left him only partial use of the other. Today he is well, but, Nancy McArdle says: "It was three, four years of just not knowing from one day to the next how he was going to do, in the hospital all the time. . . . Jill picked up on it right away and tried to make everything easy on us where she was concerned." (Jamie Matthews also grew up with a chronically ill sibling.) Beyond worrying constantly about her ill son, Nancy McArdle, whose own childhood was marked by alcoholism in her family, admits to feeling a general sense of impending catastrophe while her children were young. "I wouldn't drive on expressways—I'd take a different route," she says. "If I saw a storm coming, I'd think it was a tornado." Giggling at the memory, Jill says: "She'd make us all go into the basement with pillows and blankets. I've been petrified of storms ever since then."

Nancy McArdle has since been given a diagnosis of obsessive-compulsive disorder and is on Prozac, and she and Jill can now laugh about those old fears. But it's easy to see how Jill, as a child with a terrified mother, a chronically ill sibling and a father who kept a certain distance from the emotional upheavals in the household, might have felt isolated and imperiled. She quickly developed an unusual tolerance for pain. "I'd fall and I'd never cry. . . . I never felt any pain, really. It was there, but I pushed it back." Triumphing over physical pain was something she could excel at—distinguishing herself from her physically weak older brother, while at the same time reassuring her mother that she, anyway, would always be strong.

This mix of toughness and a hypervigilant desire to please is still the 45 engine of Jill's social persona, which mingles easy affection with an opacity that seals off her real thoughts. "She never tells anybody how she feels—ever," Nancy McArdle says. Jill agrees: "I turn it all inside. I just think I have to help myself, it all has to be up to me."

But paradoxically, the child who feels that she must be completely self-sufficient, that no one can help her or that she doesn't deserve help is uniquely ill equipped for the independence she seeks. Terrified to express emotions like sadness or rage for fear of driving everyone away from her, such a person becomes more easily overwhelmed by those feelings and turns them on herself. "I and my razors and my pieces of glass and the pins and the needles are the only things I can trust to bring relief," paraphrases Dr. Kaplan, author of *Female Perversions.* "These are their care givers. These have the power to soothe and bring relief of the tension building up inside. . . . They don't expect the environment to hold them." Tending to their own wounds, which many injurers do solicitously, is the final part of the experience. In a sense, self-injury becomes a perverse ritual of self-caretaking in which the injurer assumes all roles of an abusive relationship: the abuser, the victim and the comforting presence who soothes her afterward.

In someone like Jane C., whose childhood was severely traumatic, physiology may be partly to blame; trauma can cause lasting neurological changes, especially if it occurs while the central nervous system is still developing. Dr. Bessel van der Kolk, a professor of psychiatry at Boston University who specializes in trauma, explains: "The shock absorbers of the brain are shot. If everything is running smoothly, if it crawls along just fine—as it does in nobody's life—you're fine. But the moment you get hurt, jealous, upset, fall in love, fall out of love, your reaction becomes much stronger."

It is for this reason, many people believe, that self-injury begins during adolescence. "They go through early childhood developing very poor capacities to deal with states of internal disruption," says Dr. Karen Latza, a Chicago psychologist who does diagnostic work for SAFE. "I can't think of a single thing that involves more internal upheaval than the adolescent years. The changes that come with their menstrual cycles or with sexual arousal engender panic in the young self-injurer."

Jill fits such a model: For all her popularity, she steers clear of romance out of an apprehension she attributes to the friend who lied about her. "I just think that every boy would be like that, just make up stuff," she says. But there is a second danger for Jill: her irrepressible impulse to please, which could make her vulnerable to unwanted sexual attention. As if sensing this, Jill tends to develop a distaste for boys who take an interest in her.

The next time I see Jill at SAFE, the weather is warmer, the ice on the   50
ponds at Rock Creek is melting, and she seems antsy to resume her old life. "I'm just sick of having to wake up every morning and go to therapy, therapy, therapy," she says. Cheerleading tryouts are that night; the following week, she will begin easing back into school. The thought of facing her peers en masse fills her with anxiety. "Last Thursday I went to a hockey game and I saw all these boys, and seriously, my skin was crawling. . . . They'd give me looks, and I couldn't even look at them."

After the SAFE group, Jill and I drive to Mt. Carmel High School, in a run-down neighborhood on Chicago's South Side, for her tryouts. Her fellow cheerleaders greet her enthusiastically; Jill brings one of them a birthday present. Another girl fawns over Jill in a feigned display of unctuous sweetness. "That's the bitch I hate," Jill says matter-of-factly. The girl, still within earshot, shoots her a look. "She thinks I'm kidding, but I'm not," Jill says.

With glitter over their eyes and tiny mirrored hearts pasted to their cheeks, these incumbent cheerleaders huddle in a stairwell outside the gymnasium, awaiting the chance to defend their positions on the squad. Their coach, Suzy Davy, assures me privately that Jill will be chosen. "She was just so cute and energetic," Davy says of Jill's performance last year, which earned her the Spirit Award during the same period when she was cutting and burning herself in secret. "She wasn't fake. She was just out there and she said, 'This is me!' "

Finally the girls file into the gym, shoes squeaking on the varnished wood, and spread out on the floor to stretch. Some of them seem to be vying for Jill's attention; others keep a respectful distance. And it strikes me that by cutting herself—by getting caught and hospitalized—Jill has freed herself from her own tough persona, at least for a time. Everyone knows that something is wrong, that no matter how happy and confident she may seem, there is unhappiness, too, and a need to be cared for. She has revealed herself in the only way she was able.

There is nothing new about self-injury. As Favazza documents in *Bodies under Siege,* from the Christian flagellant cults of the 13th and 14th centuries to male Australian Aborigines who undergo subcision, or the slicing open of the penis along the urethra, as a rite of passage, the equation of bodily mortification with transcendence and healing is repeated across cultures. Many such rituals occur in the context of adolescent initiation rites—ceremonies involving youths about the same age as most boys and girls who begin cutting themselves. "We've done away with rites of passage, but the pattern can still exist," says Favazza. "And the younger teenagers who are seeking to become adults, the ones who can't make it the ordinary way, somehow tap into that."

One group that consciously seeks to tap into primitive rituals and vanished rites of passage are practitioners of what is called new tribalism or extreme body arts, who embrace such forms of body modification as tattooing, piercing and, more recently, scarification and branding. Some of these practices are performed as public rituals of a sort, particularly in gay S & M culture, where they are known as bloodsports. Ron Athey, an H.I.V.-positive performance artist, cuts and pierces himself before audiences while reading aloud from autobiographical texts. An entirely different sort of performance is practiced by Orlan, a French woman who has undergone repeated facial plastic surgeries on video. 55

More often, body modification takes place in private studios like Modern American Bodyarts in Bay Ridge, Brooklyn, a small, scrupulously clean storefront bedecked with African masks. Here, a multiply pierced and heavily tattooed artist, Keith Alexander, pierces clients, cuts designs into them using scalpels, and brands them with sheet metal bent into designs, heated up to 1,800 degrees and "pressed firmly and quickly into the flesh."

Partly, the purpose of these practices is to create a decorative scar. Raelyn Gallina, a body artist in San Francisco, takes impressions of her blood designs with Bounty paper towels and has a portfolio of hundreds. But the experience and the scar itself are also symbolic. Gallina says: "You know that you're going to endure some pain, you're going to shed your blood. . . . That act, once it happens and you come out victorious, makes you go through a trans-formation. We have so little control over what goes on around us. . . . It comes down to you and your body."

Of course "control," or the illusion of control, is perhaps the primary moti-vation behind self-injury too. And the parallels don't end there. Gallina, like many body modifiers, says that a high proportion of her female clients report having been sexually abused. Rebecca Blackmon, 35, a slim, fair-haired woman with a gentle voice, was such a person. "I wanted to heal all the sexual parts of my body," she says. She began in 1989 by having her clitoral hood pierced; now, her pubic bone and stomach are branded, her nipples, tongue and belly button are pierced and a crescent moon of thick scar tissue from repeated cut-tings encircles the lower half of both her breasts. "It's made me a lot more aware of my body; it's made me a lot more sexual," Blackmon says. Her feelings about her abuse have changed, too. "It's not so present in my mind all the time."

Clearly, body modifiers like Blackmon share the urge of many self-injurers to return to the site of their abuse—the body—and alter it in a manner that feels symbolically curative. And as with self-injury, "aftercare," or tending to one's wounds, is an important part of the process. "The ritual part to me is the daily taking care of it," says Blackmon. "The daily cleansing it, pampering it, putting heat packs on it." Among body modifiers who cut, there is great con-cern over scar enhancement, or thwarting the body's healing process. Com-mon scarring techniques include dousing the freshly cut skin in rubbing alcohol and setting it afire; rubbing cigar ash or ink into the open wounds and advising clients to pick off their newly formed scabs each day.

But the many resonances of motive and procedure between self-injurers   60
and body modifiers can obscure a crucial difference: control. Getting an occa-sional brand or cut design in the course of a functional life is not the same as slashing at one's flesh—or fighting the urge to do so—on a daily basis. One is a shared act of pride; the other a secretive act steeped in shame. And many body modifiers—perhaps the majority, now that piercing and tattooing have become so commonplace—are motivated not by the process at all but by the simple desire to belong to a group that is visibly outside the mainstream.

One of the most famous body modifiers is Fakir Musafar, 66, who spent much of his early life secretly indulging his own urges to do such things as bind his waist to 19 inches and sew together parts of himself with needle and thread. As a teen-ager in South Dakota, he assembled a photography dark room in his mother's fruit cellar so that "if she knocked and I was in there putting needles in myself or ripping flesh, I'd say, 'Sorry, I'm developing film and I can't open the door now.' " Now a certified director of a state-licensed school for branding and body piercing in San Francisco, Fakir, as he is known, has seen his secret practices embraced by a growing population of young people. He performs rit-uals around the world, including the O-Kee-Pa, in which he hangs suspended from two giant hooks that penetrate permanent holes near his pectorals.

Favazza asked Fakir to contribute an epilogue to the second edition of *Bodies under Siege,* published recently. In it, Fakir suggests that self-mutilation and body modification share a common root in a collective human uncon-scious. "There's an undercurrent in everybody that's quite universal," Fakir says, "to experience in the body self-initiation or healing. If there is some way socially that these urges can be faced, they don't overpower people and get them into mental hospitals." The argument makes a kind of sense, but there is a lot it doesn't explain: if these longings are so universal, why are those cut-ting themselves, and being cut, so often the victims of trauma and neglect? And using Fakir's logic, couldn't one argue that anorexics and bulimics are merely performing their own symbolic body manipulations? Surely the coex-istence of urges, symbolism and a sense of meaning or empowerment is not enough to make a practice healthy.

But Fakir has led a long, rich life, and Blackmon feels she has reclaimed her body, so perhaps there may be a context in which "self-injury," controlled and guided along safe paths, could serve as part of a healing process. Favazza seems to think so. "If it can be controlled and relabeled and not get out of hand, every-body would be better off," he says. "There's less shame associated with it, there's less possibility for bad accidents to occur. . . . But we're dealing with a lot of ifs, ands, and buts here."

It's a sunny, springlike St. Patrick's Day, and the McArdle household is teeming with relatives and small children eating corned beef and green-frosted cupcakes from a generous spread on the dining-room table. Jill's bed-room smells of styling gel and electric curlers, and her cheerleading outfit is heaped in one corner. Her hair, which spirals in curls down her back, is crowned with a ring of metallic green and silver shamrocks. With a friend at her side, she works the family phone, trying to figure out where the best par-ties will take place during the South Side Irish parade.

Soon we're wandering through a neighborhood awash in Irish pride. Jill and her friend sneak cans of beer from the pockets of their windbreakers and guzzle them as we walk. "I love this day," Jill says. She finished the SAFE pro-gram two weeks ago but returns twice each week to see her therapist. "I'm feeling so much better," she says, smoking a cigarette as we pass Monroe Park, where the boys used to tease her. "Usually I'd be afraid to go somewhere because maybe somebody wouldn't want me. Now I don't care. Now it's like I'm O.K. with myself. It's their own problem."

We begin a desultory journey from party to party that leads from a cramped back porch beside a half-frozen portable swimming pool to a base-ment rec room with a hanging wicker chair and a bubble-hockey set. Jill cheerfully explains my presence to anyone with an interest: "She's writing an article on self-mutilation. That's what I was in the hospital for," seeming mildly amused by the double takes this bombshell induces. An old friend of hers, a boy, informs me that Jill is "a nice, friendly person who likes to talk."

She waits for him to say more. "Remember in eighth grade when you used to say to me, 'You have a thousand faces'?" she prompts. "Remember that?"

The boy looks puzzled. "Eighth grade was a long time ago," he says.

65

Finally we head to Western Avenue for a glimpse of the parade. As we walk in the bright sunlight, I notice that Jill's friend has fresh scars covering her forearms. She tells me rather proudly that she went on a recent binge of cutting herself, but insists she did not get the idea from Jill. Jill tells me privately that she thinks her friend did it to get attention, because the day after, she wore a short-sleeved shirt in the dead of winter, and everyone saw. Jill has been urging her friend to seek help.

The riotous spectators seem almost to drown out the tail end of the *70* parade. Jill plunges into the drunken crowd, tripping over her untied shoelace, her friend straining to keep up with her. Men gape at her under her crown of shamrocks; she cheerily bellows hello at them and then swirls out of sight. We turn onto an alley, and in the sudden quiet, Jill stops a group of strangers and lights her cigarette off one of theirs. Her friend seizes this moment to kneel down and carefully tie Jill's shoelace.

Outside Jill's house, the girls hide their beers and cigarette butts in the bushes, then go inside to exchange a few pleasantries with Jill's family. The openness Jill showed toward her parents at SAFE has vanished behind a sheen of wary cheerfulness. Watching her, I find myself wondering whether self-injury will wind up as a mere footnote to her adolescence or become a problem that will consume her adulthood, as it has Jane C.'s. Often, particularly in someone with an intact family and friends, the behavior will simply fade away. "This disorder does tend to burn out, for some reason," says Cross. "Life takes over." And Jill knows where to get treatment, should she need it again. Jamie Matthews felt like a failure when she relapsed, until she talked to a friend who has repeatedly sought help with her eating disorder. "She said it's like a spiral staircase," Jamie says. "You keep going around in circles, but each time you're at a different level."

As for Jane C., she returned home shortly after Jill left SAFE and reports that the azaleas are blooming. It's hard, she says, returning to a place where she has always felt she was wearing a mask. "One night I was incredibly close," she says. "I mean, I had the blade to the skin. I sat there and I thought, It doesn't matter to anybody else. And I was just about hysterical, but I stopped myself. I thought, This isn't the only way that works."

Jill, too, seems to be making a kind of staggered progress. "I know I have to take care of myself more instead of other people," she says. "I'm at peace with myself." Since leaving the program, she says, she has had no impulses to hurt herself. "Part of me always used to want to do it, but that part of me dissolved."

Her mother, admittedly a worrier by nature, is less sure, and says she has resorted to sneaking into Jill's room in the wee hours with a penlight, lifting the covers while her daughter sleeps to check for new cuts or burns. So far, she's pleased to say, there has been nothing to report. As Jill and her friend finally burst from the house and clamber arm in arm down the block into the late afternoon, Nancy McArdle watches them from the living-room window and says, "You can't ever relax."

THE NANKING SAFETY ZONE

Iris Chang

*Iris Chang majored in journalism at the University of Illin___
a graduate fellowship in writing at the Johns Hopkins Univer___
of Nanking: The Forgotten Holocaust of World War II (199___
selection is a chapter, she is the author of* Thread of the Silk___
*awards from the John T. and Catharine D. MacArthur Found___
Foundation, and the Harry Truman Library.*

*As you prepare to read "The Nanking Safety Zone," you ___
information useful. The Japanese invaded China in 1931, ten ___
Pearl Harbor. By 1935, the Japanese had seized control of M___
they controlled such major cities as Peking (Beijing), Shanghai___
was the capital of the nationalist government of Chiang Kai-sh___
ally be defeated by the communists led by Mao Zedong in 19___
in December 1937, and historians now agree that the rape a___
who had remained in the city was brutal almost beyond belie___
often referred to as "the rape of Nanking," a handful of Weste___
and their letters and diaries have helped historians to know wh___
modern army was apparently given permission to do as it wish___
reading the following account of how three westerners struggl___
you should also know that Japan was allied to Germany in this___
tionship with the United States was deteriorating—primarily be___*

In the history of every war, there are always a few ___
emerge as beacons of hope for the persecuted. In the Un___
ers freed their own slaves and helped establish the Unde___
Europe during World War II, Oskar Schindler, a Nazi, ___
to save twelve hundred Jews from the Auschwitz gas c___
Wallenberg, a Swedish diplomat, saved more than one hu___
by giving them false passports. Who can forget Mies___
woman who together with others hid the young Anne ___
in an Amsterdam attic?

Dark times paralyze most people, but some very few ___
us will never understand, are able to set aside all caution ___
they could not imagine themselves doing in ordinary tir___
about a bright spot in the horror that is the Rape of Nan___
it is surely to shine a light on the actions of a small ban___
Europeans who risked their lives to defy the Japanese ___

QUESTIONS FOR DISCUSSION

1. In your experience, what aspects of Jill McArdle seem typical of adolescents? What is it that led her to engage in self-destructive behavior?
2. How well did Jill's parents respond to this problem? If they had asked your advice, what would you have recommended they do?
3. In paragraph 11, Egan links self-mutilation to the larger phenomenon of "body modification." What forms of body modification have you witnessed in recent years?
4. How does gender affect body modification?
5. How does Jill compare to the other women described in this report? What do they have in common, and how do they differ?
6. After leaving a program designed to help people like her, Jill claims, "I'm at peace with myself. [. . .] Part of me always used to want to do it, but that part of me dissolved." On the basis of the information reported in this article, do you believe her?

SUGGESTIONS FOR WRITING

1. What kind of resources are available on your campus or in your community to help people who are hurting themselves? Write a report that could serve as a resource guide for a woman who is either cutting herself or living with an eating disorder.
2. Egan refers in passing to the practices of Australian Aborigines and other peoples for whom some form of body modification is a ritual marking the passage from youth to adulthood. Research the nature of such practices in a non-Western culture and report your results.
3. Research the process of getting a tattoo. Then write an essay describing that process and informing readers what factors should be considered before getting tattooed.

LINKS ■ ■ ■

■ **WITHIN THE BOOK**

For another selection focused on a young woman who engages in self-damaging behavior, see "My Diagnosis" by Susanna Kaysen (pages 321–328).

■ **ELSEWHERE IN PRINT**

Alderman, Tracy. *The Scarred Soul: Understanding and Ending Self-Inflicted Violence.* Oakland: New Harbinger, 1997.

(continues)

LINKS ■ ■ ■ (continued)

■ ELSEWHERE IN PRINT

Conterio, Karen, and Wendy Lader, with Je
    ily Harm: The Breakthrough Healing Prog
    York: Hyperion, 1998.

Egan, Jennifer. *Emerald City: Stories.* New Yo

———, *Invisible Circus.* New York: Talese, 1995.

Farber, Sharon Klayman. *When the Body Is t*
    Traumatic Attachments. Northvale: Arons

Favazza, Armando. *Bodies under Siege: Self-M*
    chiatry. Baltimore: Johns Hopkins UP, 1

Kettlewell, Caroline. *Skin Game.* New York:

Levenkron, Steven. *Cutting: Understanding ar*
    New York: Norton, 1998.

Strong, Marilee. *A Bright Red Scream: Self-M*
    Pain. New York: Viking, 1998.

■ ONLINE

- Borderline Personality Disorder
    <http://www.palace.net/~llama/psych/b

- Brief Biography
    <http://www.all-story.com/search.cgi?act
    show_author&author_id=75>

- Self-Harming Behavior and Ways to Stay S
    <http://www.selfharm.com>

- Self-Injury: You Are not the Only One
    <http://www.palace.net/~llama/psych/inj

- Understanding and Preventing Suicide
    <http://www.suicideology.org>

hundreds of thousands of Chinese refugees from almost certain extermination. These courageous men and women created the International Committee for the Nanking Safety Zone. This is their story.

The decision to create a safety zone in the city of Nanking arose almost spontaneously, within weeks of the collapse of Shanghai. In November 1937, Father Jacquinot de Bessage, a French priest, established a neutral area in Shanghai to shelter 450,000 Chinese refugees whose homes had been destroyed by the invading Japanese soldiers.[1] When the Presbyterian missionary W. Plumer Mills learned of Bessage's project, he suggested to his friends that a similar zone be created in Nanking. Mills and some two dozen other people (mostly American, but also German, Danish, Russian, and Chinese) ultimately designated a region slightly west of the center of the city as a safety zone.[2] Within the zone were situated Nanking University, Ginling Women's Arts and Science College, the American embassy, and various Chinese government buildings. In setting up the zone, the committee sought to offer refuge for noncombatants caught in the crossfire between the Japanese and Chinese militaries. The foreigners had every intention of shutting the zone down a few days or weeks after the city passed safely into Japanese hands.

The idea was not universally accepted at first. The Japanese, for one, flatly refused to honor it. And as enemy troops approached the city, the zone committee heard urgent pleas not only from friends and family but from Chinese, Japanese, and Western officials to abandon the project at once and flee for their lives. In early December the American embassy staff insisted that the zone leaders join them onboard the USS *Panay,* a gunboat packed with diplomats, journalists, and Western and Chinese refugees as it prepared to move upriver away from Nanking. But the zone leaders politely declined the offer, and after giving them a final warning, the diplomats on the *Panay* sailed away on December 9, 1937, leaving the remaining foreigners to their fate.

Interestingly enough, the *Panay* would later be bombed and machine-gunned by Japanese aviators.[3] On the afternoon of December 12, Japanese aviators sank the gunboat without warning, killing two people and wounding numerous others, even circling over the area repeatedly as if they planned to exterminate the survivors, who hid under a thicket of riverbank reeds. The reasons for the attack were unclear. The Japanese later claimed that their aviators lost their cool judgment in the heat of battle and that fog or smoke prevented them from seeing the American flags on the *Panay,* but this claim was later proven to demonstrably false. (Not only was the day of the bombing sunny and cloudless, but the Japanese aviators had received explicit orders to bomb the *Panay,* orders the aviators carried out reluctantly only after vehement protests and arguments.) Today some suspect that the bombing was a test to see how the Americans would react, while others believe it was the result of internal politics within the Japanese high command. But whatever the reason behind the attack, the city of Nanking turned out to be a safer place for the remaining foreigners than the *Panay.*

5

woul
our p
100 p
I
the N
perse
true.
summ
we ar
leave
V
emba
gates
Zone
geste
prote
in the
affair
F
ing h
dren
treate
years
assur
woul
T
loyal
tions
F
tect l
team
powe
polic
hosp
I nov
I had
F
scarc
ing v
temb
Gern
kow,
suits,
more

The first refugees to enter the Nanking Safety Zone were those who had lost their homes to aerial bombardments or had abandoned homes on the outskirts of the city in the face of the approaching Japanese army. Soon these first refugees packed the camps so densely that it was said that many had to stand without sleeping for several days until new camps were added. Once the city fell, the zone housed not just thousands but hundreds of thousands of people. For the next six weeks the committee had to find a way to provide these refugees with the bare necessities of survival—food, shelter, and medical care. The committee members also had to protect them from physical harm. Often this required on-the-spot intervention to prevent the Japanese military from proceeding with some threatened action. And through it all, though no one asked them to do so, they documented and broadcasted Japanese outrages to the world. In doing so, they left a written record for posterity of what they had witnessed.

In retrospect, it seems almost miraculous that some two dozen foreigners managed to do everything they did while fifty thousand Japanese soldiers ripped apart the city. Remember, by occupation these men and women were missionaries, doctors, professors, and executives—not seasoned military officers. Their lifestyles had been sheltered and leisurely. "We were not rich," one woman said of that period, "but a little foreign money went a long way in China."[4] Many were ensconced in luxurious mansions, surrounded by teams of servants.

Strangely, because of an incident in Nanking a decade earlier, most expected to have more trouble with the Chinese than the Japanese. Those who had been in Nanking in 1927 remembered that during the Nationalist invasion of the city, Chinese troops recklessly killed foreigners and besieged a group of them, including the American consul and his wife, in a house on top of Socony Hill. ("Would they kill us?" one woman wrote of that horrible time. "Would they torture us as in the Boxer°? Would they do worse? Torture the children before our eyes? I did not let my mind touch what they might do to us as women."[5]) Indeed, one of the foreign eyewitnesses of the 1937 massacre admitted: "We were more prepared for excesses from the fleeing Chinese, particularly troops from Hsiakwan, but never, never from the Japanese. On the contrary, we had expected that with the appearance of the Japanese the return of peace, quiet and prosperity would occur."[6]

The heroic efforts of the Americans and Europeans during this period are so numerous (their diaries run for thousands of pages) that it is impossible to narrate all of their deeds here. For this reason, I have decided to concentrate on the activities of three individuals—a German businessman, an American surgeon, and an American missionary professor—before describing the committee's achievements as a whole. On the surface, the three could not have been more different.

---

the Boxer: A rebellion in 1900 prompted by the exploitation of China by foreign powers.

But his biggest concern was not for his own personal safety or well-being   20
but for the establishment of the Safety Zone. The committee members wanted
the zone to be free of all military activity, but the Japanese army refused to recognize it as neutral territory, and the committee found it next to impossible to
dislodge Chinese General Tang Sheng-chih's men from the area—especially
because Tang's own villa stood within it. For Rabe the final straw came
when the Chinese army not only refused to evacuate the area but
erected its gun turrets on streets inside the zone. Losing his patience,
Rabe threatened to quit his position as head of the Safety Zone and
tell the world the reason why unless Tang evacuated his troops from
the area immediately. "They promised me that my wishes would be
respected," Rabe said, "but the fulfillment itself took a bit longer."

Rabe sensed the need to call on higher authorities for help. On November 25, he wrote Adolf Hitler to request the Fuehrer's "kindly intercession in
asking that the Japanese government grant the building of a neutral zone for
those who are not fighting to battle for Nanking." At the same time Rabe
also sent a telegram to his friend General Counsel Mr. Kriebel: "Asking cor-
dially for support of my request of the Fuehrer . . . which otherwise would
make a terrible bloodbath unavoidable. Heil Hitler! Rabe—Siemens representative and head of the International Committee in Nanking."

Neither Hitler nor Kriebel replied, but Rabe soon noticed something
unusual in the Japanese bombing pattern in the city. Before he sent the
telegrams, Japanese planes bombed areas within Nanking indiscriminately;
afterwards they attacked only military targets, such as military schools,
airstrips, and arsenals. Wrote Rabe, "This . . . was the goal of my telegram and
it made quite a lasting impression on my American colleagues."

But his triumph was short-lived as one crisis loomed after another. Originally
Rabe and his colleagues hoped to reserve the empty buildings in the zone for
the poorest citizens of Nanking. To avoid a rush of people, the committee had
pasted posters all over the city, urging refugees to rent housing from friends.
But so many people surged into the area of two and a half square miles that
Rabe soon found himself with fifty thousand more residents than he had
expected even in the worst-case scenario. The refugees not only packed the
buildings but spilled forth onto lawns, trenches, and bomb dugouts. Entire
families slept in the open streets, while hundreds of mat dwellings mush-
roomed next to the American embassy. By the time the city fell, the Safety
Zone—its borders lined by white flags and sheets marked with the red cross
symbol within a red circle—was a swarming "human beehive" of 250,000
refugees.

Sanitation soon posed another nightmare. The filth in the camps—
especially the toilets—enraged Rabe, and it took a tirade on his part to get
the refugee center on the Siemens grounds in acceptable order. Afterwards,
when Rabe inspected the Siemens camp, he found not only were the toilets
in better shape but every wall on the Siemens grounds had been repaired.
"Nobody would tell me where the beautiful new bricks came from," Rabe

wrote. "I determined later on that many of the newer buildings in the area were considerably shorter than before."

But the shortage of food created the worst headache of all for the zone leaders. In early December the mayor of Nanking gave the International Committee thirty thousand *tan* (or two thousand tons) of rice and ten thousand bags of flour to feed the population.[9] But the food was stored outside of the city, and the committee lacked the necessary trucks to bring it into the zone. The Chinese military had already commandeered most of the vehicles in the area to transport twenty thousand men and five thousand cases of Peking Palace treasures out of the capital; desperate civilians and individual soldiers had stolen virtually all the rest. With no alternative open to them, Rabe and the remaining foreigners drove frantically through Nanking, using their own automobiles to haul as much rice as possible into the zone. As the Japanese bombarded the city, the foreigners continued the deliveries; one driver actually lost an eye from flying shrapnel.[10] In the end the zone leaders secured only a fraction of the total food available—ten thousand *tan* of rice and one thousand bags of flour—but the food went far to stave off hunger for many of the refugees in the zone.[11]

On December 9, recognizing the dire situation ahead, the committee tried to negotiate a three-day cease-fire, during which the Japanese could keep their positions and the Chinese could withdraw peacefully from the walled city. However, Chiang Kai-shek did not agree to the cease-fire, prompting the Japanese to begin a furious bombardment of Nanking the following day. On December 12, the committee was again approached by the Chinese military, this time to negotiate a surrender, but again the plan fell through.

From that point on, there was little Rabe could do that day but watch and wait for the inevitable. He recorded the events as they enfolded, hour by hour. At 6:30 P.M. on December 12 he wrote: "The cannons on the Purple Mountain fire continuously—there is lightning and thunder all around it. Suddenly, the entire mountain is in flames—some houses and munitions depots are also on fire." At that moment Rabe recalled an ancient Chinese saying that portended the city's doom: "When the Purple Mountain burns . . . then Nanking is lost."

At 8:00 P.M., Rabe watched as the skies to the south of the city glowed red with flames. Then he heard frantic knocking on both gates of his house: Chinese women and children were begging for entrance, men were scaling the garden wall behind his German school, and people were cramming themselves into the foxholes in his garden, even ducking under the giant German flag he had used to warn pilots from bombing his property. The cries and knocking increased until Rabe could bear it no longer. He flung open the gates to let the crowd in. But the noise only intensified as the night wore on. Exasperated, Rabe donned a steel helmet and ran through his garden, yelling at everyone to shut up.

At 11:30 P.M., Rabe received a surprise visitor. It was Christian Kröger, a fellow Nazi Party member in his midthirties who worked for the German engineering firm of Carlowitz & Company. The tall, blond engineer had come to China to oversee the construction of a large steel mill but found himself, like Rabe, in the midst of Nanking's insanity. The International Committee had appointed Kröger its treasurer.

Kröger had stopped by to tell Rabe that Chungshan Road was littered   30
with weapons and supplies that the Chinese military had left behind during its retreat. Someone had even abandoned a bus, offering it for sale for twenty dollars.

"Do you think someone will take it?" Kröger asked.

"But Christian, how can they?" Rabe said.

"Na. I ordered the man to come into my office in the morning."

Finally, the din around his house began to diminish. The exhausted Rabe, who had not had time even to change clothes for two days, lay back in bed, trying to relax as the society he knew and loved collapsed around him. He knew that the Ministry of Communication building was burning down and that the city would fall any minute. Rabe reassured himself that things would only get better, not worse, from this point on. "You don't have to be scared of the Japanese," his Chinese colleagues had told him. "As soon as they have taken over the city, peace and order will prevail—the rail connections with Shanghai will be quickly rebuilt and the stores will return to their normal functions." Before he fell asleep, Rabe thought, "Thank God that the worst has been overcome!"

The next morning Rabe awoke to the sound of yet another air raid. Appar-   35
ently not all of the Chinese army had been forced from the city, he thought. It was only 5:00 A.M., so he lay down again. Like most people in the city, Rabe had become so jaded by air raids that the blasts no longer bothered him.

Later that morning Rabe explored the city to check out the extent of the damage. In the streets lay numerous Chinese corpses, many of them civilians who had been shot in the back. He watched a group of Japanese soldiers push their way into a German coffeehouse. When Rabe chastised them for stealing, pointing to the German flags on the house, an English-speaking Japanese soldier snapped: "We are hungry! If you want to complain, go to the Japanese embassy. They will pay for it!" The Japanese soldiers also told Rabe that their supply column had not arrived, and they could not count on the column for any nourishment even if it did arrive. Later Rabe learned that the soldiers looted the coffeehouse, then set it afire.

Worse was to come. In the distance, Rabe saw Japanese soldiers marching north from the south side of Nanking to occupy the rest of the city. To avoid them, he immediately drove north and reached the main street of the city, Chungshan Road, stopping at the Red Cross hospital in the Foreign Ministry. The Chinese staff had fled the premises, and bodies were everywhere—clogging the rooms, corridors, and even the exits from the hospital.

That day Rabe encountered the remains of the Chinese army—hungry and exhausted stragglers who had failed to cross the Yangtze River to safety. Driving through Shansi Road Circle, he met four hundred Chinese troops, all of them still armed, marching in the direction of the advancing Japanese army. It was then that Rabe had a sudden "humanitarian impulse" that was to haunt his conscience for months, if not years, afterwards. Warning them about the Japanese troops to the south, Rabe advised the Chinese soldiers to throw away their machine guns and join the refugees in the Safety Zone. After a short discussion, they agreed and followed Rabe into the zone.

Similarly, when hundreds of Chinese soldiers found themselves trapped on the northern side of the city, unable to secure passage across the river, many broke into the Safety Zone, begging the American and European administrators to save their lives. The committee members were uncertain as to whether they should help them. After all, they had created the zone as a sanctuary for civilians, not soldiers. The committee tried to resolve the dilemma by addressing the issue with Japanese army headquarters but got no further than a captain on Han Chung Road.[12]

Moved by the plight of the soldiers, the committee eventually caved in to   40
their pleas. Like Rabe, they told the soldiers that if they laid down their arms, the Japanese might treat them mercifully. Then they helped the soldiers disarm and housed them in various buildings within the neutral area. In the confusion, many of the soldiers stripped off their uniforms and mingled with the civilians in the zone.[13]

The next day John Rabe wrote a long letter explaining the situation to a Japanese military commander. He begged the Japanese to exercise mercy toward the former soldiers and to treat them humanely according to the recognized laws of war. To Rabe's great relief, a Japanese officer promised him that the lives of the Chinese soldiers would be spared.

But relief turned into horror when the Japanese betrayed Rabe and seized the disarmed soldiers for execution. If Rabe had hoped that the Japanese would not be able to separate the troops from the hundreds of thousands of civilians, he was sorely mistaken. The Japanese detected virtually every one of the former soldiers by examining their hands, knowing that the daily use of guns caused calluses on certain areas on the fingers of soldiers. They also examined shoulders for backpack marks, foreheads and hair for indentations from military caps, and even feet for blisters caused from months of marching.

During a staff conference the night of December 14, the committee learned that the Japanese had rounded up thirteen hundred men in a Safety Zone camp near the headquarters to shoot them. "We knew that there were a number of ex-soldiers among them, but Rabe had been promised by an officer that afternoon that their lives would be spared," George Fitch, the YMCA representative, wrote in his diary of the incident. "It was now all too obvious what they were going to do. The men were lined up and roped together in groups of about 100 by soldiers with bayonets fixed; those who had hats had them roughly torn off and thrown to the ground—and then by the lights of our headlights we watched them marched away to their doom."[14]

"Did I have the right to act that way?" Rabe wrote later of his decision to quarter the soldiers in the zone. "Did I handle that correctly?"

For the next few days Rabe watched helplessly as the Japanese dragged   45
thousands more soldiers from the zone and executed them. The Japanese
killed thousands of innocent men who happened to have calluses on their
fingers, foreheads, or feet—men who were ricksha coolies, manual laborers,
and police officers. Rabe later witnessed the Red Swastika Society, a charita-
ble Buddhist organization in the city, pull more than 120 corpses from a single
pond. (In a later report, Rabe pointed out that several ponds in Nanking actually disappeared because they were so filled with corpses.)

As both head of the International Committee and local head of the Nazi
Party, a position that was certain to carry some weight with the Japanese
authorities, Rabe wrote letter after letter to the Japanese embassy. At first he
was unfailingly polite, toning down his anger because of his perceived obligation, as a German citizen and Nazi leader, to maintain the relationship
between the two embassies. He asked the American members of the committee to let him review their letters to the Japanese embassy so that he could
"put some honey" into them as well. He maintained his polite tone in his
personal visits to the embassy.

In turn, the Japanese diplomats received Rabe's letters and visits with
gracious smiles and official courtesy, but in the end he always received the
same answer: "We shall inform the military authorities." As days passed, each
bringing its own unrelenting onslaught of fresh atrocities, Rabe's written
communication to the Japanese grew increasingly hostile, punctuated with
exclamations of outrage:

> All 27 Westerners in the city at that time and our Chinese population
> were totally surprised by the reign of robbery, rapine, and killing initi-
> ated by your soldiers on the 14th![15]
>
> We did not find a single Japanese patrol either in the Zone or at the
> entrances![16]
>
> Yesterday, in broad daylight, several women at the Seminary were
> raped right in the middle of a large room filled with men, women and
> children! We 22 Westerners cannot feed 200,000 Chinese civilians and
> protect them night and day. That is the duty of the Japanese authori-
> ties. If you can give them protection, we can help feed them![17]
>
> If this process of terrorism continues, it will be next to impossible to
> locate workers to get the essential services started.[18]

Gradually Rabe and the rest of the International Committee began to
read the real message in the diplomat's answers—it was the military, not the
embassy, calling the shots. Fukuda Tokuyasu, secretary of the Japanese embassy,
told Rabe as much by saying: "The Japanese army wants to make it very bad
for the town, but we, the embassy, will try to prevent it." During the great
Rape some Japanese embassy officials actually suggested that the International Committee seek publicity in Japan directly so that public opinion
would force the Japanese government to take action.[19] But at the same time
another embassy official urged Rabe to remain silent, warning him that "if

you tell the newspaper reporters anything bad, you will have the entire Japanese army against you."[20]

Finally, with only his status as an official of an allied nation for protection, Rabe did what now seems the unthinkable: He began to roam about the city, trying to prevent atrocities himself.

Whenever he drove through Nanking, some man would inevitably leap out and stop the car to beg Rabe to stop a rape in progress—a rape that usually involved a sister, a wife, or a daughter. Rabe would then let the man climb into the car and direct him to the scene of the rape. Once there, he would chase Japanese soldiers away from their prey, on one occasion even bodily lifting a soldier sprawled on top of a young girl.[21] He knew these expeditions were highly dangerous ("The Japanese had pistols and bayonets and I . . . had only party symbols and my swastika armband," Rabe wrote in his report to Hitler), but nothing could deter him from making them—not even the risk of death.

His diary entry on January 1, 1938, is typical: "The mother of a young attractive girl called out to me, and throwing herself on her knees, crying, said I should help her. Upon entering [the house] I saw a Japanese soldier lying completely naked on a young girl, who was crying hysterically. I yelled at this swine, in any language it would be understood, 'Happy New Year!' and he fled from there, naked and with his pants in his hand."

Rabe was appalled by the rape in the city. In the streets he passed scores of female corpses, raped and mutilated, next to the charred remains of their homes. "Groups of 3 to 10 marauding soldiers would begin by traveling through the city and robbing whatever there was to steal," Rabe wrote in his report to Hitler.

> They would continue by raping the women and girls and killing anything and anyone that offered any resistance, attempted to run away from them, or simply happened to be in the wrong place at the wrong time. There were girls under the age of 8 and women over the age of 70 who were raped and then, in the most brutal way possible, knocked down and beat up. We found corpses of women on beer glasses and others who had been lanced by bamboo shoots. I saw the victims with my own eyes—I talked to some of them right before their deaths and had their bodies brought to the morgue at the Kulo hospital so that I could be personally convinced that all of these reports had touched on the truth.

As he walked through the burning wreckage of his beloved city, Rabe could read, on almost every street corner, beautiful Japanese posters that proclaimed: "Trust Our Japanese Army—They Will Protect and Feed You."

Determined to save Chinese lives, Rabe sheltered as many people as he could, turning his house and office into sanctuaries for Siemens employees and their families. Rabe also harbored hundreds of Chinese women on his property, permitting them to live in tiny straw huts in his backyard. With these women Rabe developed a warning system to protect them from Japanese

50

rapists. Whenever Japanese soldiers scaled the wall of his yard, the women would blow a whistle and send Rabe running out into the yard to chase the offenders away. This happened so frequently that Rabe rarely left his home at night, fearful that Japanese intruders would commit an orgy of rape in his absence. He complained about the situation to Japanese military officers, but they failed to take the matter seriously.[22] Even when Rabe caught a Japanese soldier raping a woman in one of the backyard straw huts, a military officer did nothing to punish the rapist except slap him across the face.

If Rabe was frustrated by the futility of the situation—by the limitations of what he and some twenty other individuals could accomplish to protect hundreds of thousands of civilians from more than fifty thousand Japanese soldiers—he did not show it. He knew it was crucial to hide any sign of weakness from the Japanese and to overwhelm them with "a domineering presence and energy." [55]

Fortunately, his status as a Nazi caused several Japanese soldiers to hesitate before committing further mayhem—at least in his presence. George Fitch, the local YMCA secretary, wrote that "when any of them objects, [Rabe] thrusts his Nazi armband in their face and points to his Nazi decoration, the highest in the country, and asks them if they know what that means. It always works!"[23] The Japanese soldiers appeared to respect—at times even fear—the Nazis of Nanking. While the Japanese privates did not hesitate to beat up the Americans, charge at them with bayonets, or even to push one American missionary down a flight of stairs, they exercised considerable restraint in their dealings with Rabe and his countrymen. Once, when four Japanese soldiers in the midst of raping and looting saw Eduard Sperling's swastika armband, they screamed "Deutsche! Deutsche!" and ran away.[24] On another occasion, the swastika probably saved Rabe's life. One evening Japanese soldiers broke into his property, and Rabe confronted them with his flashlight. One of them reached for his pistol, as if to shoot Rabe, but stopped when he realized it would be "bad business to shoot a German subject."[25]

If the Japanese respected Rabe, the Chinese refugee community revered him. To them he was the man who rescued daughters from sexual slavery and sons from machine-gun fire. Rabe's very presence sometimes touched off riots in Safety Zone camps. During one of his visits to the zone, thousands of Chinese women flung themselves to the ground before him, weeping and begging for protection, declaring they would rather commit suicide on the spot than leave the zone to be raped and tortured.[26]

Rabe tried to keep hope alive for his refugees in the midst of their terror. He hosted little birthday celebrations for the children born to refugee women living in his backyard. Each newborn received a gift: $10 for baby boys and $9.50 for baby girls. (As Rabe explained in his report to Hitler—"Girls in China aren't worth as much as boys.") Typically, when a boy was born, he received Rabe's name, and if a girl was born, she received his wife's name, Dora.

Rabe's courage and generosity ultimately won the respect of the other members of the International Committee, even those fundamentally opposed

Dr. Robert Wilson, the only surgeon in Nanking during the massacre. Yale Divinity School Library.

to Nazism. George Fitch wrote to his friends that he would "almost wear a Nazi badge" to keep fellowship with Rabe and the other Germans in Nanking.[27] Even Dr. Robert Wilson, a man thoroughly repulsed by Nazism, sang Rabe's praises in letters to his family: "He is well up in Nazi circles and after coming into such close contact with him as we have for the past few weeks and discover[ing] what a splendid man he is and what a tremendous heart he has, it is hard to reconcile his personality with his adulation of 'Der Fuhrer.'"[28]

THE ONLY SURGEON IN NANKING

It is not surprising that Robert Wilson stayed in Nanking when virtually every other surgeon left, for Nanking, the city of his birth and boyhood, had always commanded a special place in his heart. Born in 1904, Wilson was reared by a family of Methodist missionaries who had shaped many of Nanking's educational institutions.[29] His uncle, John Ferguson, founded the University of Nanking. His father worked as an ordained minister and middle-school instructor in the city, while his mother, a college-educated Greek scholar who spoke several languages fluently, ran her own school for missionary children. As a

60

teenager, Robert Wilson even learned geometry from Pearl Buck, who would later win the Nobel Prize in Literature for her novels about China. Thriving in this environment, and displaying exceptional intellectual promise, Wilson won, at age seventeen, a scholarship to Princeton University. Upon graduation from college, he taught Latin and mathematics for two years at a high school in Connecticut, enrolled in Harvard Medical School and then served as an intern at St. Luke's Hospital in New York, where he courted and married the head nurse. But rather than pursue a career in the United States, Wilson decided that his future lay in his hometown of Nanking, and taking his bride with him, he returned in 1935 to practice medicine at the University of Nanking Hospital.

The first two years for the Wilsons were perhaps the most idyllic of their lives.[30] Time was marked by a slow-paced charm—dinners with other missionary couples, elegant teas and receptions at foreign embassies, parties at sprawling country villas staffed with private cooks and coolies. In the evenings he read ancient Chinese in its original text and studied under a private tutor to expand his knowledge of the language. He also took every Wednesday afternoon off to play tennis. Sometimes he and his wife would go to the lake together and have dinner on a boat, inhaling the perfumed air as they drifted through watery lanes of red lotus blossom.

War, however, shattered forever the timeless serenity the Wilsons had enjoyed in Nanking. After the Marco Polo Bridge incident in July,° the people of Nanking began to carry gas masks in the street, along with chemical solution and layers of gauze, fearing a Japanese poison-gas attack.[31] By August 1937, when the Japanese started to bomb the capital, his wife Marjorie had boarded a gunboat with their infant daughter Elizabeth and arrived safely at Kuling. But Wilson, fearing his wife and child would starve to death if the war continued, insisted that they return to the United States. Mrs. Wilson complied with his wishes and went back to work at St. Luke's in New York while her mother cared for the baby. But there was no question that Dr. Wilson himself would stay in Nanking. "He saw this as his duty," his wife recalled, almost sixty years later. "The Chinese were his people."[32]

No doubt to dispel loneliness that autumn, Wilson moved into the house of J. Lossing Buck, the former husband of Pearl Buck, and the house soon filled up with his friends: the surgeon Richard Brady, the United Christian missionary James McCallum, and other people who would later serve as members of the International Committee for the Nanking Safety Zone.[33] Like Wilson, many of these men had sent their wives and children away from Nanking.

When he wasn't busy with patients, Wilson often wrote letters home to his family. Most contained gruesome descriptions of the victims of Japanese bombs, such as the girl who had crouched with her back to an explosion, only to have her buttocks ripped off.[34] From the casualties of war he dug out

---

Marco Polo Bridge incident: Full-scale war between Japan and China began in 1937 when a Japanese soldier was allegedly shot near this ancient bridge.

a growing heap of shrapnel and bullets—enough, he wrote cynically, to open "a respectable museum" before the war was over.[35]

Even though he knew that the Japanese had no qualms about bombing hospitals, Wilson continued to go to work. On September 25, in one of the worst air raids Nanking had ever experienced, the Japanese aimed two 1,000-pound bombs at the Central Hospital and Ministry of Health, despite the presence of a large red cross clearly painted on one of the roofs.[36] The bombs landed only fifty feet away from a dugout where one hundred doctors and nurses were hiding.

65

Wilson did everything possible in the hospital to minimize the risk of attracting Japanese bombs. Heavy black curtains were drawn over the windows to hide lit rooms from Japanese aviators.[37] But the city crawled with rumors of spies guiding pilots to key targets with red and green lanterns at night. During one raid a stranger crept into the hospital with a red-shielded flashlight instead of a green- or black-shielded one and aroused suspicions when he tried to open a window that had been securely shut to prevent the seepage of poison gas. He raised even more eyebrows when he asked a Chinese aviator patient a number of unusual questions about the flying height and range of Chinese bombers.

As autumn drew to a close, Wilson found himself tremendously overworked. More people needed medical attention than ever before—not only civilian victims of Japanese bombs but veterans from Shanghai. There were approximately one hundred thousand wounded Chinese veterans in hospitals between Shanghai and the city of Wuhu.[38] Trainload after trainload dumped them off at the station in Hsiakwan, the northern Nanking suburb. Some lay dying on the floor of the station, while others limped aimlessly through the capital. Soldiers who healed were returned to the front, but those who lost arms or legs, those crippled beyond hope, were simply turned loose with two-dollar compensations and instructions to go home.[39] Home was far away for most soldiers. Few had the money or physical energy to get there. Abandoned by their leaders, stranded in the Shanghai-Nanking area, thousands of Chinese veterans—blind, lame, rotting away from wounds and infections—were reduced to begging in the streets.

As the situation worsened, the staff at the hospital shrank. Chinese doctors and nurses fled the city, joining the hundreds of thousands of Nanking residents in their westward migration.[40] Wilson did all he could to dissuade his medical staff from leaving, insisting that under martial law they would have nothing to fear after the city fell. Ultimately, however, he was unable to convince them to stay.[41] By the end of the first week of December there were only three doctors at the University of Nanking Hospital: Robert Wilson, C. S. Trimmer, and a Chinese physician.[42] When Richard Brady, the only other American surgeon in the city, left Nanking because his little girl was seriously ill in Kuling, Wilson was the only person left to perform the hourly amputations.[43] "It is quite a sensation," he wrote on December 7, "to be the only surgeon in a big war-torn city."[44]

The following day, as Japanese soldiers roamed the streets, Wilson nearly lost his life. That afternoon he had decided to perform a delicate operation on a patient who had suffered severe eye injury from a bomb. Wilson had to remove what was left of the eye in order to save the other one. The eyeball was halfway out when a shell landed fifty yards away from Wilson and exploded, shattering the windows and spraying the room with shrapnel. No one was killed or injured, but Wilson noted that the nurses were "naturally pretty shaky" and wanted to know whether they should continue the operation.[45] "There was obviously nothing else to do," Wilson wrote, "but I don't think any eyes have come out that fast."

By nightfall of December 13, the Japanese had seized complete control of the ancient capital. Wilson saw Japanese flags fluttering all over town.[46] The following day the conquering army began to take over the hospitals in the city. They broke into the main hospital of the Chinese army—located within the Ministry of Foreign Affairs and run by Safety Zone members who had organized themselves as a chapter of the Red Cross—and trapped hundreds of Chinese soldiers inside.[47] The Japanese forbade doctors to enter the hospital or send food to the wounded soldiers, who were later marched out and systematically shot. After three out of four Red Cross hospitals fell in this manner to the Japanese, the International Committee concentrated its efforts on the University of Nanking Hospital.

During the first few days of occupation, Wilson watched the Japanese soldiers loot and burn the city. He saw them rob the University of Nanking Hospital and, frustrated that he could not stop all of the thefts, mentally aimed a "swift kick" at a soldier who tried to steal a camera from a nurse.[48] He also watched soldiers burn a heap of musical instruments in the street and wondered whether the destruction of property was a Japanese plot to compel the people of Nanking to buy Japanese goods later.[49]

Wilson even witnessed the ransacking of his own home. Venturing to his house to survey possible damage, he caught red-handed three Japanese soldiers in the process of looting it. They had broken into the attic, opened up a big trunk, and strewn its contents all over the floor. One of them was peering into a microscope when Wilson walked in. Upon seeing him, all three soldiers ran down the stairs and out the door. "The crowning insult was on the second floor where one had just finished depositing his calling card on the floor of the toilet within a foot of the toilet bowl," Wilson wrote. "He had covered it with a clean towel which had been left hanging in the room."[50]

But nothing of the looting could compare to the rape and murder that he witnessed in the city. Even Wilson, now a jaded war surgeon, found the intensity of the atrocities shocking.

December 15: The slaughter of civilians is appalling. I could go on for pages telling of cases of rape and brutality almost beyond belief.[51]

December 18: Today marks the 6th day of modern Dante's Inferno, written in huge letters with blood and rape. Murder by the wholesale and rape by the thousands of cases. There seems to be no stop to the ferocity, lust and atavism of the brutes. At first I tried to be pleasant to them to avoid arousing their ire, but the smile has gradually worn off and my stare is fully as cool and fishy as theirs.[52]

December 19: All the food is being stolen from the poor people and they are in a state of terror-stricken, hysterical panic. When will it stop![53]

Christmas Eve: Now they tell us that there are twenty thousand soldiers still in the Zone (where they get their figures no one knows), and that they are going to hunt them out and shoot them all. That will mean every able-bodied male between the ages of 18 and 50 that is now in the city. How can they ever look anybody in the face again?[54]

By the end of the year his letters carried a fatalistic air. "The only consolation is that it can't be worse," he wrote on December 30. "They can't kill as many people as there aren't any more to kill."[55]

Frequently Wilson and the others saw the Japanese round up Chinese soldiers, shoot them, and stuff the bodies in dirt air-raid shelters that doubled as mass graves.[56] But Wilson heard that many Chinese people were executed not because they posed any threat to the Japanese army but because their bodies served a practical purpose. After the fall of Nanking, the big trenches that the Chinese had built for tank traps were filled to the brim by the Japanese with the bodies of dead and wounded soldiers.[57] When the Japanese failed to find enough bodies of dead soldiers so tanks could pass over them, they shot nearby residents and threw them in the trenches as well. The witness who told Wilson the story borrowed a camera so that he could take pictures to confirm his statements.

There was very little Wilson could do to prevent these murders. The Japanese soldiers he confronted often made a point of conspicuously playing with their weapons—loading and unloading them—in order to intimidate him and other foreigners.[58] Wilson fully expected to be shot in the back at any moment.

One of the worst scenes Wilson saw in Nanking—a scene he would remember for the rest of his life—was a massive gang rape of teenage girls in the street.[59] A group of young women between the ages of fifteen and eighteen were lined up by the Japanese and then raped in the dirt, one after another, by an entire regiment. Some hemorrhaged and died, while others killed themselves shortly afterwards.

But the scenes in the hospitals were even more horrifying than those in the streets. Wilson was mortified by the women who came to the emergency room with their bellies ripped open, by the charred and horribly disfigured men whom the Japanese tried to burn alive, and by numerous other horrors he barely had time to describe on paper. He told his wife that he would never forget the woman whose head was nearly cut off, teetering from a point on her neck.[60] "This morning came another woman in a sad plight and with a horrible story," a hospital volunteer wrote of this woman in his diary on January 3, 1938.

She was one of the five women whom the Japanese soldiers had taken to one of their medical units—to wash their clothes by day, to be raped by night. Two of them were forced to satisfy from 15 to 20 men and the prettiest one as many as 40 each night. This one who came to us had been called off by three soldiers into an isolated place where they attempted to cut off her head. The muscles of the neck had been cut but they failed to sever the spinal cord. She feigned death but dragged herself to the hospital—another of the many to bear witness to the brutality of soldiers.[61]

Yet in the midst of their pain and suffering, Wilson was amazed by the willpower of some of his patients. In a letter to his family dated New Year's Day 1938, he told an incredible account of survival.[62] Chinese soldiers burned down the home of a twenty-nine-year-old woman in a tiny village south of Nanking, forcing her to head for the capital by foot with her five small children. Before nightfall a Japanese airplane dove down at them, strafing the family with machine-gun fire and sending a bullet through the mother's right eye and out her neck. She fainted in shock but awoke the next morning, lying in a pool of blood next to her crying children. Too weak to carry her youngest child, a three-month-old baby, she left it behind in an empty house. Yet she somehow found the strength to struggle on to Nanking with her four remaining children, making her way successfully to the hospital.

Wilson and other volunteers stayed in the hospital until they wavered on the verge of collapse. The International Committee could have used medical help from outside the city, but the Japanese would not permit doctors or medical volunteers to enter Nanking. So the burden of caring for the sick and administering the zone fell on this tiny beleaguered committee of no more than some twenty individuals. They worked in shifts to ensure that the hospital was guarded from the Japanese by at least one foreigner twenty-four hours a day. Some of them became so overworked that they succumbed to colds, flu, and various other illnesses. During the massacre the only other Western doctor in the city, C. S. Trimmer, struggled with a fever of 102 degrees.[63]

The University of Nanking Hospital swiftly became another refugee *80* camp because Wilson refused to discharge patients who had no place to go. Patients who did leave the hospital were accompanied by foreigners to ensure that they returned home safely. James McCallum acted as the hospital chauffeur, driving patients about town in unpainted, patched-up ambulances. Survivors of the massacre remember that the exhausted McCallum pressed cold towels against his face to stay awake as he drove patients home. But when even cold towels failed to keep his eyes open, McCallum resorted to chewing his tongue until it bled.[64]

Few people in Nanking pushed themselves as hard as Wilson did in the hospital. When the massacre and rapes gradually subsided, several of the other physicians went to Shanghai every weekend to recover from the strain.[65] But Wilson continued to operate on patients relentlessly, day and night, around the

Minnie Vautrin, "The Living Goddess of Nanking." Courtesy of Emma Lyon.

clock. His selflessness was remembered almost sixty years later by survivors who spoke of Wilson with great reverence, at least one of them discussing in detail the preparation and successful result of his operation under Wilson's hands. He operated for free, because few patients had money to pay him, but the surgeries exacted a terrible price from his own health. In the end, his family believes that only his faith as a devout Methodist, combined with his love for China, gave him the courage to survive the Rape of Nanking.

THE LIVING GODDESS OF NANKING

Wilhelmina Vautrin (or Minnie Vautrin, as most people called her), by occupation head of the Education Department and dean of studies at Ginling Women's Arts and Science College, was one of the few Western women in the city during the first few weeks of the Nanking massacre. Years later she would be remembered not only for her courage in protecting thousands of women from Japanese soldiers but also for the diary she kept, a diary that some historians believe will eventually be recognized, much like the diary of Anne Frank, for its importance in illuminating the spirit of a single witness during a holocaust of war.

Vautrin, the daughter of a blacksmith, was fifty-one years old in 1937.[66] Born in the tiny farming community of Secor, Illinois, she was sent to live with neighbors when her mother died six years later. In their homes Vautrin was often treated little better than a servant or field hand, and she found herself herding cattle during the bleakest months of winter. Despite the impoverishment of her childhood, she was able to work her way through school, graduating with honors in 1912 from the University of Illinois at Urbana-Champaign.

Tall and handsome in her youth, with long dark hair, she was a vivacious and popular woman who attracted numerous suitors. But by the time she graduated from the University of Illinois, she had made up her mind to forgo marriage. Instead, she joined the United Christian Missionary Association and moved to Hofei, a city in the Anhwei province of China, where she worked for seven years as the principal of a girls' school and learned to speak Chinese. Then Vautrin moved to Nanking, to the position she held at the time of the massacre.

Vautrin was clearly very happy in Nanking. On visits to her hometown in Illinois, she talked incessantly of China—its culture, its people, and its history. She gave her family silkworm cocoons and taught them how to cook and eat Chinese food. In her diary, she never ceased to marvel at the beauty of the Nanking landscape.[67] An avid gardener, she planted roses and chrysanthemums at Ginling College, visiting greenhouses at Sun Yat-sen Memorial Park, walking down the fragrant lanes of plum and peach trees near the Ming Tombs. 85

In the summer of 1937, while vacationing with friends in the seaside summer resort of Tsingtao, Vautrin heard that a Japanese soldier had disappeared a few miles south of Peking.[68] The disappearance triggered several battles between the Chinese and Japanese in the area, prompting a friend of hers to comment darkly that the assassination of only two people in Sarajevo in 1914° had eventually culminated in the deaths of more than 11 million people.

Still, Vautrin refused to join the other Americans evacuating Nanking, and so the American embassy lent her a new nine-foot American flag to lay flat on the center of the grassy quadrangle of Ginling College to protect the campus against Japanese pilots.[69] The embassy staff also gave her and the other International Committee members lengths of rope to knot into ladders and told them that once the *Panay* departed with the American embassy officials, and the Chinese military slammed all the gates shut, their only hope of escape would be over the city walls.[70]

But Vautrin hardly had time to think about running away. With most of the faculty gone from Nanking (most had abandoned their homes to flee to cities like Shanghai, Chengtu, and Szechwan), Vautrin was now the acting head of the institution. She labored to prepare the campus for female refugees and

---

two people in Sarajevo: Archduke Franz Ferdinand and his wife, an assassination which led to World War I.

to evacuate wounded soldiers from the area.[71] To disguise their identities, she burned their military papers and garments in the college incinerator. Under her direction, furniture was moved into attics, safes were emptied, dorms were cleaned, and valuables were wrapped in oil paper and hidden. Meanwhile, posters, signs, and armbands for the Nanking Safety Zone were created and distributed among volunteers. Vautrin also commissioned the sewing of a second American flag, this one twenty-seven-feet long, but the Chinese tailor who put it together accidentally sewed the blue field with the stars on the lower, left-hand corner instead of the upper.[72]

By the second week of December the gates of Ginling opened for women and children.[73] Thousands of people poured in. Refugees were passing through the city at the rate of one thousand a day.[74] Many of them, exhausted, bewildered, and hungry, came into the Safety Zone camps with only the clothing on their backs.[75] "From 8:30 this morning until 6 this evening, excepting for the noon meal, I have stood at the front gate while refugees poured in," she continued. "There is terror in the faces of many of the women—last night was a terrible night in the city and many young women were taken from their homes by the Japanese soldiers."[76]

Vautrin allowed the women and children to come in freely but implored older women to stay home to leave space for the younger ones.[77] Few women took her suggestion, and most begged just for a place to sit on the lawn. By the night of December 15, the population of the camps at Ginling had swelled to more than three thousand people.

The next day Japanese soldiers stormed the college. At 10:00 A.M. on December 16, more than one hundred Japanese troops burst onto the Ginling campus to inspect the buildings for hidden Chinese soldiers. They demanded that every door be opened, and if a key was not forthcoming, a Japanese soldier stood ready with an ax to break down the door by force. . . .

Twice that day the Japanese seized servants on campus and started to drag them away. They certainly would have been killed if Vautrin had not rescued them with cries of "No soldier—coolie!"[78] Only later did she learn that the Japanese had trained at least six machine guns on the campus, with many more soldiers on guard outside, ready to shoot anyone who attempted to run away.

That evening Vautrin saw women being carted away in the streets and heard their desperate pleas. A truck went by with eight to ten girls, and as it passed she heard them scream, "Jiu Ming! Jiu Ming! (Save our lives!)"[79]

The following day, December 17, 1937, was even worse. The migration of women into Ginling only intensified as Japanese soldiers flooded the city. "What a heartbreaking sight!" Vautrin wrote. "Weary women, frightened girls, trudging with children and bedding and small packages of clothes."[80] If only someone had time to write the story of each refugee who came in, she thought—especially the stories of the girls who had blackened their faces and cut their hair. As she accommodated the stream of "wild-eyed women," she heard stories of the Japanese raping girls as young as twelve and women as elderly as sixty, or raping pregnant women at bayonet point. The harried Vautrin spent the entire day trying to secure food for the refugees, direct Chinese men to other camps in the Safety Zone, and run to areas on campus where Japanese soldiers had been sighted.

But nothing prepared Vautrin for the encounter that awaited her that evening. Two Japanese soldiers were pulling at the door of the Central Building, demanding that Vautrin open it immediately, but when she insisted that she had no key and that no soldiers were hiding inside, a Japanese soldier slapped her in the face and also struck the Chinese man next to her. Then she saw two Japanese soldiers lead away three bound servants from the college. She followed them to the front gate, where the Japanese had forced a large group of Chinese to kneel beside the road. The Japanese demanded to speak to the master of the institution and, learning that it was Vautrin, ordered her to identify every kneeling person. One man in the party spoke up to help Vautrin, and for this he was slapped severely.

In the midst of this ordeal, three committee members drove up: the YMCA secretary George Fitch, the Nanking University sociology professor Lewis Smythe, and the Presbyterian missionary W. Plumer Mills. The soldiers forced the three men to stand in line and frisked them for pistols. Suddenly they heard screams and cries and saw the Japanese dragging women out of the side gate. It was only then that Vautrin realized that the entire interrogation was a ploy to keep the foreigners at the front gate while other Japanese soldiers searched the campus for women to rape. "Never shall I forget that scene," she wrote, remembering her rage and helplessness: "The people kneeling at side of road, Mary, Mrs. Tsen and I standing, the dried leaves rattling, the moaning of the wind, the cry of women being led out."[81]

For the next few months, Vautrin often found herself one of the sole defenders of the refugee camps at Ginling College. Japanese soldiers constantly harassed the refugees there by rounding up men for execution or women for military brothels. Sometimes their recruitment tactics were brazen. On at least one occasion Japanese soldiers drove up to campus with a truck and asked for girls.[82] Most of the time, however, the kidnapping of women for rape was done covertly. Soldiers jumped over bamboo fences at night or broke open the side or back gates to seize random women in the darkness—expeditions that began to be known throughout the populace as "the lottery."[83]

On New Year's Day 1938, Vautrin rescued a girl whom a soldier had dragged into a bamboo grove north of the library.[84] On several occasions her heroism nearly cost Vautrin her life. Many of the soldiers were "fierce and unreasonable" toward her, brandishing bayonets reddened with fresh bloodstains.[85] Vautrin wrote that "in some cases they are defiant and look at me with a dagger in their eyes, and sometimes a dagger in their hands." One time, when she tried to stop Japanese soldiers from looting, one of them aimed a gun at her.

Sometimes in her dealings with the Japanese, Vautrin made mistakes. Just as Rabe and the other committee members had been duped by the Japanese into handing over men for execution, Vautrin appears to have been duped into delivering innocent women into the arms of Japanese soldiers. On

December 24, Vautrin was summoned to her office to meet with a high Japanese military officer and an elderly Chinese interpreter, who discussed with her the Japanese army's need for prostitutes. "The request was that they be allowed to pick out the prostitute women from our ten thousand refugees," Vautrin later wrote of the meeting in her diary. "They said they wanted one hundred. They feel if they can start a regular licensed place for the soldiers then they will not molest innocent and decent women."[86]

Strangely enough, Vautrin granted the request. Perhaps she had no choice in the matter, or perhaps she actually believed that once the Japanese left with the prostitutes for their military brothel they would stop bothering the virgins and respectable matrons in the refugee camps. Whatever the reasons behind her decision, it is safe to assume that Vautrin made it under pressure. She waited while the Japanese conducted their search and after a long time they finally secured twenty-one women. How the Japanese were able to distinguish these women as prostitutes Vautrin does not say, but she did mention that the Japanese were dissatisfied with the result because they were convinced that more prostitutes were hiding somewhere in the zone. "Group after group of girls have asked me if they will select the other seventy-nine from among the decent girls—and all I can answer is that they will not do so if it is in my power to prevent it," she wrote.[87]

A week after the city fell, the Japanese began a systematic effort to regulate activity within the zone.[88] The commander of the military police of the Japanese army made a proclamation, effective December 24, dictating that all civilians obtain passports (also called "good citizen's papers") from the issuing office of the Japanese army. No one was allowed to get a passport for some one else, and those without passports would not be allowed to live within the Nanking city walls. The military posted bulletins in the streets notifying people to register or face the risk of being executed.

On December 28, registration of the men began. At Ginling College they formed lines of four, received copies of forms, and marched to a house at the northeast corner of the campus where the Japanese recorded their names, ages, and occupations. Vautrin noticed that the men who arrived for registration were mainly old or maimed because most of the young men had already fled the city or been killed.[89] Among those who showed up, more men were taken away as ex-soldiers, leaving behind old men and women who wept and kneeled before the Safety Zone leaders, begging them to secure the release of their husbands and sons. In a few cases the zone leaders were successful, but they noticed that the Japanese military officials were growing increasingly resentful of their interference.[90]

When the turnout of men for registration disappointed the Japanese, they tried to intimidate the populace into compliance. On December 30, they announced that all who had not been registered by 2:00 P.M. the following day would be shot. "This proved to be a bluff," one missionary wrote of the incident, "but it frightened the people."[91] The next morning huge crowds of

100

people dutifully appeared at the registration areas, many of whom had risen before 3:00 A.M. to ensure their place in line. The Draconian threats of the Japanese had instilled such fear that by January 14 the authorities succeeded in registering at least 160,000 people.[92]

Then registration began for the women. At 9:00 A.M. on December 31, thousands of Chinese women gathered in front of the Central Building of Ginling College, where a Japanese military official lectured to them. Speeches were given first in Japanese, then translated into Chinese by an interpreter: "You must follow the old customs of marriage," Vautrin recalled them saying. "You must not study English or go to theatres. China and Japan must be one."[93] The women were then marched single file in two lines through frames set up for selling rice, where they were given tickets. Vautrin observed that the Japanese soldiers seemed to get a great deal of amusement herding the women about like cattle, sometimes putting the stamp on their cheeks.[94] The soldiers also forced the women to smile and look happy for Japanese newsmen and photographers, even though the mere prospect of registration had made some women literally ill with fear.[95]

At times the Japanese registration of Chinese women seemed to Vautrin nothing less than a full-scale inspection of the most attractive candidates for rape. On the very first day of female registration, the Japanese scrutinized certain women in the zone and tried to take them away. They had singled out twenty girls, no doubt for prostitution, because they had curled hair or dressed too well. But all were released, Vautrin later wrote, "because a mother or some other person could vouch for them."[96]

After registration, the Japanese tried to eliminate the zone itself.[97] In late January the Japanese announced that they wanted everyone out of the camps and back into their homes by the end of the month. February 4 was given as the deadline for evacuation.[98] When the deadline arrived, Japanese soldiers inspected Ginling College and ordered the remaining girls and women to leave. When Vautrin told the inspectors that they could not leave because they were from other cities or their homes had burned down, the Japanese announced that the military police would assume the responsibility of protecting them. Vautrin was wary of these promises, and even the Chinese interpreter who came with the Japanese to deliver their messages whispered to Vautrin that he felt the young women were not safe and should continue to stay where they were.[99]

The sheer number of refugees overwhelmed Vautrin. Hundreds of women crammed themselves into verandas and covered ways head to feet, and many more women slept outside on the grass at night.[100] The attic of Ginling's Science Hall housed more than one thousand women, and a friend of Vautrin's noted that women "slept shoulder to shoulder on the cement floor for weeks on end during the cold winter months! Each cement step in the building was the home of one person—and those steps are not more than four feet long! Some were happy to have a resting place on the chemistry lab tables, the water pipes and other paraphernalia not interfering at all."[101]

The Rape of Nanking wore down Vautrin physically, but the mental torture she endured daily was far worse than her physical deterioration. "Oh, God, control the cruel beastliness of the soldiers in Nanking tonight . . ." she wrote in her diary. "How ashamed the women of Japan would be if they knew these tales of horror."[102]

Under such pressure, it is remarkable that Vautrin still found the spirit to comfort others and give them a renewed sense of patriotism. When an old lady went to the Red Cross kitchen at Ginling College to fetch a bowl of rice porridge, she learned that there was no porridge left. Vautrin immediately gave her the porridge she had been eating and said to her: "Don't you people worry. Japan will fail. China will not perish."[103] Another time, when she saw a boy wearing an armband marked with the Japanese symbol of the rising sun to ensure his safety, Vautrin scolded him and said: "You do not need to wear this rising sun emblem. You are a Chinese and your country has not perished. You should remember the date you wear this thing, and you should never forget."[104] Again and again, Vautrin urged the Chinese refugees on campus never to lose faith in their future. "China has not perished," she told them. "China will never perish. And Japan will definitely fail in the end."[105]

Others could see how hard she was working. "She didn't sleep from morning till night," one Chinese survivor recalled. "She kept watching and if Japanese soldiers came . . . she would try her best to push them out and went out to their officials to pray them not to do so much evil things to the Chinese women and children."[106] "It was said that once she was slapped several times by beastly Japanese soldiers," another wrote in his eyewitness account of the Nanking massacre. "Everyone was worried about her. Everyone tried to comfort her. She still fought for the cause of protecting Chinese women with courage and determination from beginning to end."[107]

The work of running the zone was not only physically taxing but psychologically debilitating. Christian Kröger, a Nazi member of the International Committee, claimed that he saw so many corpses in the streets that he soon suffered nightmares about them.[108] But in the end, under unbelievable circumstances, the zone saved lives. Here are some startling facts:

—Looting and arson made food so scarce that some Chinese refugees ate the Michaelmas daisies and goldenrod growing on the Ginling College campus or subsisted on mushrooms found in the city.[109] Even the zone leaders went hungry from lack of meals. They not only provided free rice to the refugees through soup kitchens but delivered some of it directly to refugee compounds, because many Chinese in the zone were too scared to leave their buildings.[110]

—Bookish and genteel, most of the zone leaders had little experience in handling a horde of rapists, murderers, and street brawlers. Yet they acted as bodyguards for even the Chinese police in the city and somehow, like warriors, found the physical energy and raw courage to throw themselves in the line of fire—wrestling Chinese men away from execution sites, knocking Japanese soldiers off of women, even jumping in front of cannons and machine guns to prevent the Japanese from firing.[111]

—In the process, many zone leaders came close to being shot, and some received blows or cuts from Japanese soldiers wielding bayonets and swords. For example: Charles Riggs, a University of Nanking professor of agricultural engineering, was struck by an officer when he tried to prevent him from taking away a group of Chinese civilians mistaken as soldiers. The infuriated Japanese officer "threatened Riggs with his sword three times and finally hit him hard over the heart twice with his fist."[112] A Japanese soldier also threatened Professor Miner Searle Bates with a pistol.[113] Another soldier pulled a gun on Robert Wilson when he tried to kick out of the hospital a soldier who had crawled into bed with three girls.[114] Still another soldier fired a rifle at James McCallum and C. S. Trimmer but missed.[115] When Miner Searle Bates visited the headquarters of the Japanese military police to learn the fate of a University Middle School student who had been tied up and carried off by soldiers, the Japanese shoved Bates down a flight of stairs.[116] Even the swastikas the Nazis carried about like amulets occasionally failed to protect them from assault. On December 22, John Rabe wrote that Christian Kröger and another German named Hatz were attacked when they tried to save a Chinese man who had been wounded in the throat by a drunken Japanese soldier. Hatz defended himself with a chair, but Kröger apparently ended up being tied and beaten.[117]

—The zone eventually accommodated some 200,000–300,000 refugees—almost half the Chinese population left in the city.[118]

The last is a chilling statistic when placed in the context of later studies of the Nanking massacre. Half the original inhabitants of Nanking left before the massacre. About half of those who stayed (350,000 people out of the 600,000–700,000 Chinese refugees, native residents, and soldiers in the city when it fell) were killed.

If half of the population of Nanking fled into the Safety Zone during the worst of the massacre, then the other half—almost everyone who did not make it to the zone—probably died at the hands of the Japanese.

NOTES

1. Tien-wei Wu, "Let the Whole World Know the Nanking Massacre" (Society for Studies of Japanese Aggression Against China, 1997), p. 16.
2. Angie Mills to the author, 16 February 1997. In her family archives, Mills found a copy of a speech given by John Rabe on 28 February 1938 at the Foreign YMCA in Shanghai to a group of Westerners. In it he said, "I must tell you Mr. Mills is the man who originally had the idea of creating the Safety Zone. I can say that the brains of our organization were to be found in the Ping Tsang Hsiang No. 3 [the address, according to Angie Mills, of Lossing Buck's house, where nine or ten of the Americans were

living during this period, near Nanking University]. Thanks to the cleverness of my American friends: Mr. Mills, Mr. Bates, Dr. Smythe, Mr. Fitch, Mr. Sone, Mr. Magee, Mr. Forster and Mr. Riggs, the Committee was put on its feet, and thanks to their hard work it ran as smoothly as could be expected under the dreadful circumstances we lived in."

3. "Sinking of the USS *Panay,*" Ch. 11 of *Some Phases of the Sino-Japanese Conflict* (July–December 1937), compiled from the records of the Commander in Chief, Asiatic Fleet, by Captain W. A. Angwin (MC), USN, December 1938, Shanghai, Office of the Chief of Naval Operations, Division of Naval Intelligence, general correspondence, 1929–42, folder P9–2/EF16#23, box 284, entry 81, RG 38, National Archives; "The *Panay* Incident," Records of the Office of the Chief of Naval Operations, Records of the Deputy Chief of Naval Operations, 1882–1954, Intelligence Division–Naval Attaché Reports, 1886–1939, box 438, entry 98, RG 38, National Archives; "The Bombing of the USS *Panay,*" drawn by Mr. E. Larsen after consultation with Mr. Norman Alley, 31 December 1937, box 438, entry 98, RG 38, National Archives; Weldon James, "Terror Hours on *Panay* Told by Passenger," *Chicago Daily News,* 13 December 1937; A. T. Steele, "Chinese War Horror Pictured by Reporter: *Panay* Victims Under Japanese Fire for Full Half Hour; Butchery and Looting Reign in Nanking," *Chicago Daily News;* 17 December 1937; David Bergamini, *Japan's Imperial Conspiracy* (New York: Morrow, 1971), pp. 24–28.

4. Marjorie Wilson, telephone interview with the author.

5. Alice Tisdale Hobart, *Within the Walls of Nanking* (New York: Macmillan, 1928), pp. 207–8.

6. "*Deutsche Botschaft* China," German diplomatic reports, 15 January 1938, starting on p. 214, National History Archives, Xingdian, Taipei County, Republic of China.

7. Details of John Rabe's early life come from correspondence between the author and Rabe's granddaughter, Ursula Reinhardt, and from the archives of the Siemens Company, Berlin, Germany.

8. Rabe's account of the Rape of Nanking can be found in "Enemy Planes over Nanking," report to Adolf Hitler, copies of which are now at Yale Divinity School Library, the Memorial Hall of the Victims of the Nanking Massacre by Japanese Invaders, and the Budesarchiv of the Federal Republic of Germany. Information and quotes in this section not otherwise attributed come from this report.

9. Letter from John Rabe of the International Committee for Nanking Safety Zone to the Imperial Japanese Embassy, 27 December 1937, enclosure to report "Conditions in Nanking," 25 January 1938, Intelligence Division, Naval Attaché Reports, 1886–1939, Records of the Office of the Deputy Chief of Naval Operations, 1882–1954, Office of Naval Intelligence, box 996, entry 98, RG 38, National Archives.

10. George Fitch, *My Eighty Years in China* (Taipei: Mei Ya Publications, 1974) p. 101.

11. Hsu Shuhsi, ed., *Documents of the Nanking Safety Zone* (Shanghai, Hong Kong, Singapore: Kelly & Walsh, 1939) p. 56.

12. Hsu, p. 2.

13. Letter from John Rabe to Fukuda Tokuyasa, 15 December 1937, box 996, entry 98, RG 38, National Archives.

14. George Fitch, diary entry for 14 December 1937, reprinted in *My Eighty Years in China,* p. 106. One of the original copies can be found in Commanding Officer C. F. Jeffs to

the Commander in Chief, U.S. Asiatic Fleet (letterhead marked the USS *Oahu*), 14 February 1938, intelligence summary filed for the week ending 13 February 1938, Office of the Chief of Naval Operations, Division of Naval Intelligence, general correspondence, 1929–42, p. 5, folder A8–21/FS#3, box 195, entry 81, RG 38, National Archives. In the diary, Fitch wrote: "Not a whimper came from the entire throng. Our own hearts were lead. . . . How foolish I had been to tell them the Japanese would spare their lives!"

15. Letter from Rabe to the Imperial Japanese Embassy, 17 December 1937, enclosure no. 8 to report "Conditions in Nanking," National Archives. This letter can also be found in Hsu Shuhsi.

16. Rabe to Imperial Japanese Embassy, 17 December 1937; Hsu Shuhsi, p. 12.

17. Rabe to Imperial Japanese Embassy, 17 December 1937; Hsu Shuhsi, p. 20.

18. Rabe to Imperial Japanese Embassy, 17 December 1937; Hsu Shuhsi, p. 17.

19. IMTFE judgment, National Archives. See "Verdict of the International/Military Tribunal for the Far East (IMTFE) on the Rape of Nanking," *Journal of Studies of Japanese Aggression Against China* (November 1990): p. 75.

20. Fu Kuishan's warning to Rabe, recorded in John Rabe diary, 10 February 1938, p. 723.

21. Robert Wilson, letter to family, 31 January 1938, p. 61, Yale Divinity School Library.

22. Even the Japanese embassy staff seemed secretly gleeful of the excesses of the Japanese army. When Hsu Chuang-ying caught a Japanese soldier raping a woman in a bath house and informed Fukuda, vice-consul of the Japanese embassy, of the situation, he saw that Fukuda had "a little smile on his face." Transcript of the International Military Tribunal of the Far East (IMFTE), "Testimony of Hsu Chuang-ying, witness," entry 319, pp. 2570–71, RG 311, Records of the Allied Operational/Occupation Headquarters, National Archives.

23. Copy of George Fitch diary, enclosed in file from Assistant Naval Attaché E. G. Hagen to Chief of Naval Operations (Director of Naval Intelligence), Navy Department, Washington, D.C., 7 March 1938, Office of the Chief of Naval Operations, Division of Naval Intelligence, general correspondence, 1929–42, folder P9–2/EF16#8, box 277, entry 81, RG 38, National Archives; also reprinted in Fitch, *My Eighty Years in China*, p. 114.

24. "Cases of Disorder by Japanese Soldiers in the Safety Zone," filed 4 January 1938, in Hsu Shuhsi, p. 65.

25. "Cases of Disorder by Japanese Soldiers in the Safety Zone," subenclosure to enclosure no. 1-c, Intellience Division, Naval Attaché Reports, 1886–1939, Records of the Office of the Deputy Chief of Naval Operations, 1882–1954, Office of Naval Intelligence, folder H-8-B Register#1727A, box 996, entry 98, RG 38, National Archives.

26. Minnie Vautrin, diary 1937–40, 17 February 1938, p. 198, Yale Divinity School Library.

27. George Fitch, "Nanking Outrages," 10 January 1938, George Fitch Collection, Yale Divinity School Library.

28. Robert Wilson, letter to family, Christmas Eve 1937, p. 6.

29. Early biographical information on Robert Wilson comes from Marjorie Wilson (his widow), telephone interviews with the author.

30. Ibid.

31. Robert Wilson, letter to family, 18 August 1937.

32. Marjorie Wilson, telephone interview.

33. Robert Wilson, letter to family, 12 October 1937, p. 15.

34. Ibid., 20 August 1937, p. 9.

35. Ibid., 9 December 1937, p. 35.

36. Ibid., 25 and 27 September 1937; Vautrin, diary 1937–40, 26 September 1937, p. 33.

37. Robert Wilson, letter to family, 23 August 1937.

38. Commander Yangtze Patrol E. J. Marquart to Commander in Chief, U.S. Asiatic Fleet (letterhead marked "Yangtze Patrol, USS *Luzon* [Flagship])," intelligence summary for week ending 24 October 1937, 25 October 1937, Office of the Chief of Naval Operations, Division of Naval Intelligence, general correspondence, 1929–42, folder A8-2/FS, box 194, entry 81, RG 38, National Archives; Minnie Vautrin, diary 1937–40, 26 October and 8 November 1937, pp. 55, 64 (she writes that some 100,000 soldiers have been injured or killed in the Shanghai area).

39. Ibid.

40. Vautrin, diary 1937–40, 5 December 1937, p. 96; Ernest and Clarissa Forster, letter to parents, 7 December 1937, Earnest and Clarissa Forster Collection, box 263, RG 8, Miscellaneous Personal Papers, Yale Divinity School Library.

41. Robert O. Wilson (witness), testimony, Records of the Allied Operational/Occupation Headquarters, IMTFE transcript, entry 319, RG 331, pp. 2531–32, National Archives.

42. Mrs. E. H. Forster report, 12 December 1937, from newsletter in Ernest and Clarissa Forster Collection.

43. Robert Wilson, letter to family, 2 December 1937; A. T. Steele, "Tells Heroism of Yankees in Nanking," *Chicago Daily News,* 18 December 1937.

44. Robert Wilson, letter to family, 7 December 1937.

45. Ibid., 14 December 1937.

46. Ibid.

47. Frank Tillman Durdin, "Japanese Atrocities Marked Fall of Nanking after Chinese Command Fled," *New York Times,* 22 December 1937, p. 38; Rabe, "Enemy Planes over Nanking"; an excerpt from a verbal presentation by Mr. Smith of Reuters about the events of Nanking on 9–15 December 1937, document no. 178, Hankow, 1 January 1938, in "*Deutsche Botschaft* China," German diplomatic reports, National History Archives, Republic of China.

48. Robert Wilson, letter to family, 18 December 1937.

49. Ibid., 28 December 1937.

50. Ibid., 19 December 1937.

51. Ibid., 15 December 1937.

52. Ibid., 18 December 1937.

53. Ibid., 19 December 1937.

54. Ibid., 24 December 1937.

55. Ibid., 30 December 1937.

56. Durdin, "Japanese Atrocities Marked Fall of Nanking."

57. Robert Wilson, letter to family, 24 December 1937.

58. Robert Wilson, letter to family, 21 December 1937, p. 6; Marjorie Wilson, telephone interview with the author; John Magee to "Billy" (signed "John"), 11 January 1938, Ernest and Clarissa Forster Collection.

59. Marjorie Wilson, telephone interview with the author.

60. Ibid.

61. J. H. McCallum, diary entry for 3 January 1937, reprinted in *American Missionary Eyewitnesses to the Nanking Massacre, 1937–1938,* ed. Martha Lund Smalley (New Haven: Yale Divinity School Library, 1997), p. 39.

62. Robert Wilson, letter to family, 1 January 1938, p. 11.

63. Ibid., 26 December 1937, p. 7.

64. James Yin (coauthor of *The Rape of Nanking: An Undeniable History in Photographs* [Chicago: Innovative Publishing Group]), telephone interview with the author. The information about McCallum comes from his research in China.

65. Marjorie Wilson, telephone interview with the author.

66. Early biographical details about Minnie Vautrin come from Emma Lyon (Vautrin's niece), telephone interview with the author, 28 October 1996.

67. Most of the information for this section comes directly from Minnie Vautrin's diary, 1937–40, Yale Divinity School Library. Although she used her own page-numbering system (on the top of the middle of each page), I have used the Yale Divinity School page numbers, which were stamped on the top right-hand corner of each diary page.

68. Vautrin, diary 1937–40, 2–18 July 1937, p. 2.

69. Ibid., 20 September 1937, p. 27.

70. Ibid., 1 and 8 December 1937, pp. 91, 100; Commanding Officer C. F. Jeffs to the Commander in Chief, U.S. Asiatic Fleet (letterhead marked "the USS *Oahu*"), intelligence summary for the week ending 13 February 1938, 14 February 1938 (includes excerpt of missionary letter, which was not given to the press for fear of reprisals from the Japanese); George Fitch diary (name not given in report), Office of the Chief of Naval Operations, Division of Naval Intelligence, general correspondence, 1929–42, folder A8-21/FS#3, box 195, entry 81, RG 38, National Archives.

71. Vautrin, diary 1937–40, 3, 6, and 7 December 1937, pp. 94, 97, 98.

72. Ibid., 6 October 1937, p. 41.

73. Vautrin, "Sharing 'the Abundant Life' in a Refugee Camp," 28 April 1938, box 103, RG 8, Jarvis Collection, Yale Divinity School Library.

74. Letter to parents, probably from Forster, 4 October 1937, from Hsiakwan, Ernest and Clarissa Forster Collection.

75. General Records of the Department of State, 793.94/12060, report no. 9114, 11 December 1937, restricted report, National Archives.

76. Vautrin, diary 1937–40, 15 December 1937, p. 111.

77. Ibid.

78. Ibid., 16 December 1937, p. 113.

79. Ibid., 16 December 1937, p. 114. In her diary, Vautrin records that the women screamed "gin ming," but a more accurate translation of the Chinese expression for help is "jiu ming."

80. Ibid., 17 December 1937, pp. 115–16.

81. Ibid., pp. 117–18.

82. Ibid., 27 December 1937, p. 130.

83. Committee for the Historical Materials of the Nanking Massacre and the Nanjing Tushuguan (Nanking Library), ed., *Source Materials Relating to the Horrible Massacre*

Committed by the Japanese Troops in Nanking in December 1937 (Nanking: Jiangsu Ancient Books Publisher, July 1985), pp. 9–10.

84. Vautrin, diary 1937–40, 1 January 1938, p. 137.
85. Ibid., 18 December 1937, pp. 119–20.
86. Ibid., 24 December 1937, p. 127.
87. Ibid.
88. Enclosure to report, "Conditions in Nanking"; Hu Hua-ling, "Chinese Women Under the Rape of Nanking," *Journal of Studies of Japanese Aggression Against China* (November 1991): p. 69.
89. Vautrin, diary 1937–40, 28 December 1937, p. 131.
90. Fitch, *My Eighty Years in China,* p. 117.
91. John Magee, letter to his wife, 30 December 1937, archives of David Magee.
92. Hsu Shuhsi, p. 84.
93. Vautrin, diary 1937–40, 31 December 1937, p. 135.
94. Ibid., 4 January 1938, p. 141.
95. Ibid., 6 January 1938, p. 144.
96. Ibid., 31 December 1937, p. 135.
97. Ernest Forster, letter of 21 January 1938, Ernest and Clarissa Forster Collection.
98. [Lewis Smythe?], letter of 1 February 1938, box 228, RG 8, Yale Divinity School Library.
99. Vautrin, diary 1937–40, 4 February 1938, p. 183.
100. Ibid., 8 December 1937.
101. Resident of 145 Hankow Road, letter of 12 February 1939, Ernest and Clarissa Forster Collection.
102. Vautrin, diary 1937–40, 16 December 1937, p. 114.
103. Hsu Chi-ken, *The Great Nanking Massacre: Testimonies of the Eyewitnesses* (Taipei, 1993), pp. 56–57.
104. Ibid., p. 60.
105. Hu Hua-ling, "Miss Minnie Vautrin: The Living Goddess for the Suffering Chinese People During the Nanking Massacre," *Chinese American Forum* 11, no. 1 (July 1995): 20; Ko Chi, "Recording with Blood and Tears the Fallen Capital," in *Source Materials Relating to the Horrible Massacre.*
106. Huang Shu, interview with filmmaker Jim Culp; transcript from the personal archives of Jim Culp, San Francisco.
107. Ko Chi, "Blood and Tears," p. 16; Hu Hua-ling, "Miss Minnie Vautrin," p. 18.
108. Christian Kröger, "Days of Fate in Nanking," unpublished report, 13 January 1938, archives of Peter Kröger.
109. Vautrin, diary 1937–40, 4 March 1938, p. 208; on mushrooms, see Liu Fonghua, interview with the author, Nanking People's Republic of China, 29 July 1995.
110. Lewis S. C. Smythe to Tokuyasu Fukuda, Attaché to the Japanese Embassy, enclosure no. 1 to "Conditions in Nanking."
111. James McCallum, diary, 30 December 1937, Yale Divinity School Library.
112. Hsu Shuhsi, p. 24.
113. "Cases of Disorder by Japanese Soldiers in Safety Zone," National Archives.
114. Diary of John Magee in long letter to his wife, entry for 19 December 1937, archives of David Magee.

115. "Cases of Disorder by Japanese Soldiers in Safety Zone," National Archives.

116. John Magee to "Billy" (signed "John"), 11 January 1938, Ernest and Clarissa Forster Collection.

117. Rabe diary, 22 December 1937, pp. 341–42.

118. In "Days of Fate in Nanking," Christian Kröger states his belief that 200,000–250,000 refugees fled into the zone on December 12; Miner Searle Bates ("Preliminary Report on Christian Work in Nanking," archives of Shao Tzuping) echoes the figure of 250,000; the estimate of 300,000 refugees in the zone comes from the IMTFE testimony of Hsu Chuang-ying, who was in charge of housing for the zone; see IMTFE transcript, entry 319, RG 331, p. 2561, National Archives.

QUESTIONS FOR DISCUSSION

1. What were the goals of the Nanking Safety Zone, and what obstacles did its organizers need to overcome?
2. Of the three individuals Chang chose to focus upon in this selection, she writes that John Rabe was "the most fascinating." What makes his story especially interesting?
3. What do Rabe's letters to Hitler and to the Japanese authorities reveal about him? What assumptions did he make about people in positions of power?
4. What motivated Rabe, Wilson, and Vautrin to remain in Nanking after most Westerners had fled to relative safety?
5. How does Chang account for the mistakes made by Rabe and Vautrin? Do you think they could have avoided these mistakes?
6. Although Robert Wilson chose to remain in Nanking, he sent his wife and child back to the United States. How do you respond to that decision?
7. Consider the story in paragraph 77 of the wounded woman who abandons her youngest child in order to save her oldest four. Under the same circumstances, how do you think you would behave?
8. Change chose to end this selection with a summary of what happened during the conquest of Nanking and what the International Committee was able to accomplish. Was this a good writing decision? Would your response to this selection be different if she offered this summary at the beginning?

SUGGESTIONS FOR WRITING

1. Research the Japanese view of what happened in Nanking and report your findings.
2. According to Chang, "The first two years for the Wilsons were perhaps the most idyllic in their lives. Time was marked by a slow-paced charm— dinners with other missionary couples, elegant teas at foreign embassies, parties at sprawling country villas staffed with private cooks and coolies. In the evenings he read ancient Chinese in its original texts and studied with a private tutor to expand his knowledge of the language. He also took

every Wednesday off to play tennis. Sometimes he and his wife would go to the lake together and have dinner on a boat, inhaling the perfumed air as they drifted through the watery lanes of red lotus blossoms." How typical was this kind of experience for Westerners living in China between 1890 and 1937? Research the Western presence in China during the years in question and report what you discover.

3. Locate book reviews of *The Rape of Nanking* and report what reviewers have said about the quality of Chang's scholarship.

LINKS ■ ■ ■

■ WITHIN THE BOOK

For an essay that cites Chang, see Ian Buruma's "The Joys and Perils of Victimhood" (pages 246–255).

■ ELSEWHERE IN PRINT

Ballard, J. G. *Empire of the Sun*. New York: Simon, 1984.

Chang, Iris. *The Rape of Nanking: The Forgotten Holocaust of World War II*. New York: Basic, 1997.

Fogel, Joshua A., ed. *The Nanjing Massacre in History and Historiography*. Berkeley: U of California P, 2000.

Hu, Hua-Ling. *American Goddess at the Rape of Nanking: The Courage of Minnie Vautrin*. Carbondale: Southern Illinois UP, 2000.

Rabe, John. *The Good Man of Nanking: The Diaries of John Rabe*. Trans. John E. Woods. New York: Knopf, 1998.

Xu, Zhigeng. *Lest We Forget: Nanking Massacre, 1937*. Trans. Zhang Tingquan and Lin Wusun. Beijing: Panda/Chinese Lit. P, 1995.

Yamamoto, Masahiro. *Nanking: Anatomy of an Atrocity*. Westport: Praeger, 2000.

■ ONLINE

- Interview with Iris Chang
  <http://www.pbs.org/newshour/gergen/february98/chang_2-20.html>

- Iris Chang Papers
  <http://www.library.ucsb.edu/speccoll/cema/chang.html>

- Rape of Nanking
  <http://www.bergen.org/AAST/Projects/ChinaHistory/rape.html>

3

Writing to Interpret Information

W hat does it mean to shout "Fire!" in a crowded theater? Is there a connection between gender and intelligence? Why did an ancient people abandon beautiful homes that they had built with care? Why do many people see themselves as "victims"? To answer such questions requires you to interpret information so you can help people understand what something means, what causes it to happen, and what its consequences are. In other words, you must interpret information to reveal what is not readily apparent to others. Because information can legitimately be viewed in more than one way, different writers can come to significantly different conclusions. Interpretation is an essential skill for making sense of the world around us.

When we interpret, we need to analyze or classify information, examine causes and consequences, and define concepts by distinguishing them from others that are similar. We may also need to paraphrase, which means taking someone else's words and translating them into words of our own that can be more easily understood by our audience. Any of these ways of interpreting information can be used independently or in combination with any of the others.

Suppose you are asked on a midterm exam in Earth Science to explain why there is a big desert between the Sierra Nevada and the Rockies. You could begin by describing what a desert is. You might then note some of the implications of that description: "Only a few, very hardy plants that have adapted well to going without water can grow in deserts, and animals that require large supplies of water, such as mammals, generally avoid deserts." All you will have done to this point is report information. This step is often necessary before you can interpret information, because gaps in your readers' knowledge may hinder them from understanding what you wish to convey.

But once you begin to address *why* the area became a desert, you will have moved from reporting to interpreting. Alternatively, if you explain *how* animals can adapt successfully to living in such a harsh environment, you are also offering an interpretation. Similarly, you would be interpreting information if, instead of simply listing animals living in the desert, you placed these animals into different categories (or classes) based on different strategies for survival. You would be interpreting, too, if you defined a concept about which people can disagree. For example, although most readers would agree that "a desert is a place where there is very little annual rainfall," they may not agree about the meaning of more abstract terms such as *environmentalist*. Hence the need for strategies such as definition, classification, and analysis when you write to interpret rather than to report. You will find examples of all these strategies in this chapter.

The principal difference between interpreting and reporting is the difference between knowing something and understanding it. If you were to simply describe a perfectionist named Evelyn by showing what she looks like and how she behaves, your readers would learn something about her, but they would not understand why she is the way she is. To promote an understanding of Evelyn, you would need to explain her background—considering, for example, the way she was treated by her parents as a child. You would be *reporting* if you presented information without reasons but *interpreting* if you identified the reasons underlying that information.

Although interpreting information is different from reporting information, you will find that writers often choose to do both in a single piece. Writers who are primarily interested in reporting may include brief explanations for some of the information they are conveying. And, as noted earlier, writers who are primarily interested in interpreting may need to report information before they can interpret it. For example, if you review "The Thin Red Line" in Chapter 2, you will find that Jennifer Egan focuses on reporting information about an adolescent girl engaged in self-destructive behavior and the treatment this teenager receives. Although Egan offers some possible reasons for the behavior in question, she devotes more attention to reporting information about symptoms, treatments, and the kind of people with whom this girl comes into regular contact. In contrast, Stephen Jay Gould, whose work appears in this chapter, reports information about nineteenth-century science primarily to explain how reputable scientists can come to erroneous conclusions. Similarly, you will find that Catherine Dold offers some background information about the Anasazi before focusing on why these people disappeared. Like writers such as these, you may need to combine reporting and interpreting in an essay of your own. The challenge, as in any kind of writing, is to remain mindful of your primary purpose—or motive for writing. If you are asked to explain or interpret something, make sure that you are helping your audience to understand your subject, not just gain information about it.

CONSIDERING YOUR AUDIENCE AND CONTEXT

When you write to interpret information, your aim is to change the way readers view a particular subject, not just to increase their knowledge of it.

By explaining the history of the dictum, "You can't shout 'Fire!' in a crowded theater," Alan M. Dershowitz encourages readers to resist inappropriate efforts to limit free speech. When interpreting what the Bible says about women, Peter Gomes urges his audience to understand that "feminist interpreters of scripture have much to teach us, and we ignore these lessons to the peril of scripture and of the church." "The Joys and Perils of Victimhood" also involves changing the way readers see a subject. By distinguishing between genuine victims and people who identify themselves with these victims, Ian Buruma cautions against allowing cultural identity to be determined primarily by suffering and letting feelings replace ideas in political debates.

Contexts for interpretation abound. In an American history course, for instance, you might be asked to write about the significance of Manifest Destiny or explain why the United States became involved in Vietnam. In a science course you might describe a Mandelbrot set or define what a *strange attractor* is in chaos theory. Alternatively, in a humanities course you might show how jazz developed from African music or discuss why one generation favors music that seems incomprehensible to another. You might compare an early painting by Monet with one of his later works to interpret his development as an artist. Or you might try to explain the meaning of a short story (a kind of interpretation discussed in Chapter 10).

Once you have identified a tentative topic, you should test your choice before proceeding. Ask yourself: "Will I be explaining something that my readers probably do not understand?" If the answer is yes, then you know that you are about to engage in meaningful communication. You are now ready to plan what you want to say about it.

PLANNING YOUR ESSAY

One useful way to prepare for writing interpretation is to review your topic to see what its main divisions are and then list the subtopics that develop those main points. In making decisions like these, you are analyzing. **Analysis** is a systematic way of thinking about a subject so as to divide it into the elements of which it is made. This analysis must be done consistently on some logical basis.

The opposite of analysis is **classification.** Classification is a thinking process whereby you consider a number of diverse items or pieces of information, looking for ways to group this bit with that and establish some order. As with analysis, you must have some logical basis for a classification—some principle by which you decide which things go in each group. Suppose you have a bin full of used T-shirts to sell. You need to price them, but putting a price tag on each shirt is time-consuming. So you make a sign that says:

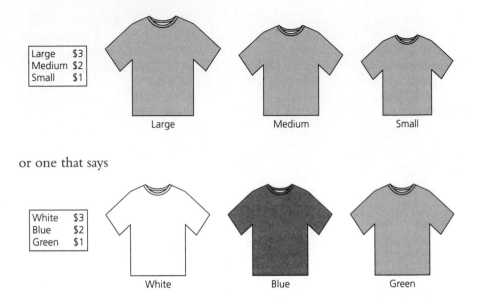

Large	$3
Medium	$2
Small	$1

Large   Medium   Small

or one that says

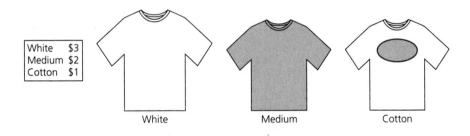

White	$3
Blue	$2
Green	$1

White   Blue   Green

But you should not make one that says

White	$3
Medium	$2
Cotton	$1

White   Medium   Cotton

Using more than one basis for classification creates confusion: How much does a white, medium-sized cotton shirt cost?

To take another example, suppose you look at an automobile and note that it has wheels, a body, a motor, a transmission, and so on; you have analyzed the automobile by dividing it into parts. Or you can look at all those parts lying on the garage floor and figure out that this part belongs to the motor, that one to the transmission, and so on—that's classification. Analysis involves taking things apart, and classification involves putting them together.

Within this chapter, Raymond L. Sickinger's "Hitler and the Occult: The Magical Thinking of Adolf Hitler" provides an example of classification. After studying how different historians have responded to Hitler's interest in the occult, Sickinger classifies these historians into two groups before offering his own interpretation of the information available to him. In his words, "The first group of writers generally ignored, rejected, or downplayed the relationship of Hitler and occult knowledge, while the second argued that such a connection was the only way to understand the true power of Hitler." In the essay that follows this introductory statement, Sickinger discusses the first group and then the second group as background for "a third position" that offers a way of reconciling the two groups he has discussed.

Another widely used approach for interpreting information is called **cause-and-effect analysis,** a strategy writers use to explain what has caused something to happen or what happens as the result of a cause. To some extent, all the writers in this chapter use cause–and–effect analysis. In "What Happened to the Anasazi?" for example, Catherine Dold discusses a new theory about what caused the disappearance of the Native American people known for the elaborate cliff dwellings they constructed at Mesa Verde and other sites in the West. And as the title of Ian Buruma's "The Joys and Perils of Victimhood" suggests, Buruma writes both about what causes people to see themselves as victims (the "joys") and about the effects of such identification (the "perils").

Cause-and-effect analysis can be undertaken in a number of ways. But if you are writing a short essay, you may find it helpful to focus on either "causes" or "effects." You will often find that you can interpret information by using either causes or effects to focus an analysis of the same subject. An essay on terrorism, for example, could focus on what causes terrorists to commit mass murder—as they did when destroying the twin towers of the World Trade Center in 2001. You might prefer, however, to focus on the effects of terrorism or the effects of a specific act—as in an essay on what happened as the result of terrorists seizing commercial aircraft and flying them into the World Trade Center. The charts on page 206 may help you see how very different essays are generated by the same subject depending on what kind of analysis you use. As you develop essays along these lines, you can explore different causes or different effects in separate paragraphs—although some causes or effects will need more than one paragraph to explain.

♦ **Definition** often plays an important role in writing to interpret information. If you are writing about terrorism, you may need to distinguish it from conventional warfare. In the essays included in this chapter, you will find that Nicholas Kristof defines the meaning of *wa* in Japanese culture, while Raymond L. Sickinger defines the meaning of *magical thinking*. Other writers might devote an entire essay to defining a complex or frequently misunderstood term.

To define what you mean by a word or phrase that requires interpretation, you must go beyond quoting a dictionary definition, for quoting by itself is simply reporting information already constructed by others. To compose your own definition of a problematic term, you can proceed as follows:

- Trace its origin and show how its meaning has evolved.
- Contrast it with whatever it might be confused with.
- Use negation to clarify what it does *not* mean.
- Provide examples.

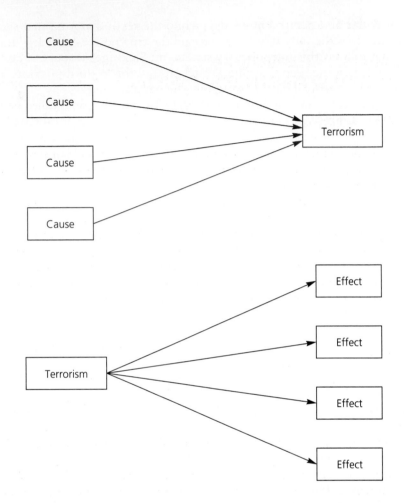

When you read the essays in this chapter, you may identify a number of terms that require interpretation, because they could mean different things to different people. How, for example, would you define *feminist, victim,* or *free speech*? Or consider some of the words that appear in public policy debates. Interpreting the meaning of *multicultural,* for example, can be not only a useful service in itself but also an important preliminary for other motives for writing—such as writing to evaluate or writing to persuade.

In short, when you get ready to interpret information for others, make a realistic appraisal of who your readers are, what they know, and what they need to be told. Remember that when you write to interpret information, you are making a conscious effort to help readers make sense of it. You are assuming the role of teacher rather than reporter. As you assume this responsibility, arrange your ideas in a pattern that will help readers understand them.

IN JAPAN, NICE GUYS
(AND GIRLS) FINISH TOGETHER

Nicholas D. Kristof

A Phi Beta Kappa graduate of Harvard who went on to study law as a Rhodes Scholar at Oxford University, Nicholas D. Kristof has lived in Tokyo since 1993 as a foreign correspondent for the New York Times.

While observing the behavior of Japanese children, Kristof was struck by how these children seemed less competitive than American children of the same age. The "information" that he wishes to interpret in this case is quite simple: Japanese children who were attending a birthday party for his son were too polite, at first, to win at playing a game of musical chairs. To interpret this information, however, Kristof needs to understand differences in cultural values. As you read, be alert for the reasons the author offers as he attempts to explain the behavior he witnessed.

My intention, honest, was not to scar these Japanese kids for life. I just wanted to give them a fun game to play.

It was the fifth birthday party last year for my son Gregory, and he had invited all his Japanese friends over from the Tokyo kindergarten that he attended. My wife and I explained the rules of musical chairs, and we started the music.

It was not so awful for the Japanese boys. They managed to fight for seats, albeit a bit lamely. But the girls were at sea.

The first time I stopped the music, Gregory's 5-year-old girlfriend, Chitose-chan, was next to him, right in front of a chair. But she stood politely and waited for him to be seated first.

So Gregory scrambled into her seat, and Chitose-chan beamed proudly   5
at her own good manners. Then I walked over and told her that she had just lost the game and would have to sit out. She gazed up at me, her luminous eyes full of shocked disbelief, looking like Bambi might after a discussion of venison burgers.

"You mean I lose because I'm polite?" Chitose-chan's eyes asked. "You mean the point of the game is to be rude?"

Well, now that I think of it, I guess that is the point. American kids are taught to be winners, to seize their opportunities and maybe the next kid's as well. Japanese children are taught to be good citizens, to be team players, to obey rules, to be content to be a mosaic tile in some larger design.

One can have an intelligent debate about which approach is better. The Japanese emphasis on consideration and teamwork perhaps explains why Japan has few armed robbers but also so few entrepreneurs. The American emphasis on winning may help explain why the United States consistently racks up Olympic gold medals but also why its hockey players trashed their rooms in Nagano.

The civility that still lingers in Japan is the most charming and delightful aspect of life here today. Taxi drivers wear white gloves, take pride in the cleanliness of their vehicles, and sometimes give a discount if they mistakenly take a long route. When they are sick, Japanese wear surgical face masks so they will not infect others. The Japanese language has almost no curses, and high school baseball teams bow to each other at the beginning of each game.

One can go years here without hearing a voice raised in anger, for when 10 Japanese are furious, they sometimes show it by becoming incredibly formal and polite. Compared with New York, it's rather quaint.

The conundrum is that Japan is perhaps too civilized for the 1990s. To revive its economy, mired in a seven-year slump, the country now needs an infusion of economic ruthlessness, a dose of the law of the jungle. Japan desperately needs to restructure itself, which is to say that it needs to create losers— companies need to lay off excess workers, Mom-and-Pop rice shops need to be replaced by more efficient supermarkets and failing banks need to go bankrupt.

But Japan is deeply uncomfortable with the idea of failures or losers. The social and economic basis of modern Japan is egalitarianism, and that does not leave much room for either winners or losers. In Japan, winning isn't everything, and it isn't the only thing; in elementary schools it isn't even a thing at all.

When Gregory and his brother Geoffrey went to Sports Day at their Japanese kindergarten, everybody told us that this was the big event of the year. So my wife and I went to cheer, but it wasn't really necessary. There were three-legged races and team basketball shoots and all kinds of games, but somehow at the end of the day no one won and no one lost. There were no blue ribbons, no prizes for the fastest runner, no cheers for the best basketball shooter, or anything else; instead, every child got a small prize.

The point of Sports Day was not to divide students by recognizing individual excellence but to unite them by giving them a shared experience. Likewise, schools do not normally break up children into "fast reading classes" and "slow reading classes," because that would stigmatize the slower ones. During recess or phys ed, there is no system of having a few captains take turns picking teams, because the last-picked might be upset; instead kids divide by class or by the Japanese equivalent of alphabetical order. When drama teachers select a play to perform, they choose one in which there is no star, just a lot of equal parts—which makes for first-rate student harmony and second-rate drama.

Of course, competition is inevitable in any society, and in Japan it is intro- 15 duced in junior high schools, when children must compete intensely to pass high school and college entrance examinations. But the emphasis remains on "wa," or harmony, on being one with the group.

Ask a traditional Japanese housewife what she wants for her child, and you will sometimes hear an answer like: "I just want my kid to grow up so as not to be a nuisance to other people." Hmmm. Not a dream often heard in America.

Even in business, the obsession with egalitarian wa goes to astonishing lengths. One Tokyo bank executive told me how he envied the Japanese subsidiary of Citibank, which waives certain fees for customers who keep a large minimum balance. That would never be tolerated in a Japanese bank, he said, because it would be regarded as discriminatory against the poor. Likewise, he said, his bank cannot easily close unprofitable branches in remote areas, because then it would be criticized for abandoning the people there.

The emphasis on wa perhaps arises because 125 million Japanese, almost half of America's population, are squeezed into an area the size of California. How else could they survive but with a passion for protocol and a web of picayune rules dictating consideration for others? If 125 million Americans were jammed into such a small space, we might have torn each other to shreds by now.

Building teamwork in Japan starts from birth. When our third child, Caroline, was born in Tokyo last fall, the hospital explained that the mothers were to nurse their babies all together in the same room at particular meal times. So on her first day of life, Caroline was effectively told to discipline her appetites to adjust to a larger scheme with others.

This civility and egalitarianism shape just about every aspect of life. When   20
the Japanese translation of a book that my wife and I wrote was published, we were pleased that the first reviews were positive. But we were frankly surprised when every single Japanese review was positive, and I remarked on that to a Japanese friend. "Oh, that's the only kind of book review there is in Japan," he explained. "There are no bad book reviews. Just nice ones."

And insipid ones, of course. Indeed, Japan itself is so polite as to be a bit bland, rather like "Mr. Rogers' Neighborhood" on a national scale. And of course Mr. Rogers' Neighborhood was never known for its hustle or economic vibrancy.

So now, Japan is trying to become nastier. Workers are being pushed out of their jobs, occasionally even laid off. Employees are no longer being automatically promoted by seniority. Pay differentials are widening. Companies are becoming more concerned with efficiency and share prices, less concerned with employee welfare.

All this will make Japan a more prosperous country but perhaps a less civil one. The changes certainly rub against the grain here, particularly of older people.

They rub just a bit against my grain, too. I bought a long scroll of calligraphy with the character "wa" in hopes that my kids will learn harmony instead of clubbing each other over toys. Yet, on the other hand, I still want them to win—at musical chairs and everything else.

That is getting tougher, because young Japanese are adapting to greater   25
competition, and they seem to be a bit more aggressive and individualist than their parents. Some young Japanese are even getting pretty good at musical chairs.

And little Chitose-chan, Gregory's girlfriend—well, she may be polite, but don't underestimate her generation's ability to catch on quickly. Thirty minutes after the game of musical chairs, Chitose-chan and her friend Naoko-chan got into an argument over a party favor. Chitose-chan slugged Naoko-chan in the mouth and grabbed the toy.

Perhaps that's globalization.

QUESTIONS FOR DISCUSSION

1. At the beginning of his essay, Kristof notes that Japanese girls seem less competitive than Japanese boys. Assuming that this information is accurate, how do you interpret it?
2. According to Kristof, "Japan is deeply uncomfortable with the idea of failures or losers." What information does he provide to support this interpretation?
3. Consider Kristof's description of Sports Day. How does it compare with your own experience in sports? How would you feel if you were participating in an athletic competition organized along the lines described by Kristof?
4. What does *wa* mean? Have you ever seen it practiced by American children?
5. On the basis of what he witnessed at his son's birthday party, what kind of future does Kristof envision for Japan?

SUGGESTIONS FOR WRITING

1. Spend an afternoon or evening in the company of American children, observing their behavior closely and taking notes if necessary. Then write an essay in which you offer your interpretation of the behavior you witnessed.
2. Observe the behavior of American college students attending a large party. Imagine that you have just arrived in this country. After the party, write an essay that describes the party and what it reveals about American values.
3. Consider how your coworkers relate to one another on the job. Then write an essay explaining conduct that enhances or interferes with efficient performance in the workplace.

LINKS ■ ■ ■

■ **WITHIN THE BOOK**

Another window into Japanese culture and the mentoring of a child is provided by Toshio Mori in "Abalone, Abalone, Abalone" (pages 680–682).

■ **ELSEWHERE IN PRINT**

Gudykunst, William B., and Tsukasa Nishida. *Bridging Japanese / North American Differences.* Thousand Oaks: Sage, 1994.

Heinrich, Amy Vladeck. *Currents in Japanese Culture: Translation and Transformations.* New York: Columbia UP, 1997.

Kristof, Nicholas, and Sheryl WuDunn. *Thunder from the East: Portrait of a Rising Asia.* New York: Knopf, 2000.

Marra, Michele, ed. *Modern Japanese Aesthetics: A Reader.* Honolulu: U of Hawai'i P, 1999.

Okakura, Kakuzo. *The Book of Tea.* 1906. Introd. Liza Dalby. Boston: Tuttle, 2000.

Schaller, Michael. *Altered States: The United States and Japan since the Occupation.* New York: Oxford UP, 1997.

Whiting, Robert. *You Gotta Have Wa.* New York: Macmillan, 1989.

■ **ONLINE**

- Child-Rearing and Educational Practices in the United States and Japan: Comparative Perspectives
  <http://www.ceser.hyogo-u.ac.jp/suzukimj/paper9_99.html>

- Japanese Customs and Traditions
  <http://www.japan-guide.com/e/e638.html>

- The Japanese Educational System
  <http://www.japaninfo.org/education/rekishi.htm>

SHOUTING "FIRE!"

Alan M. Dershowitz

Americans have often been told that freedom of speech doesn't mean being able to shout "Fire!" in a crowded theater. But where does that expression come from, and what exactly does it mean? As you read this essay, notice how Alan M. Dershowitz clarifies and interprets a common expression by placing it in a historical context. Note that, according to Oliver Wendell Holmes, "The character of every act depends on the circumstances in which it is done." Consider how Dershowitz himself uses the interrelationship of act, place, and time when writing his explanation.

First in his class at Yale Law School, where he was editor of the Yale Law Journal, *Dershowitz became a full professor at Harvard Law School when he was only twenty-eight—the youngest full professor in that school's history. Widely regarded as one of the best civil liberties lawyers in the country, he has defended such high-profile clients as O.J. Simpson, Claus von Bulow, Leona Helmsley, and Patricia Hearst. He is also the author of many books and hundreds of articles, including the following selection, which was first published by the* Atlantic Monthly *in 1989.*

When the Reverend Jerry Falwell learned that the Supreme Court had reversed his $200,000 judgment against *Hustler* magazine for the emotional distress that he had suffered from an outrageous parody, his response was typical of those who seek to censor speech: "Just as no person may scream 'Fire!' in a crowded theater when there is no fire, and find cover under the First Amendment, likewise, no sleazy merchant like Larry Flynt should be able to use the First Amendment as an excuse for maliciously and dishonestly attacking public figures, as he has so often done."

Justice Oliver Wendell Holmes's classic example of unprotected speech—falsely shouting "Fire!" in a crowded theater—has been invoked so often, by so many people, in such diverse contexts, that it has become part of our national folk language. It has even appeared—most appropriately—in the theater: in Tom Stoppard's play *Rosencrantz and Guildenstern Are Dead,* a character shouts at the audience, "Fire!" He then quickly explains: "It's all right—I'm demonstrating the misuse of free speech." Shouting "Fire!" in the theater may well be the only jurisprudential analogy that has assumed the status of a folk argument. A prominent historian recently characterized it as "the most brilliantly persuasive expression that ever came from Holmes's pen." But in spite of its hallowed position in both the jurisprudence of the First Amendment and the arsenal of political discourse, it is and was an inapt analogy, even in the context in which it was originally offered. It has lately become—despite, perhaps even because of, the frequency and promiscuousness of its invocation—little more than a caricature of logical argumentation.

The case that gave rise to the "Fire!"-in-a-crowded-theater analogy—
Schenck v. *United States*—involved the prosecution of Charles Schenck, who
was the general secretary of the Socialist Party in Philadelphia, and Elizabeth
Baer, who was its recording secretary. In 1917 a jury found Schenck and Baer
guilty of attempting to cause insubordination among soldiers who had been
drafted to fight in the First World War. They and other party members had circulated leaflets urging draftees not to "submit to intimidation" by fighting in a
war being conducted on behalf of "Wall Street's chosen few." Schenck admitted, and the Court found, that the intent of the pamphlets' "impassioned language" was to "influence" draftees to resist the draft. Interestingly, however,
Justice Holmes noted that nothing in the pamphlet suggested that the draftees
should use unlawful or violent means to oppose conscription: "In form at least
[the pamphlet] confined itself to peaceful measures, such as a petition for the
repeal of the act" and an exhortation to exercise "your right to assert your opposition to the draft." Many of its most impassioned words were quoted directly
from the Constitution.

Justice Holmes acknowledged that "in many places and in ordinary times
the defendants, in saying all that was said in the circular, would have been
within their constitutional rights." "But," he added, "the character of every act
depends upon the circumstances in which it is done." And to illustrate that
truism he went on to say,

> The most stringent protection of free speech would not protect a man
> in falsely shouting fire in a theater, and causing a panic. It does not
> even protect a man from an injunction against uttering words that
> may have all the effect of force.

Justice Holmes then upheld the convictions in the context of a wartime
draft, holding that the pamphlet created "a clear and present danger" of hindering the war effort while our soldiers were fighting for their lives and our
liberty.

The example of shouting "Fire!" obviously bore little relationship to the
facts of the Schenck case. The Schenck pamphlet contained a substantive political message. It urged its draftee readers to *think* about the message and then—
if they so chose—to act on it in a lawful and nonviolent way. The man who
shouts "Fire!" in a crowded theater is neither sending a political message nor
inviting his listener to think about what he has said and decide what to do in a
rational, calculated manner. On the contrary, the message is designed to force
action *without* contemplation. The message "Fire!" is directed not to the mind
and the conscience of the listener but, rather, to his adrenaline and his feet. It is
a stimulus to immediate *action,* not thoughtful reflection. It is—as Justice
Holmes recognized in his follow-up sentence—the functional equivalent of
"uttering words that may have all the effect of force."

Indeed, in that respect the shout of "Fire!" is not even speech, in any meaningful sense of that term. It is a *clang* sound—the equivalent of setting off a
nonverbal alarm. Had Justice Holmes been more honest about his example, he

would have said that freedom of speech does not protect a kid who pulls a fire alarm in the absence of a fire. But that obviously would have been irrelevant to the case at hand. The proposition that pulling an alarm is not protected speech certainly leads to the conclusion that shouting the word *fire* is also not protected. But the core analogy is the nonverbal alarm, and the derivative example is the verbal shout. By cleverly substituting the derivative shout for the core alarm, Holmes made it possible to analogize one set of words to another—as he could not have done if he had begun with the self-evident proposition that setting off an alarm bell is not free speech.

The analogy is thus not only inapt but also insulting. Most Americans do not respond to political rhetoric with the same kind of automatic acceptance expected of schoolchildren responding to a fire drill. Not a single recipient of the Schenck pamphlet is known to have changed his mind after reading it. Indeed, one draftee, who appeared as a prosecution witness, was asked whether reading a pamphlet asserting that the draft law was unjust would make him "immediately decide that you must erase the law." Not surprisingly, he replied, "I do my own thinking." A theatergoer would probably not respond similarly if asked how he would react to a shout of "Fire!"

Another important reason why the analogy is inapt is that Holmes emphasizes the factual falsity of the shout "Fire!" The Schenck pamphlet, however, was not factually false. It contained political opinions and ideas about the causes of the war and about appropriate and lawful responses to the draft. As the Supreme Court recently reaffirmed (in *Falwell* v. *Hustler*), "The First Amendment recognizes no such thing as a 'false' idea." Nor does it recognize false opinions about the causes of or cures for war.

A closer analogy to the facts of the Schenck case might have been provided 10 by a person's standing outside a theater, offering the patrons a leaflet advising them that in his opinion the theater was structurally unsafe and urging them not to enter but to complain to the building inspectors. That analogy, however, would not have served Holmes's argument for punishing Schenck. Holmes needed an analogy that would appear relevant to Schenck's political speech but that would invite the conclusion that censorship was appropriate.

Unsurprisingly, a war-weary nation—in the throes of a know-nothing hysteria over immigrant anarchists and socialists—welcomed the comparison between what was regarded as a seditious political pamphlet and a malicious shout of "Fire!" Ironically, the "Fire!" analogy is nearly all that survives from the Schenck case; the ruling itself is almost certainly not good law. Pamphlets of the kind that resulted in Schenck's imprisonment have been circulated with impunity during subsequent wars.

Over the past several years I have assembled a collection of instances— cases, speeches, arguments—in which proponents of censorship have main- tained that the expression at issue is "just like" or "equivalent to" falsely shouting "Fire!" in a crowded theater and ought to be banned, "just as" shout- ing "Fire!" ought to be banned. The analogy is generally invoked, often with self-satisfaction, as an absolute argument-stopper. It does, after all, claim the high authority of the great Justice Oliver Wendell Holmes. I have rarely heard it invoked in a convincing, or even particularly relevant, way. But that, too, can claim lineage from the great Holmes.

Not unlike Falwell, with his silly comparison between shouting "Fire!" and publishing an offensive parody, courts and commentators have frequently invoked "Fire!" as an analogy to expression that is not an automatic stimulus to panic. A state supreme court held that "Holmes's aphorism . . . applies with equal force to pornography"—in particular to the exhibition of the movie *Carmen Baby* in a drive-in theater in close proximity to highways and homes. Another court analogized "picketing . . . in support of a secondary boycott" to shouting "Fire!" because in both instances "speech and conduct are brigaded." In the famous Skokie case one of the judges argued that allowing Nazis to march through a city where a large number of Holocaust survivors live "just might fall into the same category as one's 'right' to cry fire in a crowded theater."

Outside court the analogies become even more badly stretched. A spokesperson for the New Jersey Sports and Exposition Authority complained that newspaper reports to the effect that a large number of football players had contracted cancer after playing in the Meadowlands—a stadium atop a landfill—were the "journalistic equivalent of shouting fire in a crowded theater." An insect researcher acknowledged that his prediction that a certain amusement park might become roach-infested "may be tantamount to shouting fire in a crowded theater." The philosopher Sidney Hook, in a letter to *The New York Times* bemoaning a Supreme Court decision that required a plaintiff in a defamation action to prove that the offending statement was actually false, argued that the First Amendment does not give the press carte blanche to accuse innocent persons "any more than the First Amendment protects the right of someone falsely to shout fire in a crowded theater."

Some close analogies to shouting "Fire!" or setting off an alarm are, of course, available: calling in a false bomb threat; dialing 911 and falsely describing an emergency; making a loud, gunlike sound in the presence of the President; setting off a voice-activated sprinkler system by falsely shouting "Fire!" In one case in which the "Fire!" analogy was directly to the point, a creative defendant tried to get around it. The case involved a man who calmly advised an airline clerk that he was "only here to hijack the plane." He was charged, in effect, with shouting "Fire!" in a crowded theater, and his rejected defense—as quoted by the court—was as follows: "If we built fireproof theaters and let people know about this, then the shouting of 'Fire!' would not cause panic."

Here are some more-distant but still related examples: the recent incident of the police slaying in which some members of an onlooking crowd urged a mentally ill vagrant who had taken an officer's gun to shoot the officer; the screaming of racial epithets during a tense confrontation; shouting down a speaker and preventing him from continuing his speech.

Analogies are, by their nature, matters of degree. Some are closer to the core example than others. But any attempt to analogize political ideas in a pamphlet, ugly parody in a magazine, offensive movies in a theater, controversial

15

newspaper articles, or any of the other expressions and actions catalogued above to the very different act of shouting "Fire!" in a crowded theater is either self-deceptive or self-serving.

The government does, of course, have some arguably legitimate bases for suppressing speech that bear no relationship to shouting "Fire!" It may ban the publication of nuclear-weapon codes, of information about troop movements, and of the identity of undercover agents. It may criminalize extortion threats and conspiratorial agreements. These expressions may lead directly to serious harm, but the mechanisms of causation are very different from that at work when an alarm is sounded. One may also argue—less persuasively, in my view—against protecting certain forms of public obscenity and defamatory statements. Here, too, the mechanisms of causation are very different. None of these exceptions to the First Amendment's exhortation that the government "shall make no law . . . abridging the freedom of speech, or of the press" is anything like falsely shouting "Fire!" in a crowded theater; they all must be justified on other grounds.

A comedian once told his audience, during a stand-up routine, about the time he was standing around a fire with a crowd of people and got in trouble for yelling "Theater, theater!" That, I think, is about as clever and productive a use as anyone has ever made of Holmes's flawed analogy.

QUESTIONS FOR DISCUSSION

1. What was the political context that led Oliver Wendell Holmes to make his famous remark about shouting "Fire!" in a crowded theater?
2. Why does Dershowitz believe that the fire analogy was inappropriate for the Schenck case? Why does he conclude that it was "not only inapt but also insulting"?
3. How important is the word *falsely* in the quotation from Holmes in paragraph 4? Would Holmes approve of calling "Fire!" when there is a fire? How would he respond to someone who calls "Fire!" out of a sincere but mistaken belief that there is a fire?
4. According to Dershowitz, what types of speech might the government have legitimate reason to suppress?
5. How convincing is the alternative analogy offered by Dershowitz in paragraph 10?
6. What evidence does Dershowitz offer to support his claim that the Holmes ruling "is almost certainly not good law"?

SUGGESTIONS FOR WRITING

1. Take a commonly used expression (such as "You can't teach an old dog new tricks," or "Don't throw the baby out with the bath water") and explain what it means. Try to define circumstances for which the expression would be both appropriate and inappropriate.

2. Research a Supreme Court decision involving censorship, abortion, gun control, or capital punishment. Then explain why the Court reached its decision and what the implications of that decision are for the future.
3. Research the trial of Claus von Bulow, and then write an essay explaining how Dershowitz secured his acquittal.

LINKS ■ ■ ■

■ WITHIN THE BOOK

If you would like to see another essay that involves interpreting the law, see "Why You Can Hate Drugs and Still Want to Legalize Them" (pages 550–561).

■ ELSEWHERE IN PRINT

Alschuler, Albert W. *Law without Values: The Life, Work, and Legacy of Justice Holmes.* Chicago: U of Chicago P, 2000.

Dershowitz, Alan. *The Best Defense.* New York: Random, 1982.

——. *Chutzpah.* Boston: Little, 1991. Eastland, Terry, ed. *Freedom of Expression in the Supreme Court.* Lanham: Rowman, 2000.

Eastland, Terry, ed. *Freedom of Expression in the Supreme Court.* Lanham: Rowman, 2000.

Farber, Daniel A. *The First Amendment.* New York: Foundation, 1998.

Rabban, David M. *Free Speech in Its Forgotten Years: 1870–1920.* New York: Cambridge UP, 1997.

Schwartz, Bernard. *A History of the Supreme Court.* New York: Oxford UP, 1993.

■ ONLINE

- First Amendment Limitations on Civil Law Liability
  <http://www.law.umkc.edu/faculty/projects/ftrials/conlaw/commonlaw.htm>
- Oliver Wendell Holmes, Jr.
  <http://www.lucidcafe.com/lucidcafe/library/96mar/holmes.html>
- Schenck v. United States
  <http://www.ukans.edu/carrie/docs/texts/schenck.htm>

WHAT *DOES* THE BIBLE SAY ABOUT WOMEN?

Peter J. Gomes

A graduate of Bates College and Harvard Divinity School, Peter J. Gomes is the Plummer Professor of Christian Morals at Harvard College, where he also serves as minister in the Memorial Church. His sermons there and elsewhere led Time *magazine to name him as one of the seven best preachers in America. In addition to writing many sermons and articles, Gomes is author of* The Good Book: Reading the Bible with Mind and Heart *(1996), which the Archbishop of Canterbury calls "easily the best contemporary book on the Bible for thoughtful people." The following selection is part of a chapter in that book. As you read it, you will find that Gomes writes with Christian concerns in mind. But whatever your own faith tradition may be, consider what you learn about the nature of reading and the value of scholarship from Gomes's discussion of how to interpret what the New Testament says about women.*

The Bible has a great deal to say about women, and the Old Testament is filled with a wide variety of female personalities and voices. There is Eve, the mother of all living. There are Sarah, Abraham's conniving wife; Hannah, the mother of Samuel; Jezebel, the foreign-born wife of Ahab; Delilah, who wormed Samson's secret from him; Ruth and Rahab, ancestresses of Jesus, and many more. In the wisdom literature, wisdom is herself feminine, and in certain of the prophetic books, Israel is feminine, and the land is fecund and maternal. The images in Hebrew scripture are many and varied, and the presence of women in these holy books has never been an issue. When Christians speak about "what the Bible says" with regard to women, however, invariably they mean the New Testament, and so is it here that we will look.

As in all the church of the saints, the women should keep silence in the churches. For they are not permitted to speak, but should be subordinate, as even the law says. If there is anything they desire to know, let them ask their husbands at home. For it is shameful for a woman to speak in church. (I Corinthians 14:34–35)

Let a woman learn in silence with all submissiveness. I permit no woman to teach or to have authority over men; she is to keep silent. (I Timothy 2:11–12)

Mary Magdalene went and said to the disciples, "I have seen the Lord," and she told them that he had said these things to her. (John 20:18)

For as many of you as were baptized into Christ have put on Christ. There is neither Jew nor Greek, there is neither slave nor free, there is neither male nor female; for you are all one in Christ Jesus. And if you are Christ's, then you are Abraham's offspring, heirs according to promise. (Galatians 3:27–29)

Those four passages from the New Testament represent the tension between the New Testament's principle of transformation and renewal in Christ, by which the old and established order is overturned and transcended, and the apostolic government of the early church, where explicit rules of conduct and patterns of relationship for specific situations are seen to be normative and definitive for Christian conduct and order in the church. For many, the problem of the New Testament and women is the reconciliation of the so-called "hard passages," with the gospel principle of participation and equality. The problem is compounded by the fact that both principles are expressed in practice, and both thereby share in the authority and primacy accorded scripture. The secular cynics may dismiss the whole dilemma with the often quoted notion that you can find any verse in the Bible to support any view you wish. The fact that this is more true than untrue does not dismiss the problem but only compounds it for persons of goodwill who genuinely seek "the mind of scripture" in the ordering of their affairs. [. . .] the more seriously one takes scripture, the more difficult becomes the problem of its several, often contradictory, voices, and therefore the more urgent becomes the development of a persuasive principle of interpretation by which the differences are reconciled, the authority of scripture maintained, and the moral and theological life developed from its teachings affirmed. As the Protestant Reformation introduced as normative the principle of *sola scriptura*, fidelity to scripture has become the normative principle for the faith and practice of most Protestant churches. For many churches of this inheritance, a case is made or lost on how one "reads" scripture.

"Reading scripture," however, is not as simple as most Protestants would like to believe. Reading is a transaction, and by no means a neutral transaction. A text does not simply "say what it says," despite the rational good intentions of a sensible reader like Alice in Wonderland. We read more like Humpty-Dumpty than we would care to admit, for in reading it is a matter not only of what is written there but what we expect to find there, what we bring to the text, and what we take away from it. Reading, then, is hardly a clinical or neutral affair. There is that bewildering battery of text, context, subtext, and pre-text with which we must contend, which we in fact do automatically and subconsciously. The scanning of these interests is so automatic and instantaneous that we are as unaware of it as we are unaware of the infinite number of physical motions and electrical impulses that it takes for us to turn the handle of a doorknob. When that simple action is reduced to slow motion and recorded, or when we find that some injury or ailment makes it difficult or impossible to do, then, and perhaps only then, do we realize the complexity that is camouflaged by the apparent natural ease with which we have performed the function before we were required to take notice of it.

Reading is such a function, and particularly the reading of scripture. The reading of contentious or difficult passages involves both an encounter with the text and an extra-textual consciousness by which we are enabled to make sense and reconcile the foreign and contrary with the familiar and accepted. This context, as opposed to the historical and literary context of the text itself, I call the culture or climate of interpretation. For most readers of scripture, or of anything else, this is the only context that counts. The very notion, for example, of "hard passages" in a discussion of women and the Bible does not necessarily presuppose that there is a "problem" with the biblical context, although there may be. The problem that makes these passages hard is that what they appear to say is at odds with what we now think. In other words, the text is out of sync with our climate or culture of interpretation. Thus, in order to make sense of what the text says, it must in some sense be made to conform to our climate of interpretation. With all due respect to the pieties addressed to the mind of scripture and to its context, as in most things our context is the only one that really counts.

Remember how our temperance friends "read" those accounts of the   5 scriptural use of wine, which clearly did not coincide with the moral content of their contemporary climate of interpretation? It was scripture that was made to conform. In the matter of slavery, each side adapted the context and content of the biblical writings on slavery to suit the moral purposes of their own contemporary climate of interpretation, and that battle was settled not by an exegetical consensus but by might of arms.

The readings of scripture in the debates about the role of women in the church today tell us as much, if not more, about the climate of interpretation within which we are willing to undertake the reading in the first place as it tells us about the content, context, and "clear meaning of scripture."

For those for whom the writings in Corinthians and in Timothy are not hard, and who take them as normative practice for the church in all places and at all times, the problem is no problem. Why? Because the texts as they read them, and the climate of interpretation within which they read them, are not in conflict—at least, they do not believe them to be. The pope is not anxious to know if scripture and his reading of scripture are at odds on the matter of women priests. He has said over and over again that the question of the ordination of women to the priesthood is settled by the fact that Jesus did not call women to serve as his disciples. The practice and principle of scripture in the mind of the pope are consistent with his reading and interpretation of it. In this view he is joined by many conservative Protestants, with what is called a high view of scripture.

There is a substantial and growing body of Christians in all communions, however, for whom the biblical texts in question and the climate of interpretation are in fact out of sync. Many of these would argue that the texts themselves are out of sync within their own context, both of the gospel and of the particular message and example of Paul himself. It is this range of interests and views, stimulated by the larger cultural revolution by which women have determined to overcome their marginalization and cultural disenfranchisement, that has generated the theological revolution in interpretation of which we have spoken earlier with profound and massive implications for the ways in which we read and understand scripture. The most interesting, creative, and demanding scholarship in the field of biblical interpretation since the translations of the Bible into English has been generated in the last twenty-five years by what may be called the feminist initiative.

This frightens people—the very notion of a feminist initiative in the interpretation of scripture—in much the same way that good Christians of varied opinions were frightened by the abolitionists of the nineteenth century. Many have been and will be put off by the sense of an aggressive set of special interests that are brought to the interpretation of scripture with destabilizing consequences to the authority of the scripture, the order of the church, and the structure of society and of civilization itself. As we have pointed out before, however, it is not just feminists who have an interest in the way in which the Bible is read these days. In their fight for the Bible and the right both to take it and themselves seriously, feminist interpreters of scripture have much to teach us, and we ignore these lessons to the peril of scripture and of the church.

It has become a habit on the part of some evangelicals and religious conservatives to dismiss the mountain of female scholarship on the Bible with the taint of the most extreme and deconstructive dimensions of that scholarship, suggesting pagans and goddesses under every hermeneutical bed. Any challenge to the language of patriarchy or the thousand years of male interpretation is understood to be a challenge to the full wealth of conviction and part of a "liberal," "feminist," or "radical" conspiracy to subvert the faith once delivered to the saints. As in politics, there is clearly a paranoid style in much of the response to the new scholarship of women on the Bible. Of course, as in physics, every action generates a reaction. When feminist scholarship concludes that it is no longer appropriate to pray to "Our Father," and such masculine titles as "Lord" and "King" are excluded both from the text and from worship, the instinctual reaction of those who feel thus deprived of the familiar and useful language of piety is to reject the possibility that any helpful insights can be provided from such scholarship.

Language has become the battlefield for the conflict between old and new ideas, and the inclusive language debates with which Christian churches have contended in the last twenty years demonstrate just how hard and bitterly people will fight for the right to their language of choice. Perhaps even more than the ordination of women, the language issue has been the place where the conflicts of inclusion have been most painfully addressed. More perhaps than through the Bible itself, the popular piety of most Christians, particularly Protestants, has been expressed in the hymns people sing in church. The late New Testament scholar and poet, Amos Niven Wilder, once said that what incense is to the Catholic, hymns are to the Protestant: an indescribable, primal association of the personal and the holy. One learns the hymns of the faith in childhood. They provide a theological vocabulary that may be supplemented and improved upon by age and experience but is never supplanted. It has been my experience time after time that what remains with

10

the dying Christian is the hymns of childhood. And it is my experience, as well as that of practically every other preacher, that worship depends upon the hymns. The sermon may be good or bad, the liturgy indifferent, but the effect of the service depends upon whether or not the people know and like the hymns. And most people like the hymns they know and on that basis know what they like. Thus to tamper with the hymns is to get perilously close to the emotional center of the worshiper.

"TEXTUAL HARASSMENT?"[1]

Women recognized this early on, knowing that the hymnic images are for most people the determining images and language of piety. Thus, to be excluded from the language was in their minds to be excluded from the fundamental experience of worship, or to be included under terms that did not affirm their particular identity as women. Women would ask, "Where am I?" when at funerals we sang Isaac Watts's great paraphrase, "Time, like an ever-rolling stream, bears all its *sons* away." Even in so basic an act of Christian praise as the Doxology, which affirms, "Praise Him all creatures here below" and closes with the Trinitarian formula of "Father, Son, and Holy Ghost," women increasingly asked where they were in these classical formulations. When the congregation is asked to sing "Rise Up, O Men of God," are the women to remain seated, or are they to think of themselves as Elizabeth I did, as a man trapped in the puny body of a woman?

Challenges in scholarship are one thing. But challenges to popular piety, which strike at the heart of the believer and the language of devotion, with all of the fond and intimate associations that language evokes, are another thing. Congregations were set at each other over the battle for the hymns. Radical inclusivists were accused of Freudian-like "pronoun envy," and the hymns, once the point of commonality, became symbols of the great divisions among people. It is difficult to say if the scholarship of women generated the dis-ease with the language of hymnody, or if the distress at the exclusive language of hymnody generated the case for a new and compelling scholarship. Whatever the answer to this particular chicken-and-egg dilemma, hymns will never be quite the same again. For my part, I have been no more willing to edit out offending passages in hymns than I have been to edit out offending passages in scripture. But while it is not possible to write new Bibles that reflect the spirit of the age, it is not only possible, but essential, that we write new hymns to add to the storehouse of piety, hymns that include more people.

It seems to me that, where the old hymns are concerned, we do not have to be like Oliver Cromwell's Puritan New Model Army, which took great delight in smashing the medieval iconography of the English cathedrals, justifying such vandalism in the name of God and of their revolution. Had they been more successful in their efforts than they were, we would be the poorer today. It was an English cleric friend of mine who, at the height of the revision of liturgical language in the English prayer book two decades ago, observed that the glories of English worship had survived Henry VIII, Oliver Cromwell, and Adolf Hitler, only to be done in by the heavy hand of the liturgical reformers of the 1970s.

Somewhere between a thoughtless veneration of the past and the total destruction of all that is out of step with the latest conclusions of the moment is where most of us within the church would like to stand, and it is possible that women may show us, at least in part, how to do this.   15

Dianne Bergant in her article "Women in the Bible: Friends or Foes?"[2] divides the biblical scholarship of women into revisionists and reformists. The revisionists, or revolutionaries, as some of the feminist theologians prefer to be called, "contend that the Bible has not only outgrown its usefulness, but is, in fact, detrimental to the development of women—and men for that matter. They often seek to reconstruct history as it *should have been* remembered, not as it *has been* remembered." The tradition for this point of view is not simply exclusive, it is destructive, and therefore irrelevant. The reformers, on the other hand, while equally opposed to patriarchy, "maintain that the message of the Bible is itself intrinsically liberating." To get at that biblical message and its liberating truth depends, of course, on how the Bible is to be read.

Bergant defines herself as a reformist, which means to her that the biblical tradition is a source of revelation for her, and remains so in its contemporary reinterpretation. She makes the telling but not so radical point that every generation, "successive communities of faith," as she calls them, has struggled with the relationship between the received tradition and the demands of its own unique experiences. Technically, this process in the field of biblical interpretation is called canonical criticism, but so technical a term should not disguise the fundamental fact that each age can read what it has received only through the lenses of its own experience.

Anyone who considers the matter will realize that eighteenth-century Christians do not necessarily interpret the texts of scripture in the same way as twelfth-century Christians. Augustine did not read scripture in the same way as Paul, and Luther repudiated centuries of Roman Catholic interpretation. American fundamentalists read scripture very differently from nonfundamentalist communions—and, in fact, very differently from the primitive church, although they would dispute that as a slander upon themselves and scripture. This is not simply a matter of relativity, as many with a high view of scripture would contend, but an unavoidable and perfectly understandable phenomenon of relevance. That women should do this is no more destructive of scripture than it was when Augustine, Luther, or Calvin did it. Scripture will survive such an inquiry, although there may be some reasonable doubt about the survivability of the exclusively male view of scripture.

Bergant's method is disarmingly simple, and I will describe it only briefly and without doing full justice to her discussion, simply to demonstrate that the best of this feminist scholarship is both accessible and constructive, taking both scripture and its interpretation as seriously today as ever it was taken in the great historical days of biblical interpretation. She calls her method "recontextualizing," and it involves: (1) Looking carefully at the received tradition; how has this text come down to us in the history of interpretation? (2) Operating out of a feminist sensitivity to the contemporary context; how is the text received now? (3) Finally, pointing out how "the dynamics within the text" can achieve a significance within the community that now reads and hears it. This is really no more than the Saturday-night method of any responsible preacher who has to stand up in the pulpit on Sunday morning, text in hand: (1) What did it mean then? (2) How do we understand it now? (3) So what do we do with it, or what does it do with us?

Rather than terrorizing scripture or subverting the faithful, this particular example of a feminist hermeneutic, one among many, I might add, actually works toward liberating both text and reader and is hardly a radical methodology—except, perhaps, in the including of perspectives hitherto excluded. Bergant concludes: "The result of such an approach is a reading that is both faithful and challenging. It is faithful because as 'word of God,' it is challenging; and it is challenging precisely because as open to God, it is faithful." *20*

OPTIONS FOR THE HARD PASSAGES

A story of W. C. Fields has the old reprobate on what he thinks may well be his deathbed. When his doctor comes in to see him, he finds Fields leafing furiously through a huge Bible. Surprised at such a sign of piety in so notoriously profane a fellow as Fields, the physician asks, "What are you looking for?" Replies Fields, "Loopholes."

That may appear to be the only paradigm available to those who would look at the hard passages here and hope to find something other than a confirmation of the status quo, but there is more to it than that, and a survey of critical literature presents us with a range of opinion on how to "read" what we find here. These are not loopholes, but they are options, and we look at them now. The options, adapted from a technical but useful study by Arthur Rowe,[3] are these:

1. Paul, a man of his time
2. Permanent principles
3. Particular problems
4. Not from Paul
5. Hermeneutical problem

The first option may well be called the principle of context. Paul writes as a man in a man's world. The roles of men and women in agrarian first-century society were prescribed by the circumstances of that society, where, with very rare exceptions, women were subordinate to men. In the three worlds of which Paul was a citizen, the Jewish, the Greek, and the Roman, women's societal roles were dictated by the subordination principle. His teachings on women, therefore, while reflecting the mores of his time, are no more relevant to an age where those mores no longer apply than, say, first-century standards of dress, of social etiquette, or of dietary rules. Paul is a social and political conservative. He does not, for example, advocate revolution against the state, and as we know, he requires that Christians obey lawful authority. Only in his theology, and in anticipation of the world to come, is he radical. So we should understand him, his social teachings, and those who imitate his teachings, such as the writer of Timothy, as writing from within the social assumptions of the age of which they are a part.

The second option sees Paul enunciating in these hard passages permanent principles of behavior, normative rules for the organization of the church and the relations between men and women within those churches. Here we should not necessarily infer that one role is better and superior to, or less good and inferior to, the other; they are simply different and distinct. The model and order of creation to which Paul himself appeals is an example: The man is made first, and the woman second. This does not mean that the man is better than the woman, or the woman inferior to the man. It does mean that they are different, by order of precedence, and by function. Harmony is assured when that order is understood and the different functions in the relationship are appreciated and affirmed.

The third option looks at the hard passages in Corinthians and Timothy   25
as addressed to particular and particularly troublesome situations in the places to which the letters are addressed. As we do not have all of the correspondence and do not necessarily know what it is that provokes Paul's response, we may well infer that women were party to some contentiousness in these churches. These then are Paul's instructions to put these troubles in those places, and at that time, to rest. These instructions are situation-oriented, and are not meant to be normative, and they certainly are not meant to inhibit the work of the Lydias, the Phoebes, and the Priscillas, and they do not negate the "equality principle" enunciated in Galatians 3:28, where all distinctions are leveled in Christ on the basis of baptism.

The fourth option is perhaps the most attractive for those who want to liberate themselves and Paul from Paul: These texts are not from Paul but from a "proto-Paul." One tempting theory, supported apparently by the earliest manuscripts, is that the instructions about women are to be found in the margin of the manuscript and not in the text, and they appear in their present places in the manuscripts by virtue of a later editorial decision on the part of a copyist. The problem remains, but at least it is not a problem of Paul's and, lacking that ultimate authority, can be "situationalized."

The fifth option is perhaps the most demanding, and that is that we must seek principles of interpretation that allow for the cultural presuppositions both of Paul and of the reader in making sense of these texts. In other words, if we expect to find women in a subordinate cultural position in Pauline times, we read that condition as normative in reading the text; and if in our own climate of interpretation we understand that subordination to be biblical, we are not surprised to find it there and affirm its presence and its application to our own time as well.

If one has no interest concerning the role of women in New Testament times, or now, for that matter, and if one does not see these hard passages as essentially inconsistent with the larger picture of the gospel as found in the New Testament, then, as we have said before, the problem is no problem. However, the last twenty-five years of New Testament studies with respect to the role of women both in the Bible and now in the churches makes this of interest, indeed, of concern, to everyone who takes the Bible and the churches seriously, even those who are opposed to any construction of these hard passages other than what they believe to be their clear, if painful, meaning. No less a resource than *The Women's Bible Commentary,* published in 1992, with the ambition, as stated in the introduction, "to gather some of the fruits of feminist biblical scholarship on each book of the Bible in order to share it with the larger community of women who read the Bible," says of I Corinthians 14:34–35: "The inclusion of these verses in the text of Paul's letter is particularly unfortunate, for their strong wording affects the way the rest of Paul's comments on women are read. They reinforce, for example, the conservative tendencies of Chapter 11, and obscure the more liberating aspects of Paul's statements about women."

From a brief review of these options we might well conclude that, rather than loopholes or ways out of a sticky situation, they are in fact variously related efforts to get into, and behind, and admittedly beyond, the texts. Women who might be expected willingly to toss out the offending passages, in much the same way as Thomas Jefferson edited out of "his" Bible all those Pauline passages not consistent with his view of the ethical and moral teachings of Jesus, have by and large done no such thing and have fought for the Bible, hard passages and all, and for the right to interpret them within and against the context of the larger principles for which Paul writes and which his own experience with women co-workers amplifies.

Although Christian traditions as diverse as the Roman Catholic Church 30 and the Mennonite Brethren Church continue to affirm that such passages as I Corinthians 14 and I Timothy 2 are normative texts whose prohibition against the teaching of women "concerns the official function of teaching in the Christian assembly"—a phrase from the "Declaration on the Question on Admission to the Ministerial Priesthood" of the Sacred Congregation for the Doctrine of the Faith of the Roman Catholic Church—the overwhelming consensus of the vast literature on these texts since 1970 suggests that they are meant to be understood situationally, contextually, and not normatively. Despite the firmly stated desire of Pope John Paul II and his allies within significant portions of the evangelical Protestant communions to put the divisive nature of this debate to rest in favor of the Pauline status quo, the issue will not go away for women, nor for those who demand for them a role at the very least as central as the roles played by Lydia, Phoebe, and Priscilla.

With women bishops in the Anglican Church, women clergy throughout the ranks of the Protestant churches, an unremitting campaign for women within the Roman Catholic Church, and the prodigious scholarship of women and men on the frontiers of biblical study, this particular fight for the Bible is by no means over, but it certainly looks nearer to 1945 for the Allies than it does to 1940 for the Germans. Let no one mistake that this is a battle still in progress, however. As one critic has pointed out, the issue for the conservative position is not women. That tradition honors and cherishes women and their unique and biblically approved gifts, for without women the churches would not function, let alone flourish. The pope's most recent pastoral letter on women makes this point. The concern is not women, but rather the authority of scripture, the teaching tradition of the church, and the social, theological, and moral upheaval that is sure to come from selective principles of interpretation that relegate the teachings of scripture to the realm of first-century sociology and the control of a cadre of experts. If we are wrong, say the more perceptive and worried among these conservatives, on so clear a matter as the biblical warrant for the subordination of women, on what else could we be wrong, and what other changes, even less agreeable than these, are in store for those who worry that a Bible diminished by interpretation is no Bible at all?

These are not new concerns or issues. They are as old as scripture itself, and they have arisen in every age when the prevailing climate of interpretation has been challenged. The conservative rabbis of biblical times raised the same issues about Jesus and Paul, and we heard the same anxious concerns expressed about the authority of scripture and the order of society in the debates about temperance, to a lesser degree, and far more urgently, about race within our own lifetimes. When Roland Bainton declared in the matter of total abstinence that he was giving precedence to biblical principle over biblical practice, and regarded doing so as biblical, he did not provide us with a way out but a way in to the fight for the Bible which is as old as the Bible itself, and as painful and new as each age's attempt to understand and appropriate that book for itself. Making that point upon a review of the New Testament discussions of women, Malcolm O. Tolbert[4] concludes that one of our most fundamental mistakes in the reading of scripture, particularly of the New Testament, is to assume that the structures and the systems it describes are as sacred and authoritative as the principles it affirms. Not only is this wrong, it is idolatrous, even blasphemous, to use the word of God to affirm and maintain human privilege. It was wrong in the interpretation that God approved and encouraged chattel slavery, it was wrong in the maintenance of a climate in which the persecution of the Jews could be regarded as biblical, and it is wrong, unequivocally wrong, in imposing first-century social standards on the participation of women in the life of the church simply to preserve the abstraction of the authority of scripture and the preservation of a status quo favorable to those already in power.

Tolbert writes, "I do not understand the pattern of male dominance reflected in the Bible as an expression of the will of God. It is rather the reflection of the culture in which Jews and Christians as well as pagans lived. I am governed rather by the insights found in various key texts which make it possible for the Christian to criticize the structures of society and the Church. These passages, Mark 10:43 and Galatians 3:28, emphasize the ideals of servanthood and mutuality in relationships rather than the ascendancy of any one person or group of persons over others." He is of a large and growing company.

As long as there are people willing to read the Bible in this way over and against the powers and principalities that would have them read it otherwise, such people will fight for the Bible and for the right to read themselves into it rather than to be read out of it. In the vanguard of this battle, perhaps the most significant battle for the Bible since the debates over slavery, at least in the United States, the women have led the way, and one would like to think that Lydia, Phoebe, and Priscilla would be pleased.

NOTES

1. The wickedly delicious concept of "textual harassment" was coined by Mary Jacobus and first appeared, I believe, in her article "Is There a Woman in This Text?" in *The New Literary History,* 1982.
2. Dianne Bergant, "Women in the Bible: Friends or Foes?" *Theology Digest* 40 (1993), pp. 103–112. Bergant cautions against the unthinking use of exemplary women in the Bible and would not necessarily approve of the use I make of Lydia, Phoebe, and Priscilla. "Just because women seem to be portrayed as self-directed and competent is no guarantee that such was the point intended by the author. In fact, they may be reinforcing patriarchal or Kyiarchal structures" (p. 106). I take her point, but mine is that the presence of these women in the Pauline text is an affirmation by Paul of a colleagueship with them that indeed transcends a purely patriarchal reading. Lydia, Phoebe, and Priscilla were included at the beginning of the gospel work and by no means should be "read out" or their presence diminished.
3. Arthur Rowe's article, "Hermeneutics and 'Hard Passages' in the NT on the Role of Women in the Church: Issues from Recent Literature," appeared in *The Epworth Review* 18 (1991), pp. 82–88.
4. Malcolm O. Tolbert's article "Searching the Scriptures" appears in *The New Has Come: Emerging Roles among Southern Baptist Women,* ed. Anne Thomas Neil and Virginia Garrett Neely (Washington, D.C.: Southern Baptist Alliance, 1989), pp. 29–39.

QUESTIONS FOR DISCUSSION

1. Why does the New Testament seem to offer conflicting statements on the role of women in the church? In what sense are "hard passages" hard?
2. What does Gomes mean when, in paragraph 3, he writes that reading is a "transaction"? How is reading shaped by what a reader brings to a text?
3. Gomes claims, "With all due respect to the pieties addressed to the mind of scripture and to its context, as in most things our context is the only one that really counts." What is "our context"? Do you agree that our context "is the only one that really counts"?
4. Why are hymns important, and to what extent are they gender based?
5. What is the difference between "revisionists" and "reformists"?
6. What are the five options identified in this selection for men and women who want to understand what the Bible says about women? Can you explain these options in your own words?

7. If you are a member of a Christian church, how do you think the other members of your congregation would respond to Gomes if you shared this selection with them?

SUGGESTIONS FOR WRITING

1. Choose one of the options Gomes identifies for interpreting the Bible, and write your own interpretation of what one of the gospels in the New Testament says about women.
2. Write an interpretation of what the Old Testament says about women.
3. Research how contemporary scholars are interpreting the Torah and the Koran. Then write a paper explaining how meaning in one of those texts is still being determined.

LINKS ■ ■ ■

■ WITHIN THE BOOK

For another selection that encourages reexamination of spiritual values, see "Sweet Chariot" by Mark Doty (pages 89–94).

■ ELSEWHERE IN PRINT

Bergant, Dianne. "Women in the Bible: Friends or Foes." *Theology Digest* 40 (1993): 103–12.

Daly, Mary. *Beyond God the Father: Toward a Philosophy of Women's Liberation.* 1973. Boston: Beacon, 1985.

Gomes, Peter J. *The Good Book: Reading the Bible with Mind and Heart.* New York: Morrow, 1996.

———. *Sermons: Biblical Wisdom for Daily Living.* New York: Morrow, 1998.

Rowe, Arthur. "Hermeneutics and 'Hard Passages' in the New Testament on the Role of Women in the Church: Issues from Recent Literature." *Epworth Review* 18 (1991): 82–88.

■ ONLINE

- Brief Biography
  <http://www.hds.harvard.edu/dpa/faculty/min/gomes.html>
- Feminist Theology: Online Bibliography
  <http://www.dike.de/hulda/fembib.html>
- Women in the Bible
  <http://www.umilta.net/bible.html>

WOMEN'S BRAINS

Stephen Jay Gould

Stephen Jay Gould (1941–2002) was the Alexander Agassiz Professor of Zoology at Harvard University, where he was also a professor of geology and Curator of Invertebrate Paleontology in the Harvard Museum of Comparative Zoology. He also served as the Vincent Astor Visiting Research Professor of Biology at New York University. During the late twentieth century, he wrote almost 300 articles about science for his monthly column in Natural History. *When asked by an interviewer, "What ultimate effect would you like your work to have?" he responded: "I hope it will be one further step in the kind of humility that would benefit humans enormously with regard to our powers and possibilities on this planet. I think we want to be around for a while. We'd better understand that we weren't meant to be, and we don't have dominion over everything, and we're not always as smart as we think."*

In the following essay, first published in 1980, Gould reports information about a French scientist named Paul Broca who falsely concluded that women are less intelligent than men. As you read this essay, consider Gould's purpose in reporting the story of Broca's research. Consider also what this essay reveals about the importance of interpreting information.

In the prelude to *Middlemarch,* George Eliot° lamented the unfulfilled lives of talented women:

> Some have felt that these blundering lives are due to the inconvenient indefiniteness with which the Supreme Power has fashioned the natures of women: if there were one level of feminine incompetence as strict as the ability to count three and no more, the social lot of women might be treated with scientific certitude.

Eliot goes on to discount the idea of innate limitation, but while she wrote in 1872, the leaders of European anthropometry were trying to measure "with scientific certitude" the inferiority of women. Anthropometry, or measurement of the human body, is not so fashionable a field these days, but it dominated the human sciences for much of the nineteenth century and remained popular until intelligence testing replaced skull measurement as a favored device for making invidious comparisons among races, classes, and sexes. Craniometry, or measurement of the skull, commanded the most attention and respect. Its unquestioned leader, Paul Broca (1824–80), professor of clinical surgery at the Faculty of Medicine in Paris, gathered a school of disciples and imitators around himself. Their

---

George Eliot: The pen name of English novelist Mary Ann Evans (1819–1880).

work, so meticulous and apparently irrefutable, exerted great influence and won high esteem as a jewel of nineteenth-century science.

Broca's work seemed particularly invulnerable to refutation. Had he not measured with the most scrupulous care and accuracy? (Indeed, he had. I have the greatest respect for Broca's meticulous procedure. His numbers are sound. But science is an inferential exercise, not a catalog of facts. Numbers, by themselves, specify nothing. All depends upon what you do with them.) Broca depicted himself as an apostle of objectivity, a man who bowed before facts and cast aside superstition and sentimentality. He declared that "there is no faith, however respectable, no interest, however legitimate, which must not accommodate itself to the progress of human knowledge and bend before truth." Women, like it or not, had smaller brains than men and, therefore, could not equal them in intelligence. This fact, Broca argued, may reinforce a common prejudice in male society, but it is also a scientific truth. L. Manouvrier, a black sheep in Broca's fold, rejected the inferiority of women and wrote with feeling about the burden imposed upon them by Broca's numbers:

> Women displayed their talents and their diplomas. They also invoked philosophical authorities. But they were opposed by *numbers* unknown to Condorcet or to John Stuart Mill. These numbers fell upon poor women like a sledge hammer, and they were accompanied by commentaries and sarcasms more ferocious than the most misogynist imprecations of certain church fathers. The theologians had asked if women had a soul. Several centuries later, some scientists were ready to refuse them a human intelligence.

Broca's argument rested upon two sets of data: the larger brains of men in modern societies, and a supposed increase in male superiority through time. His most extensive data came from autopsies performed personally in four Parisian hospitals. For 292 male brains, he calculated an average weight of 1,325 grams; 140 female brains averaged 1,144 grams for a difference of 181 grams, or 14 percent of the male weight. Broca understood, of course, that part of this difference could be attributed to the greater height of males. Yet he made no attempt to measure the effect of size alone and actually stated that it cannot account for the entire difference because we know, a priori, that women are not as intelligent as men (a premise that the data were supposed to test, not rest upon):

> We might ask if the small size of the female brain depends exclusively upon the small size of her body. Tiedemann has proposed this explanation. But we must not forget that women are, on the average, a little less intelligent than men, a difference which we should not exaggerate but which is, nonetheless, real. We are therefore permitted to suppose that the relatively small size of the female brain depends in part upon her physical inferiority and in part upon her intellectual inferiority.

In 1873, the year after Eliot published *Middlemarch,* Broca measured the cranial capacities of prehistoric skulls from L'Homme Mort cave. Here he found ₅ a difference of only 99.5 cubic centimeters between males and females, while modern populations range from 129.5 to 220.7. Topinard, Broca's chief disciple, explained the increasing discrepancy through time as a result of differing evolutionary pressures upon dominant men and passive women:

> The man who fights for two or more in the struggle for existence, who has all the responsibility and the cares of tomorrow, who is constantly active in combating the environment and human rivals, needs more brain than the woman whom he must protect and nourish, the sedentary woman, lacking any interior occupations, whose role is to raise children, love, and be passive.

In 1879, Gustave Le Bon, chief misogynist of Broca's school, used these data to publish what must be the most vicious attack upon women in modern scientific literature (no one can top Aristotle). I do not claim his views were representative of Broca's school, but they were published in France's most respected anthropological journal. Le Bon concluded:

> In the most intelligent races, as among the Parisians, there are a large number of women whose brains are closer in size to those of gorillas than to the most developed male brains. This inferiority is so obvious that no one can contest it for a moment; only its degree is worth discussion. All psychologists who have studied the intelligence of women, as well as poets and novelists, recognize today that they represent the most inferior forms of human evolution and that they are closer to children and savages than to an adult, civilized man. They excel in fickleness, inconstancy, absence of thought and logic, and incapacity to reason. Without doubt there exist some distinguished women, very superior to the average man, but they are as exceptional as the birth of any monstrosity, as, for example, of a gorilla with two heads; consequently, we may neglect them entirely.

Nor did Le Bon shrink from the social implications of his views. He was horrified by the proposal of some American reformers to grant women higher education on the same basis as men:

> A desire to give them the same education, and, as a consequence, to propose the same goals for them, is a dangerous chimera. . . . The day when, misunderstanding the inferior occupations which nature has given her, women leave the home and take part in our battles: on this day a social revolution will begin, and everything that maintains the sacred ties of the family will disappear.

Sound familiar?*

_____

*When I wrote this essay, I assumed that Le Bon was a marginal, if colorful, figure. I have since learned that he was a leading scientist, one of the founders of social psychology, and best known for a seminal study on crowd behavior, still cited today (*La psychologie des foules,* 1895), and for his work on unconscious motivation.

I have reexamined Broca's data, the basis for all this derivative pronounce-ment, and I find his numbers sound but his interpretation ill-founded, to say the least. The data supporting his claim for increased difference through time can be easily dismissed. Broca based his contention on the samples from L'Homme Mort alone—only seven male and six female skulls in all. Never have so little data yielded such far-ranging conclusions.

In 1888, Topinard published Broca's more extensive data on the Parisian hospitals. Since Broca recorded height and age as well as brain size, we may use modern statistics to remove their effect. Brain weight decreases with age, and Broca's women were, on average, considerably older than his men. Brain weight increases with height, and his average man was almost half a foot taller than his average woman. I used multiple regression, a technique that allowed me to assess simultaneously the influence of height and age upon brain size. In an analysis of the data for women, I found that, at average male height and age, a woman's brain would weigh 1,212 grams. Correction for height and age reduces Broca's measured difference of 181 grams by more than a third, to 113 grams.

I don't know what to make of this remaining difference because I cannot   10
assess other factors known to influence brain size in a major way. Cause of death has an important effect: Degenerative disease often entails a substantial diminution of brain size. (This effect is separate from the decrease attributed to age alone.) Eugene Schreider, also working with Broca's data, found that men killed in accidents had brains weighing, on average, 60 grams more than men dying of infectious diseases. The best modern data I can find (from Amer-ican hospitals) records a full 100-gram difference between death by degenera-tive arteriosclerosis and by violence or accident. Since so many of Broca's subjects were elderly women, we may assume that lengthy degenerative dis-ease was more common among them than among the men.

More importantly, modern students of brain size still have not agreed on a proper measure for eliminating the powerful effect of body size. Height is partly adequate, but men and women of the same height do not share the same body build. Weight is even worse than height, because most of its variation reflects nutrition rather than intrinsic size—fat versus skinny exerts little influ-ence upon the brain. Manouvrier took up this subject in the 1880s and argued that muscular mass and force should be used. He tried to measure this elusive property in various ways and found a marked difference in favor of men, even in men and women of the same height. When he corrected for what he called "sexual mass," women actually came out slightly ahead in brain size.

Thus, the corrected 113-gram difference is surely too large; the true fig-ure is probably close to zero and may as well favor women as men. And 113 grams, by the way, is exactly the average difference between a 5 foot 4 inch and a 6 foot 4 inch male in Broca's data. We would not (especially us short folks) want to ascribe greater intelligence to tall men. In short, who knows what to do with Broca's data? They certainly don't permit any confident claim that men have bigger brains than women.

To appreciate the social role of Broca and his school, we must recognize that his statements about the brains of women do not reflect an isolated prejudice toward a single disadvantaged group. They must be weighed in the context of a general theory that supported contemporary social distinctions as biologically ordained. Women, blacks, and poor people suffered the same disparagement, but women bore the brunt of Broca's argument because he had easier access to data on women's brains. Women were singularly denigrated, but they also stood as surrogates for other disenfranchised groups. As one of Broca's disciples wrote in 1881: "Men of the black races have a brain scarcely heavier than that of white woman." This juxtaposition extended into many other realms of anthropological argument, particularly to claims that, anatomically and emotionally, both women and blacks were like white children—and that white children, by the theory of recapitulation, represented an ancestral (primitive) adult stage of human evolution. I do not regard as empty rhetoric the claim that women's battles are for all of us.

Maria Montessori did not confine her activities to educational reform for young children. She lectured on anthropology for several years at the University of Rome, and wrote an influential book entitled *Pedagogical Anthropology* (English edition, 1913). Montessori was no egalitarian. She supported most of Broca's work and the theory of innate criminality proposed by her compatriot Cesare Lombroso. She measured the circumferences of children's heads in her schools and inferred that the best prospects had bigger brains. But she had no use for Broca's conclusions about women. She discussed Manouvrier's work at length and made much of his tentative claim that women, after proper correction of the data, had slightly larger brains than men. Women, she concluded, were intellectually superior, but men had prevailed heretofore by dint of physical force. Since technology has abolished force as an instrument of power, the era of women may soon be upon us: "In such an epoch there will really be superior human beings, there will really be men strong in morality and in sentiment. Perhaps in this way the reign of women is approaching, when the enigma of her anthropological superiority will be deciphered. Woman was always the custodian of human sentiment, morality and honor."

This represents one possible antidote to "scientific" claims for the constitutional inferiority of certain groups. One may affirm the validity of biological distinctions but argue that the data have been misinterpreted by prejudiced men with a stake in the outcome, and that disadvantaged groups are truly superior. In recent years, Elaine Morgan has followed this strategy in her *Descent of Woman,* a speculative reconstruction of human prehistory from the woman's point of view—and as farcical as more famous tall tales by and for men.

I prefer another strategy. Montessori and Morgan followed Broca's philosophy to reach a more congenial conclusion. I would rather label the whole enterprise of setting a biological value upon groups for what it is: irrelevant and highly injurious. George Eliot well appreciated the special tragedy that biological labeling imposed upon members of disadvantaged groups. She expressed it for people like herself—women of extraordinary talent. I would apply it more widely—not only to those whose dreams are flouted but also to those who never realize that they may dream—but I cannot match her prose. In conclusion, then, the rest of Eliot's prelude to *Middlemarch:*

15

The limits of variation are really much wider than anyone would imagine from the sameness of women's coiffure and the favorite love stories in prose and verse. Here and there a cygnet is reared uneasily among the ducklings in the brown pond, and never finds the living stream in fellowship with its own oary-footed kind. Here and there is born a Saint Theresa, foundress of nothing, whose loving heartbeats and sobs after an unattained goodness tremble off and are dispersed among hindrances instead of centering in some long-recognizable deed.

QUESTIONS FOR DISCUSSION

1. Why do you think Mary Ann Evans chose to publish under a man's name? And why do you think Gould chose to open and close his article with references to one of her books?
2. When reporting the accomplishments of the French scientist Paul Broca, Gould declares that information was carefully collected and that the numbers are reliable. But he then observes, "Numbers, by themselves, specify nothing. All depends upon what you do with them." How was Broca misled by his numbers? What did he fail to take into account?
3. What does Gould mean when he supports the claim that "women's battles are for all of us"?
4. What is the significance of Gould's note on the bottom of page 232?
5. This article includes several long quotations. Are they all necessary? Which affected you the most?

SUGGESTIONS FOR WRITING

1. Research the status of women in a country of your choice. Then write an essay in which you explain the reasons for that status.
2. Do research on either George Eliot or Paul Broca, and interpret the data you gather to explain why she or he became a respected authority. Be sure to reveal your sources, and try to consult at least one work written by the person you are investigating.
3. In paragraph 14, Gould refers to the work of Maria Montessori. Research how Montessori Schools operate within the United States, and write an essay explaining what makes them distinctive.

LINKS ■ ■ ■

■ **WITHIN THE BOOK**

In "What *Does* the Bible Say about Women?" (pages 218–228), Peter Gomes explains other reasons why women were once considered inferior to men.

■ **ELSEWHERE IN PRINT**

Belenky, Mary Field, Blythe Clinchy, Nancy Goldberger, and Jill Tarule. *Women's Ways of Knowing: The Development of Self, Voice, and Mind.* New York: Basic, 1986.

Eliot, George. *Middlemarch.* 1872. Ed. Gordon S. Haight. Boston: Houghton, 1956.

Gould, Stephen Jay. *Dinosaur in a Haystack: Reflections on Natural History.* New York: Harmony, 1995.

———. *Ever Since Darwin: Reflections in Natural History.* New York: Norton, 1977.

———. *The Flamingo's Smile: Reflections in Natural History.* New York: Norton, 1985.

Jolly, Allison. *Lucy's Legacy: Sex and Intelligence in Human Evolution.* Cambridge: Harvard UP, 1999.

Morgan, Elaine. *The Descent of Woman.* New York: Stein, 1972.

■ **ONLINE**

- Anthropometry
  <http://skepdic.com/anthropo.html>
- Brief Biography
  <http://www.annonline.com/interviews/961009/biography.html>
- George Eliot: Middlemarch
  <http://etext.lib.virginia.edu/english/eliot/middlemarch>
- Paul Broca
  <http://www.epub.org.br/cm/n02/historia/broca.htm>
- Science and Feminism
  <http://www.cddc.vt.edu/feminism/sci.html>

WHAT HAPPENED TO THE ANASAZI?

Catherine Dold

Some of the most beautiful houses in our country were built almost a thousand years ago by the Anasazi, an Indian tribe that briefly flourished in the Southwest when Europe was still climbing out of the Dark Ages. The ruins of these houses, which were often built into the sides of cliffs (as shown by the illustration on page 241), have inspired considerable speculation about the fate of this vanished tribe. The following article explains how scholars are interpreting recent findings at archeological digs in the area. As you read, remember that you are reading about an ancient people struggling to survive during desperate times.

Catherine Dold lives in Boulder, Colorado. Formerly a senior editor at Audubon *magazine, she has also written for* Smithsonian, Discover, *and the* New York Times *in addition to being a staff writer for the National Resources Defense Council.*

Life in the southwestern corner of Colorado can be difficult in the best of times. Rainfall is scarce, making growth hard even for the scrubby sagebrush and tough piñon and juniper trees that dot the arid land. In summer the heat is oppressive on the flatlands, and only slightly more tolerable on top of the flat, high mesas that jut above the horizon. Winter is not much better.

Chapin Mesa, one of the largest features in the area, dominates the landscape and the imagination. Tucked away within its hidden canyons are the famous cliff dwellings built long ago by the Anasazi Indians. Sheltered by enormous natural overhangs, each village is a dense cluster of brick-walled rooms stacked two or three stories high, fronted by sunny plazas. Tiny windows in some rooms yield glimpses of paintings on inside walls; subterranean gathering rooms—called kivas—feature benches and elaborate ventilation systems. Everything is constructed of reddish-gold sandstone, which seems to glow in the unforgiving southwestern sun. Magnificent as these homes were, however, the Anasazi lived in them for fewer than a hundred years. For some unknown reason, they completely abandoned the area around A.D. 1300. Today, most of the cliff dwellings are preserved in Mesa Verde National Park, and every summer throngs of visitors ponder the mysterious departure of the Anasazi. Drought, warfare, and the harsh environment are all cited as possible explanations.

But another, deeper mystery lies just a dozen or so miles west of Mesa Verde, in an area known as Cowboy Wash, a broad, flat floodplain in the shadow of Sleeping Ute Mountain. A century and a half before the abandonment of Mesa Verde, Cowboy Wash was home to another group of people, probably Anasazi as well. Recently archeologists discovered several piles of human bones at the site. These bones, they say, show clear evidence of cannibalism. What's more, they maintain that this find does not represent an isolated incident. In the last few years, at least 30 nearby digs have yielded similar evidence of humans eating humans. Some archeologists speculate, naturally, that only people forced to desperate measures by starvation in this harsh environment would resort to cannibalism. The excavators of Cowboy Wash, however, propose a new theory. The cannibalism that occurred there, they say, was an act of prehistoric terrorism.

Traditionally, the Anasazi have been portrayed as peaceful farmers who quietly tended their corn and bean crops. Archeological records indicate that they occupied the Four Corners area—the juncture of present-day Colorado, Utah, Arizona, and New Mexico—from the beginning of the first millennium to around 1300. During that time they developed complex societies, farming methods, and architectural styles, culminating in life among the cliff dwellings. But recent work hints that the Anasazi world was far more turbulent than suspected.

The clues come from an archeological dig conducted by Soil Systems,   *5* Inc., a private consulting firm in Phoenix, Arizona. Under contract to the Ute Mountain Ute Tribe, SSI excavated several ruins in the Cowboy Wash area so the tribe could relocate any ancient human remains before the launch of a new irrigation project. The site where the bones were found, a dwelling known as 5MT10010, is believed to have been occupied between the years 1125 and 1150. It includes three pit structures, the roofed, semi-sunken rooms typical of Anasazi homes at that time, as well as other rooms and trash heaps known as middens. Some 15 to 20 people, divided into three households, probably lived there.

The telltale bones were found scattered about the floors of two of the pit structures. In one, known as Feature 3, SSI archeologists found more than 1,100 bones and bone fragments, including shoulder blades, skulls, vertebrae, ribs, arm bones, hand and foot bones, and teeth. Nearly all were broken. Most were found in a heap at the bottom of an air shaft. In the other pit structure, Feature 13, the bones were found scattered on the floor and in side chambers.

"This was in no way a burial," says Patricia Lambert, a bioarcheologist from Utah State University in Logan who was hired to analyze the bones. "There was no reverence for these remains." Lambert's job was to try to reconstruct complete skeletons from the fractured pieces and decipher the clues left behind. "It was a big puzzle," she says. "The elements were all mixed together and broken." Many bones, particularly large leg bones, were missing. Eventually Lambert established that at least five people had been disposed of at Feature 3—three adult males, one adult female, and an 11-year-old child. Two children were found in the other pit structure, one a 7-year-old, the other 14.

Evidence of trauma was not hard to find. Most of the bones were broken, and many looked scraped and scorched. The marks looked like those left on the bones of large game animals after butchering. According to many archeologists, the presence of such marks on human bones is a clear indication of cannibalism. Someone who is planning to eat a human body part, the theory goes, would naturally prepare it in the same manner as he would an elk or a deer. And that is exactly what Lambert found.

"I found cut marks at muscle attachment sites, such as where the femur is attached to the hipbone," she says. "It's pretty clear they were disarticulating the body, cutting tendons and soft tissues that connect various parts." The cut marks occur when cutting tools slip and strike bone instead of tissue, she explains, and they cannot be mistaken for the gnawing marks an animal might leave. The relatively pristine condition of the bones is yet another clue. If the flesh had been left to rot away rather than being deliberately removed, says Lambert, the bones would be discolored and pitted instead of white, smooth, and dense. And some bones look as though they were broken open so the nutritious marrow could be extracted. They bear the complex fractures that occur in living bone—not the simple, smooth fractures of decaying bone. Moreover, they show flake scars, the marks that are left when a hammering tool chips bone.

Perhaps most disturbing was the evidence of burning and cooking—even a mere summation of it, 850 years after the fact, is enough to make one queasy: Some bones appear to have been browned by heat exposure when they were still covered with flesh, and the skulls of both children in Feature 13 were obviously burned. "The burning clearly happened while the head was intact," says Lambert. "The back of the cranial vault was down around the coals, and the flames licked up and browned the side and blackened the back. Sometime later the head was taken apart—we found the pieces in two separate piles. They were putting the head on the fire. They were not incinerating it, but they did put it on there long enough to have cooked the brains.

"I can't say that they were eating these people, but they were certainly processing them in a way that suggests they were," says Lambert.

The victims and alleged perpetrators also left behind a few other clues. In one pit structure, archeologists found a set of tools, including two axes, that might have been used to butcher the bodies. "Sort of like leaving a calling card," muses archeologist Brian Billman, project director for SSI. Not only were cooking pots, ladles, and lids left behind, but so were tools, beads, and some jewelry. Leaving behind such valuables suggests that the sites were suddenly abandoned, says Billman, and sediment deposits on top of the bones and pots provide clues that the homes remained vacant. Furthermore, three other sites in the immediate area yielded the same type of remains, from the same time period: human bones irreverently scattered about deserted homes.

The evidence, Billman concludes, all points to an outbreak of cannibalism designed to terrorize and intimidate a group of people, most likely some foreigners who posed competition for scarce food resources. "It was a time of severe drought, as well as social and political upheaval," he says. "People were moving into new areas and mixing up alliances." Billman believes that people from about 60 miles south moved into Cowboy Wash and replaced the local community, as evidenced by several pots found there bearing the style of a more southern culture. But the immigrants' arrival apparently did not sit well with the local Anasazi.

10

"We think that certain groups in the Mesa Verde area, out of desperation, then turned to a strategy of warfare and cannibalism. One or more of the communities in this area decided on this as a political strategy, to push the new groups back out of the area and give themselves more resources. Plus, the message would be delivered to other communities that 'You'd better not mess with us.' It would so terrorize people that they would never think of messing with you." The carnage was indeed extensive. Billman estimates that between 60 and 100 people lived in the nine dwellings at Cowboy Wash. In the four dwellings he has excavated so far, he turned up the remains of 24 people.

Billman says two distinct patterns of human remains at several suspected cannibalism sites support his terrorism theory. In one pattern, which was also observed at Cowboy Wash, human remains were scattered on floors and the dwellings abandoned soon after. In the other, remains were not left lying about but were dumped into trash pits or unused rooms. Billman thinks the first pattern occurred in victims' homes, where they were cut up and consumed. The second pattern occurred in sites belonging to the perpetrators, who continued to use their homes after processing the bodies. "At the Mancos Canyon site, which is only 12 miles from Cowboy Wash, 30 to 40 people were found in trash dumps. They might have been people who were taken back to that village and consumed there." Likewise, the meat-laden leg bones missing from Cowboy Wash were probably carried off to be eaten later at secondary sites. At any rate, that is what Billman suspects, based on how hunters typically handle large game. 15

At least half the suspected incidents of cannibalism at the sites he reviewed occurred around 1150. "We call this an 'outbreak' of cannibalism. It looks like before this there was a very low level of cannibalism, then with this severe drought and social turmoil a few groups turned to terroristic violence." By the early 1200s, he notes, climatic conditions were back to normal and there were very few incidents of cannibalism. Around this time, too, the inhabitants of Mesa Verde moved from the pueblos on top of the mesa to the cliff dwellings in the sheltered cliff alcoves, a move some say was taken because the cliff dwellings were more easily defended.

Researchers have proposed other motivations for the alleged cannibalism, but they just don't fit the scenario, he adds. If the perpetrators had been goaded by hunger, he says, they would have been more likely to leave the area and search for food rather than resort to such drastic measures. Hunger-induced cannibalism typically occurs in groups that are trapped, such as the Donner party, which was caught by a snowstorm in the Sierra Nevada in 1846. The people of the Cowboy Wash site had no such constraints. And besides, most of the victims appear to have been done away with in one fell swoop—not a prudent use of resources if you're starving.

Christy Turner, a bioarcheologist at Arizona State University in Tempe, agrees with the terrorism theory but thinks the explanation for it is even more complex. Anasazi culture bears signs of trade with Mexico, such as copper bells, macaws, and corn. During this time central Mexico was in social turmoil, says

Cliff Place, constructed A.D. 1209–1270s, has 250 rooms and 23 kivas.

Turner, and hundreds of cults sprang up. Some members may have fled north, bringing not only distinctive trade goods but, possibly, flesh-eating rituals too. Plenty of evidence for such rituals occurs in historical accounts and in the archeological record of central Mexico, says Turner, and the practice was often used to intimidate neighboring tribes. Another possibility is that cannibalism might have developed independently—but for similar reasons—in the Four Corners region. It may, for example, be linked to a strategy for social control by inhabitants of Chaco Canyon, a New Mexico community of several thousand Anasazi that lay some 80 miles south of Mesa Verde. Chaco Canyon was a hub of Anasazi culture, and many scholars think it had great political and social influence over outlying communities.

The details of that particular scenario are sketchy, and Turner, who is at work on a book about the subject, won't elaborate. But Billman doesn't think the evidence supports that theory. He contends that the major outbreak of cannibalism actually occurred *after* Chaco Canyon was abandoned in the 1140s. Moreover, nobody knows where the former residents of Chaco Canyon went. Billman thinks it more likely that the victims at Cowboy Wash came from the Chuska Mountains, some 60 miles south of the site. What both hypotheses share, however, is the idea that neighboring groups were using cannibalism as a terrorist strategy to drive out competition for scarce resources.

There is no shortage of speculation on the causes of the suspected canni-   20
balism. But do the bones really tell a tale of cannibalism? With no eyewitnesses, can anyone really be sure of what happened at Cowboy Wash eight and a half centuries ago?

"How do you tell that a person committed a murder when nobody saw it?" asks Tim White, a physical anthropologist at the University of California at Berkeley. "Evidence." White has closely examined the bones found at Mancos Canyon, and both he and Turner have proposed criteria that they say must be met to make a finding of cannibalism. Among them are cut marks, burn patterns, broken bones, and "pot polish," the way sharply fragmented bone gets rounded by rattling around in a pot of boiling water. "The question we need to ask is, Do people prepare other mammals in this fashion in this culture? Because humans are large animals. If you find that the patterning matches, then that becomes evidence," says White.

Turner, Billman, and others agree that, by these criteria, evidence from many southwestern sites, including Cowboy Wash, clearly indicates cannibalism. But Peter Bullock, a staff archeologist at the Museum of New Mexico in Santa Fe, is not ready to convict. He says that basing such studies on animal-butchering practices biases the results toward a consumption conclusion and fails to consider human motivations. Bones could end up being scraped, shattered, and scorched as a result of warfare, mutilation, or burial practices, he says. As an example, Bullock cites human remains recovered from the Battle of Little Bighorn, where General George Custer and his troops were slain.

"The results looked pretty similar to this cannibalism stuff, but we know from historical accounts that no cannibalism took place," he says. Kurt Dongoske, an archeologist employed by the Hopi, agrees. "To say that these disarticulated remains have been cannibalized is a real stretch."

"We've got folks who are processing humans in exactly the same way they process animals and we're supposed to believe that the end result was not consumption?" White asks incredulously. "Why does it look exactly like consumption?"

Native American representatives are silent on the matter. A spokesman for the Ute Mountain Ute Tribe, on whose land the Cowboy Wash bones were found, declined to comment either on that site or on the possibility of any incidents of cannibalism among the Anasazi. The tribe also refused to allow outsiders to visit the excavated site or to view the bones. Their reaction is understandable, some say. How would other people feel if scientists dug up bodies at Arlington National Cemetery and declared the soldiers cannibals? Not surprisingly, Park Service brochures handed out at Mesa Verde make no mention of the possibility of cannibalism either. The bones will eventually be reburied by a Ute religious leader.

"We can't get the meat from the hand into the mouth," concedes Bill-   25
man. "But there is now a possibility that we may be able to do that. One of the last things that was done on our site—once the hearth had gone cold and was filled with ash—was someone squatted down in the hearth and defecated." A preliminary analysis of the coprolite, as the preserved specimen is called, indicates that its owner's last meal was almost entirely animal protein. Determining just what type of animal—elk, deer, or human—the protein came from will be the job of Richard Marlar, a professor of molecular biology at the University of Colorado at Denver. He heard about the Cowboy Wash coprolite and offered to analyze its contents.

It might seem that Marlar could just look for human blood or cells in the coprolite, but humans often shed their own intestinal cells in feces. So he will test for the presence of myoglobin, a protein found in human skeletal muscle but not in the intestines. He will dissolve samples of the coprolite in a buffer solution and then add antibodies that recognize myoglobin. If myoglobin is present, reactions with the antibodies will tint the solution. Marlar also plans to test residues from cooking vessels found at the site.

Although such tests have been routinely used to identify bison, antelope, and human blood at archeological sites, no one has used the technique yet to address the question of humans eating humans. But Marlar predicts that it "could really answer if cannibalism occurred, once and for all." And, if the test is positive, archeologists will have even more reason to speculate on scenarios about social turmoil in the Southwest. Of course, if the test is negative, the case is still not closed. The abundance of evidence points to cannibalism among the Anasazi. But without clear historical records, the precise reason for that cannibalism—if it occurred—will probably never be known.

QUESTIONS FOR DISCUSSION

1. What are the traditional explanations for the disappearance of the Anasazi? If scholars confirm evidence that the Anasazi practiced cannibalism, how would that information help us understand the past?
2. What evidence has led investigators to believe that there was an outbreak of cannibalism near Mesa Verde some 850 years ago?
3. In your opinion, are there any circumstances under which eating human flesh could be morally justifiable?
4. Where does Dold indicate that claims of cannibalism have not yet been entirely proven? What does she achieve by doing so?
5. How would you describe the tone of this article? How respectful is Dold of the culture she is interpreting?
6. In the years that have passed since the Anasazi disappeared, has warfare become more civilized or less so?

SUGGESTIONS FOR WRITING

1. Do research on the art and architecture of the Anasazi. Then write an essay interpreting what these artistic achievements reveal about Anasazi culture.
2. In paragraph 17, Dold mentions the Donner party—a group of white settlers who practiced cannibalism when they were stranded by a snowstorm while traveling to California. Research how this trip was planned and write an essay explaining what went wrong.
3. Taken from their original sites, Native American objects—and even the remains of human bodies—are held in the collections of many American museums. Write an essay explaining why some of these holdings have become controversial.

LINKS ■ ■ ■

■ WITHIN THE BOOK

For another work addressing the relationship between Native Americans and the environment, see "The New Gold Rush" by Rebecca Solnit (pages 115–120).

■ ELSEWHERE IN PRINT

Billman, Brian, and Gary M. Feinman, eds. *Settlement Pattern Studies in the Americas.* Washington, DC: Smithsonian, 1999.
Ferguson, William M. *The Anasazi of Mesa Verde and the Four Corners.* Niwot: U of Colorado P, 1996.

■ **ELSEWHERE IN PRINT** *(continued)*

Goldman, Laurence, ed. *The Anthropology of Cannibalism*. Westport:
  Bergin, 1999.
Noble, David Grant. *Understanding the Anasazi of Mesa Verde and Hoven-
  weep*. Santa Fe: Ancient City P, 1985.
Turner, Christy G., II, and Jacqueline Turner. *Man Corn: Cannibalism
  and Violence in the Prehistoric American Southwest*. Salt Lake City: U of
  Utah P, 1999.

■ **ONLINE**

- Anasazi
  <http://www.cia-g.com/~rockets/anasazi.htm>
- Archeological Sites on Chapin Mesa
  <http://www.swcolo.org/tourism/archaeology/chapin.html>
- Cannibalism in the Ancient Southwest
  <http://www.unc.edu/news/newsserv/research/sep00/
  billman090600.htm>
- Ute Mountain Tribe
  <http://www.utemountainute.com>

THE JOYS AND PERILS OF VICTIMHOOD

Ian Buruma

A Fellow at St. Anthony's College, Oxford, Ian Buruma is the author of a novel, Playing the Game, *and several books of nonfiction, including* God's Dust, The Wages of Guilt, A Japanese Mirror, *and* Anglomania. *Culture editor for the* Far Eastern Review, *he also writes frequently for* The New Yorker *and* The New Republic *as well as* The New York Review of Books, *which published the following essay in 2000. Read primarily by well-educated Americans with a serious interest in ideas,* The New York Review of Books *includes not only reviews of specific books but also articles like Buruma's that explain the significance of ideas that have surfaced in numerous sources. As you read "The Joys and Perils of Victimhood," be alert for how Buruma sympathizes with the suffering of Holocaust victims—and victims of other violence—while questioning the extent to which this suffering should shape the identities of subsequent generations.*

In his book *The Seventh Million,* the Israeli journalist Tom Segev describes a visit to Auschwitz and other former death camps in Poland by a group of Israeli high school students. Some students are from secular schools, others from religious ones. All have been extensively prepared for the visit by the Israeli Ministry of Education. They have read books, seen films, and met survivors. Nonetheless, after their arrival in Poland, Segev notes a degree of apprehension among the students: Will they suddenly collapse? Will they reemerge from the experience as "different people"? The fears are not irrational, for the students have been prepared to believe that the trip will have a profound effect on their "identities," as Jews and as Israelis.

These regular school tours to the death camps are part of Israeli civic education. The political message is fairly straightforward: Israel was founded on the ashes of the Holocaust, but if Israel had already existed in 1933, the Holocaust would never have happened. Only in Israel can Jews be secure and free. The Holocaust was proof of that. So the victims of Hitler died as martyrs for the Jewish homeland, indeed as potential Israeli citizens, and the state of Israel is both the symbol and the guarantor of Jewish survival.

This message is given further expression, on those wintry spots where the Jewish people came close to annihilation, by displays of the Israeli flag and singing of the national anthem. But Segev noticed a peculiarly religious, or pseudo-religious, aspect to the death camp visits as well. The Israeli students in Poland, in his view, were like Christian pilgrims in Jerusalem, oblivious to everything except the sacred places. They marched along the railway tracks in Auschwitz-Birkenau like Christians on the Via Dolorosa. They brought books of prayers, poems, and psalms, which they recited in front of the ruined gas chambers. They played cassette tapes of music composed by a Holocaust survivor named Yehuda Poliker. And at one of the camps, a candle was lit in the crematorium, where the students knelt in prayer.

Some call this a form of secular religion. The historian Saul Friedlander was harsher and called it a union of kitsch and death. I felt the pull of kitsch emotion myself on my only visit to Auschwitz, in 1990. By kitsch I don't mean gaudiness or camp, but rather an expression of emotion that is displaced, focused on the wrong thing, or, to use that ghastly word properly for once, inappropriate. I am not the child of Holocaust survivors. My mother was Jewish, but she lived in England, and no immediate relations were killed by the Nazis. And yet even I couldn't escape a momentary feeling of vicarious virtue, especially when I came across tourists from Germany. They were the villains, I the potential victim. But for the grace of God, I thought, I would have died here too. Or would I? An even more grotesque calculation passed through my mind: How did I fit into the Nuremberg laws? Was I a *Mischling* of the first degree or the second? Was it enough to have two Jewish grandparents, or did you need more to qualify for the grim honor of martyrdom? When would I have been deported? Would I have been deported at all? And so on, until I was woken from these smug and morbid thoughts by the sight of a tall man in American Indian dress, followed by young Japanese, Germans, and others of various nationalities banging on tambourines, yelling something about world peace.

All this seems far away from Primo Levi's° fears of oblivion. One of the cruelest curses flung at the Jewish victims by an SS officer at Auschwitz was the promise that, even if one Jew survived the camp, no one would believe what had happened to him or her. The SS man was quite wrong, of course. We cannot imagine the victims' torment, but we believe it. And far from forgetting the most recent and horrible chapter in the long book of Jewish suffering, the remembrance of it grows in volume the further the events recede into the past. Holocaust museums and memorials proliferate. Holocaust movies and television soap operas have broken box office records. More and more people visit the camps, whose rotting barracks have to be carefully restored to serve as memorials and movie sets.

In a curious way, the Jewish Holocaust has been an inspiration for others, for almost every community, be it a nation or a religious or ethnic or sexual minority, has a bone to pick with history. All have suffered wrongs, and to an increasing and in my view alarming extent, all want these wrongs to be recognized, publicly, ritually, and sometimes financially. What I find alarming is not the attention we are asked to pay to the past. Without history, including its most painful episodes, we cannot understand who we are, or indeed who others are. A lack of historical sense means a lack of perspective. Without perspective we flounder in the dark and will believe anything, no matter how vile. So history is

---

Primo Levi: Italian chemist and writer who survived internment at Auschwitz.

good, and it is right that victims who died alone and in misery should be remembered. Also, some minorities are still being victimized—the Tibetans, for example. What is alarming, however, is the extent to which so many minorities have come to define themselves above all as historical victims. What this reveals, in my view, is precisely a lack of historical perspective.

Sometimes it is as if everyone wants to compete with the Jewish tragedy, in what an Israeli friend once called the Olympics of suffering. Am I wrong to detect a hint of envy when I read that Iris Chang, the Chinese-American author of a recent bestseller about the 1937 rape of Nanking, wishes for a Steven Spielberg to do justice to that event? (Her book bears the subtitle *The Forgotten Holocaust of World War II*.)° It is, it appears, not enough for Chinese-Americans to be seen as the heirs of a great civilization; they want to be recognized as heirs of their very own Holocaust. In an interview about her celebrity, Chang related how a woman came up to her in tears after a public reading and said that Chang's account of the massacre had made her feel proud to be Chinese-American. It seems a very peculiar source of pride.

Chinese-Americans are not the only ones to be prey to such emotions. The idea of victimhood also haunts Hindu nationalists, Armenians, African-Americans, American Indians, Japanese-Americans, and homosexuals who have adopted AIDS as a badge of identity. Larry Kramer's book on AIDS, for example, is entitled *Reports from the Holocaust*. Even the placid, prosperous Dutch, particularly those now in their teens and twenties, much too young to have experienced any atrocity at all, have narrowed down their historical perspective to the hardship suffered under German occupation in World War II. This is no wonder, since pre-twentieth-century history has been virtually abolished from the curriculum as irrelevant.

The use of Spielberg's name is of course telling, for the preferred way to experience historical suffering is at the movies. Hollywood makes history real. When Oprah Winfrey played a slave in the movie *Beloved,* she told the press, she collapsed on the set, crying and shaking. "I became so hysterical," she said, "that I connected to the raw place. That was the transforming moment. The physicality, the beatings, going to the field, being mistreated every day, was nothing compared to the understanding that you didn't own your life." And remember, this was just a movie.

My intention is not to belittle the suffering of others. The Nanking mas- 10 sacre, during which tens and perhaps hundreds of thousands of Chinese were slaughtered by Japanese troops, was a terrible event. The brutal lives and violent deaths of countless men and women from Africa and China who were traded as slaves must never be forgotten. The mass murder of Armenians in the Ottoman Empire cannot be denied. Many Hindu temples and Hindu lives were destroyed by Muslim invaders. Women and homosexuals have been discriminated against. The recent murder of a gay college student in Laramie, Wyoming, is a brutal reminder of how far we have yet to go. And whether or not they are right to

---

For an excerpt from this book, see pages 167–192.

call Columbus a mass murderer on his anniversary day, there is no doubt that the American Indians were decimated. All this is true. But it becomes questionable when a cultural, ethnic, religious, or national community bases its communal identity almost entirely on the sentimental solidarity of remembered victimhood, for that way lies historical myopia and, in extreme circumstances, even vendetta.

Why has it come to this? Why do so many people wish to identify themselves as vicarious victims? There is of course no general answer. Histories are different, and so are their uses. Memories, fictionalized or real, of shared victimhood formed the basis of much nineteenth-century nationalism. But nationalism, though not always absent, does not seem to be the main driving force for vicarious victims today. There is something else at work. First there is the silence of the actual victims: the silence of the dead, but also of the survivors. When the survivors of the Nazi death camps arrived in Israel on rusty, overloaded ships, shame and trauma prevented most of them from talking about their suffering. Victims occupied a precarious place in the new state of Jewish heroes. It was as though victimhood were a stain that had to be erased or overlooked. And so by and large the survivors kept quiet. A similar thing happened in Western Europe, particularly in France. De Gaulle built a roof for all those who had come through the war, former resistants, Vichyistes, *collabos,* Free French, and Jewish survivors: Officially all were citizens of eternal France, and all had resisted the German foe. Since the last thing French Jews wanted was to be singled out once again as a separate category, the survivors acquiesced in this fiction and kept quiet.

Even though the suffering of Japanese-Americans, interned by their own government as "Japs," cannot be compared to the destruction of European Jews, their reaction after the war was remarkably similar. Like the French Jews, they were happy to be reintegrated as citizens and to blanket the humiliation they had suffered with silence. The situation in China was more political. Little was made in the People's Republic of the Nanking massacre because there were no Communist heroes in the Nationalist capital in 1937. Indeed, there had been no Communists there at all. Many of those who died in Nanking, or Shanghai, or anywhere in southern China, were soldiers in Chiang Kai-shek's army. Survivors with the wrong class or political backgrounds had enough difficulty surviving Maoist purges to worry too much about what had happened under the Japanese.

It was left up to the next generation, the sons and daughters of the victims, to break the silence. In the case of China, it took a change of politics: Deng Xiaoping's open-door policy toward Japan and the West had to be wrapped in a nationalist cloak; dependency on Japanese capital was compensated for by stabs at the Japanese conscience. It was only after 1982 that the Communist government paid any attention to the Nanking massacre at all. But leaving China aside for the moment, why did the sons and daughters of other survivors decide to speak up in the sixties and seventies? How do we explain the doggedness of a man like Serge Klarsfeld, whose father was killed at Auschwitz and who has done more than any Frenchman to bring the history of French Jews to public notice?

There is a universal piety in remembering our parents. It is a way of honoring them. But remembering our parents, especially if their suffering remained mute and unacknowledged, is also a way of asserting ourselves, of telling the world who we are. It is understandable that French Jews or Japanese-Americans wished to slip quietly into the mainstream by hiding their scars, as though their experiences had been like everyone else's, but to their children and grandchildren this was not good enough. It was as if part of themselves had been amputated by the silence of their parents. Speaking openly about the communal suffering of one's ancestors—as Jews, Japanese-Americans, Chinese, Hindus, etc.—can be a way of "coming out," as it were, of nailing the colors of one's identity to the mast. The only way a new generation can be identified with the suffering of previous generations is for that suffering to be publicly acknowledged, over and over again. This option is especially appealing when few or indeed no other tags of communal identity remain, often precisely because of the survivors' desire to assimilate. When Jewishness is reduced to a taste for Woody Allen movies and bagels, or Chineseness to Amy Tan novels and dim sum on Sundays, the quasi-authenticity of communal suffering will begin to look very attractive.

The Harvard scholar K. Anthony Appiah made this point beautifully in   15
an analysis of identity politics in contemporary America ("The Multiculturalist Misunderstanding," *New York Review of Books,* Oct. 9, 1997). The languages, religious beliefs, myths, and histories of the old countries tend to fade away as the children of immigrants become Americans. This often leads to defensive claims of Otherness, especially when there is little Otherness left to defend. As Appiah said about hyphenated Americans, including African-Americans, "Their middle-class descendants, whose domestic lives are conducted in English and extend eclectically from *Seinfeld°* to Chinese takeout, are discomfited by a sense that their identities are shallow by comparison with those of their grandparents; and some of them fear that, unless the rest of us acknowledge the importance of their difference, there soon won't be anything worth acknowledging." He goes on to say that "the new talk of 'identity' offers the promise of forms of recognition and of solidarity that could make up for the loss of the rich, old kitchen comforts of ethnicity." Alas, however, those forms too often resemble the combination of kitsch and death described by Saul Friedlander. Identity more and more rests on the pseudo-religion of victimhood. What Appiah says about ethnic minorities might even be applied to women: The more emancipated women become, the more some extreme feminists begin to define themselves as helpless victims of men.

But surely nationalities are not the same as ethnic minorities in America, let alone women. Indeed, they are not. By and large, people of different

---

Seinfeld: A popular television comedy in the 1990s.

nations still speak different languages, have different tastes in food, and share distinct histories and myths. These distinctions, however, are becoming fuzzier all the time. To a certain extent, especially in the richer countries, we are all becoming minorities in an Americanized world, where we watch *Seinfeld* while eating Chinese takeout. Few nations are defined by religion anymore, even though some, such as Iran and Afghanistan, are busy reviving that definition. And national histories, celebrating national heroes, are abolished in favor of social studies, which have replaced national propaganda based on historical continuity with celebrations of contemporary multiculturalism. Literary canons, though perhaps less under siege in Europe than they are in the United States, are also becoming increasingly obsolete. Combined with a great deal of immigration to such countries as Britain, Germany, France, and Holland, these developments have eroded what kitchen comforts of ethnicity remained in European nation-states.

Perhaps the strongest, most liberating, and most lethal glue that has bound national communities together is the way we choose or are forced to be governed. Some nations have been defined mainly by their political systems. The United States is such a place. Sometimes politics and religion are combined in monarchies. Nowhere is politics entirely devoid of irrational elements: Customs, religion, and historical quirks all leave their marks. It was an extreme conceit born of the Enlightenment and the French Revolution that political utopias could be based on pure reason. Nationalism, in the sense of worshipping the nation-state as an expression of the popular will, was part of this. Politics was destined to replace the bonds of religion, or region, or race. This did some good. It also did a great deal of harm. The twin catastrophes of communism and fascism showed how dangerous it is to see the nation-state as a pure expression of the people's will. In any event, the ideological split between left and right, which was spawned by the division in the French National Assembly in 1789 and was eventually hardened by the cold war, effectively collapsed with the end of the Soviet Union. And the effects of global capitalism and multinational political arrangements, especially in Europe, have to some extent undermined the perception that nations are defined by the way they are governed. It doesn't seem to matter anymore how they are governed: decisions always appear to be made somewhere else. The current English obsession with the culture of Englishness has come just at the time of increasing integration into European institutions.

So where do we go in this disenchanted world of broken-down ideologies, religions, and national and cultural borderlines? From a secular, internationalist, cosmopolitan point of view, it may not seem such a bad world. That is, of course, if one is living in the wealthy, liberal West. It is surely good that nationalistic historical narratives have been discarded, that homosexuals can come out and join the mainstream, that women can take jobs hitherto reserved for men, that immigrants from all over the world enrich our cultures, and that we are no longer terrorized by religious or political dogma. A half-century of secular, democratic, progressive change has surely been a huge success. We have finally been liberated from irrational ethnic comforts. And yet, after all that, a growing number of people seek to return to precisely such comforts, and the form they often take is the pseudo-religion of kitsch and death. Tom Segev argues that the modern Israeli tendency to turn the Holocaust into a civic religion is a reaction against secular Zionism. The "new man"—socialist, heroic, pioneering—turned out to be inadequate. More and more, people want to rediscover their historical roots. To be serious about religion is demanding, however. As Segev says, "Emotional and historical awareness of the Holocaust provides a much easier way back into the mainstream of Jewish history, without necessarily imposing any real personal moral obligation. The 'heritage of the Holocaust' is thus largely a way for secular Israelis to express their connection to Jewish heritage."

The same is true for many of us, whether Jewish, Chinese-American, or whatnot. The resurgence of Hindu nationalism in India, for instance, is especially strong among middle-class Hindus, who are reacting against the Nehruvian° vision of a socialist, secular India. Since many urban, middle-class Hindus have only a superficial knowledge of Hinduism, aggressive resentment of Muslims is an easier option. And so we have the peculiar situation in India of a majority feeling set upon by a poorer, much less powerful minority. But there is a larger context too, particularly in the West. Just as the Romantic idealism and culture worship of Herder and Fichte° followed the secular rationalism of the French *philosophes,* our attraction to kitsch and death heralds a new Romantic age, which is antirational, sentimental, and communitarian. We see it in the politics of Clinton and Blair, which have replaced socialist ideology with appeals to the community of feeling, where we all share one another's pain. We saw it in the extraordinary scenes surrounding the death of Princess Diana, when the world, so TV reporters informed us, united in mourning. Princess Diana was in fact the perfect embodiment of our obsession with victimhood. Not only did she identify with victims, often in commendable ways, hugging AIDS patients here and homeless people there, but she was seen as a suffering victim herself: of male chauvinism, royal snobbery, the media, British society, and so on. Everyone who felt victimized in any way identified with her, especially women and members of ethnic minorities. And it says something about the state of Britain, changed profoundly by immigration, Americanization, and Europeanization, yet unsure of its status in Europe, that so many people felt united as a nation only when the princess of grief had died.

This sharing of pain has found its way into the way we look at history, too. Historiography is less and less a matter of finding out how things really were or trying to explain how things happened, for not only is historical truth irrelevant, but it has become a common assumption that there is no such thing. Everything is subjective or a sociopolitical construct. And if the civics lessons

20

Nehruvian: From Jawaharlal Nehru, prime minister of India (1950–64).
Herder and Fichte: German philosophers Johann Gottfried von Herder (1744–1803) and Johann Gottlieb Fichte (1762–1814).

we learn at school teach us anything, it is to respect the truths constructed by others, or, as it is more usually phrased, the Other. So we study memory, that is to say, history as it is felt, especially by its victims. By sharing the pain of others, we learn to understand their feelings and get in touch with our own.

Vera Schwarcz, a professor of East Asian studies at Wesleyan University, recently wrote a book entitled *Bridge Across Broken Time,* in which she links her own memories as the child of Jewish Holocaust survivors with those of Chinese victims of the Nanking massacre and the violent crackdown in 1989 in Tiananmen Square. With images of 1989 fresh in her mind, Schwarcz visits Yad Vashem, the Holocaust memorial outside Jerusalem. There she realizes

> the immensity both of the suffering that could not be commemorated in China after 1989 and of the Nanking Massacre of 1937 with its countless dead that had yet to become imprinted upon communal memory in Japan and the United States. I also sensed the magnitude of my own loss that could not be assuaged by the light of a candle, even if it was reflected one million times.

Now, I don't doubt the nobility of Professor Schwarcz's sentiments, but I do wonder whether this sort of thing—even Maya Angelou's poetry makes a cameo appearance in her book—is enlightening in any historical sense. In fact it is ahistorical, because the actual experiences of historical victims get blended in a kind of soup of pain. Although it is undoubtedly true that Chinese, Jews, gays, and others have suffered, it is not so that they all suffered in the same way. The distinctions tend to get lost. It is all too typical of our neo-Romantic age that a well-known Dutch ballet dancer and novelist named Rudi van Dantzig should announce in a pamphlet issued by the Resistance Museum in Amsterdam that homosexuals and other minorities in the Netherlands should take anti-Nazi resisters as models for their struggle against social discrimination.

But enlightenment is probably not the issue here. Instead there is authenticity. When all truth is subjective, only feelings are authentic, and only the subject can know whether his or her feelings are true or false. One of the most remarkable statements along these lines was written by the novelist Edmund White. In an article about AIDS literature (*The Nation,* May 12, 1997), he argues that literary expressions of the disease cannot be judged by critical standards. As he puts it, a trifle histrionically, "I can scarcely defend my feelings beyond saying that it strikes me as indecent to hand out grades to men and women on the edge of the grave." He then stretches AIDS literature to encompass multiculturalism in general, and states not only that multiculturalism is incompatible with a literary canon but that "I'd go even further and say multiculturalism is incompatible with the whole business of handing out critical high and low marks." In other words, our critical faculties cannot be applied to novels, poems, essays, or plays expressing the pain of Others. As White says about the AIDS genre, "We will not permit our readers to evaluate us; we want them to toss and turn with us, drenched in our night sweats."

What makes us authentic, then, as Jews, homosexuals, Hindus, or Chinese, is our sense of trauma, and thus our status as victims, which cannot be questioned. The vulgar Freudianism of the view is remarkable in an age of debunking Freud. In fact, Freud's endeavors were themselves a brilliant product of late-nineteenth-century identity politics. To secular, bourgeois, assimilated German and Austrian Jews, psychoanalysis was a logical route to self-discovery. What Freud did for his Viennese patients is in a way what Edmund White and other identity politicians are now doing for their various "communities," and real politicians are borrowing their language.

Apart from the sentimentality that this injects into public life, the new religions of kitsch and death are disturbing for other reasons. Vera Schwarcz's talk of building bridges between mourning communities notwithstanding, I think the tendency to identify authenticity in communal suffering actually impedes understanding among people, for feelings can only be expressed, not discussed or argued about. This cannot result in mutual understanding, but only in mute acceptance of whatever people wish to say about themselves, or in violent confrontation. The same is true of political discourse. Ideology has caused a great deal of suffering, to be sure, particularly in political systems where ideologies were imposed by force. But without any ideology, political debate becomes incoherent, and politicians appeal to sentiments instead of ideas. And this can easily result in authoritarianism, for again, you cannot argue with feelings. Those who try are denounced not for being wrong but for being unfeeling, uncaring, and thus bad people who don't deserve to be heard.   25

The answer to these problems is not to tell people to go back to their traditional places of worship, in an attempt to supplant pseudo-religions with established ones. I am not opposed to organized religion on principle, but as a secular person myself it is not my place to promote it. Nor am I against building memorials for victims of wars or persecution. The decision by the German government (subject to parliamentary approval) to build a Holocaust museum in Berlin is laudable, because it will also contain a library and document center. Without such a center, it would just be a colossal monument. In the new plan, memory will go together with education. Literature, of fact and fiction, about individual and communal suffering should have its place. History is important. Indeed, there should be more of it. And it would be perverse to take issue with the aim of fostering tolerance and understanding of other cultures and communities. But the steady substitution of political argument in public life with the soothing rhetoric of healing is disturbing.*

So how do we deal with this? We can make a start toward resolving the problem by drawing distinctions where few are made now. Politics is not the same as religion or psychiatry, even though it may be influenced by both.

---

*But it is hard to see which ideologies will bring some clarity back to politics. The prevailing ideology in the United States is market liberalism. Free trade in an unstable global market is breeding discontents. But its opponents, on the right and the left, have yet to come up with a coherent alternative.

Memory is not the same as history, and memorializing is different from writing history. Sharing a cultural heritage is more than "negotiating an identity." It is perhaps time for those of us who have lost religious, linguistic, or cultural ties with our ancestors to admit to that and let go. Finally, and I think this goes to the heart of the matter, we should recognize that truth is not just a point of view. There are facts that are not made up but real. And to pretend there is no difference between fact and fiction, or that all writing is fiction, is to paralyze our capacity to distinguish truth from falsehood. And that is the worst betrayal of Primo Levi and all those who suffered in the past. For Levi's fear was not that future generations would fail to share his pain, but that they would fail to recognize the truth.

QUESTIONS FOR DISCUSSION

1. Why does Buruma believe that minorities should not base their identities on their perception of themselves as victims?
2. According to Buruma, what motivates people to see themselves as victims even if they have not been victimized in their own lives?
3. Where does Buruma establish that he respects the suffering of others, and why is it useful for him to make this point?
4. Consider Buruma's definition of *kitsch* in paragraph 4. What examples of kitsch can you find in popular culture?
5. According to Buruma, "We cannot imagine the victims' torment, but we believe it." How is it possible to believe what we cannot imagine?
6. Why is it important to know history? How does history differ from memory?

SUGGESTIONS FOR WRITING

1. Write an essay in which you explain a positive aspect of your communal identity (as determined by race, religion, geography, gender, sexual orientation, or social class).
2. What role does "victimhood" play in American politics today? Write an essay explaining why a specific group of Americans considers itself to be victims.
3. Research how the victims of terror or war can be helped, and explain the kind of treatment that seems most effective.

LINKS ■ ■ ■

■ WITHIN THE BOOK

For other views of victims, see "Conveying Atrocity in Image" by Barbie Zelizer (pages 428–438).

(continues)

LINKS ■ ■ ■ *(continued)*

■ **ELSEWHERE IN PRINT**

Appiah, K. Anthony. "The Multiculturalist Misunderstanding." *New York Review of Books,* 9 Oct. 1997: 30–36.

Buruma, Ian. *Images of Guilt: Memories of War in Germany and Japan.* New York: Farrar, 1994.

---. *The Missionary as the Liberator: Love and War in East and West.* New York: Farrar, 1991.

Levi, Primo. *The Periodic Table.* New York: Schocken, 1995.

Segev, Tom. *The Seventh Million: The Israelis and the Holocaust.* New York: Hill, 1994.

■ **ONLINE**

- Holocaust History Project
  <http://www.holocaust-history.org>

- Israeli Ministry of Education
  <http://www.info.gov.il/eng/mainpage.asp>

- Primo Levi
  <http://www.inch.com/~ari/levi1.html>

HITLER AND THE OCCULT: THE MAGICAL THINKING OF ADOLF HITLER°

Raymond L. Sickinger

In 1918, Adolf Hitler was a corporal in the German army. Fifteen years later, he was leader of Germany and beginning a period in which he would come to dominate most of Europe and parts of North Africa. When seeking to understand why Hitler gained so much power, historians point to numerous factors—among them, harsh economic conditions in Germany and Hitler's willingness to use illegal force to subdue opposition. Nevertheless, the question remains: "Why Hitler?" How did he become one of the most powerful people in the world when there were other potential leaders who were better educated and more experienced in both the military and the government? And why were Germans moved by rhetoric that was often crude and repetitive? In "Hitler and the Occult: The Magical Thinking of Adolf Hitler," Raymond L. Sickinger argues that, although Hitler did not have supernatural powers, he could nevertheless have a magical effect on others—and that "magical thinking" accounts for some of his successes as well as his ultimate destruction.

Sickinger teaches history at Providence College in Providence, Rhode Island. In 2000, he published the following article in the Journal of Popular Culture, *a journal that publishes scholarly articles about issues, products, and events that reflect the interests of the general public. As you read, note how he draws on the work of other historians but nevertheless offers his own interpretation of the information in question.*

Because the name Adolf Hitler evokes so many images and provokes so many responses, it is difficult, if not impossible, to sort through them and arrive at the real Hitler. Hitler's character and career, however, have remained consistently popular subjects.[1] Many people have tried to give insights into his character and personality. But some of the most controversial have been those writers who have claimed a strong connection between Hitler and occult practices. In fact, over the past thirty years two radically different positions on the subject have formed. The first group of writers generally ignored, rejected, or downplayed the relationship of Hitler and occult knowledge, while the second argued that such a connection was the only way to understand the true power of Hitler.

The first group includes some of the major biographers of Hitler: Bullock, Toland, and Fest. Alan Bullock rejected any suggestions that Hitler was fascinated with occult knowledge and practices. He maintained that there was

---

This piece illustrates the use of MLA-style documentation. For a discussion of MLA style, see pages 38–44 and 47.

no "evidence to substantiate the once-popular belief that he resorted to astrology. His secretary says categorically that he had nothing but contempt for such practices, although faith in the stars was certainly common among some of his followers like Himmler." According to Bullock, "Hitler was a rationalist and materialist. [. . .] What interested Hitler was power, and his belief in Providence or Destiny was only a projection of his own sense of power" (389–90). Yet he still made references to Hitler's "magic" and to his "magic circle" (563, 722, 776), suggesting that even Bullock may have perceived an inexplicable side of Hitler.

Unlike Bullock, John Toland documented some of Hitler's superstitious beliefs and practices. Laying the cornerstone of a modern art museum in Munich during the fall of 1933, Hitler broke a silver hammer when he struck the cornerstone with it. According to Toland, "There was an awkward silence because of a superstition that the architect would die if the hammer broke. Goebbels tried to make light of it. [. . .] But it was no joke to Hitler, who was convinced that it was a bad omen." Interestingly, the architect, Troost, was hospitalized a few days later and died within a few months (Toland 296, 384, 565). Toland also recounted a Teutonic Divination Ceremony which took place early in the morning of January 1, 1939, and which involved the pouring of molten lead in water to determine the future. In his view, "Hitler did not seem satisfied with his results, for afterwards he sat down in an armchair, gazing dejectedly at the fire, and hardly spoke for the rest of the evening" (695).

Although Toland revealed a superstitious side of Hitler, he did not support claims of any greater occult interests or powers. For example, after describing Hitler's body language lessons provided by Erik Jan Hanussen, "one of the most renowned seers and astrologists in Europe," Toland reported that Hitler asked Hanussen to cast his horoscope. The horoscope indicated certain "hindrances to his rise to power" that could be removed only by "a mandrake (a root in the shape of a man) found in a butcher's yard in the town of Hitler's birthplace by the light of the full moon." But whether or not Hitler gave any credence to what Hanussen said was openly questioned by Toland. H. R. Knickerbocker's interview with Dr. Carl Gustav Jung° was also treated in Toland's work. Jung expressed his conviction that Hitler was like a shaman; his power was magic. Toland, however, made no comment about whether or not he accepted Jung's thesis. As regards matters of astrology, Toland was clear that "astrological speculation concerning the Führer° was *verboten*.°" Moreover, although Hess and Himmler experimented with a variety of esoteric, occult practices, Toland argued that Hitler did not approve of such things (384–85, 682, 806, 909, 1047).

The third biographer, Joachim Fest, rejected "that school of thought which attributes superhuman abilities to Hitler." According to Fest, Hitler's "career depended not so much on demonic traits as on his typical, 'normal' characteristics. The course of his life reveals the weaknesses and ideological

5

Carl Gustav Jung: Influential Swiss psychiatrist (1875–1961).
Führer: German for "leader."
verboten: German word for "forbidden."

bias of all the theories that represent Hitler as a fundamental antithesis to the age and its people. He was not so much the great contradiction of the age as its mirror" (Fest 7). To be sure, Fest made references to Hitler's "demagogic magic," his "mediumistic powers," his "magical self-reassurance," and his "phrases from the realm of magic" (149, 367, 646), but these Fest used primarily for emphasis and dramatic effect; they were not to be taken literally.

Unlike the first group, the second group of writers posited the undeniable connection between Hitler and the occult. Included in this latter group are Louis Pauwels, Jacques Bergier, Jean-Michel Angebert, Dusty Sklar, and Trevor Ravenscroft. In the mystical, and sometimes esoteric, work entitled *The Morning of the Magicians,* Pauwels and Bergier chastised historians for reducing "one of the most fantastic episodes of contemporary history to the level of an elementary history lesson on evil instincts." To understand fully Hitler and the Nazi Movement, both argued that historians must decide "to abandon our positive way of looking at things and try to enter a Universe where Cartesian reason and reality are no longer valid" (133, 139). Claiming that Hitler believed in "a magic relationship between Man and the Universe,"[2] Pauwels and Bergier contended that Hitler wanted "to bring about, by scientific or pseudo-scientific means, a return to the beliefs of a bygone age according to which Man, Society and the Universe all obey the same Laws, and there is a close connection between soul-states and the movements of the stars" (209, 172).

In *The Occult and the Third Reich: The Mystical Origins of Nazism and the Search for the Holy Grail,* Jean-Michel Angebert[3] described the roots of the Nazi Movement:

> It is, therefore, an analysis of National Socialist thought by way of the labyrinth of esoteric tradition that we propose to the reader. The central theme being Gnosis,° with its most significant thrust represented by the prophet Mani, its evolution necessarily brings us to Catharism, a neo-Gnostic sect of the Middle Ages, and thence to Templarism. Subsequently, Gnosis goes underground, degenerating with the Rosicrucians and the Illuminati of Bavaria, and finally culminates, after many detours, in the mysterious Thule Society.

Portraying Hitler as an initiate of the Thule Society, this work maintained that Hitler eventually became the "new imperial Messiah" and "the master of the Third Reich, an adept in that black magic in which he had been initiated." Hitler's mesmerizing powers did not surprise Angebert, because the Führer "doubtless owes it to his Bavarian origins. Southern Germany is a hotbed of mediums [. . .] and other occultists [. . .] born, like Adolf Hitler, in the little town of Branau-am-Inn" (53, 160, 232).

In the hands of Dusty Sklar, Hitler emerged as a person with a "penchant for the occult." Maintaining that the Viennese bookseller Ernst Pretzsche "introduced Hitler to consciousness-expanding drugs, as well as to astrological

---

Gnosis: Understanding spiritual truths intuitively—from the Gnostics, an early Christian sect who believed that a select few could transcend matter.

and alchemical symbolism," Sklar emphasized that "[b]y daring to break taboos against acts which would disgust other people, one might gain powers of which ordinary men did not dream." She concluded that "Hitler's later reputation for unnatural practices [. . .] may well have been deserved." Hitler's will to power, according to Sklar, "has not been given its proper due. [. . .] But this early will to power betrays the interests of a potential occultist." After examining Hitler's youth and career, she was convinced that Hermann Rauschning's memorable assessment of Hitler was accurate:

> Black magic, white magic—Hitler is the typical person with no firm foundation, with all the shortcomings of the superficial, of the man without reverence, quick to judge and quick to condemn. He is one of those with no spiritual tradition, who, being caught by the first substitute for it that they meet, hold tenaciously to that, lest they fall back into Nothingness. [. . .] For all those who have been unsuccessful in the battle of life National Socialism is the great worker of magic. And Hitler himself is the first of these; thus he has become the master-enchanter and the high priest of the religious mysteries of Nazidom.

For Sklar there was no doubt that Hitler was the "supreme magician" (16, 23–24, 49, 125).[4]

Of all the writers in this second group, the most controversial was Trevor Ravenscroft. In his highly popular work, *The Spear of Destiny,* Ravenscroft contended that the Holy Lance which pierced Christ's side was the "talisman of power" and "was to become the central pivot in the life of Adolf Hitler and the very source of his ambitions to conquer the world." According to this account, when, as a young man, Hitler first saw the lance, he thought it was "some sort of magical medium of revelation. [. . .] 'I felt as though I myself had held it in my hands before in some earlier century of history—that I myself had once claimed it as my talisman of power and held the destiny of the world in my hands.'" While viewing the lance in the Hapsburg museum, the young Hitler had a vision of his future role in service to the Superman. The person to whom Hitler confided this story was an associate of Ravenscroft, Dr. Walter Stein, who insisted that he had numerous conversations with Hitler and who in turn reported them to Ravenscroft. The latter, however, made no formal notes of these talks. Moreover, Ravenscroft asserted that Hitler entered into an occult world of magic which was the key to his power. In his view, Dietrich Eckart introduced Hitler to a "world of cosmology and magic" in the Thule Society, recognizing Hitler as the Anti-Christ who would eventually control the power of the lance. During the *Anschluss*° in 1938, Hitler seized the lance and its powers for his own and transported it and other treasures to Nuremberg. In fact, Ravenscroft clearly believed that Hitler wanted magical power and that "monstrous sexual perversion was the very core of his whole existence, the source of

---

Anschluss: German for "connection" or "union"; used to describe Germany's annexation of Austria in 1938.

his mediumistic and clairvoyant powers and the motivation behind every act through which he reaped a sadistic vengeance on humanity" (xx–xxi, 8–9, 60–61, 92, 155, 160, 315–16, 330).

Most of the claims of the second group of authors are intriguing, but gen- 10
erally unsubstantiated. In fact, a recent work by an Australian journalist, Ken Anderson, ripped apart the claims of Ravenscroft and other occult historians. In Anderson's view, it is necessary "to reject claims that Hitler had supernatural powers of his own [. . .]. The occult influences he is said to have been open to [. . .] are unproven [. . .] and he remains an enigma! However, allowing false and fanciful claims about Hitler to go unchallenged will not help to unwrap that enigma" (233–36).

There is, however, a third position that needs to be considered. Must we either accept completely or reject completely the thesis that Hitler had super-natural powers? Can we instead suggest that Hitler thought and acted in a magical way and that he found a magical approach to difficult problems to be efficacious rather than insist that Hitler really had supernatural powers? It is this latter thesis that needs to be explored further, because one of the best ways to gain insight into Hitler and to interpret his actions both before and during the war is to understand that he thought and acted in a magical way.

It has already been indicated by one biographer that Hitler had a super-stitious nature (Toland 565, 695), and there is little doubt that Hitler's person-ality was one prone to "believing in magic" (Vyse 25–57). In his youth, Hitler lived in a fantasy world. For example, Hitler had a fantasy relationship with a young girl named Stephanie Jansten. Although Hitler never directly commu-nicated with her, he believed in their common destiny. In Toland's words, Hitler "was immersed [. . .] in Norse and German mythology where the women were anything but ordinary, and he probably had a romanticized, knightly concept of all things sexual. No prosaic introduction for this young Siegfried!° Fantasy built on fantasy" (30–31). As Hitler's friend, August Kubizek, stated in his recollections: "For such exceptional human beings as himself and Stephanie, he said, there was no need for the usual communica-tion by word of mouth; extraordinary human beings would understand each other by intuition. [. . .] This mixing of dream and reality is characteristic of the young Hitler" (58–69). Such "intuition" would later become a hallmark of Hitler's thinking and the inspiration for many of his decisions.

Although Kubizek commented that Hitler "was absolutely skeptical about occultism and more than rational in these matters," he also gave further insights into the development of magical thinking in his friend. Hitler con-vinced Kubizek to join him in the purchase of a lottery ticket. He was certain that they would win: "Never did it occur to Adolf to reproach himself for having taken for granted that the first prize belonged to him by right." In another recollection, Kubizek shared his belief that Hitler would "prefer to

---

Siegfried: A character in operas by Richard Wagner (1813-83) initially believed to be invincible and capable of recovering the lost treasure of his people.

stick to his wishful thinking rather than unbosom himself with real people." Neither did Hitler have an open mind nor did he engage in critical reflection: "I never felt [. . .] that he was seeking anything concrete in his piles of books, such as principles and ideas for his own conduct; on the contrary, he was looking only for confirmation of those principles and ideas he already had." While listening to Wagner, Adolf willingly "let himself be carried away into the mystical universe which was more real to him than the actual workaday world" (93–95, 129, 184, 191–92). These descriptions are not just those of an aimless young dreamer; they represent a form of magical thinking in which the world is thought to be manipulated by will.

A wartime report developed for the Allies during World War II includes information which not only corroborates Kubizek's statement about Hitler's lack of critical reflection but which also reinforces this point about magical thinking:

> [Hitler] does not think out in a logical and consistent fashion, gathering all available information pertinent to the problem, mapping out alternative courses of action, and then weighing the evidence pro and con for each of them before reaching a decision. His mental processes operate in reverse. Instead of studying the problem as an intellectual would do, he avoids it and occupies himself with other things until unconscious processes furnish him with a solution. Having the solution he then begins to look for facts that will prove that it is correct. [. . .] [But he] becomes dependent on his inner guide, which makes for unpredictability on the one hand and rigidity on the other. (Langer 74–75)

His wartime experiences from 1914 to 1918 had reinforced these magical elements in his personality. Hitler saw front-line action and frequently volunteered for dangerous duty. Saved at least once, if not more times, by his "inner voice" or intuition, Hitler came to believe that he was blessed, that he was earmarked by Providence for a special mission. There was some kind of magical destiny for him (Toland 79–97).

In his early life, Hitler indeed thought and acted in a magical way and his   15
experiences taught him to trust, rather than to discredit, this magical approach to life. For many people, however, the word "magic" unfortunately raises images of Houdini and other illusionists. Although Hitler was certainly a master of illusion, that is not the meaning intended here. The magical tradition has very deep roots in the human past. Magic was once an essential part of life and certainly an essential part of political life, because its primary purpose was to give human beings power: "As a belief, [magic] is the recognition of the existence of occult power, impersonal or only vaguely personal, mystically dangerous and not lightly to be approached, but capable of being channeled, controlled, and directed by man. As a practice, magic is the utilization of this power for public or private ends." In the magical tradition, the role of the person who practices magic or acts magically is clearly defined. That designated person identifies or predicts "what is otherwise hidden in time or in

space from human eyes; he influences and manipulates the objects and phenomena of nature and all creatures so that they may satisfy actual or assumed needs; and, finally, he combats, neutralizes, and remedies the onslaught of evils, real or imaginary, afflicting mankind." The extent of magic is "almost as wide as the life of man. All things under heaven, and even the inhabitants of heaven, become the subject of its sway" (Webster 55).

This description perfectly fits the role of Der Führer. He claimed to know *what is otherwise hidden*. According to Werner Maser, "Hitler [. . .] was convinced that he had discovered and grasped what historians and philosophers had sought for millennia—the 'eternal course of history'. [. . .] early on he came to see himself as a political genius, as someone who had lifted the veil of history and discovered the final truth" (280). *Mein Kampf*° was just one of the ways Hitler revealed what was hidden; his speeches were another. As Fest indicated, "Significantly, he trusted inspiration more than he did thought and genius more than diligence. [. . .] 'Geniuses of the extraordinary type,' he remarked, with a side glance at himself, 'can show no consideration for normal humanity'" (531). Ernst Roehm was also quick to recognize this magical trait in Hitler: "What he wants is to sit on the hilltop and pretend he's God. [. . .] He wants to let things run their course. He expects a miracle" (qtd. in Rauschning 153–54). Although highly critical of Hitler, Hermann Rauschning gave witness to Hitler's tendency to act as if he were providing profound revelations into mysteries: "Pronounced with the authority of the recognized leader [. . .] , such *dicta* [. . .] gave the impression of deep revelations. [. . .] He regarded it as belittling of his stature if we mentioned similar opinions [. . . and] was unaware that the ideas that seemed to him to be mysterious inspirations were the product of the general intellectual outlook." According to Rauschning, Hitler believed that a "new age of magic interpretation of the world is coming, of interpretation in terms of the will and not of the intelligence." Hitler was the voice of that new age (223–25).

Hitler claimed to be able to *manipulate the objects and phenomena of nature and all creatures in order to satisfy needs*. His twenty-five-point program for the Nazi Party in 1920 and his *Mein Kampf* in 1923 constituted his magic formula for the ills and the needs of his Germany. Throughout his career he remained faithful to most of these original principles, because a true magician never deviates from the formula or the precise set of rituals needed to achieve the desired result.[5] In fact, Hitler was quite adamant about fidelity to the formula:

> Therefore, the program of the new movement was summed up in a few guiding principles, twenty-five in all. [. . .] the so-called *program of the movement* is absolutely correct in its ultimate aims, [. . .] but in the course of time the conviction may well arise that in individual instances certain of the guiding principles ought perhaps to be framed differently. [. . .] Every attempt to do this, however, usually works out

---

Mein Kampf: German for *my struggle,* the title of Hitler's political manifesto, published in 1925.

catastrophically. For in this way something which should be unshake-able is submitted to discussion. (Hitler, *Kampf* 458)

Hitler finally claimed that he was the person who *combats, neutralizes, and remedies the onslaught of evils, real or imaginary, afflicting mankind.* The Jews in particular became the chief scapegoat (Webster 54)[6] for all of Germany's problems—past, present, and future. They were the most significant "taboo." In a magical world, "Crises are generally engendered by breaches of taboo" (Balikci 199). As Robert Waite remarks, "'The Jew' was the single, simple answer to all problems. Who had stabbed Germany in the back during the war and caused disastrous defeat? Who had signed the armistice? [. . .] Who had accepted the 'Treaty of Shame'? Who were the profiteers and exploiters who caused the inflation and the Great Depression? The answer was clear and compelling; 'always and only the Jew!'" (368). In a speech in Munich on July 28, 1922, Hitler contended that "[t]he Jew has never founded any civilization, though he has destroyed hundreds. [. . .] In the last resort it is the Aryan alone who can form States and set them on their path to future greatness. [. . .] the Jew [. . .] with his envious instinct for destruction [. . .] seeks to disintegrate the national spirit of the Germans and to pollute their blood."[7] Hitler believed that he was "called" and that he was the only one to save Germany from this evil threat (Toland 197).

The famous Swiss psychologist Carl Gustav Jung recognized that Hitler thought and acted magically. As indicated earlier, Toland's biography included Jung's insights. But the actual interview was conducted by an American journalist named H. R. Knickerbocker in 1941. In this interview, Jung defined the nature of Hitler's power:

> There were two types of strong men in primitive society. One was the chief who was physically powerful, [. . .] and another was the medicine man who was not strong in himself but was strong by reason of the power which the people projected into him. [. . .] Hitler belongs in the category of the truly mystic medicine man. His body does not suggest strength. The outstanding characteristic of his physiognomy is its dreamy look. I was especially struck by that when I saw pictures taken of him in the Czechoslovakian crisis; there was in his eyes the look of a seer.

Knickerbocker further questioned Jung about Hitler's powerful effect upon Germans and his inability to impress many foreigners in the same way. Jung was quick to respond: 20

> It is because Hitler is the mirror of every German's unconscious. But of course he mirrors nothing from a non-German. [. . .] Hitler's power is not political; it is magic. To understand magic you must understand what the unconscious is. It is that part of our mental constitution over which we have little control and which is stored with all sorts of impressions and sensations; [. . .] Now the secret of Hitler's power is [. . .] twofold; first, that his unconscious has exceptional access to his con-

sciousness, and second, that he allows himself to be moved by it. He is like a man who listens intently to a stream of suggestions in a whispered voice from a mysterious source, and then acts upon them. In our case, [. . .] we have too much rationality, [. . .] to obey it—but Hitler listens and obeys. (Knickerbocker 45–47)

In the ancient world, the medicine man or the shaman served a political function by advising political leaders. In fact, in the shamanistic, magical tradition, the shaman is said to possess special insights and mystical visions, but is too unstable to be handed the reins of power (Cavendish 1: 63). As described by Richard Cavendish,

> The shaman or sorcerer-priest [. . .] is frequently classed as a psychopath. In spirit he flies up to heaven, descends to hell, and dives to the nethermost regions of the sea. He receives messages from the dead, communes with spirits. But his mental balance is insecure and he is easily "unhinged." If suddenly angered or startled he loses his self-control completely. His eyes redden and bulge out, his face goes through the most hideous contortions, and unless restrained he will not hesitate to maim or to murder the person who provoked him.

Such a person is believed to be touched by the divine and to have special insights and magical powers which can be very valuable to the community in which he lives. Considered holy, he brings healing to those who are sick and protects the whole community from evil (12: 1765, 1678).

Does Jung's description of Hitler have any merit? There are indeed similarities between Hitler and the medicine man/shaman of magical lore. Rauschning attested that Hitler "is simply a sort of great medicine-man. He is literally that, in the full sense of the term. We have gone back so far toward the savage state that the medicine-man has become king among us." He further observed that "it is the Shaman's drum that beats round Hitler. Asiatic, African cults and bewitchments are the true element of his spell, and furious dances to the point of exhaustion. The primitive world has invaded the West" (Rauschning 259). There were others who attested to this shaman-like quality: "For us this man was a whirling dervish. But he knew how to fire up the people, not with arguments, [. . .] but with the fanaticism of his whole manner, screaming and yelling, and above all by his deafening repetition, and a certain contagious rhythm. This he has learned to do and it has a fearfully exciting and barbaric effect" (Zuckmayer 384). Kubizek once referred to Hitler as a person of "ecstatic creativeness" (200). Apparently some German people saw what Jung had seen.

As Rauschning pointed out, what is peculiar is that Hitler seemed to combine the role of political leader and shaman. The Führer, a title which is vague in definition, mystical in quality, and magical in its powers, highlights this very point. No one questioned the insight of a shaman. No one questioned Der Führer. Hitler's anger, like the anger of the magical shaman, was notorious. He would lash out, sometimes verbally, sometimes physically, against those who questioned his insights, insights often derived from no official sources of authority (Waite 8–10). His fluctuation between laziness and bursts of energy were also shaman-like (Waite 42; Fest 535). In earlier periods of time, a shaman could be ignored or appeased by a leader, but his words were never absolute commands. With Hitler, however, the visions and magic formulae of the shaman become absolute commands. The shaman was now the leader who divined the future.

Essential to magic is the power of words. In magical theory, just as someone of strong personality can use words to control other people, "so the magician armed with the lightning of concentrated will–power and the thunder of overwhelming language can dominate anything in the universe. [. . .] 'In magic,' according to the French magician Eliphas Levi, '[. . .] to affirm and will what ought to be is to create; to affirm and will what ought not to be is to destroy.' " The person who utters the words must have a very strong will and the words that he utters must be valid by virtue of being revered as sacred by time and tradition (Cavendish 11:1418). There is no doubt that Adolf Hitler believed in the magic power of words. As he said in *Mein Kampf,* "But the power which has always started the greatest religious and political avalanches in history rolling has from time immemorial been the magic power of the spoken word, and that alone" (107). He believed that if he uttered the same message over and over that it would become reality. His speeches were like incantations. A magician delivering an incantation does so with a rising intensity as he proceeds: "This contributes to a rising state of intoxication, in which the magician convinces himself that the words he utters are charged with invincible power and are actually taking effect. [. . .] the words are put together deliberately [. . .] and are rhythmical. [. . .] their impressive sound and beat influence the supernatural forces which he attempts to control" (Cavendish 11: 1419–20). Hitler's speeches exhibited this same quality. Heinz Haushofer recalled: "It was terrible [. . .] shouting and arm waving. He was not interrupted. He just spoke and spoke, like a record in a groove, for an hour or an hour and a half until he became absolutely exhausted [. . .] and when he was finished and breathless, he just sat down once more a simple and nice man" (Toland 284). Hitler's speeches repeated the same themes again and again. And his voice would rise with excitement, sweeping his audience along with him. The businessman Kurt Ludecke described his response to a speech by Hitler: "Presently my critical faculty was swept away. [. . .] The intense will of the man, the passion of his sincerity seemed to flow from him into me. I experienced an exaltation that could be likened only to a religious conversion. I felt sure that no one who had heard Hitler that afternoon could doubt that he was a man of destiny, the vitalizing force in the future of Germany" (Ludecke 13–14; Fest 323–24). The power of Hitler's words was indeed magical.

Ritual is still another important dimension of the magical tradition. 25 Doing things in a precise way is an essential part of successful magic. By nature Hitler was a man of ritual. According to Robert Waite, "Intimates all agreed that Hitler's daily routine was followed to the smallest detail. As chancellor, when taking his dog for a walk, Hitler went through the same field every time, and each time he threw a piece of wood from exactly the same spot in exactly the same direction. Any attempt to persuade him to deviate from the pattern would result in considerable agitation and anger on his part" (15). Hitler wanted to maintain control; ritual gives a person a sense of control, while magic ritual promises actual control. The yearly Nuremburg rallies provide an excellent example of ritual which was intended to produce magical results. The use of special symbols, fire, incense, repetition of phrases and words were all intended to do just what magic ritual intends to do: to control nature, humans, even the divine forces, and ultimately to give Hitler power (Toland 492–97).[8]

The presence of Hitler and his personal will was essential to the whole ritual process. As one historian of the supernatural notes, "If the magician is not present (and not only physically but emotionally present) he can achieve nothing. For this reason, spells and incantations tend to look inert and meaningless when printed, like a cross between a cookbook and the jottings of a madman" (Hill and Williams 138–39). Hitler was fanatical about his role. Everything was orchestrated carefully; no detail was left to chance. The 1938 rally captured on film by Leni Riefenstahl gives ample evidence of the power of ritual and the importance of Hitler's role. It is indeed a magical ceremony at which Hitler presides and to which he brings the full force of his will and emotions (Bullock 379; Toland 492–97). Without the presence of Hitler, there would be no future for Germany. In fact, there would simply be no Germany. As Hitler once remarked, "I must in all modesty say that my own person is indispensable. Neither a military nor a civilian personality could replace me [. . .]. I am convinced of the strength of my brain and my resolution [. . .]. The fate of the Reich is dependent entirely upon me" (Waite 46).

For magic to work, it needs a receptive audience whose members believe in its efficacy. There is evidence that Hitler's Germany provided him with such an audience. As H. G. Baynes pointed out in 1941, Hitler's "apparent belief in his own divine gift lends him an arrogant air of certainty which had a paralyzing effect upon the suggestible minds of the Germans" (Baynes 16). Otto Strasser remarked on Hitler's uncanny ability to connect with his audience: "A clairvoyant, face-to-face with his public, goes into a trance. That is his moment of real greatness [. . .]. He believes what he says; carried away by a mystic force, he cannot doubt the genuineness of his mission." Strasser likened Hitler to a wireless receiving set which enabled him, "with a certainty with which no conscious gift would endow him, to act as a loudspeaker, proclaiming the most secret desires, the least admissible instincts, the sufferings and personal revolts of a whole nation" (Strasser 62–66). Konrad Heiden in his introduction to *The Memoirs of Felix Kersten* (Heinrich Himmler's masseur) declared that in Germany between the wars, there were "so many 'miracles' performed, so many ghosts conjured, so many illnesses cured by magnetism, so many horoscopes read" that it seemed like a "veritable mania of superstition had seized the country, and all those who made a living by exploiting human stupidity thought the millennium had come."[9] Germany was ripe for such a person, because it was ripe for magical thinking.

Hitler not only had an audience open to his magical thinking, but his magical solutions also seemed to be successful in practice. Success confirmed to him the genuineness of his approach. As a result, Hitler learned not to question his way of thinking, but rather to blame those who were unfaithful to following it precisely.[10] And his success was based in part on his magical belief that he could divine the future.[11] Believing that he knew the future of Germany, Hitler thought that he could lead the German people into the future, if they would only listen to and obey him. In fact, it was this confidence about knowing the future that created tensions with the German military. For example, Hitler's attempt to remilitarize the Rhineland was opposed by the military. The military feared that the army was not ready for any retaliation from the French and British. Hitler, however, believed that success comes to the daring and he proved to himself that his instincts were superior. This incident convinced Hitler that his insight into the future outcome of present actions was sound: "You can serve God only as a hero [. . .]. I go the way that Providence dictates with the assurance of a sleepwalker" (Toland 525–31). Hitler moved his foreign policy forward with intensity. By March of 1939, Hitler had obtained many of the foreign policy objectives he had proposed as early as the 1920s for the regeneration of Germany. This repeated success reinforced Hitler's belief that he had a special "intuition" and could predict the future: "I am [. . .] convinced that the secret of the greatest successes in history was that based, not on human logic, but on inspirations of the moment. [. . .] intuition [. . .] plays a major part [. . . in] politics, statecraft, and military strategy."[12] Yet Hitler could still be apprehensive under the right set of circumstances. On August 24, 1939, Hitler met with a group of trusted people at *Eagle's Nest* above Berchtesgaden. While watching a display of northern lights that night, Hitler saw an omen in the predominantly red light cast on him and his friends. He indicated to an aide that the omen clearly meant that without force, Germany would not make it this time (Toland 752). Within a few short days, the invasion of Poland occurred and World War II had begun.

By the time war broke out in 1939, Hitler was firmly in control of the army, because he trusted only his own insights. In February of 1938, Hitler became the official supreme commander-in-chief of the armed forces. He created the Oberkommando der Wehrmacht (OKW), which served as his military staff under his direct command. The air force and the navy were already subject to him. By December of 1941, Hitler assumed control of the army as commander-in-chief and imposed strategy on the Oberkommando des Heeres (OKH), the Army High Command. Hitler had virtually complete control of military affairs and he was in large part responsible for the successes of 1939 and 1940 (Fest 625–34). Most historians concede that he had some military talents.[13] But his successes in 1939 and 1940 were his undoing. He believed that his willpower was sufficient; he merely had to will what he wanted to happen and it would happen (Spielvogel 222; Toland 762; Wagener 150–154). By 1941, according to Fest, Hitler was "sustained by the certainty [. . .] that Providence presided over all his decisions. This growing effort to invoke irrational support strikingly reflected his state of uneasiness. Quite often his gestures of magical self-assurance occurred as abrupt interjections in matter-of-fact conversations" (647). By 1942 Hitler even turned his thoughts to India and had already planned a vast naval base at Trondheim to serve future needs (Lewin 34; Toland 891). This is clearly a magical, not a rational, approach to wartime operations.

This approach became even more pronounced after 1942. Hitler would not allow retreat, because retreat would indicate that his insights and his magic formula for Germany were not infallible. Any deviation from his plans, like the deviation from a precise set of magic rituals, would spell disaster, he thought. As the military historian, Ronald Lewin, argued, from June of 1943, "in the conduct of military operations [Hitler's] procedure was [. . .] irrational, holding-out-to-the-last, flawed conceptually and in execution because its pattern was shaped by the flaws in his own personality" (151). 30

There were numerous attempts to end Hitler's reign of power from 1938 to 1944, but all ended in failure. The last and, perhaps, most famous plot occurred during the end stages of the war in July of 1944. A huge explosion in the staff meeting room at Wolfschanze bruised and shook Hitler, but it did not kill him. His vengeance against the military personnel who were implicated was swift and brutal. The effect of each of these successful escapes from death only served to confirm Hitler's belief that he was a special person with magical power to control his fate and that of Germany. It also brought him sympathy from many Germans who did not support the resistance (Fest 707–15; Toland 1092–1127; Bullock 743–52).[14]

Hitler ended his career in a grand magical gesture, remaining consistent to the last. Hitler was fascinated with the theories of Dr. Hörbiger, who talked of the universe as the creation of the conflict between fire and ice (Hitler, *Secret Conversations* 263). Perhaps he was attracted to this theory because it was so closely related to the Norse myth of creation (Hamilton 312–13). But the myth also promised a day of doom (Ragnarok), when the world and the gods would be destroyed by "Armaggedon, the destroying fire followed by the renewal of life." According to the myth,

> First will come [. . .] winters [. . .] accompanied by great wars throughout the whole world. Brothers will kill each other for the sake of gain, and no one will spare father or son in manslaughter or in incest. [. . .] The stars will disappear from heaven. [. . .] the whole surface of the earth and the mountains will tremble so [. . .] that the trees will be uprooted from the ground, mountains will crash down, and all fetters and bonds will be snapped and severed. [. . .] The wolf Fenfir will advance with wide open mouth [. . .] and his eyes and nostrils will blaze with fire. [. . .] fire will [be flung] over the earth and burn up the whole world.

Out of this universal destruction, however, will come new life and rebirth (Leeming 85–88). Hitler, the "fortunate wolf" (Toland 130–31),[15] knew the legends of German mythology, reading about them often in his early years (Kubizek 182; Waite 102) and was fascinated by the "interplay of destruction and creativity." Moreover, Hitler was "fascinated by fire [. . .]. He worked himself into a frenzy of delight over the pictures of great capitals of Europe in flames" (Waite 34). His insistence on a scorched-earth policy and on his own immolation represented a magical fulfillment of both the destruction and the hope of *Götterdämmerung,* "The Twilight of the Gods."° As Robert Waite has suggested, "in ordering the *Götterdämmerung* for his world, [. . .] Hitler envisaged himself as a Teutonic god fulfilling ancient myth" (425). In fact, a recent psychological study of suicide described it as a "magical act, actuated to achieve irrational, illusional ends" (Wahl 23). Whatever way you look at it, Hitler's last act was indeed a magical one.

In conclusion, the opposing claims of the two different camps of writers explored in this paper can be reconciled. We neither have to accept fully that Hitler had supernatural, occult powers, nor do we have to reject totally his connection with occult matters. Instead, we can view Hitler as a person who developed a pattern of magical thinking and who was confirmed in this kind of thinking by the successes which he was convinced were caused by it. As one scholar has noted of magical thinking, "Thus the belief in magic, far from appearing unreasonable and illogical to those who hold it, seems to be confirmed over and over again by the experiences of daily life" (Webster 489). Confident in his own ability to divine the future direction of Germany, Hitler had no need of astrologers and others who claimed special insights. In fact, such people were a genuine threat to his own power.[16] Moreover, interpretations of Hitler's foreign policy movements as a death wish and as a need to destroy (Waite 386–411) overlook the genuinely hopeful attitude of Hitler that his magical formula and his magical intuition would surmount all obstacles. As Fest noted, "We might say: only unreality made him real. In his comments to his entourage, even in those weary, toneless monologues in the last phase of the war, his voice became animated only when he spoke of the 'gigantic tasks,' the 'enormous plans' for the future. Those were his real reality" (677).

In 1942, Hitler remarked that if the German people lost faith in him, "if the German people were no longer inclined to give itself body and soul in order to survive—then the German people would have nothing to do but disappear" (*Secret Conversations* 210)! Less than one year before his suicide, Hitler expressed his faith that the "gods love those whom they ask the impossible and who ask the impossible of them."[17] Such delusions were fatal:

> Magic must rank among the greatest of man's delusions. In the presence of the unknown and the disconcerting the magician does not investigate critically, but is content with an explanation that appeals to imagination. He builds an airy fabric of fancy and discovers in the external world sequences of cause and effect which are nonexistent. He thinks

Götterdämmerung: An 1876 opera by Richard Wagner (1813–83).

that he understands them and, self-reliant and imperturbable, would turn them to his own benefit. [. . .] magical beliefs and practices have operated to discourage intellectual acquisitiveness, to nourish vain hopes that can never be realized, and to substitute unreal for real achievement. (Webster 506–7)

Such a person was Adolf Hitler. Until the bitter end, he deluded himself with the belief that he, and he alone, was Germany's magical savior.

NOTES

1. They have even been particularly popular features on the History Channel, which has also aired programs on Hitler's and the Nazi Party's connections with occult practices.
2. The quote is actually taken from Hermann Rauschning's statement: "It is impossible to understand Hitler's political plans unless one is familiar with his basic beliefs and his conviction that there is a magic relationship between Man and the Universe." Pauwels and Bergier think that he was one of the few to understand what was actually transpiring in Hitler's Germany.
3. The name Jean-Michel Angebert is a pen name formed from the names of two individuals who actually authored the work in question.
4. Sklar's quotation from Rauschning is found on p. 125.
5. Fest supports this view (122–24, 199–220) and so does Toland (12–130, 265–71). Bullock, however, does not view the twenty-five points as a program which Hitler would not alter. He actually claimed that Hitler was later embarrassed by them (74–77).
6. Ironically, a scapegoat was part of Jewish folklore and magic. To ward off evil or a demon, it would be driven into a goat by means of a ritual.
7. Quoted in Bullock 407. His statement about the Jews in 1922 is repeated nearly verbatim at later points in his career. See *Mein Kampf* 305–8. See also *Hitler's Secret Conversations* 97. Even at the very end of his life, the same message prevailed. See also Genoud 50–57.
8. According to Webster (77), "a magical rite normally involves a manual act, a verbal expression (spell or incantation), and the use of some material, inanimate object (charm or 'medicine') possessing occult power either original with it or ascribed to it." This description fits the "blood flag" ceremony, among others, performed by Hitler.
9. Quoted in Sklar 3. Heiden's points are certainly reinforced and developed more extensively in Rhodes.
10. To the very end this is true. His *Last Will and Testament* gives ample proof of this. See Genoud. See also Schwaab 143–45.
11. In the magical tradition, although shamans were considered too unpredictable to be entrusted with power, their potential to see into the future (to divine) was very valuable and was used by leaders to evaluate policies or tactics. See Cavendish 1: 63.
12. Quoted in Wagener. See also Toland 984, Anderson 113–20.
13. See Toland 745–46; Fest 63. Bullock (582) holds a lower view of Hitler on this score. For more discussion of Hitler as a military leader, see Gilbert, Schramm, Lewin.
14. See Hoffmann 135–47. See also Baigent and Leigh. Baigent and Leigh contend that Stauffenberg believed that Hitler was practicing "black magic" and saw the opposition to Hitler in grand mystical terms of good against evil.

15. This is the meaning of the name Hitler. For Hitler's interests in wolves, see Waite 26–27, 166–67, 425.
16. For an insight into the issue of astrologers and the Third Reich, see Wilhelm Wulff.
17. Speech of 5 July 1944 in Domarus 2 (4):2233; quoted in Maser 207–8.

WORKS CITED

Anderson, Ken. *Hitler and the Occult.* New York: Prometheus, 1995.

Angebert, Jean-Michel. *The Occult and the Third Reich: The Mystical Origins of Nazism and the Search for the Holy Grail.* New York: Macmillan, 1974.

Baigent, Michael, and Richard Leigh. *Secret Germany: Stauffenberg and the Mystical Crusade against Hitler.* London: Penguin, 1995.

Balikci, Asen. "Shamanistic Behavior among Netsilik Eskimos." *Magic, Witchcraft, and Curing.* Ed. John Middleton. American Museum Sourcebooks in Anthropology. New York: Natural History, 1967.

Baynes, H. G. *Germany Possessed.* London: Cape, 1941.

Bullock, Alan. *Hitler: A Study in Tyranny.* New York: Harper, 1964.

Cavendish, Richard, ed. *Man, Myth, Magic: An Illustrated Encyclopedia of the Supernatural.* 24 vols. New York: Marshall, 1970.

Domarus, Max, ed. *Hitler: Reden und Proklamationen 1932–1945.* 2 vols. in 4. Munich: Süddeutscher, 1965.

Fest, Joachim. *Hitler.* Trans. Richard and Clara Winston. New York: Vintage, 1975.

Genoud, François, ed. *The Testament of Adolf Hitler: The Hitler-Bormann Documents February–April 1945.* Trans. Colonel R. H. Stevens. London: Cassell, 1959.

Gilbert, Felix, ed. *Hitler Directs His War.* New York: Oxford UP, 1950.

Hamilton, Edith. *Mythology.* New York: NAL, 1962.

Hill, Douglas, and Pat Williams. *The Supernatural.* New York: Hawthorn, 1965.

Hitler, Adolf. *Hitler's Secret Conversations 1941–1944.* Trans. Norman Cameron and R. H. Stevens. New York: Farrar, 1953.

---. *Mein Kampf.* Trans. Ralph Manheim. Boston: Houghton, 1971.

Hoffmann, Peter. "Generals and the German Resistance." *The Nazi Revolution.* Ed. Allan Mitchell. Boston: Heath, 1997.

Knickerbocker, H. R. *Is Tomorrow Hitler's?* New York: Reynal, 1941.

Kubizek, August. *The Young Hitler I Knew.* Trans. E. V. Anderson. Boston: Houghton, 1955.

Langer, Walter. *The Mind of Adolf Hitler: The Secret Wartime Report.* New York: Stein, 1972.

Leeming, David Adams. *The World of Myth.* New York: Oxford UP, 1990.

Lewin, Ronald. *Hitler's Mistakes: New Insights into What Made Hitler Tick.* New York: Morrow, 1984.

Ludecke, Kurt. *I Knew Hitler.* New York: Scribner's, 1937.

Maser, Werner. *Hitler's Letters and Notes.* Trans. Arnold Pomerans. London: Heinemann, 1974.

Pauwels, Louis, and Jacques Bergier. *The Morning of the Magicians.* Trans. Rollo Myers. New York: Stein, 1964.

Rauschning, Hermann. *The Voice of Destruction.* New York: Putnam's, 1940.

Ravenscroft, Trevor. *The Spear of Destiny.* York Beach: Weiser, 1982.

Rhodes, James M. *The Hitler Movement: A Modern Millenarian Revolution.* Stanford: Hoover, 1980.

Schramm, Percy. *Hitler: The Man and the Military Leader.* Trans. and ed. Donald S. Detwiler. Chicago: Quadrangle, 1971.

Schwaab, Edleff H. *Hitler's Mind: A Plunge into Madness.* New York: Praeger, 1992.

Sklar, Dusty. *The Nazis and the Occult.* New York: Dorset, 1989.

Spielvogel, Jackson J. *Hitler and Nazi Germany: A History.* 3rd ed. Englewood Cliffs: Prentice-Hall, 1996.

Strasser, Otto. *Hitler and I.* Trans. Gwenda David and Eric Mossbacher. Boston: Houghton, 1940.

Toland, John. *Adolf Hitler.* New York: Doubleday, 1977.

Vyse, Stuart A. *Believing in Magic: The Psychology of Superstition.* New York: Oxford UP, 1997.

Wagener, Otto. *Hitler: Memoirs of a Confidant.* Ed. Henry Ashby Turner, Jr. Trans. Ruth Hein. New Haven: Yale UP, 1985.

Wahl, Charles William. "Suicide As a Magical Art." *Clues to Suicide.* Ed. Edwin S. Schneidman and Norman L. Farberow. New York: McGraw, 1957. 22–30.

Waite, Robert G. L. *The Psychopathic God: Adolf Hitler.* 1977. New York: Da Capo, 1993.

Webster, Hutton. *Magic: A Sociological Study.* 1948. New York: Octagon, 1973.

Wulff, Wilhelm. *Zodiac and Swastika: How Astrology Guided Hitler's Germany.* New York: Coward, 1973.

Zuckmayer, Carl. *Als wär's ein Stück von mir.* Frankfurt: Fischer, 1966.

QUESTIONS FOR DISCUSSION

1. Before offering his own views, Sickinger summarizes the views of other historians. What does he accomplish by doing so? Are there any risks to using this strategy?
2. What does Sickinger mean by "magical thinking"?
3. Why would anyone think that Hitler "thought and acted in a magical way"?
4. What is the difference between magic as a "belief" and magic as a "practice"?
5. What role does rhetoric play in magic?
6. In paragraph 18, Sickinger quotes anti-Semitic statements by Hitler without responding to them. What do you think of Hitler's words? Why do you think Sickinger choose to let these words speak for themselves?
7. Sickinger claims that magic requires "a receptive audience whose members believe in its efficacy." Drawing upon your knowledge of history, what events could have made Germans receptive to Hitler's message?
8. What are the dangers of magical thinking?

SUGGESTIONS FOR WRITING

1. Sickinger claims that as supreme commander-in-chief of the German military, Hitler "was in large part responsible" for Germany's success early in the war but made bad military decisions after 1940. Research how Hitler waged war and then explain why his military thinking was flawed.
2. Interest in the occult has resurfaced in recent years. Write an essay explaining why some Americans are drawn to magical thinking and practice.
3. In paragraphs 21–25, Sickinger discusses the work of Carl Jung. Research Jung and explain why his work has appealed to psychoanalysts.

LINKS ■ ■ ■

■ WITHIN THE BOOK

As a young man, Hitler saw himself as a victim, and he later encouraged Germans to believe that they were victims of World War I. In "The Joys and Perils of Victimhood" (pages 246–255), Ian Buruma discusses what happens when people see themselves as victims of Hitler and other oppressive rulers.

■ ELSEWHERE IN PRINT

Eliade, Mircea. *Occultism, Witchcraft, and Cultural Fashions: Essays in Comparative Religions.* Chicago: U of Chicago P, 1978.
Jung, Carl. *The Basic Writings of Carl Jung.* Ed. Violet De Laszlo. Trans. R. F. C. Hull. Princeton: Princeton UP, 1991.
Redlich, Fritz. *Hitler: Diagnosis of a Destructive Prophet.* New York: Oxford UP, 1998.
Rosenbaum, Ron. *Explaining Hitler: The Search for the Origins of His Evil.* New York: Random, 1998.
Weinberg, Gerhard L. *Germany, Hitler, and World War II: Essays in Modern German and World History.* Cambridge: Cambridge UP, 1995.

■ ONLINE

- Brief Biography
  <http://homer.providence.edu/web/schools/PCI/his/rsicking/rsicking.html>
- Occult Beliefs and Nazi Politics
  <http://users.powernet.co.uk/orion/aryan.htm>
- The Swastika and the Nazis
  <http://www.intelinet.org/swastika>

4

Writing to Evaluate Something

When you are trying to decide whether you want to buy a wool sweater or a cotton one, when you bet your brother that your team will win the game this weekend, when you decide which dictionary to buy or make a decision to vote for a particular candidate—when you do any of these things, you are *evaluating*. Evaluating means thinking critically so that you can make intelligent choices—and, when you make your evaluation public, influence others to accept your judgments.

Evaluation requires that you determine the nature or the quality of what you are judging. For instance, if you decide to consume less caffeine, that decision is probably based on a judgment that caffeine can be bad for you. Your purchase of a name-brand lawn mower rather than a store brand rests on your evaluation of the quality of the two brands to assure yourself that you will have a reliable, well-made machine; in this situation your concern is with quality. Evaluation also means determining importance, benefit, or worth. For example, importance would be the issue if you were trying to determine which in a long list of tasks you absolutely had to get done before the weekend. You are concerned with benefit if you decide that a course in art history would be more useful to you as an architecture major than would a course in music history. When you buy a house or a car, you will most likely ask yourself if it is worth what you have to pay for it.

In the preceding examples, you are trying to convince yourself of something. But there will be plenty of times when your evaluation must convince someone else: Which supplier should you recommend to your employer? What should you say when asked to write a letter of recommendation? Whose opinion should prevail when a couple disagree about which of two apartments to rent? Addressing situations like these means you have to define your assumptions, anticipate opposition, and draw conclusions.

When writing an evaluation, you also need to assure your readers that you have the credentials to make judgments about the subject you're addressing. Demonstrating that you know what you're talking about is essential if you want your readers to take your evaluation seriously. The more your readers think you know about your subject, the more likely they are to follow your advice. But no matter how knowledgeable you may be, try not to sound as if you have a monopoly on good advice. People can take perverse pleasure in not following the advice of a critic who seems arrogant. Consider how Mark Twain just barely avoids the charge of arrogance in his essay on James Fenimore Cooper. Much of Twain's credibility rests on his own reputation as a master of the craft of fiction; but he also disposes readers to agree with his attack on Cooper by allowing his trademark folksy tone to show through. Thinking, "This person who seems so unpretentious couldn't possibly be an ill-tempered, arrogant boor," many readers acquit Twain and find Cooper guilty as charged. Like Twain, you can often benefit from sounding engaging as well as knowledgeable. Although the extent to which you allow your personality to come through will depend on your rhetorical situation, evaluations are seldom impersonal.

PLANNING YOUR ESSAY

When you are ready to choose a subject for evaluation, consider what you have some experience in and knowledge of, as well as what you are interested in. If you are knowledgeable about a subject, you will usually have a good idea of what criteria people use when evaluating it. This knowledge will help you focus on how to make your evaluation satisfy your readers' needs. For example, if you recently bought a stationary exercise bicycle for home use and think that your written evaluation of the available models will help others decide which one to buy, make sure you don't base your evaluation only on which bicycle is cheapest. Readers also need to know what they are getting for their money. Report what you know about features such as mileage counters and tension adjustment; then discuss how well different bikes perform and how likely they are to hold up under use. Otherwise, a reader may wind up with a bicycle that was cheap because it lacked important features or because it was difficult to use.

If you have the time to do research, writing an evaluation can be an excellent way to prepare for a decision you need to make. Thus, if you are planning to buy exercise equipment but cannot decide between a stationary bicycle and a stair stepper, you can use evaluation as a way to decide what to buy. Careful shoppers go through this process routinely. They may visit a number of stores, question salespeople and friends who have experience with the product, and—if the purchase is large—search for information on the World Wide Web or go to the library and consult one or more of the magazines available for consumers. Writing an evaluation of a product you expect to purchase is a way of discovering and reporting the results of this process.

In this chapter, an article from *Consumer Reports* on bottled water illustrates how shoppers can benefit from evaluations of a product based on factors such as cost and taste. Similarly, a review by Dara Moskowitz shows how an evaluation can help diners decide whether or not to try a specific restaurant and, if they go, what to order. But, as the article by Jonathan Rowe demonstrates, the evaluation of a product does not have to focus on the cost and features of the product itself. In "Reach Out and Annoy Someone," Rowe evaluates cell phones by discussing the consequences of using them in public. He finds that cell phones have harmful effects regardless of which brand is being used—a very different approach from evaluating several specific models to determine which to buy. You could write an evaluation along these lines by deciding to discuss the effects of such products as coffee, computer games, or sport utility vehicles.

Writing to evaluate can also help readers to understand the merits of a particular activity or the product that results from that activity. In "She: Portrait of the Essay as a Warm Body," Cynthia Ozick discusses why she likes to read and write essays. She is not trying to convince readers that one essayist is better than another or that writing essays is better than writing fiction. Instead, she focuses on why essays are worth reading and writing by offering a positive evaluation of what can be accomplished through this kind of nonfiction. If you are interested in writing an evaluation along these lines, you might consider subjects such as the merits of a particular type of music or the benefits of studying chemistry. You could also address subjects such as these when writing to understand experience (as in Chapter 1). But in that case, the emphasis would be on experience involving the subject rather than the subject itself. In "Levi's" (pages 57–59), for example, Marilyn Schiel focuses on what a pair of jeans meant to her as a child—which is different from evaluating the quality of Levi's or evaluating the impact of jeans on American culture. When writing to evaluate, you need to focus on the subject itself—as you would when writing to report information or writing to interpret information (see Chapters 2–3). Your experience with that subject may be part of the evaluation you compose, but you should emphasize the subject rather than yourself (unless you are the subject, as in a self-assessment required by a teacher or employer).

Writers like Moskowitz, Rowe, and Ozick all use a kind of **cause-and-effect analysis** (see pages 293–295 and 307–318) when evaluating their subjects. Other situations require other strategies. But whatever your subject, you should examine what kind of information you have about it and assess whether you have to do research. Information is essential, because you must support your evaluation with specific evidence. For instance, when evaluating a novel by James Fenimore Cooper, Twain supports the claims he makes with evidence from the novel. But he also places his evaluation in a critical context by demonstrating, at the beginning of his essay, that he is familiar with prevailing views on Cooper. His evaluation thus required reading more than one text. Similarly, Susanna Kaysen needed to obtain copies of her medical records and consult a medical handbook to evaluate the accuracy of the diagnosis she received when hospitalized for mental illness. And when doing research on Bing Crosby, Gary Giddins listened to "more than 2,000 recordings (including radio broadcasts)" in addition to consulting print sources ranging from an

1899 issue of *Popular Science Monthly* to a memoir written by Crosby's eldest son. Whatever strategy you need to employ when preparing to write an evaluation, be sure to present readers with enough information so they can decide whether your judgment is worth taking seriously.

A good way to begin an evaluation is to think about your subject analytically. (See pages 203–204.) Here is a four-step process for using analysis to plan an evaluation:

1. Divide your subject by identifying its major components. For example, if you are evaluating a movie, you might address plot, acting, and special effects. Or if you are evaluating a book, you can judge it according to content, style, and organization.

2. Consider what information you have (or can obtain) to discuss the divisions you have identified.

3. Ask yourself which of these divisions are most likely to be important to readers, and consider whether you have overlooked any important part of your subject that your readers would probably want information about. Unless you are writing for your own benefit, eliminate any division that seems to be a personal interest unlikely to concern other readers.

4. Decide whether to discuss all the important divisions that you have identified or to focus on only one if you have enough information about it and feel sure that you would be focusing on something important. An evaluation of a restaurant, for example, can be limited to a discussion of its food (although you would probably end up subdividing that subject somehow—according to appetizers, entrees, and desserts or according to selection, presentation, and taste).

When planning an evaluation, you should also consider how strongly you feel about your subject. Some people believe that you should always write about something you have a real investment in, because your enthusiasm will make your writing lively. Others think this approach leads to one-sided evaluation. If you've just bought a new car and really love it, you may lack the objectivity to evaluate it fairly. But if you've driven the car for a year and still love it, you probably have enough distance from your purchase to offer a balanced judgment. One of the strengths of Dara Moskowitz's "The Sad Comedy of Really Bad Food" is that she looks for things to praise even though she's disappointed by the restaurant she's reviewing. When you read her evaluation, you will find that she made several visits to the restaurant in question to make sure that her evaluation was fair.

DEFINING YOUR CRITERIA

Effective, accurate evaluations are not the result of whim; they are based on standards that most people agree with, that the authority of the writer bolsters, or that can be independently verified. Evaluation requires you to make the criteria you use for judging absolutely clear—as Twain does when he provides a list of eighteen "rules governing literary art." Clear criteria can also be found in almost any issue of *Consumer Reports*—criteria involving tangible qualities (such as size and price) and functional criteria (such as performance and reliability). If an article in this magazine declares that brand X is both less expensive and more reliable than brand Y, you might purchase brand X because these criteria are important to you. But if price does not concern you and performance matters more than reliability, you might decide to purchase brand Y. In either case, you would be basing your decision on a combination of personal values and information obtained through empirical testing in a research laboratory. Moreover, you might be guided by the evaluation you read in *Consumer Reports* because you came to that article with a positive evaluation of the magazine itself—an evaluation based on another set of criteria that may or may not be verifiable. If someone is trying to sell you a product that received a poor evaluation in *Consumer Reports,* that person might challenge the magazine's reliability.

In many cases, a writer's criteria are implied by the evaluation without being specifically stated. When reviewing a restaurant in Minneapolis, Dara Moskowitz complains about the service, the atmosphere, and the quality of most of the food she sampled—while praising the wine list and several desserts. From this, we can infer that she appreciates being offered a nice selection of wine and desserts but places greater emphasis on service, atmosphere, and the quality of the menu as a whole—hence her negative review of the restaurant in question. In other words, her implicit criteria are that a restaurant should offer good food and good service in a pleasant setting. Another writer with different criteria (such as the size of the servings or whether or not the restaurant draws a fashionable crowd) could come to a different assessment of the same place. As a general rule, subjective criteria, which are based on someone's values, are easier to challenge than objective criteria, which can be confirmed through empirical testing. But an evaluation based on subjective criteria can be persuasive if the evaluator seems well informed and fair minded. (For additional information on persuasion, see pages 497–509.)

Whether subjective or objective, criteria should be appropriate for your audience. Suppose that your criterion for evaluating a magazine for entrepreneurs is that each issue should include an article on how to dress in the workplace. This criterion is inappropriate because entrepreneurs are more likely to be interested in how to acquire capital, attract clients, and generate profits. Similarly, if you base your judgment of stocks on which ones will double your money the fastest, your standard is inappropriate for advising retirees whose primary interest in stocks is securing a safe income. Or to take another example, if you are evaluating local housing for an audience of college students who want to party, you will not want to rate housing higher because playgrounds and day-care facilities are available, whereas that information could be vital for married couples or single parents. You should set criteria you think your readers will agree with—or at least will not reject.

Examine your criteria and ask yourself if they justify the evaluation you plan to make. You may be furious at one of the local apartment complexes for charging you two months' rent as a deposit because you have a pet, but your sense of having been victimized is not necessarily a legitimate criterion for giving that complex a negative rating in your guide to local housing. It would be much better to simply state the policy; perhaps other prospective tenants would not object to such a high deposit—or may even approve of it. Base your evaluation of the apartment complex on more objective criteria. For example, what is the rent per square foot? Are the apartments furnished? What appliances are included? Is there a fireplace? What kind of storage is available? Does the rent include access to a swimming pool and party facility? Have there been complaints about how the complex is maintained? What about late-payment policies?

You also need to consider the kind of evidence that will persuade your audience to accept your evaluation. If you want the single students on campus to accept your negative evaluation of the apartment complex with the high deposit for pets, you might consider investigating what the management's policies about parties are, whether guests can use the pool, and how management handles summer sublets. If these policies are strict, single students should be informed, and they may choose to rent elsewhere, even though there is a great party room, every unit has a fireplace, and the rent is reasonable. You should offer evidence according to what you think your readers expect to find out and how knowledgeable they are. It is rare that any subject will elicit the kind of universal agreement that will permit you to use the same criteria and information for all audiences.

Readers expect to find enough information to reconstruct the reasoning you used to arrive at your evaluation. Be sure to provide adequate information for readers unfamiliar with the subject you are evaluating. When readers are unfamiliar with a complex subject, a thorough evaluation can take many pages. But whatever the level of expertise your audience possesses, you are responsible for making sure they understand the information you give them— and the criteria you are using to interpret that information—so the judgment you reach will be both clear and credible.

ORGANIZING YOUR ESSAY

However you choose to proceed, you should state your judgment clearly and place it prominently. It is your main point and, depending on other decisions you have made, may appear near the beginning or the end of your piece. Generally, it is useful to put it in both places. By placing it near the beginning, you prepare readers for the conclusion you will draw; by placing it near the end, you demonstrate how specific evidence has led to that conclusion. It is also usually wise to show your readers that you have considered both the strengths and the weaknesses of your subject. To do so, you may wish to adapt the following pattern of classical oration for evaluations:

- Present your subject. (This discussion includes background information, description, acknowledgment of weaknesses, and so forth.)
- State your criteria. (If your criteria are controversial, be sure to justify them.)
- Make your judgment. (State it as clearly and emphatically as possible.)
- Give your reasons. (Be sure to present evidence for each one.)
- Refute opposing evaluations. (Let your reader know you have given thoughtful consideration to opposing views, when they exist.)
- State your conclusion. (Restate your judgment, and make recommendations for improvement if your evaluation is negative.)

Notice that the refutation comes near the end, after the judgment is well established. An alternative strategy is to refute opposing evaluations early in the essay; this strategy can be especially effective when opposing views are already widely held and you intend to advance a new point of view. In this case, recognizing views that your audience may already hold can clear the way for a fresh evaluation. This is the strategy Twain used when writing about Cooper at a time when Cooper was much praised. (For additional information on refutation, see pages 506–508.)

When deciding how to present your evaluation, you should also consider the possibility of developing your position through the use of **comparison or contrast.** Comparative judgments focus on similarities, and contrasting judgments focus on differences, but the two can be combined. In any comparison or contrast, you must find a point of significant similarity between what you are evaluating and another item. In this chapter, *Consumer Reports* compares and contrasts several different kinds of bottled water, Gary Giddins compares and contrasts Bing Crosby and Frank Sinatra, and Cynthia Ozick contrasts the nature of an essay with the nature of fiction. In an essay of your own, you might incorporate comparison or contrast into almost any plan that you choose for organizing your ideas.

In some cases, however, you may find it helpful to organize an entire essay in terms of a comparison or contrast. Doing so is especially useful when the purpose of your evaluation is to help you—and your audience—make a choice between different products or options, as in deciding which of two cars to buy or which of two schools to attend. This strategy can also be useful when evaluating the abilities of different people, as in deciding which of two teachers to recommend or determining which of two senators is doing the better job of representing your state. If you want to use comparison or contrast as the primary means for organizing your evaluation, you might use one of two common patterns for arranging comparisons and contrasts to organize your evaluation: (1) subject by subject or (2) point by point.

When two subjects are evaluated in a subject-by-subject pattern, the first subject is discussed thoroughly before the second is discussed at all. In a point-by-point pattern, both subjects are discussed throughout the essay, with the discussion organized around different aspects (or points) of evaluation. If you want to evaluate the pizza served at two local restaurants, for example, you might use a subject-by-subject approach and complete your discussion of the first restaurant before beginning your discussion of the second. But if you are comparing two subjects with many components, then you might choose a point-by-point comparison. A comparison of two similar cars made by different manufacturers might be organized along the following lines: standard features of both vehicles, available options for both vehicles, performance of both vehicles, and reliability of both vehicles. This kind of organization has the advantage of not requiring the reader to keep the whole subject in mind, but the frequent switches between the subjects compared can sometimes seem choppy. Only one switch is necessary in subject-by-subject comparison, but readers must keep a whole subject in mind. For a long or complicated comparison, this can become difficult.

Comparison and contrast are by no means limited to evaluations; elsewhere in this book, you will find writers using these strategies for other motives. But comparison and contrast are especially useful for evaluation, because placing two subjects alongside each other can lead to a better understanding of both—and can often help you decide whether one is superior. If offered two different jobs, both of which seem attractive, you can probably clarify which is preferable by comparing them carefully.

It would be a mistake, however, to assume that evaluation must always lead to a rating of some sort. Although criticism usually leads to a judgment on quality or worth, it is also concerned with improving our knowledge of what is being evaluated. In this chapter, "Bing Crosby: The Unsung King of Song" provides the clearest example of how evaluation can be informative. Believing that Crosby "is the ideal figure for tracking the rise of popular culture," Gary Giddins provides extensive information about Crosby's success as a singer and film star. Moreover, he locates this success within a historical context by discussing other singers who were popular during Crosby's long career. A critic reviewing a book or movie in a newspaper is expected to give the work an overall rating, because that is what newspaper readers most want to know: Is this work worth reading or seeing? But evaluation isn't always a matter of getting people to do (or not do) something. Sometimes it's simply devoted to getting people to see something that they might otherwise miss, as in Cynthia Ozick's tribute to the essay. Understanding that there is more to something than we had realized can lead us to reappraise our valuation of it, even if we do not need to make a choice or decide upon a specific action (as, for example, by reading more essays or buying Bing Crosby's CDs).

As we have seen before, motives for writing can overlap. You will usually need to report and interpret information to show readers how you reached a particular judgment—and if you want your evaluation to be persuasive, you may need to draw on some of the strategies discussed in the introduction to Chapter 7. The selections that follow in this chapter were chosen to give you a sense of different types of evaluation. As you read them, try to evaluate the extent to which each succeeds in accomplishing what it sets out to do.

IT'S ONLY WATER, RIGHT?

Consumer Reports

Bottled water has become increasingly popular in the United States. Indeed, it is not unusual to see urban Americans carrying bottled water with them as move through the day—so water bottles now frequently appear in the hands not only of walkers and bicy-clists but also of shoppers wandering into stores and students showing up for class. The following evaluation by a much-trusted consumer magazine evaluates several brands for taste, purity, and price. The article was first published in 2000. As you read, think about what the public consumption of bottled water says about American values and manners.

Consumer Reports is available both in print and online from Consumers Union, which describes itself as "an independent, nonprofit testing and information organization" providing "unbiased advice about products and services, personal finance, health and nutrition, and other consumer concerns."

Every minute of every day, Americans shell out more than $10,000 for something many don't even have to buy: water. The figures are no Y2K blip, either. Sales of bottled water have been rising steadily for years. In 1976, Americans drank 1.5 gallons of bottled water per person; in 1999, they drank 15.5 gallons.

You might think that all bottled waters taste pretty much alike and that none could harbor the kind of contaminants occasionally found in tap water. They don't, and they can. In fact, a four-year study of 103 bottled waters released last year by the National Resources Defense Council, an environmental group, revealed concerns. Among them: Several waters had levels of chlorine by-products or arsenic that were above the threshold set by California, though within limits set by the U.S. Food and Drug Administration (FDA).

For our report, we bought multiple samples of 39 bottled waters—still (noncarbonated), carbonated, and mineral. We focused mainly on taste but also had a lab analyze the waters for harmful substances that can occur naturally or stem from treatment procedures or bottling. In a nutshell, we found:

- The major differences in taste were due to the type of plastic in the water's bottle. In most cases, waters in clear PET plastic (usually bottles of 1.5 liters or smaller) tasted better than those in cloudy, softer HDPE plastic (usually 1-gallon bottles).

- None of the waters we tested harbored contaminants above current standards. That said, some occasionally had a bit more than we'd like to see of one or more substances that shouldn't be prevalent in drinking water.

- Although the top-rated water costs 29 cents per 8-fluid-ounce glass, some waters that cost half as much tasted very good.

Taste-test results are in the Ratings on page 291; a glossary of contaminants occasionally found in water is in "A Contaminant Compendium" on pages 287–288.

Finally, we spot-checked the quality of tap water from seven U.S. cities. [. . .]   5

THE TERMS, THE SOURCES

Technically, there are more choices in bottled water than just with fizz or without:

Spring water comes from an underground formation and must flow naturally to the earth's surface. Water is collected at the spring or through a hole that taps the source, and the source must be stated on the label. Spring water is typically protected from microorganisms sometimes found in surface water. Carbon dioxide can be added to make it "sparkling."

Purified drinking water has been processed by reverse osmosis, distillation, or similar procedures that remove minerals and contaminants. The source need not be named and is often tap water.

Naturally sparkling water is naturally carbonated and often comes from a spring. Bubbles lost during treatment or collection may be replaced with the same amount of carbon dioxide the water held originally.

Soda water and seltzer are not considered bottled water. The FDA reg-   10
ulates them as soft drinks, under rules less strict than those for bottled water, and some products may have added sugar, flavors, or salts. They're often carbonated municipal water, sometimes with extra filtration.

Mineral water contains at least 250 parts per million of dissolved solids— usually calcium, magnesium, sodium, potassium, silica, and bicarbonates. Minerals must occur naturally. Mineral water is typically spring water and can be sparkling or still.

Despite formal definitions, labels can be confusing. *Aquafina Purified Drinking Water,* one of America's top-selling bottled waters, sounds like an Italian import, and its label favors the deep blues and snow-capped mountains many brands use to telegraph the idea of faraway glacial springs. In fact, *Aquafina* is produced by the Pepsi Cola Company. Its name? From "the marketing folks," says Pepsi spokesman Larry Jabbonsky. The water originates from 16 sources— mainly municipal water supplies. Sources include venues no more exotic than Cheraw, S.C.; Detroit; Fresno, Calif.; and Munster, Ind. *Aquafina* is "not in the high end of water," Jabbonsky concedes.

Pepsi is now being challenged by—who else?—Coca-Cola. Coke's water, *Dasani,* is purified from municipal sources, "enhanced with a mix of minerals for a crisp taste," a Coke spokesman told us. (*Aquafina* and *Dasani* fell in the middle of our Ratings.)

Something else the label may not reveal is that a single brand of spring water can come from many sources. *Dannon Natural Spring Water,* another recent entry into the national market, taps four springs, in Florida, Pennsylvania, Utah, and Quebec. Different sources can mean different tastes.

THE TASTE OF TASTELESS

Good drinking water should taste like nothing. However, nothing can   *15*
still taste a little like *something,* and water should taste clean, fresh, lively, and a
little crisp.

Waters bottled in PET plastic generally tasted better than those bottled in
HDPE. That was true even within the same brand. *Arrowhead Mountain Spring
Water,* for example, was very good when bottled in PET, which imparted a hint
of sweet, fruity plastic flavor (imagine the scent when you blow up a beachball).
But *Arrowhead* was only fair when bottled in HDPE, which made it taste a bit
like melted plastic (imagine the smell when you get a plastic container too close
to a flame). For waters that come in both kinds of bottle, the Ratings list two
scores (and two prices—water is apt to cost more in PET). The only water bottled in PVC plastic, Winn-Dixie's *Prestige Premium 100% Spring Water,* rated
good overall.

Why did different plastics impart different tastes? There's no one answer.
Some plastics more easily allow nearby odors and tastes into water. Small
amounts of chemicals in the plastic itself could leach into the water. Even the
process used in making the plastic could affect taste. For details, see "Bottle
Basics" on page 286.

Still waters. Only *Volvic Natural Spring Water* was excellent. A French
import, *Volvic* comes from an area rich in volcanic rock, a company spokesman
said. Several other waters were very good and cost much less.

Carbonated waters. All are bottled in PET, and differences among the
seven brands we tasted were subtle. The best—*Vintage Old Original Seltzer
Water* and *Canada Dry Original Seltzer*—were very good. Both were less bitter
than others.

Mineral waters. Each of the five we tried has a different taste. Which   *20*
you choose will depend on whether you like mineral water more or less fizzy
or mineral-y. For that reason, we didn't rate these waters, but we list tasters'
comments on page 291.

TROUBLED WATER?

The nation's thirst for bottled water, we suspect, has grown at least in part
because its confidence in tap water has been shaken. Concerns were fueled in
1993, when cryptosporidium, a parasite from animal waste, entered Milwau-
kee's water supply. It killed more than 50 people, sent 4,400 to hospitals, and
sickened hundreds of thousands.

The U.S. Environmental Protection Agency (EPA) has standards for some
80 contaminants in public drinking water and maintains that the U.S. enjoys
some of the safest water in the world. You can check for yourself: Since 1999,
Federal law has required local water utilities to send "consumer confidence
reports" to their customers each year. The reports detail ongoing laboratory
testing, name system trouble spots, and outline measures being taken to fix

BOTTLE BASICS

Bottles can actually affect a water's taste and chemical content. Here are advantages and disadvantages of common bottle materials.

PET (Also Called PETE)

Short for polyethylene terephthalate, PET is a clear, strong plastic that leaves nothing more than a faint sweet or fruity plastic flavor, if that. Labels for some brands packed in PET play up the "clear" taste of the water inside.

HDPE

High-density polyethylene is the opaque, flexible material of milk containers. It's less expensive than PET but often imparts a slight melted-plastic taste to water. Taste may also be affected by excessive heat or flavors from foods stored nearby.

Glass

Chemically, glass is inert and imparts no taste whatsoever. But it's heavy and breakable and is seldom used nowadays except for pricey mineral waters and water bottled for bars, restaurants, and hotels.

Polycarbonate

Strong and rigid, it's used for compact discs as well as 5-gallon water-cooler jugs. The three water-cooler waters we sampled—*Great Bear, Deer Park,* and *Poland Spring*—had no funny flavors. In fact, those waters tasted better than the same products in PET or HDPE bottles. But our analyses showed that polycarbonate sometimes leaves residues of a worrisome chemical, bisphenol-A (see "A Contaminant Compendium," pages 287–288).

■ ■ ■

problems. If you haven't received one, contact your local water department, call the Safe Drinking Water Hotline at (800) 426-4791, or visit <*www.epa.gov/safewater/dwinfo.htm*>.

The bottled-water industry falls under the jurisdiction of the FDA, which has borrowed from the EPA's standards for tap water. The International Bottled Water Association, the industry's trade group, has its own model code, with some standards stricter than the FDA's. Member companies, which produce 85 percent of the bottled water sold in the U.S., must also allow annual surprise inspections at processing plants by an independent nonprofit group.

Bottlers often imply their product is purer than tap water. Some play up "protected sources," often underground springs whose output the company tests regularly. Others say their waters have undergone ozonation (it disinfects but leaves no chlorine aftertaste) or "one-micron absolute" filtration (water is strained through pores small enough to catch cryptosporidium).

We tested all the bottled waters for trihalomethanes (THMs), a potentially harmful by-product of the chlorine treatment to which tap water is subjected. 25

A CONTAMINANT COMPENDIUM

Bottled waters must meet U.S. Food and Drug Administration standards for a roster of contaminants, and companies must hew to "good manufacturing practices"—rules for sanitary production. Nevertheless, contaminants crop up occasionally in both tap water and bottled water. Below are details about some that have been in the news.

Arsenic

Source. A poisonous element in the earth's crust, arsenic can enter water naturally or through factory runoff, animal-feed additives, herbicides, and refineries. Water systems that depend on underground sources are especially at risk for arsenic.

Health effects. Long-term exposure to even low concentrations may cause lung, skin, and bladder cancer as well as diseases of the blood vessels, liver, and other organs.

Limit. The current standard—50 parts per billion (ppb) in tap water and bottled water—dates from the 1940s. In May, the EPA proposed lowering the limit in tap water to 5 ppb. The agency is now soliciting public comments on a range of limits: 20 ppb, 10 ppb, 5 ppb, and 3 ppb. A decision is to be made within a year. Whatever the eventual limit, the FDA will probably set a similar standard for bottled water.

Our findings. Nearly all the waters had no detectable arsenic, and all met the current standard. However, some samples of a few waters were above the possible future standard of 5 ppb. Among them: all three bottles of *Vittel* (they averaged 14 ppb), one of three bottles of *Calistoga Sparkling Mineral Water* (18 ppb), one of three bottles of *American Fare Natural Spring Water* (10 ppb), and one of three bottles of *Apollinaris Naturally Sparkling Mineral Water* (10 ppb).

Trihalomethanes (THMS)

Source. THMs are produced when chlorination chemicals (for disinfection) combine with organic matter in water supplies. Cities sometimes use more chlorine in warm weather, so THM levels can fluctuate season to season and even day to day.

Health effects. If consumed over long periods, THMs may increase the risk of bladder and rectal cancers and of miscarriage. But risks must be weighed against benefits: Chlorination kills harmful germs.

Limit. It's now 100 ppb for tap water and bottled water. The tap-water standard will fall to 80 ppb next year for large systems; the bottled-water standard may follow.

Our findings. Some seltzers had levels of about 50 ppb. Other types of bottled waters from municipal sources have often been treated or filtered; they had few or no THMs. Companies usually don't chlorinate spring waters, and those, too, had few or no THMs.

(continues)

■ ■ ■

A CONTAMINANT COMPENDIUM *(continued)*

Fluoride

Source. It's a naturally occurring element and is often added to municipal water to prevent tooth decay.

Health effects. Too little can reduce dental benefits; too much can discolor or mottle tooth enamel in children.

Limit. The FDA limit ranges from 0.8 to 2.4 parts per million (ppm). The American Dental Association says the optimal level is 0.7 to 1.2 ppm.

Our findings. Most bottled water has little or no fluoride. Waters with added fluoride will say so on the label. Too little fluoride can be a concern for people—especially for children—who don't drink fluoridated tap water. For information about specific products, contact manufacturers.

Heterotrophic Plate Count (HPC)

Source. HPC tallies a mix of bacteria in the water.

Health effects. The germs counted are not necessarily harmful, but large numbers of them may point to poor sanitation practices.

Limit. Counted as "colony-forming units per milliliter," or cfu/ml. There are no official standards; one guideline is 500 cfu/ml or less.

Our findings. Two brands of eight we checked had at least one bottle over the guideline. Those were waters that the Natural Resources Defense Council had found no problems with in its study last year; conversely, two waters in which NRDC had found high HPC were free of it in our tests. The inconsistencies suggest that problems are sporadic.

Plastic Components

Source. Bisphenol-A (BPA) is the building block of polycarbonate and can leach from there into water or food.

Health effects. BPA is a carcinogen and mimics the hormone estrogen in animal studies.

Limit. There is none.

Our findings. Eight of the ten 5-gallon polycarbonate jugs we checked leached bisphenol-A into water—from 0.5 ppb to 11 ppb. Any health effects would be most likely to occur in developing fetuses, judging from animal research.

■■■

We confined tests for other contaminants to waters in which they would most likely be found. Without comprehensive nationwide tests, no one can say how much cleaner bottled water might be than tap water. We do know that none of the waters in our analyses—bottled or tap—harbored contaminants at levels above current standards. However, several samples of bottled water were above the EPA's *proposed* standard for arsenic, a couple of samples had a fairly high level of bacteria that can indicate spotty sanitation, and eight of ten polycarbonate jugs leached a potentially problematic plastic component into water.

MINERALS ON THE ROCKS

Each mineral water has a unique "fingerprint" owing to the rocks and earth it passes by. Here's how five of the leading mineral waters tasted. Prices are per 8-fluid-ounce glass.

Apollinaris Naturally Sparkling Mineral Water (37 cents): Moderate fizz, slight mineral and baking-soda flavors.

Calistoga Sparkling Mineral Water (23 cents): Little fizz, slight earthy, mineral, and baking-soda flavors.

Perrier Sparkling Mineral Water (36 cents): Moderate fizz, slight baking-soda flavor, trace of mineral flavor.

S. Pellegrino Natural Sparkling Mineral Water (47 cents): Very little fizz, slight mineral and baking-soda flavors.

Vittel Mineral Water (23 cents): No fizz, slight mineral flavor.

▪ ▪ ▪

RECOMMENDATIONS

It's important to drink enough water—eight glasses per day; more in hot weather or if you're especially active. Drinking too little water can cause fatigue, weakness, dizziness, and headaches. Over the long term, drinking too little water has been linked to constipation, kidney stones, and even some cancers. Yet despite the rise in consumption of bottled water, one American in ten doesn't typically drink water at all, according to a recent survey for the bottled-water industry and Rockefeller University.

Where should that water come from? You can take it from the tap, of course, and incidents of contamination by harmful chemicals or parasites in public drinking water are very rare. Taste is another matter. Some of the tap waters we sampled tasted almost swampy. (Bad taste doesn't necessarily mean water is unhealthful, however.)

Some carafe filters and faucet-mounted filters improve tap water's taste—for far less money than a bottle or two of water per day. [. . .]

If you prefer bottled water, you have plenty of choices in a wide price range. One overall finding to keep in mind: Water in PET plastic bottles generally tasted better than water in HDPE plastic, though water in HDPE is usually cheaper. Note also that taste differences are most obvious when water is at room temperature. When the water is icecold, differences will be less noticeable.

Volvic Natural Spring Water, 29 cents per 8-fluid-ounce glass, was excellent, with no off-tastes. Next best was *Dannon Natural Spring Water,* 14 cents. Very good when bottled in PET (but not in HDPE) were *Arrowhead Mountain Spring Water, American Fare Natural Spring Water* (Kmart), and *Albertson's A + Natural Spring Water,* all 12 cents.

30

BOTTLED WATER

In addition to the products covered in this report, there are flavored waters with hints of watermelon, ginger, even peach–ginseng; "baby water" brands like *Beech-Nut* and *Gerber,* to mix with formula, juice, and cereal (sometimes with fluoride, and highly purified); and water with vitamins or caffeine. Newer national brands include *Aquafina, Dannon,* and *Dasani.* Older regional brands include *Calistoga, Zephyrhills,* and *Poland Spring,* which has flowed from Maine since 1845.

The Tests Behind the Ratings

The **flavor score** is an average of several lots for each product, based on judgments of our trained sensory panelists. An excellent still water should taste clean and fresh, with no off-tastes or aromas to detract from it. Carbonated water should be effervescent and can be a little sour (from dissolved carbon dioxide) and have a slight soda-like taste, a touch of bitterness, and a faint impression of saltiness. **Source** tells whether a water comes from a single place (S), often a particular spring, or from multiple sources (M), which means taste can vary, depending on where it's purchased. A dash means the water does not specify its source. Federal regulations allow purified drinking water to omit its source from labels; much of it is reprocessed tap water drawn from a variety of municipal water systems. **Plastic** shows the type used, typically clear PET (officially, polyethylene terephthalate) or cloudier HDPE (high-density polyethylene). One water came in PVC (polyvinyl chloride). Where waters of the same brand are bottled in two kinds of plastic, we've given two flavor scores, and the waters are rated by the higher score (generally, the PET score). To complicate matters, the names of two waters, *American Fare* and *Prestige,* varied with the type of bottle. **Cost per glass** is for an 8-fluid-oz. serving, based on the approximate retail price. For PET bottles, cost is usually based on the 1.5 liter size; for HDPE bottles, 1 gallon; for carbonated waters, 1 liter.

■ ■ ■

The best carbonated water, *Vintage Old Original Seltzer Water,* was also the cheapest, at 11 cents a glass.

Mineral waters have very individual tastes. *Vittel* and *Calistoga* were less expensive than the others, at 23 cents per serving.

QUESTIONS FOR DISCUSSION

1. Why do you think so many Americans are buying bottled water?
2. How do you respond to the information, in paragraph 12, that the Pepsi Cola company uses municipal water supplies for its bottled water?
3. Consider the information in paragraph 14. If a company is marketing water from four different regions under a single label, how consistent would you expect the product to be?
4. How does the nature of the container affect the taste of bottled water?
5. What are the consequences of drinking too little water each day?

Overall Ratings — Within types, in order of flavor score

PET ▬▬ HDPE ▬▬ PVC ▬▬

PRODUCT	SOURCE	COST PER GLASS	PLASTIC	FLAVOR SCORE	COMMENTS
STILL WATER					
Volvic Natural Spring Water	S	29¢	PET		Very clean, no off-flavors.
Dannon Natural Spring Water	M	14	PET		Relatively clean; hint of sweet, fruity plastic flavor.
Arrowhead Mountain Spring Water	M	12	PET		Hint of sweet, fruity plastic flavor.
		7	HDPE		Pronounced melted-plastic flavor; hint of wet-dust flavor.
American Fare Natural Spring Water	M	12	PET		Hint of sweet plastic flavor.
American Fare Spring Water		4	HDPE		Pronounced melted-plastic flavor.
Albertson's A+ Natural Spring Water	M	12	PET		Hint of sweet plastic flavor.
		5	HDPE		Hint of melted-plastic flavor; hint of wet-dust flavor in some samples.
Prestige Premium 100% Spring Water	M	8	PVC		Hint of plastic flavor.
Prestige Natural Spring Water		12	PET		Hint of sweet plastic flavor.
Crystal Geyser Natural Alpine Spring Water	M	12	PET		Hint of sweet plastic flavor.
Zephyrhills Natural Spring Water	S	6	HDPE		Hints of plastic and mineral flavors.
		14	PET		Hint of sweet plastic flavor.
Evian Natural Spring Water	S	28	PET		No plastic flavor; hint of mineral flavor.
Sparkletts Crystal-Fresh Drinking Water[1]	–	12	PET		Hint of sweet plastic flavor.
		7	HDPE		Pronounced melted-plastic flavor.
Dasani Purified Water	–	23	PET		Hint of sweet, fruity plastic flavor.
Pure American Spring Water	M	12	PET		Hint of sweet, fruity plastic flavor.
		5	HDPE		Pronounced melted-plastic flavor.
Poland Spring Natural Spring Water	S	7	HDPE		Hint of melted-plastic flavor.
		15	PET		Hint of sweet plastic flavor.
Kroger Natural Spring Water	M	11	PET		Hint of plastic flavor.
		6	HDPE		Hint of melted-plastic flavor.
Deer Park Spring Water	M	13	PET		Hint of sweet plastic flavor.
		6	HDPE		Pronounced melted-plastic flavor; hint of wet-dust flavor in some samples.
Aquafina Purified Drinking Water	–	19	PET		Hint of sweet, fruity plastic flavor.
Naya Canadian Natural Spring Water	M	19	PET		Hints of sweet, fruity plastic and mineral flavors.
Ozarka Natural Spring Water	M	14	PET		Hint of sweet plastic flavor.
		6	HDPE		Pronounced melted-plastic flavor.
Aberfoyle Springs Imported Natural Spring Water	M	11	PET		Hints of sweet plastic and mineral flavors.
Great Bear Natural Spring Water	M	6	HDPE		Hint of melted-plastic flavor.
Calistoga Mountain Spring Water	M	14	PET		Pronounced sweet, fruity plastic flavor.
Safeway Drinking Water	M	6	HDPE		Hint of melted-plastic flavor.
Crystal Springs Mountain Spring Water[2]	M	13	PET		Hint of melted-plastic flavor.
		7	HDPE		Pronounced melted-plastic flavor.
Pathmark Natural Spring Water	M	5	HDPE		Hints of melted-plastic and wet-dust flavors.
		12	PET		Pronounced plastic flavor.
Great Value Spring Water	M	4	HDPE		Hints of melted-plastic and mineral flavors.
Walgreens Drinking Water	M	5	HDPE		Pronounced melted-plastic flavor.
America's Choice Natural Spring Water[3]	M	5	HDPE		Pronounced melted-plastic flavor; hint of wet-dust flavor.
CARBONATED WATER					
Vintage Old Original Seltzer Water	–	11	PET		Strong effervescence; hint of bitterness and occasional hint of fruity flavor; cleaner-tasting than most.
Canada Dry Original Seltzer[4]	–	23	PET		Strong effervescence; hint of bitterness and occasional hint of fruity flavor.
Albertson's A+ Original Seltzer	–	16	PET		Occasional hint of fruity flavor.
Safeway Select Seltzer Water	–	18	PET		Strong effervescence; occasional hint of fruity flavor.
Schweppes Original Seltzer Water	–	26	PET		Strong effervescence; occasional hint of fruity flavor.
Kroger Golden Crown Sparkling Seltzer Water	–	19	PET		Occasional hint of fruity flavor.
Poland Spring Sparkling Spring Water	–	22	PET		Hint of mineral flavor, and occasional hint of fruity flavor.

Flavor score scale: 0 — 100 (P F G VG E)

[1] Also sold as Alhambra Crystal-Fresh Drinking Water. [2] Also sold as Crystal Springs Spring Water. [3] As of 2000, mfr. says, water will also be bottled in PET. [4] Also sold as Canada Dry Original Sparkling Water.

6. Based on the information in this evaluation, which products are you most likely to buy and which are you most likely to avoid?

SUGGESTIONS FOR WRITING

1. Evaluate the quality of research behind this evaluation of bottled water as well as the clarity with which testing results are conveyed to the public.
2. Evaluate for taste and value the four or five bottled waters you see most frequently on your campus.
3. Choose another consumer product and consult sources about it on the World Wide Web and in print. Then write an evaluation of which form is easier to consult: a Web page or an article in print.

LINKS ■ ■ ■

■ WITHIN THE BOOK

For another evaluation that focuses on taste and value, see "The Sad Comedy of Really Bad Food" by Dara Moskowitz (pages 293–295).

■ ELSEWHERE IN PRINT

Cooper, Ann, with Lisa N. Holmes. *Bitter Harvest: A Chef's Perspective on the Hidden Dangers in the Foods We Eat and What You Can Do about It.* New York: Routledge, 2000.

Senior, Dorothy A. G., and Philip R. Ashurst, eds. *Technology of Bottled Water.* Boca Raton: CRC, 1998.

Simontacchi, Carol. *The Crazy Makers: How the Food Industry Is Destroying Our Brains and Harming Our Children.* New York: Tarcher, 2000.

Von Wiesenberger, Arthur. *H_2O: The Guide to Quality Bottled Water.* Santa Barbara: Woodbridge, 1988.

■ ONLINE

- Bottled Water: Pure Drink or Pure Hype
  <http://www.nrdc.org/water/drinking/nbw.asp>
- History of Fresh Water Resources
  <http://www.iwha.net>
- International Bottled Water Association
  <http://www.bottledwater.org>

THE SAD COMEDY OF REALLY BAD FOOD

Dara Moskowitz

*No matter how many people enjoy eating out, some restaurants never succeed in
attracting business. Others become so popular that customers will wait in line for a table.
Food critics play a significant role in determining where people choose to go when
they're looking for a good meal. Responsible critics visit a restaurant anonymously at
least twice before reporting on it to make sure that their experience is representative of
what other people can expect. If you have ever been disappointed by bad service or
bad food, you may have wished to make your views known to others. Dara Moskowitz
does just that in the following review of a fashionable restaurant in Minnesota.*

A weekly columnist for the City Pages *in Minneapolis, Moskowitz was awarded first
prize in restaurant criticism by the Association of Food Journalists in 2000.*

Mpls. Cafe
1110 Hennepin Ave., Mpls.; 672-9100

When people find out what I do for a living, they invariably ask whether
restaurateurs know when I'm coming. The answer is that, no, they never do,
because I want to get the same treatment that any Josie Blow coming in off
the street would get. This policy presents several major benefits: First, it makes
me feel ethically smug; second, it means I can write off my many wig and
prosthetic-nose purchases; and third, it makes me laugh. Or at least it makes
me laugh through what would ordinarily be a merely painful meal. For example, consider the terrible times I've endured recently at the Mpls. Cafe.

There I was, withered to my bones with dehydration. Tumbleweeds rat-
tled around in the bone-dry mesa of my water glass. My waiter had apparently given up the profession and lit out for a better life. The floor manager
was busy giving free drinks to another, louder table, to apologize to them for
all the things they wanted that they couldn't have—like food, and for them
wine, since no one thought to entrust the floor manager with the key to the
tantalizing wine cellar. It had been a long hour since I placed an appetizer
order, and I might as well have been waiting for a bus for all the fine dining I
was doing. I felt like Pamela Anderson° at a NAMBLA° convention. Had I
not been a food critic—and in this case, incredibly, dining with *another* local
food critic—I would have wept.

Yet instead, when our waiter, apparently having met disappointment on
the coasts, returned at one hour 10 minutes (sans H$_2$O), and asked, incredibly,

---

Pamela Anderson: Actress who drew attention for her role as a swimsuit-clad lifeguard on *Baywatch.*
NAMBLA: North American Man–Boy Love Association.

whether we needed more *bread*—well, that was merely the beginning of the hilarity. I laughed. When I said no, we had plenty of bread, the waiter, not trusting me—and why should he, with me sneaking into his section and marring a life of vagabond adventure—unwrapped the focaccia in its napkin-nest, peeked in at it, rewrapped it, and strode off again to his lair. I laughed so hard I thought I'd rupture something. Actually, I'm still laughing about it. Because it's not just me getting the worst service in the world: It's me getting the worst service in the world while taking notes. I'm Allen Funt in my own private *Candid Camera*. (By the way, focaccia here isn't mere bread, it's "farm-fresh focaccia," freshly hoed up from the focaccia fields.)

When the food eventually arrived, one of the dishes, the Turkey Mediterranean Tulips (turkey wings baked and finished on the grill with a jerk sauce, $6.75) was the best thing I had at the Mpls. Cafe. They were smoky, tender, spicy. The Potato Cakes with Balsamic Syrup ($6.25) were dull as paint—simply giant patties of underseasoned mashed potatoes served in a watery balsamic-vinegar sauce that eventually soaked into the potatoes, leaving them soggy and brownish. It seemed like ill-conceived leftovers.

After so many hours the entrées, of course, arrived just on the heels of the appetizers, and things went downhill from there. The bouillabaisse-style Soupe Canoise ($5.95/$9.95) tasted burnt and had a little black hot-pepper-looking thing lolling suspiciously to one side. I asked my bus-friend, the only person who ever attended the table, what it was, and, as he didn't know, he set out in pursuit of our waiter, who it took another 15 minutes to track down. Flyboy had never seen it either; it's been my experience that, if you ask any member of the wait staff at Mpls. Cafe what anything on the menu is, they become startled and disappear for maddening amounts of time in search of answers—so he went looking for a manager.

When the young, key-free manager arrived and he identified the little stem-on vegetable as a Japanese eggplant, I couldn't stop giggling. Then I tasted it, and I stopped laughing. It was bitter, charred, and awful—it made me want to spit. (If you ever wondered why people salt and drain eggplants, take a cute little past-prime Japanese eggplant, char it over an open flame, and pop it into your mouth. You'll salt forevermore.)

Of course, one bad experience does not make a bad restaurant. So I returned. And returned again. Each time the service was comical, and the food, while conceptually interesting, often seemed as though no one had tasted it after the idea was put to paper. The Salmon Tartar ($11.25), minced salmon served in a pool of cayenne-infused olive oil, tasted dusty and inedibly oily; Wood Roasted Quail Provençale ($17.95) was teeth-achingly salty; Casablanca Risotto with Saffron Infused Chicken Kabob ($13.25) was a pair of painfully over-salted kabobs resting on a mountain of gummy risotto; New Zealand Rack of Lamb ($21.50) was virtually ruined, as each small lamb chop was heaped with a spoon of raw, biting sorrel-garlic pesto; Chicken Garlic Basil Rigatoni ($10.75) was dull and undifferentiated; and worst of all was a special of lobster ravioli with fresh blueberries. I imagined puffs of tender lobster meat with a dozen or so blueberries thrown in for color and contrast. I got raviolis enriched with crunchy bits of shell, drowning in a thick, sour, jam-like paste.

On the up side, I liked the Caesar salad ($3.95/$6.95), which was lemony, spare, and honest; the pizzas are very good, wood-roasted, crisp, and simple; and the Planked Cochonnailles—a trio of pâtés served with spicy French gherkins and oil-cured olives—were fine. But I could have, in good conscience, sent back three out of four dishes that arrived from the Mpls. Cafe kitchen. It was hilarious, in its fashion.

It was also really funny when I went to order dessert on another visit and my waitress said, "That's the only good thing here." Then she backpedaled and clarified, saying, "What I mean is, in my opinion, it's my favorite part of the menu." She's right, many of the desserts are spectacular: I loved the crème brûlée ($4.95), which is presented in a glamorous haze of smoke as your server brands the top with a hot iron plate. The Pear Obsession ($5.95), poached pear slices on a layer of flaky, almond-laced pastry drizzled with a cinnamon-caramel sauce, is also truly wonderful. And the Crepe à la Gundel ($5.95), a tender crepe filled with warm fresh berries and dressed with two spectacular sauces, a crème anglaise and a Grand Marnier caramel syrup, is absolutely perfect; for everything I didn't like about the Mpls. Cafe, I'll be back for this wonder.

Mpls. Cafe also takes the prize for the most artful, ample, and delicious sauce-painting I've ever seen. It also must be said that its wine list is masterful. Champagnes and sparkling wines are nicely represented, and premium bottles can be had at reasonable prices. The rest of the list is global in scope, arranged in an exceedingly user-friendly manner, and considerately showcases many wines in every price range. Mpls. Cafe has only been open for two months, and perhaps the time will come when the food lives up to the strengths of the desserts. Until then it's a fine place for music, late-night gatherings, post-theater, pre-Holidazzle,° and the like—as long as you bring your sense of humor.

But wait—I totally forgot to tell you about how the rice in the Moroccan rice salad arrives as a large, ice-cold dome surrounded by hot, delicate seafood that (predictably) turns icy in a matter of moments. And how there are four televisions showing sports in a place with $175 bottles of champagne on the menu. Oh, and get this: One time, at a neighboring table, a customer spilled a glass of water, and it splashed all over the floor, and no one ever came to wipe it up, leaving patrons to pick their purses up off the floor to avoid the streaming rivulets; and then this one bus-guy actually told a waitress to watch out for the spilled water, because she might slip on it, and so they both avoided the spot for the rest of the night but never wiped it up. Man, was that funny. Oh, and the time I went by the open kitchen and a chef had this magazine spread out over his cutting board, and this other time . . .

Oh well. I guess it was just one of those things where you had to be there. But it was really funny.

10

Holidazzle: A nightly parade in downtown Minneapolis during the Christmas shopping season.

QUESTIONS FOR DISCUSSION

1. Moskowitz opens her review by discussing her life as a restaurant critic. What is her purpose in doing so?
2. The service at this restaurant is clearly a disappointment to Moskowitz. What does it take to be a good server? In your experience, why does service sometimes break down?
3. According to Moskowitz, she could have "in good conscience, sent back three out of four dishes that arrived from the Mpls. Cafe kitchen." If she's disappointed in the food, why doesn't she send it back to the kitchen? Under what circumstances would you ask a server to return your meal?
4. Although this is an unusually negative review, Moskowitz does find some things to praise. What does she achieve by reporting that the restaurant in question had a good wine list and good desserts?
5. How would you describe the tone of this review? Does it seem appropriate under the circumstances?

SUGGESTIONS FOR WRITING

1. Visit a new restaurant in your area with two or three other people with whom you can share impressions. Then write a review in which you let readers know what they can expect if they decide to go there for a meal.
2. Choose a kind of food—like hamburgers or pizza—that is available at several restaurants in your area. Within no more than a week, sample this item at several sites. Then write a review in which you describe where you went and rank what you ate.
3. Write an evaluation of the food served on your campus that would help visitors learn where to go and what to order.

LINKS ■ ■ ■

■ WITHIN THE BOOK

In "Breakfast at the FDA Café" (pages 593–595), John R. Alden envisions a restaurant where the service is too attentive.

■ ELSEWHERE IN PRINT

Fisher, M. F. K. *The Gastronomical Me.* 1943. San Francisco: North Point, 1989.
———. *How to Cook a Wolf.* 1942. San Francisco: North Point, 1988.
Trillin, Calvin. *Travels with Alice.* New York: Ticknor, 1989.
———. *The Tummy Trilogy: American Fried/Alice, Let's Eat/Third Helpings.* New York: Farrar, 1994.

■ ELSEWHERE IN PRINT *(continued)*

Warde, Alan, and Lydia Martens. *Eating Out: Social Differentiation, Consumption and Pleasure.* New York: Cambridge UP, 2000.

■ ONLINE

- Brief Biography
  <http://www.hermenaut.com/autindex.html>
- Critiquing Restaurant Critics
  <http://www.restaurantreport.com/greatdebates/critics.html>
- Regrettable Food
  <http://www.lileks.com/institute/gallery>

BING CROSBY, THE UNSUNG KING OF SONG

Gary Giddins

If you have ever heard the sound of Bing Crosby's voice, it is probably because you have heard his much-loved recording of White Christmas, *which is still played by many radio stations every December. Or, if you like old movies, you may remember seeing him in* Going My Way, The Bells of St. Mary's *or* High Society. *But as Gary Giddins notes in the following evaluation, Crosby fell out of fashion thirty years ago. As a result, many Americans are unfamiliar with the work that made Crosby one of the most widely admired American performers during the 1930s, 1940s, and 1950s. Giddins, a columnist for the* Village Voice *in New York City, is the author of* Visions of Jazz *and* Bing Crosby: Pocketful of Dreams. *In "Bing Crosby: The Unsung King of Song," first published by the* New York Times *in 2001, he offers a survey of Crosby's career so that his readers can understand his own admiration for Crosby's many accomplishments. As you read, try to put out of mind the singers who dominate popular music today, and consider whether the time has come for a Crosby revival.*

For the last decade, whenever I mentioned to anyone that I was working on a life of Bing Crosby, the usual response was, "Why?" I can't say I was surprised. For 30 years, between 1927 and 1956, Crosby was a looming presence in America's cultural landscape. At the peak of his career, in the 1930s and 1940s, he was thought by many to be the most famous American alive. For much of that period, he was undoubtedly the most admired. The cycle of "Road" pictures with Bob Hope established Crosby as a great comic actor. Yet by the 1960s, the ocean began to roll over Der Bingle°, and though he continued to sell millions of records—chiefly holiday songs—he had morphed into a grand old man while retaining little of the bite of his contemporary, Louis Armstrong, or his aging offspring, Frank Sinatra. Crosby's reputation faltered along with his music after his death in 1977. When his eldest son, Gary Crosby, published a bitter memoir describing the unflappable Bing administering vigorous corporal punishment, his halo tilted and crashed. Soon the afterlife of his career imploded. Jazz lovers kept his memory alive, mainly because of his early records and the later collaborations with Armstrong, Louis Jordan, Les Paul, and others. But jazz lovers are by nature classicists, and Crosby had spent most of his life on the other side of the divide: the pop world, where success is measured in numbers—a world remade by rock, in which even the oldest of oldies postdate "Heartbreak Hotel."

Der Bingle: A nickname for Crosby.

Yet consider this: In 1946, three of the five top-grossing Hollywood pictures (*The Bells of St. Mary's, Blue Skies, Road to Utopia*) were Crosby vehicles; for five years running (1944 to 1948), he was No. 1 at the box office; his radio programs (1931 to 1962) attracted at their wartime peak as many as 50 million listeners; he recorded nearly 400 hit singles, an achievement no one—not Sinatra, Elvis or the Beatles—has come close to matching. Could a man who spoke so deeply to so many for so long have nothing to say to us now? For a biographer, Crosby's career offers more incentive than mere statistics. He is the ideal figure for tracking the rise of American popular culture. He played pivotal roles in the development of the recording, radio and film industries, while virtually defining the microphone as a singer's instrument. His influence on other singers—including Sinatra, Elvis and John Lennon, avowed fans all—would be hard to overstate, and he managed to maintain his popularity through several major cultural upheavals in 20th-century American history: Prohibition, Depression, World War II, the cold war and the affluent society.

Like many in my generation, I was drawn to the enunciated clarity, effortless swing, and insouciant scat-singing° of Crosby in his jazz years while ignoring his later work as meretricious. After listening to his exhaustive discography, more than 2,000 recordings (including radio broadcasts), it became apparent that his voice and style peaked not in the 1920's, when he joined Paul Whiteman's orchestra as the first ever full-time band singer, but a decade later, in Hollywood. Jazz-born prejudices are often inadequate in evaluating a popular idol. Irving Berlin once said he wrote music for the "mob" and that as far as he was concerned, the mob was always right.

Crosby's Dickensian appetite for every kind of song obliges us to savor the validity and verve of music created not by or for the elect but for the delectation of the millions. The mob is not always right. Its infinite longing for rote repetition and screwy novelties ("Three Little Fishies," anyone?) is matched by its impatience with music that demands concentration. Yet the ability of the millions to discriminate is not negligible. Examine the pop records released between 1934 and 1954, and compare the major hits to the numberless misses: You cannot help admiring the mob's batting average.

The public had little trouble distinguishing between Crosby and his rivals   5
in the 1920s. His first solo record, though not a hit, showed those who were paying attention that the times were changing. A year after Armstrong recorded "Heebie Jeebies," the explosive scat-driven number that put his vocal style on the map, and three months after Crosby had begun touring with Whiteman, he was allotted a chorus on "Muddy Water." The session took place on March 7, 1927, at Leiderkranz Hall in New York. Crosby's record, unlike Armstrong's, no longer seems as radical as it once did—unless you listen to it in tandem with the other white pop records of the time, in which case his debut seems absolutely astonishing. The song itself is a conventional

---

scat-singing: A way of vocalizing, in jazz, by using sounds instead of words.

idyll about life "down Dixie way," created by an integrated team, the white composer Peter DeRose and the black lyricist Jo Trent.

In Matty Malneck's arrangement, "Muddy Water" opens with a trombone and a bold unison ensemble chorus, promising a jazz performance; yet only the vocal, backed by viola and rhythm, makes good on that promise. Compared to his mature work, Crosby's chorus is stilted, almost formal. But his rhythm and articulation are sure, especially on the bridge, in which he emphasizes "there" and "care" with a trilling vibrato that displays his innate affinity for swing. Giving each word its due, his winged phrasing banishes sentimentality. The sound of his voice is unlike that of any of his contemporaries: a vibrant, virile baritone, completely at odds with the effete tenors and semifalsetto warblers who dominated male popular singing in that era. After hearing him, Duke Ellington vowed not to hire a male vocalist until he found one who sounded like Crosby.

The modern style of American popular singing, as distinct from the theatrical emoting of the minstrel and vaudeville eras, was originated by four performers, each to some degree rooted in jazz and blues. All but one were African-American: Bessie Smith, Ethel Waters, Armstrong, and Crosby. In their day, Smith, who was born in 1894, in Chattanooga, Tenn., was the least widely known. Yet as the finest heavy-voiced blues singing (some said shouting) contralto of the era, she established vocal techniques intrinsic to the American style, most notably an undulating attack in which notes are stretched, bent, curved, moaned and hollered. She perfected and popularized an old style of melisma that had been described by the writer Jeannette Robinson Murphy in an 1899 issue of *Popular Science Monthly*. Trying to instruct white singers in the art of "genuine Negro melodies," Murphy insisted it was necessary "that around every prominent note [the singer] place a variety of small notes, called 'trimmings.'" She said the singer "must sing tones not found in our scale [. . .] careful to divide many of his monosyllabic words in two syllables." Smith had a limited range, but she proved that emotional power does not depend on conventional vocal abilities.

Ethel Waters, born in Chester, Pa., in 1896, was another story. Though initially characterized as a blues singer, she came to embody the aspirations of black performers determined to make it on "white time." With her higher range and light supple voice, she lacked the weighty sonority of Smith, but her superb enunciation, gift for mimicry, and versatility allowed her to switch between irrepressible eroticism (she was the queen of double entendre) and high-toned eloquence. Smith and Waters dazzled the young white jazz acolytes of the 1920s, and Crosby was exposed to their records early on by another highly influential singer, Mildred Bailey, the benefactress of his apprentice years. What's more, Bailey told him that if he was really serious about singing, he would have to find out about Louis Armstrong, a young trumpet player and singer in Chicago; the grapevine was buzzing about him, though he had made few records—none of them vocals.

Armstrong, born in New Orleans in 1901, was the most extreme force American music had ever known. Having absorbed every valuable tradition in the 19th-century vernacular, sacred or secular, he offered a new vision that liberated American music vocally and instrumentally. Armstrong transformed everyone who heard him; musicians who came under his spell felt freer, more optimistic and ambitious, willing to take risks. He anchored, as Bessie Smith could not, the blues as the foundation for a new American music; and he revealed, as Ethel Waters could not, that swing, a seductive canter as natural and personal as a heartbeat, would be its irreducible rhythmic framework.

Harry Lillis Crosby—nicknamed Bing at the age of 7 because of his fond-   *10* ness for a syndicated newspaper parody, "The Bingville Bugle"—was born in Tacoma, Wash., in 1903, the fourth of seven children in a working-class family governed by a strict Irish Catholic mother. It was their easygoing Protestant father, however, who brought home the appliance that changed Bing's life: an Edison phonograph, purchased to commemorate the family's move to Spokane in 1906. Bing listened to every record he could get his hands on, especially those by Al Jolson; when he got to watch Jolson in action a few years later, he began to contemplate the life of an entertainer. He eventually dropped out of law school to play drums and sing with a local band, before leaving Spokane with his partner, Al Rinker (Bailey's brother), to try for the big time.

When he encountered Armstrong in Chicago in 1926, Crosby had barely a year of vaudeville under his belt, and he was utterly transfixed. Crosby was the first and, for a while, the only singer who fully assimilated the shock of Armstrong's impact; Crosby would later call Armstrong "the beginning and the end of music in America." One of the most important things Crosby learned from Armstrong was that the contagious pulse known as swing did not have to be exclusive to jazz. It was a universally applicable technique that deepened the interpretation of any song in any setting. Crosby's uncanny ability to hear "the one"—the downbeat of each measure—was unheard of among white singers in the 1920s, and it never left him. Jake Hanna, Crosby's drummer in the 1970s, observed: "Bing had the best time, the absolute best time. And I played with Count Basie, and that's great time." Most singers who imitated Crosby in the 1920s and 1930s—Russ Columbo, Perry Como, Dick Todd—took the superficial aspects of his style without the jazz foundation, which is why so much of their work is antiquated.

To the mix as developed by Smith, Waters and Armstrong, Crosby added three elements that were crucial to the fulfillment of pop singing: his expansive repertory, expressive intimacy, and spotless timbre. He grew up in a time and place when young music lovers were not concerned with the snobberies of high versus low, hip versus square, in versus out. The phonograph was a new invention, and each record was a mystery until it was played. Every record collection was a canon unto itself. Crosby saw no contradiction in his love for the great Irish tenor John McCormack, the Broadway minstrel Al Jolson, and the jazz and blues groups that excited his contemporaries. Yet he offered something different from them.

Crosby had begun his career just as the condenser microphone was perfected, replacing the silly-looking megaphones he had used in his school band. He realized that the mike was an instrument. He understood instinctively the modernist paradox: electrical appliances made singing more human, more expressive, more personal. They also enriched his unique style: rich, strong, intimate, and smart. Listeners who were put off by vernacular growls and moans could enjoy his relatively immaculate approach. His focus on the meaning of lyrics helped reshape the popular song. With his combination of intelligence and rhythmic acuity, Crosby could transfigure trite songs tritely arranged ("I Found a Million Dollar Baby"), but also underscore the banality of June/moon bromides, hymns to a mother's tears and "dark town" caricatures. A new generation of lyricists—Larry Hart, Cole Porter, Leo Robin, Al Dubin, Mitchell Parish, Yip Harburg and the self-renewing Irving Berlin—found in Crosby an interpreter who brought their subtlest verbal conceits to life.

Everything came together during the Depression, when Crosby proved you could be all things to all men and all women. At the same time that he reached jazz peaks in his flights on "Sweet Georgia Brown" and "Some of These Days," he transformed other songs into Depression anthems, including the vivid protest song "Brother, Can You Spare a Dime?" and "Home on the Range," a little-known saddle song that he turned into the most renowned of western ballads. As the most popular singer in the world, he recorded an unparalleled variety of songs: hymns, minstrel arias, singspiel, rhythm and blues—not even Sinatra, who would deepen the interpretation of lyrics, could handle such a spectrum.

On a 1943 edition of "Command Performance," a radio series recorded   15
on transcription discs for shipment to overseas forces, the M.C., Dinah Shore, remarked, "You know, Bing, a singer like Frank Sinatra comes along only once in a lifetime." Bing's famous response: "Yeah, and he has to come along in my lifetime." From 1931, when Crosby first triumphed on network radio and his rivals faded, through 1940, when Tommy Dorsey took the country by storm with "I'll Never Smile Again" and other records featuring vocals by Sinatra, Crosby ruled mainstream pop. Armstrong, Bailey, Billie Holiday, and Jimmy Rushing prospered in jazz, just as other singers found audiences in country, gospel and other idioms. But Crosby was king of the mountain—the national voice, America's troubadour. In Sinatra, he had at long last a worthy heir, a contender. By the end of 1943, Sinatra beat him in the Down Beat poll of popular singers. High school and college clubs as well as professional pundits routinely debated their respective merits.

Yet, contrary to the Sinatra myth, at no time in the 1940s did Sinatra seriously crimp Crosby's popularity. This was the period when Bing was twice nominated for best-actor Oscars (he won in 1944 for "Going My Way"), when he recorded the most successful record of all time, "White Christmas," and when he was named in a poll of servicemen as the man who had done most for Army morale. (Enlisted men had little use for Sinatra, who was disparaged as a draft dodger and seducer.) When the troops came home, Crosby enjoyed a new crest in popularity, while Sinatra's career dimmed and almost faded to black. It was Crosby who best captured the tenor of the times in recordings like "It's Been a Long, Long Time," a definitive home-from-war anthem, which never mentions the war.

Bing Crosby, left, and Frank
Sinatra in 1944.

By 1955, things began to change. The previous year had been a glorious
one for Crosby. He had starred in the top-grossing picture of the year, *White
Christmas,* and scored his third Oscar nomination for his stunning portrayal of
an alcoholic has-been in *The Country Girl.* Yet what a difference a year made.
Sinatra revived himself, retooled as a jet-age hipster balladeer, with a deepened voice and style and a poise fine-tuned by tribulation. Elvis Presley was
knocking them dead in the South and about to break nationally. Crosby's
vocal style had changed little. He could still croon with swinging élan, as
demonstrated on his 1957 album, *Bing With a Beat,* and he continued to enjoy
other triumphs. He joined with Sinatra, Armstrong, and Grace Kelly for the
musical film *High Society* in 1956, and was widely thought to have outshone
his rival—he once chose his duet with Sinatra ("Well, Did You Evah?") as his
favorite movie scene. Crosby's television specials through the mid-1960s were
highly musical and invariably successful. Yet in this new climate, his greatest
strength was considered a liability. Sinatra rang the rafters, Tony Bennett
poured out his heart, and Presley rocked, but Crosby's preternatural cool, his
canny gentleness, was too laid-back, too easy for the nuclear age.

By then he had begun to retreat from the stage. He now had a young wife,
Kathryn Grant, and three small children, and he was determined not to repeat
the mistakes of his first marriage to Dixie Lee, when his work kept him away
for long stretches and he tried to compensate by imposing strict disciplinary

BING, FOR STARTERS

One obstacle to a serious reconsideration of Bing Crosby's music has been availability: Many of the best performances were never reissued on LP, let alone on CD. Here are 10 splendid avenues into the immense labyrinth of Crosby's recorded legacy.

Bing Crosby 1926–1932 (*Timeless CBC 1-004*). A representative sampling of the Whiteman years, expertly remastered.

Bing—His Legendary Years 1931–1957 (*MCA MCAD4-10887*). An essential four-disc survey of Crosby's most fruitful period—with Decca Records.

Bing Crosby 1928–1945 (*L'Art Vocal 20*). A French import and the best single-disc introduction to Crosby in print.

Bing Crosby and Some Jazz Friends (*Decca/MCA GRD-603*). A one-volume anthology of the Decca years, focusing on jazz collaborations.

Bing's Gold Records (*MCA MCAD-11719*). Also from Decca, a collection of all 26 Crosby million-sellers.

I'm an Old Cowhand (*ASV AJA 5160*). Western songs, including his hymnlike "Home on the Range," a favorite of Franklin Roosevelt.

Bing Crosby Kraft Shows (*Lost Gold Records LGR 7598*). Two complete radio broadcasts, with Duke Ellington and Nat (King) Cole as guests.

Havin' Fun (*Jazz Unlimited JUCD 2034*). Highlights from Crosby's radio broadcasts with Louis Armstrong.

Bing with a Beat (*RCA Victor LTM-1473*). A masterly 1957 album with Bob Scobey's Frisco Jazz Band, long out of print. Write BMG or your congressman.

The Voice of Christmas (*MCA MCAD2-11840*). The ultimate mistletoe collection, two discs, complete with a rejected take of "White Christmas."

—Gary Giddins

■ ■ ■

measures on his four sons. He continued to broadcast Christmas specials, which led to a famous duet with David Bowie ("The Little Drummer Boy") and was seen frequently on the variety show *Hollywood Palace*. Yet his film career came to an end with *Stagecoach* in 1966, and American record companies no longer wanted to record him; his 1970s comeback was fueled with albums made and released in England, including a treasurable 1975 duet with Fred Astaire, "A Couple of Song and Dance Men." At Crosby's death, two years later, his contemporaries mourned him, but to a younger generation he had become a Norman Rockwell poster, an irrelevant holdover from another world.

His art, however, retains its power in unexpected ways. His versions of late-19th-century and early-20th-century songs are oddly compelling, and it is difficult to imagine another singer—Sinatra, for example—attempting them; I once saw an opera expert reduced to tears by Crosby's "Sweetheart of Sigma Chi." His great Depression waltzes ("Mexicali Rose," "The One Rose") recapture the dark side of that era as nothing else does. Crosby's early collaborations with Bix Beiderbecke and Ellington and later ones with Armstrong, Eddie Condon, Connie Boswell, Johnny Mercer, Woody Herman, Bob Crosby (his kid brother), Eddie Heywood, Bob Scobey, Rosemary Clooney, and many others retain their ingenuity and rhythmic zest. No matter how popular he became, his prowess and his jazz beat kept him honest. For that reason, he continues to speak to us, and in that sense, he remains our contemporary.

QUESTIONS FOR DISCUSSION

1. What qualities made Crosby such an admired singer during his lifetime? What were his strengths?
2. According to Giddins, why did Crosby fall out of fashion? What were his weaknesses?
3. In paragraph 2, Giddins asks, "Could a man who spoke so deeply to so many for so long have nothing to say to us now?" How would you answer this question?
4. How does Giddins justify his focus on Crosby?
5. Consider Irving Berlin's use of "mob" in paragraph 3, which Giddins carries over into paragraph 4. What does this word imply about the American public? If you find his term objectionable, what words would you use to describe Americans with mainstream taste?
6. Although he is focusing on Crosby, Giddins includes discussion of Ethel Waters, Louis Armstrong, and Frank Sinatra. Why does he do so? Was this a good writing decision?

SUGGESTIONS FOR WRITING

1. Listen to recordings of Bing Crosby, and write your own evaluation of his voice.
2. Rent the video of *High Society,* and compare Crosby's performance with Frank Sinatra's in that film.
3. Define the criteria that determine how you evaluate contemporary music.

LINKS ■ ■ ■

■ WITHIN THE BOOK

For another view of popular culture, an analysis rather than an evaluation, see Susan Bordo's "Beauty (Re)discovers the Male Body," pages 392–409.

(continues)

LINKS ■ ■ ■ *(continued)*

■ **ELSEWHERE IN PRINT**

Barnes, Ken. *The Crosby Years.* New York: St. Martin's, 1980.

Crosby, Bing, as told to Pete Martin. *Call Me Lucky.* Introd. Gary Giddins. New York: Da Capo, 1993.

Crosby, Gary, and Ross Firestone. *Going My Own Way.* Garden City: Doubleday, 1983.

Giddins, Gary. *Bing Crosby: A Pocketful of Dreams—The Early Years, 1903–1940.* Boston: Little, 2001.

———. *Visions of Jazz: The First Century.* New York: Oxford UP, 1998. Gioia, Ted. *The History of Jazz.* New York: Oxford UP, 1997.

Thompson, Charles. *Bing: The Authorized Biography.* New York: McKay, 1975.

■ **ONLINE**

- Bessie Smith
  <http://alt.venus.co.uk/weed/bessie/welcome.htm>
- Bing Crosby
  <http://www.kcmetro.cc.mo.us/pennvalley/biology/lewis/crosby/bing.htm>
- Ethel Waters
  <http://www.redhotjazz.com/waters.html>
- Frank Sinatra
  <http://www.sinatra.com>
- Louis Armstrong
  <http://www.satchmo.net/index1.html>

REACH OUT AND ANNOY SOMEONE

Jonathan Rowe

*Cell phones seem almost everywhere these days—in schools, offices, airports, restau-
rants, cars, buses, and on the street. How do all these cell phones affect the quality of
public life? Jonathan Rowe believes that increasing reliance on cell phones has had negative effects on both the users of these phones and the people who are near them. If you
enjoy the use of your own cell phone, you may think his evaluation is too one-sided. But
as you prepare to read, understand that Rowe chose to focus on the social consequences
of cell phone use—not the convenience of such phones for the individuals who use them.*

Rowe is a contributing editor of The Washington Monthly, *which published "Reach
Out and Annoy Someone" in 2000. He has also written for* The Christian Science Monitor *and* The Atlantic Monthly. *Currently, he is a senior fellow at Redefining Progress,
which describes itself as "a public policy organization that seeks to ensure a more sus-
tainable and socially equitable world for our children and our children's children."*

In the latter 1990s, in the midst of the high-tech boom, I spent a lot of
time in a coffee shop in the theater district in San Francisco. It was near Union
Square, the tourist hub, and I observed a scene play out there time and time
again. Mom is nursing her mocha. The kids are picking at their muffins, feet
dangling from their chairs. And there's Dad, pulled back slightly from the
table, talking into his cell phone.

I would watch the kids' faces, vacant and a little forlorn, and wonder what
happens to kids whose parents aren't there even when they are. How can we
expect kids to pay attention if we are too busy to pay attention to them? Peter
Breggin, the psychiatrist, says much "attention deficit disorder" is really "dad
deficit disorder." Maybe he's right.

As I sat there, I would think, too, about the disconnect between the way
we talk about the economy in the U.S. and the way we actually experience it.
The media were enthusing daily about the nation's record "expansion," and
here were these kids staring off into space. It was supposed to be a "communications revolution," and yet here, in the technological epicenter, the members of this family were avoiding one another's eyes.

With technology in particular, we can't seem to acknowledge the actual
content of our economic experience; and we discuss the implications only
within a narrow bandwidth of human concern. Is there a health risk? Might
the thing cause cancer? That's about it with cell phones, computers, genetic
engineering, and a host of other new developments. As a result, we must await
the verdict of the doctors to find out whether we are permitted to have
qualms or reservations. Jacob Needleman, the contemporary philosopher, says

that we Americans are "metaphysically repressed," and the inability to discuss the implications of technology—except in bodily or stock market terms—is a case in point.

I don't discount the significance of cancer. But there is something missing 5 from a discussion that can't get beyond the most literal and utilitarian concerns. Actually, some of the problems with cell phones aren't at all squishy or abstract. If you've been clipped by a car tooling around the corner while the driver sits gabbing, cell phone in hand, then you are aware of this. The big problem, of course, is the noise. For sheer intrusiveness, cell phones rank with mega-amp car stereoes and political commercials, and they are harder to escape.

We all know the drill. First the endearing beep, which is like an alarm clock going off at 5:30 a.m. Then people shout into the things, as though they are talking across the Cross Bronx Expressway. It's become a regular feature at movies and ball games, restaurants and parks. I've heard the things going off in men's room stalls. They represent more than mere annoyances. Cell phones affect life in ways that are, I suspect, beyond the capacity of the empirical mind to grasp.

Travel is an example. Thomas Carlyle° once advised Anthony Trollope° to use travel as a time to "sit still and label his thoughts." For centuries, travel played this quiet role. I have a hunch that the eloquence and depth of this nation's founders had partly to do with their mode of travel. Madison, Jefferson, and the others had that long ride to Philadelphia in which to sort out their thoughts and work over their sentences in their minds. There was time in which thought could expand; we can hear the echoes today in the spaciousness and considered quality of such documents as the *Federalist Papers*—a quality that political argument today rarely achieves.

In more recent times, trains have served as a link to that kind of travel. I used to look forward to Amtrak rides almost as a sanctuary. They provided precious hours in which to work or read or simply muse without the interruptions of the telephone and office. But now, cell phones have caught up with me. They have turned Amtrak into a horizontal telephone booth; on a recent trip to New York my wife and I were besieged by cell phones and their cousins, high-powered Walkmen, literally on all sides. The trip, which used to be a pleasure, has become one long headache.

I wrote the president of Amtrak to tell him this. I tried to be constructive. There is a real opportunity here for Amtrak to get ahead of the curve, I said. Why not provide "Quiet Cars" the way they provided No Smoking cars when smoking first became an issue? Amtrak could give riders a choice, which is what America is supposed to be about—and which Amtrak's main competitors, the airlines, cannot do. This seemed like a no-lose proposition. The yakkers could yak, others could enjoy the quiet, and Amtrak could have

---

Thomas Carlyle: Scottish historian and social critic (1795–1881) who influenced many important thinkers in the nineteenth century.   *Anthony Trollope:* British novelist (1815–1882) best known for *Barchester Towers* and *The Warden*.

a PR coup. (In a just world, the cell phoners would have to sit together in Noise Cars, but I was trying to be accommodating.)

The argument seemed pretty convincing. As the weeks passed, I imag- ined my letter circulating at the highest levels. Perhaps I'd even be called in as a consultant. Now that I have the reply, I'm not holding my breath. But the reasons that Amtrak offered for inaction are worth a few moments, since they suggest how quickly a technology invokes its own system of rationalization.

For example, the letter said that Amtrak does not want to inconvenience the "responsible" users of cell phones. That's typical; try to isolate a few aberrant users and so legitimate the rest. But cell phones are like cigarettes in this respect—they are intrusive when used normally, as intended. They beep like a seat belt warning or play a tinny melody like a musical toilet seat. People usually shout into them. They produce secondhand noise, just as cigarettes produce secondhand smoke; and from the standpoint of the forced consumer of this noise, the only responsible use is non-use.

Then the letter turned the issue upside down. "We hesitate to restrict responsible users of cell phones," it said, "especially since many customers find train travel to be an ideal way to get work done." But that is exactly why cell phones should be restricted—because many travelers are trying to get work done. For one thing, the notion that people are busily working on cell phones is New Economy hype. I have been a coerced eavesdropper on more conversations than I could count. I have listened to executives gab about their shopping hauls and weekend conquests. I once had to endure, between Philadelphia and New York, an extended brag from an associate sports agent regarding the important people he was meeting. It is not often that I hear anyone actually discussing work.

But more importantly, consider the assumption here. We have two people who arguably are trying to get some work done. There's the cell phone user, who wants to make noise. And there's myself (and probably numerous others), who would appreciate a little quiet. Why does the noise automatically take precedence over the quiet? Why does the polluter get first dibs on the air?

This is where the trail starts to get warm, I think. There is something about technology that enables it to take front seat in any situation it enters; which is to say, there is something in ourselves that seeks to give it this seat. A Maine essayist by the name of John Gould once noted this about the ordinary telephone. He was up on his roof one day when his wife called to him about something. "Later," he said, "Can't you see I'm working?" Later came, and this time the phone rang. Gould scrambled down the ladder in a frantic attempt to get to that phone.

Afterwards he reflected upon what had happened. His wife could wait, he thought, but the phone rang with the authority of Mussolini in a bad mood. Most of us probably have had this experience. We've been making a purchase when the phone rang and the clerk dropped us cold and got into a long conversation on the phone. Or perhaps we had a visitor in our own office and interrupted the conversation to pick up the phone. Whatever is happening, the

10

15

telephone comes first. Call waiting ratchets up the authority structure like a dictatorship that adds minions at the top. Now there are intrusions upon the intrusions; how many of us hear that click and think, "Oh, just let it ring."

What is it about these things that makes us so obedient, and so oblivious to that which lies outside them—such as actual people? I once asked a man who was bellowing into a cell phone in the coffee shop in San Francisco why he was talking so loudly. A bad connection, he said. It had not crossed his mind that anything else mattered at that moment. Like computers and television, cell phones pull people into their own psychological polar field, and the pull is strong. I've watched people complete a conversation, start to put the thing away, and then freeze. They sit staring at it, as though trying to think of someone else to call. The phone is there. It demands to be used, almost the way a cigarette demands to be smoked. Does the person own the cell phone, or is it the other way around?

And what does that suggest about where this "communications revolution" is taking us? When I was in Hong Kong a year and a half ago, it was becoming a cell-phone hell. The official statistics said there was one phone for every two people, but it often felt like two for one. They were everywhere; the table scenes in the splendid food courts in the high-rise malls were San Francisco to the second or third power. At a table with four people, two or three might be talking on the phone. You'd see a couple on a date, and one was talking on the phone.

In a way, I could understand the fixation. Hong Kong is crowded almost beyond belief. It makes parts of Manhattan feel like Kansas, and I suspect that a cell phone offers an escape, a kind of crack in space. It is an entrance to a realm in which you are the center of attention, the star. Access becomes a status symbol in itself. A lawyer friend of mine there described the new ritual at the start of business meetings. Everyone puts their cell phone on the conference table, next to their legal pad, almost like a gun. My power call against yours, *gweilo* (Chinese for foreigner; literally "ghost"). The smallest ones are the most expensive and therefore have the most status.

In places like Hong Kong, moreover, most people live in cramped quarters, which means consumption must take less space-consuming forms. That's all understandable. To a lesser degree, such considerations apply in places such as Washington and New York.

There is something lonely about a wired world. The more plugged in everyone else is, the more we feel we have to be there too. But then effect becomes cause. The very thing that pulls us away from live public spaces begins to make those spaces uninhabitable. It is the pollution of the aural commons, the enclosure of public space by giant telecommunications firms, and the result is to push us all towards private space—if we can afford it.

This is technological Reaganism, a world in which personal desires are all that matters and to hell with everything else. So everything else starts to go to hell. The libertarian dogmatics of the computer crowd thus become self-fulfilling prophecies. But there's this, too. Not only are they saying, "Get out of my face." They are also saying, "I can't stop myself. I'm hooked." It is a communications revolution all right, but one that requires psychologists and anthropologists to understand. Economists just don't get it. They couch these events in the language of Locke and Smith—of rational people seeking a rational self-interest. But in reality it's the old dark stuff: the vagrant passions and attachments of the human heart.

But forgive me. I forgot. This is the longest economic expansion on record we are talking about here, so we aren't supposed to get too deep. So I'll just close with a prediction. Secondhand noise is going to become a bigger issue in the next decade than secondhand smoke was in the last. It will be part of the big second wave of environmentalism—the fight against cognitive pollution, the despoiling of the aural and visual commons, whether by cell phones and Walkmen or by advertising everywhere.

It's going to be a wrenching battle, but I predict at least one early victory. Quiet cars on Amtrak within five years. Meanwhile, I have my eye on a company in Israel, called NetLine Technologies, that makes small portable devices to block cell phones. Technically, they are illegal, and I doubt that more technology ultimately is the answer. But they do raise a useful question. If some people can use technology to pollute the air we share, why can't other people use technology to clean it up again?

QUESTIONS FOR DISCUSSION

1. Rowe claims that Americans rarely discuss the implications of technology. Do you agree?
2. Why does Rowe believe that cell phones "represent more than mere annoyances"? Why is the public use of cell phones problematic?
3. In paragraph 15, Rowe notes that salespeople sometimes take phone calls even when they are already working with someone in the store—giving the caller priority over the shopper. His this ever happened to you? What do managers assume when they train salespeople to work this way?
4. How would you respond if someone you were dating took a call when you were having dinner together in a restaurant?
5. Why can technology become addictive?
6. How fair is Rowe's assessment of cell phones? Do you think he should have discussed how cell phones can make a positive contribution to society? Or was he wise to stay focused on the negative aspects of these phones?

SUGGESTIONS FOR WRITING

1. In paragraphs 7 and 8, Rowe comments on how noisy travel has become. Consider your own travel experience, especially trips made by bus, train, or plane. Then write an evaluation of a specific journey.
2. Imagine that you are writing for an audience of people interested in purchasing a cell phone. Compare three cell phones that are widely used today, evaluating their quality and value.

3. How does the public use of the Walkman and other portable CD players affect social life? Write an evaluation in which you appraise both the positive and negative aspects of this form of technology.

LINKS ■ ■ ■

■ WITHIN THE BOOK

For a humorous essay on technology, see Patricia Volk's "Technology Makes Me Mad" (pages 585–586).

■ ELSEWHERE IN PRINT

Carter, Stephen. *Civility: Manners, Morals, and the Etiquette of Democracy.* New York: Basic, 1998.

Dresser, Norine. *Multicultural Manners: New Rules of Etiquette for a Changing Society.* New York: Wiley, 1996.

Post, Peggy, *Emily Post's Etiquette.* 16th ed. New York: Harper, 1997.

■ ONLINE

- Cellular Telecommunications and Internet Association (CTIA) <http://www.wirelessdata.org/front.asp>

- Does Cell Phone Conversation Impair Driving Performance? <http://www.nsc.org/library/shelf/inincell.htm>

- The Ten Commandments of Cell Phone Etiquette <http://www.infoworld.com/articles/op/xml/00/05/26/000526opwireless.xml>

SHE: PORTRAIT OF THE ESSAY AS A WARM BODY

Cynthia Ozick

One of the most widely admired American essayists writing today, Cynthia Ozick is also the author of finely crafted short stories. A frequent contributor to the New York Review of Books, *among other periodicals, she published the following essay in a 1998 issue of* The Atlantic Monthly. *Instead of evaluating the work of a specific writer, she chose to evaluate the merit of a specific genre: the essay. As you read, be alert for how Ozick distinguishes an "essay" from other genres such as "a tract" and "a novel." Bearing her distinctions in mind could help you to determine which of the selections in this book are essays and which are articles—as well as understand how fiction differs from nonfiction.*

When discussing writing in an interview with Katie Bolick for Atlantic Unbound, *the online version of* The Atlantic Monthly, *Ozick stated, "I don't agree with the sentiment 'write what you know.' That recommends circumspection. I think one should write what one doesn't know. The world is bigger and wider and more complex than our small subjective selves. One should prod, goad the imagination. That's what it's there for." Consider what goads your own imagination as you read the following essay.*

An essay is a thing of the imagination. If there is information in an essay, it is by-the-by, and if there is an opinion, one need not trust it for the long run. A genuine essay rarely has an educational, polemical, or sociopolitical use; it is the movement of a free mind at play. Though it is written in prose, it is closer in kind to poetry than to any other form. Like a poem, a genuine essay is made of language and character and mood and temperament and pluck and chance.

I speak of a "genuine" essay because fakes abound. Here the old-fashioned term *poetaster* may apply, if only obliquely. As the poetaster is to the poet—a lesser aspirant—so the average article is to the essay: a look-alike knockoff guaranteed not to wear well. An article is often gossip. An essay is reflection and insight. An article often has the temporary advantage of social heat—what's hot out there right now. An essay's heat is interior. An article can be timely, topical, engaged in the issues and personalities of the moment; it is likely to be stale within the month. In five years it may have acquired the quaint aura of a rotary phone. An article is usually Siamese-twinned to its date of birth. An essay defies its date of birth—and ours, too. (A necessary caveat: Some genuine essays are popularly called "articles"—but this is no more than an idle, though persistent, habit of speech. What's in a name? The ephemeral is the ephemeral. The enduring is the enduring.)

A small historical experiment. Who are the classic essayists who come at once to mind? Montaigne, obviously. Among the nineteenth-century English masters, the long row of Hazlitt, Lamb, De Quincey, Stevenson, Carlyle,

Ruskin, Newman, Martineau, Arnold. Of the Americans, Emerson. Nowadays, admittedly, these are read only by specialists and literature majors, and by the latter only under compulsion. However accurate this observation, it is irrelevant to the experiment, which has to do with beginnings and their disclosures. Here, then, are some introductory passages:

> One of the pleasantest things in the world is going a journey; but I like to go by myself. I can enjoy society in a room; but out of doors, nature is company enough for me. I am then never less alone than when alone.
> —William Hazlitt, "On Going a Journey"

> To go into solitude, a man needs to retire as much from his chamber as from society. I am not solitary whilst I read and write, though nobody is with me. But if a man would be alone, let him look at the stars.
> —Ralph Waldo Emerson, "Nature"

> . . . I have often been asked, how I first came to be a regular opium-eater; and have suffered, very unjustly, in the opinion of my acquaintance, from being reputed to have brought upon myself all the sufferings which I shall have to record, by a long course of indulgence in this practice purely for the sake of creating an artificial state of pleasurable excitement. This, however, is a misrepresentation of my case.
> —Thomas De Quincey,
> "Confessions of an English Opium-Eater"

> The human species, according to the best theory I can form of it, is composed of two distinct races, *the men who borrow, and the men who lend.*
> —Charles Lamb, "The Two Races of Men"

> I saw two hareems in the East; and it would be wrong to pass them over in an account of my travels; though the subject is as little agreeable as any I can have to treat. I cannot now think of the two mornings thus employed without a heaviness of heart greater than I have ever brought away from Deaf and Dumb Schools, Lunatic Asylums, or even Prisons.
> —Harriet Martineau, "The Hareem"

> The future of poetry is immense, because in poetry, where it is worthy of its high destinies, our race, as time goes on, will find an ever surer and surer stay. There is not a creed which is not shaken, not an accredited dogma which is not shown to be questionable, not a received tradition which does not threaten to dissolve. . . . But for poetry the idea is everything; the rest is a world of illusion, of divine illusion.
> —Matthew Arnold, "The Study of Poetry"

> The changes wrought by death are in themselves so sharp and final, and so terrible and melancholy in their consequences, that the thing

stands alone in man's experience, and has no parallel upon earth. It outdoes all other accidents because it is the last of them. Sometimes it leaps suddenly upon its victims, like a Thug; sometimes it lays a regular siege and creeps upon their citadel during a score of years. And when the business is done, there is sore havoc made in other people's lives, and a pin knocked out by which many subsidiary friendships hung together.

—Robert Louis Stevenson, "*Aes Triplex*"

It is recorded of some people, as of Alexander the Great, that their sweat, in consequence of some rare and extraordinary constitution, emitted a sweet odour, the cause of which Plutarch and others investigated. But the nature of most bodies is the opposite, and at their best they are free from smell. Even the purest breath has nothing more excellent than to be without offensive odour, like that of very healthy children.

—Michel de Montaigne, "Of Smells"

What might such a little anthology of beginnings reveal? First, that language differs from one era to the next: archaism intrudes, if only in punctuation and cadence. Second, that splendid minds may contradict each other (outdoors, Hazlitt never feels alone; Emerson urges others to go outdoors in order to feel alone). Third, that the theme of an essay can be anything under the sun, however trivial (the smell of sweat) or crushing (the thought that we must die). Fourth, that the essay is a consistently recognizable and venerable—or call it ancient—form. In English, Addison and Steele in the eighteenth century, Bacon and Browne in the seventeenth, Lyly in the sixteenth, Bede in the eighth. And what of the biblical Koheleth (Ecclesiastes), who may be the oldest essayist reflecting on one of the oldest subjects—world-weariness?

So the essay is ancient and various; but this is a commonplace. Something else, more striking yet, catches our attention—the essay's power. By "power" I mean precisely the capacity to do what force always does: coerce assent. Never mind that the shape and inclination of any essay is against coercion or suasion, or that the essay neither proposes nor purposes to get us to think like its author—at least not overtly. If an essay has a "motive," it is linked more to happenstance and opportunity than to the driven will. A genuine essay is not a doctrinaire tract or a propaganda effort or a broadside. Thomas Paine's "Common Sense" and Emile Zola's "*J'Accuse . . . !*" are heroic landmark writings; but to call them essays, though they may resemble the form, is to misunderstand. The essay is not meant for the barricades; it is a stroll through someone's mazy mind. This is not to say that no essayist has ever been intent on making a moral argument, however obliquely—George Orwell is a case in point. At the end of the day the essay turns out to be a force for agreement. It co-opts agreement; it courts agreement; it seduces agreement. For the brief hour we give to it, we are sure to fall into surrender and conviction. And this will occur even if we are intrinsically roused to resistance.

To illustrate: I may not be persuaded by Emersonianism as an ideology, but Emerson—his voice, his language, his music—persuades me. When we look for words of praise, not for nothing do we speak of "commanding" or "compelling" prose. If I am a skeptical rationalist or an advanced biochemist, I may regard (or discard) the idea of the soul as no better than a puff of warm vapor. But here is Emerson on the soul: "When it breathes through [man's] intellect, it is genius; when it breathes through his will, it is virtue; when it flows through his affection, it is love." And then—well, I am in thrall; I am possessed; I believe.

The novel has its own claims on surrender. It suspends our participation in the society we ordinarily live in, so that for the time we are reading, we forget it utterly. But the essay does not allow us to forget our usual sensations and opinions. It does something even more potent: it makes us deny them. The authority of a masterly essayist—the authority of sublime language and intimate observation—is absolute. When I am with Hazlitt, I know no greater companion than nature. When I am with Emerson, I know no greater solitude than nature.

And what is oddest about the essay's power to lure us into its lair is how it goes about this work. We feel it when a political journalist comes after us with a point of view—we feel it the way the cat is wary of the dog. A polemic is a herald complete with feathered hat and trumpet. A tract can be a trap. Certain magazine articles have the scent of so much per word. What is indisputable is that all of these are more or less in the position of a lepidopterist with his net: They mean to catch and skewer. They are focused on prey—us. The genuine essay, in contrast, never thinks of us; the genuine essay may be the most self-centered (the politer word would be subjective) arena for human thought ever devised.

Or else, though still not having us in mind (unless as an embodiment of common folly), it is not self-centered at all. When I was a child, I discovered in the public library a book that enchanted me then, and the idea of which has enchanted me for life. I have no recollection of either the title or the writer—and anyhow, very young readers rarely take note of authors; stories are simply and magically *there*. The characters include, as I remember them, three or four children and a delightful relation who is a storyteller, and the scheme is this: each child calls out a story element, most often an object, and the storyteller gathers up whatever is supplied (blue boots, a river, a fairy, a pencil box) and makes out of these random, unlikely and disparate offerings a tale both logical and surprising. An essay, it seems to me, may be similarly constructed—if so deliberate a term applies. The essayist, let us say, unexpectedly stumbles over a pair of old blue boots in a corner of the garage, and this reminds her of when she last wore them—twenty years ago, on a trip to Paris, where on the bank of the Seine she stopped to watch an old fellow sketching, with a box of colored pencils at his side. The pencil wiggling over his sheet is a grayish pink, which reflects the threads of sunset pulling westward in the sky, like the reins of a fairy cart . . . and so on. The mind meanders, slipping from one impression to another, from reality to memory to dreamscape and back again.

In the same way Montaigne, when contemplating the unpleasantness of   *10*
sweat, ends with the pure breath of children. Stevenson, starting out with
mortality, speaks first of ambush, then of war, and finally of a displaced pin.
No one is freer than the essayist—free to leap out in any direction, to hop
from thought to thought, to begin with the finish and finish with the middle, or to eschew beginning and end and keep only a middle. The marvel is
that out of this apparent causelessness, out of this scattering of idiosyncratic
seeing and telling, a coherent world is made. It is coherent because, after all,
an essayist must be an artist, and every artist, whatever the means, arrives
at a sound and singular imaginative frame—call it, on a minor scale, a
cosmogony.

Into this frame, this work of art, we tumble like tar babies, and are held
fast. What holds us there? The authority of a voice, yes; the pleasure—sometimes the anxiety—of a new idea, an untried angle, a snatch of reminiscence,
bliss displayed or shock conveyed. An essay can be the product of intellect or
memory, lightheartedness or gloom, well-being or disgruntlement. But always
we sense a certain quietude, on occasion a kind of detachment. Rage and
revenge, I think, belong to fiction. The essay is cooler than that. Because it so
often engages in acts of memory, and despite its gladder or more antic incarna-
tions, the essay is by and large a serene or melancholic form. It mimics that
low electric hum, which sometimes rises to resemble actual speech, that all
human beings carry inside their heads—a vibration, garrulous if somewhat
indistinct, that never leaves us while we are awake. It is the hum of perpetual
noticing: the configuration of someone's eyelid or tooth, the veins on a hand, a
wisp of string caught on a twig; some words your fourth-grade teacher said, so
long ago, about the rain; the look of an awning, a sidewalk, a bit of cheese left
on a plate. All day long this inescapable hum drums on, recalling one thing and
another, and pointing out this and this and this. Legend has it that Titus,
Emperor of Rome, went mad because of the buzzing of a gnat that made her
home in his ear; and presumably the gnat, flying out into the great world and
then returning to her nest, whispered what she had seen and felt and learned
there. But an essayist is more resourceful than an Emperor, and can be relieved
of this interior noise, if only for the time required to record its murmurings. To
seize the hum and set it down for others to hear is the essayist's genius.

It is a genius bound to leisure, and even to luxury, if luxury is measured
in hours. The essay's limits can be found in its own reflective nature. Poems
have been wrested from the inferno of catastrophe or war, and battlefield letters, too; these are the spontaneous bursts and burnings that danger excites.
But the meditative temperateness of an essay requires a desk and a chair, a
musing and a mooning, a connection to a civilized surround; even when the
subject itself is a wilderness of lions and tigers, mulling is the way of it. An
essay is a fireside thing, not a conflagration or a safari.

This may be why, when we ask who the essayists are, we discover that
though novelists may now and then write essays, true essayists rarely write

novels. Essayists are a species of metaphysician: They are inquisitive, and analytic, about the least grain of being. Novelists go about the strenuous business of marrying and burying their people, or else they send them to sea, or to Africa, or at the least out of town. Essayists in their stillness ponder love and death. It is probably an illusion that men are essayists more often than women, especially since women's essays have in the past frequently assumed the form of unpublished correspondence. (Here I should, I suppose, add a note about maleness and femaleness as a literary issue—what is popularly termed "gender," as if men and women were French or German tables and sofas. I *should* add such a note—it is the fashion, or, rather, the current expectation or obligation—but nothing useful can be said about any of it.) Essays are written by men. Essays are written by women. That is the long and the short of it. John Updike, in a genially confident discourse on maleness ("The Disposable Rocket"), takes the view—though he admits to admixture—that the "male sense of space must differ from that of the female, who has such interesting, active, and significant inner space. The space that interests men is outer." Except, let it be observed, when men write essays, since it is only inner space—interesting, active, significant—that can conceive and nourish the contemplative essay. The "ideal female body," Updike adds, "curves around centers of repose," and no phrase could better describe the shape of the ideal essay—yet women are no fitter as essayists than men. In promoting the felt salience of sex, Updike nevertheless drives home an essayist's point. Essays, unlike novels, emerge from the sensations of the self. Fiction creeps into foreign bodies: The novelist can inhabit not only a sex not his own but also beetles and noses and hunger artists and nomads and beasts. The essay is, as we say, personal.

And here is an irony. Though I have been intent on distinguishing the marrow of the essay from the marrow of fiction, I confess that I have been trying all along, in a subliminal way, to speak of the essay as if it—or she—were a character in a novel or a play: moody, fickle, given to changing her clothes, or the subject, on a whim; sometimes obstinate, with a mind of her own, or hazy and light; never predictable. I mean for her to be dressed—and addressed—as we would Becky Sharp, or Ophelia, or Elizabeth Bennet, or Mrs. Ramsay, or Mrs. Wilcox, or even Hester Prynne. Put it that it is pointless to say (as I have done repeatedly, disliking it every time) "the essay," or "an essay." The essay—an essay—is not an abstraction; she may have recognizable contours, but she is highly colored and individuated; she is not a type. She is too fluid, too elusive, to be a category. She may be bold, she may be diffident, she may rely on beauty or cleverness, on eros or exotica. Whatever her story, she is the protagonist, the secret self's personification. When we knock on her door, she opens to us; she is a presence in the doorway; she leads us from room to room. Then why should we not call her "she"? She may be privately indifferent to us, but she is anything but unwelcoming. Above all, she is not a hidden principle or a thesis or a construct: She is *there,* a living voice. She takes us in.

QUESTIONS FOR DISCUSSION

1. According to Ozick, what is the difference between an "essay" and an "article"? Why does Ozick prefer the essay?
2. How do essays differ from fiction?
3. What is your personal response to the introductory passages quoted by Ozick in paragraph 3? Based on these quotations, which essay would most interest you? And which would interest you the least?
4. In paragraph 8, Ozick writes, "A tract can be a trap." What do you think she means by this?
5. Why does Ozick believe that "No one is freer than the essayist"?
6. What do you think of Ozick's use of gender in characterizing the essay? If the essay is a "she," what assumptions are being made about what it means to be a woman?

SUGGESTIONS FOR WRITING

1. Write an essay defining the criteria with which you evaluate either essays or articles.
2. Read one of the essays quoted in paragraph 3, and write an evaluation of it.
3. Evaluate a literary genre or other art form that strikes you as a "he" rather than a "she."

LINKS ■ ■ ■

■ WITHIN THE BOOK

In "Monologue to the Maestro" (pages 626–631), Ernest Hemingway offers ideas about writing fiction.

■ ELSEWHERE IN PRINT

Anderson, Chris, ed. *Literary Nonfiction: Theory, Criticism, Pedagogy.* Carbondale, Southern Illinois UP, 1989. Ozick, Cynthia. *The Cannibal Galaxy.* New York: Knopf, 1983.
———. *Fame and Folly.* New York: Knopf: 1996.
———. *Metaphor and Memory.* New York: Knopf, 1989.
———. *Quarrel and Quandary: Essays.* New York: Knopf, 2000.

■ ONLINE

■ Charles Lamb
    <http://www.ucs.louisiana.edu/~jer6616>

(continues)

LINKS ■ ■ ■ *(continued)*

- Michel de Montaigne
  <http://www. orst.edu/instruct/phl302/philosophers/
  montaigne.html>
- Ralph Waldo Emerson
  <http://www.rwe.org>
- Thomas De Quincey
  <http://www.ace.acadiau.ca/english/morrison/dequincey/
  welcome.htm>

MY DIAGNOSIS

Susanna Kaysen

A common form of assessment is a personal evaluation. An evaluation of this sort could take the form of a letter of recommendation, an annual job review, or notes written in the record of a hospital patient. "My Diagnosis" is an excerpt from Girl, Interrupted *(1993), Susanna Kaysen's memoir of what it was like to be hospitalized for mental illness when she was eighteen—an experience that was by then more than twenty years in her past. After studying the notes written in her chart, as well as the definition of her diagnosis published by the American Psychiatric Association, Kaysen writes a self-evaluation that is, among other things, an evaluation of her evaluation.*

In an interview about Girl, Interrupted, *Kaysen told* Publisher's Weekly *that she decided to incorporate hospital records in her memoir "because the contrast between their language and my language was interesting" and "provided a viewpoint on the experience that I couldn't provide." Although* Girl, Interrupted *is her best-known work and became a movie starring Winona Ryder and Angelina Jolie, Kaysen is also the author of two novels:* Asa: As I Knew Him *(1987) and* Far Afield *(1990).*

McLEAN HOSPITAL   Page _____   F-90

№. 22 201   **Name**   KAYSEN, Susanna

1968
9-4   DISCHARGE ON VISIT SUMMARY:

             G.   Formal Diagnosis:
             Schizophrenic reaction, paranoid type (borderline)--
             currently in remission. Patient is functioning on
             a passive-aggressive personality, passive-dependent
             type.

                                                        12
KAYSEN, Susanna N.
Hospital No. 22201
                    CASE REPORT--CONT'D

B. Prognosis: The resolution of the depressive effect
and suicidal drive should be expected as a result of the
hospitalization. The degree of personality integration and ego
function which may be achieved for the long term is hard to
predict. We may say that with a good intensive working relationship in therapy and a successful relationship to
the hospital the patient may be able to achieve a more
satisfactory means of adapting. Nevertheless because of
the chronicity of the illness and the basic deficiencies
involved in personality structuring, a more complete
recovery is not to be expected at this time. However, the
patient may learn to make more wise choices for herself within
the boundaries of her personality so that she is
able to achieve a satisfactory dependent relationship if necessary which will sustain her for a long period of time.

BORDERLINE PERSONALITY DISORDER*

*From the *Diagnostic and Statistical Manual of Mental Disorders,*
3rd edition, revised (1987), pages 346–47

An essential feature of this disorder is a pervasive pattern of instability of self-image, interpersonal relationships, and mood, beginning in early adulthood and present in a variety of contexts.

A marked and persistent identity disturbance is almost invariably present. This is often pervasive, and is manifested by uncertainty about several life issues, such as self-image, sexual orientation, long-term goals or career choice, types of friends or lovers to have, and which values to adopt. The person often experiences this instability of self-image as chronic feelings of emptiness and boredom.

Interpersonal relationships are usually unstable and intense, and may be characterized by alternation of the extremes of overidealization and devaluation. These people have difficulty tolerating being alone, and will make frantic efforts to avoid real or imagined abandonment.

Affective instability is common. This may be evidenced by marked mood shifts from baseline mood to depression, irritability, or anxiety, usually lasting a few hours or, only rarely, more than a few days. In addition, these people often have inappropriately intense anger with frequent displays of temper or recurrent physical fights. They tend to be impulsive, particularly in activities that are potentially self-damaging, such as shopping sprees, psychoactive substance abuse, reckless driving, casual sex, shoplifting, and binge eating.

Recurrent suicidal threats, gestures, or behavior and other self-mutilating behavior (e.g., wrist-scratching) are common in the more severe forms of the disorder. This behavior may serve to manipulate others, may be a result of intense anger, or may counteract feelings of "numbness" and depersonalization that arise during periods of extreme stress. . . .

Associated Features. Frequently this disorder is accompanied by many features of other Personality Disorders, such as Schizotypal, Histrionic, Narcissistic, and Antisocial Personality Disorders. In many cases more than one diagnosis is warranted. Quite often social contrariness and a generally pessimistic outlook are observed. Alternation between dependency and self-assertion is common. During periods of extreme stress, transient psychotic symptoms may occur, but they are generally of insufficient severity or duration to warrant an additional diagnosis.

Impairment. Often there is considerable interference with social or occupational functioning.

Complications. Possible complications include Dysthymia [depressive neurosis], Major Depression, Psychoactive Substance Abuse, and psychotic disorders such as Brief Reactive Psychosis. Premature death may result from suicide.

Sex Ratio. The disorder is more commonly diagnosed in women.

Prevalence. Borderline Personality Disorder is apparently common.

Predisposing and Familial Pattern. No information.

Differential Diagnosis. In Identity Disorder there is a similar clinical picture, but Borderline Personality Disorder preempts the diagnosis of Identity Disorder if the criteria for Borderline Personality Disorder are met, the disturbance is sufficiently pervasive and persistent, and it is unlikely that it will be limited to a developmental stage. . . .

So these were the charges against me. I didn't read them until twenty-five years later. "A character disorder" is what they'd told me then.

I had to find a lawyer to help me get my records from the hospital; I had to read line 32a of form A1 of the Case Record, and entry G on the Discharge on Visit Summary, and entry B of Part IV of the Case Report; then I had to locate a copy of the *Diagnostic and Statistical Manual of Mental Disorders* and look up Borderline Personality to see what they really thought about me.

It's a fairly accurate picture of me at eighteen, minus a few quirks like reckless driving and eating binges. It's accurate but it isn't profound. Of course, it doesn't aim to be profound. It's not even a case study. It's a set of guidelines, a generalization.

I'm tempted to try refuting it, but then I would be open to the further charges of "defensiveness" and "resistance."

All I can do is give the particulars: an annotated diagnosis.   5

"[U]ncertainty about several life issues, such as self-image, sexual orientation, long-term goals or career choice, types of friends or lovers to have . . ." I relish that last phrase. Its awkwardness (the "to have" seems superfluous) gives it substance and heft. I still have that uncertainty. Is this the type of friend or lover I want to have? I ask myself every time I meet someone new. Charming but shallow; good-hearted but a bit conventional; too handsome for his own good; fascinating but probably unreliable; and so forth. I guess I've had my share of unreliables. More than my share? How many would constitute more than my share?

Fewer than for somebody else—somebody who'd never been called a borderline personality?

That's the nub of my problem here.

If my diagnosis had been bipolar illness, for instance, the reaction to me and to this story would be slightly different. That's a chemical problem, you'd say to yourself, manic-depression, Lithium, all that. I would be blameless, somehow. And what about schizophrenia—that would send a chill up your spine. After all, that's real insanity. People don't "recover" from schizophrenia. You'd have to wonder how much of what I'm telling you is true and how much imagined.

I'm simplifying, I know. But these words taint everything. The fact that I   10 was locked up taints everything.

What does *borderline personality* mean, anyhow?

It appears to be a way station between neurosis and psychosis: a fractured but not disassembled psyche. Though to quote my post-Melvin° psychiatrist: "It's what they call people whose lifestyles bother them."

He can say it because he's a doctor. If I said it, nobody would believe me.

Melvin: Kaysen's psychiatrist when she was a patient at McLean Hospital.

An analyst I've known for years said, "Freud and his circle thought most people were hysterics, then in the fifties it was psychoneurotics, and lately, everyone's a borderline personality."

When I went to the corner bookstore to look up my diagnosis in the *Manual,* it occurred to me that I might not find it in there anymore. They do get rid of things—homosexuality, for instance. Until recently, quite a few of my friends would have found themselves documented in that book along with me. Well, they got out of the book and I didn't. Maybe in another twenty-five years I won't be in there either.

"[I]nstability of self-image, interpersonal relationships, and mood . . . uncertainty about . . . long-term goals or career choice . . ." Isn't this a good description of adolescence? Moody, fickle, faddish, insecure: in short, impossible.

"[S]elf-mutilating behavior (e.g., wrist-scratching) . . ." I've skipped forward a bit. This is the one that caught me by surprise as I sat on the floor of the bookstore reading my diagnosis. Wrist-scratching! I thought I'd invented it. Wrist-banging, to be precise.

This is where people stop being able to follow me. This is the sort of stuff you get locked up for. Nobody knew I was doing it, though. I never told anyone, until now.

I had a butterfly chair. In the sixties, everyone in Cambridge had a butterfly chair. The metal edge of its upturned seat was perfectly placed for wrist-banging. I had tried breaking ashtrays and walking on the shards, but I didn't have the nerve to tread firmly. Wrist-banging—slow, steady, mindless—was a better solution. It was cumulative injury, so each bang was tolerable.

A solution to what? I quote from the *Manual:* "This behavior may . . . counteract feelings of 'numbness' and depersonalization that arise during periods of extreme stress."

I spent hours in my butterfly chair banging my wrist. I did it in the evenings, like homework. I'd do some homework, then I'd spend half an hour wrist-banging, then finish my homework, then back in the chair for some more banging before brushing my teeth and going to bed. I banged the inside, where the veins converge. It swelled and turned a bit blue, but considering how hard and how much I banged it, the visible damage was slight. That was yet one more recommendation of it to me.

I'd had an earlier period of face-scratching. If my fingernails hadn't been quite short, I couldn't have gotten away with it. As it was, I definitely looked puffy and peculiar the next day. I used to scratch my cheeks and then rub soap on them. Maybe the soap prevented me from looking worse. But I looked bad enough that people asked, "Is something wrong with your face?" So I switched to wrist-banging.

I was like an anchorite with a hair shirt. Part of the point was that nobody knew about my suffering. If people knew and admired—or abominated—me, something important would be lost.

I was trying to explain my situation to myself. My situation was that I was in pain and nobody knew it; even I had trouble knowing it. So I told

15

20

myself, over and over, You are in pain. It was the only way I could get through to myself ("counteract feelings of 'numbness'"). I was demonstrating, externally and irrefutably, an inward condition.

"Quite often social contrariness and a generally pessimistic outlook are   *25* observed." What do you suppose they mean by "social contrariness"? Putting my elbows on the table? Refusing to get a job as a dental technician? Disappointing my parents' hope that I would go to a first-rate university?

They don't define "social contrariness," and I can't define it, so I think it ought to be excluded from the list. I'll admit to the generally pessimistic outlook. Freud had one too.

I can honestly say that my misery has been transformed into common unhappiness, so by Freud's definition I have achieved mental health. And my discharge sheet, at line 41, Outcome with Regard to Mental Disorder, reads "Recovered."

Recovered. Had my personality crossed over that border, whatever and wherever it was, to resume life within the confines of the normal? Had I stopped arguing with my personality and learned to straddle the line between sane and insane? Perhaps I'd actually had an identity disorder. "In Identity Disorder there is a similar clinical picture, but Borderline Personality . . . preempts the diagnosis . . . if the disturbance is sufficiently pervasive and . . . it is unlikely that it will be limited to a developmental stage." Maybe I was a victim of improper preemption?

I'm not finished with this diagnosis.

"The person often experiences this instability of self-image as chronic   *30* feelings of emptiness or boredom." My chronic feelings of emptiness and boredom came from the fact that I was living a life based on my incapacities, which were numerous. A partial list follows. I could not and did not want to: ski, play tennis, or go to gym class; attend to any subject in school other than English and biology; write papers on any assigned topics (I wrote poems instead of papers for English; I got F's); plan to go or apply to college; give any reasonable explanation for these refusals.

My self-image was not unstable. I saw myself, quite correctly, as unfit for the educational and social systems.

But my parents and teachers did not share my self-image. Their image of me was unstable, since it was out of kilter with reality and based on their needs and wishes. They did not put much value on my capacities, which were admittedly few, but genuine. I read everything, I wrote constantly, and I had boyfriends by the barrelful.

"Why don't you do the assigned reading?" they'd ask. "Why don't you write your papers instead of whatever you're writing—what is that, a short story?" "Why don't you expend as much energy on your schoolwork as you do on your boyfriends?"

By my senior year I didn't even bother with excuses, let alone explanations.

"Where is your term paper?" asked my history teacher.   *35*

"I didn't write it. I have nothing to say on that topic."

"You could have picked another topic."

"I have nothing to say on any historical topic."

One of my teachers told me I was a nihilist. He meant it as an insult but I took it as a compliment.

Boyfriends and literature: How can you make a life out of those two things? As it turns out, I did; more literature than boyfriends lately, but I guess you can't have everything ("a generally pessimistic outlook [is] observed").

Back then I didn't know that I—or anyone—could make a life out of boyfriends and literature. As far as I could see, life demanded skills I didn't have. The result was chronic emptiness and boredom. There were more pernicious results as well: self-loathing, alternating with "inappropriately intense anger with frequent displays of temper. . . ."

What would have been an appropriate level of intensity for my anger at feeling shut out of life? My classmates were spinning their fantasies for the future: lawyer, ethnobotanist, Buddhist monk (it was a very progressive high school). Even the dumb, uninteresting ones who were there to provide "balance" looked forward to their marriages and their children. I knew I wasn't going to have any of this because I knew I didn't want it. But did that mean I would have nothing?

I was the first person in the history of the school not to go to college. Of course, at least a third of my classmates never finished college. By 1968, people were dropping out daily.

Quite often now, people say to me, when I tell them I didn't go to college, "Oh, how marvelous!" They wouldn't have thought it was so marvelous back then. They didn't; my classmates were just the sorts of people who now tell me how marvelous I am. In 1966, I was a pariah.

What was I going to do? a few of my classmates asked.

"I'm going to join the WACs,°" I told one guy.

"Oh, yeah? That will be an interesting career."

"Just kidding," I said.

"Oh, uh, you mean you're not, really?"

I was stunned. Who did they think I was?

I'm sure they didn't think about me much. I was that one who wore black and—really, I've heard it from several people—slept with the English teacher. They were all seventeen and miserable, just like me. They didn't have time to wonder why I was a little more miserable than most.

Emptiness and boredom: what an understatement. What I felt was complete desolation. Desolation, despair, and depression.

Isn't there some other way to look at this? After all, angst of these dimensions is a luxury item. You need to be well fed, clothed, and housed to have time for this much self-pity. And the college business: My parents wanted me to go, I didn't want to go, and I didn't go. I got what I wanted. Those who

WACs: Women's Army Corps.

don't go to college have to get jobs. I agreed with all this. I told myself all this over and over. I even got a job—my job° breaking au gratin dishes.

But the fact that I couldn't hold my job was worrisome. I was probably crazy. I'd been skirting the idea of craziness for a year or two; now I was closing in on it.

Pull yourself together! I told myself. Stop indulging yourself. There's   55
nothing wrong with you. You're just wayward.

One of the great pleasures of mental health (whatever that is) is how much less time I have to spend thinking about myself.

I have a few more annotations to my diagnosis.

"The disorder is more commonly diagnosed in women."

Note the construction of that sentence. They did not write, "The disorder is more common in women." It would still be suspect, but they didn't even bother trying to cover their tracks.

Many disorders, judging by the hospital population, were more com-   60
monly diagnosed in women. Take, for example, "compulsive promiscuity."

How many girls do you think a seventeen-year-old boy would have to screw to earn the label "compulsively promiscuous"? Three? No, not enough. Six? Doubtful. Ten? That sounds more likely. Probably in the fifteen-to-twenty range, would be my guess—if they ever put that label on boys, which I don't recall their doing.

And for seventeen-year-old girls, how many boys?

In the list of six "potentially self-damaging" activities favored by the borderline personality, three are commonly associated with women (shopping sprees, shoplifting, and eating binges) and one with men (reckless driving). One is not "gender-specific," as they say these days (psychoactive substance abuse). And the definition of the other (casual sex) is in the eye of the beholder.

Then there is the question of "premature death" from suicide. Luckily, I avoided it, but I thought about suicide a lot. I'd think about it and make myself sad over my premature death, and then I'd feel better. The idea of suicide worked on me like a purgative or a cathartic. For some people it's different— Daisy,° for instance. But was her death really "premature"? Ought she to have sat in her eat-in kitchen with her chicken and her anger for another fifty years? I'm assuming she wasn't going to change, and I may be wrong. She certainly made that assumption, and she may also have been wrong. And if she'd sat there for only thirty years, and killed herself at forty-nine instead of at nineteen, would her death still be "premature"?

I got better and Daisy didn't and I can't explain why. Maybe I was just   65
flirting with madness the way I flirted with my teachers and my classmates. I wasn't convinced I was crazy, though I feared I was. Some people say that having any conscious opinion on the matter is a mark of sanity, but I'm not sure that's true. I still think about it. I'll always have to think about it.

---

my job: A position in a cookware store, where Kaysen accidentally dropped things.
Daisy: Another patient on the ward who gorged on chicken and eventually committed suicide.

I often ask myself if I'm crazy. I ask other people too.

"Is this a crazy thing to say?" I'll ask before saying something that probably isn't crazy.

I start a lot of sentences with "Maybe I'm totally nuts," or "Maybe I've gone 'round the bend."

If I do something out of the ordinary—take two baths in one day, for example—I say to myself: Are you crazy?

It's a common phrase, I know. But it means something particular to me: the tunnels, the security screens, the plastic forks, the shimmering, ever-shifting borderline that like all boundaries beckons and asks to be crossed. I do not want to cross it again.   70

QUESTIONS FOR DISCUSSION

1. According to the chart reprinted on page 321, Kaysen was said to be in "remission" when she was discharged from the hospital. What are the implications of this? If you thought you had recovered from a mental illness, how would it feel to be told you were in remission?
2. What are the characteristics of Borderline Personality Disorder? Why does Kaysen believe that the description of this disorder contains gender bias?
3. In your experience, to what extent do the characteristics of Borderline Personality Disorder seem to apply to the typical American teenager?
4. Why does Kaysen mention that homosexuality is no longer listed as an illness in the *Diagnostic and Statistical Manual of Mental Disorders*? What is she implying?
5. Recalling her adolescence, Kaysen writes, "My self-image was not unstable. I saw myself, quite correctly, as unfit for the educational and social systems." How would you describe Kaysen's self-image now that she is middle-aged?
6. What do you think would motivate someone to research how she was seen in the past? What is Kaysen trying to accomplish?

SUGGESTIONS FOR WRITING

1. Imagine that you are someone who had authority over you at some point in your past. Write an evaluation of yourself at that age based on how you imagine that person saw you.
2. Evaluate the quality of medical treatment you have received in recent years.
3. Write a self-assessment of your academic performance this year.

LINKS ▪ ▪ ▪

▪ WITHIN THE BOOK

In "The Thin Red Line" (pages 151–166), Jennifer Egan provides a detailed profile of a teenage girl who engages in behavior associated with Borderline Personality Disorder.

▪ ELSEWHERE IN PRINT

Beam, Alex. *Gracefully Insane: The Rise and Fall of America's Premier Mental Hospital.* New York: Public, 2001.

Kaysen, Susanna. *Far Afield.* New York: Vintage, 1990.

—. *Girl, Interrupted.* New York: Turtle Bay, 1993.

Moskovitz, Richard A. *Lost in the Mirror: An Inside Look at Borderline Personality Disorder.* Dallas: Taylor, 1996.

Plath, Sylvia. *The Bell Jar.* 1963 New York: Harper, 2000.

Santoro, Joseph, with Ronald Cohen. *The Angry Heart: Overcoming Borderline and Addictive Disorders: An Interactive Self-Help Guide.* Oakland: New Harbinger, 1997.

▪ ONLINE

▪ Borderline Personality Disorder
  <http://www.palace.net/~llama/psych/bpd.html>

▪ Interview with Susanna Kaysen
  <http://www.ivillage.com/books/intervu/nonfict/articles/
  0,11872,167230_62470,00.html>

▪ Understanding and Preventing Suicide
  <http://www.suicideology.org>

FENIMORE COOPER'S LITERARY OFFENSES

Mark Twain

During the first half of the nineteenth century, James Fenimore Cooper wrote a series of novels that made him internationally famous as an American writer—one of the first Americans to achieve literary celebrity. Although much of his work is uneven, showing signs that Cooper often wrote quickly to earn money, several of his novels continue to engage both readers and critics.

By the time Mark Twain published the following evaluation of Cooper's work in 1895, Cooper had been dead for forty-four years, and Twain was at the height of his own popularity—well known for such works as The Adventures of Tom Sawyer *(1876),* The Prince and the Pauper *(1882),* Life on the Mississippi *(1883),* The Adventures of Huckleberry Finn *(1884–85), and* The Tragedy of Pudd'nhead Wilson *(1894). Twain continues to be widely read and taught today, much more widely than Cooper. As you read "Fenimore Cooper's Literary Offenses," ask yourself what could have motivated this negative evaluation of a dead writer from an earlier era. Consider how it affects you. Does Twain's evaluation convince you that Cooper is not worth reading, or does it lead you to wonder whether Cooper could possibly be as bad as Twain claims?*

The Pathfinder and *The Deerslayer* stand at the head of Cooper's novels as artistic creations. There are others of his works which contain parts as perfect as are to be found in these, and scenes even more thrilling. Not one can be compared with either of them as a finished whole.

The defects in both of these tales are comparatively slight. They were pure works of art.

—PROF. LOUNSBURY

The five tales reveal an extraordinary fulness of invention.

. . . One of the very greatest characters in fiction, Natty Bumppo. . . .

The craft of the woodsman, the tricks of the trapper, all the delicate art of the forest, were familiar to Cooper from his youth up.

—PROF. BRANDER MATTHEWS

Cooper is the greatest artist in the domain of romantic fiction yet produced by America.

—WILKIE COLLINS

It seems to me that it was far from right for the Professor of English Literature in Yale, the Professor of English Literature in Columbia, and Wilkie Collins to deliver opinions on Cooper's literature without having read some of it. It would have been much more decorous to keep silent and let persons talk who have read Cooper.

Cooper's art has some defects. In one place in *Deerslayer,* and in the restricted space of two-thirds of a page, Cooper has scored 114 offenses against literary art out of a possible 115. It breaks the record.

There are nineteen rules governing literary art in the domain of romantic fiction—some say twenty-two. In *Deerslayer* Cooper violated eighteen of them. These eighteen require:

1. That a tale shall accomplish something and arrive somewhere. But the *Deerslayer* tale accomplishes nothing and arrives in the air.

2. They require that the episodes of a tale shall be necessary parts of the tale, and shall help to develop it. But as the *Deerslayer* tale is not a tale, and accomplishes nothing and arrives nowhere, the episodes have no rightful place in the work, since there was nothing for them to develop.

3. They require that the personages in a tale shall be alive, except in the cases of corpses, and that always the reader shall be able to tell the corpses from the others. But this detail has often been overlooked in the *Deerslayer* tale.

4. They require that the personages in a tale, both dead and alive, shall exhibit a sufficient excuse for being there. But this detail also has been overlooked in the *Deerslayer* tale.

5. They require that when the personages of a tale deal in conversation, the talk shall sound like human talk, and be talk such as human beings would be likely to talk in the given circumstances, and have a discoverable meaning, also a discoverable purpose, and a show of relevancy, and remain in the neighborhood of the subject in hand, and be interesting to the reader, and help out the tale, and stop when the people cannot think of anything more to say. But this requirement has been ignored from the beginning of the *Deerslayer* tale to the end of it.

6. They require that when the author describes the character of a personage in his tale, the conduct and conversation of that personage shall justify said description. But this law gets little or no attention in the *Deerslayer* tale, as Natty Bumppo's case will amply prove.

7. They require that when a personage talks like an illustrated, gilt-edged, tree-calf, hand-tooled, seven-dollar Friendship's Offering in the beginning of a paragraph, he shall not talk like a negro minstrel in the end of it. But this rule is flung down and danced upon in the *Deerslayer* tale.

8. They require that crass stupidities shall not be played upon the reader as "the craft of the woodsman, the delicate art of the forest," by either the author or the people in the tale. But this rule is persistently violated in the *Deerslayer* tale.

9. They require that the personages of a tale shall confine themselves to possibilities and let miracles alone; or, if they venture a miracle,

the author must so plausibly set it forth as to make it look possible and reasonable. But these rules are not respected in the *Deerslayer* tale.

10. They require that the author shall make the reader feel a deep interest in the personages of his tale and in their fate; and that he shall make the reader love the good people in the tale and hate the bad ones. But the reader of the *Deerslayer* tale dislikes the good people in it, is indifferent to the others, and wishes they would all get drowned together.

11. They require that the characters in a tale shall be so clearly defined that the reader can tell beforehand what each will do in a given emergency. But in the *Deerslayer* tale this rule is vacated.

In addition to these large rules there are some little ones. These require that the author shall:

12. *Say* what he is proposing to say, not merely come near it.

13. Use the right word, not its second cousin.

14. Eschew surplusage.

15. Not omit necessary details.

16. Avoid slovenliness of form.

17. Use good grammar.

18. Employ a simple and straightforward style.

Even these seven are coldly and persistently violated in the *Deerslayer* tale.

Cooper's gift in the way of invention was not a rich endowment; but such as it was he liked to work it, he was pleased with the effects, and indeed he did some quite sweet things with it. In his little box of stage-properties he kept six or eight cunning devices, tricks, artifices for his savages and woodsmen to deceive and circumvent each other with, and he was never so happy as when he was working these innocent things and seeing them go. A favorite one was to make a moccasined person tread in the tracks of the moccasined enemy, and thus hide his own trail. Cooper wore out barrels and barrels of moccasins in working that trick. Another stage-property that he pulled out of his box pretty frequently was his broken twig. He prized his broken twig above all the rest of his effects, and worked it the hardest. It is a restful chapter in any book of his when somebody doesn't step on a dry twig and alarm all the reds and whites for two hundred yards around. Every time a Cooper person is in peril, and absolute silence is worth four dollars a minute, he is sure to step on a dry twig. There may be a hundred handier things to step on, but that wouldn't satisfy Cooper. Cooper requires him to turn out and find a dry twig; and if he can't do it, go and borrow one. In fact, the Leather Stocking Series ought to have been called the Broken Twig Series.

I am sorry there is not room to put in a few dozen instances of the delicate art of the forest, as practiced by Natty Bumppo and some of the other Cooperian experts. Perhaps we may venture two or three samples. Cooper 5 was a sailor—a naval officer; yet he gravely tells us how a vessel, driving toward a lee shore in a gale, is steered for a particular spot by her skipper because he knows of an *undertow* there which will hold her back against the gale and save her. For just pure woodcraft, or sailorcraft, or whatever it is, isn't that neat? For several years Cooper was daily in the society of artillery, and he ought to have noticed that when a cannon-ball strikes the ground it either buries itself or skips a hundred feet or so; skips again a hundred feet or so—and so on, till finally it gets tired and rolls. Now in one place he loses some "females"—as he always calls women—in the edge of a wood near a plain at night in a fog, on purpose to give Bumppo a chance to show off the delicate art of the forest before the reader. These mislaid people are hunting for a fort. They hear a can-non-blast, and a cannon-ball presently comes rolling into the wood and stops at their feet. To the females this suggests nothing. The case is very different with the admirable Bumppo. I wish I may never know peace again if he doesn't strike out promptly and *follow the track* of that cannon-ball across the plain through the dense fog and find the fort. Isn't it a daisy? If Cooper had any real knowledge of Nature's ways of doing things, he had a most delicate art in con-cealing the fact. For instance: one of his acute Indian experts, Chingachgook (pronounced Chicago, I think), has lost the trail of a person he is tracking through the forest. Apparently that trail is hopelessly lost. Neither you nor I could ever have guessed out the way to find it. It was very different with Chicago. Chicago was not stumped for long. He turned a running stream out of its course, and there, in the slush in its old bed, were that person's moccasin-tracks. The current did not wash them away, as it would have done in all other cases—no, even the eternal laws of Nature have to vacate when Cooper wants to put up a delicate job of woodcraft on the reader.

We must be a little wary when Brander Matthews tells us that Cooper's books "reveal an extraordinary fulness of invention." As a rule, I am quite will-ing to accept Brander Matthews's literary judgments and applaud his lucid and graceful phrasing of them; but that particular statement needs to be taken with a few tons of salt. Bless your heart, Cooper hadn't any more invention than a horse; and I don't mean a high-class horse, either; I mean a clothes-horse. It would be very difficult to find a really clever "situation" in Cooper's books, and still more difficult to find one of any kind which he has failed to render absurd by his handling of it. Look at the episodes of "the caves"; and at the cel-ebrated scuffle between Maqua and those others on the table-land a few days later; and at Hurry Harry's queer water-transit from the castle to the ark; and at Deerslayer's half-hour with his first corpse; and at the quarrel between Hurry Harry and Deerslayer later; and at—but choose for yourself; you can't go amiss.

If Cooper had been an observer his inventive faculty would have worked better; not more interestingly, but more rationally, more plausibly. Cooper's proudest creations in the way of "situations" suffer noticeably from the absence of the observer's protecting gift. Cooper's eye was splendidly inaccurate. Cooper seldom saw anything correctly. He saw nearly all things as through a glass eye, darkly. Of course a man who cannot see the commonest little every-day matters accurately is working at a disadvantage when he is constructing a "situation." In the *Deerslayer* tale Cooper has a stream which is fifty feet wide where it flows out of a lake; it presently narrows to twenty as it meanders along for no given reason, and yet when a stream acts like that it ought to be required to explain itself. Fourteen pages later the width of the brook's outlet from the lake has suddenly shrunk thirty feet, and become "the narrowest part of the stream." This shrinkage is not accounted for. The stream has bends in it, a sure indication that it has alluvial banks and cuts them; yet these bends are only thirty and fifty feet long. If Cooper had been a nice and punctilious observer he would have noticed that the bends were oftener nine hundred feet long than short of it.

Cooper made the exit of that stream fifty feet wide, in the first place, for no particular reason; in the second place, he narrowed it to less than twenty to accommodate some Indians. He bends a "sapling" to the form of an arch over this narrow passage, and conceals six Indians in its foliage. They are "laying" for a settler's scow or ark which is coming up the stream on its way to the lake; it is being hauled against the stiff current by a rope whose stationary end is anchored in the lake; its rate of progress cannot be more than a mile an hour. Cooper describes the ark, but pretty obscurely. In the matter of dimensions "it was little more than a modern canal-boat." Let us guess, then, that it was about one hundred and forty feet long. It was of "greater breadth than common." Let us guess, then, that it was about sixteen feet wide. This leviathan had been prowling down bends which were but a third as long as itself, and scraping between banks where it had only two feet of space to spare on each side. We cannot too much admire this miracle. A low-roofed log dwelling occupies "two-thirds of the ark's length"—a dwelling ninety feet long and sixteen feet wide, let us say—a kind of vestibule train. The dwelling has two rooms—each forty-five feet long and sixteen feet wide, let us guess. One of them is the bedroom of the Hutter girls, Judith and Hetty; the other is the parlor in the daytime, at night it is papa's bed-chamber. The ark is arriving at the stream's exit now, whose width has been reduced to less than twenty feet to accommodate the Indians—say to eighteen. There is a foot to spare on each side of the boat. Did the Indians notice that there was going to be a tight squeeze there? Did they notice that they could make money by climbing down out of that arched sapling and just stepping aboard when the ark scraped by? No, other Indians would have noticed these things, but Cooper's Indians never notice anything. Cooper thinks they are marvelous creatures for noticing, but he was almost always in error about his Indians. There was seldom a sane one among them.

The ark is one hundred and forty feet long; the dwelling is ninety feet long. The idea of the Indians is to drop softly and secretly from the arched sapling to the dwelling as the ark creeps along under it at the rate of a mile an hour, and butcher the family. It will take the ark a minute and a half to pass under. It will take the ninety-foot dwelling a minute to pass under. Now, then, what did the six Indians do? It would take you thirty years to guess, and even then you would have to give it up, I believe. Therefore, I will tell you what the Indians did. Their chief, a person of quite extraordinary intellect for a Cooper Indian, warily watched the canal-boat as it squeezed along under him, and when he had got his calculations fined down to exactly the right shade, as he judged, he let go and dropped. And *missed the house!* That is actually what he did. He missed the house, and landed in the stern of the scow. It was not much of a fall, yet it knocked him silly. He lay there unconscious. If the house had been ninety-seven feet long he would have made the trip. The fault was Cooper's, not his. The error lay in the construction of the house. Cooper was no architect.

There still remained in the roost five Indians. The boat has passed under and is now out of their reach. Let me explain what the five did—you would not be able to reason it out for yourself. No. 1 jumped for the boat, but fell in the water astern of it. Then No. 2 jumped for the boat, but fell in the water still farther astern of it. Then No. 3 jumped for the boat, and fell a good way astern of it. Then No. 4 jumped for the boat, and fell in the water *away* astern. Then even No. 5 made a jump for the boat—for he was a Cooper Indian. In the matter of intellect, the difference between a Cooper Indian and the Indian that stands in front of the cigar-shop is not spacious. The scow episode is really a sublime burst of invention; but it does not thrill, because the inaccuracy of the detail throws a sort of air of fictitiousness and general improbability over it. This comes of Cooper's inadequacy as an observer.

The reader will find some examples of Cooper's high talent for inaccurate observation in the account of the shooting-match in *The Pathfinder*.

> A common wrought nail was driven lightly into the target, its head having been first touched with paint.

The color of the paint is not stated—an important omission, but Cooper deals freely in important omissions. No, after all, it was not an important omission; for this nailhead is *a hundred yards from* the marksmen, and could not be seen by them at that distance, no matter what its color might be. How far can the best eyes see a common house-fly? A hundred yards? It is quite impossible. Very well; eyes that cannot see a housefly that is a hundred yards away cannot see an ordinary nail head at that distance, for the size of the two objects is the same. It takes a keen eye to see a fly or a nail-head at fifty yards—one hundred and fifty feet. Can the reader do it?

The nail was lightly driven, its head painted, and game called. Then the Cooper miracles begin. The bullet of the first marksman chipped an edge of the nail-head; the next man's bullet drove the nail a little way into the target—and removed all the paint. Haven't the miracles gone far enough now? Not to suit Cooper; for the purpose of this whole scheme is to show off his prodigy, Deerslayer-Hawkeye-Long-Rifle-Leather-Stocking-Pathfinder-Bumppo before the ladies.

> "Be all ready to clench it, boys!" cried out Pathfinder, stepping into his friend's tracks the instant they were vacant. "Never mind a new nail; I can see that, though the paint is gone, and what I can see I can hit at a hundred yards, though it were only a mosquito's eye. Be ready to clench!"

> The rifle cracked, the bullet sped its way, and the head of the nail was buried in the wood, covered by the piece of flattened lead.

There, you see, is a man who could hunt flies with a rifle, and command a ducal salary in a Wild West show today if we had him back with us.

The recorded feat is certainly surprising just as it stands; but it is not sur- 15 prising enough for Cooper. Cooper adds a touch. He has made Pathfinder do this miracle with another man's rifle; and not only that, but Pathfinder did not have even the advantage of loading it himself. He had everything against him, and yet he made that impossible shot; and not only made it, but did it with absolute confidence, saying, "Be ready to clench." Now a person like that would have undertaken that same feat with a brick-bat, and with Cooper to help he would have achieved it, too.

Pathfinder showed off handsomely that day before the ladies. His very first feat was a thing which no Wild West show can touch. He was standing with the group of marksmen, observing—a hundred yards from the target, mind; one Jasper raised his rifle and drove the center off the bull's-eye. Then the Quartermaster fired. The target exhibited no result this time. There was a laugh. "It's a dead miss," said Major Lundie. Pathfinder waited an impressive moment or two; then said, in that calm, indifferent, know-it-all way of his, "No, Major, he has covered Jasper's bullet, as will be seen if anyone will take the trouble to examine the target."

Wasn't it remarkable! How *could* he see that little pellet fly through the air and enter that distant bullet-hole? Yet that is what he did; for nothing is impossible to a Cooper person. Did any of those people have any deep-seated doubts about this thing? No; for that would imply sanity, and these were all Cooper people.

> The respect for Pathfinder's skill and for his *quickness and accuracy of sight* [the italics are mine] was so profound and general, that the instant he made this declaration the spectators began to distrust their own opinions, and a dozen rushed to the target in order to ascertain the fact. There, sure enough, it was found that the Quartermaster's bullet had gone through the hole made by Jasper's, and that, too, so accurately as to require a minute examination to be certain of the circumstance, which, however, was soon clearly established by discovering one bullet over the other in the stump against which the target was placed.

They made a "minute" examination; but never mind, how could they know that there were two bullets in that hole without digging the latest one out? for neither probe nor eyesight could prove the presence of any more than one bullet. Did they dig? No; as we shall see. It is the Pathfinder's turn now; he steps out before the ladies, takes aim, and fires.

But, alas! here is a disappointment; an incredible, an unimaginable disappointment—for the target's aspect is unchanged; there is nothing there but that same old bullet-hole!

"If one dared to hint at such a thing," cried Major Duncan, "I should say that the Pathfinder has also missed the target!"

As nobody had missed it yet, the "also" was not necessary; but never mind about that, for the Pathfinder is going to speak. 20

"No, no, Major," said he, confidently, "that *would* be a risky declaration. I didn't load the piece, and can't say what was in it; but if it was lead, you will find the bullet driving down those of the Quartermaster and Jasper, else is not my name Pathfinder."

A shout from the target announced the truth of this assertion.

Is the miracle sufficient as it stands? Not for Cooper. The Pathfinder speaks again, as he "now slowly advances towards the stage occupied by the females":

"That's not all, boys, that's not all; if you find the target touched at all, I'll own to a miss. The Quartermaster cut the wood, but you'll find no wood cut by that last messenger."

The miracle is at last complete. He knew—doubtless *saw*— at the distance of a hundred yards that his bullet had passed into the hole *without fraying the edges*. There were now three bullets in that one hole—three bullets embedded processionally in the body of the stump back of the target. Everybody knew this—somehow or other—and yet nobody had dug any of them out to make sure. Cooper is not a close observer, but he is interesting. He is certainly always that, no matter what happens. And he is more interesting when he is not noticing what he is about than when he is. This is a considerable merit.

The conversations in the Cooper books have a curious sound in our modern ears. To believe that such talk really ever came out of people's mouths would be to believe that there was a time when time was of no value to a person who thought he had something to say; when it was the custom to spread a two-minute remark out to ten; when a man's mouth was a rolling-mill, and busied itself all day long in turning four-foot pigs of thought into thirty-foot bars of conversational railroad iron by attenuation; when subjects were seldom faithfully stuck to, but the talk wandered all around and arrived nowhere; when conversations consisted mainly of irrelevancies, with here and there a relevancy, a relevancy with an embarrassed look, as not being able to explain how it got there.

Cooper was certainly not a master in the construction of dialogue. Inaccurate observation defeated him here as it defeated him in so many other enterprises of his. He even failed to notice that the man who talks corrupt English six days in the week must and will talk it on the seventh, and can't help himself. In the *Deerslayer* story he lets Deerslayer talk the showiest kind of book-talk sometimes, and at other times the basest of base dialects. For instance, when someone asks him if he has a sweetheart, and if so, where she abides, this is his majestic answer:

"She's in the forest—hanging from the boughs of the trees, in a soft rain—in the dew on the open grass—the clouds that float about in the blue heavens—the birds that sing in the woods—the sweet springs where I slake my thirst—and in all the other glorious gifts that come from God's Providence!"

And he preceded that, a little before, with this:

"It consarns me as all things that touches a fri'nd consarns a fri'nd."

And this is another of his remarks:

"If I was Injin born, now, I might tell of this, or carry in the scalp and boast of the expl'ite afore the whole tribe; or if my inimy had only been a bear."

—and so on.

We cannot imagine such a thing as a veteran Scotch Commander-in-Chief   25 comporting himself in the field like a windy melodramatic actor, but Cooper could. On one occasion Alice and Cora were being chased by the French through a fog in the neighborhood of their father's fort:

"Point de quartier aux coquins!" cried an eager pursuer, who seemed to direct the operations of the enemy.

"Stand firm and be ready, my gallant 60ths!" suddenly exclaimed a voice above them; "wait to see the enemy; fire low, and sweep the glacis."

"Father! father!" exclaimed a piercing cry from out the mist; "it is I! Alice! thy own Elsie! spare, O! save your daughters!"

"Hold!" shouted the former speaker, in the awful tones of parental agony, the sound reaching even to the woods, and rolling back in solemn echo. "'Tis she! God has restored me my children! Throw open the sally-port; to the field, 60ths, to the field! pull not a trigger, lest ye kill my lambs! Drive off these dogs of France with your steel!"

Cooper's word-sense was singularly dull. When a person has a poor ear for music he will flat and sharp right along without knowing it. He keeps near the tune, but it is *not* the tune. When a person has a poor ear for words, the result is a literary flatting and sharping; you perceive what he is intending to say, but you also perceive that he doesn't *say* it. This is Cooper. He was not a word-musician. His ear was satisfied with the *approximate* word. I will furnish some circumstantial evidence in support of this charge. My instances are gathered from half a dozen pages of the tale called *Deerslayer*. He uses "verbal," for "oral"; "precision," for "facility"; "phenomena," for "marvels"; "necessary," for "predetermined"; "unsophisticated," for "primitive"; "preparation," for "expectancy"; "rebuked," for "subdued"; "dependent on," for "resulting from"; "fact," for "condition"; "fact," for "conjecture"; "precaution," for "caution"; "explain," for "determine"; "mortified," for "disappointed"; "meretricious," for "factitious"; "materially," for "considerably"; "decreasing," for "deepening"; "increasing," for "disappearing"; "embedded," for "enclosed"; "treacherous," for "hostile"; "stood," for "stooped"; "softened," for "replaced"; "rejoined," for "remarked"; "situation," for "condition"; "different," for "differing"; "insensible," for "unsentient"; "brevity," for "celerity"; "distrusted," for "suspicious"; "mental imbecility," for "imbecility"; "eyes," for "sight"; "counteracting," for "opposing"; "funeral obsequies," for "obsequies."

There have been daring people in the world who claimed that Cooper could write English, but they are all dead now—all dead but Lounsbury. I don't remember that Lounsbury makes the claim in so many words, still he makes it, for he says that *Deerslayer* is a "pure work of art." Pure, in that connection, means faultless—faultless in all details—and language is a detail. If Mr. Lounsbury had only compared Cooper's English with the English which he writes himself—but it is plain that he didn't; and so it is likely that he imagines until this day that Cooper's is as clean and compact as his own. Now I feel sure, deep down in my heart, that Cooper wrote about the poorest English that exists in our language, and that the English of *Deerslayer* is the very worst that even Cooper ever wrote.

I may be mistaken, but it does seem to me that *Deerslayer* is not a work of art in any sense; it does seem to me that it is destitute of every detail that goes to the making of a work of art; in truth, it seems to me that *Deerslayer* is just simply a literary *delirium tremens*.

A work of art? It has no invention; it has no order, system, sequence, or result; it has no lifelikeness, no thrill, no stir, no seeming of reality; its characters are confusedly drawn, and by their acts and words they prove that they are not the sort of people the author claims that they are; its humor is pathetic; its pathos is funny; its conversations are—oh! indescribable; its love-scenes odious; its English a crime against the language.

Counting these out, what is left is Art. I think we must all admit that.   *30*

QUESTIONS FOR DISCUSSION

1. Why does Twain preface his evaluation with quotes from two prominent professors and an important English novelist?
2. Consider the eighteen rules that Twain provides for "literary art." Do any of them overlap? Which seem the most important to you? Are the last seven really "little ones"? Which of these rules is appropriate for nonfiction?
3. Why is it important for writers to be good observers? Why does Twain believe that Cooper "seldom saw anything correctly"? Does he persuade you that this is so?
4. Twain points out that Cooper always called women "females." What is the difference between these two words? Why would anyone find it objectionable to call a woman a female?
5. Consider the second sentence in paragraph 6. Do you detect a shift in diction at some point in this sentence? Do you think it was deliberate? What is its effect?
6. According to Twain, what is wrong with Cooper's dialogue? How useful are the examples he provides?
7. Cooper had been dead for forty-four years when Twain wrote this essay, and Twain later went on to write another essay attacking him. What would motivate someone to make such a detailed and sustained attack on a dead writer?

SUGGESTIONS FOR WRITING

1. Use Twain's criteria to evaluate a novel that you have recently read.
2. Read *Deerslayer* and evaluate how fairly Twain treated Cooper. Be sure to make your evaluation criteria clear.
3. Read a story or novel by Mark Twain and determine how well he honors his own criteria for writing fiction.

LINKS ■ ■ ■

■ WITHIN THE BOOK

For additional criteria used in evaluating literature, see Cynthia Ozick's "She: Portrait of the Essay as a Warm Body" (pages 313–319).

■ ELSEWHERE IN PRINT

Clymer, William B. *James Fenimore Cooper.* 1900. St. Clair Shores: Scholarly, 2000.

Collins, Wilkie. *The Woman in White.* 1860. Ed. and introd. John Sutherland. New York: Oxford UP, 1996.

Cooper, James Fenimore. *The Deerslayer.* 1841. Introd. H. Daniel Peck. New York: Oxford UP, 1993.

———. *The Last of the Mohicans.* 1826. New York: Modern, 2001.

Kelly, William P. *Plotting America's Past: Fenimore Cooper and the Leatherstocking Tales.* Carbondale: Southern Illinois UP, 1983.

Rans, Geoffrey. *Cooper's Leather-Stocking Novels: A Secular Reading.* Chapel Hill: U of North Carolina P, 1991.

Twain, Mark. *Collected Tales, Sketches, Speeches, and Essays, 1852–1910.* Ed. Louis J. Budd. New York: Library of America, 1992.

■ ONLINE

- Brander Matthews
  <http://www.litgothic.com/Authors/matthews.html>

- Fenimore Cooper Society
  <http://www.webserver1.oneonta.edu/external/cooper>

- The Mark Twain Papers and Project Site
  <http://www.lib.berkeley.edu/BANC/MTP>

- Wilkie Collins
  <http://www.deadline.demon.co.uk/wilkie/wilkie.htm>

Writing to Analyze Images

Because you learn through what you see, as well as by what you read or write, the ability to analyze images can help you to determine why some images are memorable while others pass unnoticed, how some facilitate learning while others foster misconceptions. Instead of a passive recipient subconsciously influenced by the images your eye takes in, you become a critic who can understand how images are composed and what can be learned from these compositions. In other words, you understand their design and purpose, analyzing images as texts that can be "read" and interpreted. As you proceed, you will discover that different viewers have different responses to images. This is because individuals notice different aspects of an image and respond with different degrees of thoughtfulness to the pictures before them.

Images are visual representations of people, animals, objects, and concepts. An image can be a painting, drawing, sculpture, map, logo, or photograph (in which there is no written text to accompany the image) or an advertisement, cartoon, or Web page (in which pictures are combined with text). Of course, variations on these possibilities exist: A map may have place names inscribed upon it; a newspaper photograph may have a caption; and even a logo or painting may have words or phrases embedded within it. When you write to analyze an image that includes written as well as visual text, take both into account. Within this chapter, the selections by Susan Bordo and Jean Kilbourne provide the clearest examples of how to analyze works in which visual and written texts are combined.

Both Bordo and Kilbourne focus on the images conveyed through advertising. As one of the principal means by which Americans are exposed to images, advertisements shape markets and even identity in some cases (as, for example, when the use of unusually thin models makes some people believe that self-worth is tied to body weight). Bordo and Kilbourne address issues such as these by focusing on how gender is used to sell products ranging from underwear to ice cream. Bordo discusses the use of the male body in advertising, Kilbourne the use of the female. As with many ads, most of those featured in their analyses use photographs, one of the most important ways images are conveyed to viewers.

Photographs, of course, are not limited to advertising. In addition to the images you keep on your desk or in your album, photographs appear in newspapers, magazines, and books as well as in galleries and museums. When deciding which photographic images to publish or display, editors and curators usually sort through many possibilities before making their selections. In her book *Remembering to Forget: Holocaust Memory through the Camera's Eye,* Barbie Zelizer discusses how photographers tried to communicate the horror of Nazi concentration camps to American and British audiences and how newspaper editors decided what kind of images could be printed. She also discusses how the captions for these images helped shape the way the images were perceived upon publication. In the excerpt from that book reprinted in this chapter, "Conveying Atrocity in Image," Zelizer provides a model analysis that you can use to discuss a series of closely related photographs.

UNDERSTANDING THE PURPOSE OF ANALYSIS

Like writing to evaluate, writing to analyze images requires the ability to discern the difference between the effective and the ineffective and to explain why you have made this judgment. Accordingly, it requires criteria that guide your analysis as well as a structure for clearly conveying your ideas. Writers who analyze images often indicate their criteria within their analyses so that their audiences will understand their approach. For example, within "Designing a Web Page," Patrick J. Lynch and Sarah Horton establish that the design of a Web page should reflect "your overall purpose, the nature of your content, and most important, the expectations of your readers." They then go on to discuss *layout, length,* and *aesthetics*—the structure of their analysis being determined by these components, which derive from their criteria that Web pages should be attractively designed and easy to navigate. In this case, the application of clearly defined criteria to the analysis of Web pages serves the purpose of teaching readers how to create effective Web pages of their own. Analysis is almost always instructive to some extent. As in writing to interpret information, as well as in writing to evaluate something, writing an analysis helps readers to increase their understanding of the subject you have chosen. Moreover, in writing an analysis you will probably increase your own understanding of your subject.

As the article by Lynch and Horton shows, the analysis of images often serves a business interest. An effective Web page design can help generate income for the company that sponsors it or, in the case of Web pages designed by university libraries and other institutions, increase the efficiency with which users learn and work. Similarly, producing an appealing and easily identifiable logo can help make a business or institution seem attractive and memorable. On the other hand, understanding how companies and institutions use images can also help make investors, customers, clients, and service users understand that a handsome image does not necessarily prove that a reliable product is behind that image.

Advertising provides an especially clear example of how images are tied to dollars and cents. In a competitive marketplace, companies that can afford it will invest great sums to foster the creation of advertisements and the wide circulation of these images. Good choices can make a company profitable. Consider, for example, how the entrepreneurs behind Abercrombie & Fitch captured a large part of the clothing market for young Americans. Founded in 1892, Ambercrombie & Fitch specialized in high-quality outdoor gear. In 1988, the store's parent company was acquired by the owners of The Limited, a chain of casual clothing stores. The new owners then used the distinguished-sounding name of "Ambercrombie & Fitch" to launch another chain of casual clothing stores. Although the clothing sold in these stores is unremarkable, it has been successfully tied to images of clean-cut, handsome, and muscular young men who are often partially undressed—with a woman occasionally included in a group scene to suggest that the men in question are heterosexual. Sensible people should understand that wearing clothes from this store will not make them look like the images linked to the brand. But the ads continue to appear, and the clothes continue to sell because effective advertisements often appeal to desire rather than to intelligence.

The need to analyze images is often independent of the marketplace, however. A psychologist, for example, may need to analyze drawings by a young child to help that child therapeutically. An astronomer may need to analyze photographs sent back to Earth from a spacecraft thousands of miles away. A radiologist may need to analyze an x-ray when giving a presentation at a professional conference or teaching younger physicians. And a cartographer, anthropologist, or historian may need to analyze ancient maps to determine how another culture understood the rest of the world.

Moreover, writing to analyze images plays an important role in the humanities and fine arts, most notably art history. When you write about a painting, sculpture, or photograph, your purpose may be to show your instructor that you have made a careful study of a specific work of art. But if you do so successfully, you will be achieving a higher purpose: understanding what makes a work of art a thing of beauty or horror, why it haunts the imagination or soothes the spirit. Similarly, a theater major trying to understand why a specific production of a play was successful may need to study photographs of its sets or of the actors at work. An English major may need to analyze the illustrations included in the original edition of a novel, especially if the illustrations in question were made or selected by the novelist.

The full range of how writers in various disciplines analyze images is beyond the reach of this chapter. What matters is that you understand that such writers always have a purpose for analysis, and that purpose is usually educational. A thoughtful analysis of a compelling advertisement may help others become wiser consumers. An accurate analysis of scientific images can help save lives. And a scholarly analysis of art can help readers understand the nature of aesthetics as well as gain knowledge of diverse cultures. As you plan your own essay, remember that you will be assuming the role of a teacher, and decide what you most want your audience to learn from your work.

ESTABLISHING A FRAMEWORK FOR ANALYSIS

To analyze is to separate something into parts and to determine how these parts function together or how one part contributes to the whole. (See pages 203–204.) Accordingly, you must identify the components of the image you wish to analyze, and arrange them in a coherent, easy-to-follow order. The selections in this chapter will help you understand how other writers have met this challenge.

Barbie Zelizer discusses Holocaust photographs in terms of where evidence of atrocity is *placed* within a photograph, the *number* of people in each shot, and the *gaze* of the people portrayed, having established through her research that "near identical images arrived over the wires within hours and days of each other, differing only slightly in focus, distance, exposure, and perspective." This being the case, she decided to analyze these images in terms of what elements they had in common, and these elements provide the structure for her analysis: After discussing *placement,* she discusses *number,* and after number she discusses *gaze.*

As in Zelizer's analysis, photographs and other images can be analyzed in terms of placement, number, and gaze. But other factors are also relevant. Consider the following questions:

- **Subject**   Who or what is in this image? If more than one person, animal, or object appear, what is their relationship to one another?

- **Number**   How many figures or objects appear in this image?

- **Placement**   How are these figures or objects arranged? What appears in the foreground? What appears in the background? What is most prominent in the image? What is of secondary or tertiary importance?

- **Pose**   Do figures appear naturally, or do they seem posed? If posed, what does the pose suggest about the purpose of the image?

- **Gaze**   If there are people or animals in the picture, where are they looking? If they are looking toward the viewer, what does the expression in their eyes convey to you? If they are looking at someone or something else, what does this reveal?

- **Mouth**   Are figures smiling or unsmiling? If smiling, do the smiles seem genuine or forced? Does the smiling mouth correspond to the gaze? Why are these figures smiling? If unsmiling, do the figures seem serious, thoughtful, or unhappy?

- **Clothing**   How are the people in this image dressed? What does their clothing indicate about them? If a person appears partially undressed or nude, what does this indicate? Does the lack of clothing make this figure seem natural, artistic, silly, or seductive?

- **Color**   If the image is in color, what does the color communicate? Do some colors seem warm or cold—and others neutral? Does color emphasize any specific parts of the image? If the image is in black and white, how do these colors—as well as shades of gray—influence what you see? Are some images more effective in color and others more effective in black and white?

- **Light**   How is this image illuminated? Are all parts of the image equally bright, or does lighting draw your eye in a specific direction? Is the light subtle or harsh? Where is it coming from?

- **Size**   How large is this image? If you are analyzing an image reprinted in a book, newspaper, or magazine, are you seeing the image in its original size, or has the image been reduced or enlarged? How does the size you are seeing influence your perception of the image? How would the image change if its size were changed (for example, if a magazine advertisement were used to fill a large billboard)?

- **Context**   Where and when did this image originally appear? How would this context affect the choice of subject and how the subject is treated? How does the image appear when studied outside its original context?

- **Association** Does this image seem similar in any way to other images you have seen? If so, do you think the image-maker was influenced directly by work done by someone else? Or are you making a comparison on your own that could help readers understand the work in question?

Most of these questions are also appropriate for the analysis of paintings and photographs that do not include human figures. If writing about a landscape, for example, you could analyze that image by discussing *subject, placement, color, light, size, context,* and *association.* These factors are also useful when analyzing abstract contemporary art (or other images such as a map or logo). Although there may be occasions when you can benefit from considering all the factors in the foregoing list, do not think that you must always do so. Work with those that seem best suited to the specific image you wish to analyze.

Within this chapter, "Images of Women in European Art" by John Berger is an example of how works of art can be analyzed. Because Berger's purpose is to show how male artists have treated their female subjects, he discusses many different paintings. He could not make his point if he discussed only one or two images, but because he needs to discuss many images, he can discuss each of them only briefly. In order to discuss a work in depth, art historians often focus on a single image, writing twenty or thirty pages about a specific painting, sculpture, or photograph. You can find examples of such works by browsing through the art history section of your college or university library—or by looking through recent issues of such periodicals as *American Art, Journal of Contemporary Art,* and *Oriental Art.* If you have a serious interest in art history, you can research an artist or a specific work by using the print or electronic versions of the *Art Index.*

CHOOSING A SUBJECT

Images are broadcast to you throughout the day, and you discover other images by leading the life you want to live. If you choose to visit a museum, for example, you will encounter images that differ from those in a general-circulation magazines. And if you spend much of your time in cyberspace, you will see images that may never reach someone who does not use a computer. When choosing a subject, consider what kinds of images you have the most familiarity with or what kinds you most want to learn about. Remember also that the nature of an image ultimately matters less than what you have to say about it. While a painting may be worth millions of dollars in terms of market value and a photograph only a dollar or two, a thoughtful analysis of a photograph can be much more educational than a superficial analysis of a great work of art. But be sure to consider the needs and expectations of your audience as well: What kind of image would your readers be most likely to enjoy? What might be new for them and helpful to understand?

Look for images that catch your attention because you find them compelling or disturbing. Choosing as your subject an image that evokes a strong personal response can help get you get started, because you know that the image made you react to it. As you analyze the image, you can then determine what elements of it provoked your response. You might even include this personal response in the introduction or conclusion of your essay. Remember, however, that you will be analyzing an image, not analyzing yourself. You must be able to focus on the image itself, discussing its different components rather than dwelling on your feelings. In other words, look closely at the image you choose, and write about its design and purpose. Include your feelings about the image only if you can tie these feelings to details in the image, and devote most of your essay to these details.

Several of the writers in this chapter discuss multiple images because they want to show how a pattern emerges—a pattern that can help readers to analyze similar images that they discover on their own. Undertaking work of this kind requires extensive research and limits the extent to which any single image can be analyzed. When planning a short essay of your own, you will usually benefit from focusing on a single image, or on two images that can become more easily understood when compared.

Experienced though you may be in seeing images, the experience of writing about an image may be new to you. If so, you may benefit from choosing an image that has some complexity. For example, an image of two or three people who seem to have some kind of relationship to each other may give you more to write about than an image of a single person. On the other hand, the image of a single person may generate lots of ideas if this person's appearance or setting is noteworthy. Similarly, a painting done in many colors may give you more to say than a painting done in two. A Web page with interesting colors and other design elements may be easier to discuss than a page that consists entirely of text laid out in an unremarkable pattern. As you gain experience in analyzing images, you will find that you are able to see complexity in images that seem simple at first glance, because you are learning to read visual texts as closely as you read written texts. But if you begin with a simple image (such as a conventional head-and-shoulders photograph in a high school year book), you may be undertaking too great a challenge at first. Give yourself the opportunity to develop an essay on a subject about which much can be said.

ORGANIZING YOUR ESSAY

Considering the elements listed on pages 344–345 can help you decide how to organize your essay. The first step is to determine which elements will help you analyze the image you have chosen; the second is to decide on the order in which you wish to arrange the discussion of these elements. There is no single pattern that is appropriate for every analysis. The sequence in which you arrange your ideas should be determined by what you want to say and what pattern will help you to move easily from one part of your analysis to another.

The following guidelines may be useful, however:

■ **Introduction** Because your readers will need some kind of orientation before they can appreciate your analysis, you would help them by introducing your *subject*. This is the time to define the subject and to identify who created it (if the artist or designer is known to you). The introduction is also a good place to explain where you found the image and why you have chosen to work with it. Moreover, if you plan to provide information about *context,* the introduction may be the best place to do so because details about the work's history can give readers useful background. Finally, information about *size* is also helpful when placed early in an analysis.

- **Body** Discussion of *number* should usually proceed discussion of *placement* because it is easier to discuss how figures, objects, and space are arranged after you have established how many components exist in the image. In other words, number provides information that can help you to introduce placement. When discussing number, do not settle for identifying the number in question. Name each of the figures, objects, or other elements in the image you are analyzing, and arrange this list in the order you will follow when discussing placement. If your image includes human figures, keep your discussion of elements such as pose, gaze, mouth, and clothing together rather than discussing pose, then color, and then moving back to gaze. Similarly, color and lighting are closely related, so if you are planning to discuss both of these, it would probably be best to locate them next to each other.

- **Conclusion** Although *association* can form the body of an essay when your purpose is to compare or contrast two works, it can contribute to the conclusion of an essay about a single image. People often learn new ideas when these ideas are linked to something they already know. Considering the nature and expectations of your audience, you might decide that it would be helpful to conclude your essay with a paragraph linking the image you have been discussing with other images that may be more familiar to your readers. Of course, the conclusion also provides a good opportunity to summarize your main points or indicate why you think readers can benefit from your analysis. If you have not done so in your introduction (and even perhaps if you have), the conclusion also provides an opportunity to emphasize the most important point you want your audience to understand about the image or images in question.

ADDITIONAL TIPS

As you draft your analysis, remember that you are writing about an image, not about the reality that may have inspired the image. If you are analyzing a painting of Niagara Falls, you are writing about the painting—not the actual waterfall. Similarly, if you are writing about an advertisement for an automobile, you are writing about the ad—not the car. Information about the reality behind the image is relevant only if it helps readers better understand the image. For example, "In order to emphasize the grandeur of the falls, the artist has made them appear larger than they actually are." Or: "Photographed from this angle, the car seems to have a larger interior than it actually has." In most cases, however, you must stay focused on the image. If you are writing about an image of a person or place you care about, or perhaps an advertisement for some product you long to acquire, you could easily drift away from the image to your own memories and dreams. If you accidentally do so when drafting, eliminate these passages when you revise, unless a brief discussion along these lines helps you to introduce or conclude your essay. The body of the essay must address the elements you identify in the image.

Because writers often benefit from narrowing their focus, you may decide to address only one or two elements in a short essay. For example, you could write an essay focused exclusively on an artist's use of color in a specific painting or on a photographer's use of placement. When narrowing your focus, however, think twice before eliminating any element that is closely related to your focus. If you are discussing the foreground of a photograph, for example, your readers may expect you to balance this discussion with analysis of the background. If you are analyzing a painting of a woman and child seated in a garden, you might decide to focus on the human figures rather than on the setting in which they are located. But if you write about the woman, your audience will probably expect you to write about the child as well.

When you have drafted and revised your essay, be sure to attach a copy of the image or images you are analyzing. You can attach photocopies of the work in question at the end of your essay as a kind of appendix, including an image of the work as a whole and, if useful, an enlargement of parts of the work you want your audience to see clearly. If you have the necessary software and skills, you can communicate better with your audience by locating the image (and various parts of the image) within the text of your essay. If the work you are analyzing appeared in color, and you are discussing the use of color in your analysis, use a color printer or a color photocopier, and check the accuracy of the color reproduction you have achieved. If there is any variation of the color in the image you originally encountered and the image copy you are including in your essay, be sure to alert your audience to this difference.

NeXT: UNDERSTANDING A CORPORATE LOGO

Steven Heller and Karen Pomeroy

A senior art director at The New York Times, *Steven Heller is the author of more than sixty books on graphic design. He is also editor of* AIGA Journal of Graphic Design *as well as a contributing editor to* Print, ID, *and* Eye *magazines. Based in Los Angeles, Karen Pomeroy is a writer and graphic designer who is the co-author of* Designing with Illustration. *The following article is from* Design Literacy: Understanding Graphic Design, *which Heller and Pomeroy published in 1997. If the subject of the design of a corporate logo seems remote from your daily concerns, bear in mind that how corporations present themselves through design plays a role in how they are perceived by the public. Given the power that many corporations enjoy and the importance of presentation in business life, good design can affect a company's income and status.*

It is difficult enough to invent a meaningful corporate logo, sign, or mark to express conventional business issues without having to depict the future as well. However, that is what was demanded of Paul Rand (1914–1996) when in 1988 he was commissioned to design a logo for NeXT, an educational computer company headed by Steven Jobs, the founder of Apple Computer Company. Although NeXT's new product was cast in secrecy, the corporate name alluded to its futuristic positioning—not simply a *new* computer, but the *next* wave of information processing for the educational market. With only a few clues, Rand was given a month to devise a logo that would embody as much symbolic power as the memory of a silicon chip.

Rand had made identity systems out of whole cloth many times before. He created time-honored marks for IBM, UPS, and ABC. In each he found the most identifiable graphic forms: stripes for IBM, a gift box atop a shield for UPS, the repetition of circles for the lowercase letters *abc*. Designing such charged—and lasting—logos is not magic, but it does take an acute understanding of the nature of perception and the ability to translate that into a visual form. "Logos are *aides de mémoire* that give you something to hook onto when you see it, and especially when you don't see it," explained Rand. And the problem with the word NeXT was that it was not depictable. "What are you going to show? A barber shop with somebody pointing, 'You're next'? It's simply not describable in typographic terms."

Graphic devices that represent the future, such as the arrow, were made meaningless by overuse, but the NeXT computer was contained in a black cube, which gave Rand the idea he needed. He decided to frame the word in a cube to evoke the product itself. However, at the time the logo was introduced to the public, the computer's shape and form were completely secret.

"It was understandable only as a cube, nothing else," he explained. "But without that reference point, I would have had to devise something out of the blue." In fact, for Rand it was not so much a question of having a reference point as using that reference point. "The client mentioned the cube to me when I was given the problem, and I'm sure the other designers who worked on the logo must also have heard about it," Rand presumed.

The NeXT logo was successful in part because the cube was symbolically related to the product itself, but Rand insisted that the shape was only important in sparking the idea. "Some reference was made to it being like a child's block," he continued. "I really think that is one of its virtues and part of its charm. However, the logo is not designed to be charming, it is designed to identify."

Before the logo could do the job, however, Rand had to sell the mark to   5
Jobs. For this he had a pronged strategy. The first was to present only one logo. This underscored his own confidence in the solution and deflected indecision on the part of the client. The second was to "speak" only through a presentation booklet that concisely explained the rationale and showed the applications of the logo. Jobs had seen all the timeworn futuristic clichés—arrows, clouds, lightning bolts—in the book. However, he was unprepared for Rand's twenty-page book entitled "The Sign of the Next Generation of Computers *for Education.* . . ."

From the beginning of this limited (fifty copies), Platonic document, Rand announced his premise: "What should a logo for NeXT look like?" he

asked in text set in Caslon, which led into a concise narrative that condensed decades of communications history into ten minutes of reading time.

First he introduced the concept of type itself: "Choosing a typeface as the basis for the design of a logo is a convenient starting point. Here are two examples: Caslon and Bifur. Caslon is an alphabet designed as far back as 1725 by William Caslon. It appears to be a good choice because it is both elegant and bookish, qualities well suited for educational purposes. . . ." He described the nature of his faces, their quirks and virtues, and concluded by admitting, "Attributing certain magical qualities to particular typefaces is, however, largely a subjective matter."

Next he defused the client's need to sample a variety of typefaces: "One reason for looking at a number of possible typefaces is to satisfy one's curiosity. Another, and perhaps more meaningful one, is to study the relationship of different letter combinations, to look for visual analogies, and to try to elicit ideas that the design of a letter or group of letters might inspire." He offered some examples that were intended to pique the reader's interest, and offered this warning: "Personal preferences, prejudices, and stereotypes often dictate what a logo looks like, but it is *needs,* not wants, *ideas,* not type styles, which determine what its form should be. . . ."

Then Rand took a representative typeface and set it in caps to explain why this particular iteration was unsuccessful: "Set in all capitals, the word NEXT is sometimes confused with EXIT, possibly because the EXT grouping is so dominant. A combination of capitals and lowercase letters alleviates this problem." And after winning the argument, he provided a textbook example of a more successful application: "Here are some possibilities which explore the use of lowercase letters. The *e* is differentiated so as to provide a focal point and visual contrast among the capital letters which, otherwise, consist only of straight lines. Happily the *e* also could stand for: education, excellence, expertise, exceptional, excitement, $e = mc^2$, etc."

This brief lesson in typographic style segued into an explanation of how a mark should function: "Ideally, a logo should explain or suggest the business it symbolizes, but this is rarely possible or even necessary. There is nothing about the IBM symbol, for example, that suggests computers, except what the viewer reads into it. Stripes are now associated with computers because the initials of a great computer company happen to be striped. . . ." And then he introduced the idea underlying his version of NeXT: "A logo takes on meaning, only if over a period of time it is linked to some product or service of a particular organization. What is essential is finding a meaningful device, some idea—preferably product-related—that reinforces the company name. The cube, in which the computer will be housed, can be such a device because it has visual impact and is easy to remember. Unlike the word *Next,* it is depictable, possesses the *promise of meaning* and the *pleasure of recognition.*"

Understanding that questions would arise concerning the application of the cube, Rand talked about versatility: "This idea in no way restricts its appli- 10 cation to any one product or concept. The three-dimensional effect functions as an underscore to attract the viewer's attention." Once established that the cube was the appropriate form, Rand addressed the basic structure of the logo: "Splitting the logo into two lines accomplishes several things: It startles the viewer and gives the word a new look, thus making it easier to separate from common usage. And even more importantly, it increases the letter size twofold, within the framework of the cube. For small space use, a one-line logo would have been too small to fit within this same framework." Rand showed that readability was not affected because the word was too simple to be misread. "Moreover, people have become accustomed to this format with such familiar four-letter word combinations as LOVE."

He concluded his primer with a down-to-earth analysis: "The adaptation of this device to miniaturization—tie tacks, charm bracelets, paperweights, stickers, and other promotional items—is endless. It lends itself as well to large-scale interpretation—signs, exhibits in the shape of cubes, in which the actual exhibit is housed, as well as exhibit stands. For printed matter, its infinite adaptability and attention-compelling power is self-evident."

Upon presentation, Rand did not utter a word, he just sat silently watching as Jobs read. "The book itself was a big surprise." Jobs recalled, "I was convinced that each typographic example on the first few pages was the final logo. I was not quite sure what Paul was doing until I reached the end. And at that moment I knew we had the solution. . . . Rand gave us a jewel, which in retrospect seems so obvious." Moreover, as it turned out, Rand's user-friendly teaching aid underscored Jobs' own commitment to the process of education.

QUESTIONS FOR DISCUSSION

1. What does this article reveal about the principles that determined the way Paul Rand approached assignments for designing corporate logos?
2. What were the challenges that faced Rand in designing a logo for NeXT?
3. What does Heller mean when he describes the booklet Rand prepared as a "Platonic document"?
4. What specific arguments did Rand advance on behalf of his design?
5. Heller quotes Steven Jobs as saying, "Rand gave us a jewel, which in retrospect seems obvious." Is this a compliment? In what sense is the NeXT logo "obvious"?

SUGGESTIONS FOR WRITING

1. Write an analysis of the logo that appears on the stationery of your college or university.
2. Choose a commercial emblem (such as the Morton Salt girl or the image of Betty Crocker) and research how it has evolved since first published. Then analyze the significance of the changes you discover.

3. Heller notes that Paul Rand also designed the logos for IBM and UPS. Choose one of these logos, analyze its components, and explain what the image communicates.

LINKS ■ ■ ■

■ **WITHIN THE BOOK**

For another view of American business, see Eric Schlosser's "Why McDonald's Fries Taste So Good" (pages 122–131).

■ **ELSEWHERE IN PRINT**

Bierut, Michael, William Drenttel, Steven Heller, and D. K. Holland, eds. *Looking Closer: Critical Writings on Graphic Design.* New York: Allworth, 1994.

Heller, Steven, and Marie Finamore, eds. *Design Culture: An Anthology of Writing from the AIGA Journal of Graphic Design.* New York: Allworth, 1997. Sparkman, Don. *Selling Graphic Design.* 2nd ed. New York: Allworth, 1999.

Votolato, Gregory. *American Design in the Twentieth Century: Personality and Performance.* New York: Manchester UP, 1998.

■ **ONLINE**

■ Design Literacy
   <http://www.education.canberra.edu.au/education/centres/acae/literacy/litpapers/deslit.htm>

■ NeXT Computer Links
   <http://www.jlc.net/~jmeacham/next.html>

■ Paul Rand Tribute
   <http://www.dlsdesign.com/rndtrib1.htm>

DESIGNING A WEB PAGE

Patrick J. Lynch and Sarah Horton

Given the frequency with which millions of people turn to the World Wide Web for information and the huge number of Web sites that can be accessed, the design of a Web page can help determine whether or not it will prove popular and useful. Good design can also affect profitability when the site in question is tied to a business. What then, makes the difference between good design and poor design when creating Web pages? And how can you create an engaging Web page of your own? These are among the questions answered by Patrick J. Lynch and Sarah Horton in the following chapter from their book Web Style Guide *(1999), which was described upon publication as the "essential guide for Web site designers." Lynch is director of the Center for Advanced Instructional Media at Yale University School of Medicine. Horton works at Dartmouth College, where she is a multimedia applications specialist in Curricular Computing.*

Clutter and confusion are failures of design, not attributes of information.

—EDWARD TUFTE, 1997 interview

We seek clarity, order, and trustworthiness in information sources, whether traditional paper documents or Web pages. Effective page design can provide this confidence. The spatial organization of graphics and text on the Web page can engage readers with graphic impact, direct their attention, prioritize the information they see, and make their interactions with your Web site more enjoyable and efficient.

Visual logic   Graphic design creates visual logic and seeks an optimal balance between visual sensation and graphic information. Without the visual impact of shape, color, and contrast, pages are graphically boring and will not motivate the viewer. Dense text documents without contrast and visual relief are also harder to read, particularly on the relatively low-resolution screens of personal computers. But without the depth and complexity of text, highly graphical pages risk disappointing the user by offering a poor balance of visual sensation, text information, and interactive hypermedia links. In seeking this ideal balance, the primary design constraints are the restrictions of html and the bandwidth limitations on user access speeds that range from 28.8 kbps (kilobits per second) modems to Ethernet.

Visual and functional continuity in your Web site organization, graphic design, and typography are essential to convince your audience that your Web site offers them timely, accurate, and useful information. A careful, systematic approach to page design can simplify navigation, reduce user errors, and make it easier for readers to take advantage of the information and features of the site.

VISUAL HIERARCHY

The primary task of graphic design is to create a strong, consistent visual hierarchy in which important elements are emphasized and content is organized logically and predictably.

Graphic design is visual information management, using the tools of layout, typography, and illustration to lead the reader's eye through the page. Readers first see pages as large masses of shape and color, with foreground elements contrasted against the background field. Only secondarily do they begin to pick out specific information, first from graphics if they are present, and only then do they start parsing the harder medium of text and begin to read individual words and phrases. (See Figure 1.)

Contrast is essential   The overall graphic balance and organization of the page is crucial to drawing the reader into your content. A dull page of solid text will repel the eye as a mass of undifferentiated gray, without obvious cues to the structure of your information. A page dominated by poorly designed or overly bold graphics or typography also will distract or repel users looking for substantive content. You will need to strike an appropriate balance between attracting the eye with visual contrast and providing a sense of organization. (See Figure 2.)

Visual balance and appropriateness to the intended audience are the keys to successful design decisions. The most effective designs for general (mostly modem-based) Internet audiences use a careful balance of text and links with relatively small graphics. These pages load into viewers quickly, even when accessed from 28.8 modems, yet still achieve substantial graphic impact. (See Figure 3.)

When establishing a page design for your Web site, consider your overall purpose, the nature of your content, and, most important, the expectations of your readers.

CONSISTENCY

Establish a layout grid and a style for handling your text and graphics, then apply it consistently to build rhythm and unity across the pages of your site. Repetition is not boring; it gives your site a consistent graphic identity that creates and then reinforces a distinct sense of "place" and makes your site distinct and memorable. A consistent approach to layout and navigation allows readers to adapt quickly to your design and predict with confidence the loca-

Visual scanning of page structure over time

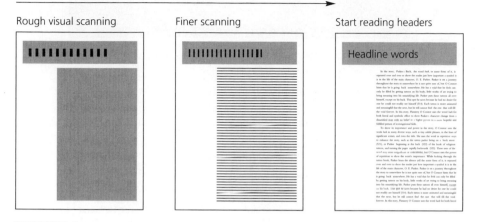

FIGURE 1

FIGURE 2

tion of information and navigation controls across the pages of your site. (See Figure 4.)

If you choose a graphic theme, use it throughout your Web site. Meta-Design's home page banner (Figure 5) sets the graphic theme for the site and introduces distinctive typography and a set of navigation icons.

Figure 6 is a banner at the top of an interior page in MetaDesign's site. Note how the typography and the icon theme are carried through to the interior banners. There is no confusion about whose site you are navigating through.

10

The Curricular Computing division of Dartmouth's department of Academic Computing was established to assist faculty in creating and using computer-based curricular resources. Our services include consulting, design, and programming for custom multimedia applications, digitization of educational resources, and providing and maintaining public work spaces created specifically for faculty curricular development use. CC staff are available for individual consultation and also offer workshops and presentations of the latest uses of technology in the classroom. Curricular Computing also maintains membership in the New Media Centers program.

Stay tuned to our site for workshop schedules, new and/or noteworthy resources at Dartmouth and around the world, and information on the latest tools for curricular computing.

Curricular Computing also provides the Didactic Web, a Web site with information and tutorials on creating Web sites, creating graphics for the Web, digital video, and other topics.

Curricular Computing, Dartmouth College, copyright 1997

FIGURE 3

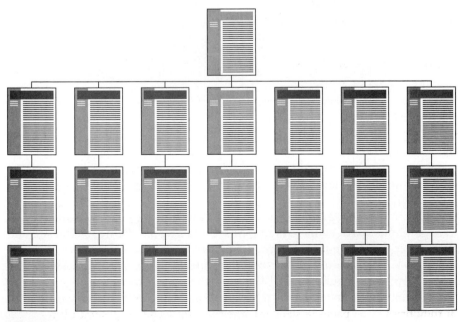

FIGURE 4

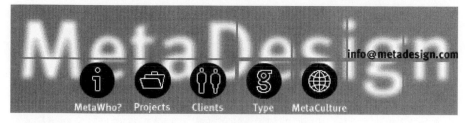

FIGURE 5

FIGURE 6

PAGE DIMENSIONS

Although Web pages and conventional print documents share many graphic, functional, and editorial similarities, the computer screen, not a printed page, is the primary delivery site for Web-based information, and the computer screen is very different from the printed page. Computer screens are typically smaller than most opened books or magazines. A common mistake in Web design is spreading the width of page graphics beyond the area most viewers can see on their fourteen- or fifteen-inch display screens. (See Figure 7.)

Graphic Safe Areas

The "safe area" for Web page graphics is determined by two factors: the minimum screen size in common use today (640 × 480 pixels) and the width of paper used to print Web pages.

Most monitors used in academia and business are fourteen to fifteen inches (thirty-five to thirty-eight centimeters) in size, and they are usually set to display a 640 × 480-pixel screen. Web page graphics that exceed the width dimension of these small monitors look amateurish and will inconvenience many readers by forcing them to scroll both horizontally and vertically to see the full page layout. It's bad enough to have to scroll in one (vertical) direction; having to scroll in two directions is intolerable.

Even on small monitors it is possible to display graphics that are too wide to print well on common letter-size, legal-size, or A4 paper widths. However, in many Web pages printing is a secondary concern. Just be aware that your readers will lose the right three-quarters of an inch (two centimeters) of your layout if they print wide pages in standard vertical print layout. Pages with lots of text should *always* be designed to print properly, because most readers will print

15

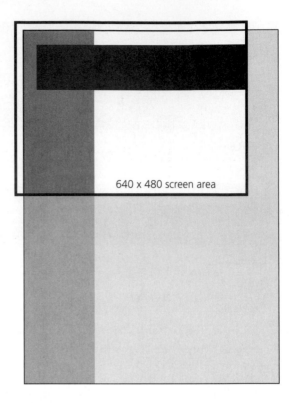

640 x 480 screen area

FIGURE 7

those pages to read them more comfortably, and if the layout page is too wide, readers will lose several words from each line of text down the right margin.

The graphic safe area dimensions for printing layouts and for page layouts designed to use the maximum width of a 640 × 480-pixel screen are shown in Figure 8.

Graphic "safe area" dimensions for layouts designed to print well:

Maximum width = 535 pixels

Maximum height = 295 pixels

Graphic "safe area" dimensions for layouts designed to maximize screen usage:

Maximum width = 595 pixels

Maximum height = 295 pixels

PAGE LENGTH

Determining the proper length for any Web page requires balancing four factors:

1. The relation between page and screen size
2. The content of your documents

3. Whether the reader is expected to browse the content online or to print or download the documents for later reading

4. The bandwidth available to your audience

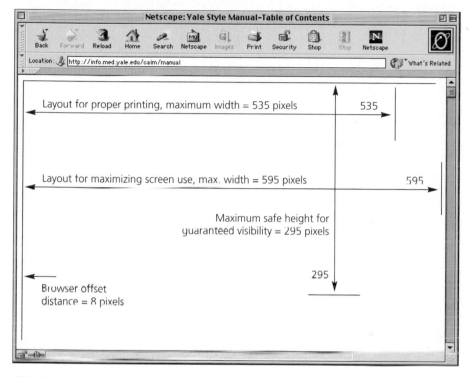

FIGURE 8 Graphic safe areas, 640 × 480 screens. Dimensions account for both Netscape Navigator and Internet Explorer, in both Windows95/NT and Macintosh versions. Note that if you choose to maximize the width of your page layout, you may lose about two centimeters off the right edge of the page when it is printed.

Researchers have noted the disorientation that results from scrolling on computer screens. The reader's loss of context is particularly troublesome when such basic navigational elements as document titles, site identifiers, and links to other site pages disappear off-screen. This effect argues for the creation of navigational Web pages (especially home pages and menus) that contain no more than one or two 640 × 480 screens' worth of information and that feature local navigational links at the beginning and end of the page layout. Long Web pages require the user to remember too much information that scrolls off the screen; users easily lose their sense of context when the navigational buttons or major links are not visible. (See Figure 9.)

Scrolling   In long Web pages, the user must depend on the vertical scroll bar slider (the little box within the scroll bar) to navigate. In some graphic

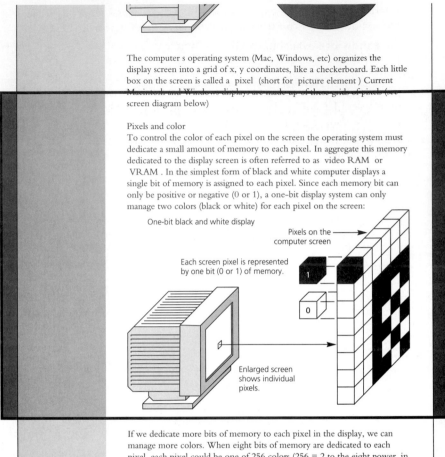

The computer s operating system (Mac, Windows, etc) organizes the display screen into a grid of x, y coordinates, like a checkerboard. Each little box on the screen is called a pixel (short for picture element) Current Macintosh and Windows displays are made up of these grids of pixels (see screen diagram below)

Pixels and color
To control the color of each pixel on the screen the operating system must dedicate a small amount of memory to each pixel. In aggregate this memory dedicated to the display screen is often referred to as video RAM or VRAM . In the simplest form of black and white computer displays a single bit of memory is assigned to each pixel. Since each memory bit can only be positive or negative (0 or 1), a one-bit display system can only manage two colors (black or white) for each pixel on the screen:

One-bit black and white display

Pixels on the computer screen

Each screen pixel is represented by one bit (0 or 1) of memory.

1

0

Enlarged screen shows individual pixels.

If we dedicate more bits of memory to each pixel in the display, we can manage more colors. When eight bits of memory are dedicated to each pixel, each pixel could be one of 256 colors (256 = 2 to the eight power, in other words, 256 is the maximum number of unique combinations of 0 s and 1 s you can make with eight bits). This kind of computer display is called an eight-bit or 256-color display, and is very common in current microcomputing, especially on lap-top computers and older desktop machines.

FIGURE 9

interfaces (Macintosh, Windows 3.1), the scroll bar slider is fixed in size and provides little indication of the document length relative to what's visible on the screen, so the reader gets no visual cue to page length. In very long Web pages, small movements of the scroll bar can completely change the visual contents of the screen, leaving the reader no familiar landmarks to orient by. This gives the user no choice but to crawl downward with the scroll bar arrows or risk missing sections of the page. [20]

Long Web pages do have their advantages, however. They are often easier for managers to organize and for users to download. Web site managers don't have to maintain as many links and pages with longer documents, and users don't need to download multiple files to collect information on a topic. Long pages are particularly useful for providing information that you don't expect users to read online (realistically, that means any document longer than two printed pages). You can make long pages friendlier by positioning "jump to top buttons" at intervals equivalent to one small screenful of page (about 295 vertical pixels). That way the user will never have to scroll more than about half a screen to find a navigation button that quickly brings him or her back to the top of the page. (See Figure 10.)

All Web pages longer than two vertical screens should have a jump button at the foot of the page (Figure 11).

If a Web page is too long, however, or contains too many large graphics, the page can take too long for users with slow connections to download. Very large Web pages with many graphics may also overwhelm the RAM (random access memory) limitations of the user's Web browser, causing the browser to crash or causing the page to display and print improperly.

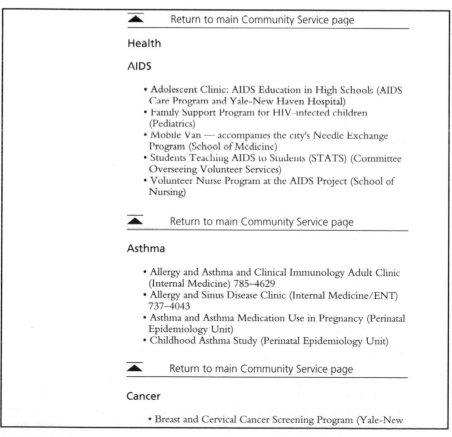

FIGURE 10

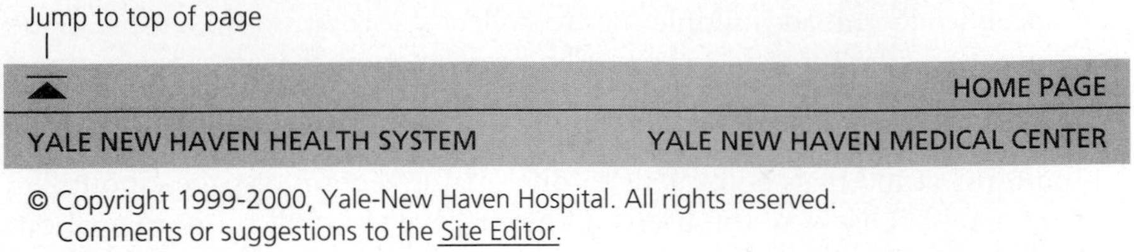
Jump to top of page
HOME PAGE
YALE NEW HAVEN HEALTH SYSTEM
YALE NEW HAVEN MEDICAL CENTER
© Copyright 1999-2000, Yale-New Haven Hospital. All rights reserved.
Comments or suggestions to the Site Editor.

FIGURE 11

Content and Page Length

It makes sense to keep closely related information within the confines of a single Web page, particularly when you expect the user to print or save the text. Keeping the content in one place makes printing or saving easier. But more than four screens' worth of information forces the user to scroll so much that the utility of the online version of the page begins to deteriorate. Long pages often fail to take advantage of the linkages available in the Web medium.

If you wish to provide both a good online interface for a long page and easy printing or saving of its content:

- Divide the page into chunks of no more than one to two printed pages' worth of information, including inlined graphics or figures. Use the power of hypertext links to take advantage of the Web medium.
- Provide a link to a separate file that contains the full-length text combined as one page, designed so the reader can print or save all the related information in one step. Don't forget to include the URL of the online version within the text of that page so that users can find updates and correctly cite the source.

In general, you should favor shorter Web pages for:

- Home pages and menu or navigation pages elsewhere in your site
- Documents to be browsed and read online
- Pages with very large graphics

In general, longer documents are:

- Easier to maintain (content is in one piece, not in linked chunks)
- More like the structure of their paper counterparts (not chopped up)
- Easier for users to download and print

DESIGN GRIDS FOR WEB PAGES

Consistency and predictability are essential attributes of any well-designed 25
information system. The design grids that underlie most well-designed paper publications are equally necessary in designing electronic documents and

online publications, where the spatial relations among on-screen elements are constantly shifting in response to the user's input and system activity.

Grids bring order to the page   Current implementations of HyperText Markup Language do not allow the easy flexibility or control that graphic designers routinely expect from page layout software or multimedia authoring tools. Yet HTML can be used to create complex and highly functional information systems if it is used thoughtfully. When used inappropriately or inconsistently, the typographic controls and inlined graphics of Web pages can create a confusing visual jumble without apparent hierarchy of importance. Haphazardly mixed graphics and text decrease usability and legibility, just as they do in paper pages. A balanced and consistently implemented design scheme will increase readers' confidence in your site. (See Figure 12.)

No one design grid system is appropriate for all Web pages. Your first step is to establish a basic layout grid. With this graphic "backbone," you can determine how the major blocks of type and illustrations will regularly occur in your pages and set the placement and style guidelines for major screen titles, subtitles, and navigation links or buttons. To start, gather representative examples of your text, along with some graphics, scans, or other illustrative material, and experiment with various arrangements of the elements on the page. In larger projects it isn't possible to predict how every combination of text and graphics will interact on the screen, but examine your Web layout "sketches" against both your most complex and your least complex pages.

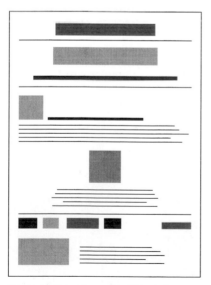

Poor page layout, no visual hierarchy   Better layout, balanced

FIGURE 12

Your goal is to establish a consistent, logical screen layout, one that allows you to "plug in" text and graphics without having to stop and rethink your basic design approach on each new page. Without a firm underlying design grid, your project's page layout will be driven by the problems of the moment, and the overall design of your Web site will seem patchy and confusing.

Vertical stratification in Web pages   A Web page can be almost any length, but you've only got about thirty square inches "above the fold"—at the top of your page—to capture the average reader, because that is all he or she will see as the page loads. One crucial difference between Web page design and print page design is that, when readers turn a book or magazine page, they see not only the whole next page but the whole two-page spread, all at the same time. In print design, therefore, the two-page spread is the fundamental graphic design unit.

Print design can achieve a design unity and density of information that   30
Web page design cannot emulate. Regardless of how large the display monitor is, the reader still sees one page at a time, and even a twenty-one-inch monitor will display only as much information as is found in a typical magazine spread. (See Figure 13.)

Design for screens of information   Most Web page designs can be divided vertically into zones with different functions and varying levels of graphics and text complexity. As the page is progressively revealed by vertical scrolling, new content appears and the upper content disappears. A new graphic context is established each time the reader scrolls down the page. Web page layouts should thus be judged not by viewing the whole page as a unit but by dividing the

Book pages

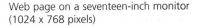
Web page on a seventeen-inch monitor
(1024 x 768 pixels)

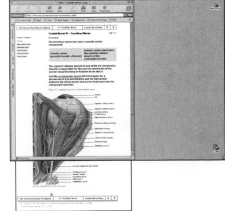

Book spreads are seen as units of two pages;
Web pages are always single units, regardless
of monitor size

FIGURE 13

page into visual and functional zones and judging the suitability of each screen of information. Notice the vertical structure of Yale–New Haven Hospital's home page (Figure 14). The top screen of information is much denser with links because it is the only area sure to be visible to all users.

FIGURE 14

Sample page grid When we designed our online Web style manual <info.med.yale.edu/caim/manual>, we used a basic Web page grid that incorporates an image map with paging buttons at the top and bottom of each page. A "scan column" along the left side of the page does two jobs: It provides space for local links to related material, and it gives visual relief by narrowing the right text column to about sixty to seventy characters per line. The diagram below shows the major repeating components of the style manual pages. (See Figure 15.)

In Figure 16, we show the "invisible" table (BORDER = "0") that underlies the column structure of the page, with the critical page dimensions.

We chose 535 pixels as the maximum dimension for the page layout because that is the widest table that will print on a standard letter-size page. With a few exceptions, all graphics for the online manual were designed to fit within the 365-pixel "safe area" of the text column.

PAGE HEADERS AND FOOTERS

Many Web authors surrender to the giddy thrills of large home page graphics, forgetting that a Web page is not just a visual experience—it has to function efficiently to retain its appeal to the user. Remember that the page builds its graphic impact only gradually as it is downloaded to the user. The best measure of the efficiency of a page design is the number of options available for readers within the top four inches of the page. A big, bold graphic

35

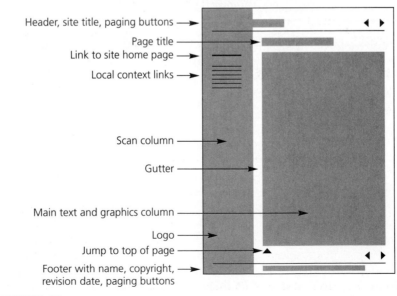

Header, site title, paging buttons →
Page title →
Link to site home page →
Local context links →
Scan column →
Gutter →
Main text and graphics column →
Logo →
Jump to top of page →
Footer with name, copyright, → revision date, paging buttons

FIGURE 15

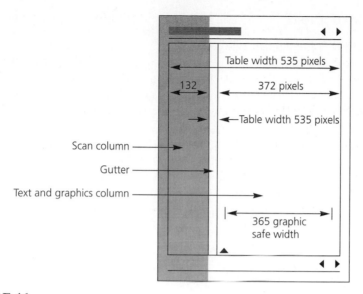

Table width 535 pixels

132

372 pixels

Table width 535 pixels

Scan column

Gutter

Text and graphics column

365 graphic
safe width

FIGURE 16

may tease casual Web surfers, but if it takes the average reader a full minute to download the top of your page, and there are few links to be seen until he or she scrolls down the page (causing even longer delays), then you may lose a big part of your audience before you offer them links to the rest of your site.

Page Headers: Site Identity

Careful graphic design will give your Web site a unique visual identity. A "signature" graphic and page layout allow the reader to grasp immediately the purpose of the document and its relation to other pages. Graphics used within headers can also signal the relatedness of a series of Web pages. Unlike designers of print documents, designers of Web systems can never be sure what other pages the reader has seen before linking to the current page. Yale–New Haven Hospital's many Web pages and subsites all include a signature header graphic that is also an imagemap with basic navigation links included. (See Figure 17.)

Even if you choose not to use graphics on your pages, the header area of every Web page should contain a prominent title at or near its top. Graphics placed above the title line should not be so large that they force the title and introductory text off the page on standard office-size monitors. In a related series of documents, there may also be subtitles, section titles, or other text elements that convey the relation of the displayed document to others in the series. To be effective, these title elements must be standardized across all the pages in your site.

NEED A DOCTOR?	HOME PAGE	SEARCH	COMMENTS
Directions & parking	Staff directory	Online resources	Calendar

FIGURE 17

Page Footers: Provenance

Every Web page should contain basic data about the origin and age of the page, but this repetitive and prosaic information does not need to be placed at the top of the page. Remember, too, that by the time readers have scrolled to the bottom of your Web page the navigation links you might have provided at the top may no longer be visible. Well-designed page footers offer the user a set of links to other pages in addition to essential data about the site.

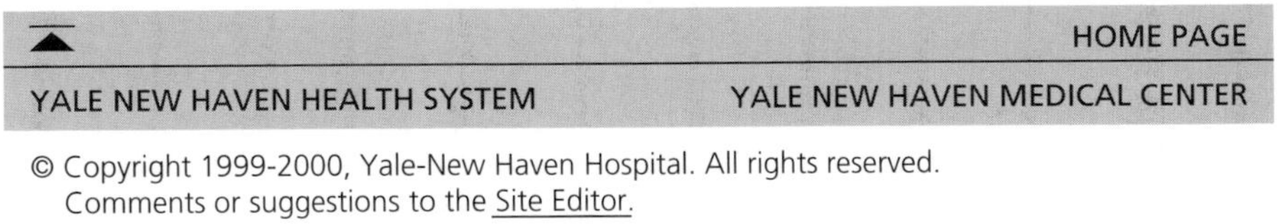

▲	HOME PAGE
YALE NEW HAVEN HEALTH SYSTEM	YALE NEW HAVEN MEDICAL CENTER

© Copyright 1999-2000, Yale-New Haven Hospital. All rights reserved.
Comments or suggestions to the Site Editor.

FIGURE 18

The pages in Yale–New Haven Hospital's Web site all carry a distinctive footer graphic with a consistent visual and functional identity (Figure 18).

GENERAL DESIGN CONSIDERATIONS

- *Understand the medium*   Readers experience Web pages in two ways: as a direct medium where pages are read online and as a delivery medium to access information that is downloaded into text files or printed onto paper. Your expectations about how readers will typically use your site should govern your page design decisions. Documents to be read online should be concise, with the amount of graphics carefully "tuned" to the bandwidth available to your mainstream audience. Documents that will most likely be printed and read offline should appear on one page, and the page width should be narrow enough to print easily on standard paper sizes. 40

- *Include fixed page elements*   Each page should contain a title, an author, an institutional affiliation, a revision date, copyright information, and a link to the "home page" of your site. Web pages are often printed or saved to disk, and without this information there is no easy way to determine where the document originated. Think of each page in your site as a newspaper clipping, and make sure that the information required to determine its provenance is included.

■ *Don't impose style* Don't set out to develop a "style" for your site, and be careful about simply importing the graphic elements of another Web site or print publication to "decorate" your pages. The graphic and editorial style of your Web site should evolve as a natural consequence of consistent and appropriate handling of your content and page layout.

■ *Maximize prime real estate* In page layout the top of the page is always the most dominant location, but on Web pages the upper page is especially important because the top four inches of the page are all that is visible on the typical monitor. Use this space efficiently and effectively.

■ *Use subtle colors* Subtle pastel shades of colors typically found in nature make the best choices for background or minor elements. Avoid bold, highly saturated primary colors except in regions of maximum emphasis, and even there use them cautiously.

■ *Beware of graphic embellishments* Horizontal rules, graphic bullets, icons, and other visual markers have their occasional uses, but apply each sparingly (if at all) to avoid a patchy and confusing layout. The same consideration applies to the larger sizes of type on Web pages. [. . .] The tools of graphic emphasis are powerful and should be used only in small doses for maximum effect. Overuse of graphic emphasis leads to a "clown's pants" effect in which everything is garish and nothing is emphasized. 45

QUESTIONS FOR DISCUSSION

1. Why is it useful to design a Web page carefully?
2. What criteria do Lynch and Horton establish for the evaluation of Web pages?
3. How is designing a Web page like composing a written text? How does the design of a Web page differ from the design of a work intended for print publication?
4. Consider the use of bullets in paragraph 24. How does this design feature affect your reading of the text?
5. What does this article reveal about the nature of reading?
6. Consider the advice with which Lynch and Horton conclude this selection. Can any of this advice be applied to other media?

SUGGESTIONS FOR WRITING

1. Download two Web pages from different sites, one you think is well designed and one you think is poorly designed. Then, applying the criteria established by Lynch and Horton, analyze why one site is effective and the other is not.

2. Drawing on your own experience with Web page design, evaluate the work of Lynch and Horton in terms of its clarity and relevance.
3. Write a short "manual" for teaching others how to understand and apply design principles appropriate for laying out retail space, a home office, a banquet facility, or the living room in a small apartment.

LINKS ■ ■ ■

■ WITHIN THE BOOK

In "Privacy, the Workplace, and the Internet" (pages 563–577), Seumas Miller and John Weckert discuss another aspect of life in cyberspace.

■ ELSEWHERE IN PRINT

Krug, Steven. *Don't Make Me Think: A Common Sense Approach to Web Usability.* Indianapolis: Que, 2000.

Lynch, Patrick J., and Sarah Horton. *Web Style Guide: Basic Design Principles for Creating Web Sites.* New Haven: Yale UP, 1999.

Niederst, Jennifer. *Web Design in a Nutshell.* 2nd ed. Sebastopol: O'Reilly, 2001.

Nielsen, Jakob. *Designing Web Usability.* Indianapolis: Riders, 2000.

Rosenfeld, Louis, and Peter Morville. *Information Architecture for the World Wide Web.* Sebastopol: O'Reilly, 1998.

■ ONLINE

- A Beginner's Guide to HTML
  <http://archive.ncsa.uiuc.edu/Genral/Internet/WWW/HTMLPrimer.html>

- Evaluating Web Sites
  <http://www.library.cornell.edu/okuref/research/webeval.htm>

- Writing for the Web
  <http://www.useit.com/papers/webwriting>

- Yale Web Style Guide
  <http://www.info.med.yale.edu/caim/manual>

IMAGES OF WOMEN IN EUROPEAN ART

John Berger

John Berger is a British art critic, novelist, and screenwriter who has published and translated many works on diverse subjects. Assessing Berger's achievement in an article for The New York Times Book Review, *Robert Boyers writes, "To read Mr. Berger over the last thirty years has been to feel oneself in the presence of an intelligence utterly un-moved by literary or political fashion and unfailingly committed to its own clear vision of what is decent and important, in art and in life."*

The following selection is based on part of a television series created by Berger for the British Broadcasting Company. Material from this program was subsequently pub-lished as a book, Ways of Seeing, *in 1972. John Berger appears as the "author" of this text, but a note opposite the title page states that the book was "made by John Berger, Sven Blomberg, Chris Fox, Michael Dibb, Richard Hollis"—indicating his respect for col-leagues and his commitment to collaboration. "Images of Women in European Art" comes from this text. Like the original presentation on television, it emphasizes visual images with relatively little analysis. But the analysis is provocative and helped shape the way educated viewers have come to see the female nude in Western art. As you read, pay close attention to both images and text.*

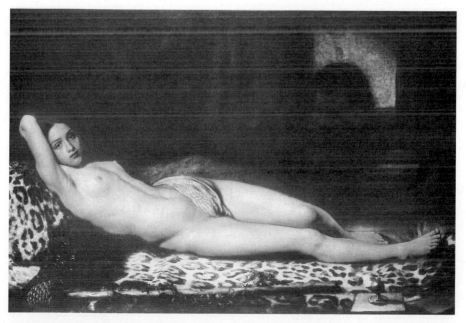

Reclining Bacchante by Trutat 1824–1848

According to usage and conventions which are at last being questioned but have by no means been overcome, the social presence of a woman is different in kind from that of a man. A man's presence is dependent upon the promise of power which he embodies. If the promise is large and credible, his presence is striking. If it is small or incredible, he is found to have little presence. The promised power may be moral, physical, temperamental, economic, social, sexual—but its object is always exterior to the man. A man's presence suggests what he is capable of doing to you or for you. His presence may be fabricated, in the sense that he pretends to be capable of what he is not. But the pretense is always toward a power which he exercises on others.

By contrast, a woman's presence expresses her own attitude to herself, and defines what can and cannot be done to her. Her presence is manifest in her gestures, voice, opinions, expressions, clothes, chosen surroundings, taste—indeed there is nothing she can do which does not contribute to her presence. Presence, for a woman, is so intrinsic to her person that men tend to think of it as an almost physical emanation, a kind of heat or smell or aura.

To be born a woman has been to be born, within an allotted and confined space, into the keeping of men. The social presence of women has developed as a result of their ingenuity in living under such tutelage within such a limited space. But this has been at the cost of a woman's self being split into two. A woman must continually watch herself. She is almost continually accompanied by her own image of herself. Whilst she is walking across a room or whilst she is weeping at the death of her father, she can scarcely avoid envisaging herself walking or weeping. From earliest childhood she has been taught and persuaded to survey herself continually.

And so she comes to consider the *surveyor* and the *surveyed* within her as the two constituent yet always distinct elements of her identity as a woman.

She has to survey everything she is and everything she does because how   5
she appears to others, and ultimately how she appears to men, is of crucial importance for what is normally thought of as the success of her life. Her own sense of being in herself is supplanted by a sense of being appreciated as herself by another.

Men survey women before treating them. Consequently how a woman appears to a man can determine how she will be treated. To acquire some control over this process, women must contain it and interiorize it. That part of a woman's self which is the surveyor treats the part which is the surveyed so as to demonstrate to others how her whole self would like to be treated. And this exemplary treatment of herself by herself constitutes her presence. Every woman's presence regulates what is and is not "permissible" within her presence. Every one of her actions—whatever its direct purpose or motivation—is also read as an indication of how she would like to be treated. If a woman throws a glass on the floor, this is an example of how she treats her own emotion of anger and so of how she would wish it to be treated by others. If a man does the same, his action is only read as an expression of his anger. If a woman makes a good joke, this is an example of how she treats the joker in herself and accordingly of how she as a joker-woman would like to be treated by others. Only a man can make a good joke for its own sake.

One might simplify this by saying: *Men act* and *women appear.* Men look at women. Women watch themselves being looked at. This determines not only most relations between men and women but also the relation of women to themselves. The surveyor of woman in herself is male: the surveyed female. Thus she turns herself into an object—and most particularly an object of vision: a sight.

In one category of European oil painting women were the principal, ever-recurring subject. That category is the nude. In the nudes of European painting we can discover some of the criteria and conventions by which women have been seen and judged as sights.

The first nudes in the tradition depicted Adam and Eve. It is worth referring to the story as told in Genesis:

> And when the woman saw that the tree was good for food, and that it was a delight to the eyes, and that the tree was to be desired to make one wise, she took of the fruit thereof and did eat; and she gave also unto her husband with her, and he did eat.
>
> And the eyes of them both were opened, and they knew that they were naked; and they sewed fig-leaves together and made themselves aprons. . . . And the Lord God called unto the man and said unto him, "Where are thou?" And he said, "I heard thy voice in the garden, and I was afraid, because I was naked; and I hid myself. . . ."
>
> Unto the woman God said, "I will greatly multiply thy sorrow and thy conception; in sorrow thou shalt bring forth children; and thy desire shall be to thy husband and he shall rule over thee."

What is striking about this story? They became aware of being naked   10
because, as a result of eating the apple, each saw the other differently. Nakedness was created in the mind of the beholder.

The second striking fact is that the woman is blamed and is punished by being made subservient to the man. In relation to the woman, the man becomes the agent of God.

In the medieval tradition the story was often illustrated, scene following scene, as in a strip cartoon.

During the Renaissance the narrative sequence disappeared, and the single moment depicted became the moment of shame. The couple wear fig leaves or make a modest gesture with their hands. But now their shame is not so much in relation to one another as to the spectator.

Later the shame becomes a kind of display.

When the tradition of painting became more secular, other themes also   15
offered the opportunity of painting nudes. But in them all there remains the implication that the subject (a woman) is aware of being seen by a spectator.

She is not naked as she is.

She is naked as the spectator sees her.

Fall and Expulsion from Paradise
by Pol de Limbourg, early
15th Century

Adam and Eve by Mabuse, early
16th Century

Susannah and the Elders by Tintoretto

Often—as with the favourite subject of Susannah and the Elders—this is the actual theme of the picture. We join the Elders to spy on Susannah taking her bath. She looks back at us looking at her.

In another version of the subject by Tintoretto, Susannah is looking at herself in a mirror. Thus she joins the spectators of herself.

The mirror was often used as a symbol of the vanity of woman. The mor-   *20*
alizing, however, was mostly hypocritical.

You painted a naked woman because you enjoyed looking at her, you put a mirror in her hand and you called the painting *Vanity,* thus morally condemn-ing the woman whose nakedness you had depicted for your own pleasure.

The real function of the mirror was otherwise. It was to make the woman connive in treating herself as, first and foremost, a sight.

The judgment of Paris was another theme with the same inwritten idea of a man or men looking at naked women.

But a further element is now added. The element of judgment. Paris awards the apple to the woman he finds most beautiful. Thus Beauty becomes competi-tive. (Today The Judgment of Paris has become the Beauty Contest.) Those who are not judged beautiful are *not beautiful.* Those who are, are given the prize.

The prize is to be owned by a judge—that is to say to be available for him.   *25*
Charles the Second commissioned a secret painting from Lely. It is a highly typical image of the tradition. Nominally it might be a *Venus and Cupid.* In fact it is a portrait of one of the King's mistresses, Nell Gwynne. It shows her passively looking at the spectator staring at her naked. (See page 380.)

Susannah and the Elders by Tintoretto 1518–1594

This nakedness is not, however, an expression of her own feelings; it is a sign of her submission to the owner's feelings or demands. (The owner of both woman and painting.) The painting, when the King showed it to others, demonstrated this submission and his guests envied him.

It is worth noticing that in other non-European traditions—in Indian art, Persian art, African art, Pre-Columbian art—nakedness is never supine in this way. And if, in these traditions, the theme of a work is sexual attraction, it is likely to show active sexual love as between two people, the woman as active as the man, the actions of each absorbing the other. (See pages 380–381.)

We can now begin to see the difference between nakedness and nudity in the European tradition. In his book *The Nude*, Kenneth Clark maintains that to be naked is simply to be without clothes, whereas the nude is a form of art. According to him, a nude is not the starting point of a painting but a way of seeing which the painting achieves. To some degree, this is true—although the way of seeing "a nude" is not necessarily confined to art: There are also nude photographs, nude poses, nude gestures. What is true is that the nude is always conventionalized—and the authority for its conventions derives from a certain tradition of art.

What do these conventions mean? What does a nude signify? It is not sufficient to answer these questions merely in terms of the art form, for it is quite clear that the nude also relates to lived sexuality.

To be naked is to be oneself.

Vanity by Memling
1435–1494

The Judgement of Paris by Rubens 1577–1640

Nell Gwynne by Lely
1618–1680

Vishnu and Lakshmi
11th Century

To be nude is to be seen naked by others and yet not recognized for one-self. A naked body has to be seen as an object in order to become a nude. (The sight of it as an object stimulates the use of it as an object.) Nakedness reveals itself. Nudity is placed on display.

To be naked is to be without disguise.

To be on display is to have the surface of one's own skin, the hairs of one's own body, turned into a disguise which, in that situation, can never be discarded. The nude is condemned to never being naked. Nudity is a form of dress.

Mochica Pottery

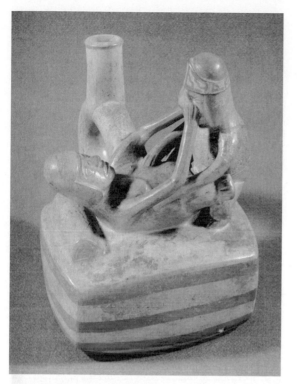

In the average European oil painting of the nude, the principal protagonist is never painted. He is the spectator in front of the picture, and he is presumed to be a man. Everything is addressed to him. Everything must appear
to be the result of his being there. It is for him that the figures have assumed
their nudity. But he, by definition, is a stranger—with his clothes still on.

Consider the *Allegory of Time and Love* by Bronzino. The complicated   35
symbolism which lies behind this painting need not concern us now, because
it does not affect its sexual appeal—at the first degree. Before it is anything
else, this is a painting of sexual provocation. (See page 382.)

The painting was sent as a present from the Grand Duke of Florence to
the King of France. The boy kneeling on the cushion and kissing the woman
is Cupid. She is Venus. But the way her body is arranged has nothing to do
with their kissing. Her body is arranged in the way it is, to display it to the
man looking at the picture. This picture is made to appeal to *his* sexuality. It
has nothing to do with her sexuality. (Here and in the European tradition
generally, the convention of not painting the hair on a woman's body helps
towards the same end. Hair is associated with sexual power, with passion. The
woman's sexual passion needs to be minimized so that the spectator may feel
that he has the monopoly of such passion.) Women are there to feed an
appetite, not to have any of their own. [. . .]

It is true that sometimes a painting includes a male lover.

Venus, Cupid, Time and Love by
Bronzino 1503–1572

Bacchus, Ceres and Cupid by
Von Aachen 1552–1615

But the woman's attention is very rarely directed towards him. Often she looks away from him, or she looks out of the picture toward the one who considers himself her true lover—the spectator-owner.

There was a special category of private pornographic paintings (especially in the eighteenth century) in which couples making love make an appearance. But even in front of these it is clear that the spectator-owner will in fantasy oust the other man, or else identify with him. By contrast the image of the couple in non-European traditions provokes the notion of many couples making love. "We all have a thousand hands, a thousand feet and will never go alone."

Almost all post-Renaissance European sexual imagery is frontal—either   40
literally or metaphorically—because the sexual protagonist is the spectator-owner looking at it.

The absurdity of this male flattery reached its peak in the public academic art of the nineteenth century. (See page 384.)

Men of state, of business, discussed under paintings like this. When one of them felt he had been outwitted, he looked up for consolation. What he saw reminded him that he was a man.

There are a few exceptional nudes in the European tradition of oil painting to which very little of what has been said above applies. Indeed they are no longer nudes—they break the norms of the art form; they are paintings of loved women, more or less naked. Among the hundreds of thousands of nudes which make up the tradition, there are perhaps a hundred of these exceptions. In each case the painter's personal vision of the particular woman he is painting is so strong that it makes no allowance for the spectator. The painter's vision binds the woman to him so that they become as inseparable as couples in stone. The spectator can witness their relationship—but he can do no more: He is forced to recognize himself as the outsider he is. He cannot deceive himself into believing that she is naked for him. He cannot turn her into a nude. The way the painter has painted her includes her will and her intentions in the very structure of the image, in the very expression of her body and her face.

The typical and the exceptional in the tradition can be defined by the simple naked/nude antinomy, but the problem of painting nakedness is not as simple as it might at first appear.

What is the sexual function of nakedness in reality? Clothes encumber con-   45
tact and movement. But it would seem that nakedness has a positive visual value in its own right: we want to *see* the other naked: The other delivers to us the sight of themselves, and we seize upon it—sometimes quite regardless of whether it is for the first time or the hundredth. What does this sight of the other mean to us, how does it, at that instant of total disclosure, affect our desire?

Their nakedness acts as a confirmation and provokes a very strong sense of relief. She is a woman like any other: or he is a man like any other: we are overwhelmed by the marvellous simplicity of the familiar sexual mechanism.

We did not, of course, consciously expect this to be otherwise: Unconscious homosexual desires (or unconscious heterosexual desires if the couple

Les Oréades by Bouguereau 1825–1905

concerned are homosexual) may have led each to half expect something different. But the "relief" can be explained without recourse to the unconscious.

We did not expect them to be otherwise, but the urgency and complexity of our feelings bred a sense of uniqueness which the sight of the other, as

Danäe by Rembrandt 1606–1669

she is or as he is, now dispels. They are more like the rest of their sex than they are different. In this revelation lies the warm and friendly—as opposed to cold and impersonal—anonymity of nakedness.

One could express this differently: At the moment of nakedness first perceived, an element of banality enters: an element that exists only because we need it.   50

Up to that instant the other was more or less mysterious. Etiquettes of modesty are not merely puritan or sentimental: It is reasonable to recognize a loss of mystery. And the explanation of this loss of mystery may be largely visual. The focus of perception shifts from eyes, mouth, shoulders, hands—all of which are capable of such subtleties of expression that the personality expressed by them is manifold—it shifts from these to the sexual parts, whose formation suggests an utterly compelling but single process. The other is reduced or elevated— whichever you prefer—to their primary sexual category: male or female. Our relief is the relief of finding an unquestionable reality to whose direct demands our earlier, highly complex awareness must now yield.

We need the banality which we find in the first instant of disclosure because it grounds us in reality. But it does more than that. This reality, by promising the familiar, proverbial mechanism of sex, offers, at the same time, the possibility of the shared subjectivity of sex.

The loss of mystery occurs simultaneously with the offering of the means for creating a shared mystery. The sequence is: subjective—objective—subjective to the power of two.

We can now understand the difficulty of creating a static image of sexual nakedness. In lived sexual experience nakedness is a process rather than a state. If one moment of that process is isolated, its image will seem banal, and its banality, instead of serving as a bridge between two intense imaginative states, will be chilling. This is one reason why expressive photographs of the naked are even rarer than paintings. The easy solution for the photographer is to turn the figure into a nude, which, by generalizing both sight and viewer and making sexuality unspecific, turns desire into fantasy.

Let us examine an exceptional painted image of nakedness. It is a paint-   55 ing by Rubens of his young second wife, whom he married when he himself was relatively old.

We see her in the act of turning, her fur about to slip off her shoulders. Clearly she will not remain as she is for more than a second. In a superficial sense her image is as instantaneous as a photograph's. But, in a more profound sense, the painting "contains" time and its experience. It is easy to imagine that a moment ago, before she pulled the fur round her shoulders, she was entirely naked. The consecutive stages up to and away from the moment of total disclosure have been transcended. She can belong to any or all of them simultaneously.

Her body confronts us, not as an immediate sight but as experience—the painter's experience. Why? There are superficial anecdotal reasons: her dishevelled hair, the expression of her eyes directed toward him, the tenderness with which the exaggerated susceptibility of her skin has been painted. But the profound reason is a formal one. Her appearance has been literally re-cast by the painter's subjectivity. Beneath the fur that she holds across herself, the upper part of her body and her legs can never meet. There is a displacement sideways of about nine inches: her thighs, in order to join onto her hips, are at least nine inches too far to the left.

Rubens probably did not plan this: The spectator may not consciously notice it. In itself it is unimportant. What matters is what it permits. It permits the body to become impossibly dynamic. Its coherence is no longer within itself but within the experience of the painter. More precisely, it permits the upper and lower halves of the body to rotate separately, and in opposite directions, round the sexual center which is hidden: the torso turning to the right, the legs to the left. At the same time this hidden sexual center is connected by means of the dark fur coat to all the surrounding darkness in the picture, so that she is turning both around and within the dark, which has been made a metaphor for her sex.

Helene Fourment in a Fur Coat
by Rubens 1577–1640

Apart from the necessity of transcending the single instant and of admitting subjectivity, there is, as we have seen, one further element which is essential for any great sexual image of the naked. This is the element of banality which must be undisguised but not chilling. It is this which distinguishes between voyeur and lover. Here such banality is to be found in Rubens's compulsive painting of

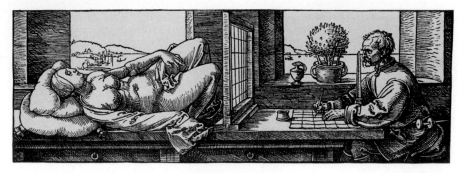

Man Drawing Reclining Woman by Dürer 1471–1528

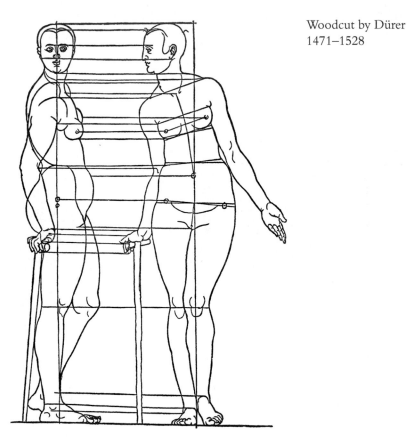

Woodcut by Dürer
1471–1528

the fat softness of Hélène Fourment's flesh, which continually breaks every ideal convention of form and (to him) continually offers the promise of her extraordinary particularity.

The nude in European oil painting is usually presented as an admirable expression of the European humanist spirit. This spirit was inseparable from individualism. And without the development of a highly conscious individual-

60

The Venus of Urbino by Titian c. 1487–1576

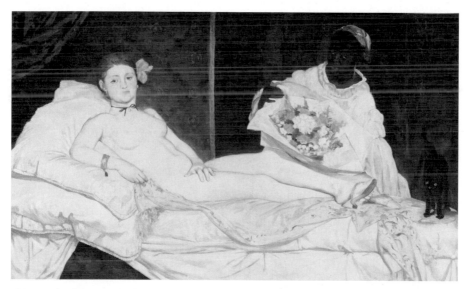

Olympia by Manet 1832–1883

ism, the exceptions to the tradition (extremely personal images of the naked), would never have been painted. Yet the tradition contained a contradiction which it could not itself resolve. A few individual artists intuitively recognized this and resolved the contradiction in their own terms, but their solutions could never enter the tradition's *cultural* terms.

The contradiction can be stated simply. On the one hand the individual-ism of the artist, the thinker, the patron, the owner: on the other hand, the person who is the object of their activities—the woman—treated as a thing or an abstraction.

Dürer believed that the ideal nude ought to be constructed by taking the face of one body, the breasts of another, the legs of a third, the shoulders of a fourth, the hands of a fifth—and so on.

The result would glorify Man. But the exercise presumed a remarkable indifference to who any one person really was.

In the art form of the European nude, the painters and spectator-owners were usually men and the persons treated as objects, usually women. This unequal relationship is so deeply embedded in our culture that it still struc-tures the consciousness of many women. They do to themselves what men do to them. They survey, like men, their own femininity.

In modern art the category of the nude has become less important. Artists themselves began to question it. In this, as in many other respects, Manet rep-resented a turning point. If one compares his *Olympia* with Titian's original, one sees a woman, cast in the traditional role, beginning to question that role, somewhat defiantly. (See page 389.)

The ideal was broken. But there was little to replace it except the "real-ism" of the prostitute—who became the quintessential woman of early avant-garde twentieth-century painting. (Toulouse-Lautrec, Picasso, Rouault, German Expressionism, etc.) In academic painting the tradition continued.

Today the attitudes and values which informed that tradition are expressed through other, more widely diffused media—advertising, journal-ism, television.

But the essential way of seeing women, the essential use to which their images are put, has not changed. Women are depicted in a quite different way from men—not because the feminine is different from the masculine—but because the "ideal" spectator is always assumed to be male, and the image of the woman is designed to flatter him. If you have any doubt that this is so, make the following experiment. Choose [. . .] an image of a traditional nude. Transform the woman into a man, either in your mind's eye or by drawing on the reproduction. Then notice the violence which that transformation does–not to the image, but to the assumptions of a likely viewer.

QUESTIONS FOR DISCUSSION

1. Why does Berger believe that "a woman must continually watch herself"?
2. Writing over thirty years ago, Berger claims: "*men act* and *women appear.*" Putting aside how men and women behave in their daily lives, is Berger's claim still true for pictures of men and women?
3. Is Berger right to assume that men are the most likely audience to enjoy representations of the female nude?
4. What is the difference between being "naked" and being "nude"?

5. According to Berger, what is the effect of seeing someone "naked"? Do you agree?
6. What does Berger mean by "banality," and why is it important when viewing "nakedness"?

SUGGESTIONS FOR WRITING

1. Berger describes the image on page 384 as a "peak" in "male flattery [...] in the public academic art of the nineteenth century." Write a paper explaining how this image flatters men.
2. Consider the painting by Rembrandt on page 385. Write about how you see this image and what makes it an exception from the dominant tradition discussed by Berger.
3. Write an essay contrasting the two images that appear on page 389.

LINKS   ■ ■ ■

■ WITHIN THE BOOK

For another discussion of visual representations of women, see "Please, Please, You're Driving Me Wild" by Jean Kilbourne (pages 413–426).

■ ELSEWHERE IN PRINT

Berger, John. *About Looking.* 1980. New York: Vintage, 1991.
———. *Ways of Seeing.* 1972. New York: Viking, 1995.
Broude, Norma, and Mary D. Garrad, eds. *Feminism and Art History.* New York: Harper, 1982.
McDonald, Helen. *Erotic Ambiguities: The Female Nude in Art.* New York: Routledge, 2001.
Nochlin, Linda. *Representing Women.* New York: Thames, 1999.

■ ONLINE

- Images of Women in Ancient Art
  <http://www.arthistory.sbc.edu/imageswomen>
- Images of Women in Art
  <http://www.womenshistory.about.com/cs/artimages>
- Interpreting Images
  <http://www.aber.ac.uk/media/Documents/gaze/gaze.html>
- John Berger, *Ways of Seeing*
  <http://www.lcc.gatech.edu/~takacs/Fall2001/berger>

BEAUTY (RE)DISCOVERS THE MALE BODY

Susan Bordo

A professor of English and women's studies, Susan Bordo holds the Otis A. Singletary Chair in the Humanities at the University of Kentucky. A feminist philosopher who is especially interested in the nature of gender, she has been credited with having created an interdisciplinary interest in "body studies." Bordo also lectures widely on the relationship between popular culture and how people perceive their bodies, addressing such issues as eating disorders and cosmetic surgery. Her books include Unbearable Weight: Feminism, Western Culture, and the Body; Twilight Zones: The Hidden Life of Cultural Images from Plato to O.J.; *and* The Male Body *(1999), in which the following selection (illustrated with additional advertisements) appears as a chapter.*

Reviewers across the country praised The Male Body *upon its initial publication, using words such as "provocative," "unexpected," "funny," and "compelling." Excerpts appeared in* Mademoiselle, Elle, Vanity Fair, *and* The New York Times Magazine. *As you read the following excerpt, be prepared for some frank language as well as erotically charged images. But be alert for how Bordo provides thoughtful analysis of what these images reveal about the use of eroticism in marketing.*

Putting classical art to the side for the moment, the naked and near-naked female body became an object of mainstream consumption first in *Playboy* and its imitators, then in movies, and only then in fashion photographs. With the male body, the trajectory has been different. Fashion has taken the lead, the movies have followed. Hollywood may have been a chest-fest in the fifties, but it was male clothing designers who went south and violated the really powerful taboos—not just against the explicit depiction of penises and male bottoms but against the admission of all sorts of forbidden "feminine" qualities into mainstream conceptions of manliness.

It was the spring of 1995, and I was sipping my first cup of morning coffee, not yet fully awake, flipping through *The New York Times Magazine,* when I had my first real taste of what it's like to inhabit this visual culture as a man. It was both thrilling and disconcerting. It was the first time in my experience that I had encountered a commercial representation of a male body that seemed to deliberately invite me to linger over it. Let me make that stronger—that seemed to reach out to me, interrupting my mundane but peaceful Sunday morning, and provoke me into erotic consciousness, whether or not I wanted it. Women—both straight and gay—have always gazed covertly, of course, squeezing our illicit little titillations out of representations designed for—or pretending to—other purposes than to turn us on. *This* ad made no such pretense. It caused me to knock over my coffee cup, ruining the more cerebral pleasures of the *Book Review*. Later, when I had regained my equilibrium, I made a screen-saver out of him, so I could gaze at my leisure.

I'm sure that many gay men were as taken as I was, and perhaps some gay women too. The erotic charge of various sexual styles is not neatly mapped onto sexual orientation (let alone biological sex). Brad Pitt's baby-butch looks are a turn-on to many lesbians, while I—regarded by most of my gay friends as a pretty hard-core heterosexual—have always found Anne Heche irresistible (even before Ellen did). [. . .] Despite such complications, until recently only heterosexual men have continually been inundated by popular cultural images *designed* with their sexual responses (or, at least, what those sexual responses are imagined to be) in mind. It's not entirely a gift. On the minus side is having one's composure continually challenged by what Timothy Beneke has aptly described as a culture of "intrusive images," eliciting fantasies, emotions, and erections at times and in places where they might not be appropriate. On the plus side is the cultural permission to be a voyeur.

Some psychologists say that the circuit from eyes to brain to genitals is a quicker trip for men than for women. "There's some strong evidence," popular science writer Deborah Blum reports, citing studies of men's responses to pictures of naked women, "that testosterone is wired for visual response." Maybe. But who is the electrician here? God? Mother Nature? Or Hugh Hefner? Practice makes perfect. And women have had little practice. The Calvin Klein ad made me feel like an adolescent again, brought me back to that day when I saw Barry Resnick on the basketball court of Weequahic High and realized that men's legs could make me weak in the knees. Men's legs? I knew that *women's* legs were supposed to be sexy. I had learned that from all those hose-straightening scenes in the movies. But men's legs? Who had ever seen a woman gaga over some guy's legs in the movies? Or even read about it in a book? Yet the muscular grace of Barry's legs took my breath away. Maybe something was wrong with me. Maybe my sex drive was too strong, too much like a man's. By the time I came across that Calvin Klein ad, several decades of feminism and life experience had left me a little less worried about my sex drive. Still, the sight of that model's body made me feel that my sexual education was still far from complete.

I brought the ad to classes and lectures, asking women what they thought of him. Most began to sweat the moment I unfolded the picture, then got their bearings and tried to explore the bewitching stew of sexual elements the picture has to offer. The model—a young Jackson Browne look-alike—stands there in his form-fitting and rip-speckled Calvin Klein briefs, head lowered, dark hair loosely falling over his eyes. His body projects strength, solidity; he's no male waif. But his finely muscled chest is not so overdeveloped as to suggest a sexuality immobilized by the thick matter of the body. Gay theorist Ron Long, describing contemporary gay sexual aesthetics—lean, taut, sinuous muscles rather than Schwarzenegger bulk—points to a "dynamic tension" that the incredible hulks lack. Stiff, engorged Schwarzenegger bodies, he says, seem to *be* surrogate penises—with nowhere to go and nothing to do but stand there

5

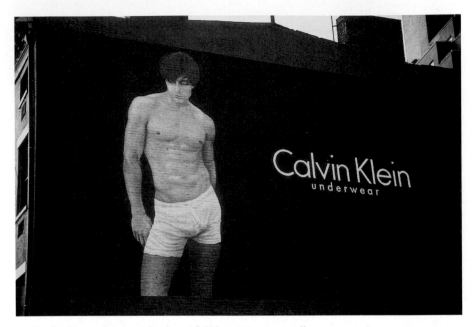

An invitation to linger: a body with "dynamic tension."

looking massive—whereas muscles like this young man's seem designed for movement, for sex. His body isn't a stand-in phallus; rather, he *has* a penis—the real thing, not a symbol, and a fairly breathtaking one, clearly outlined through the soft jersey fabric of the briefs. It seems slightly erect, or perhaps that's his nonerect size; either way, there's a substantial presence there that's palpable (it looks so touchable, you want to cup your hand over it) and very, very male.

At the same time, however, my gaze is invited by something "feminine" about the young man. His underwear may be ripped, but ever so slightly, subtly; unlike the original ripped-underwear poster boy Kowalski°, he's hardly a thug. He doesn't stare at the viewer challengingly, belligerently, as do so many models in other ads for male underwear, facing off like a street tough passing a member of the rival gang on the street. ("Yeah, this is an underwear ad and I'm half naked. But I'm still the one in charge here. Who's gonna look away first?") No, this model's languid body posture, his averted look are classic signals, both in the "natural" and the "cultural" world, of willing subordination. He offers himself nonaggressively to the gaze of another. Hip cocked in the snaky S-curve usually reserved for depictions of women's bodies, eyes downcast but not closed, he gives off a sultry, moody, subtle but undeniably seductive consciousness of his erotic allure. Feast on me, I'm here to be looked at, my body is for your eyes. Oh my.

Kowalski: Stanley Kowalski, lead character in *A Streetcar Named Desire* by Tennessee Williams—a role first played by Marlon Brando. (See photograph on page 411.)

Such an attitude of male sexual supplication, although it has (as we'll see) classical antecedents, is very new to contemporary mainstream representations. Homophobia is at work in this taboo, but so are attitudes about gender that cut across sexual orientation. For many men, both gay and straight, to be so passively dependent on the gaze of another person for one's sense of self-worth is incompatible with being a real man. As we'll see, such notions about manliness are embedded in Greek culture, in contemporary visual representation, and even (in disguised form) in existentialist philosophy. "For the woman," as philosopher Simone de Beauvoir° writes, ". . . the absence of her lover is always torture; he is an eye, a judge . . . away from him, she is dispossessed, at once of herself and of the world." For Beauvoir's sometime lover and lifelong soul mate Jean-Paul Sartre°, on the other hand, the gaze (or the Look, as he called it) of another person—including the gaze of one's lover—is the "hell" that other people represent. If we were alone in the world, he argues, we would be utterly free—within physical constraints—to be whomever we wanted to be, to be the creatures of our own self-fantasies, to define our behavior however we like. Other people intrude on this solipsism, and have the audacity to see us from their own perspective rather than ours. The result is what Sartre calls primordial Shame under the eyes of the Other, and a fierce desire to reassert one's freedom. The other person has stolen "the secret" of who I am. I must fight back, resist their attempts to define me.

I understand, of course, what Sartre is talking about here. We've all, male and female alike, felt the shame that another pair of eyes can bring. Sartre's own classic example is of being caught peeking through a keyhole by another person. It isn't until those other eyes are upon you that you truly feel not just the "wrongness" of what you are doing, but—Sartre would argue—the very fact that you are doing it. Until the eyes of another are upon us, "catching us" in the act, we can deceive ourselves, pretend. Getting caught in moments of fantasy or vanity may be especially shameful. When I was an adolescent, I loved to pretend I was a radio personality, and talking into an empty coffee can created just the right sound. One day, my mother caught me speaking in the smooth and slightly sultry tones that radio personalities had even in those days. The way I felt is what Sartre means when he describes the Look of another person as the fulcrum of shame-making. My face got hot, and suddenly I saw how ridiculous I must have seemed, my head in the Chock Full O' Nuts, my narcissistic fantasies on full display. I was caught, I wanted to run.

The disjunction between self-conception and external judgment can be especially harsh when the external definitions carry racial and gender stereotypes with them. Sartre doesn't present such examples—he's interested in capturing the contours of an existential situation shared by all rather than in analyzing the cultural differences that affect that situation—but they are surely relevant to understanding the meaning of the Look of the Other. A black man

---

Simone de Beauvoir: French writer (1908–1986) best known for *The Second Sex.*
Jean-Paul Sartre: French philosopher (1905–1980) who is widely associated with Existentialism.

jogs down the street in sweat clothes, thinking of the class he is going to teach later that day; a white woman passes him, clutches her handbag more tightly, quickens her step; in her eyes, the teacher is a potentially dangerous animal. A Latin American student arrives early the first day of college; an administrator, seeing him in the still-deserted hall, asks him if he is the new janitor. The aspiring student has had his emerging identity erased, a stereotype put in its place by another pair of eyes. When women are transformed from professionals to "pussies" by the comments of men on the street, it's humiliating, not so much because we're puritans as because we sense the hostility in the hoots, the desire to bring an uppity woman down to size by reminding her that she's just "the sex" (as Beauvoir put it).

We may all have felt shame, but—as the different attitudes of Beauvoir   10
and Sartre suggest—men and women are socially sanctioned to deal with the gaze of the Other in different ways. Women learn to anticipate, even play to the sexualizing gaze, trying to become what will please, captivate, turn shame into pride. (In the process, we also learn how sexy being gazed at can feel— perhaps precisely because it walks the fine edge of shame.) Many of us, truth be told, get somewhat addicted to the experience. I'm renting a video, feeling a bit low, a bit tired. The young man at the counter, unsolicited, tells me I'm "looking good." It alters everything, I feel fine, alive; it seems to go right down to my cells. I leave the store feeling younger, stronger, more awake. When women sense that they are not being assessed sexually—for example, as we age, or if we are disabled—it may feel like we no longer exist.

Women may dread being surveyed harshly—being seen as too old, too fat, too flat-chested—but men are not supposed to enjoy being surveyed *period*. It's feminine to be on display. Men are thus taught—as my uncle Leon used to say—to be a moving target. Get out of range of those eyes, don't let them catch you—even as the object of their fantasies (or, as Sartre would put it, don't let them "possess," "steal" your freedom). This phobia has even distorted scientific research [. . .]. Evolutionary theorists have long acknowledged display as an important feature of courting behavior among primates—except when it comes to *our* closest ancestors. With descriptions of hominid behavior, male display behavior "suddenly drops out of the primate evolutionary picture" (Sheets-Johnstone) and is replaced by the concept of year-round female sexual receptivity. It seems that it has been intolerable, unthinkable for male evolutionary theorists to imagine the bodies of their male ancestors being on display, sized up, dependent on selection (or rejection) by female hominids.

Scientists and "ordinary guys" are totally in synch here, as is humorously illustrated in Peter Cattaneo's popular 1997 British film *The Full Monty*. In the film, a group of unemployed metalworkers in Sheffield, England, watch a Chippendale's show and hatch the money-making scheme of presenting their own male strip show in which they will go right down to the "full Monty." At the start of the film, the heroes are hardly pillars of successful manliness (Gaz, their leader, refers to them as "scrap"). Yet even they have been sheltered by their guyhood, as they learn while putting the show together. One gets a penis pump. Another borrows his wife's face cream. They run, they wrap their bellies in plastic, they do jumping jacks, they get artificial tans. The most over-weight one among them (temporarily) pulls out of the show. Before, these guys hadn't lived their lives under physical scrutiny but in male action mode, in which men are judged by their accomplishments. Now, anticipating being on display to a roomful of spectators, they suddenly realize how it feels to be judged as women routinely are, sized up by another pair of eyes. "I pray that they'll be a bit more understanding about us" than they've been with women, David (the fat one) murmurs.

They get past their discomfort, in the end, and their show is greeted with wild enthusiasm by the audience. The movie leaves us with this feel-good end-ing, not raising the question obvious to every woman watching the film: Would a troupe of out-of-shape women be received as warmly, as affectionately? The climactic moment when the men throw off their little pouches is demurely shot from the rear, moreover, so we—the audience—don't get "the full Monty." Nonetheless, the film gently and humorously makes an important point: For a heterosexual man to offer himself up to a sexually evaluating gaze is for him to make a large, scary leap—and not just because of the anxieties about size [. . .](the guy who drops out of the show, remember, is embarrassed by his fat, not his penis). The "full Monty"—the naked penis—is not merely a body part in the movie (hence it doesn't really matter that the film doesn't show it). It's a symbol for male exposure, vulnerability to an evaluation and judgment that women—clothed or naked—experience all the time.

I had to laugh out loud at a 1997 *New York Times Magazine* "Style" col-umn, entitled "Overexposure," which complained of the "contagion" of nudity spreading through celebrity culture. "Stars no longer have private parts," the author observed, and fretted that civilians would soon also be mea-sured by the beauty of their buns. I share this author's concern about our body-obsessed culture. But, pardon me, he's just noticing this now??? Actresses have been baring their breasts, their butts, even their bushes, for some time, and ordinary women have been tromping off to the gym in pursuit of com-parably perfect bodies. What's got the author suddenly crying "overkill," it turns out, is Sly Stallone's "surreally fat-free" appearance on the cover of *Van-ity Fair,* and Rupert Everett's "dimpled behind" in a Karl Lagerfeld fashion spread. Now that *men* are taking off their clothes, the culture is suddenly going too far. Could it be that the author doesn't even "read" all those naked female bodies as "overexposed"? Does he protest a bit too much when he declares in the first sentence of the piece that he found it "a yawn" when Dirk Diggler unsheathed his "prosthetic shillelagh" ("penis" is still a word to be avoided whenever possible) at the end of *Boogie Nights?* A yawn? My friend's palms were sweating profusely, and I was not about to drop off to sleep either.

As for dimpled behinds, my second choice for male pinup of the decade is the Gucci series of two ads in which a beautiful young man, shot from the rear, puts on a pair of briefs. In the first ad, he's holding them in his hands, contemplating them. Is he checking out the correct washing-machine temp? It's odd, surely, to stand there looking at your underwear, but never mind. The

15

point is: His underwear is in his hands, not on his butt. *It*—his bottom, that is—is gorgeously, completely naked—a motif so new to mainstream advertising (but since then catching on rapidly) that several of my friends, knowing I was writing about the male body, e-mailed me immediately when they saw the ad. In the second ad, he's put the underwear on and is adjusting it to fit. Luckily for us, he hasn't succeeded yet, so his buns are peeking out the bottom of the underwear, looking biteable. For the *Times* writer, those buns may be an indecent exposure of parts that should be kept private (or they're a boring yawn, I'm afraid he can't have it both ways), but for me—and for thousands of gay men across the country—this was a moment of political magnitude, and a delicious one. The body parts that *we* love to squeeze (those plastic breasts, they're the real yawn for me) had come out of the closet and into mainstream culture, where *we* can enjoy them without a trip to a specialty store.

But all this is very new. Women aren't used to seeing naked men frankly portrayed as "objects" of a sexual gaze (and neither are heterosexual men, as that *Times* writer makes clear). So pardon me if I'm skeptical when I read arguments about men's greater "biological" responsiveness to visual stimuli. These "findings," besides being ethnocentric (no one thinks to poll Trobriand Islanders), display little awareness of the impact of changes in cultural representations on our capacities for sexual response. Popular science writer Deborah Blum, for example, cites a study from the Kinsey Institute which showed a group of men and women a series of photos and drawings of nudes, both male and female:

> Fifty-four percent of the men were erotically aroused versus 12 percent of the women—in other words, more than four times as many men. The same gap exists, on a much larger scale, in the business of pornography, a $500-million-plus industry in the U.S. which caters almost exclusively to men. In the first flush of 1970s feminism, two magazines—*Playgirl* and *Viva*—began publishing male centerfolds. *Viva* dropped the nude photos after surveys showed their readers didn't care for them; the editor herself admitted to finding them slightly disgusting.

Blum presents these findings as suggestive of a hard-wired difference between men and women. I'd be cautious about accepting that conclusion. First of all, there's the question of which physiological responses count as "erotic arousal" and whether they couldn't be evidence of other states. Clearly, too, we can *learn* to have certain physiological responses—and to suppress them—so nothing biologically definitive is proved by the presence or absence of physical arousal.

Studies that rely on viewers' *own* reports need to be carefully interpreted too. I know, from talking to women students, that they sometimes aren't all that clear about *what* they feel in the presence of erotic stimuli, and even when they are, they may not be all that comfortable admitting what they feel. Hell, not just my students! Once, a lover asked me, as we were about to part for the evening, if there was anything that we hadn't done that I'd really like to do. I knew immediately what that was: I wanted him to undress, very slowly, while

I sat on the floor and just watched. But I couldn't tell him. I was too embarrassed. Later, alone in my compartment on the train, I sorely regretted my cowardice. The fact is that I love to watch a man getting undressed, and I especially like it if he is conscious of being looked at. But there is a long legacy of shame to be overcome here, for both sexes, and the cultural models are only now just emerging which might help us move beyond it.

Perhaps, then, we should wait a bit longer, do a few more studies, before we come to any biological conclusions about women's failure to get aroused by naked pictures. A newer (1994) University of Chicago study found that 30 percent of women ages eighteen to forty-four and 19 percent of women ages forty-five to fifty-nine said they found "watching a partner undress" to be "very appealing." ("Not a bad percentage," Nancy Friday° comments, "given that Nice Girls didn't look.") There's still a gender gap—the respective figures for men of the same age groups were 50 percent and 40 percent. We're just learning, after all, to be voyeuses. Perhaps, too, heterosexual men could learn to be less uncomfortable offering themselves as "sexual objects" if they realized the pleasure women get from it. Getting what you have been most deprived of is the best gift, the most healing gift, the most potentially transforming gift—because it has the capacity to make one more whole. Women have been deprived not so much of the *sight* of beautiful male bodies as the experience of having the male body *offered* to us, handed to us on a silver platter, the way female bodies—in the ads, in the movies—are handed to men. Getting this from her partner is the erotic equivalent of a woman's coming home from work to find a meal prepared and ready for her. Delicious—even if it's just franks and beans.

THANKS, CALVIN!

Despite their bisexual appeal, the cultural genealogy of the ads I've been discussing and others like them is to be traced largely through gay male aesthetics, rather than a sudden blossoming of appreciation for the fact that women might enjoy looking at sexy, well-hung young men who don't appear to be about to rape them. Feminists might like to imagine that Madison Avenue heard our pleas for sexual equality and finally gave us "men as sex objects." But what's really happened is that women have been the beneficiaries of what might be described as a triumph of pure consumerism—and with it, a burgeoning male fitness and beauty culture—over homophobia and the taboos against male vanity, male "femininity," and erotic display of the male body that have gone along with it.

Throughout this century, gay photographers have created a rich, sensuous, and dramatic tradition which is unabashed in eroticizing the male body, male sensuousness, and male potency, including penises. But until recently,

Nancy Friday: Contemporary feminist writer best known for *My Secret Garden.*

such representations have been kept largely in the closet. Mainstream responses to several important exhibits which opened in the seventies—featuring the groundbreaking early work of Wilhelm von Gloeden, George Dureau, and George Platt Lynes as well as then-contemporary artists such as Robert Mapplethorpe, Peter Hujar, and Arthur Tress—would today probably embarrass the critics who wrote about them when they opened. John Ashbery, in *New York* magazine, dismissed the entire genre of male nude photography with the same sexist tautology that covertly underlies that *Times* piece on cultural "overexposure": "Nude women seem to be in their natural state; men, for some reason, merely look undressed . . . When is a nude not a nude? When it is male." (Substitute "blacks" and "whites" for "women" and "men" and you'll see how offensive the statement is.)

For other reviewers, the naked male, far from seeming "merely undressed," was unnervingly sexual. *New York Times* critic Gene Thompson wrote that "there is something disconcerting about the sight of a man's naked body being presented as a sexual object"; he went on to describe the world of homoerotic photography as one "closed to most of us, fortunately." Vicki Goldberg, writing for the *Saturday Review,* was more appreciative of the "beauty and dignity" of the nude male body, but concluded that so long as its depiction was erotic in emphasis, it will "remain half-private, slightly awkward, an art form cast from its traditions and in search of some niche to call its home."

Goldberg needed a course in art history. It's true that in classical art, the naked human body was often presented as a messenger of spiritual themes, and received as such. But the male bodies sculpted by the Greeks and Michelangelo were not exactly nonerotic. It might be more accurate to say that in modernity, with the spiritual interpretation of the nude body no longer a convention, the contemporary homophobic psyche is not screened from the sexual charge of the nude male body. Goldberg was dead wrong about something else too. Whatever its historical lineage, the frankly sexual representation of the male body was to find, in the next twenty years, a far from private "niche to call its home": Consumer culture discovered its commercial potency.

Calvin Klein had his epiphany, according to one biography, one night in 1974 in New York's gay Flamingo bar:

> As Calvin wandered through the crowd at the Flamingo, the body heat rushed through him like a revelation; this was the cutting edge. . . . [The] men! The men at the Flamingo had less to do about sex for him than the notion of portraying men as gods. He realized that what he was watching was the freedom of a new generation, unashamed, in-the-flesh embodiments of Calvin's ideals: straight-looking, masculine men, with chiseled bodies, young Greek gods come to life. The vision of shirtless young men with hardened torsos, all in blue jeans, top button opened, a whisper of hair from the belly button disappearing into the denim pants, would inspire and inform the next ten years of Calvin Klein's print and television advertisements.

Klein's genius was that of a cultural Geiger counter; his own bisexuality *25* enabled him to see that the phallic body, as much as any female figure, is an enduring sex object within Western culture. In America in 1974, however, that ideal was still largely closeted. Only gay culture unashamedly sexualized the lean, fit body that virtually everyone, gay and straight, now aspires to. Sex, as Calvin Klein knew, sells. He also knew that gay sex wouldn't sell to straight men. But the rock-hard, athletic gay male bodies that Klein admired at the Flamingo did not advertise their sexual preference through the feminine codes—limp wrists, raised pinkie finger, swishy walk—which the straight world then identified with homosexuality. Rather, they embodied a highly masculine aesthetic that—although definitely exciting for gay men— would scream "heterosexual" to (clueless) straights. Klein knew just the kind of clothing to show that body off in too. As Steven Gaines and Sharon Churcher tell it:

> He had watched enough attractive young people with good bodies in tight jeans dancing at the Flamingo and Studio 54 to know that the "basket" and the behind was what gave jeans sex appeal. Calvin sent his assistants out for several pairs of jeans, including the classic five-button Levi's, and cut them apart to see how they were made. Then he cut the "rise," or area from the waistband to under the groin, much shorter to accentuate the crotch and pull the seam up between the buttocks, giving the behind more shape and prominence. The result was instant sex appeal—and a look that somehow Calvin just *knew* was going to sell.

So we come to the mainstream commercialization of the aesthetic legacy of Stanley Kowalski and those inspired innovations of Brando's costumer in *A Streetcar Named Desire*. When I was growing up, jeans were "dungarees"—suitable for little kids, hayseeds, and juvenile delinquents, but not for anyone to wear on a date. Klein transformed jeans from utilitarian garments to erotic second skins. Next, Klein went for underwear. He wasn't the first, but he was the most daring. In 1981, Jockey International had broken ground by photographing Baltimore Oriole pitcher Jim Palmer in a pair of briefs (airbrushed) in one of its ads—selling $100 million worth of underwear by year's end. Inspired by Jockey's success, in 1983 Calvin Klein put a forty-by-fifty-foot Bruce Weber photograph of Olympic pole vaulter Tom Hintinauss in Times Square, Hintinauss's large penis clearly discernible through his briefs. The Hintinauss ad, unlike the Palmer ad, did not employ any of the usual fictional rationales for a man's being in his underwear—for example, the pretense that the man is in the process of getting dressed—but blatantly put Hintinauss's body on display, sunbathing on a rooftop, his skin glistening. The line of shorts "flew off the shelves" at Bloomingdale's, and when Klein papered bus shelters in Manhattan with poster versions of the ad, they were all stolen overnight.

Images of masculinity that will do double (or triple or quadruple) duty with a variety of consumers, straight and gay, male and female, are not difficult to create in a culture like ours, in which the muscular male body has a long and glorious aesthetic history. That's precisely what Calvin Klein was the

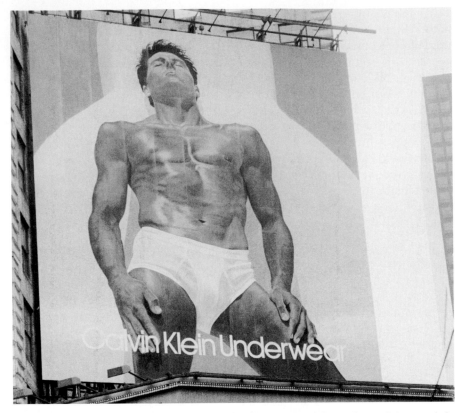

Bronzed and beautiful Tom Hintinauss: a breakthrough ad for Calvin Klein—and the beginning of a new era for the unabashed erotic display of the male body.

first to recognize and exploit—the possibility and profitability of what is known in the trade as a "dual marketing" approach. Since then, many advertisers have taken advantage of Klein's insight. A recent Abercrombie & Fitch ad, for example, depicts a locker room full of young, half-clothed football players getting a postmortem from their coach after a game. Beautiful, undressed male bodies doing what real men are "supposed to do." Dirty uniforms and smudged faces, wounded players, helmets. What could be more straight? But as iconography depicting a culture of exclusively male bodies, young, gorgeous, and well-hung, what could be more "gay"?

It required a Calvin Klein to give the new vision cultural form. But the fact is that if we've entered a brave, new world of male bodies it is largely because of a more "material" kind of epiphany—a dawning recognition among advertisers of the buying power of gay men. For a long time prejudice had triumphed over the profit motive, blinding marketers to just how sizable—and well-heeled—a consumer group gay men represent. (This has been the case with other "minorities" too. Hollywood producers, never bothering to do any demographics on middle-class and professional African-American women—or the issues that they share with women of other races and classes in this culture—were shocked at the tremendous box office success of *Waiting to Exhale*. They won't make that particular mistake again.) It took a survey conducted by *The Advocate* to jolt corporate America awake about gay consumers. The survey, done between 1977 and 1980, showed that 70 percent of its readers aged twenty to forty earned incomes well above the national median. Soon, articles were appearing on the business pages of newspapers, like one in 1982 in *The New York Times Magazine,* which described advertisers as newly interested in "wooing . . . the white, single, well-educated, well-paid man who happens to be homosexual."

"Happens to be homosexual": the phrasing—suggesting that sexual identity is peripheral, even accidental—is telling. Because of homophobia, dual marketing used to require a delicate balancing act, as advertisers tried to speak to gays "in a way that the straight consumer will not notice." Often, that's been accomplished through the use of play and parody, as in Versace's droll portraits of men being groomed and tended by male servants, and Diesel's overtly narcissistic gay posers. "Thanks, Diesel, for making us so very beautiful," they gush. Or take the ad [. . .] with its gorgeous, mechanically inept model admitting that he's "known more for my superb bone construction and soft, supple hair than my keen intellect." The playful tone reassures heterosexual consumers that the vanity (and mechanical incompetence) of the man selling the product is "just a joke." For gay consumers, on the other hand, this reassurance is *itself* the "joke"; they read the humor in the ad as an insider wink, which says, "This is for *you,* guys." The joke is further layered by the fact that they know the model in the ad is very likely to be gay.

Contrast this ad to the ostentatious heterosexual protest of a Perry Ellis ad which appeared in the early 1990s (and no, it's not a parody):
30

> I hate this job. I'm not just an empty suit who stands in front of a camera, collects the money and flies off to St. Maarten for the weekend.
>
> I may model for a living, but I hate being treated like a piece of meat. I once had a loud-mouthed art director say "Stand there and pretend you're a human." I wanted to punch him, but I needed the job.
>
> What am I all about? Well, I know I'm very good-looking, and there are days when that is enough. Some nights, when I'm alone, it's not.
>
> I like women—all kinds.
>
> I like music—all kinds.
>
> I like myself so I don't do drugs.
>
> Oh yeah, about this fragrance. It's good. Very good.
>
> When I posed for this picture, the art director insisted that I wear it while the pictures were being taken. I thought it was silly, but I said "What the hell? It's their money."
>
> After a while, I realized I like this fragrance a lot. When the photo shoot was over, I walked right over, picked up the bottle, put it in my pocket and said "If you don't mind, I'd like to take this as a souvenir." Then I smiled my best f— you smile and walked out.

Next time, I'll pay for it.
It's that good.

Today, good-looking straight guys are flocking to the modeling agencies, much less concerned about any homosexual taint that will cleave to them. It's no longer necessary for an ad to plant its tongue firmly in cheek when lavishing erotic attention on the male body—or to pepper the ad with proofs of heterosexuality. It used to be, if an advertisement aimed at straight men dared to show a man fussing over his looks with seemingly romantic plans in mind, there had better be a woman in the picture, making it clear just *whom* the boy was getting pretty for. To sell a muscle-building product to heterosexuals, of course, you had to link it to virility and the ability to attract women on the beach. Today, muscles are openly sold for their looks; Chroma Lean nutritional supplement unabashedly compares the well-sculpted male body to a work of art (and a gay male icon, to boot)—Michelangelo's "David." Many ads display the naked male body without shame or plot excuse, and often exploit rather than resolve the sexual ambiguity that is generated.

Today, too, the athletic, muscular male body that Calvin plastered all over buildings, magazines, and subway stops has become an aesthetic norm, for straights as well as gays. "No pecs, no sex," is how the trendy David Barton gym sells itself: "My motto is not 'Be healthy'; it's 'Look better naked,'" Barton says. The notion has even made its way into that most determinedly heterosexual of contexts, a Rob Reiner film. In *Sleepless in Seattle,* Tom Hanks's character, who hasn't been on a date in fifteen years, asks his friend (played by Rob) what women are looking for nowadays. "Pecs and a cute butt," his friend replied without hesitation. "You can't even turn on the news nowadays without hearing about how some babe thought some guy's butt was cute. Who the first woman to say this was I don't know, but somehow it caught on." Should we tell Rob that it wasn't a woman who started the craze for men's butts?

ROCKS AND LEANERS

We "nouvelles voyeuses" thus owe a big measure of thanks to gay male designers and consumers, and to the aesthetic and erotic overlap—not uniform or total, but significant—in what makes our hearts go thump. But although I've been using the term for convenience, I don't think it's correct to say that these ads depict men as "sex objects." Actually, I find that whole notion misleading, whether applied to men or women, because it seems to suggest that what these representations offer is a body that is inert, depersonalized, flat, a mere thing. In fact, advertisers put a huge amount of time, money, and creativity into figuring out how to create images of beautiful bodies that are heavy on attitude, style, associations with pleasure, success, happiness. The most compelling images are suffused with "subjectivity"—they *speak* to us, they seduce us. Unlike other kinds of "objects" (chairs and tables, for example), they don't let us use them in any way we like. In fact, they exert considerable power over us—over our psyches, our desires, our self-image.

How do male bodies in the ads speak to us nowadays? In a variety of ways. Sometimes the message is challenging, aggressive. Many models stare coldly at the viewer, defying the observer to view them in any way other than how they have chosen to present themselves: as powerful, armored, emotionally impenetrable. "I am a rock," their bodies (and sometimes their genitals) seem to proclaim. Often, as in the Jackson Browne look-alike ad, the penis is prominent, but *unlike* the penis in that ad, its presence is martial rather than sensual. Overall, these ads depict what I would describe as "face-off masculinity," in which victory goes to the dominant contestant in a game of will against will. Who can stare the other man down? Who will avert his eyes first? Whose gaze will be triumphant? Such moments—"facing up," "facing off," "staring down"—as anthropologist David Gilmore has documented, are a test of macho in many cultures, including our own. "Don't eyeball me!" barks the sergeant to his cadets in training in *An Officer and a Gentleman;* the authority of the stare is a prize to be won only with full manhood. Before then, it is a mark of insolence—or stupidity, failure to understand the codes of masculine rank. In *Get Shorty,* an unsuspecting film director challenges a mob boss to look him in the eye; in return, he is hurled across the room and has his fingers broken.

"Face-off" ads, except for their innovations in the amount of skin exposed, 35
are pretty traditional—one might even say primal—in their conception of masculinity. Many other species use staring to establish dominance, and not only our close primate relatives. It's how my Jack Russell terrier intimidates my male collie, who weighs over four times as much as the little guy but cowers under the authority of the terrier's macho stare. In the doggie world, size doesn't matter; it's the power of the gaze—which indicates the power to stand one's ground—that counts. My little terrier's dominance, in other words, is based on a convincing acting job—and it's one that is very similar, according to William Pollack, to the kind of performance that young boys in our culture must learn to master. Pollack's studies of boys suggest that a set of rules—which he calls "The Boy Code"—govern their behavior with each other. The first imperative of the code—"Be a sturdy oak"—represents the emotional equivalent of "face-off masculinity": Never reveal weakness. Pretend to be confident even though you may be scared. Act like a rock even when you feel shaky. Dare others to challenge your position.

The face-off is not the only available posture for male bodies in ads today. Another possibility is what I call "the lean"—because these bodies are almost always reclining, leaning against, or propped up against something in the fashion typical of women's bodies. James Dean was probably our first pop-culture "leaner"; he made it stylish for teenagers to slouch. Dean, however, never posed as languidly or was as openly seductive as some of the high-fashion leaners are today. A recent Calvin Klein "Escape" ad depicts a young, sensuous-looking man leaning against a wall, arm raised, dark underarm hair exposed. His eyes seek out the imagined viewer, soberly but flirtatiously. "*Take Me,*" the copy reads.

"Face-off masculinity."

Languid leaners have actually been around for a long time. Statues of sleeping fauns, their bodies draped languorously, exist in classical art alongside more heroic models of male beauty. I find it interesting, though, that Klein has chosen Mr. Take Me to advertise a perfume called "Escape." Klein's "Eternity" ads usually depict happy, heterosexual couples, often with a child. "Obsession" has always been cutting-edge, sexually ambiguous erotica. This ad, featuring a man offering himself up seductively, invitingly to the observer, promises "escape." From what? *To* what? Men have complained, justly, about the burden of always having to be the sexual initiator, the pursuer, the one of whom sexual "performance" is expected. Perhaps the escape is from these burdens, and toward the freedom to indulge in some of the more receptive pleasures traditionally reserved for women. The pleasures, not of staring someone down but of feeling one's body caressed by another's eyes, of being the one who receives the awaited call rather than the one who must build up the nerve to make the call, the one who doesn't have to hump and pump, but is permitted to lie quietly, engrossed in reverie and sensation.

Some people describe these receptive pleasures as "passive"—which gives them a bad press with men, and is just plain inaccurate too. "Passive" hardly describes what's going on when one person offers himself or herself to another. Inviting, receiving, responding—these are active behaviors too, and rather thrilling ones. It's a macho bias to view the only *real* activity as that which takes, invades, aggresses. It's a bias, however, that's been with us for a long time, in both straight and gay cultures. In many Latin cultures, it's not a disgrace to sleep with other men, so long as one is *activo* (or *machista*)—the penetrator rather than the penetratee. To be a *pasivo*, on the other hand, is to be socially stigmatized. It's that way in prison cultures too—a good indication of the power hierarchies involved. These hierarchies date back to the ancient Greeks, who believed that passivity, receptivity, penetrability were marks of inferior feminine being. The qualities were inherent in women; it was our nature to be passively controlled by our sexual needs. (Unlike us, the Greeks viewed women—not men—as the animalistic ones.) Real Men, who unlike women had the necessary rationality and will, were expected to be judicious in the exercise of their desires. But being judicious and being "active"—deciding when to pursue, whom to pursue, making advances, pleading one's case—went hand in hand.

Allowing oneself to be pursued, flirting, accepting the advances of another, offering one's body—these behaviors were permitted also (but only on a temporary basis) to still-developing, younger men. These young men—not little boys, as is sometimes incorrectly believed—were the true "sex

A "languid leaner."

objects" of elite Greek culture. Full-fledged male citizens, on the other hand, were expected to be "active," initiators, the penetrators not the penetratees, masters of their own desires rather than the objects of another's. Plato's *Symposium* is full of speeches on the different sexual behaviors appropriate to adult men with full beards and established professions and glamorous young men still revered more for their beauty than their minds. But even youth could not make it okay for a man to behave *too much* like a woman. The admirable youth was the one who—unlike a woman—was able to remain sexually "cool" and remote, to keep his wits about him. "Letting go" was not seemly.

Where does our culture stand today with respect to these ideas about   40 men's sexuality? Well, to begin with, consider how rarely male actors are shown—on their faces, in their utterances, and not merely in the movements of their bodies—having orgasms. In sex scenes, the moanings and writhings of the female partner have become the conventional cinematic code for heterosexual ecstasy and climax. The male's participation is largely represented by caressing hands, humping buttocks, and—on rare occasions—a facial expression of intense concentration. She's transported to another world; he's the pilot of the ship that takes her there. When men are shown being transported themselves, it's usually been played for comedy (as in Al Pacino's shrieks in *Frankie and Johnny,* Eddie Murphy's moanings in *Boomerang,* Kevin Kline's contortions in *A Fish Called Wanda*), or it's coded to suggest that something is not quite normal about the man—he's sexually enslaved, for example (as with Jeremy Irons in *Damage*). Mostly, men's bodies are presented like action-hero toys—wind them up and watch them perform.

Hollywood—still an overwhelmingly straight-male-dominated industry—is clearly not yet ready to show us a man "passively" giving himself over to another, at least not when the actors in question are our cultural icons. Too feminine. Too suggestive, metaphorically speaking, of penetration by another. But perhaps fashion ads are less uptight? I decided to perform an experiment. I grouped ads that I had collected over recent years into a pile of "rocks" and a pile of "leaners" and found, not surprisingly, that both race and age played a role. African-American models, whether in *Esquire* or *Vibe,* are almost always posed facing-off. And leaners tend to be younger than rocks. Both in gay publications and straight ones, the more languid, come-hither poses in advertisements are of boys and very young men. Once a certain maturity line is crossed, the challenging stares, the "face-off" postures are the norm. What does one learn from these ads? Well, I wouldn't want to claim too much. It used to be that one could tell a lot about gender and race from looking at ads. Racial stereotypes were transparent, the established formulas for representing men and women were pretty clear (sociologist Erving Goffman even called ads "gender advertisements"), and when the conventions were defied it was usually because advertisers sensed (or discovered in their polls) that social shifts had made consumers ready to receive new images. In this "postmodern" age, it's more of a free-for-all, and images are often more reactive to each other than to social change. It's the viewers' jaded eye, not their social prejudices, that is the prime consideration of every ad campaign, and advertisers are quick to tap into taboos, to defy expectations, simply in order to produce new and arresting images. So it wouldn't surprise me if we soon find languid black men and hairy-chested leaners in the pages of *Gentlemen's Quarterly.*

But I haven't seen any yet. At the very least, the current scene suggests that even in this era of postmodern pastiche racial clichés and gender taboos persist; among them, we don't want grown men to appear too much the "passive" objects of another's sexual gaze, another's desires. We appear, still, to have somewhat different rules for boys and men. As in ancient Greece, boys are permitted to be seductive, playful, to flirt with being "taken." *Men* must still be in command. Leonardo DiCaprio, watch out. Your days may be numbered.

WORKS CONSULTED°

Beauvoir, Simone de. *The Second Sex.* 1953. Trans. H. M. Parshley. New York: Vintage, 1974.

Berger, John. *Ways of Seeing.* Harmondsworth, Eng.: Penguin, 1972.

Blum, Deborah. *Sex on the Brain: The Biological Differences between Men and Women.* New York: Viking, 1997.

Boyd, Herbert, and Robert Allen, eds. *Brotherman.* New York: Ballantine, 1995.

Clark, Danae. "Commodity Lesbianism." *Free Spirits.* Ed. Kate Meuhuron and Gary Persecute. Englewood Cliffs: Prentice, 82–94.

Clarkson, Wensley. *John Travolta: Back in Character.* Woodstock, NY: Overlook, 1997.

Ellenzweig, Allen. *The Homoerotic Photograph.* New York: Columbia UP, 1992.

Farnham, Alan. "You're So Vain." *Fortune* 12 Sept. 1996: 66–82.

Foucault, Michel. *The Use of Pleasure.* Trans. Robert Hurley. New York: Vintage, 1985.

Friday, Nancy. *The Power of Beauty.* New York: Harper, 1996.

Gaines, Steven, and Sharon Churcher. *Obsession: The Lives and Times of Calvin Klein.* New York: Avon, 1994.

Gilmore, David. *Manhood in the Making.* New Haven: Yale UP, 1990.

Gladwell, Malcolm. "Listening to Khakis." *The New Yorker* 28 July 1997: 54–58.

Hollander, Anne. *Sex and Suits: The Evolution of Modern Dress.* New York: Kodansha, 1994.

Long, Ron. "The Fitness of the Gym." *Harvard Gay and Lesbian Review* 4.3 (Summer 1997): 20–22.

Majors, Richard, and Janet Mancini Billson. *Cool Pose: The Dilemmas of Black Manhood in America.* New York: Lexington, 1992.

This MLA-style bibliography is called "Works Consulted" rather than "Works Cited" because Bordo did not provide internal documentation by using either parenthetical citations or endnotes—probably because her work was published by a commercial publisher and marketed for the general public, even though it draws upon a substantial body of scholarship. Like other writing decisions, how to document the use of sources is determined by the author's purpose, audience, and context (see pages 2–7). In academic discourse (pages 34–49), such as papers for most college courses, you would be expected to provide parenthetical citations as well as a bibliography. For an example, see pages 257–273.

Peiss, Kathy. *Hope in a Jar: The Making of America's Beauty Culture.* New York: Metropolitan, 1998.

Pieterse, Jan Nederveen. *White on Black: Images of Africa and Blacks in Western Popular Culture.* New Haven: Yale UP, 1900.

Plato. *Symposium.* Trans. Alexander Nehama. Indianapolis: Hackett, 1989.

Pollack, William. *Real Boys: Rescuing Our Sons from the Myths of Boyhood.* New York: Random, 1998.

Richmond, Peter. "How Do Men Feel About Their Bodies?" *Glamour* Apr. 1987: 312+.

Rotundo, E. Anthony. *American Manhood: Transformation in Masculinity from the Revolution to the Modern Era.* New York: Basic, 1993.

Sartre, Jean-Paul. *Being and Nothingness.* 1943. Trans. Hazel E. Barnes. New York: Washington, 1966.

Shaw, Dan. "Mirror, Mirror." *New York Times* 29 May 1994, sec. 9: 1+.

Sheets-Johnstone, Maxine. *The Roots of Power: Animate Form and Gendered Bodies.* Chicago: Open, 1994.

Spindler, Amy. "It's a Face-Lifted Tummy-Tucked Jungle Out There." *New York Times* 9 June 1996: F1.

Taylor, John. "The Long Hard Days of Dr. Dick." *Esquire* Sept. 1995: 120–130.

White, Shane, and Graham White. *Stylin'.* Ithaca: Cornell UP.

QUESTIONS FOR DISCUSSION

1. What makes certain images "intrusive"? Can you identify any that have intruded upon your own consciousness?
2. What role have "gay male aesthetics" played in the development of ads that are directed, at least in part, to heterosexuals?
3. Consider the discussion of Jean-Paul Sartre in paragraph 7. What does this discussion of looking (and being seen) have to do with the advertisements discussed by Bordo?
4. What does Bordo disclose about herself in this piece, and how do these disclosures influence your response to her work?
5. How is the response to naked bodies determined by gender? To what extent do other factors determine how men and women respond to images of the naked male body?
6. Why does Bordo believe that the images she analyzes do not treat men as "objects"?

SUGGESTIONS FOR WRITING

1. Study images of the female body in magazine advertisements, and analyze how these images are designed to inspire consumption of specific products.
2. Consider how either men or women most frequently dress on your campus, and analyze what this clothing conveys about the people in question.
3. Write an analysis of one of the male images reprinted on page 411.

Marlon Brando as Stanley Kowalski.

Gordon Hanson, 1954, by George Platt Lynes.

LINKS ■ ■ ■

■ **WITHIN THE BOOK**

For another article on advertising, see the selection by Jean Kilbourne (pages 413–426) on how advertisements are designed to appeal to women.

■ **ELSEWHERE IN PRINT**

Bordo, Susan. *The Male Body: A New Look at Men in Public and Private.* New York: Farrar, 1999.

Faludi, Susan. *Stiffed: The Betrayal of the American Man.* New York: Morrow, 1999.

Kimmel, Michael. *Manhood in America.* New York: Free, 1996.

Pope, Harrison G., Katharine A. Phillips, and Roberto Olivardia. *The Adonis Complex.* New York: Free, 2000.

■ **ONLINE**

- Brief Biography
  <http://www.cddc.vt.edu/feminism/Bordo.html>
- Masculinity and Representation
  <http://www.newcastle.edu.au/department/so/kibby.htm>
- Queer Theory
  <http://www.queertheory.com/queer_theory_site_index.htm>

"PLEASE, PLEASE, YOU'RE DRIVING ME WILD"

Jean Kilbourne

Named by the New York Times *as one of the three most popular speakers on campuses across the country, Jean Kilbourne has done groundbreaking work on the effects of using images of women in advertisements for tobacco, alcohol, and food. Drawing upon her research, Kilbourne has produced three award-winning documentaries:* Killing Us Softly, Slim Hopes, *and* Pack of Lies. *Currently a visiting scholar at Wellesley College, she has also served as an advisor to the U.S. Surgeon General.*

The following selection is a chapter in her book Deadly Persuasion: Why Women and Girls Must Fight the Addictive Power of Advertising *(1999). As you read it, note how Kilbourne is careful to give credit to the creativity of the advertising industry even though she is deeply concerned about the addictive behaviors she believes are encouraged by advertisements for food and diets. You should also know that the companies responsible for the advertisements discussed in this work refused permission to allow these ads to appear in this textbook. You can find these advertisements in Kilbourne's book, bibliographical information about which appears on page 427. When you finish this excerpt from her book, you may be able to explain why the companies in question decided as they did.*

While men are encouraged to fall in love with their cars, women are more often invited to have a romance, indeed an erotic experience, with something even closer to home, something that truly does pump the valves of our hearts—the food we eat. And the consequences become even more severe as we enter into the territory of compulsivity and addiction.

Women have always been closely linked with food—with its gathering, preparation, and serving. We're called peaches, tomatoes, pieces of meat, dishes . . . honey, sugar, sweetie. Beautiful women, especially those who accompany playboys and older men, are "arm candy." And increasingly, as with ads for cars and other products, the thing becomes the lover, as in the ad in a Thai publication featuring two scoops of ice cream as a woman's breasts.

Food is intertwined with love throughout our culture. We give chocolates on Valentine's Day. We say that we are "starved for affection." We think of certain foods, such as custard, ice cream, and macaroni and cheese, as "comfort foods." In infancy and early childhood, food was a major way we were connected to someone else, the most important way that we were nurtured. Many of us had caregivers who used food as a reward or a punishment. Others suffered terrible trauma in childhood and learned to use food for solace and escape. No wonder feeding ourselves can sometimes be an attempt to re-create some sense of wholeness and connection. No wonder it is so easy to confuse food and love.

Food has long been advertised as a way for women both to demonstrate our love and to ensure its requital. Countless television commercials feature a woman trying to get her husband and children to love her or just to pay attention to her via the cakes and breakfast cereals and muffins she serves them. "Bake a Comstock pie," one ad says, "they'll love you for it." Instant oatmeal "warms your heart and soul," a print ad tells us, "like a hug that lasts all day." "Awesome Mom" is the tagline for an ad featuring a little boy smiling widely, obviously delighted to find prepackaged junk food in his lunchbox. "Skip the Zip on my little girl's sandwich and give up one of her bear hugs? Not in her lifetime," says a mother hugging her daughter in a mayonnaise ad. The implication, of course, is that the child won't hug her mother unless she gets the right kind of mayonnaise on her sandwich. As always, the heartfelt connection, the warm relationship is simply a device to sell something—and even our children's love for us is contingent upon our buying the right product.

Very few ads feature women being given food by men or even by other women. More often, when a woman is being fed, she is feeding herself. A television commercial for candy features a series of vignettes in which what a woman does for others (such as making a costume for her daughter) is ignored and unappreciated. At the end of each vignette, the woman pops a piece of candy in her mouth and says, "I thank me very much with Andy's Candies." Another commercial featuring a woman feeding herself candy has the tagline "From you to you."

In many of these commercials, the woman is not only rewarding herself, she also is coping with her disappointment at being unappreciated. Advertisers often offer food as a way to repress anger, resentment, and hurt feelings. "What to do for dinner after a long day of eating your words and swallowing your pride" says an ad for frozen chicken. "Got a big mouth?" asks an ad for caramel candies, "Put a soft chewy in it." "Not satisfied with your payday?" asks an ad for Payday candy bars. "Try ours." And an ice cream ad featuring a young woman walking her dog says, "He never called. So Ben and I went out for a pint of Frusen Glädjé. Ben's better looking anyway." Another ad features the empty foil wrappings of twelve pieces of candy with statements beneath them, from "I didn't sleep late" to "I didn't call him" to "I didn't buy it," "I didn't put off the laundry," "I didn't get upset" to "I didn't skip gym," ending with "He called."

It is interesting that the ad includes so many ways that people escape from difficulties with relationships (shopping, sleeping, watching television) and yet encourages one of the most common escape routes of all, overeating. I am especially struck by "I didn't get upset." Sometimes getting upset is the healthiest and most appropriate response. Certainly it is better to get upset than to numb one's feelings with an overdose of chocolate. Better for us, that is—not better for candy manufacturers. No wonder they run ads like the one that says, "Whatever mood you're in, you're always in the mood for chocolate."

A 1995 Häagen-Dazs ad features a large spoon dipping into a pint of ice cream and the copy, "Your fiance agreed to have a big wedding. *Have a Häagen-*

Dazs. He wants to have it in a Sports Bar. *Have some more."* Again the message to women is clear. When your man upsets you, don't make trouble, don't argue, just eat something—or have a drink or a tranquilizer or a cigarette. "At least one thing in your day will go smoothly," says an ad for a candy bar. Sadly, many women do eat compulsively in an attempt to assuage loneliness and disappointment within relationships (from the past as well as in the present). Family therapist Jill Harkaway says, "When you are lonely, you can't count on people, but you can count on your refrigerator or the nearby 7-Eleven not to let you down." Of course, this fails to address the real problems, thus ensuring continued feelings of isolation and alienation, while breeding eating disorders.

Advertisers spend a lot of money on psychological research. They know that many people, especially women, use food to help us deal with loneliness and disappointment and also as a way to connect. The ads play on this. "You know that empty feeling you have when you're watching what you eat?" asks a four-page ad featuring an empty dessert bowl on the first page. "Start filling up," the ad continues on the next two pages, which picture a variety of sugar-free puddings. A 1999 Burger King commercial features flashes of food and the Burger King logo while Leslie Gore's old hit "It's My Party" plays in the background—"It's my party and I'll cry if I want to." The final caption reads "Stop crying and start eating," and the burger disappears in three large bites.

Advertisers especially offer food as a way to relate romantically and sexu-   10
ally. A television commercial for a pasta sauce features a couple eating and gazing intensely at each other while "I don't know why I love you like I do" plays in the background. "In the mood for something really intense?" asks the sexy female voiceover. The couple feed each other while the words "Unexpected . . . Intense . . . Bold" appear onscreen. In the last shot, the woman is suggestively licking the man's finger while the voiceover says, "You're gonna love it." And an ad for a frozen mousse dessert features Dr. Ruth Westheimer, America's sexual guru, digging in and advising the reader, "Achieving mutual satisfaction is easy. Just share some Mousse du Jour."

One of my favorite ads of all time ran in the early 1980s in many women's magazines. It showed a closeup of a woman's face. She was smiling very seductively, and the copy said, "Whatever you're giving him tonight, he'll enjoy it more with rice." As I said to my audiences at the time, "I don't think I'm particularly naive, but I haven't figured out what the hell you do with rice." "Maybe it's wild rice," someone suggested. Another woman called out, "Let's just hope it isn't Minute Rice." The 1990s version of using sex to sell rice is much more explicit, of course: an ad for Uncle Ben's rice shows a woman feeding a man a forkful of rice by candlelight. The copy says, "Passion Lesson #13. From now on every night would be different . . . filled with endless variety."

One of the most erotic commercials I have ever seen is a British one (no doubt too racy for America) that features a man and a woman making love while feeding each other something. Because the commercial is shot with infrared film, we see only their shapes and intense patterns of red and yellow and blue. "Make Yourself Comfortable" is playing on the record player. They lick some substance off each other's bodies, while an elderly man below bangs on the ceiling with a broomstick, shouting "Mr. Rogers" (thus playing on the British slang "to roger," meaning to have intercourse, and also implying that the man is single and that this is a tryst, not a marriage). At the very end of the commercial we see that the couple's erotic toy is a pint of Häagen-Dazs ice cream. "Dedicated to pleasure" is the slogan.

This campaign ran in print too, with erotic black and white photographs by French photographer Jeanloup Sieff. In just a few months after the campaign broke in upscale magazines such as *Tatler* and *Vogue,* sales of Häagen-Dazs in Great Britain rose 400 percent. This spectacular success indicates that advertisers do indeed sometimes know what they are doing.

Of course, we are not stupid. We don't for a minute believe that we're actually going to improve our relationships with ice cream or pasta sauce. But these ads do contribute to a cultural climate in which relationships are constantly trivialized and we are encouraged to connect via consumption. An obsession with food interferes with real relationships just as any other obsession does, yet food advertising often normalizes and glamorizes such an obsession.

We are not only offered connection via the product, we are offered connection *with* the product. Food becomes the lover. "Rich, impeccable taste and *not an ounce of fat.* Wow, if only I could find a guy like that," says a woman holding a candy bar. "Looking for a light cheesy relationship?" asks an ad for macaroni and cheese, which concludes with a shot of the package and the copy, "Oh, baby, where have you been all my life?" And another ad features an extreme closeup of potatoes with the headline, "Potatoes that get more oohs and aahs than a supermodel." This ad ran in women's magazines and clearly targets women, so the promise is that the woman can distract her husband's attention from supermodels by cooking the right food. ¹⁵

Men are sometimes also targeted, however, with the message that food is love. In a commercial broadcast on Valentine's Day, romantic music plays as we see a couple coming out of the Tunnel of Love at an amusement park, embracing passionately. A voiceover says, "Can you put a price on love?" As the next boat comes out of the tunnel, carrying a man alone, eating a large hamburger, the voiceover continues, "You betcha—if the object of your affection is a McDonald's Big Mac!" The man seems delirious with happiness as he eats his burger, and the voiceover gives some details about the price and says, "Taste that makes you swoon. Or, if you're a two-timer, get cozy with two Big Mac sandwiches. But hurry—your love may be eternal but these prices aren't." The commercial ends with the old man who is running the ride looking with envy at the man with the burger while saying to his helper, "Where does one find such love?"

However, women and girls are targeted far more often. A television commercial broadcast during *Sabrina, the Teenage Witch,* a show popular with teenage girls, features a woman reading a book by a window. "You are my destiny, you share my reverie, you're more than life can be" plays in the background. The woman takes a bite of a cookie and fantasizes a handsome man on a white horse coming to her, riding his horse into her house. "Ah," a female voiceover says, "the new moister–than–ever devil's food cookie from Snack-Well." The man reaches for the cookie and the woman turns him into a frog. "Passion, desire, devotion?" says the voiceover while the words appear on screen. "Nah, it goes way beyond that." This is funny, of course, but it also normalizes an obsession with food that takes precedence over human connection.

Another television commercial goes even further. It begins with an extreme closeup of the peaks and swirls of frosting on a cake. A woman's voice passionately says, "Oh, my love." A man's voice says, "Huh?" and the woman replies, "Not you—the frosting!" With increasing excitement, she continues, "It's calling my name!" and the man replies, "Janet?" The woman cries out, "I'm yours!" as a male voiceover says, "Give in to the rich and creamy temptation of Betty Crocker frosting." As one of the peaks of the frosting peaks, so to speak, and then droops, the woman says, in a voice rich with satisfaction, "That was great." As is often the case, this ad is very funny and seemingly harmless. But also, as is often the case, it is frightful upon reflection. A human relationship is trivialized and ignored ("Not you—the frosting!") while someone connects passionately with a product. Imagine if this were an ad for alcohol ("Not you—the bourbon!"). Perhaps we'd understand how sad and alienating it is.

"I had a dream about salad dressing. Is that weird?" asks a woman lifting a lettuce leaf to her mouth. Of course it's weird! A Cool Whip ad shows a manicured hand plunging a strawberry into whipped cream and the caption, "Go skinny dippin'." And an ad for frozen yogurt features a closeup of a woman's face in what looks like sexual ecstasy and the copy, "Vanilla so pure it sends chills down your spine and back up again." Another version of the ad shows the same ecstatic face and the copy, "Your tastebuds cry out yes yes. Oh, yes." Shades of Molly Bloom!°

Certainly food can be an important part of loving ourselves and others. It [20] can be comforting as well as nourishing, and indeed it can be sexy. When a friend of mine told her husband on the phone that she had just eaten a persimmon, he said, "You had sex without me!" Who can forget the erotic feasting scene in the film *Tom Jones,* the characters looking hungrily at each other, grease glistening on their lips, while ripping meat from bones? This scene, which shocked many people back in 1963, would be tame compared to many food advertisements today.

Often food is shot in extreme closeup and is very sensually inviting. "Bet this little lite will turn you on," says an ad that features a very suggestive closeup of the inside of a candy bar. Another ad featuring a Fudgsicle oozing its chocolate filling is headlined, "Introducing our deep, dark secret," and an ad for a cereal bar says, "Trapped inside this wholesome rolled oats crust is a sultry little French pastry struggling to get out."

Molly Bloom: Character in *Ulysses* by James Joyce who speaks the final words in the novel, words that signify her willingness to have sex: "yes I said yes I will Yes."

A hilarious ad for sour cream features a baked potato begging for the sour cream's touch, "Please . . . please . . . you're driving me wild." Another baked potato is brought to ecstasy by a bottle of tabasco sauce (named "The Exciter"). Indeed there were a series of ads featuring tabasco sauce as a stud. At the end of what must have been a wild night in the kitchen, the bottle is on its side, empty, and the copy says, "A good time was had by all." These ads are powerful examples of the wit, humor, and sheer cleverness one sometimes finds in advertising. There is no harm and indeed much delight in them individually, but their cumulative impact is another story.

Just what is this cumulative impact? What's the problem? For one thing, when food is sex, eating becomes a moral issue—and thinness becomes the equivalent of virginity. The "good girl" today is the thin girl, the one who keeps her appetite for food (and power, sex, and equality) under control. "I'm a girl who just can't say no. I insist on dessert," proclaims a thin woman in an ad for a sugar-free gelatin. It used to be that women who couldn't say no were talking about something other than food. Women were supposed to control their sexual appetites. Now we're supposed to control our appetite for food. If a woman comes back from a weekend and says she was "bad," we assume she broke her diet, not that she did something interesting sexually. The *ménage à trois* we are made to feel ashamed of is with Ben and Jerry.

"Pizza without guilt," declares an ad featuring a heavyset woman tied up to keep her from eating regular pizza. Weight Watchers ads feature extreme closeups of rich foods and the slogan, "Total indulgence. Zero guilt." As if women should feel guilty about eating!

In the old days, bad girls got pregnant. These days they get fat—and are   25
more scorned, shamed, and despised than ever before. Prejudice against fat people, especially against fat women, is one of the few remaining prejudices that is socially acceptable. This strikes fear into the hearts of most women, who are terrified of inspiring revulsion and ridicule. And this contributes mightily, of course, to the obsession with thinness that has gripped our culture for many years, with devastating consequences for many women and girls.

A television commercial for ice cream features actor Bernadette Peters in slinky pajamas in her kitchen at night. "I love being naughty," she says in her little-girl voice, "especially when I can get away with it. Like with Breyer's light ice cream. It has less fat so I can indulge in sinful fudge . . . real vanilla." Her voice is rising as she becomes more excited and builds to an orgasmic crescendo—"Mmmm, pure true taste!" Almost out of breath, she slides down the refrigerator door, saying, "I feel like I'm cheating, but I'm not . . . what a shame."

This moral tone shows up again and again, often with religious connotations. A rich chocolate sundae is labeled "Temptation" on one side of a page. On the other is the "Salvation," a low-calorie shake. "40% Sin 60% Forgiveness," proclaims an ad featuring a priest eating a blend of butter and margarine. And an ad for pork, touting its leanness, says, "We lead you to temptation but deliver you from evil."

However, unlike traditional religious morality in which one has to suffer, to do penance in order to be saved, we are offered products that will allow us to sin without consequence. Just as advertising constantly offers us sex without the burdens and responsibilities of a relationship, it offers us the pleasure of consuming rich foods without having to "pay the price." Now that we have birth control, to eliminate the "sin" of pregnancy but not the joy of sex, all we need is girth control, to eliminate the "sin" of obesity but not the joy of overeating. It doesn't matter if we are "guilty" as long as we don't look it. If we can remain thin by taking laxatives or diet pills or chugging artificially sweetened colas and eating low-fat ice cream rather than exercising moderately and eating healthfully or joining a recovery program, so much the better. In fact, bulimia is the ultimate solution.

Another problematic aspect of the cumulative impact of food advertising is that many ads normalize and glamorize harmful and often dangerous attitudes toward food and eating. And we suffer drastically as a culture from the negative consequences of these attitudes. About eighty million Americans are clinically obese, and nearly three out of four are overweight. Indeed, in a culture seemingly obsessed with thinness and fitness, Americans are fatter than ever and fatter than people in most other cultures. Eight million Americans suffer from an eating disorder and as many as 10 percent of all college-age women are bulimic. Eating disorders are the third most common chronic illness among females. In fact, they are so common it really is misleading to refer to them as "disorders." More accurately, they are a common way that women cope with the difficulties in their lives and with the cultural contradictions involving food and eating. Few of us aren't touched by some kind of problem with food (not to mention the thirty million at risk for hunger and malnutrition).

There are many reasons for these problems, ranging from the decrease in *30*
physical education in our schools to our use of the automobile to the development of the TV remote control to fear of crime, which keeps people indoors, often in front of the television set with its blaring litany of commercials for junk food and diet products. American children see over ten thousand commercials for food on television each year. Ninety-five percent are for four food groups: soft drinks, candy, fast food, and sugar-coated cereal. There's a lot of money at stake: Americans spend an estimated $14 billion a year on snack foods, $15 billion on chocolate, and $86 billion on fast food restaurants.

The commercials are only one part of the problem, but they are a significant part. Just as alcohol ads teach us that drinking leads inevitably to good times, great sex, athletic prowess, and success, without any risks or negative consequences whatsoever, so do the food ads associate eating and overeating with only good things. The negative consequences are obliterated. Indeed, in order to maximize their profits, the junk food and the diet industries need to normalize and glamorize disordered and destructive attitudes toward food and eating.

One of the clearest examples of this is the advertising campaigns for Häagen-Dazs ice cream over a period of several years. In 1990 "Enter the state of Häagen-Dazs" was the slogan for this popular ice cream. The ads featured blissful men and women eating Häagen-Dazs. Sometimes the container was empty, but the people seemed calm and happy, somewhat smug, maybe even slightly stoned. The focus was on the smiling person in the ad, not the product, and the ad was in full color.

In 1991 a new Häagen-Dazs campaign featured ghostly black-and-white photographs of people with copy inscribed over their faces. In one a man is saying, "Maybe I'm a bit of a perfectionist. My CD's are in alphabetical order. . . . Yet everytime I have Häagen-Dazs I seem to lose control. . . . Each creamy spoonful was a moment suspended in time. I would have stopped before I finished the whole pint. Only problem was, I couldn't find the lid."

In another, a woman says, "I pride myself on my level-headed approach to life. . . . But all it takes is one smooth taste of Häagen-Dazs Strawberry ice cream and I find myself letting go. . . . I must do something about this Häagen-Dazs passion. Maybe I could organize it, structure it or control it . . . tomorrow." The campaign slogan is "Tääste the Passion." What an invitation to binge this is! People who feel too controlled in their lives, with too few avenues to real passion, often turn to food or other potentially addictive products as a way to loosen up, to relax. This campaign normalizes and legitimizes this process.

By 1992 there were no longer people in the ads at all, simply a large photograph of the pint of ice cream, with copy beginning in small letters and gradually growing larger and larger. "Wow have you seen it? Another outrageous Exträs ice cream from Häagen-Dazs. . . . Oh my gosh! Luscious fudge chunks too. Give me the entire pint of Cookie Dough Dynamo!"   35

These few years of Häagen-Dazs advertising perfectly illustrate the progression of addiction. The first ad features a woman nibbling on an ice cream bar, somewhat spaced-out but still in control. In the second, a man talks about losing control and unintentionally finishing a pint. In the third, someone is shouting "I need it" and "Give me the entire pint." Granted, this is not heroin we're talking about. But compulsive overeaters will certainly say that their addiction rules and ruins their lives as completely as any other.

Although addiction to food is often trivialized, it is in fact a major problem for many women and men. People who binge on food and overeat compulsively say this has the same effect on their minds and lives as does addiction to alcohol and other drugs. They experience the terror of loss of control, diminished self-esteem, damaged relationships, and even such consequences as hangovers and blackouts. In *Make the Connection,* her best-selling book about overcoming a lifelong eating problem, Oprah Winfrey writes about a binge she had when all she could find in her kitchen was salt, Tabasco sauce, starch, maple syrup, and frozen hot dog buns. "Quickly I turned the oven on broil, threw the buns in to thaw out, and even before they could, I grabbed the syrup and smeared it over the partly burnt, partly frozen buns. Looking back, I see no difference between myself and a junkie, scrambling for a needle and whatever dope might be around. Food was my drug."

There are those who question whether food can be truly addictive. They believe that compulsive overeaters simply lack willpower. Some people still feel this way about alcoholics, although there is much more evidence these days that alcoholism is a disease. Scientists increasingly are discovering physiological and biochemical bases for eating disorders just as for alcoholism. A 1999 study, published in the American Medical Association's *Archives of General Psychiatry,* found that bulimia springs at least in part from a chemical malfunction in the brain resulting in low levels of serotonin, a mood-and-appetite-regulating chemical.

These days many people are cross-addicted. In fact, it is rare to find someone with a single addiction. Most alcoholics are addicted to other drugs too, especially nicotine. Women often wash their tranquilizers down with alcohol or become addicted to amphetamines in an attempt to control their obsession with food. The frequency of eating disorders is significantly higher in alcoholic women than in the general population. Many women with eating disorders come from alcoholic homes. Current research indicates that alcoholism and eating disorders often occur together but are transmitted independently in families. Whatever the origins, it is clear that neither alcoholism nor eating disorders are linked with any character weaknesses.

Advertisers are clearly aware of the psychology of food addiction and com-   40
pulsive overeating. Since food addicts spend a lot of money on food, it is to the advertisers' advantage to make their obsessive and addictive attitudes seem normal and appropriate. An ad featuring a suggestive closeup of a candy bar says, "What you do in the dark is nobody else's business." Compulsive eaters almost always binge alone and feel terribly ashamed. This ad is clearly meant both to tempt and to assuage guilt feelings, to help the eater rationalize his or her behavior, to create the climate of denial so essential for addictions to flourish.

A 1998 SnackWell's campaign cuts right to the heart of the matter by openly declaring that eating cookies will boost a woman's self-esteem. The commercials show scenes of women in warm family embraces, while a voiceover says that eating SnackWell's isn't about feeding yourself but "feeding your self-esteem," "treating yourself well," and "fulfilling yourself." Even Bob Garfield of *Advertising Age* responded to this campaign with "Women of America, feel better about yourselves: Pig out on crap!" He continues, "Feeling a bit down on yourself? Have a cookie. Career stagnating and love life not working out? Have 28 cookies. Suicidal depression? Get the caramel filled one, melt it in a spoon and inject it directly into your vein." Eating to feel better about oneself is not a healthy idea—it is a symptom of a problem.

A recent candy commercial further illustrates this normalization of problematic attitudes. The commercial begins with a middle-aged man seated in an armchair, holding a piece of candy in his hand. He says, "What a combination—crunchy Werther's toffee and delicious milk chocolate . . . mmm." The scene switches to a beautiful young blond woman standing beside her car. She is holding a bag of the candy and says, "I keep one bag in the car, one in my desk, one in the living room, and one next to my bed." Hoarding the supply is one of the signs of addiction. Although alcoholics are best known for this (hiding bottles in toilet tanks and linen closets), most addicts do it. Surely a woman who can't be far from her stash of candy has got a problem.

The next scene in the commercial features a man in a suit holding up one piece of candy, almost as if it were a cigar, and saying, "Now that's where there's quality." Next we see a middle-aged woman pouring the candy into a dish in her kitchen. She says, "Nothing but the best for my guests." Next, a woman in a slinky black dress is seated in an armchair beside a blazing fire. A bag of chocolates is cuddled up against her. She slowly unwraps one piece and pops it in her mouth, saying suggestively, "It's going to be a *nice* evening." At this point, we see a closeup of a bowl of candy, and a male voiceover touts its virtues. The commercial ends with another attractive young blond woman, sitting barefoot on a bench outdoors and holding a bag of the candy. Pulling one from the bag, she says, giggling, "I start on them right after breakfast."

This commercial normalizes some potentially dangerous attitudes toward food in some rather subtle ways. The women in trouble—the two young blondes and the woman by the fireplace—are sandwiched between people with more healthful attitudes. These three women are holding the entire bag of candy, whereas the men are holding only one piece and the middle-aged woman is pouring the candy into a bowl to serve to others. The first troubled woman is hoarding her supply, the second is seemingly preparing for a binge, and the third is rationalizing eating the candy all day long, beginning in the morning.

Thus, women with disordered attitudes toward food, women who seem to be compulsive eaters, are presented as normal, desirable, and even especially attractive. Why would the candy manufacturers want to do this? Because the compulsive eaters, obviously, are going to spend a great deal more on the candy than are the people who eat it infrequently, a piece or two at a time. No matter what a company is selling, the heavy user is their best customer. Thus, it is always in their best interest to normalize and encourage heavy use, even if that might have destructive or even deadly consequences. 45

Obsession with food is also presented as normal and even as attractive in an ad for sugar-free pudding that features a pretty young woman with a spoonful of pudding in her mouth and the headline, "Dessert? It's always on the tip of my tongue." The copy continues, "Really. I mean, if I'm not eating dessert, I'm talking about it. If I'm not talking about it, I'm eating it. And I'm always thinking about it. . . . It's just always on my mind." Like the women who obsess about candy, this young woman has a problem.

And, as is always the case in the world of advertising, the solution to her problem is a product, in this case a diet product. The ad promises her, as almost all the diet ads do, that she can have her pudding and eat it too. How odd this is, when we think about it. Here we are surrounded by all these tempting, luscious ads for food. We are told, on the one hand, give in, reward yourself, indulge. But, on the other hand, we (especially women) are told that we must be thin, indeed that there is no greater sin than being fat.

It might seem strange that there so many ads for diet products interspersed with ads for rich foods. It might seem stranger still that it is often so difficult to tell the difference between the junk food ads and the diet ads. However, this is not strange at all. The tempting food ads do not contradict the message of the diet culture. They are an integral part of it. The junk food industry and the diet industry depend on each other.

In order to be profitable, both these industries require that people be hooked on unhealthy and mostly unsatisfying food, high in fat and sugar. In addition, the diet industry depends upon a rigid cultural mandate for women to be thin. If we ate and took pleasure in basically healthy food and were physically active, if we recognized that bodies come in many different sizes and shapes, and we did not consider it necessary for women to be bone-thin to be attractive—the junk food industry would lose a great deal of money, and there would be no diet industry.

The success of the diet industry primarily depends on women being dis-   50
satisfied with their bodies. Many people say that advertising simply reflects the society. But certainly the body images of women that advertising reflects today are as distorted as the reflections in a funhouse mirror. Since advertising cashes in on women's body-hatred and distorted self-images, it sometimes deliberately promotes such distortion. A yogurt ad says, "How to go from see-ing yourself like this . . . to seeing yourself like this," and portrays the "before" image with a pear. In fact, it is perfectly normal for a woman to be pear-shaped. Many more women have pear-shaped bodies than have the V-shaped bodies of the models, but we don't see them in the media. Instead, we get the message that this shape is unacceptable.

The use of body doubles in films and commercials makes it even less likely that we'll see real women's bodies. A photograph of Julia Roberts and Richard Gere that was widely used to advertise the hit film *Pretty Woman* fea-tured Julia Roberts's head but not her body. Apparently, even *her* body wasn't good enough or thin enough to be in the ad. A body double was also used for Roberts when she was nude or partially nude in the film. This is common practice in the industry. Not surprisingly, at least 85 percent of body doubles have breast implants.

Unfortunately, the obsession with thinness is becoming a problem through-out the developed world. "Le diete S.O.S.," the title of an article featured on the cover of an Italian magazine, is understood in many languages. Italy used to be a country where voluptuous women could still feel desirable, but the model on the cover shown measuring her waist is extremely thin by any standards.

The dieter, even more than the addict, is the ideal consumer. She (most dieters are women) will spend a lot on food and then spend even more to lose weight—and the cycle never stops. Sales of low-fat frozen yogurt soar, but so do sales of high-fat premium ice cream. The diet industry, which includes diet drugs and other products, diet workshops and books, health spas, and more, has tripled in recent years, increasing from a $10 billion to a $36 billion-a-year industry. No one loses, especially the dieter (although she doesn't win either).

Some research indicates that thin people do live longer than overweight people. Some people have latched on to this as proof that we needn't worry about people dieting—in fact, we should worry more if they don't diet. The truth, however, is that fatness is related to the obsession with thinness. Chronic dieting is part of the generally bad eating and exercise habits that make so many Americans overweight and unhealthy. Although being thin is good for one's heart, dieting is bad for everyone.

The fat-free products we consume in great quantities are often bad for us. We eat them instead of eating healthy foods, drinking Coke and Pepsi instead of water, lunching on low-fat cold cuts instead of grains and vegetables and snacking on cholesterol-free cookies instead of fruit. We welcome artificial sweeteners and fake fats, even if they have unpleasant or unhealthy side effects. Olestra, the latest fake fat, not only removes some fat-soluble vitamins from the body, it also sometimes causes bloating, diarrhea, and cramping, as well as what is referred to as "rectal leakage." 55

Sometimes the ads themselves acknowledge the dangers of dieting. As is typical of advertising, however, the solution is not to stop the dangerous practice: The solution is another product. One ad for yogurt features a very young, very thin woman, and the headline "A body like this could be missing out on a lot." The ad acknowledges that the dieting required to keep this teenager so thin is robbing her body of necessary minerals and vitamins. Similarly, another ad reminds us that dieting damages skin tone. The solution, as always, is the product, a skin cream. Neither ad questions the practice of dieting.

An ad featuring a beautiful blonde says, "Christina is a 5′10″, 125 lb. fashion model of Scandinavian heritage. Everyone thinks she has the most marvelous bone structure. She doesn't. She is on her way to osteoporosis." The copy continues, "Her cheekbones are to die for, but not her vertebrae. Too many diets and too little calcium have left her bone density below average. If she doesn't do something, she'll shrink. Her spine will compact. Her clothes won't fit. Looking up at the sky will be impossible." The solution to this impending catastrophe? Certainly not for Christina to stop dieting. Rather, she simply should take calcium supplements. Maybe she should just buy a periscope so she can continue to see the sky.

Christina is five feet ten inches tall and weighs 125 pounds! She is a genetic freak. It's hard not to be a dieter when this is the ideal body type reflected throughout the media and the consequences for not having it are so extreme. Ninety-five percent of all women are excluded from this ideal, which is virtually unattainable by most women, yet it is *they* who feel abnormal and deviant. As an ad for the Body Shop, featuring a voluptuous Barbie-type doll, says, "There are 3 billion women who don't look like supermodels and only 8 who do." As a result, more than half the adult women in the United States are currently dieting, and over three-fourths of normal-weight American women think they are "too fat."

Certainly this delusion comes at least in part from the media images that surround us. Yesterday's sex symbols by today's standards would be considered fat: Betty Grable, Jane Russell, Marilyn Monroe—or just the pretty young woman on the beach featured on a cover of *Life* magazine in 1970. To be sure, there are some large women today, such as Rosie O'Donnell, the plus-size model Emme, and Delta Burke, who are very successful. However, it has been estimated that twenty years ago the average model weighed 8 percent less than the average woman; today she weighs 23 percent less.

Ironically, what is considered sexy today is a look that almost totally sup- 60 presses female secondary sexual characteristics, such as large breasts and hips. Thinness is related to decreased fertility and sexuality in women. Indeed, many of the ultrathin models have ceased to menstruate. Chronic dieting is damaging to one's health and upsets the body's natural metabolism. In 1997 the drug combination of fenfluramine and phentermine, known as fen/phen, was pulled off the market by the FDA because of a high incidence of heart problems among patients who take it. Not surprisingly, research has also found that dieters often experience a temporary drop in mental abilities and thus have less energy to focus on tasks other than controlling their food.

Although the dangers of dieting are sometimes mentioned in women's magazines, the warning is certainly diminished, if not entirely negated, by the ads surrounding the articles. The May 1997 issue of *Vogue* contained an article about the dangers of diet pills called "Dying to Lose Weight." However, on the opposite page is an ad for Special K, a low-caloric cereal, featuring a tiny bikini and the tagline, "It's not doing you any good tucked away in your bottom drawer." To Kellogg's credit, it completely revamped the Special K campaign in 1998 and ran ads and commercials that explicitly challenged the emphasis on thinness and uniformity. The funniest was a commercial featuring several men sitting around talking about their bodies in the way that women often do— "Do these jeans make my butt look big?" and "I have to face it—I have my mother's thighs." The commercial made it obvious how absurd this kind of conversation is and how different are the cultural expectations for women and men. Unfortunately, commercials like this are very few and far between.

In addition to all the psychic and physical damage the diet products do, they don't even fulfill their purpose, at least not for long. Ninety-five percent of dieters are even fatter after five years of dieting than before they began. This information, if widely disseminated throughout the mass media, could be as damaging to corporate profits as is the information that cigarette smoking causes lung cancer. It is no surprise that, in both cases, there is widespread distortion and suppression of such information. Indeed, the only thing that could destroy the diet industry faster than the truth about the failure rates of diets would be a diet that did work.

A Weight Watchers ad features a Boston cream pie, oozing its creamy filling, and the caption, "Feel free to act on impulse." Why would Weight Watchers, of all companies, use such tempting images? Because it is, after all, in Weight Watchers' best interest for its customers to fail, to relapse, to have to return again and again. If people really lost weight and kept it off, Weight Watchers and other such programs would quickly go out of business.

Food ads are often funny, clever, highly entertaining. But food that is heavily advertised is seldom nourishing and rarely deeply satisfying. Often it is sold in a way that exploits and trivializes our very basic human need for love and connection. It is wonderful to celebrate food, to delight in it. Food can nourish us and bring us joy . . . but it cannot love us, it cannot fill us up emotionally. If we turn to food as a substitute for human connection, we turn away from that which could fill up the emptiness we sometimes feel inside—authentic, mutual, satisfying relationships with other human beings. And when people use food as a way to numb painful feelings, to cope with a sense of inner emptiness, and as a substitute for human relationships, for living fully, many of them end up with eating problems that can destroy them and that certainly, ironically, destroy any pleasure they might get from food.°

QUESTIONS FOR DISCUSSION

1. In paragraph 3, Kilbourne notes that "it is so easy to confuse food and love." In your experience, what circumstances are likely to generate this confusion?
2. What cultural factors, aside from advertising, encourage women to use food to cope with anxiety or disappointment?
3. Are ads wrong to suggest that food plays a role in romance?
4. Where does Kilbourne recognize that there is a positive dimension to the ads she discusses? Why is it useful for her to recognize this?
5. Consider Kilbourne's claim in paragraph 25: "Prejudice against fat people, especially against fat women, is one of the few remaining prejudices that is socially acceptable." Do you agree?
6. What is the relationship between ads that promote junk food such as ice cream and candy and those that promote diet products?
7. Why do you think the companies responsible for the advertisements discussed in this work refused permission to reprint them?

SUGGESTIONS FOR WRITING

1. Go through recent issues of a magazine directed towards an audience of women and examine advertisements for food and diet products. Select an image that illustrates the concerns Kilbourne has raised. Then write a detailed analysis of that advertisement.
2. Analyze how images are used to persuade women to purchase a product unrelated to food.
3. In her opening sentence, Kilbourne claims that advertising encourages men "to fall in love with their cars." Review car ads during the past year in magazines directed to an audience of men, and analyze one of the images that you discover.

The original version of this work included both notes and an extensive bibliography that have been omitted here to conserve space. For examples of notes, see pages 192–198 and 228. For examples of bibliographies, see pages 272–273 and 575–577. For additional information on documentation, see pages 38–46.

LINKS ■ ■ ■

■ WITHIN THE BOOK

For information about a woman who is engaging in addictive behavior, see "The Thin Red Line" by Jennifer Egan (pages 151–164).

■ ELSEWHERE IN PRINT

Bartos, Rena. *Marketing to Women around the World*. Boston: Harvard Business School P, 1989.

Cortese, Anthony J. *Provocateur: Images of Women and Minorities in Advertising*. Lanham: Rowman, 1999.

Kilbourne, Jean. *Can't Buy Me Love: How Advertising Changes the Way We Think and Feel*. Fwd. Mary Pipher. New York: Touchstone, 2000.

———. *Deadly Persuasion: Why Women and Girls Must Fight the Addictive Power of Advertising*. New York: Free, 1999.

Pipher, Mary. *Reviving Ophelia: Saving the Souls of Adolescent Girls*. New York: Putnam, 1994.

Schutzman, Mady. *The Real Thing: Performance, Hysteria, and Advertising*. Hanover: UP of New England, 1999.

■ ONLINE

- Brief Biography
  <http://www.jeankilbourne.com>

- Economic Research Service
  <http://www.ers.usda.gov/publications>

- Gender and Advertising
  <http://www.aber.ac.uk/media/Sections/advert04.html>

- Responsible Food Advertising
  <http://www.mcspotlight.org/media/reports/rfa.html>

CONVEYING ATROCITY IN IMAGE
Barbie Zelizer

A columnist for the Nation, *Barbie Zelizer teaches at the highly respected Annenberg School of Communication at the University of Pennsylvania. She has also taught at Columbia University, Princeton University, and the Hebrew University in Jerusalem. Her books include* Covering the Body: The Kennedy Assassination, the Media, and the Shaping of Collective Memory. *She is also the co-author of* Almost Midnight: Reforming the Late-Night News.

The following selection is an abridgement of one of her chapters in Remembering to Forget: Holocaust Memory through the Camera's Eyes, *published by the University of Chicago Press in 1998. As you prepare to read this piece, it might be useful to bear in mind that more than six million Jews were killed during the Nazi regime (1933–1945), most of them in concentration camps during the Second World War. Millions of other victims perished as well. The images in the following selection may disturb you, but if you find them distressing, you might consider the huge difference between viewing images of the Holocaust and being one of its direct victims.*

When discussing her interest in analyzing photographs, Zelizer cautions that "visual memory is deceptive" and that photos seen out of context can "undermine our ability to understand the contingent details of Holocaust atrocity" as well as "our capacity to respond to atrocities today in Rwanda, Bosnia, Cambodia, and elsewhere." As you read this example of her work, be alert for how images become more meaningful through analysis.

Using images to bear witness to atrocity required a different type of representation than did words. Images helped record the horror in memory after its concrete signs had disappeared, and they did so in a way that told a larger story of Nazi atrocity. As the U.S. trade journal *Editor and Publisher* proclaimed, "the peoples of Europe, long subjected to floods of propaganda, no longer believe the written word. Only factual photographs will be accepted."[1]

While words produced a concrete and grounded chronicle of the camps' liberation, photographs were so instrumental to the broader aim of enlightening the world about Nazi actions that when Eisenhower proclaimed, "Let the world see," he implicitly called upon photography's aura of realism to help accomplish that aim. Through its dual function as carrier of truth-value and symbol, photography thus helped the world bear witness by providing a context for events at the same time as it displayed them.

ATROCITY PHOTOS AS TOOLS OF DOCUMENTATION

The photographs that became available on the liberation of the western camps were too numerous and varied to be published together by any one

U.S. or British publication. This was because scores of photographers in different capacities—professional, semiprofessional, and amateur photographers as well as soldiers bearing cameras—accompanied the liberating forces into the camps, and most were placed immediately under the aegis of the U.S. Signal Corps, the British Army Film and Photographic Unit, and other military units. Making available numerous atrocity photos already in the first days after the camps' liberation, these photographers displayed horror so wide-ranging and incomprehensible that it enhanced the need to bear witness, forcing an assumption of public responsibility for the brutality being depicted.

How did photographers record the scenes of barbarism that they encountered? Like reporters, photographers accompanying the liberating forces received few instructions concerning which camps they were entering or what they should do once they arrived; they were given even fewer guidelines about which shots to take or how to take them. This meant that for many the so-called professional response to the event was simply one of "making do," an improvisory reaction to often faulty equipment, bad weather, and uneven training and experience. As one photographer with the British Army Film and Photographic Unit said simply, "we did what [we] saw at the time."[2]

The atrocity photos played a complex role in recording the atrocities. Like words, the images were of limited representativeness, providing only a partial picture of the consequences of years of forced torture, harassment, and eventual death—not the Holocaust per se but a partial depiction of its final phase. As British M.P. Mavis Tate commented, "you can photograph results of suffering but never suffering itself." But photography also offered graphic representations of atrocity that were more difficult to deny than with words. Photographers, one reporter claimed, sent pictures bearing such "irrefutable evidence of Nazi degradation and brutality" that were "so horrible that no newspaper normally would use them, but they were less horrible than the reality." Photographs thus pushed the authenticity of unbelievable camp scenes by pitching depictions closely to the events being described at the same time as they signaled a broader story of Nazi atrocity. It is no surprise, then, that photographs flourished for the press as an effective mode of documenting what was happening.[3] [...]

Practices of Composition: Placement, Number, and Gaze

Though numerous and wide-ranging in their depictions of horror, the atrocity photos were somewhat unusual due to the repetitive scenes reproduced by different photographers, regardless of their degree of professional training. While varying the depiction—by changing the camera position, camera angle, focal length of the lens, light, and length of exposure—might have lent an individualized signature to the photos, this was generally not characteristic of these photos. Instead, near identical images arrived over the wires within hours and days of each other, differing only slightly in focus, distance, exposure, and perspective.

Placement   The decision of where to place evidence of atrocity in a photo created a layering between the atrocity photos' foreground and background, for the two often communicated different levels of specificity about what was being depicted. Witnesses and bodies were depicted in many of the images, and one was used as context for the other.

Evidence of atrocity usually meant pictures of corpses, and it often alternated with witnesses in either the shot's foreground or background. One widely circulated image portrayed General Eisenhower and other ranking generals at Ohrdruf viewing corpses strewn across the camp's forecourt [Figure 1]. Eisenhower and company faced the camera from the back of the shot while they overlooked the dead bodies in its foreground that spilled into the camera. Taken by an unidentified photographer, the photograph appeared in the *Washington Post* on April 16 and resurfaced frequently over the next two weeks. It played in the *Illustrated London News* as a full front-page photo whose legend told readers that "the usually genial General Eisenhower shows by his grim aspect his horror of German brutality." The photo not only heightened the role of the American GI as witness to atrocity but juxtaposed the reader with the GI across the space of the bodies. It was impossible to contemplate the GI's act of witnessing without first contemplating the corpses.[4]

Elsewhere the foreground and background were switched, with the corpses positioned in the back of the shot. The British *News Chronicle* ran a front-page picture of Belsen that showed women cooking and peeling potatoes in the foreground and heaps of dead bodies in the background. Another frequently circulated triangular shot of the Buchenwald courtyard depicted a visual confrontation juxtaposing U.S. soldiers, a stack of dead bodies on a wagon, and the backs of German civilians [Figure 2]. The bodies occupied the back right-hand corner of the shot, soldiers the back left-hand corner, and civilians the foreground. In viewing the shot, the reader had to look over the shoulders of the German civilians in order to see the bodies, creating a layering between the shot's foreground (where the Germans were standing) and the background (where the victims and liberators stood). The effect was magnified by the middle of the shot, where a seemingly impassable white space kept the groups at a distance from each other. That aesthetic was reproduced in other atrocity photos.[5]

Number   A second practice of composition had to do with the numbers   10
of people who were depicted in atrocity photos. The photos oscillated between pictures of the many and pictures of the few. Pictures of the many portrayed mass graves, where bodies had been thrown together so indiscriminately that it was difficult, if not impossible, to discern which appendage belonged to which body; pictures of the few portrayed single individual bodies frozen in particularly horrific poses—a starved man stretched out in rigor mortis on the grounds of one of the camps. Taken together, the images portrayed both individual agony and the far-reaching nature of mass atrocity,

FIGURE 1. General Eisenhower and other officers examine corpses at Ohrdruf, April 12, 1945, by NARA.°

suggesting that the depiction of each individual instance of horror represented thousands more who had met the same fate. The photos functioned not only referentially but as symbolic markers of atrocity in its broadest form.[6]

On the whole, the press presented collective images of atrocity more frequently than it did those of individuals. Perhaps because the group shots suggested a collective status that helped offset public disbelief, group shots appeared frequently regardless of the type of collective represented—groups of victims, survivors, or witnesses. Group images tended to be less graphic than those of individuals, partly because the rarely visible eyes and faces worked against the possibility of identifying the victims being depicted. Foremost here was a famous shot by Margaret Bourke-White, captioned simply "Victims of the Buchenwald Concentration Camp." Unaccredited at the time it originally appeared, the photo portrayed piles of human feet and heads angled away from the camera; the pile gave viewers the impression that it was

NARA: National Archives and Records Administration.

FIGURE 2. German civilians view corpses at Buchenwald, April 16, 1945, by NARA.

about to spill over onto the photographer, and that it was barred from doing so only by a length of chain at the bottom of the picture [Figure 3]. Other photographs, less renowned than Bourke-White's, showed the same pile of bodies from a long shot, a perspective that revealed them to be stacked atop a wagon in the camp's courtyard. That same wagon, portrayed from an even further distance, was featured in the aforementioned triangular shot of the Buchenwald courtyard [Figure 2].[7]

Images of other kinds of groups—survivors, German civilians, German perpetrators, and official witnesses—also proliferated, each displayed with repeated visual characteristics. Groups of witnesses were nearly always portrayed at one side of the frame, looking sideways at corpses that were either inside or outside the field of the camera. Groups of German perpetrators, for instance, were almost always portrayed at harsh angles to the camera and in rigid and upright postures [Figure 4]. These individuals looked angry and cruel, almost maniacal. That perception was upheld in the captions that accompanied images of this type, as when the *Illustrated London News* labeled a group of perpetrators "The Female Fiends."[8]

FIGURE 3. Corpses of civilians killed at Buchenwald, April–May 1945, by NARA.

Often the shots depicted confrontations between groups—German civilians and victims or news editors and survivors. One image—which circulated under the caption "Slave Laborer Points Finger of Guilt"—depicted a survivor of an unidentified camp pointing at a German guard [Figure 5]. The guard stood at the right-hand corner of the image, his contorted face twisting away from both the camera lens and the accusing, outstretched finger of the former prisoner. Although the prisoner was portrayed sideways to the camera, the photographer's empathy with him was clear.[9] Behind the two figures stood other officials, one of whom was witnessing the confrontation.

Thus, in each case framing the depiction as an act of collective, not individual, contemplation reflected a need to collectively address and understand the atrocities. While the emphasis on collective representation may have worked against a recognition of the individual tragedies that lay underneath each photo, the emphasis on groups fit more effectively than did an individual focus on Eisenhower's aim to use the photos as persuasive tools for the war effort. Groups, more than individuals, lent the war effort urgency. Understanding the scope and magnitude of atrocity, in this sense, was equally important to recognizing its individual cases.

FIGURE 4. Women SS guards at Belsen, April 17, 1945, courtesy of The Imperial War Museum, London.

Gaze   Yet a third compositional practice had to do with the gaze of those being depicted. The gaze of emaciated, near-dead survivors, whose eyes seemed not to comprehend the target of vision, tended to be frontal and appeared to signify frankness—though, as one British Army Film and Photographic Unit photographer of Belsen recalled, many of the same people were "incapable of coherent thought. . . . It was a very quiet, silent business. They sat about, very little movement. Some of them were too far gone to move." The survivors were almost always represented in frontal gazes that stared directly at the camera or at a short distance behind the photographer [see Figure 6].[10] In a sense, atrocity survivors appeared to see without seeing. One such photo, which appeared in *PM,* depicted two young adult women in a close shot that echoed their hollowed cheekbones and vacant eyes [Figure 7]. "Here's How Nazis Treat Their Captives . . . ," read the caption to the photo, as it implored readers to look at the "faces of these women."[11] [. . .]

German perpetrators generally were depicted in side views or three-quarter gazes, their eyes averted and narrowed [Figure 8]. Often they were depicted looking sideways at a survivor or soldier, who nearly always stared either directly at them or toward the camera. One such widely circulated image was that of Belsen commander Josef Kramer. It portrayed him walking in Belsen, his mouth pursed and features tight, under a guard's watchful eye, who stared at him intently from the right-hand corner of the photograph.

FIGURE 5. Russian survivor identifies former camp guard at Buchenwald, April 14, 1945, by NARA.

FIGURE 6. Former prisoners of Buchenwald, April 16, 1945, by NARA.

FIGURE 7. Two survivors in Bergen-Belsen, April 30, 1945, courtesy of The Imperial War Museum, London.

The same figures were portrayed from a greater distance in the *Daily Mail,* where Kramer was shown to be accompanied on his stroll not only by a soldier at his side but by another soldier prodding a rifle into his back.[12]

CONCLUSION

In composition, then, the published photos depicted a level of horror that went beyond one specific instance of brutality so as to present it as a representative incident. The combination of corpses and witnesses in the photos facilitated both the display of a particular act of barbarism and its more general context of atrocity; the number of individuals depicted in atrocity photos facilitated an emphasis on the collectives involved in atrocity—either as victims, survivors, perpetrators, or witnesses; and the gaze of those associated with atrocity opened the photographic document to the act of bearing witness in different configurations for victims, survivors, and perpetrators. In each case, on the level of composition photographs offered more than just the

FIGURE 8. Former women guards at Bergen–Belsen, April 1945, courtesy of The Imperial War Museum, London.

referential depiction of one specific event, action, or camp. Compositional practices suggested a broader level of the story that went beyond the concrete target of photographic depiction. [. . .]

All of this suggests that by capitalizing on the symbolic dimensions of images, the press set in place a broader interpretive scheme for comprehending and explaining the atrocities. Playing to the symbolic dimensions of these images had an important effect on publics, not only because they may have been the most effective and least uncomfortable way to comprehend the tragedies of Nazi Europe, but also because they framed events in such a way that all who saw the photos could bear witness to the atrocities. Within that frame, the exact details of the atrocities mattered less than the response of bearing witness. For those inundated with a guilt that came from not having responded earlier, this was no small aim.

NOTES°

1. Jack Price, " 'Doormat' Label Develops Ire of Cameramen," *Editor and Publisher,* March 10, 1945, p. 44.

2. Interview with Sgt. W. Lawrie, Department of Sound Records, IWM; cited in Martin Caiger-Smith, *The Face of the Enemy: British Photographers in Germany, 1944–1952* (Berlin: Nishen, 1988), p. 11.

3. "Europe's Problem: What M.P.s Say of the Nazi Horror Camps," *Picture Post,* May 12, 1945, p. 25; Edward R. Murrow, "Despatch by Ed Murrow—CBS," transcription, April 15, 1945, p. 2 (Templeton Peck Papers, Box 1, HIA).

4. Picture captioned " 'Ike' at Scene of Atrocity," *Washington Post,* April 16, 1945, p. 4; picture appended to "German Atrocities."

5. "There Was Fuel in Plenty," *News Chronicle,* April 21, 1945, p. 1. The British photographer who snapped this shot later wrote home of the difficulties he experienced in doing so. "There were hundreds of bodies lying about, in many cases piled 5 or 6 high," he wrote. "Amongst them sat women peeling potatoes and cooking scraps of food. They were quite unconcerned when I lifted my camera to photograph them. They even smiled" (letter from Sgt. Midgley, IWM, cited in Caiger-Smith, *Face of the Enemy,* p. 14). The triangular shot of Buchenwald, taken on April 16, appeared in numerous newspapers, including a picture captioned "At Buchenwald," *London Times,* April 19, 1945, p. 6, and a picture captioned "German Civilians See Truckload of Bodies," *Boston Globe,* April 25, 1945, p. 13.

6. Such pictures were typical of a two-page pictorial spread entitled "When You Hear Talk of a Soft Peace for the Germans—Remember These Pictures," *PM,* April 26, 1945, pp. 12–13. The journal displayed an additional page of atrocity photos the next day.

7. Picture appended to "This Was Nazi Germany—Blood, Starvation, the Stench of Death," *Stars and Stripes,* April 23, 1945, pp. 4–5. A long shot of the same wagon was used by photographers to depict the witnessing activities of different groups, such as Weimar civilians facing Allied troops in the aforementioned triangular shot of Buchenwald or official delegations inspecting the bodies. See "Nazi Barbarism," *Philadelphia Inquirer,* April 26, 1945, p. 14, and "Penna. Congressman Sees Evidence of Foe's Cruelty," *Philadelphia Inquirer,* April 26, 1945, p. 14.

8. Shot captioned "Study in Evil: The S.S. Women of Belsen," *Daily Mail,* April 23, 1945, p. 3; picture appended to a set of pictures entitled "Like a Doré Drawing of Dante's Inferno: Scenes in Belsen," *Illustrated London News,* April 28, 1945, supplement, p. iii.

9. Picture captioned "Slave Laborer Points Finger of Guilt," *Washington Post,* April 26, 1945, p. 9.

20

In addition to providing notes, Zelizer includes an extensive bibliography in her book (information about which appears on page 442). This bibliography has been omitted here to conserve space.

10. "Dachau—a Grisly Spectacle," *Washington Post,* May 2, 1945, p. 3. The image was taken on April 16 (Document #208AA-206K-31, file "German Concentration Camps—Buchenwald and Dachau," NA) and appeared as "Crowded Bunks in the Prison Camp at Buchenwald," *New York Times Magazine,* May 6, 1945, p. 42. One exception to the anonymity rule was a Dachau survivor named Margit Schwartz, who insisted on being photographed in the same upright pose she had assumed in her only prewar possession—a photograph of herself standing. Despite the protestations of those around her, she dragged herself to her feet and prodded the photographer to take her image. British Official Photo (Document #208-AA-129G-3, file "Atrocities–Germany–Belsen," NA).

11. Interview with Sgt. M. Lawrie, cited in Caiger-Smith, *Face of the Enemy,* p. 11; picture appended to "Here's How Nazis Treat Their Captives . . . ," *PM,* May 1, 1945, p. 8.

12. Picture appended to Peter Furst, "Anti-Nazi Bavarians Helped to Seize Munich," *PM,* May 1, 1945, p. 12, and to Hibbs, "Journey to Shattered World," p. 21; *Lest We Forget: The Horrors of Nazi Concentration Camps Revealed for All Time in the Most Terrible Photographs Ever Published* (London: Daily Mail, 1945), p. 73.

QUESTIONS FOR DISCUSSION

1. Why did photographs play such an important role in conveying the nature of the Holocaust? Why might people in the 1940s and later have doubted the reality of the Holocaust?

2. Why did newspapers and magazines publish "images of witnessing"? Why were these images significant? What kind of context had to be established before such images could be understood?

3. How did photographers decide to frame images of victims? What role did "placement" have in influencing how viewers responded to these images?

4. Why were "collective images of atrocity" published more frequently than images of individuals?

5. How are the images included in this selection "symbolic"? To what extent are historical details—such as the names of individuals or the precise sites where the pictures were taken—important?

6. Zelizer notes that newspapers used captions for atrocity pictures, such as "The Female Fiends," which differ from those used in this text. If a newspaper editor asked you to write new captions for the images reproduced here, what words would you write?

7. If you were given the responsibility of sorting through thousands of photographs of an atrocity and deciding which images to select for publication, how would you proceed?

SUGGESTIONS FOR WRITING

1. The photographs reprinted within this reading as Figures 2 and 3 were taken at the same site. Consider how they differ. Supplement Zelizer's analysis by writing your own.

2. Write an analysis of Figure 6 in which you discuss number, placement, and gaze.
3. Analyze the composition of one of the following photographs:

LINKS ■ ■ ■

■ **WITHIN THE BOOK**

For another view of Holocaust victims, see Ian Buruma's "The Joys and Perils of Victimhood" (pages 246–255).

■ **ELSEWHERE IN PRINT**

Amishai-Maisels, Ziva. *Depiction and Interpretation: The Influence of the Holocaust on the Visual Arts.* New York: Pergamon, 1993.

Caiger-Smith, Martin, ed. *The Face of the Enemy: British Photographers in Germany, 1944–1952.* London: Nishen, 1988.

Connerton, Paul. *How Societies Remember.* New York: Cambridge UP, 1989.

Friedländer, Saul. *Memory, History, and the Extermination of the Jews of Europe.* Bloomington: Indiana UP, 1993.

Lipstadt, Deborah. *Beyond Belief: The American Press and the Coming of the Holocaust, 1944–1945.* New York: Free, 1986.

Tagg, John. *The Burden of Representation: Essays on Photographies and Histories.* Amherst: U of Massachusetts P, 1988.

Zelizer, Barbie. *Remembering to Forget: Holocaust Memory through the Camera's Eyes.* Chicago: U of Chicago P, 1998.

■ **ONLINE**

- Genocide Research Project
  <http://www.people.memphis.edu/~genocide/index.html>
- Holocaust Documentation
  <http://www.holocaust.fiu.edu/history1.html>
- Holocaust Cybrary
  <http://www.remember.org>
- Visual Rhetorics and Rhetorical Visions
  <http://www.indiana.edu/~rhetid/lookout.html>

6

Writing to Move Others

The desire to move an audience has been a major motive of rhetoric since ancient times. *Ceremonial speech,* as conceived by classical rhetoric, did not need to inspire a specific decision or action; its purpose was simply to strengthen beliefs that were already held. The ancient Greeks even had contests in which speakers were judged by how successful they were in moving their audience. Such contests are rare today and are more likely to feature students than professional speakers, but it is still useful to think of "writing to move" as a type of public performance.

THINKING ABOUT AUDIENCE

You will be familiar with this kind of rhetorical situation if you have ever been addressed as part of a crowd that has something in common—the shared values that writing to move assumes. Graduation speeches, for instance, are usually written to inspire loyalty to one's old school and to exhort graduates to live productive lives. The eulogy at a funeral is usually designed to inspire admiration or respect for the dead. And churches offer sermons aimed at reinforcing beliefs that are, in theory at least, already held. In each of these cases the audience has a common bond: graduation from the same school, acquaintance with the same person, or membership in the same church. The reinforcement of common ties is one of the things that writing to move has in common with writing to amuse (which is discussed in Chapter 8). In both, writers aim to trigger a specific response from their audience. But while writing to amuse is designed to make readers enjoy themselves, writing to move is designed to inspire strong feelings. When amused, readers are usually able to relax; when moved, they are most likely to be invigorated.

Consider, for example, the purpose of a keynote speech at a political convention. Everyone at the convention already belongs to the same party; no one has to be persuaded to join or be informed about what the party stands for. The speaker can usually assume that the audience will support the party's candidates in the next election and that this support will be given with varying degrees of enthusiasm. Some people at the convention may have reservations about language in the party's platform; others may be feeling hot, tired, and eager to get back home where they have other obligations to fulfill—obligations that may take precedence over helping the party win the election. The primary purpose of this keynote speech is to inspire enthusiasm—to make the delegates forget their other concerns, rise to their feet, and feel certain that they are part of a noble cause. The speaker in this case may benefit from reinforcement unavailable to writers: At key moments, carefully selected video images may flash across screens surrounding the podium. But this speech began as a written speech employing rhetorical strategies that take advantage of communal values—strategies that we can adapt for other occasions in which community is important.

PURPOSE AND STYLE

Martin Luther King's "I Have a Dream" provides an example of political exhortation at its best. The words on the page and the care with which they are arranged make it a moving piece of prose without the benefit of our hearing King's voice or being present at the scene where this speech was delivered. Visualizing the situation for which this speech was designed, however, can help you understand King's purpose and the techniques he used to arouse his audience's emotions. The occasion was the hundredth anniversary of the Emancipation Proclamation; the scene was the steps of the Lincoln Memorial, from which King faced an audience of more than two hundred thousand people who had marched to Washington on behalf of civil rights for African Americans. King did not need to persuade that audience that African Americans deserved civil rights. If they didn't already believe this, they would not have come to Washington. What King needed to do was to reinforce the beliefs his audience already shared—to vindicate whatever hardships they had endured and to help them lift up their hearts.

Although the entire speech deserves close reading, a short excerpt illustrates a number of points essential to our understanding of writing to move. Here are paragraphs 9 and 10 from the eighteen-paragraph-long speech.

> I am not unmindful that some of you have come here out of great trials and tribulations. Some of you have come fresh from narrow jail cells. Some of you have come from areas where your quest for freedom left you battered by the storms of persecution and staggered by the winds of police brutality. You have been the veterans of creative suffering. Continue to work with the faith that unearned suffering is redemptive.
>
> Go back to Mississippi, and go back to Alabama. Go back to South Carolina. Go back to Georgia. Go back to Louisiana. Go back to the

slums and ghettos of our Northern cities, knowing that somehow this situation can and will be changed. Let us not wallow in the valley of despair.

When we look closely at these paragraphs, we see that King is not attempting to persuade his audience to undertake a specific action. It is true that he advises his listeners to go back home and keep on working, but the promise that "somehow this situation can and will be changed" is short on details and unlikely to satisfy someone who has not been moved by the speech as a whole.

A paraphrase focusing only on the content of these two paragraphs might read: "I know you've all had a rough time, but go back home and cheer up. Things are going to get better." Reducing King's prose to this paraphrase is grotesque but illuminating: We have stripped these paragraphs of their beauty and their power to move—deprived them of their reason for being. What is it, then, that makes King's prose moving?

In the first place, King was a gifted prose stylist with a fine ear for rhythm; his sentences are so nicely cadenced that they can engage the attention of an audience by the quality of their music. The previous short excerpt uses two techniques that can be found in much of King's work. When he writes "trials and tribulations," he is using a simple form of *parallel construction,* which means putting similar ideas in similar form for the sake of balance. In this case a plural noun is balanced with a plural noun.

The third sentence in the first paragraph provides another example of parallelism: "battered by the storms of persecution and staggered by the winds of police brutality." "Battered" is balanced against "staggered," "storms" against "winds," and "persecution" against "police brutality"—as can be easily seen when we reformat these lines:

<u>battered</u>	<u>by the storms</u>	<u>of persecution</u>
and		
<u>staggered</u>	<u>by the winds</u>	<u>of police brutality</u>

Only "police" keeps this example from being perfectly parallel. It is being used here as an adjective describing "brutality," but there is no equivalent adjective describing "persecution." From this example we can conclude two things.

- Parallelism does not necessarily require a word-for-word balance—although the more words that are balanced, the stronger the parallel will be.

- A word or phrase that does not fit within a parallel will receive increased emphasis because it interferes with the prevailing rhythm. In this case it is quite possible that King wanted "police" to have this extra emphasis. His original audience would have believed that the police were interfering with much more than parallel construction.

Although the second paragraph of the excerpt also features a strong parallel structure in which patterns repeat and harmonize with one another, it also illustrates another rhetorical device: *anaphora,* or deliberate repetition at the beginning of sentences or clauses for the purpose of affecting the reader. King emphasizes *Go back* to such an extent here that the words no longer seem as simple as they would in another context (e.g., "Go back to your room and get a sweater."). As the *Go backs* accumulate, they become a type of song in which the words mean more than they say. Behind these *Go backs* is a meaning that can be felt even though it is unstated. *Go back* becomes "Go back and don't give up; go back and keep on fighting."

The rhetorical use of repetition for emphasis can be thought of as a more sophisticated version of how a cheerleader uses repetition when trying to move a crowd ("*Go* team *go; fight* team *fight*"). Unlike the simple chants you hear at a pep rally, King's prose draws on a variety of techniques and does so for a serious end. Nevertheless, one way of reading "I Have a Dream" is to read it as a type of rallying cry. King's purpose, after all, was to move his listeners to continued struggle by reaffirming the importance of their common cause.

Neither parallel construction nor deliberate repetition is limited to exhortation, and you will find examples of both in works that have other motives behind them. But because writing to move has strong links to oratory, it is especially likely to draw on strategies like these that make sentences easy to read and easy to remember. When you read "I Have a Dream," you will find that King uses both parallelism and repetition many times. You will also find that he keeps his diction simple. With the possible exception of two words ("tribulations" and "redemptive"), the words of the passage quoted previously could be understood by almost any English-speaking person. King, an experienced speaker, understood that we cannot be moved by what we do not understand. On this occasion eloquence required simplicity because he was addressing a large and diverse audience.

Style, however, is only one of the factors that explain why King's prose is so much more effective than the paraphrase of it (on page 445). Writing to move requires creating a bond between the writer and the reader. It is one thing to say "I know you've had a rough time." It is something else to show that you mean it and to leave your audience feeling personally addressed. Many of the people in King's audience would have been touched personally by the sympathetic reference to "narrow jail cells." And almost everyone in that audience would have had some experience with "persecution" and "police brutality." King then makes specific references to five southern states and a more general reference to northern cities. Anyone from Mississippi, Alabama, South Carolina, Georgia, or Louisiana would have felt as if King were addressing him or her as an individual. Furthermore, the list of five is long enough to be understood as representing other states that pass unmentioned. And references to different states remind the people in the crowd that they have friends and allies elsewhere because they are part of a nationwide struggle.

As "I Have a Dream" suggests, writing to move requires more than eloquent phrasing. It also requires a strong sense of audience, which, in turn, ultimately depends on understanding human nature and the types of experiences that evoke different emotions.

WRITING TIPS

When analyzing "I Have a Dream" and the other readings in this chapter, you can benefit from principles laid down in the eighteenth century by Hugh Blair, a professor at the University of Edinburgh, to determine what makes language moving. He offers seven principles that can help you understand the work of other writers and write moving essays of your own.°

- *Choose a topic that is suitable for writing to move.* In the pages that follow, King addresses the subject of social injustice, George Orwell raises questions about capital punishment, Dorothea Dix calls for humane treatment of the mentally ill, Alice Walker reflects on the treatment of an animal, and Jonathan Swift writes about poverty. Depending on how a writer proceeds, topics such as these can inspire a number of emotions—including anger, indignation, pity, or grief. There are, of course, many other topics suitable for this type of writing. Larry Carlat, for example, uses writing as a way to help his adopted son understand how much he is loved, and George W. Bush uses rhetoric designed to fortify a nation under attack. However, there are also topics (such as an explanation of how the brain functions) that would be inappropriate for writing to move. If you try to inspire an emotion that seems unrelated to the topic, your prose may seem overwrought rather than moving.

- *Get right into the topic without warning readers of your intention.* If you begin by writing, "I am going to tell you a sad story" (or words to that effect), you are weakening your work in at least two ways. By telling readers how you want them to respond—as opposed to letting the response grow naturally out of the work—you are giving them a ready-made standard for evaluating your work; and you may find someone who responds, "Well, I didn't think that was so sad." More-over, by putting readers on guard, you lose the strategic advantage of surprise. Readers alerted in advance to "a sad story" could brace themselves against feeling sad or decide to put your work aside to read something more cheerful. When you read "A Hanging," for example, you will find that Orwell never tells us how to feel about the execution he describes. And anyone reading "A Modest Proposal" for the first time may find it shocking at first because Swift conceals his intention for several paragraphs.

- *Include details that can evoke the response you intend.* Although supporting detail is important in almost all types of writing, it is especially important when writing to move. And the details that you choose should

---

These principles are adapted from Blair's *Lectures on Rhetoric and Belles Lettres,* first published in 1783. A modern edition edited by Harold E. Harding is available (Carbondale: Southern Illinois University Press, 1965).

have emotional appeal. For example, a specific description of a homeless person sleeping on a sidewalk is likely to be more moving than several paragraphs of statistics. Consider, in this regard, how Orwell focuses on a specific prisoner at the hour of his death rather than on providing statistics on capital punishment. Or to choose another example, consider how Dorothea Dix describes a series of individuals and the rooms in which they live to convey the horrific conditions she discovers when visiting mental asylums.

■ *Be moved yourself.* Although there are many rhetorical situations in which writers need to keep their feelings to themselves, writing to move requires that you yourself feel the emotion that you want others to share. This does not mean that you have to come out and tell readers how you feel; on the contrary, you should try to keep the focus on your subject rather than on yourself. It happens that all of the writers in this chapter use the first person at some point. In a piece such as Dix's "On Behalf of the Insane Poor," it's hard not to notice that Dix is angry. But even if you never mention yourself, readers should be able to tell how you feel about your subject. The main thing is to avoid insincerity. If you really don't care about poverty but think it would be proper to sound as if you do, you are unlikely to succeed at moving others. Write about what you care about, and don't try to fake emotion.

■ *Write simply and directly.* When you feel something strongly, you are likely to use language that is simple, direct, and bold. Formal diction and long, complicated sentences will seem artful rather than direct and will diminish the sense that you are moved by the subject you are writing about. Here, for example, is Walker describing her response to eating meat: "I am eating misery, I thought, as I took the first bite. And spit it out." These two sentences may be the result of several drafts, for the words that first occur to writers are not necessarily those that are the simplest and most direct. But the apparent simplicity of these sentences helps convey emotion. The force of "And spit it out" would be lost if, afraid to use a word like *spit,* Walker consulted a thesaurus and tried using something like *expectorated.* Because of the directness necessary for writing to move, you should find all the selections in this chapter easy to read, with the possible exception of "A Modest Proposal." Swift's essay is the most difficult to read—in part because words written almost three hundred years ago often seem less natural than those written last year, and in part because Swift deliberately violates the rule here as part of his strategy to surprise readers with a proposal that turns out to be anything but modest.

■ *Be faithful to your purpose.* When writing to move, you need to avoid any digression that would interrupt the flow of feeling you are trying to inspire. Had King paused in the middle of "I Have a Dream" to offer an analysis of congressional legislation affecting civil rights, he would have weakened the emotional power of his speech. King knew a great deal about his topic, but the context of "I Have a Dream" was one that called for inspiration rather than information. As you revise an essay designed to move, be prepared to cut not only digressions but also any sentence that seems too fancy. As Blair put it, "Sacrifice all beauties, however bright and showy, which would divert the mind from the principal object, and which would amuse the imagination, rather than touch the heart."

■ *Know when to stop.* As a general rule, writing designed to move needs to be kept fairly short. It is difficult to sustain intensity of feeling at any great length; and if you write too much about your subject, you run the risk of readers deciding that you are making too much of a fuss. Most of the readings in this chapter are only about four pages long, and on an important historic occasion, George W. Bush takes only six. "Knowing when to stop" cannot be measured by word count alone, however. It is also a matter of understanding where you can afford to linger and where it is best to let a few carefully chosen words convey a sense of things unsaid. When your material is strong, you can often benefit from handling it with restraint, letting readers' imagination fill in the gaps along lines you have merely suggested. Consider, for example, how George Orwell concludes his detailed description of an execution that took place in Burma when that country was part of the British Empire. Francis, the head jailer, remembers cases in which someone had to pull on the legs of a man being hanged to make him die. Here are the last two paragraphs of Orwell's essay:

> I found that I was laughing quite loudly. Everyone was laughing. Even the superintendent grinned in a tolerant way. "You'd better all come out and have a drink," he said quite genially. "I've got a bottle of whiskey in the car. We could do with it."
>
> We went through the big double gates of the prison into the road. "Pulling at his legs!" exclaimed a Burmese magistrate suddenly, and burst into a loud chuckling. We all began laughing again. At that moment Francis' anecdote seemed extraordinarily funny. We all had a drink together, native and European alike, quite amicably. The dead man was a hundred yards away.

A conclusion like this is considered an "open" conclusion because the writer has not "closed" with an ending that ties everything together and states or restates the main point of the essay. Open conclusions are frequently found in fiction, but they can be appropriate for nonfiction as well if a writer has given readers enough detail so they can "complete" the essay for themselves. When you read "A Hanging," you should be able to understand why these men are laughing immediately after witnessing an execution. And you should also be able to understand why Orwell moves directly from reporting this laughter to the short, simple sentence with which he concludes: "The dead man was a hundred yards away." There is irony in this situation—irony that would almost certainly be less moving if the writer explained it neatly away. Orwell wisely recognized that his material called for a mixture of frankness and restraint.

Of course, writing to move cannot be mastered by simply memorizing a few rules. Whatever the reason you may want to move people, you should not only practice the techniques outlined here but also watch and listen to other people. You may already know how to touch the hearts of those close to you. By reading the work of other writers and practicing the techniques of writing to move, you can ultimately learn to touch people you haven't met. The ability to inspire emotion is one of the most useful achievements of rhetoric. But like any other type of writing, it takes study and practice.

YOU ARE ME

Larry Carlat

How can a father convey to his son the depth of his love, especially in a culture that often discourages men from expressing their feelings? And why might this message be especially important for a child who knows he was adopted? In the following letter, first published in Esquire *in 1998, Larry Carlat tries to make his feelings clear. As you read, imagine that you are the recipient of this letter and note whether you are moved by it. Based in Woodbury, New York, Carlat is editor of* Toy & Hobby World.

Dear Robbie,

You were born a poet. Let me quote a few of your best lines:

I bet my birth mother is still crying.
I wish God would take the sadness off me.
If she kept me, I never would've known you.
I have a space in my heart that never closes.

As I sit here wrestling with words that invariably elude my grasp, I wish I could write like that. But what do I expect? You are seven, and I am only forty-two.

Before you read any further, you should know that your mom doesn't want me to write this. She doesn't want me to write anything that might one day awaken any doubt in you. So I made a deal with her. I promised that if she feels the same way after I've finished, I'll punt on the whole thing. That's how intensely she feels about you, how fiercely protective she is of you. She doesn't want me to write this letter, because she loves you so much, and I love you so much that I have to write it, even if I don't show it to you until you have kids of your own.

Here are the words your mom fears: *I didn't want to adopt you.* 5

I know that sounds like powerful stuff, but to me those words are as trifling as the ants that march across the kitchen floor before you put your thumb to them. They mean nothing because I can't even remember feeling that way. I've searched my heart and can't find any trace of not wanting you. It would be like not wanting air. Still, just as I can't imagine not wanting you now, there was a time when I couldn't imagine *you.* I didn't know that you were going to be you. I knew only that you were not going to be *me.*

Your mom says I was hung up on this crazy little thing called genetics, which should never be mistaken for that crazy little thing called love. It all seems so bizarre, given that my family background includes everything from cancer and heart disease to criminal behavior. Your mom says that I was worried that you wouldn't be perfect, that we would be inheriting somebody else's problem, and that nurture would be revealed as nothing more than nature's cheap consolation prize. Your mom says I can't recollect any of these gory details because sometimes I can be a stubborn bastard.

That must be where you get it from.

Because, Rob, when all is said and done, you are me—only way better looking. You are me if I looked like Brad Pitt and your mom looked like Sharon Stone. You're more like me than Zachary, who inherited torn genes from me and Mom. You and I are both the eldest son, moderately shy, and exceedingly anxious. We love Michael Jordan, movies, scallion pancakes, and the occasional doody joke. We're natural-born outsiders who share the same thin skin.

And there's something else that you and I have in common: I once had a   *10* space in my heart that wouldn't close. I still remember the cause. When I was four years old, two very large men wearing very large hats came into our house and hauled my father away. He didn't come back for eight years, and even after he returned, he couldn't repair what had been ripped apart. My dad, like yours, was a sad schmuck, sad in that he never tried to change himself into a dad.

For me, everything changed the moment I saw you.

After four years of infertility and a bout with cancer thrown in for good luck (if I hadn't had it, I never would have known you), I was finally ready to entertain alternatives to producing a mirror image. I tend to arrive at places in my heart long after your mom has moved in and decorated. Your mom always knew that she wanted to be a mom, while I was just beginning to understand what it meant to be a dad. You know the next part from your baby book that you keep under your pillow:

> *They met a wonderful young lady who was growing a baby boy in her belly.*
> *But she wasn't able to give her baby all the good things the world had to offer,*
> *and she wanted that for him very, very much.*

Seven months later, I found myself in the hospital, scanning the blue IT'S A BOY! stickers on the bassinets until I saw your birth mother's last name neatly printed in black ink. And at that moment, the space in my heart was filled. It was either magic or God—I've forgotten what I believed in at the time. "You're my son, you're my son," I quietly mouthed to you through the glass again and again, trying to convince myself that you were real. Then I went to your mom, and we hugged and cried while you kept sleeping, our little boy, Robbie James Carlat, unaware of how much joy you could bring to two people.

And the reason I can no longer recall not wanting to adopt you is simple: That feeling completely vanished on the day you were born. "I know, I know. It was love at first sight," you like to say, sounding like a cartoon version of me anytime I bring up the subject of your birth. But it wasn't like that between my dad and me. I don't remember my father ever kissing me or, for that matter, me kissing him. The thought of saying "I love you" to each other, even when he came back from prison or as he lay dying, would have cracked both of us up. In fact, the closest my father ever came to a term of endearment was calling me "kiddo" (which is the full extent of his parental legacy and why I usually answer, "Ditto, kiddo" when you say, "I love you").

There's a black-and-white photograph of my dad holding me up high 15 above his head—I must have been six months old—and it's the only time that I can recall him looking genuinely happy to be with me. I used to think of that picture in the months after you were born, when I danced you to sleep. I never dance, not even with your mom ("They're all going to laugh at you!" from *Carrie* pretty much sums up why), but I loved dancing with you. While you sucked on your bottle, I savored the feeling of your tiny heartbeat against mine. Joni Mitchell's *Night Ride Home* CD was on just loud enough so we wouldn't wake up your mom, and I'd gently sing to you, "All we ever wanted was just to come in from the cold, come in, come in, come in from the cold."

Still, the space you were coming in from was far colder than mine had ever been. It's the original black hole, and all of our kissing and hugging are not enough. All of your incessant *I love yous* and *I love the familys*—words you repeated as if to convince yourself, the same way I did when I first set eyes on you—are not enough. All of the times that you asked me to pick you up and I happily obliged because I knew a day would come when you would stop asking are not enough. Every night when we read your baby book, which desperately tries to explain whose belly you grew in and how you got to us, is not enough.

Nothing is enough, for there's nothing that approaches the clear and direct poetry of "I hate myself because I'm adopted" or "I'm only happy when I'm hugging and kissing you—all the other times I just make-believe." If anything, you get the prize for coming closest to the pin with "Being adopted is hard to understand." And what do you win for saying the darndest things? A profound sadness. And let's not forget its little brother, anger, which you direct at *your* little brother for no apparent reason other than that he serves as a constant reminder that you are the one who is not like the others.

The irony is that Zachy, the prototypical little bro, only wants to be you, while you'd do anything to be him.

I hope that one day God grants your wish and takes the sadness off you, because your mom and I know how truly blessed we are to have two beautiful sons—one chosen by us and one chosen for us. It's like we wrote at the end of your baby book:

> *Mommy and Daddy waited a long time for a baby—a baby boy just like you. And though it might have been nice to have you grow in Mommy's belly . . . always remember that you grew in our hearts!*

Perhaps the only thing we neglected to consider at the time was *your* 20 heart. Which reminds me of sand castles. A few summers ago, you and I built a beauty on Uncle Stephen's beach, and you wanted to surround it with a moat, so we started to dig a hole with your big yellow bucket. We kept digging faster and faster until the hole got so deep that you jumped in. "Daddy, get the water," you said, and I ran into the waves, filled the bucket, dragged it back, and dumped it into the hole. The sand quickly drank it up, so I kept going back and forth, trying to fill the hole with water, but it was like pouring the water down a drain. After a while, we finally said the hell with it and ran into the ocean.

You are the sand, little boy, and I will always be the water.

And that was where I intended to end this letter, until you came padding into the room in your G.I. Joe pajamas. "What are you writing about?" you asked. And when I told you that it was a story about you, you asked, "Is it going to be in a big magazine?"

And I said, "Yeah. How do you feel about that?"

And you said, "Scared."

And I said, "How come?"   25

And you said, "Because I'm going to be in it alone."

And I said, "No you won't. I'll be in it with you."

And you said, "I love you, Daddy."

And that's when I had to stop writing.

QUESTIONS FOR DISCUSSION

1. What do you think Carlat means when he writes, "You are seven, and I am only forty-two"? Why "only"? What is he implying about the relationship between children and adults?
2. Why did Carlat's wife discourage him from writing this letter? What does Carlat achieve by stating the very words she feared he might say: "*I didn't want to adopt you*"?
3. What worried Carlat before meeting his son? Do his anxieties have anything in common with what other parents might experience when expecting the birth of a child?
4. Why does Carlat mention his own father and reveal that he had been sent to prison?
5. Consider the conclusion to this letter. Why does Carlat reach a point where he "had to stop writing"? How well does this point serve as a conclusion?
6. How would you feel if you received a letter like this from a parent or stepparent: embarrassed, indifferent, annoyed, or pleased?

SUGGESTIONS FOR WRITING

1. Write a letter to someone you care about in which you describe your feelings and try to touch his or her heart.
2. Remember what you were like when you were seven, and write a letter to your seven-year-old self in which you convey empathy for the person you used to be.
3. Research conditions in orphanages in a foreign country. Then write an essay that would move a married couple in the United States to adopt a child from one of these orphanages.

LINKS ■ ■ ■

■ WITHIN THE BOOK

For an essay on the relationship between a father and his daughter, told from the daughter's point of view, see Itabari Njeri's "Life with Father" (pages 68–72).

■ ELSEWHERE IN PRINT

Klose, Robert. *Adopting Alyosha: A Single Man Finds a Son in Russia.* Jackson: UP of Mississippi, 1999.

Lifton, Betty Jean. *Journey of the Adopted Self: A Quest for Wholeness.* New York: Basic, 1994.

Russell, Marlou. *Adoption Wisdom: A Guide to the Issues and Feelings of Adoption.* Santa Monica: Broken, 1996.

Silber, Kathleen, and Phyllis Speedlin. *Dear Birthmother: Thank You for Our Baby.* San Antonio: Corona, 1983.

Turner, Carole S. *Adoption Journeys: Parents Tell Their Stories.* Ithaca: McBooks, 1999.

■ ONLINE

- Adoption Issues
  <http://www.adoption.org>

- National Adoption Information Clearinghouse
  <http://www.calib.com/naic>

- National Foster Parent Association
  <http://www.nfpainc.org>

I HAVE A DREAM

Martin Luther King, Jr.

An ordained Baptist minister with a Ph.D. from Boston University, Martin Luther King, Jr. (1929–1968) was arguably the single most important figure in the struggle for civil rights for African Americans during the mid-twentieth century. Founder and President of the Southern Christian Leadership Conference, he was a powerful speaker as well as an effective organizer who inspired many of his contemporaries to see how racial injustice was pervasive throughout the United States. In 1964, he became the youngest man to win the Nobel Peace Prize. He was only thirty-nine years old when he was assassinated in 1968. Although many of the problems King addressed remain unresolved, his memory is honored by a national holiday.

"I Have a Dream" is one of King's most famous speeches, and you may have read it as a document in American history earlier in your education. King gave his speech before a huge audience gathered on the Mall in Washington, D.C. as he stood upon the steps of the Lincoln Memorial with the figure of Lincoln behind him. The speech was also recorded and televised. Whether or not you have read it before, read it now as writing designed to move the heart and spirit. As you read, be alert for language that strikes you as especially effective.

I am happy to join with you today in what will go down in history as the greatest demonstration for freedom in the history of our nation.

Five score years ago, a great American, in whose symbolic shadow we stand today, signed the Emancipation Proclamation. This momentous decree came as a great beacon of light of hope to millions of Negro slaves who had been seared in the flames of withering injustice. It came as a joyous daybreak to end the long night of their captivity. But one hundred years later, the Negro still is not free. One hundred years later, the life of the Negro is still sadly crippled by the manacles of segregation and the chains of discrimination. One hundred years later, the Negro lives on a lonely island of poverty in the midst of a vast ocean of material prosperity. One hundred years later, the Negro is still anguished in the corners of American society and finds himself in exile in his own land. And so we have come here today to dramatize a shameful condition.

In a sense we have come to our nation's capital to cash a check. When the architects of our republic wrote the magnificent words of the Constitution and the Declaration of Independence, they were signing a promissory note to which every American was to fall heir. This note was the promise that all men—yes, Black men as well as white men—would be guaranteed the inalienable rights of life, liberty, and the pursuit of happiness.

It is obvious today that America has defaulted on this promissory note insofar as her citizens of color are concerned. Instead of honoring this sacred obligation, America has given the Negro people a bad check, a check which has come back marked "insufficient funds." But we refuse to believe that the bank of justice is bankrupt. We refuse to believe that there are insufficient funds in the great vaults of opportunity of this nation; and so we have come to cash this check, a check that will give us upon demand the riches of freedom and the security of justice.

We have also come to this hallowed spot to remind America of the fierce   5
urgency of *now*. This is no time to engage in the luxury of cooling off or to take the tranquilizing drug of gradualism. *Now* is the time to make real the promises of democracy. *Now* is the time to rise from the dark and desolate valley of segregation to the sunlit path of racial justice. *Now* is the time to lift our nation from the quicksands of racial injustice to the solid rock of brotherhood. *Now* is the time to make justice a reality for all of God's children.

It would be fatal for the nation to overlook the urgency of the moment. This sweltering summer of the Negro's legitimate discontent will not pass until there is an invigorating autumn of freedom and equality. Nineteen sixtythree is not an end, but a beginning. And those who hope that the Negro needed to blow off steam and will now be content will have a rude awakening if the nation returns to business as usual. There will be neither rest nor tranquility in America until the Negro is granted his citizenship rights. The whirlwinds of revolt will continue to shake the foundations of our nation until the bright day of justice emerges.

But there is something that I must say to my people who stand on the warm threshold which leads into the palace of justice. In the process of gaining our rightful place, we must not be guilty of wrongful deeds. Let us not seek to satisfy our thirst for freedom by drinking from the cup of bitterness and hatred. We must forever conduct our struggle on the high plane of dignity and discipline. We must not allow our creative protest to degenerate into physical violence. Again and again we must rise to the majestic heights of meeting physical force with soul force. And the marvelous new militancy which has engulfed the Negro community must not lead us to a distrust of all white people; for many of our white brothers, as evidenced by their presence here today, have come to realize that their destiny is tied up with our destiny, and they have come to realize that their freedom is inextricably bound to our freedom.

We cannot walk alone. And as we walk we must make the pledge that we shall always march ahead. We cannot turn back. There are those who are asking the devotees of civil rights, "When will you be satisfied?" We can never be satisfied as long as the Negro is the victim of the unspeakable horrors of police brutality. We can never be satisfied as long as our bodies, heavy with the fatigue of travel, cannot gain lodging in the motels of the highways and the hotels of the cities. We cannot be satisfied as long as the Negro's basic mobility is from a smaller ghetto to a larger one. We can never be satisfied as long as our children are stripped of their selfhood and robbed of their dignity by signs stating "For Whites Only." We cannot be satisfied as long as the Negro in Mississippi cannot vote and a Negro in New York believes he has nothing for which to vote. No, no, we are not satisfied, and we will not be satisfied until justice rolls down like waters and righteousness like a mighty stream.

I am not unmindful that some of you have come here out of great trials and tribulations. Some of you have come fresh from narrow jail cells. Some of you have come from areas where your quest for freedom left you battered by the storms of persecution and staggered by the winds of police brutality. You have been the veterans of creative suffering. Continue to work with the faith that unearned suffering is redemptive.

Go back to Mississippi, and go back to Alabama. Go back to South Car-   10
olina. Go back to Georgia. Go back to Louisiana. Go back to the slums and ghettos of our Northern cities, knowing that somehow this situation can and will be changed. Let us not wallow in the valley of despair.

I say to you today, my friends, even though we face the difficulties of today and tomorrow, I still have a dream. It is a dream deeply rooted in the American dream. I have a dream that one day this nation will rise up and live out the true meaning of its creed: "We hold these truths to be self-evident, that all men are created equal." I have a dream that one day, on the red hills of Georgia, sons of former slaves and the sons of former slave owners will be able to sit down together at the table of brotherhood. I have a dream that one day even the state of Mississippi, a state sweltering with the heat of injustice, sweltering with the heat of oppression, will be transformed into an oasis of freedom and justice. I have a dream that my four little children will one day live in a nation where they will not be judged by the color of their skin, but by the content of their character.

I have a dream today. I have a dream that one day down in Alabama—with its vicious racists, with its governor's lips dripping with the words of interposition and nullification—one day right there in Alabama, little Black boys and Black girls will be able to join hands with little white boys and white girls as sisters and brothers.

I have a dream today. I have a dream that one day every valley shall be exalted and every hill and mountain shall be made low, the rough places will be made plain and the crooked places will be made straight, and the glory of the Lord shall be revealed, and all flesh shall see it together.°

This is our hope. This is the faith that I go back to the South with. And with this faith we will be able to hew out of the mountain of despair a stone of hope. With this faith we will be able to transform the jangling discords of our nation into a beautiful symphony of brotherhood. With this faith we will be able to work together, to play together, to struggle together, to go to jail together, to stand up for freedom together, knowing that we will be free one day.

───────

every valley shall be . . . see it together: A quotation from the Old Testament, Isaiah 40:4–5.

And this will be the day—this will be the day when all of God's children   15
will be able to sing with new meaning:

> My country, 'tis of thee,
> Sweet land of liberty,
>   Of thee I sing;
> Land where my fathers died,
> Land of the Pilgrims' pride,
> From every mountainside
>   Let freedom ring.

And if America is to be a great nation, this must become true.

And so let freedom ring from the prodigious hilltops of New Hampshire. Let freedom ring from the mighty mountains of New York. Let freedom ring from the heightening Alleghenies of Pennsylvania. Let freedom ring from the snow-capped Rockies of Colorado. Let freedom ring from the curvaceous slopes of California.

But not only that. Let freedom ring from Stone Mountain of Georgia. Let freedom ring from Lookout Mountain of Tennessee. Let freedom ring from every hill and molehill of Mississippi. "From every mountainside let freedom ring."

And when this happens—when we allow freedom to ring, when we let it ring from every village and every hamlet, from every state and every city— we will be able to speed up that day when all of God's children, Black men and white men, Jews and Gentiles, Protestants and Catholics, will be able to join hands and sing in the words of the old Negro spiritual: "Free at last! Free at last! Thank God Almighty. We are free at last!"

QUESTIONS FOR DISCUSSION

1. Why was the Lincoln Memorial an appropriate setting for this speech? Can you identify any references in the speech that link it to the setting in which it was originally presented?
2. Why does King begin paragraph 2 with "Five score years ago" instead of simply saying "one hundred years ago"?
3. *Anaphora*, as noted earlier, is a term that means "the use of repetition at the beginning of sentences, clauses, or verses for rhetorical effect." Examples are the three sentences beginning "One hundred years later" in paragraph 2. Can you identify any other examples?
4. What do you think King meant by "the tranquilizing drug of gradualism" in paragraph 5?
5. Paragraph 13 concludes with a quotation from the Bible. Why was it appropriate for King to use the Bible in this speech?
6. What evidence in this work suggests that King recognized that he was speaking to an audience already committed to the importance of racial equality?

SUGGESTIONS FOR WRITING

1. A *metaphor* is a figure of speech that makes a comparison between two unlike things without using *like* or *as*. When King writes "we have come to our nation's capital to cash a check," he does not mean these words to be taken literally. Instead, he is making an implied comparison between an uncashed check and unfulfilled promises to African Americans. Reread "I Have a Dream" identifying other metaphors King uses. Then paraphrase any five successive paragraphs, eliminating all metaphors and all anaphora.

2. Using both anaphora and metaphors, write a short speech that calls attention to a current social problem that concerns you.

3. Research the conditions under which King composed and delivered "I Have a Dream." Then write an essay in which you provide background information that would help other students understand the rhetorical context of this famous speech.

LINKS ■ ■ ■

■ WITHIN THE BOOK

To see how moving an audience differs from persuading one, compare "I Have a Dream" with King's "Letter from Birmingham Jail" (pages 534–548).

■ ELSEWHERE IN PRINT

Carson, Clayborne, and Kris Shepard, eds. *A Call to Conscience: The Landmark Speeches of Dr. Martin Luther King, Jr.* New York: Warner, 2001.

King, Martin Luther, Jr. *Strength to Love.* 1963. Philadelphia: Fortress, 1986.

——. *Why We Can't Wait.* 1964. New York: Signet, 2000.

Miller, Keith D. *Voice of Deliverance: The Language of Martin Luther King, Jr., and Its Sources.* New York: Free, 1992.

Ward, Brian, and Tracy Badger, eds. *The Making of Martin Luther King and the Civil Rights Movements.* New York: New York UP, 1996.

■ ONLINE

- The Civil Rights Museum
  <http://www.civilrightsmuseum.org>
- The King Center
  <http://www.thekingcenter.org>
- Martin Luther King National Historic Site
  <http://www.nps.gov/malu>
- Martin Luther King Papers Project
  <http://www.stanford.edu/group/king>

A HANGING

George Orwell

Born in India when it was still part of the British Empire, George Orwell (1903–1950) joined the Indian Imperial Police after graduating from Eton College. From 1922–1927, he was stationed in Burma—an experience upon which he drew for his first novel, Burmese Days *(1934) and for several of his essays, including "A Hanging." Although Orwell is best known for two novels he wrote late in his life,* Animal Farm *(1945) and* Nineteen Eighty-Four *(1949), he is also widely respected for his nonfiction. "Good prose is like a window-pane," he once wrote, and his essays have been praised for their clarity of style. But like his novels, Orwell's essays also demonstrate a strong commitment to social justice. In "Why I Write," Orwell declares, "My starting point is always a feeling of partisanship, a sense of injustice. When I sit down to write a book, I do not say to myself, 'I am going to produce a work of art.' I write because there is some lie I want to expose, some fact to which I want to draw attention, and my initial concern is to get a hearing." Bearing in mind Orwell's motive for writing, consider what "lie" he is trying to expose in "A Hanging."*

It was Burma, a sodden morning of rains. A sickly light, like yellow tinfoil, was slanting over the walls into the jail yard. We were waiting outside the condemned cells, a row of sheds fronted with double bars, like small animal cages. Each cell measured about ten feet by ten and was quite bare within except for a plank bed and a pot for drinking water. In some of them brown silent men were squatting at the inner bars, with their blankets draped round them. These were the condemned men, due to be hanged within the next week or two.

One prisoner had been brought out of his cell. He was a Hindu, a puny wisp of a man, with a shaven head and vague liquid eyes. He had a thick, sprouting moustache, absurdly too big for his body, rather like the moustache of a comic man on the films. Six tall Indian warders were guarding him and getting him ready for the gallows. Two of them stood by with rifles and fixed bayonets, while the others handcuffed him, passed a chain through his handcuffs and fixed it to their belts, and lashed his arms tight to his sides. They crowded very close about him, with their hands always on him in a careful caressing grip, as though all the while feeling him to make sure he was there. It was like men handling a fish which is still alive and may jump back into the water. But he stood quite unresisting, yielding his arms limply to the ropes, as though he hardly noticed what was happening.

Eight o'clock struck and a bugle call, desolately thin in the wet air, floated from the distant barracks. The superintendent of the jail, who was standing apart from the rest of us, moodily prodding the gravel with his stick, raised his head at the sound. He was an army doctor, with a grey toothbrush moustache and a gruff voice. "For God's sake hurry up, Francis," he said irritably. "The man ought to have been dead by this time. Aren't you ready yet?"

Francis, the head jailer, a fat Dravidian° in a white drill suit and gold spectacles, waved his black hand. "Yes sir, yes sir," he bubbled. "All iss satisfactorily prepared. The hangman iss waiting. We shall proceed."

"Well, quick march, then. The prisoners can't get their breakfast till this job's over."   5

We set out for the gallows. Two warders marched on either side of the prisoner, with their rifles at the slope; two others marched close against him, gripping him by arm and shoulder, as though at once pushing and supporting him. The rest of us, magistrates and the like, followed behind. Suddenly, when we had gone ten yards, the procession stopped short without any order or warning. A dreadful thing had happened—a dog, come goodness knows whence, had appeared in the yard. It came bounding among us with a loud volley of barks, and leapt round us wagging its whole body, wild with glee at finding so many human beings together. It was a large woolly dog, half Airedale, half pariah. For a moment it pranced round us, and then, before any-one could stop, it had made a dash for the prisoner and, jumping up, tried to lick his face. Everyone stood aghast, too taken aback even to grab at the dog.

"Who let that bloody brute in here?" said the superintendent angrily. "Catch it, someone!"

A warder, detached from the escort, charged clumsily after the dog, but it danced and gambolled just out of his reach, taking everything as part of the game. A young Eurasian jailer picked up a handful of gravel and tried to stone the dog away, but it dodged the stones and came after us again. Its yaps echoed from the jail walls. The prisoner, in the grasp of the two warders, looked on incuriously, as though this was another formality of the hanging. It was several minutes before someone managed to catch the dog. Then we put my handkerchief through its collar and moved off once more, with the dog still straining and whimpering.

It was about forty yards to the gallows. I watched the bare brown back of the prisoner marching in front of me. He walked clumsily with his bound arms, but quite steadily, with that bobbing gait of the Indian who never straightens his knees. At each step his muscles slid neatly into place, the lock of hair on his scalp danced up and down, his feet printed themselves on the wet gravel. And once, in spite of the men who gripped him by each shoulder, he stepped slightly aside to avoid a puddle on the path.

It is curious, but till that moment I had never realized what it means to   10
destroy a healthy, conscious man. When I saw the prisoner step aside to avoid the puddle I saw the mystery, the unspeakable wrongness, of cutting a life short when it is in full tide. This man was not dying, he was alive just as we are alive. All the organs of his body were working—bowels digesting food, skin renew-

---

Dravidian: A member of a race of people living in southern India and Ceylon.

ing itself, nails growing, tissue forming—all toiling away in solemn foolery. His nails would still be growing when he stood on the drop, when he was falling through the air with a tenth-of-a-second to live. His eyes saw the yellow gravel and the grey walls, and his brain still remembered, foresaw, reasoned—reasoned even about puddles. He and we were a party of men walking together, seeing, hearing, feeling, understanding the same world; and in two minutes, with a sudden snap, one of us would be gone—one mind less, one world less.

The gallows stood in a small yard, separate from the main grounds of the prison, and overgrown with tall prickly weeds. It was a brick erection like three sides of a shed, with planking on top, and above that two beams and a crossbar with the rope dangling. The hangman, a grey-haired convict in the white uniform of the prison, was waiting beside his machine. He greeted us with a servile crouch as we entered. At a word from Francis, the two warders, gripping the prisoner more closely than ever, half led half pushed him to the gallows and helped him clumsily up the ladder. Then the hangman climbed up and fixed the rope round the prisoner's neck.

We stood waiting, five yards away. The warders had formed in a rough circle round the gallows. And then, when the noose was fixed, the prisoner began crying out to his god. It was a high, reiterated cry of "Ram! Ram! Ram! Ram!" not urgent and fearful like a prayer or cry for help, but steady, rhythmical, almost like the tolling of a bell. The dog answered the sound with a whine. The hangman, still standing on the gallows, produced a small cotton bag like a flour bag and drew it down over the prisoner's face. But the sound, muffled by the cloth, still persisted, over and over again: "Ram! Ram! Ram! Ram! Ram!"

The hangman climbed down and stood ready, holding the lever. Minutes seemed to pass. The steady, muffled crying from the prisoner went on and on. "Ram! Ram! Ram!" never faltering for an instant. The superintendent, his head on his chest, was slowly poking the ground with his stick; perhaps he was counting the cries, allowing the prisoner a fixed number—fifty, perhaps, or a hundred. Everyone had changed color. The Indians had gone grey like bad coffee, and one or two of the bayonets were wavering. We looked at the lashed, hooded man on the drop, and listened to his cries—each cry another second of life; the same thought was in all our minds: oh, kill him quickly, get it over, stop that abominable noise!

Suddenly the superintendent made up his mind. Throwing up his head he made a swift motion with his stick. "Chalo°!" he shouted almost fiercely.

There was a clanking noise, and then dead silence. The prisoner had vanished, and the rope was twisting on itself. I let go of the dog, and it galloped immediately to the back of the gallows; but when it got there it stopped short, barked, and then retreated into a corner of the yard, where it stood among the weeds, looking timorously out at us. We went around the gallows to inspect the prisoner's body. He was dangling with his toes pointed straight downwards, very slowly revolving, as dead as a stone.

———————

Chalo: Hindi for "Let's go."

The superintendent reached out with his stick and poked the bare brown body; it oscillated slightly. "*He's* all right," said the superintendent. He backed out from under the gallows, and blew out a deep breath. The moody look had gone out of his face quite suddenly. He glanced at his wrist-watch. "Eight minutes past eight. Well, that's all for this morning, thank God."

The warders unfixed bayonets and marched away. The dog, sobered and conscious of having misbehaved itself, slipped after them. We walked out of the gallows yard, past the condemned cells with their waiting prisoners, into the big central yard of the prison. The convicts, under the command of warders armed with lathis°, were already receiving their breakfast. They squatted in long rows, each man holding a pannikin, while two warders with buckets marched round ladling out rice; it seemed quite a homely, jolly scene, after the hanging. An enormous relief had come upon us now that the job was done. One felt an impulse to sink, to break into a run, to snigger. All at once every one began chattering gaily.

The Eurasian boy walking beside me nodded towards the way we had come, with a knowing smile: "Do you know, sir, our friend (he meant the dead man) when he heard his appeal had been dismissed, he pissed on the floor of his cell. From fright. Kindly take one of my cigarettes, sir. Do you not admire my new silver case, sir? From the boxwalah, two rupees eight annas. Classy European style."

Several people laughed—at what, nobody seemed certain.

Francis was walking by the superintendent, talking garrulously: "Well, sir, all hass passed off with the utmost satisfactoriness. It was all finished—flick! like that. It iss not always so—oah, no! I have known cases where the doctor wass obliged to go beneath the gallows and pull the prissoner's legs to ensure decease. Most disagreeable!" 20

"Wriggling about, eh? That's bad," said the superintendent.

"Ach, sir, it iss worse when they become refractory! One man, I recall, clung to the bars of hiss cage when we went to take him out. You will scarcely credit, sir, that it took six warders to dislodge him, three pulling each leg. We reasoned with him. 'My dear fellow,' we said, 'think of all the pain and trouble you are causing to us!' But no, he would not listen! Ach, he wass very troublesome!"

I found that I was laughing quite loudly. Everyone was laughing. Even the superintendent grinned in a tolerant way. "You'd better all come out and have a drink," he said quite genially. "I've got a bottle of whiskey in the car. We could do with it."

We went through the big double gates of the prison into the road. "Pulling at his legs!" exclaimed a Burmese magistrate suddenly, and burst into a loud chuckling. We all began laughing again. At that moment Francis' anecdote seemed extraordinarily funny. We all had a drink together, native and European alike, quite amicably. The dead man was a hundred yards away.

---

lathis: Heavy sticks bound with iron.

QUESTIONS FOR DISCUSSION

1. Consider the scene Orwell describes in his opening paragraph. How does his description of the weather and the cells contribute toward inspiring sympathy for the prisoner who is about to be executed?
2. Around what type of contrast has Orwell constructed his second paragraph?
3. What role does the dog play in this essay? Why does Orwell describe its presence at the execution as "dreadful"?
4. Why does Orwell consider it significant that the condemned man stepped aside to avoid a puddle?
5. Orwell describes the prisoner's prayer as "steady, rhythmical, almost like the tolling of a bell." Why is he calling attention to the prayer? Do you recognize an allusion in the reference to the bell?
6. How did witnessing this execution affect the men in the essay? How did it affect you?
7. Some critics have claimed that Orwell never witnessed the execution described in this selection. In that case what is usually considered an "essay" would become a "story." Would that limit its effectiveness? Would your own response change if you considered the piece fiction?

SUGGESTIONS FOR WRITING

1. If you have ever witnessed a disturbing event that you were powerless to stop, narrate the story of that event so that other people will feel as you do about what you saw.
2. For many people capital punishment is simply an abstract social issue, but an essay or story focused on a specific execution can make people see the issue differently. Identify a social issue that concerns you, and then dramatize it by using narration.
3. Research a capital case that is controversial because of the age, race, gender, or intelligence of the person convicted. Incorporate what you discover in a letter to the governor of the state in which the prisoner is held, moving him or her to grant clemency.

LINKS ■ ■ ■

■ WITHIN THE BOOK

For another example of Orwell's work, see "Marrakech" (pages 638–643).

■ ELSEWHERE IN PRINT

Baird-Murray, Maureen. *A World Overturned: A Burmese Childhood, 1933–1947.* Brooklyn: Interlink, 1998.

(continues)

LINKS ■ ■ ■ *(continued)*

Harvey, Godfrey. *British Rule in Burma, 1824–1942.* 1946. New York: AMS, 1992.

Orwell, George. *Burmese Days: A Novel.* 1934. New York: Harcourt, 1989.

---. *The Lion and the Unicorn: Socialism and the English Genius.* 1941. New York: AMS, 1976.

Prejean, Helen. *Dead Man Walking: An Eyewitness Account of the Death Penalty in the United States.* New York: Random, 1993.

Said, Edward W. *Culture and Imperialism.* New York: Knopf, 1993.

■ **ONLINE**

- Animal Farm
  <http://www.ddc.net/ygg/etext/animal.htm>

- George Orwell Archive
  <http://www.codoh.com/thoughtcrimes/tcportorw.html>

- Key Writings and Links
  <http://www.resort.com/~prime8/Orwell>

AM I BLUE?

"Ain't these tears in these eyes tellin' you?"°

Alice Walker

Alice Walker is best known as the author of The Color Purple, *which was turned into a popular film by Stephen Spielberg. But Walker is also the author of several other novels—as well as poems and essays, many of which focus on issues of race, family, and gender. In addition to winning the Pulitzer Prize for fiction in 1983, she has received the Lillian Smith Award from the National Endowment for the Arts, the Rosenthal Award from the National Institute of Arts and Letters, and a Guggenheim Fellowship.*

"Am I Blue?" was first published in 1986 by Ms. magazine. *In this piece, Walker writes about a stallion named Blue living in a pasture near her home. She describes how his life changed when he was given a companion and how it changed again when that companion was taken away. But as the title suggests, Walker is not interested in the horse alone. You will find that she uses Blue's story to convey feelings about a number of concerns.*

For about three years my companion and I rented a small house in the country that stood on the edge of a large meadow that appeared to run from the end of our deck straight into the mountains. The mountains, however, were quite far away, and between us and them there was, in fact, a town. It was one of the many pleasant aspects of the house that you never really were aware of this.

It was a house of many windows, low, wide, nearly floor to ceiling in the living room, which faced the meadow, and it was from one of these that I first saw our closest neighbor, a large white horse, cropping grass, flipping its mane, and ambling about—not over the entire meadow, which stretched well out of sight of the house, but over the five or so fenced-in acres that were next to the twenty-odd that we had rented. I soon learned that the horse, whose name was Blue, belonged to a man who lived in another town, but was boarded by our neighbors next door. Occasionally, one of the children, usually a stocky teenager, but sometimes a much younger girl or boy, could be seen riding Blue. They would appear in the meadow, climb up on his back, ride furiously for ten or fifteen minutes, then get off, slap Blue on the flanks, and not be seen again for a month or more.

There were many apple trees in our yard, and one by the fence Blue could almost reach. We were soon in the habit of feeding him apples, which he relished, especially because by the middle of summer the meadow grasses—so green and succulent since January—had dried out from lack of rain, and Blue stumbled about munching the dried stalks half-heartedly. Sometimes he would stand very still just by the apple tree, and when one of us came out he would whinny, snort loudly, or stamp the ground. This meant, of course: I want an apple.

It was quite wonderful to pick a few apples, or collect those that had fallen to the ground overnight, and patiently hold them, one by one, up to his large, toothy mouth. I remained as thrilled as a child by his flexible dark lips, huge, cubelike teeth that crunched the apples, core and all, with such finality, and his high, broad-breasted *enormity;* beside which, I felt small indeed. When I was a child, I used to ride horses, and was especially friendly with one named Nan until the day I was riding and my brother deliberately spooked her and I was thrown, head first, against the trunk of a tree. When I came to, I was in bed and my mother was bending worriedly over me; we silently agreed that perhaps horseback riding was not the safest sport for me. Since then I have walked, and prefer walking to horseback riding—but I had forgotten the depth of feeling one could see in horses' eyes.

I was therefore unprepared for the expression in Blue's. Blue was lonely. 5 Blue was horribly lonely and bored. I was not shocked that this should be the case; five acres to tramp by yourself, endlessly, even in the most beautiful of meadows—and his was—cannot provide many interesting events, and once rainy season turned to dry that was about it. No, I was shocked that I had forgotten that human animals and nonhuman animals can communicate quite well; if we are brought up around animals as children we take this for granted. By the time we are adults we no longer remember. However, the animals have not changed. They are in fact *completed* creations (at least they seem to be, so much more than we) who are not likely to change; it is their nature to express themselves. What else are they going to express? And they do. And, generally speaking, they are ignored.

After giving Blue the apples, I would wander back to the house, aware that he was observing me. Were more apples not forthcoming then? Was that to be his sole entertainment for the day? My partner's small son had decided he wanted to learn how to piece a quilt; we worked in silence on our respective squares as I thought . . .

Well, about slavery: about white children, who were raised by black people, who knew their first all-accepting love from black women, and then, when they were twelve or so, were told they must "forget" the deep levels of communication between themselves and "mammy" that they knew. Later they would be able to relate quite calmly, "My old mammy was sold to another good family." "My old mammy was _____." Fill in the blank. Many more years later a white woman would say: "I can't understand these Negroes, these blacks. What do they want? They're so different from us."

And about the Indians, considered to be "like animals" by the "settlers" (a very benign euphemism for what they actually were), who did not understand their description as a compliment.

And about the thousands of American men who marry Japanese, Korean, Filipina, and other non-English-speaking women and of how happy they report they are, "*blissfully,*" until their brides learn to speak English, at which point the marriages tend to fall apart. What then did the men see, when they looked into the eyes of the women they married, before they could speak English? Apparently only their own reflections.

I thought of society's impatience with the young. "Why are they playing the music so loud?" Perhaps the children have listened to much of the music of oppressed people their parents danced to before they were born, with its passionate but soft cries for acceptance and love, and they have wondered why their parents failed to hear.

I do not know how long Blue had inhabited his five beautiful, boring acres before we moved into our house; a year after we had arrived—and had also traveled to other valleys, other cities, other worlds—he was still there.

But then, in our second year at the house, something happened in Blue's life. One morning, looking out the window at the fog that lay like a ribbon over the meadow, I saw another horse, a brown one, at the other end of Blue's field. Blue appeared to be afraid of it, and for several days made no attempt to go near. We went away for a week. When we returned, Blue had decided to make friends and the two horses ambled or galloped along together, and Blue did not come nearly as often to the fence underneath the apple tree.

When he did, bringing his new friend with him, there was a different look in his eyes. A look of independence, of self-possession, of inalienable *horse*ness. His friend eventually became pregnant. For months and months there was, it seemed to me, a mutual feeling between me and the horses of justice, of peace. I fed apples to them both. The look in Blue's eyes was one of unabashed "this is *it*ness."

It did not, however, last forever. One day, after a visit to the city, I went out to give Blue some apples. He stood waiting, or so I thought, though not beneath the tree. When I shook the tree and jumped back from the shower of apples, he made no move. I carried some over to him. He managed to half-crunch one. The rest he let fall to the ground. I dreaded looking into his eyes—because I had of course noticed that Brown, his partner, had gone—but I did look. If I had been born into slavery, and my partner had been sold or killed, my eyes would have looked like that. The children next door explained that Blue's partner had been "put with him" (the same expression that old people used, I had noticed, when speaking of an ancestor during slavery who had been impregnated by her owner) so that they could mate and she conceive. Since that was accomplished, she had been taken back by her owner, who lived somewhere else.

Will she be back? I asked.

They didn't know.

Blue was like a crazed person. Blue *was*, to me, a crazed person. He galloped furiously, as if he were being ridden, around and around his five beautiful acres. He whinnied until he couldn't. He tore at the ground with his hooves. He butted himself against his single shade tree. He looked always and always toward the road down which his partner had gone. And then, occasionally, when he came up for apples, or I took apples to him, he looked at me. It was a look so piercing, so full of grief, a look so *human*, I almost laughed (I felt too sad to cry) to think there are people who do not know that animals suffer. People like me who have forgotten, and daily forget, all that animals try to tell us. "Everything you do to us will happen to you; we are your teachers, as you are ours. We are one lesson" is essentially it, I think. There are those who never once have even considered animals' rights: those who have been taught that animals actually want to be used and abused by us, as small children "love" to be frightened, or women "love" to be mutilated and raped. . . . They are the great-grandchildren of those who honestly thought, because someone taught them this: "Women can't think," and "niggers can't faint." But most disturbing of all, in Blue's large brown eyes was a new look, more painful than the look of despair: the look of disgust with human beings, with life; the look of hatred. And it was odd what the look of hatred did. It gave him, for the first time, the look of a beast. And what that meant was that he had put up a barrier within to protect himself from further violence; all the apples in the world wouldn't change that fact.

And so Blue remained, a beautiful part of our landscape, very peaceful to look at from the window, white against the grass. Once a friend came to visit and said, looking out on the soothing view: "And it *would* have to be a *white* horse; the very image of freedom." And I thought, yes, the animals are forced to become for us merely "images" of what they once so beautifully expressed. And we are used to drinking milk from containers showing "contented" cows, whose real lives we want to hear nothing about, eating eggs and drumsticks from "happy" hens, and munching hamburgers advertised by bulls of integrity who seem to command their fate.

As we talked of freedom and justice one day for all, we sat down to steaks. I am eating misery, I thought, as I took the first bite. And spit it out.

QUESTIONS FOR DISCUSSION

1. Consider the opening paragraph of this essay, a paragraph that sets the scene but does not mention the horse that provides the focus for the paragraphs that follow. Why does Walker write that the mountains were farther away than they seemed and that an unseen town intervened?
2. Why is it significant that the horse is named Blue? How has Walker attempted to make readers sympathize with him?
3. The title of this essay, which comes from a song popular in the 1920s, can be read in more than one way. How do you interpret it?
4. Walker refers to her "companion" and "partner"; later, she refers to Blue's "friend." Why do you think she has chosen these words when there are other alternatives?
5. Walker writes that she looked into Blue's eyes and found them lonely, grief-stricken, and, eventually, filled with hatred. Do you think an animal can express these emotions? Or do you think that Walker is projecting her own feelings on the horse?
6. Consider the transition between paragraphs 6 and 7, where Walker moves temporarily away from the story of Blue to reflect on other types of oppression. How successfully has she managed this transition? How would

the essay change if she kept Blue's story together and added social commentary only in her final paragraphs?

7. Explain the last paragraph of this essay. Is Walker bothered by eating meat? Or is something else upsetting her?

SUGGESTIONS FOR WRITING

1. Write about a neglected or abandoned animal so that people can begin to understand what happens to an animal that has been mistreated.
2. Write an essay about racial injustice that would move members of one race to overcome prejudice they have toward another.
3. Write an essay comparing Walker's essay with Annie Dillard's "The Deer at Providencia" (pages 633–636). Both Dillard and Walker have looked closely at a member of another species. How does their point of view differ?

LINKS ■ ■ ■

■ WITHIN THE BOOK

To see how a poet can move readers when addressing social injustice, see "Power" by Audre Lorde (pages 712–713).

■ ELSEWHERE IN PRINT

Regan, Tom. *The Case for Animal Rights.* Berkeley: U of California P, 1983.
Singer, Peter. *Animal Liberation.* New York: Ecco, 2002.
Spiegel, Marjorie. *The Dreaded Comparison: Human and Animal Slavery.* Pref. Alice Walker. Rev. ed. New York: Mirror, 1996.
Walker, Alice. *By the Light of My Father's Smile: A Novel.* New York: Random, 1998.
———. *The Color Purple.* 1982. New York: Harcourt, 1992.
———. *Horses Make a Landscape More Beautiful: Poems.* San Diego: Harcourt, 1984.
———. *In Search of Our Mothers' Gardens: Womanist Prose.* San Diego: Harcourt, 1983.

■ ONLINE

- Center to Study Human-Animal Relationships and Environments <http://www.censhare.umn.edu>
- The Life Cycle of Familiar Relationships <http://www.trinity.edu/~mkearl/fam-life.html>
- Sited Related to Animal Companionship <http://www.vachss.com/help_text/animal_companion.html>

THE STATE OF OUR UNION

George W. Bush

On September 11, 2001, terrorists seized planes from four commercial airlines and used them to cause massive destruction. Two of these planes flew directly into the twin towers of the World Trade Center, the tallest buildings in New York City, causing them to collapse. A third plane destroyed part of the Pentagon in Washington, D.C. A fourth crashed in rural Pennsylvania, its target unknown. Thousands of people died as the result of these attacks, which stunned the nation and horrified much of the world. A week after the attack, President George W. Bush addressed a joint session of Congress—as millions of Americans watched a live television broadcast—to draw the nation together and provide direction for the future. The transcript of that speech is included here as an example of writing to move, given at a critical moment in American history when feelings of shock, sorrow, anger, and anxiety prevailed throughout the country.

The 43rd president of the United States and the son of another president, George W. Bush graduated from Yale University and Harvard Business School. Before becoming president, he worked in the oil industry and served as governor of Texas.

Mr. Speaker, Mr. President pro tempore, members of Congress, and fellow Americans:

In the normal course of events, presidents come to this chamber to report on the state of the union. Tonight, no such report is needed. It has already been delivered by the American people.

We have seen it in the courage of passengers who rushed terrorists to save others on the ground, passengers like an exceptional man named Todd Beamer. Please help me to welcome his wife, Lisa Beamer, here tonight.

We have seen the state of our union in the endurance of rescuers working past exhaustion. We have seen the unfurling of flags, the lighting of candles, the giving of blood, the saying of prayers—in English, Hebrew, and Arabic. We have seen the decency of a loving and giving people, who have made the grief of strangers their own.

My fellow citizens, for the last nine days, the entire world has seen for itself the state of our union—and it is strong.

Tonight we are a country awakened to danger and called to defend freedom. Our grief has turned to anger and anger to resolution. Whether we bring our enemies to justice or bring justice to our enemies, justice will be done.

I thank the Congress for its leadership at such an important time. All of America was touched on the evening of the tragedy to see Republicans and Democrats joined together on the steps of this Capitol, singing "God Bless America." And you did more than sing; you acted, by delivering $40 billion to rebuild our communities and meet the needs of our military.

Speaker Hastert and Minority Leader Gephardt, Majority Leader Daschle and Senator Lott, I thank you for your friendship and your leadership and your service to our country.

And on behalf of the American people, I thank the world for its outpouring of support. America will never forget the sounds of our national anthem playing at Buckingham Palace and on the streets of Paris and at Berlin's Brandenburg Gate. We will not forget South Korean children gathering to pray outside our embassy in Seoul, or the prayers of sympathy offered at a mosque in Cairo. We will not forget moments of silence and days of mourning in Australia and Africa and Latin America.

Nor will we forget the citizens of eighty other nations who died with our own. Dozens of Pakistanis. More than 130 Israelis. More than 250 citizens of India. Men and women from El Salvador, Iran, Mexico, and Japan. And hundreds of British citizens. America has no truer friend than Great Britain. Once again, we are joined together in a great cause. The British prime minister has crossed an ocean to show his unity of purpose with America, and tonight we welcome Tony Blair. *10*

On September 11, enemies of freedom committed an act of war against our country. Americans have known wars, but for the past 136 years, they have been wars on foreign soil, except for one Sunday in 1941. Americans have known the casualties of war, but not at the center of a great city on a peaceful morning. Americans have known surprise attacks, but never before on thousands of civilians. All of this was brought upon us in a single day, and night fell on a different world, a world where freedom itself is under attack.

Americans have many questions tonight. Americans are asking, "Who attacked our country?"

The evidence we have gathered all points to a collection of loosely affiliated terrorist organizations known as Al Qaeda. They are the same murderers indicted for bombing American embassies in Tanzania and Kenya and responsible for the bombing of the *U.S.S. Cole.*

Al Qaeda is to terror what the Mafia is to crime. But its goal is not making money; its goal is remaking the world and imposing its radical beliefs on people everywhere.

The terrorists practice a fringe form of Islamic extremism that has been rejected by Muslim scholars and the vast majority of Muslim clerics, a fringe movement that perverts the peaceful teachings of Islam. The terrorists' directive commands them to kill Christians and Jews, to kill all Americans, and [to] make no distinctions among military and civilians, including women and children. *15*

This group and its leader, a person named Osama bin Laden, are linked to many other organizations in different countries, including the Egyptian Islamic Jihad and the Islamic Movement of Uzbekistan.

There are thousands of these terrorists in more than sixty countries. They are recruited from their own nations and neighborhoods and brought to camps in places like Afghanistan, where they are trained in the tactics of terror. They are sent back to their homes or sent to hide in countries around the world to plot evil and destruction.

The leadership of Al Qaeda has great influence in Afghanistan and supports the Taliban regime in controlling most of that country. In Afghanistan, we see Al Qaeda's vision for the world.

Afghanistan's people have been brutalized; many are starving and many have fled. Women are not allowed to attend school. You can be jailed for owning a television. Religion can be practiced only as their leaders dictate. A man can be jailed in Afghanistan if his beard is not long enough.

The United States respects the people of Afghanistan—after all, we are currently its largest source of humanitarian aid—but we condemn the Taliban regime. It is not only repressing its own people, it is threatening people everywhere by sponsoring and sheltering and supplying terrorists. By aiding and abetting murder, the Taliban regime is committing murder. And tonight, the United States of America makes the following demands on the Taliban:

- Deliver to United States authorities all the leaders of Al Qaeda who hide in your land.

- Release all foreign nationals, including American citizens you have unjustly imprisoned, and protect foreign journalists, diplomats, and aid workers in your country.

- Close immediately and permanently every terrorist training camp in Afghanistan and hand over every terrorist, and every person in their support structure, to appropriate authorities.

- Give the United States full access to terrorist training camps, so we can make sure they are no longer operating.

These demands are not open to negotiation or discussion. The Taliban must act and act immediately. They will hand over the terrorists, or they will share in their fate.

I also want to speak tonight directly to Muslims throughout the world. We respect your faith. It is practiced freely by many millions of Americans and by millions more in countries that America counts as friends. Its teachings are good and peaceful, and those who commit evil in the name of Allah blaspheme the name of Allah. The terrorists are traitors to their own faith, trying, in effect, to hijack Islam itself. The enemy of America is not our many Muslim friends; it is not our many Arab friends. Our enemy is a radical network of terrorists and every government that supports them.

Our war on terror begins with Al Qaeda, but it does not end there. It will not end until every terrorist group of global reach has been found, stopped, and defeated.

Americans are asking, "Why do they hate us?"

They hate what we see right here in this chamber, a democratically elected government. Their leaders are self-appointed. They hate our freedoms—our freedom of religion, our freedom of speech, our freedom to vote and assemble and disagree with each other.

They want to overthrow existing governments in many Muslim countries, such as Egypt, Saudi Arabia, and Jordan. They want to drive Israel out of the Middle East. They want to drive Christians and Jews out of vast regions of Asia and Africa.

These terrorists kill not merely to end lives, but to disrupt and end a way of life. With every atrocity, they hope that America grows fearful, retreating from the world and forsaking our friends. They stand against us, because we stand in their way.

We are not deceived by their pretenses to piety. We have seen their kind before. They are the heirs of all the murderous ideologies of the 20th century. By sacrificing human life to serve their radical visions, by abandoning every value except the will to power, they follow in the path of fascism and Nazism and totalitarianism. And they will follow that path all the way to where it ends in history's unmarked grave of discarded lies.

Americans are asking, "How will we fight and win this war?"

We will direct every resource at our command—every means of diplomacy, every tool of intelligence, every instrument of law enforcement, every financial influence, and every necessary weapon of war—to the disruption and defeat of the global terror network.

This war will not be like the war against Iraq a decade ago, with its decisive liberation of territory and its swift conclusion. It will not look like the air war above Kosovo two years ago, where no ground troops were used and not a single American was lost in combat.

Our response involves far more than instant retaliation and isolated strikes. Americans should not expect one battle, but a lengthy campaign unlike any other we have seen. It may include dramatic strikes visible on television, and covert operations secret even in success. We will starve terrorists of funding, turn them one against another, drive them from place to place until there is no refuge or rest. And we will pursue nations that provide aid or safe haven to terrorism. Every nation in every region now has a decision to make. Either you are with us or you are with the terrorists. From this day forward, any nation that continues to harbor or support terrorism will be regarded by the United States as a hostile regime.

Our nation has been put on notice: We are not immune from attack. We will take defensive measures against terrorism to protect Americans.

Today, dozens of federal departments and agencies, as well as state and local governments, have responsibilities affecting homeland security. These efforts must be coordinated at the highest level. So tonight I announce the creation of a Cabinet-level position reporting directly to me—the Office of Homeland Security.

These measures are essential. But the only way to defeat terrorism as a threat to our way of life is to stop it, eliminate it, and destroy it where it grows.

Many will be involved in this effort, from F.B.I. agents to intelligence operatives to the reservists we have called to active duty. All deserve our thanks, and all have our prayers. And tonight, a few miles from the damaged Pentagon, I have a message for our military: Be ready. I have called the armed forces to alert, and there is a reason. The hour is coming when America will act, and you will make us proud.

This is not, however, just America's fight. And what is at stake is not just America's freedom. This is the world's fight. This is civilization's fight. This is the fight of all who believe in progress and pluralism, tolerance and freedom.

We ask every nation to join us. We will ask, and we will need, the help of police forces, intelligence services, and banking systems around the world. The United States is grateful that many nations and many international organizations have already responded with sympathy and with support. Nations from Latin America, to Asia, to Africa, to Europe, to the Islamic world. Perhaps the NATO Charter reflects best the attitude of the world: An attack on one is an attack on all.

The civilized world is rallying to America's side. They understand that, if this terror goes unpunished, their own cities, their own citizens may be next. Terror, unanswered, can not only bring down buildings, it can threaten the stability of legitimate governments. And we will not allow it.

Americans are asking, "What is expected of us?"   40

I ask you to live your lives and hug your children. I know many citizens have fears tonight, and I ask you to be calm and resolute, even in the face of a continuing threat.

I ask you to uphold the values of America and remember why so many have come here. We are in a fight for our principles, and our first responsibility is to live by them. No one should be singled out for unfair treatment or unkind words because of their ethnic background or religious faith.

I ask you to continue to support the victims of this tragedy with your contributions. Those who want to give can go to a central source of information, <libertyunites.org>, to find the names of groups providing direct help in New York, Pennsylvania and Virginia.

The thousands of F.B.I. agents who are now at work in this investigation may need your cooperation, and I ask you to give it.

I ask for your patience with the delays and inconveniences that may accompany tighter security—and for your patience in what will be a long struggle.   45

I ask your continued participation and confidence in the American economy. Terrorists attacked a symbol of American prosperity. They did not touch its source. America is successful because of the hard work and creativity and enterprise of our people. These were the true strengths of our economy before September 11, and they are our strengths today.

Finally, please continue praying for the victims of terror and their families, for those in uniform, and for our great country. Prayer has comforted us in sorrow, and will help strengthen us for the journey ahead.

Tonight I thank my fellow Americans for what you have already done and for what you will do. And ladies and gentlemen of the Congress, I thank you, their representatives, for what you have already done and for what we will do together.

Tonight, we face new and sudden national challenges. We will come together to improve air safety, to dramatically expand the number of air marshals on domestic flights, and take new measures to prevent hijacking. We will come together to promote stability and keep our airlines flying with direct assistance during this emergency.

We will come together to give law enforcement the additional tools it *50* needs to track down terror here at home. We will come together to strengthen our intelligence capabilities to know the plans of terrorists before they act, and find them before they strike.

We will come together to take active steps that strengthen America's economy and put our people back to work.

Tonight we welcome here two leaders who embody the extraordinary spirit of all New Yorkers: Governor George Pataki and Mayor Rudy Giuliani. As a symbol of America's resolve, my administration will work with the Congress and these two leaders to show the world that we will rebuild New York City.

After all that has just passed—all the lives taken and all the possibilities and hopes that died with them—it is natural to wonder if America's future is one of fear. Some speak of an age of terror. I know there are struggles ahead and dangers to face. But this country will define our times, not be defined by them. As long as the United States of America is determined and strong, this will not be an age of terror; this will be an age of liberty, here and across the world.

Great harm has been done to us. We have suffered great loss. And in our grief and anger we have found our mission and our moment. Freedom and fear are at war. The advance of human freedom—the great achievement of our time and the great hope of every time—now depends on us. Our nation, this generation, will lift a dark threat of violence from our people and our future. We will rally the world to this cause by our efforts and by our courage. We will not tire, we will not falter, and we will not fail.

It is my hope that in the months and years ahead, life will return almost *55* to normal. We'll go back to our lives and routines, and that is good. Even grief recedes with time and grace. But our resolve must not pass. Each of us will remember what happened that day and to whom it happened. We will remember the moment the news came—where we were and what we were doing. Some will remember an image of fire or a story of rescue. Some will carry memories of a face and a voice gone forever.

And I will carry this. It is the police shield of a man named George Howard, who died at the World Trade Center trying to save others. It was given to me by his mom, Arlene, as a proud memorial to her son. This is my reminder of lives that ended and a task that does not end.

I will not forget this wound to our country or those who inflicted it. I will not yield, I will not rest, I will not relent in waging this struggle for the freedom and security of the American people.

The course of this conflict is not known, yet its outcome is certain. Freedom and fear, justice and cruelty, have always been at war, and we know that God is not neutral between them.

Fellow citizens, we will meet violence with patient justice, assured of the rightness of our cause and confident of the victories to come. In all that lies before us, may God grant us wisdom, and may He watch over the United States of America.

Thank you. *60*

QUESTIONS FOR DISCUSSION

1. At the beginning of his speech, Bush draws attention to one of the passengers who died on the plane that crashed in Pennsylvania before it could hit its target—and to the passenger's wife, who was present for the speech. What does he accomplish by this rhetorical strategy?
2. Bush addresses his remarks to his "fellow Americans." Where does he demonstrate that he understands that Americans come from diverse cultural backgrounds, and why is it important for him to do so?
3. In the weeks following the attacks of September 11, the Bush administration worked to forge an international coalition to oppose terrorism. How does this speech contribute to that effort?
4. In paragraphs 20–21, Bush makes a series of demands that are, he states, "not open to negotiation." What is the purpose of making nonnegotiable demands? How do these demands sound to you if you are an American citizen? How would they sound to you if you were a citizen of another country?
5. In paragraph 25, Bush claims the attacks of September 11 were inspired by hatred of the freedoms Americans enjoy. How does this claim support his purpose? Do you agree with it?
6. What do you think Bush means when he refers to the "civilized world"? What countries are part of this world? Which ones would be excluded?
7. At the end of this speech, Bush displayed the police shield he refers to in paragraph 56. What role does this shield play in the speech?

SUGGESTIONS FOR WRITING

1. Write an essay that could inspire people to work on behalf of world peace.
2. Write a eulogy paying tribute to the firefighters who died when trying to rescue people from the World Trade Center.
3. Research the events that led to the September 11 attack upon America, and write an essay that would move readers to care about one of the problems you discover.

LINKS ■ ■ ■

■ WITHIN THE BOOK

For another example of political oratory, see Martin Luther King's "I Have a Dream" (pages 456–459).

■ ELSEWHERE IN PRINT

Bulliet, Richard W. *Islam*. New York: Columbia UP, 1995.

▪ ELSEWHERE IN PRINT *(continued)*

Bush, George W. *A Challenge to Keep: My Journey to the White House.* New York: HarperCollins, 2001.

Goldziher, Ignaz. *Introduction to Islamic Theology and Law.* Trans. Andras Hamori and Ruth Hamori. Ed. Bernard Lewis. Princeton: Princeton UP, 1981.

Kaplan, David. *The Accidental President: How 413 Lawyers, 9 Supreme Court Justices, and 5,963,110 Floridians (Give or Take a Few) Landed George W. Bush in the White House.* New York: Morrow, 2001.

Reich, Walter. Ed. *Origins of Terrorism: Pyschologies, Ideologies, States of Mind.* Washington: Wilson, 1998.

▪ ONLINE

- Brief Biography
  <http://www.texas-on-line.com/graphic/georgewbush.htm>
- The Bush Presidency
  <http://www.whitehouse.gov>
- The Department of Defense
  <http://www.defenselink.mil>
- The Library of Congress
  <http://www.loc.gov>

ON BEHALF OF THE INSANE POOR

Dorothea Dix

One of the great reformers of the nineteenth century, Dorothea Dix (1802–1887) is best remembered for her work on behalf of the mentally ill—a project that began in 1841 when she volunteered to teach Sunday School in a jail near Boston. Appalled by the conditions she discovered there, Dix subsequently traveled throughout Massachusetts investigating how the mentally ill were locked away in prisons and workhouses, rarely getting care and often abused. Eventually she visited every state east of the Mississippi and helped to found thirty-two mental hospitals, fifteen schools for the developmentally disabled, a school for the blind, and numerous training facilities for nurses.

The following selection is excerpted from a longer work that Dix addressed to the Massachusetts legislature in 1843—a time when women were discouraged from taking an interest in public affairs. As you read, note how Dix uses gender expectations to stir feeling in men. And if any of her language seems old-fashioned today, consider what this language reveals about the culture in which Dix worked and what kind of language you would use if addressing your own state legislature on an issue of urgent importance.

I respectfully ask to present this Memorial, believing that the *cause,* which actuates to and sanctions so unusual a movement, presents no equivocal claim to public consideration and sympathy. Surrendering to calm and deep convictions of duty my habitual views of what is womanly and becoming, I proceed briefly to explain what has conducted me before you unsolicited and unsustained, trusting, while I do so, that the memorialist will be speedily forgotten in the memorial.

About two years since, leisure afforded opportunity, and duty prompted me to visit several prisons and alms-houses in the vicinity of this metropolis. I found, near Boston, in the Jails and Asylums for the poor, a numerous class brought into unsuitable connexion with criminals and the general mass of Paupers. I refer to Idiots and Insane persons, dwelling in circumstances not only adverse to their own physical and moral improvement, but productive of extreme disadvantages to all other persons brought into association with them. I applied myself diligently to trace the causes of these evils, and sought to supply remedies. As one obstacle was surmounted, fresh difficulties appeared. Every new investigation has given depth to the conviction that it is only by decided, prompt, and vigorous legislation the evils to which I refer, and which I shall proceed more fully to illustrate, can be remedied. I shall be obliged to speak with great plainness, and to reveal many things revolting to the taste, and from which my woman's nature shrinks with peculiar sensitiveness. But truth is the highest consideration. *I tell what I have seen*—painful and shocking as the details often are—that from them you may feel more deeply the imperative obligation which lies upon you to prevent the possibility of a repetition or continuance of such outrages upon humanity. If I inflict pain upon you, and move you to horror, it is to acquaint you with sufferings which you have the power to alleviate, and make you hasten to the relief of the victims of legalized barbarity.

I come to present the strong claims of suffering humanity. I come to place before the Legislature of Massachusetts the condition of the miserable, the desolate, the outcast. I come as the advocate of helpless, forgotten, insane and idiotic men and women; of beings, sunk to a condition from which the most unconcerned would start with real horror; of beings wretched in our Prisons, and more wretched in our Alms-Houses. And I cannot suppose it needful to employ earnest persuasion, or stubborn argument, in order to arrest and fix attention upon a subject, only the more strongly pressing in its claims, because it is revolting and disgusting in its details.

I must confine myself to few examples, but am ready to furnish other and more complete details, if required. If my pictures are displeasing, coarse, and severe, my subjects, it must be recollected, offer no tranquil, refined, or composing features. The condition of human beings, reduced to the extremest states of degradation and misery, cannot be exhibited in softened language, or adorn a polished page.

I proceed, Gentlemen, briefly to call your attention to the *present* state of   5
Insane Persons confined within this Commonwealth, in *cages, closets, cellars, stalls, pens! Chained, naked, beaten with rods,* and *lashed* into obedience!

As I state cold, severe *facts,* I feel obliged to refer to persons, and definitely to indicate localities. But it is upon my subject, not upon localities or individuals, I desire to fix attention; and I would speak as kindly as possible of all Wardens, Keepers, and other responsible officers, believing that *most* of these have erred not through hardness of heart and wilful cruelty, so much as want of skill and knowledge, and want of consideration. Familiarity with suffering, it is said, blunts the sensibilities, and where neglect once finds a footing other injuries are multiplied. This is not all, for it may justly and strongly be added that, from the deficiency of adequate means to meet the wants of these cases, it has been an absolute impossibility to do justice in this matter. Prisons are not constructed in view of being converted into County Hospitals, and Alms-Houses are not founded as receptacles for the Insane. And yet, in the face of justice and common sense, Wardens are by law compelled to receive, and the Masters of Alms-Houses not to refuse, Insane and Idiotic subjects in all stages of mental disease and privation.

It is the Commonwealth, not its integral parts, that is accountable for most of the abuses which have lately, and do still exist. I repeat it, it is defective legislation which perpetuates and multiplies these abuses.

In illustration of my subject, I offer the following extracts from my Note-Book and Journal:— . [. . .]

Danvers. November; visited the almshouse; a large building, much out of repair; understand a new one is in contemplation. Here are from fifty-six to sixty inmates; one idiotic; three insane; one of the latter in close confinement at all times.

Long before reaching the house, wild shouts, snatches of rude songs, 10 imprecations, and obscene language, fell upon the ear, proceeding from the occupant of a low building, rather remote from the principal building to which my course was directed. Found the mistress, and was conducted to the place, which was called *'the home'* of the *forlorn* maniac, a young woman, exhibiting a condition of neglect and misery blotting out the faintest idea of comfort, and outraging every sentiment of decency. She had been, I learnt, "a respectable person; industrious and worthy; disappointments and trials shook her mind, and finally laid prostrate reason and self-control; she became a maniac for life! She had been at Worcester Hospital for a considerable time, and had been returned as incurable." The mistress told me she understood that, while there, she was "comfortable and decent." Alas! what a change was here exhibited! She had passed from one degree of violence and degradation to another, in swift progress; there she stood, clinging to, or beating upon, the bars of her caged apartment, the contracted size of which afforded space only for increasing accumulations of filth, a *foul* spectacle; there she stood with naked arms and dishevelled hair; the unwashed frame invested with fragments of unclean garments, the air so extremely offensive, though ventilation was afforded on all sides save one, that it was not possible to remain beyond a few moments without retreating for recovery to the outward air. Irritation of body, produced by utter filth and exposure, incited her to the horrid process of tearing off her skin by inches; her face, neck, and person, were thus disfigured to hideousness; she held up a fragment just rent off; to my exclamation of horror, the mistress replied, "oh, we can't help it; half the skin is off sometimes; we can do nothing with her; and it makes no difference what she eats, for she consumes her own filth as readily as the food which is brought her."

It is now January; a fortnight since, two visitors reported that most wretched outcast as "wallowing in dirty straw, in a place yet more dirty, and without clothing, without fire. Worse cared for than the brutes, and wholly lost to consciousness of decency!" Is the whole story told? What was seen, is; what is reported is not. These gross exposures are not for the pained sight of one alone; all, all, coarse, brutal men, wondering, neglected children, old and young, each and all, witness this lowest, foulest state of miserable humanity. And who protects her, that worse than Paria° outcast, from other wrongs and blacker outrages? I do not *know* that such *have been*. I do know that they are to be dreaded, and that they are not guarded against.

Some may say these things cannot be remedied; these furious maniacs are not to be raised from these base conditions. I *know* they are; could give *many* examples; let *one* suffice. A young woman, a pauper, in a distant town, *Sandis-*

Paria: Variation of *pariah,* a person who is widely despised.

field, was for years a raging maniac. A cage, chains, and *the whip,* were the agents for controlling her, united with harsh tones and profane language. Annually, with others (the town's poor) she was put up at auction, and bid off at the lowest price which was declared for her. One year, not long past, an old man came forward in the number of applicants for the poor wretch; he was taunted and ridiculed; "what would he and his old wife do with such a mere beast?" "My wife says yes," replied he, "and I shall take her." She was given to his charge; he conveyed her home; she was washed, neatly dressed, and placed in a decent bed-room, furnished for comfort and opening into the kitchen. How altered her condition! As yet *the chains* were not off. The first week she was somewhat restless, at times violent, but the quiet kind ways of the old people wrought a change; she received her food decently; forsook acts of violence, and no longer uttered blasphemous or indecent language; after a week, the chain was lengthened, and she was received as a companion into the kitchen. Soon she engaged in trivial employments. "After a fortnight," said the old man, "I knocked off the chains and made her a free woman." She is at times excited, but not violently; they are careful of her diet; they keep her very clean; she calls them "father" and "mother." Go there now and you will find her "clothed," and though not perfectly in her "right mind," so far restored as to be a safe and comfortable inmate.

Newburyport. Visited the almshouse in June last; eighty inmates; seven insane, one idiotic. Commodious and neat house; several of the partially insane apparently very comfortable; two very improperly situated, namely, an insane man, not considered incurable, in an out-building, whose room opened upon what was called "the dead room," affording in lieu of companionship with the living, a contemplation of corpses! The other subject was a woman in a *cellar.* I desired to see her; much reluctance was shown. I pressed the request; the Master of the House stated that she was *in the cellar;* that she was *dangerous to be approached;* that "she had lately attacked his wife;" and *was often naked.* I persisted; "if you will not go with me, give me the keys and I will go alone." Thus importuned, the outer doors were opened. I descended the stairs from within; a strange, unnatural noise seemed to proceed from beneath our feet; at the moment I did not much regard it. My conductor proceeded to remove a padlock, while my eye explored the wide space in quest of the poor woman. All for a moment was still. But judge my horror and amazement, when a door to a closet *beneath* the *staircase* was opened, revealing in the imperfect light a female apparently wasted to a skeleton, partially wrapped in blankets, furnished for the narrow bed on which she was sitting; her countenance furrowed, not by age, but suffering, was the image of distress; in that contracted space, unlighted, unventilated, she poured forth the wailings of despair: mournfully she extended her arms and appealed to me, "why am I consigned to hell? dark—dark—I used to pray, I used to read the Bible—I have done no crime in my heart; I had friends, why have all forsaken me!—my God! my God! why hast *thou* forsaken me!" Those groans, those wailings come up daily, mingling, with how many others, a perpetual and sad memorial. When the good Lord shall require an account of our stewardship, what shall all and each answer!

Perhaps it will be inquired how long, how many days or hours was she imprisoned in these confined limits? *For years!* In another part of the cellar were other small closets, only better, because higher through the entire length, into one of which she by turns was transferred, so as to afford opportunity for fresh whitewashing, &c.

Saugus. December 24; thermometer below zero; drove to the poorhouse; walls garnished with was conducted to the master's family-room by himself; walls garnished with handcuffs and chains, not less than five pair of the former; did not inquire how or on whom applied; thirteen pauper inmates; one insane man; one woman insane; one idiotic man; asked to see them; the two men were shortly led in; appeared pretty decent and comfortable. Requested to see the other insane subject; was denied decidedly; urged the request, and finally secured a reluctant assent. Was led through an outer passage into a lower room, occupied by the paupers; crowded; not neat; ascended a rather low flight of stairs upon an open entry, through the floor of which was introduced a stove pipe, carried along a *few feet,* about six inches above the floor, through which it was reconveyed below. From this entry opens a room of moderate size, having a sashed-window; floor, I think, painted; apartment ENTIRELY unfurnished; no chair, table, nor bed; neither, what is seldom missing, a bundle of straw or lock of hay; cold, very cold; the first movement of my conductor was to throw open a window, a measure imperatively necessary for those who entered. *On the floor* sat a woman, her limbs immovably contracted, so that the knees were brought upward to the chin; the face was concealed; the head rested on the folded arms; for clothing she appeared to have been furnished with *fragments* of many discharged garments; these were folded about her, yet they little benefitted her, if one might judge by the constant shuddering which almost convulsed her poor crippled frame. Woful was this scene; language is feeble to record the misery she was suffering and had suffered! In reply to my inquiry if she could not change her position, I was answered by the master in the negative, and told that the contraction of limbs was occasioned by "neglect and exposure in former years," but *since she had been crazy,* and before she fell under the charge, as I inferred, of her present *guardians.* Poor wretch! she, like many others, was an example of what humanity becomes when the temple of reason falls in ruins, leaving the mortal part to injury and neglect, and showing how much can be endured of privation, exposure, and disease, without extinguishing the lamp of life.

Passing out, the man pointed to a something, revealed to more than one sense, which he called "her bed; and we throw some blankets over her at night." Possibly this is done; others, like myself, might be pardoned a doubt, if they could have seen all I saw, and heard abroad all I heard. The *bed,* so called, was about *three* feet long, and from a half to three-quarters of a yard wide; of old ticking or tow cloth was the case; the contents might have been a *full handful* of hay or straw. My attendant's exclamations on my leaving the house were emphatic, and can hardly be repeated.

The above case recalls another of equal neglect or abuse. Asking my way to the almshouse in Berkeley, which had been repeatedly spoken of as greatly neglected, I was answered as to the direction, and informed that there were "plenty of insane people and idiots there." "Well taken care of?" "Oh, well enough for such sort of creatures." "Any violently insane?" "Yes; my sister's son in there, a real tiger. I kept him here at my house awhile, but it was too much trouble to go on; so I carried him there." "Is he comfortably provided for?" "Well enough." "Has he decent clothes?" "Good enough; wouldn't wear them if he had more." "Food?" "Good enough; good enough for him." "One more question, has he the comfort of a fire?" "Fire? fire, indeed! what does a crazy man need of fire? red–hot iron wants fire as much as he!" And such are sincerely the ideas of not a few persons in regard to the actual wants of the insane. Less regarded than the lowest brutes! no wonder they sink even lower. [. . .]

Violence and severity do but exasperate the Insane: the only availing influence is kindness and firmness. It is amazing what these will produce. How many examples might illustrate this position: I refer to one recently exhibited in Barre. The town Paupers are disposed of annually to some family who, for a stipulated sum agree to take charge of them. One of them, a young woman, was shown to me well clothed, neat, quiet, and employed at needle-work. Is it possible that this is the same being who, but last year, was a raving madwoman, exhibiting every degree of violence in action and speech; a very tigress wrought to fury; caged, chained, beaten, loaded with injuries, and exhibiting the passions which an iron rule might be expected to stimulate and sustain? It is the same person; another family hold her in charge who better understand human nature and human influences; she is no longer chained, caged, and beaten; but if excited, a pair of mittens drawn over the hands secures from mischief. Where will she be next year, after the annual sale?

It is not the insane subject alone who illustrates the power of the all prevailing law of kindness. A poor idiotic young man, a year or two since, used to follow me at times through the prison as I was distributing books and papers: at first he appeared totally stupid, but cheerful expressions, a smile, a trifling gift, seemed gradually to light up the void temple of the intellect, and by slow degrees some faint images of thought passed before the mental vision. He would ask for books, though he could not read. I indulged his fancy and he would appear to experience delight in examining them; and kept them with a singular care. If I read the Bible, he was reverently, wonderingly attentive; if I talked, he listened with a half-conscious aspect. One morning I passed more hurriedly than usual, and did not speak particularly to him. "Me, me, me a book." I returned; "good morning, Jemmy; so you will have a book today? well, keep it carefully." Suddenly turning aside he took the bread brought for his breakfast, and passing it with a hurried earnestness through the bars of his iron door—"Here's bread, a'nt you hungry?" Never may I forget the tone and grateful affectionate aspect of that poor idiot. How much might we do to bring back or restore the mind, if we but knew how to touch the instrument with a skilful hand! [. . .]

Of the dangers and mischiefs sometimes following the location of insane persons in our almhouses, I will record but one more example. In Worcester, has 20 for several years resided a young woman, a lunatic pauper of decent life and respectable family. I have seen her as she usually appeared, listless and silent, almost or quite sunk into a state of dementia, sitting one amidst the family, "but not of them." A few weeks since, revisiting that almshouse, judge my horror and amazement to see her negligently bearing in her arms a young infant, of which I was told she was the unconscious parent! Who was the father, none could or would declare. Disqualified for the performance of maternal cares and duties, regarding the helpless little creature with a perplexed, or indifferent gaze, she sat a silent, but O how eloquent, a pleader for the protection of others of her neglected and outraged sex! Details of that black story would not strengthen the cause; needs it a weightier plea, than the sight of that forlorn creature and her wailing infant? Poor little child, more than orphan from birth, in this unfriendly world! a demented Mother—a Father, on whom the sun might blush or refuse to shine!

Men of Massachusetts, I beg, I implore, I demand, pity and protection, for these of my suffering, outraged sex!—Fathers, Husbands, Brothers, I would supplicate you for this boon—but what do I say? I dishonor you, divest you at once of christianity and humanity—does this appeal imply distrust. If it comes burthened with a doubt of your righteousness in this Legislation, then blot it out; while I declare confidence in your honor, not less than your humanity. Here you will put away the cold, calculating spirit of selfishness and self-seeking; lay off the armor of local strife and political opposition; here and now, for once, forgetful of the earthly and perishable, come up to these halls and consecrate them with one heart and one mind to works of righteousness and just judgment. Become the benefactors of your race, the just guardians of the solemn rights you hold in trust. Raise up the fallen; succor the desolate; restore the outcast; defend the helpless; and for your eternal and great reward, receive the benediction. . . . "Well done, good and faithful servants, become rulers over many things!"

QUESTIONS FOR DISCUSSION

1. What feelings does Dix appeal to in this essay? What assumptions has she made about her audience?
2. How does Dix use gender to inspire feeling?
3. Why was it useful for Dix to emphasize that she was reporting conditions she had seen with her own eyes?
4. Of all the abuses recorded by Dix, which made the strongest impression on you?
5. Consider the use of italics in this essay. How do you account for the words and phrases that Dix decided to italicize?
6. How does Dix demonstrate that the insane poor would benefit from better treatment?

SUGGESTIONS FOR WRITING

1. Many of the homeless living on our streets today are mentally ill people who in an earlier era might have been institutionalized. Research the conditions under which such people live, and write a plea on their behalf that

would touch the hearts of men and women who believe that the poor are well provided for.

2. Visit a nursing home, and draw on this experience to move readers to sympathize with the people you have seen. Remember that the patients you see are entitled to privacy and respect. Ask permission to visit the institution you have chosen, and ask permission of any patient you wish to visit. If you engage in conversation and learn data you would like to include in your essay, explain that you are writing a paper about nursing homes and ask if you can include what you have been told.

3. Write a speech that would move members of your state legislature to pay attention to a group of people who are suffering from neglect or abuse.

LINKS ▪ ▪ ▪

▪ WITHIN THE BOOK

Mental health issues are also addressed by Jennifer Egan in "The Thin Red Line" (pages 151–164) and Susanna Kaysen in "My Diagnosis" (pages 321–328).

▪ ELSEWHERE IN PRINT

Brown, Thomas J. *Dorothea Dix: New England Reformer.* Cambridge: Harvard UP, 1998.

Dix, Dorothea. *On Behalf of the Insane Poor: Selected Reports, 1843–1852.* New York: Arno, 1971.

———. *Remarks on Prisons and Prison Discipline in the United States. 1845.* Montclair: Patterson, 1984.

Gollaher, David. *Voice for the Mad: The Life of Dorothea Dix.* New York: Free, 1995.

Herstek, Amy Paulson. *Dorothea Dix: Crusader for the Mentally Ill.* Berkeley Heights: Enslow, 2001.

Lightner, David, L., ed. *Asylum, Prison, and Poorhouse: The Writings and Reform Work of Dorothea Dix in Illinois.* Carbondale: Southern Illinois UP, 1999.

▪ ONLINE

- Brief Biography
  <http://www.webster.edu/~woolflm/dorotheadix.html>
- Historic Asylums
  <http://www.darkspire.org/asylums>
- Ignoring Serious Mental Illness
  <http://www.apa.org/monitor/nov99/pi.html>

A MODEST PROPOSAL FOR PREVENTING THE CHILDREN OF POOR PEOPLE IN IRELAND FROM BEING A BURDEN TO THEIR PARENTS OR COUNTRY, AND FOR MAKING THEM BENEFICIAL TO THE PUBLIC

Jonathan Swift

Born to English parents who had immigrated to Ireland, Jonathan Swift (1667–1745) is widely considered one of the most important British writers of the eighteenth century. Although he lived in England for many years and had close ties to the ruling class there, he nevertheless cared deeply for the country of his birth. Ordained a priest in the Church of Ireland, he served as Dean of St. Patrick's Cathedral in Dublin for more than thirty years. A prolific writer who took an active role in politics, Swift is best remembered today as the author of Gulliver's Travels *(1726) and "A Modest Proposal" (1729).*

As you prepare to read "A Modest Proposal," you should bear in mind that Ireland was an English colony during Swift's lifetime. Following a series of rebellions there, the English had imposed increasingly strict laws upon the Irish—many of which caused great hardship, especially for Catholics and tenant farmers. Indeed, Oliver Cromwell (a British general who eventually ran the British government) had invaded Ireland and suppressed a major uprising there in 1649—only eighteen years before Swift's birth. When Swift wrote "A Modest Proposal," he was keenly aware of how the Irish people were suffering under British rule. You should also understand that Swift was a great satirist. So if the proposal he offers in the following essay strikes you as extreme rather than modest, think about what motivated Swift to write as he did. You might also consider what can be learned from the epitaph on Swift's grave: "He has gone where fierce indignation can lacerate his heart no more—depart, wayfarer, and imitate if you are able one who to the utmost strenuously championed liberty."

It is a melancholy object to those who walk through this great town° or travel in the country, when they see the streets, the roads, and cabin doors, crowded with beggars of the female sex, followed by three, four, or six children, all in rags and importuning every passenger for an alms. These mothers, instead of being able to work for their honest livelihood, are forced to employ all their time in strolling to beg sustenance for their helpless infants: who as they grow up either turn thieves for want of work, or leave their dear native country to fight for the Pretender° in Spain, or sell themselves to the Barbadoes.°

---

great town: Dublin. *Pretender:* James Stuart, son of James II and a Catholic. In 1688 the throne had gone to his sister Mary, a Protestant who ruled with her husband, William of Orange. *Barbadoes:* To get out of Ireland, many people went as indentured servants to Barbados and other British colonies.

I think it is agreed by all parties that this prodigious number of children in the arms, or on the backs, or at the heels of their mothers, and frequently of their fathers, is in the present deplorable state of the kingdom a very great additional grievance; and, therefore, whoever could find out a fair, cheap, and easy method of making these children sound, useful members of the commonwealth, would deserve so well of the public as to have his statue set up for a preserver of the nation.

But my intention is very far from being confined to provide only for the children of professed beggars; it is of a much greater extent, and shall take in the whole number of infants at a certain age who are born of parents in effect as little able to support them as those who demand our charity in the streets.

As to my own part, having turned my thoughts for many years upon this important subject, and maturely weighed the several schemes of other projectors, I have always found them grossly mistaken in their computation. It is true, a child just dropped from its dam may be supported by her milk for a solar year, with little other nourishment; at most not above the value of 2s., which the mother may certainly get, or the value in scraps, by her lawful occupation of begging; and it is exactly at one year old that I propose to provide for them in such a manner as instead of being a charge upon their parents or the parish, or wanting food and raiment for the rest of their lives, they shall on the contrary contribute to the feeding, and partly to the clothing, of many thousands.

There is likewise another great advantage in my scheme, that it will prevent those voluntary abortions, and that horrid practice of women murdering their bastard children, alas! too frequent among us! sacrificing the poor innocent babes I doubt more to avoid the expense than the shame, which would move tears and pity in the most savage and inhuman breast.

The number of souls in this kingdom being usually reckoned one million and a half, of these I calculate there may be about 200,000 couples whose wives are breeders; from which number I subtract 30,000 couples who are able to maintain their own children (although I apprehend there cannot be so many, under the present distress of the kingdom); but this being granted, there will remain 170,000 breeders. I again subtract 50,000 for those women who miscarry, or whose children die by accident or disease within the year. There only remain 120,000 children of poor parents annually born. The question therefore is, how this number shall be reared and provided for? which, as I have already said, under the present situation of affairs, is utterly impossible by all the methods hitherto proposed. For we can neither employ them in handicraft or agriculture; we neither build houses (I mean in the country) nor cultivate land; they can very seldom pick up a livelihood by stealing, till they arrive at six years old, except where they are of towardly parts; although I confess they learn the rudiments much earlier; during which time they can, however, be properly looked upon only as probationers; as I have been informed by a principal gentleman in the country of Cavan, who protested to me that he never knew above one or two instances under the age of six, even in a part of the kingdom so renowned for the quickest proficiency in that art.

I am assured by our merchants, that a boy or a girl before twelve years old is no saleable commodity; and even when they come to this age they will not yield above *3l.* or *3l. 2s. 6d.*° at most on the Exchange; which cannot turn to account either to the parents or kingdom, the charge of nutriment and rags having been at least four times that value.

I shall now therefore humbly propose my own thoughts, which I hope will not be liable to the least objection.

I have been assured by a very knowing American of my acquaintance in London, that a young healthy child well nursed is at a year old a most delicious, nourishing, and wholesome food, whether stewed, roasted, baked, or broiled; and I make no doubt that it will equally serve in a fricassee or a ragout.

I do therefore humbly offer it to public consideration that of the 120,000 children already computed, 20,000 may be reserved for breed, whereof only one-fourth part to be males; which is more than we allow to sheep, black cattle, or swine; and my reason is, that these children are seldom the fruits of marriage, a circumstance not much regarded by our savages; therefore one male will be sufficient to serve four females. That the remaining 100,000 may, at a year old, be offered in sale to the persons of quality and fortune through the kingdom; always advising the mother to let them suck plentifully in the last month, so as to render them plump and fat for a good table. A child will make two dishes at an entertainment for friends; and when the family dines alone, the fore or hind quarter will make a reasonable dish, and seasoned with a little pepper or salt will be very good boiled on the fourth day, especially in winter.

I have reckoned upon a medium that a child just born will weigh 12 pounds, and in a solar year, if tolerably nursed, will increase to 28 pounds.

I grant this food will be somewhat dear, and therefore very proper for landlords, who, as they have already devoured most of the parents, seem to have the best title to the children.

Infant's flesh will be in season throughout the year, but more plentiful in March, and a little before and after: for we are told by a grave author, an eminent French physician, that fish being a prolific diet, there are more children born in Roman Catholic countries about nine months after Lent than at any other season; therefore, reckoning a year after Lent, the markets will be more glutted than usual, because the number of popish infants is at least three to one in this kingdom: and therefore it will have one other collateral advantage, by lessening the number of papists among us.

I have already computed the charge of nursing a beggar's child (in which list I reckon all cottagers, laborers, and four-fifths of the farmers) to be about *2s.* per annum, rags included; and I believe no gentleman would repine to give *10s.* for the carcass of a good fat child, which, as I have said, will make four dishes of excellent nutritive meat, when he has only some particular friend or his own family to dine with him. Thus the squire will learn to be a

_____

3l. 2s. 6d.: Three pounds, two shillings, and six pence.

10

good landlord, and grow popular among the tenants; the mother will have *8s.* net profit, and be fit for work till she produces another child.

Those who are more thrifty (as I must confess the times require) may flay the carcass; the skin of which artificially dressed will make admirable gloves for ladies, and summer boots for fine gentlemen.

As to our city of Dublin, shambles° may be appointed for this purpose in the most convenient parts of it, and butchers we may be assured will not be wanting: although I rather recommend buying the children alive, and dressing them hot from the knife as we do roasting pigs.

A very worthy person, a true lover of his country, and whose virtues I highly esteem, was lately pleased in discoursing on this matter to offer a refinement upon my scheme. He said that many gentlemen of this kingdom, having of late destroyed their deer, he conceived that the want of venison might be well supplied by the bodies of young lads and maidens, not exceeding fourteen years of age nor under twelve; so great a number of both sexes in every country being not ready to starve for want of work and service; and these to be disposed of by their parents, if alive, or otherwise by their nearest relations. But with due deference to so excellent a friend and so deserving a patriot, I cannot be altogether in his sentiments; for as to the males, my American acquaintance assured me from frequent experience that their flesh was generally tough and lean, like that of our schoolboys by continual exercise, and their taste disagreeable; and to fatten them would not answer the charge. Then as to the females, it would, I think, with humble submission be a loss to the public, because they soon would become breeders themselves: and besides, it is not improbable that some scrupulous people might be apt to censure such a practice (although indeed very unjustly), as a little bordering upon cruelty; which, I confess, has always been with me the strongest objection against any project, howsoever well intended.

But in order to justify my friend, he confessed that this expedient was put into his head by the famous Psalmanazar, a native of the island Formosa, who came from thence to London about twenty years ago: and in conversation told my friend, that in his country when any young person happened to be put to death, the executioner sold the carcass to persons of quality as a prime dainty; and that in his time the body of a plump girl of fifteen, who was crucified for an attempt to poison the emperor, was sold to his imperial majesty's prime minister of state, and other great mandarins of the court, in joints from the gibbet, at 400 crowns. Neither indeed can I deny, that if the same use were made of several plump girls in this town, who without one single groat to their fortunes cannot stir abroad without a chair, and appear at the playhouse and assemblies in foreign fineries which they never will pay for, the kingdom would not be the worse.

Some persons of a desponding spirit are in great concern about that vast number of poor people, who are aged, diseased, or maimed, and I have been

---

shambles: Slaughterhouses.

desired to employ my thoughts what course may be taken to ease the nation of so grievous an encumbrance. But I am not in the least pain upon that matter, because it is very well known that they are every day dying and rotting by cold and famine, and filth and vermin, as fast as can be reasonably expected. And as to the young laborers, they are now in as hopeful a condition: they cannot get work, and consequently pine away for want of nourishment, to a degree that if at any time they are accidentally hired to common labor, they have not strength to perform it; and thus the country and themselves are happily delivered from the evils to come.

I have too long digressed, and therefore shall return to my subject. I think   *20* the advantages by the proposal which I have made are obvious and many, as well as the highest importance.

For first, as I have already observed, it would greatly lessen the number of papists, with whom we are yearly overrun, being the principal breeders of the nation as well as our most dangerous enemies; and who stay at home on purpose to deliver the kingdom to the Pretender, hoping to take their advantage by the absence of so many good Protestants, who have chosen rather to leave their country than stay at home and pay tithes against their conscience to an Episcopal curate.

Secondly, the poor tenants will have something valuable of their own, which by law may be made liable to distress and help to pay their landlord's rent, their corn and cattle being already seized, and money a thing unknown.

Thirdly, whereas the maintenance of 100,000 children from two years old and upward, cannot be computed at less than *10s.* a-piece per annum, the nation's stock will be thereby increased £50,000 per annum, beside the profit of a new dish introduced to the tables of all gentlemen of fortune in the kingdom who have any refinement in taste. And the money will circulate among ourselves, the goods being entirely of our own growth and manufacture.

Fourthly, the constant breeders, beside the gain of *8s.* sterling per annum by the sale of their children, will be rid of the charge of maintaining them after the first year.

Fifthly, this food would likewise bring great custom to taverns, where the   *25* vintners will certainly be so prudent as to procure the best receipts for dressing it to perfection, and consequently have their houses frequented by all the fine gentlemen, who justly value themselves upon their knowledge in good eating; and a skillful cook, who understands how to oblige his guests, will contrive to make it as expensive as they please.

Sixthly, this would be a great inducement to marriage, which all wise nations have either encouraged by rewards or enforced by laws and penalties. It would increase the care and tenderness of mothers toward their children, when they were sure of a settlement for life to the poor babes, provided in some sort by the public, to their annual profit instead of expense. We should see an honest emulation among the married women, which of them would bring the fattest child to the market. Men would become as fond of their wives during the time of their pregnancy as they are now of their mares in foal, their cows in calf, their sows when they are ready to farrow; nor offer to beat or kick them (as is too frequent a practice) for fear of a miscarriage.

Many other advantages might be enumerated. For instance, the addition of some thousand carcasses in our exportation of barreled beef, the propagation of swine's flesh, and improvement in the art of making good bacon, so much wanted among us by the great destruction of pigs, too frequent at our table; which are no way comparable in taste or magnificence to a well-grown, fat, yearling child, which roasted whole will make a considerable figure at a lord mayor's feast or any other public entertainment. But this and many others I omit, being studious of brevity.

Supposing that 1,000 families in this city would be constant customers for infants' flesh, besides others who might have it at merry-meetings, particularly at weddings and christenings, I compute that Dublin would take off annually about 20,000 carcasses; and the rest of the kingdom (where probably they will be sold somewhat cheaper) the remaining 80,000.

I can think of no one objection that will possibly be raised against this proposal, unless it should be urged that the number of people will be thereby much lessened in the kingdom. This I freely own, and it was indeed one principal design in offering it to the world. I desire the reader will observe, that I calculate my remedy for this one individual kingdom of Ireland and for no other that ever was, is, or I think ever can be upon earth. Therefore let no man talk to me of other expedients: of taxing our absentees at 5s. a pound: of using neither clothes nor household furniture except what is of our own growth and manufacture: of utterly rejecting the materials and instruments that promote foreign luxury: of curing the expensiveness of pride, vanity, idleness, and gaming in our women: of introducing a vein of parsimony, prudence, and temperance: of learning to love our country, in the want of which we differ even from Laplanders and the inhabitants of Topinamboo°: of quitting our animosities and factions, not acting any longer like the Jews, who were murdering one another at the very moment their city° was taken: of being a little cautious not to sell our country and conscience for nothing: of teaching landlords to have at least one degree of mercy toward their tenants: lastly, of putting a spirit of honesty, industry, and skill into our shopkeepers; who, if a resolution could now be taken to buy only our native goods, would immediately unite to cheat and exact upon us in the price, the measure, and the goodness, nor could ever yet be brought to make one fair proposal of just dealing, though often and earnestly invited to it.

Therefore I repeat, let no man talk to me of these and the like expedients, till he has at least some glimpse of hope that there will be ever some hearty and sincere attempt to put them in practice.   30

But as to myself, having been wearied out for many years with offering vain, idle, visionary thoughts, and at length utterly despairing of success, I

Topinamboo: Swift's name for the land of the Tobinambou, a tribe of Indians in Brazil. *their city:* Jerusalem, conquered by the Roman army during the first century.

fortunately fell upon this proposal; which, as it is wholly new, so it has something solid and real, of no expense and little trouble, full in our own power, and whereby we can incur no danger of disobliging England. For this kind of commodity will not bear exportation, the flesh being of too tender a consistence to admit a long continuance in salt, although perhaps I could name a country which would be glad to eat up our whole nation without it.

After all, I am not so violently bent upon my own opinion as to reject any offer proposed by wise men, which shall be found equally innocent, cheap, easy, and effectual. But before something of that kind shall be advanced in contradiction to my scheme, and offering a better, I desire the author or authors will be pleased maturely to consider two points. First, as things now stand, how they will be able to find food and raiment for 100,000 useless mouths and backs. And secondly, there being a round million of creatures in human figure throughout this kingdom, whose subsistence put into a common stock would leave them in debt 2,000,000*l*. sterling, adding those who are beggars by profession to the bulk of farmers, cottagers, and laborers, with the wives and children who are beggars in effect; I desire those politicians who dislike my overture, and may perhaps be so bold as to attempt an answer, that they will first ask the parents of these mortals, whether they would not at this day think it a great happiness to have been sold for food at a year old in the manner I prescribe, and thereby have avoided such a perpetual scene of misfortunes as they have since gone through by the oppression of landlords, the impossibility of paying rent without money or trade, the want of common sustenance, with neither house nor clothes to cover them from the inclemencies of the weather, and the most inevitable prospect of entailing the like or greater miseries upon their breed for ever.

I profess, in the sincerity of my heart, that I have not the least personal interest in endeavoring to promote this necessary work, having no other motive than the public good of my country, by advancing our trade, providing for infants, relieving the poor, and giving some pleasure to the rich. I have no children by which I can propose to get a single penny; the youngest being nine years old, and my wife past child-bearing.

QUESTIONS FOR DISCUSSION

1. At what point in this essay did you first become aware that Swift is being ironic?
2. What steps has Swift taken to make his proposal seem "modest" and his voice reasonable?
3. Why does the speaker in this essay believe that his proposal would be unsuitable for adolescents? Why isn't he worried about the problem of the elderly poor?
4. What does this essay reveal about Ireland under British domination?
5. Does Swift offer any alternative to eating the children of the poor? If there are alternatives to cannibalism, why devote so many paragraphs to a proposal that most people would quickly reject?

6. What is the function of the concluding paragraph?
7. Writers of textbooks often reprint this essay as an example of writing to persuade, and the essay does incorporate such persuasive strategies as anticipating and responding to points that might be raised by one's opponents. How would you define Swift's purpose? Is he writing to persuade readers to adopt specific proposals? Or is he writing primarily to shock people out of complacency?

SUGGESTIONS FOR WRITING

1. Use irony to write a "modest" solution to a contemporary social problem.
2. Would you be willing to sell your child on the black market? Imagine yourself to be desperately poor, and write a response to someone who has offered to buy your child.
3. Research conflicts between Catholics and Protestants in contemporary Ireland. Then write an essay that would move an Irish audience to overcome religious prejudice.

LINKS ■ ■ ■

■ WITHIN THE BOOK

For another famous example of eighteenth-century prose, see "The Declaration of Independence" (pages 529–532).

■ ELSEWHERE IN PRINT

Mahony, Robert. *Jonathan Swift: The Irish Identity.* New Haven: Yale UP, 1995.

McMinn, Joseph. *Jonathan's Travels: Swift and Ireland.* New York: St. Martin's, 1994.

Ogborn, Jane, and Peter Buckroyd. *Satire.* Cambridge: Cambridge UP, 2000.

Pittock, Murray. *Inventing and Resisting Britain: Cultural Identities in Britain and Ireland, 1685–1789.* New York: St. Martin's, 1997.

Swift, Jonathan. *Gulliver's Travels.* 1726. Ed. and introd. Paul Turner. New York: Oxford UP, 1998.

———. *A Modest Proposal and Other Satires.* 1729. Introd. George Levine. Amherst: Prometheus, 1995.

———. *A Tale of a Tub and Other Works.* 1704. Eds. Angus Ross and David Woolley. New York: Oxford UP, 1986.

(continues)

LINKS ■ ■ ■ *(continued)*

■ **ONLINE**

- Brief Biography
  <http://www.english.upenn.edu/~jlynch/Frank/People/swift.html>
- Crticism Collection
  <http://www.ipl.org/cgi-bin/ref/litcrit/litcrit.out.pl?au=swi-23>
- Eighteenth-Century Studies
  <http://eserver.org/18th/>
- Irish History on the Web
  <http://www.vms.utexas.edu/~jdana/irehist.html>

7

Writing to Persuade Others

As the previous chapter has shown, writers are sometimes motivated to move readers simply for the sake of producing an emotion from which some unspecified good may follow. The evocation of feeling may be necessary when working for change—be it civil rights or the elimination of poverty. But when we want to argue for a specific change, we must do more than move our audience. We must persuade them to support a proposal or undertake an action.

Persuasion ranges from advertising to scholarly arguments. Between these extremes lie dozens of situations in which persuasion is fundamental to everyday life. When you apply for a job, propose marriage, try to borrow money, or ask your landlord to fix the plumbing, you are using persuasion in an attempt to get someone to do something you want for yourself. At other times you use persuasion to achieve benefits for others—as in trying to raise money for the victims of a famine or trying to persuade the government to protect an endangered species of wildlife. And on other occasions you use persuasion when there is no question of benefits but there is a problem that needs to be resolved—as in trying to improve the functioning of a committee on which you serve when it cannot accomplish anything because of personal conflicts. What all of these examples have in common is that they assume as a given the need to change someone's mind. We need to persuade others only when differences of opinion exist. Persuasion is unnecessary when there is already widespread agreement, and it is inappropriate when questions allow for only one correct answer.

Classical rhetoric recognized that persuasion was accomplished through three means: the credibility of the writer/speaker (*ethos*), the logic of the argument (*logos*), and the skill with which appropriate feelings are inspired (*pathos*). This threefold approach to persuasion has prevailed in the West for almost two thousand years, but its practitioners vary in what they emphasize and what strategies they recommend. Aristotle, for example, believed that ethos is the most important aspect of persuasion and that we make ourselves believable by how we present ourselves in what we say and write. But Aristotle defined ethos as something created within the work (from which it would follow that a bad person could seem to be credible because of his skill in arguing). Other rhetoricians have argued that ethos cannot be created artificially and that only good people (or people who are actively trying to be good) can write truly persuasive arguments. Still others have emphasized the role of pathos. Cicero, one of the greatest speakers of the ancient world, argued that nothing is more important than being able to move an audience: "For men decide far more problems by hate, or love, or lust, or rage, or sorrow, or joy, or hope, or fear, or illusion, or some other inward emotion, than by reality, or authority, or any legal standard, or judicial precedent, or statute."

In short, there has been—and there still is—no universal agreement about how to persuade others. Different opinions prevailed in the classical world, and the debate is still going on. But you can be guided by two basic principles:

- Your strategy may vary depending on the topic and your audience, but you should always consider the extent to which you have employed ethos, logos, and pathos. As a general rule, an argument depending on only one of these methods probably won't be as persuasive as an argument using more than one.

- Although people sometimes make decisions on impulse, and some forms of persuasion (like television commercials) are designed to inspire unreasoned decisions, the most persuasive arguments are those that still make sense after we have thought about them for a while. It follows that persuasion should appeal to the mind as well as the heart.

USING LOGIC

Appealing to the mind requires at least some familiarity with logic. Classical rhetoric teaches two types of logic, inductive and deductive reasoning. Modern rhetoric has explored alternative forms of reasoning designed to complement traditional approaches. Whatever type of logic you decide best suits your needs in a specific argument, you should realize that writers are usually free to use one or more of the following options.

Inductive Reasoning

To reason inductively means to use examples to discover what seems to be true. In an inductive argument, a writer presents a series of examples (or pieces of evidence) and draws a conclusion from their significance. Reaching this conclusion means going beyond the accumulated evidence and making a reasonable guess, the *inductive leap*. Induction is persuasive when the evidence is sufficient to justify the conclusion. Writers who make the inductive leap from insufficient evidence are said to be jumping to conclusions, a failure in reasoning so common that it has become a cliché.

When you use *induction* carefully, you will reach a conclusion that is probably true. But you should recognize that your conclusion is probable rather than absolute. It is always possible that other evidence, which you haven't considered, could lead to a different conclusion. For example, suppose that it is the first week of classes and you are taking a math course from a professor with whom you have never worked before. For each of the first three classes, the professor arrives late and lectures in a disorganized manner that is difficult to understand. Tomorrow is the last day you can drop the class and still add a new one in its place. Concluding that you are dealing with a bad math teacher, you decide to drop his course and substitute another in its place. Within the constraints of daily life, which often require us to make decisions quickly, you have used induction to make a decision that seems reasonable under the circumstances. However, it is possible that the professor had a bad week because he was staying up all night with a sick child and that his performance will improve dramatically in the following weeks.

As a rule, your conclusions will be the strongest when they rest on a foundation built of many separate pieces of evidence. When a serious conclusion is arrived at inductively, it will almost certainly have extensive information behind it. The scientific method illustrates induction at its best. Researchers conduct hundreds and sometimes thousands of experiments before arguing for a new type of medical treatment, and after results are published, other researchers seek to verify them independently. But however solid these conclusions seem to be, they are often challenged by new studies that take a different approach. So no matter how many examples support an inductively derived conclusion, you can never be certain that you have managed to discover an absolute truth.

Deductive Reasoning

To reason deductively means to identify assumptions that are already believed to be true and to discover an additional truth that follows from these widely accepted beliefs. A deductive argument reflects the logic of a *syllogism* in which a major and a minor premise lead to a conclusion that is necessarily true:

Major premise: All men have hearts.
Minor premise: Bill is a man.
Conclusion: Bill has a heart.

In this case the reasoning is both valid and true. It is *valid* because it follows the conventions of logic: If we accept the major and minor premises, then we must recognize that the conclusion follows logically from them. Occasionally, however, you will find syllogisms that are valid but untrue.

Major premise: All chemistry professors are boring.
Minor premise: Veronica is a chemistry professor.
Conclusion: Veronica is boring.

Although this syllogism follows the same pattern as the previous one and is valid, it is untrue because it rests on a highly questionable major premise. For a syllogism to be *true* as well as valid, both the major and minor premises must be universally accepted.

Unfortunately, there are relatively few propositions that everyone accepts as true—or "self-evident," as Thomas Jefferson declares at the beginning of the Declaration of Independence. And the number seems to be decreasing. Consider what happens if we modify our first example:

Major premise:	All men have functioning kidneys.
Minor premise:	Bill is a man.
Conclusion:	Bill has functioning kidneys.

A hundred years ago, this syllogism would have been both valid and true; today, it is valid but untrue, since dialysis machines allow people to live without functioning kidneys. Conceivably, the day may come when people can function without hearts. (We have already seen several attempts to support life with artificial hearts.)

Consider, also, that different readers have different responses to language and that the same reader can respond differently to the same words in different contexts. To put it simply, words can (and do) change meaning. The major premise of our first example ("All men have hearts") is already more questionable than it would have been fifty years ago. A writer beginning with this statement could face such questions as "What do you mean by *men*? Does that include women?" and "What about *hearts*? Do you mean a body organ or a capacity for feeling emotion?"

But writing an essay is not the same as writing a syllogism: You have more than three sentences to make your case. If you want to organize an essay deductively because your position derives from a fundamental principle that you are confident your audience will share, you should pace yourself according to the needs of the situation. On some topics, for some audiences, you may need to spend several paragraphs establishing your premise. At other times, you may be able to take your premise for granted and offer what is called an *enthymeme,* or two-part deductive argument from which the major premise has been omitted. Abbreviating an argument in this way does not necessarily mean that it will be shorter; it just means that you have omitted one step in order to emphasize other aspects of your case.

Substantive Reasoning

Over the years, philosophers have favored deductive reasoning because it seemed to be the type of logic most likely to lead to truth. But many writers find it ill-suited for argumentation, and philosophers increasingly acknowledge other forms of reasoning. After spending many years analyzing arguments in practical fields such as politics and law, Chaim Perelman concluded that formal logic is seldom appropriate, because argument is more concerned with gaining the adherence of an audience than with demonstrating the truth of abstract propositions:

> What are we to think of this reduction to two forms of reasoning of all the wide variety of arguments that men use in their discussions and in pleading a cause or in justifying an action? Yet, since the time of Aristotle, logic has confined its study to deductive and inductive reasoning. [. . .] As a result, an argument that cannot be reduced to canonical form is regarded as logically valueless. (*The New Rhetoric and the Humanities* [Dordrecht, Holland: Reidel, 1979], 26)

Perelman showed that, when we actually examine arguments that we find persuasive, we realize that many of them seem reasonable even though they do not conform strictly to the conventions of induction or deduction.

At about the same time that Perelman was conducting his research in Belgium, the British philosopher Stephen Toulmin was reaching a conclusion similar to Perelman's. Analyzing arguments made within various fields, Toulmin discovered that they had certain features in common. This discovery led him to offer a new model of argument that is easy for writers to use. *Substantive logic* was the term he preferred for his system, a working logic suitable for the needs of the diverse range of arguments identified by Perelman and other theorists.

According to Toulmin, every argument includes a **claim,** which is the assertion or conclusion the argument is trying to prove. The claim is supported by **data,** which describe the various types of evidence (such as facts, personal experience, or appeals to authority) that lead an audience to decide that the claim is reasonable. Both the claim and the data are stated explicitly in the argument. Underlying them, however, and not necessarily made explicit (although they can be) are what Toulmin called **warrants.** He described warrants as "bridges [that] authorize the sort of step to which our argument commits us." Warrants may be directly stated, but very often (especially when they are obvious) they are not.

Here is one of the examples that Toulmin used to illustrate his model:

Claim: Harry is a British subject.
Data: Harry was born in Bermuda.
Warrant: A man born in Bermuda will be a British subject.

As you can see from this example, the claim is based directly on its data. The warrant is simply explanatory; its function is to show why the claim follows from the data. A good way to understand the warrant, especially when it has not been explicitly stated, is to imagine a statement beginning with either *since* or *because.* In the example just cited, the data support the claim, since people born in Bermuda are British subjects. If you were making this argument in Bermuda or in England, you could probably assume that your audience would understand the warrant even if you did not state it. On the other hand, if you were making this argument in Tibet, you would probably need to make sure that the warrant was clearly understood.

Behind any warrant is what Toulmin called **backing.** The backing, or grounds, for a warrant will vary from argument to argument and from field to field. For the example about Bermuda, the backing consists of the specific pieces of legislation that determine British citizenship. Like the warrant, backing may be either explicit or implicit in an argument. But unlike the warrant, which is a generalization, backing consists of facts. If you use Toulmin's model for writing persuasive essays, you should always ask yourself if you could come up with backing for your warrant if someone were to question its legitimacy.

For writers, one of the advantages of Toulmin's model is that it does not require a fixed pattern of organization. You can arrange your ideas in whatever sequence seems best suited for your work, as long as you are careful to provide data for any claim you make and are able to explain why the data support the claim when the link between them is not immediately clear. Another advantage of Toulmin's model is that it easily incorporates **qualifiers,** such as *probably* or *unless,* that protect the overall integrity of your arguments from exceptions that could be used to challenge what you are arguing. When arguing about Harry's citizenship, for example, you could point out that the data support the claim unless Harry's parents were aliens in Bermuda or unless he has become a naturalized citizen of another country.

The Toulmin model for reasoning provides a useful means of analyzing the arguments you write and read. However an argument is organized, and whatever rhetorical strategies are used within it, the work should include a clear assertion or proposition (the claim), evidence to support that claim (or data), and a principle or assumption that gives further support to the claim (the warrant). The warrant should be easy to understand even if it is not explicitly stated, and there should be additional support (or backing) that could be introduced if the warrant might be challenged. Consider, for example, the argument in this chapter on racial profiling by Stuart Taylor, Jr. His claim is that "racial profiling involves real discrimination." He backs this claim with data from states such as New Jersey, Maryland, Florida, and Louisiana. Although he does not state his warrant, it can be inferred from the argument: American citizens of any race should enjoy equal protection under the law. Even if this warrant is not always honored, backing for it can be found in the U.S. Constitution, Supreme Court decisions, laws passed by Congress, and the laws of many states.

LOGICAL FALLACIES

Whatever type of reasoning you use, you should try to be alert for certain errors that can undermine your case. The detailed study of logic reveals many different ways arguments can break down. Dwelling on these *logical fallacies,* as they are called, can sometimes make writers feel that writing to persuade is more difficult than it really is. Nevertheless, having some familiarity with a few of the most common fallacies can help you evaluate the arguments you read and revise those you write.

Ad Hominem Argument

Latin for "to the man," an *ad hominem* argument is a personal attack on someone whose view differs from that of the arguer. Writers who make *ad hominem* arguments undermine their credibility in at least two ways: To attack an opponent, rather than what an opponent has argued, is to ignore the real issues under consideration. Personal attacks also appear to be mean-spirited, and such attacks can alienate an impartial audience. When a writer arguing for gun control attacks members of the National Rifle Association as "macho men who don't understand the definition of a civilized society," she is offending the people she most needs to persuade and probably is making unbiased readers sympathize with the opponents she just attacked.

There are, of course, some situations in which it can be legitimate to question the personal integrity of an opponent. In a political campaign, for example, voters might decide that a candidate who has cheated on his income tax cannot be trusted to govern, no matter how appealing his positions on various issues are. But even in politics, where personal attacks can sometimes be justified, people quickly tire of a campaign that seems to consist of nothing but *ad hominem* arguments. As a general rule, it is more honorable to focus argument on ideas rather than personalities.

Appeal to False Authority

A good way to support an argument is to cite testimony from authorities in the field you are writing about. If you are writing about child care, for instance, you may wish to incorporate the views of a respected pediatrician. But knowledge in one field does not make someone expert in another. Citing the pediatrician in an argument about the space program is an appeal to a false authority. Advertisements offer many examples of this fallacy by attempting to persuade us to buy products that have been endorsed by well-known actors or athletes who probably know no more about the product than we do.

But *appeals to false authority* also appear in written arguments—in part because well-known people sometimes enjoy making public statements on anything that happens to interest them. Quote a novelist on writing novels, and you will have appealed to a legitimate authority. Quote that same novelist on the conduct of American foreign policy, and, unless the novelist happens to be an expert on international affairs as well, you will have appealed to a false authority.

Begging the Question

Writers *beg the question* when they begin an argument by assuming what they actually need to prove. At its most obvious, begging the question takes the form of a statement that leads nowhere because it goes around in a circle: "College is too expensive because it costs more than it is worth." This statement simply makes the same assertion two ways. An argument could be written to show that college is too expensive, but it would need to be supported with evidence rather than repetition. Begging the question can also take more subtle forms, such as introducing a word (like *unfair*) that expresses an unsupported value judgment.

Hasty Generalization

This fallacy, sometimes called *jumping to conclusions*, occurs when a writer draws a conclusion based on insufficient evidence. Consider, for example, a personnel director who decides, "I don't think we should hire any other graduates of that school; we hired Randy, and he couldn't do anything right." To judge all the graduates of a school by one person is to jump to a conclusion. People often jump to conclusions in daily life, especially when decisions are influenced by feeling: "I know you two are going out together. I saw you talking after class today!"

Writers sometimes make hasty generalizations because they lack evidence or because they are anxious to complete an assignment. Rather than jumping to a conclusion your argument has not supported, you should either search for additional evidence or modify your claim in such a way that your evidence does support it.

Post Hoc, Ergo Propter Hoc

The name of this fallacy is Latin for "after this, therefore because of this." *Post hoc* arguments, as they are called for short, confuse cause with coincidence. Examples of *post hoc* reasoning are often found in discussions of large social questions: "Since MTV began broadcasting, the number of teenage pregnancies has risen sharply." This statement assumes that MTV is causing teenagers to get pregnant. Although the lyrics of rock music and the sensual imagery of rock videos may contribute to an atmosphere that encourages sexual activity, there are almost certainly many causes for the rise of teenage pregnancy during the same period that MTV happened to be broadcasting.

Superstitions can embody a type of *post hoc* reasoning: "I failed the quiz because I walked under a ladder yesterday." It is important to realize that every event is preceded by many unrelated events: The sun may come up shortly after the rooster crows, but that doesn't prove that the rooster is making the sun come up.

Slippery Slope

Although it is reasonable to consider the probable effects of any change that is being argued for, it is fallacious to base one's opposition to that change entirely on the prediction of some future result that is, at best, a guess. Writers who use *slippery slope* arguments are using what is almost always a type of fear tactic: "Give them an inch, and they'll take a mile." An argument like this shifts attention away from the issue at hand. Because the future is hard to predict, and one change does not necessarily have to lead to another, it is wiser to consider the immediate effects of what is being debated than to draw frightening pictures of what could happen someday.

ORGANIZING YOUR ESSAY

By using logical reasoning, you can determine the organization of your essay. When you use inductive reasoning, you could present several pieces of evidence and then draw a conclusion from them. When you use deductive reasoning, you could begin by establishing a principle that you expect your readers to agree with and then move on to show how this principle leads to a certain conclusion. And when using substantive reasoning, you can make your claim at the beginning or at the end of your essay, as long as you provide sufficient evidence to support it and establish a reasonable warrant.

But while your writing can benefit from an understanding of logic, you need not confine yourself to a single method of reasoning or follow the pattern of organization called for by that method. Many writers choose to combine inductive and deductive reasoning within a single essay, and we have already seen how substantive reasoning does not demand a specific pattern of organization. Here, then, is additional advice for organizing a persuasive essay.

You may adapt a type of organization used in debates and sometimes called *presenting the stock issues*. This method of arrangement calls for showing that there is a problem and then moving on to propose a solution. In the first part of your essay, you would establish a need for change by demonstrating how the status quo is unacceptable. In the second part, you would propose a solution to the problem and demonstrate that your solution would work. Within the essays in this chapter, the clearest example of this approach is provided by Louis Barbash in "Clean Up or Pay Up." After providing evidence of corruption in college sports, Barbash asks, "Well then, is there any way out of this mess?" He then offers two possible solutions and emphasizes the one he thinks is better.

Unfortunately, writers do not always have a solution for problems; sometimes they can offer a useful service simply by persuading others that a problem exists. But when you have a specific proposal in mind, you can follow the time-honored pattern recommended by classical rhetoric:

- *Introduction:* Identify your issue and capture the attention of your audience by opening with a vivid example, dramatic anecdote, memorable quotation, or appeal to common values.

- *Statement of background facts:* Report the information you think your audience needs to know before it can understand your position.

- *Exposition:* Interpret the information you have reported, and define key terms.

- *Proposition:* Introduce the specific proposal you want to advance.

- *Proof:* Provide evidence to support your thesis. These paragraphs will be the heart of your essay, for you cannot be persuasive unless you prove that your position is sound.

- *Refutation of opposing arguments:* Show why you are not convinced by the arguments of people who disagree with you.

- *Conclusion:* Summarize your most important points, excite emotions appropriate for the context, and make your audience personally well disposed toward you.

However you choose to proceed, refutation is an important part of persuasive writing. Unfortunately, many writers are so firmly committed to their own positions that they fail to demonstrate that they have considered the views of others. Even if they are credible sources advancing sound positions, their ethos suffers because they seem one-sided. Your own writing will benefit if you respond thoughtfully to opposition, and you do not need to wait until the end of your essay to do so. When you are taking an unpopular position, you may need to respond to prevailing views before you can gain a fair hearing for your own. The standard arrangement associated with classical rhetoric can be modified in order to allow you to address prevailing views immediately. (See page 281.)

RESPONDING TO OPPOSITION

Because persuasion assumes the existence of an audience with views different from yours, it is essential to recognize these differences and respond to them fairly. One-sided arguments are almost never convincing. To be persuasive, writers must show that they have considered views that differ from their own. After anticipating the arguments most likely to be advanced by opponents, you can respond by either refuting these arguments or conceding that they have merit.

Of these two strategies, rhetoric has traditionally emphasized refutation. By introducing an opposition argument into your own essay, and then showing why that argument is faulty, you demonstrate good credibility or ethos if you respond fairly to that view. You also improve the logos of your case by resolving concerns that readers may have. Many writers find that the easiest way to introduce opposition arguments without obscuring their own position is to begin a paragraph with an argument offered by opponents and then devote the rest of the paragraph to providing a counterargument. By following this method, they get the chance to have the last word.

When you consider opposition arguments, you may very well find that there is one that you cannot refute. Controversy usually exists because there is at least one good argument that can be made on different sides. If you want to be persuasive, you should be prepared to concede any point you cannot refute. By admitting that you see merit in one of the arguments made by your opponents, you show that you are fair minded and make it easier for opponents to recognize merit in your own case. Saying that "I am completely right, and you are completely wrong" is more likely to annoy people than persuade them. But when you say, in effect, "I admit that you have a good point there," you create a bridge over which people can cross to your side.

Martin Luther King's "Letter from Birmingham Jail" provides examples of both refutation and concession. King responds to specific charges that had been brought against him and demonstrates why these charges were unfair. Writing at a time when the nation was badly divided over the cause he represented, King also anticipates a number of other arguments that could be raised against him and answers them eloquently. At other points, however, he reaches out to establish common ground with his opponents. In the very first paragraph, for example, he states that his critics are "men of genuine good will" who have expressed their views sincerely; later, he tells them, "You express a great deal of anxiety over our willingness to break laws. This is certainly a legitimate concern."

Strategies like these demonstrate that the purpose of "Letter from Birmingham Jail" is very different from the purpose of "I Have a Dream" (which is reprinted in Chapter 6). In "I Have a Dream," King speaks to his supporters and inspires them to hold fast to their beliefs; in "Letter from Birmingham Jail," he addresses people who disagree with him and seeks to change their minds. Comparing these two pieces can help you understand the difference between writing designed primarily to move others and writing designed primarily to persuade others. Like other motives for writing, these two may overlap—hence, the role of pathos within persuasion. But if you choose to inspire feelings as a strategy for persuading people to change their minds about something, remember that persuasion requires other strategies as well—such as reasoning logically, presenting evidence to support claims, and responding thoughtfully to the views of people who disagree with you.

By attempting to overcome the differences that exist between you and your opponents, you are using what Kenneth Burke called *identification*. According to Burke, identification is the necessary corrective to the divisions that exist between people. Even though individuals are distinct and may disagree strongly about a particular issue, they can be united by some principle they share. Persuasion is achieved by identifying your cause with the interests of your audience. Responding to the clergy of Birmingham, Alabama, King emphasizes that he too is a clergyman and makes numerous theological references. But the principle of identification goes far beyond such overt statements. Once you begin to think about what you have in common with others, including your opponents, you can often detect ties that you had not previously recognized—an important discovery if you are genuinely interested in solving problems and not simply in chalking up points in a debate.

ROGERIAN ARGUMENT

An emphasis on identification and problem solving shapes a kind of persuasion known as *Rogerian argument,* which incorporates the principles put forth by Carl Rogers—a psychotherapist who believed in the importance of "listening with understanding." Rogers developed his model as a kind of dialogue that could operate between individuals who are in conflict. Imagine, for example, that you are having a serious disagreement with a close friend, a disagreement that could easily escalate into a quarrel if you increase tension by either attacking your friend's position or appearing to ignore it as you move ahead with your own ideas. At a moment like this, Rogers would have recommended calming down and restating—*as clearly and fairly as possible*—what you heard your friend say to you. By demonstrating that you have really heard what your friend said (as opposed to missing half of it as you focused on what you wanted to say next), you help defuse tension. If your friend agrees that you have represented her position fairly, she might then restate your position—or ask you to state it and then restate, when you are finished, what she has heard you say. When restating another person's position in this way, it is essential to avoid judging it. After both parties in a disagreement agree that their views have been restated fairly, each can then move on to noting what he or she can agree with and what the other needs to agree to in order to resolve the conflict.

Because it operates as a dialogue, rather than a monologue, Rogerian argument is especially effective when you can engage in oral, face-to-face problem solving. But it can also be adapted for written arguments. If you want to write an argument organized along Rogerian lines, you could be guided by the following plan°:

- State the nature of the problem.
- Summarize what opponents have argued.
- Recognize those elements of the opposition's argument that have merit.
- Summarize your own position.
- Demonstrate why your position has merit.
- Conclude with a proposal that can appeal to the self-interest of both sides in the conflict.

In other words, a Rogerian argument emphasizes the importance of concession rather than refutation and places these concessions in a relatively early position.

---

plan: Adapted from Richard Coe's *Form and Substance* (New York: Wiley, 1981).

Ideally, it leads to a win–win situation rather than a win–lose situation. Instead of making your view prevail in a way that could leave people who held different views feeling as if they lost a debate, you help conflicting parties to feel that differences have been valued and some reconciliation has been achieved.

However you choose to structure your own arguments, it is important to treat your opponents with respect and to use persuasion as a means of overcoming division and drawing people together. At its crudest levels, persuasion may draw people together superficially through manipulative rather than honorable means: A successful advertising campaign can convince thousands of people to buy a product they really don't need. (For a discussion of advertising, see pages 392–427.) But when you write about ideas and treat your opponents respectfully, you open the way for long-lasting agreements built on shared beliefs.

Persuasion should thus be conducted honorably. You should never overlook important evidence that operates against your conclusion, and you should never exaggerate or misrepresent views that differ from yours. You will find that some writers follow these principles and others lose sight of them, but try not to be influenced by the bad habits of others. Whenever you attempt to write persuasively, show that you are fair minded, and be sure that your own position is clear, sincerely held, and well supported.

CLEAN UP OR PAY UP

Louis Barbash

Louis Barbash believes that college sports are a "mess" and proposes a way to clean them up. If you are a fan of college sports, you may not like his proposal, but try not to let a love for sports keep you from evaluating this essay as an argument. It was published by The Washington Monthly *in 1990. As you read, consider whether college sports have changed since Barbash wrote—or whether a writer today could add new data that would reinforce the case Barbash makes in this piece.*

Barbash is a senior program officer at the Corporation for Public Broadcasting, where he specializes in history and science programming. As an independent producer, he has also written and developed programs for the New York Times, *the AFL-CIO, and the Smithsonian Institution. He has also served as supervisor of investigation and conciliation at the U.S. Equal Employment Opportunity Commission and as assistant counsel to the U.S. Banking and Urban Affairs Committee.*

Tom Scates is one of the lucky ones. He has a bachelor's degree from Georgetown University, where he played basketball under the fabled John Thompson, one of the best college basketball coaches in the country, and one of the few who insist that their players go to class. Ninety percent of Thompson's players at Georgetown receive degrees, about three times the national average.

More than a decade after Tom Scates received his diploma, he has managed to parlay his Georgetown degree and education, his athletic skills, and the character he developed during his career in intercollegiate athletics, into a job as a doorman at a downtown Washington hotel.

Still, Scates *is* one of the lucky ones. He played for a good team at a good school, under a moral coach, and under a president, Father Timothy Healy, who believed that Georgetown was a school with a basketball team, not a basketball team with a school. He was not implicated in drug deals, shoplifting, violence, grade altering, point shaving, or under-the-table money scandals. He didn't have his scholarship yanked. He didn't emerge from school functionally illiterate. He got a job.

Many of the men Scates played against when he was at Georgetown, and their basketball and football counterparts at major colleges and universities, have not been so fortunate. Less than half the football and basketball scholarship athletes will graduate from college. And what education athletes do get is often so poor that it may be irrelevant whether they graduate or not.

In addition to corrupting the university's basic academic mission, big-time sports have been a lightning rod for financial corruption. College ath-

5

letes are cash-poor celebrities. Although their performance on the field or court produces millions in revenue for the university, they receive in return only their scholarships—tuition, room, and board—and no spending money. They are forbidden from working part-time during the season. Athletes have been caught trying to make money by getting loans from coaches and advisers, selling the shoes and other gear they get as team members, taking allowances from agents, and getting paid for no-show summer jobs provided by jock-sniffing alumni—all violations of National Collegiate Athletic Association (NCAA) rules.

Things might be different if the NCAA would show some real inclination to clean up the college sports mess. But that organization has a well-developed instinct for the capillaries: instead of attacking the large-scale academic, financial, and criminal corruption in college sports, too often the investigators from Mission, Kansas, put their energies into busting athletes for selling their complimentary tickets and coaches for starting their practices a few weeks ahead of schedule. Meanwhile, the real problems of college athletics continue to fester.

Will the NCAA change? And if so, would that matter? Earlier this year, NCAA Executive Director Dick Schultz proposed new rules to stem college sports corruption. Schultz's reforms included "quality academic advising and career-counseling programs," restriction of recruiting, long-term contracts for coaches, reduced pressure and time demands on athletes, and the elimination of athletic dormitories to "make the athlete as indistinguishable from the rest of the student body as is humanly possible."

It's illegal to bet on sports except in Nevada, so bet on this instead: Schultz's proposals will not pass an NCAA dominated by college sports officials whose careers rest on winning games. Recall what has happened to much weaker suggestions. Even Georgetown's Coach Thompson boycotted his own team's games to protest as too severe the timid requirements of the NCAA's Proposition 48, which would have barred entering freshmen from athletic scholarships and competition if they did not have a 2.0 high school GPA and SAT scores totaling 700 points. Interested in even better odds? Take this to the bank: Even if Schultz gets every one of his proposals put in exactly as he outlined them, they—like everything else the NCAA has tried—will not work.

Well then, is there any way out of this mess? Yes. Actually, there are *two* ways out. Because the NCAA has so utterly failed, because in the present system the big-money pressures to cheat are so enormous, and because, like it or not, sports have such a widespread impact on the country's moral climate, there should be a federal law that requires schools *either* to return to the Ivy League ideal in which players are legitimate members of the student body, judged by the same standards as everybody else, *or* to let players on their teams be non-student professionals. All the trouble comes from trying to mix these two alternatives—from trying to achieve big revenues while retaining the veneer of purity.

The pure alternative doesn't have to ignore athletic ability among prospective students—there were plenty of good football teams before today's   *10* double-standard disaster got firmly entrenched. You want to consider the athletic ability of college applicants for the same reason you want to consider musical or theatrical ability; a university should be a wonderfully diverse collection of talents that together stimulate people to develop in all sorts of positive ways. Athletic skill is one such talent—one that even academic purists ought to look at. But the key is that universities must consider athletic ability as only *part* of what they take into account when they accept a student. The fundamental mistake of today's college sports system is that it supposes a student could be at a university *solely* because of his athletic skill.

While the purely amateur option is probably the more desirable of the two, the professional one isn't nearly as horrible as it might seem at first. After all, coaches were originally volunteers, and now they're paid. (Army's first head coach, Dennis Michie, received no pay. Jess Hawley coached for free at Dartmouth from 1923–28. His 1925 team went undefeated and was the national champion.) So why not players?

Sweat Equity

How much would a salaried college athlete make? If the example of minor league baseball is anything to go on—and such authorities as Roger Meiners, a Clemson University economist who specializes in the economics of college sports, and Ed Garvey, the former head of the NFL Players Association, think that it is—college salaries would be enough for a young athlete to live on, but not so much as to bust college budgets. Minor league baseball players start at around $11,000 for their first full professional season and range upward to the neighborhood of $26,000 for players on AAA teams under major league option. So it seems fair to estimate a salary of about $15,000 for an average player on an average team.

The professional option's chief virtue is honesty. The current student–athlete system requires both students and universities to pretend that the young athletes are not full-time professionals, but rather full-time students who play sports in their spare time. But does anyone suppose that high school athletes reading four and five years below grade level would be considered for college admission, much less recruited and given full scholarships, if they were not football or basketball stars? Can the abuses of NCAA rules that have been uncovered at almost half of its biggest schools have any other meaning than that giving these athletes a real education is not what universities are trying to do?

The hypocrisy begins with the fundamental relationship between the players and the university: 18- to 20-year-olds, many of them poorly educated, inner-city blacks, coerced and deceived into playing four years of football or basketball without pay so that the university can sell tickets and television rights.

The coercion comes from the colleges' control of access to professional football or basketball: It is virtually impossible to go to the pros without play-

15

ing college ball first. Colleges open that opportunity only to athletes who will agree to perform for the college for four years without getting a salary or even holding an outside part-time job. The athlete does receive a four-year scholarship and room and board while he is enrolled, a package the NCAA values at about $40,000. The deception lies in the fact that the inducements held out to athletes by colleges—the chance to play pro ball and getting a college education—are essentially worthless, and the schools know it.

The athlete's first priority is to play pro ball. Forty-four percent of all black scholarship athletes, and 22 percent of white athletes, entertain hopes of playing in the pros. That's why they will play four years for nothing. But in fact, the lure of sports that keeps kids in school is a false hope and a cruel hoax. "The dream in the head of so many youngsters that they will achieve fame and riches in professional sports is touching, but it is also overwhelmingly unrealistic," says Robert Atwell, president of the American Council on Education. The would-be pro faces odds as high as 400–1. Of the 20,000 "students" who play college basketball, for example, only 50 will make it to the NBA. The other 19,950 won't. Many of them will wind up like Tom Scates, in minimum wage jobs, or like Reggie Ford, who lost his football scholarship to Northwest Oklahoma State after he injured his knee and now collects unemployment compensation in South Carolina.

The scholarships and promises of education are also worthless currency. Of every 10 young men who accept scholarships to play football at major schools, according to NCAA statistics, just 4 will graduate. Only 3 of every 10 basketball players receive degrees.

Not only are these athletes being cheated out of a promised education, but they and their universities are forced to erect elaborate, meretricious curricula to satisfy the student-athlete requirement, so of those who *do* get degrees, many receive diplomas that are barely worth the parchment they're printed on. Running back Ronnie Harmon majored in computer science at the University of Iowa but took only one computer course in his three years of college. Another Iowa football player also majored in computer science but in his senior year took only courses in billiards, bowling, and football; he followed up by getting a D in a summer school watercolor class. Transcripts of the members of the basketball team at Ohio University list credit for something called "International Studies 69B"—a course composed of a 14-day, 10-game trip to Europe.

As things stand now, athletically gifted students who genuinely want an education are often steered away by eligibility-conscious advisers. Jan Kemp, the University of Georgia academic adviser for athletes who won a lawsuit after the university fired her for insisting on the athletes' right to be educated, recalls how a Georgia athlete was always placed in "dummy" classes despite his efforts to take "real" ones. "There's nothing wrong with his mind," says Kemp. "But the situation is magnified for athletes because there is so much money involved. There is too much control over who gets in and who takes what courses."

No case illustrates the cynicism that poisons big-time college sports bet-   20
ter than that of former Washington Redskins star defensive end Dexter Manley. Manley spent four years as a "student-athlete" at Oklahoma State
University only to emerge, as he admitted years later, functionally illiterate.
But OSU President John Campbell was not embarrassed: "There would be
those who would argue that Dexter Manley got exactly what he wanted out
of OSU. He was able to develop his athletic skills and ability, he was noticed
by the pros, he got a pro contract. So maybe we did him a favor by letting
him go through the program."

One scarcely knows where to start in on a statement like that. It's
appalling that an accredited state university would admit a functional illiterate, even recruit him, and leave him illiterate after four years as a student. It's
shocking that it would do all this in order to make money from his unpaid
performance as an athlete. And it is little short of grotesque that an educator,
entrusted with the education of 20,000 young men and women, would argue
that the cynical arrangement between an institution of higher learning and an
uneducated high school boy was, after all, a fair bargain.

The infection of hypocrisy spreads from the president's office to the athletic department and coaching staff. This may be the saddest betrayal in the
system. These are 17-year-olds, dreaming of a lucrative career in sports. They
have placed their faith in the coaches who have visited their homes, solicited
their trust, and gotten to know their parents. But those coaches, as Robert
Atwell points out, "may have a vested interest in perpetuating the myth rather
than pointing out its inherent fallacy." That vested interest, of course, is that if
they do not produce winning teams, at whatever cost, they will lose their jobs.

So instead, to recruit highly sought-after high-school athletes, coaches
promise playing time, education, and exposure to national TV audiences and
professional scouts. But once the player arrives on campus, coaches are under
strong pressure to treat him like what he is: an employee, whose needs must
be subordinated to the needs of the enterprise, i.e., winning.

Sports without Strings

Gary Ruble, a former scholarship football player at the University of
North Carolina, told a House subcommittee investigating college athletics
that North Carolina "came to me and offered me, basically, the world. They
came to me and said come to our school. Be a student athlete. We will guarantee that you graduate. We will promise you to be a star, et cetera, et cetera,
et cetera." But once in Chapel Hill, Ruble found himself riding the bench.
"You go in as an offensive lineman, which I was, at 240 pounds, and you go
into a system where you have offensive linemen who are 285 and they are
telling you that you are going to play. That's an impossibility," Ruble told the
subcommittee. After three years, "my position coach called me into his office
and stated that I should consider either transferring to another school or drop-

ping out gracefully. I was no longer to be considered in their plans for our team," Ruble says. When he reported back to school anyway, he was told "I had no option of whether to stay or go. They were not allowing me to retain my scholarship."

A system of sports without strings—releasing college athletes and their universities from the pretense that they are students, and instead paying them for their services—would cure the student-athlete system's chief vices: its duplicity and its exploitiveness.

Athletes who want to get started on careers in sports, including those whose only way out of the ghetto may be the slam dunk and the 4.4–40, would find paying jobs in their chosen field. Overnight, thousands of new jobs as professional football and basketball players would be created. Players with the ability to get to the NFL and NBA would get paid during their years of apprenticeship. For those of lesser abilities, playing for college teams would be a career in itself, a career they could start right out of high school and continue as long as skills and bodies allowed. And as they matured and their playing careers drew to a close, the prospect of a real college education might seem more inviting than it did at 17.

Releasing athletes from having to be students would, ironically, make it easier for those who want an education to get it. Even with the best intentions, today's college athletes have little hope of being serious students. Basketball practice, for instance, begins October 15, and the season does not end for the most successful teams until after the NCAA championships in early April; in other words the season starts one month after school begins and ends one month before school is out. During the season, athletes spend six or more hours a day, 30 to 40 hours a week, on practice, viewing game-films, at chalk talks, weight lifting, conditioning, and attending team meetings. The best-prepared students would have difficulty attending to their studies while working 34 hours a week—and these are not the best-prepared students.

But under no-strings sports, athletes who want educations will fare better than they do now, because the pace of their education need not be governed by their eligibility for athletic competition. A football player could play the fall semester and study in the spring. Basketball players, whose season spans the two semesters, might enroll at schools with quarter or trimester systems, or study summers and after their sports careers are over. Instead of being corralled into courses rigged to provide high grades like "Theory of Volleyball," "Recreation and Leisure," "Jogging," and "Leisure Alternatives," athletes would be in a position to take only the courses they want and need. This would be even more likely if, as part of the pro option, universities were still required to offer full scholarships to athletes, to be redeemed whenever the athletes wanted to use them.

Under these changes, those athletes who end up going to college would be doing so because they were pursuing their own educational goals. This reform would replace today's phony jock curriculum with the kind of mature academic choices that made the G.I. Bill such a success.

Such considerations make it clear that it's time for schools to choose   *30*
between real amateurism and real professionalism. They can't have a little of
both. From now on, in college sports, it's got to be either poetry or pros.

QUESTIONS FOR DISCUSSION

1. Consider the introduction to this essay. Why does Barbash begin his argument by providing information about Tom Scates? Why does he wait until
   the end of paragraph 2 before revealing that Scates is a hotel doorman?
2. Barbash charges that the NCAA concerns itself only with minor rules
   infractions while "the real problems of college athletics continue to fester."
   In his view, what are those real problems? How are colleges guilty of
   "duplicity and exploitiveness" in their dealings with student athletes?
3. Why don't most gifted athletes go directly from high school to professional sports? Why are few college athletes likely to become pros?
4. How convincing is the evidence Barbash provides to support his case?
   How representative are his examples?
5. What would the advantages of paying student athletes be? Can you think
   of any disadvantages?
6. Explain the pun with which this essay concludes. How well does it work
   as a concluding line?

SUGGESTIONS FOR WRITING

1. Argue for a change in the sports program at your school that would benefit either the program or the school.
2. Barbash claims that many schools have a "jock curriculum" that enables
   athletes to keep playing even if they are not learning anything important.
   Imagine a situation in which someone has asked you to identify the easiest
   courses at your own school, then write an essay that would persuade that
   person to take more challenging courses.
3. Identify a change that you think would benefit a professional sport. Write
   an argument that would persuade anyone active in that sport to accept the
   change you have·in mind.

LINKS ■ ■ ■

■ WITHIN THE BOOK

Barbash concludes his argument by offering his audience a choice
between two options. For an argument that considers different options
but argues on behalf of one, see "Why You Can Hate Drugs and Still
Want to Legalize Them" by Joshua Wolf Shenk (pages 550–561).

▪ ELSEWHERE IN PRINT

Sack, Allen L. and Ellen J. Staurowsky. *College Athletes for Hire: The Evolution and Legacy of the NCAA's Amateur Myth.* Westport: Praeger, 1998.

Sperber, Murray. *Beer and Circus: How Big-Time Sports is Crippling Undergraduate Education.* New York: Holt, 2000.

Telander, Rick, Richard Wauch, and Murray Sperber. *The Hundred Yard Lie: The Corruption of College Football and What We Can Do to Stop it.* Champaign: U of Illinois P, 1996.

Wheeler, Dion. *A Parent's and Student Athlete's Guide to Athletic Scholarships: Getting Money Without Being Taken for a (Full) Ride.* Raleigh: Contemporary, 2000.

▪ ONLINE

- Big-Time Athletics vs. Academic Values
  <http://chronicle.com/free/v47/i20/20b00701.htm>

- Knight Commission on Intercollegiate Athletics
  <http://www.knightfdn.org/default.asp?story=news_at_knight/special_reports/coi_athletics.html#>

- National College Athletic Association
  <http://www.ncaa.org>

FLUNK THE ELECTORAL COLLEGE, PASS INSTANT RUNOFFS

John B. Anderson

From 1961 to 1981, John B. Anderson represented Illinois in the U.S. House of Representatives. A long-time Republican, he ran for President in 1980 as an Independent, winning 6.6% of the vote in a three-way race with Ronald Reagan and Jimmy Carter. Now serving as president of the Center for Voting and Democracy in Washington, D.C., Anderson published the following argument early in 2001, shortly after George W. Bush had been elected President in a close race with Al Gore—an election in which close to three million votes went to Ralph Nader, who, like Anderson, offered a choice outside the major political parties. Writing for The Progressive, *a magazine read primarily by liberal-minded citizens who are likely to favor making elections more democratic, Anderson establishes his position at the very beginning of his argument. As you read this argument, be alert for the reasons Anderson offers in support of his position.*

The Presidential controversy in Florida has had one virtue: It has shown that too many of our electoral rules and practices are antiquated and unexamined. We must seize this once-in-a-generation opportunity to modernize and fully democratize our elections.

There is no better place to start than that peculiar institution, the Electoral College. The Electoral College fails to provide for majority rule and political equality. The Electoral College divides us on regional lines, undercuts accountability, dampens voter participation, and can trump the national popular vote. With current plurality rules, it can turn third party candidates into "spoilers," where voting for your favorite candidate can help elect your least favorite. All forward-looking Americans should embrace direct election of the President by a majority vote.

The candidate with the most votes is elected in every other federal contest—and in nearly all elections of any consequence here and abroad. But instead of a simple national vote, the Presidency is decided by fifty-one separate elections in each state and the District of Columbia, with electoral votes allocated according to the size of each state's Congressional delegation. To maximize their clout, states have chosen to allocate their electoral votes by winner-take-all—the candidate who wins the most votes in a state, no matter what the margin or how small the percentage, wins all that state's electoral votes. (Maine and Nebraska also allocate some of their electors according to the popular vote winner in U.S. House districts.)

A majority of Americans consistently support direct election of the President. Their concern about the anti-democratic nature of the Electoral College is grounded in history. Our framers distrusted democracy and saw the Electoral College as a deliberative body able to correct bad choices made by the people. They had the misplaced fear that, after the consensus election of George Washington, future Presidential elections would be divided along state lines, with candidates having only regional appeal and unable to win a majority of the electoral vote. The Electoral College, then, would convene and pick the best candidate among the people's "nominees." The belief of some of our framers that the College would check the excesses of majority rule is founded on a wildly mistaken understanding of how politics would evolve in the United States.

The rule for apportioning electoral votes according to the number of 5 each state's members of Congress also was anti-democratic. It made electoral power in the Presidential race dependent on the *population* of a state rather than on its number of voters. For this reason, there is no national incentive to spur turnout in a state and expand the franchise. The initial impact was to give slave states additional weight. The infamous constitutional provision counting slaves as three-fifths of a person for the purpose of apportioning Representatives was designed to favor Southern states. Slaves couldn't vote, but they could give their owners extra power in both Congressional and Presidential elections. It is no accident that slave-owning Virginians served as President for thirty-two of the nation's first thirty-six years.

By factoring in a state's number of Senators, the Electoral College gives small states disproportionate weight, as the fewest number of electors a state can have is three—two Senators and one House member. As a result, the total number of votes cast in Wyoming this year for three electoral votes was fewer than the number of popular votes it took to win a single electoral vote in ten states that are bigger or had high turnout, such as Florida, Michigan, Minnesota, and Wisconsin. In 2000, if states had electors equal to the number of House members, Al Gore would have turned his plurality win in the national popular vote into an Electoral College win even without victories in Florida and New Mexico.

But small states should not be too quick to celebrate. Because of winner-take-all rules, big states swing far more electoral votes and gain far more attention if races are close there. This year, competitive small states did get attention from the campaigns, as both parties realized that the election could be decided by a mere handful of electoral votes. But in most elections, even the competitive small states are overlooked as the candidates focus on competitive large states.

Ironically, Electoral College defenders often express worry that the candidates will spend time only in the big states. But to win a national direct election with a majority vote would require active campaigns in far more parts of the country than under current rules.

Electoral patterns and polling allow the candidates to know precisely which states are competitive, and that is where candidates put their resources to mobilize voters and, increasingly, to pitch their messages about their national priorities. In the November election, most states—including twelve of the eighteen smallest—were won by comfortable margins, and a majority already can be judged as noncompetitive in 2004. Voter turnout increased in all but one of the closely decided states, often on the order of 10 percent, but it was down in the rest of the nation. In a national election, however, your vote would have the same power no matter where you lived. All potential voters would be treated equally, with at least some grassroots organizing activity likely to take place everywhere rather than in the fractured, piecemeal fashion we see today.

The fissures in the Electoral College map have the potential to further divide our nation. With candidates focusing only on where wins are possible, it becomes all the harder to reverse these trends. In 2000, the parties tended to strengthen their grips on their strongholds, meaning that in 2004, a candidate could become President without devoting any time or energy to whole regions of the country. Yet even the most lopsided states still have significant numbers of voters who oppose the majority choice. For example, Bill Clinton won at least 25 percent of the vote in every Congressional district in 1996. With direct election, campaigns would have an incentive to mobilize supporters no matter where they lived.

Direct election would have another enjoyable by-product: No partisan results in exit polls in the Presidential race could be discussed by a credible news agency until everyone had voted. On election night, analysts would need to focus on Congressional races and analysis of voter attitudes until polls closed on the West Coast—making it all the more likely that Westerners would see their votes as meaningful.

The Electoral College has been the subject of more proposed amendments to the Constitution than any part of that venerable document. Some have suggested awarding electoral votes in states in proportion to the candidates' share of the vote. Some would allocate electoral votes by Congressional district—a plan that sounds attractive on the surface but has serious problems. It accepts the reality of gerrymandered Congressional districts, and this year would have given George W. Bush a big victory despite his loss in the popular vote, as Republican support is more evenly dispersed across states and Democratic support more concentrated in cities. Some support amendments to ensure that if no candidate wins an electoral-vote majority, voters would pick the winners in a second-round runoff election. Others would replace actual electors with fixed numbers to avoid the chicanery of "faithless electors" overturning the will of the people.

But direct election is the only viable solution that could gain the support necessary to amend the Constitution. Nevertheless, there are important questions to resolve in proposals for direct election. The most important one—indeed, a defining demand for many reformers—is the establishment of a majority standard. Ensuring that the President can gain the votes of at least half of Americans better assures that the Presidency will have national appeal. It also would once and for all liberate voters to support the candidate of their choice by eliminating the "spoiler" problem, where a third party candidacy can fracture one major party's majority vote and allow another candidate to win with a mere plurality.

This year, I joined nearly three million Americans in casting my ballot for Ralph Nader. Nader's positions in favor of proportional representation, instant runoff voting, and other pro-democracy reforms made him by far the most attractive candidate. But that vote for Nader meant that I had no ability to express my choice between Republican George W. Bush and Democrat Al Gore. For this reason, our current plurality system tends to suppress third party candidacies and the voter participation they could generate.

We can solve this problem by instituting a far more efficient, empower- 15 ing method called instant runoff voting. Used in several nations, instant runoff voting ensures majority rule in one election. For voters, the demands are simple, and the rewards great. Rather than selecting only one choice, voters should be allowed to indicate their runoff choices by rank-ordering the candidates: first, second, third, and so on. If no candidate wins a majority of first choices, the election is not over. Instead, the weakest candidates are eliminated, and a second "runoff" round of counting takes place. Ballots count for each voter's top-ranked candidate still in the race. Rounds continue until there is a majority winner. Modern ballot machines can handle this quickly and efficiently. They also can ensure that any need for a national recount with a direct election system would be far easier than the difficult recount in Florida this year with current antiquated machines.

Instant runoff voting is enjoying a welcome rise in interest in the United States. In Alaska, supporters have turned in more than enough signatures to qualify it for a ballot initiative in 2002. If the initiative passes, Alaska would institute instant runoff voting for state and federal offices, including the Presidential race. Other states are considering it seriously. Vermont may have the best chance for a legislative win in 2001; backers there include the League of Women Voters, Common Cause, Vermont Grange, and leaders in all parties.

Majority rule and political equality are fundamental tenets of democracy. The power of one's vote should be equal no matter where one lives, and candidates for our one national office should have incentives to speak to everyone. Since the last popular-vote winner was defeated by the Electoral College in 1888, we have amended the Constitution to elect Senators directly, to guarantee women's right to vote, and to lower the voting age to eighteen. We have passed the Voting Rights Act to provide access to the ballot regardless of race or ethnicity.

The Electoral College has escaped the move to greater democracy only because of institutional inertia and states' misguided, parochial considerations. But a twenty-first century pro-democracy movement must take private money out of elections, institute proportional representation in legislatures, and bring about the direct election of the President with instant runoff voting.

Let's send a message to American voters that it is their votes alone that count when electing our leaders.

QUESTIONS FOR DISCUSSION

1. Anderson writes, "All forward-looking Americans should embrace direct election of the President by a majority vote." What do you think he means by "forward-looking"? Are any Americans "backward-looking"?
2. Why was the Electoral College created? According to Anderson, what is wrong with its design?
3. Why does Anderson believe that campaigns designed to win electoral votes have an adverse affect on voter turnout?
4. What is the difference between a majority and a plurality?
5. Consider Anderson's decision to disclose how he voted in the 2000 presidential election. How do you think his original audience was likely to respond to this disclosure? How does it influence your own response to this argument?
6. Instead of arguing for a single proposition (such as eliminating the Electoral College), Anderson argues for two (eliminating the Electoral College and implementing instant runoff voting). Was this a good writing decision?

SUGGESTIONS FOR WRITING

1. Write an argument on behalf of preserving the Electoral College.
2. Write an argument on the importance of voting, directed to the millions of eligible voters who stay away from the polls each election.
3. Argue on behalf of a Constitutional amendment that in your opinion would improve the lives of American citizens.

LINKS ■ ■ ■

■ WITHIN THE BOOK

See "The Declaration of Independence" (pages 529–532), and consider whether the Electoral College is consistent with the ideals expressed in that document.

■ ELSEWHERE IN PRINT

Abbott, David W., and James P. Levine. *Wrong Winner: The Coming Debacle in the Electoral College*. Westport: Praeger, 1991.

Best, Judith A. *The Choice of the People? Debating the Electoral College*. Lanham: Rowman, 1996.

Glennon, Michael J. *When No Majority Rules: The Electoral College and Presidential Succession*. Washington, D.C.: Cong. Quarterly, 1992.

Hardaway, Robert M. *The Electoral College and the Constitution*. Westport: Praeger, 2001.

■ **ONLINE**

- Center for Voting and Democracy
  <http://www.fairvote.org/op_eds/media.htm>
- The Electoral College
  <http://www.fec.gov/pages/ecmenu2.htm>
- Electoral College Results
  <http://www.nara.gov/fedreg/elctcoll>
- Presidential Elections
  <http://www.multied.com/elections>

RACIAL PROFILING: THE LIBERALS ARE RIGHT

Stuart Taylor, Jr.

"Racial Profiling" describes a controversial law-enforcement procedure in which police target people of color as potential criminals. In its most common practice, racial profiling leads police officers to stop and search black and Hispanic American drivers much more frequently than white drivers. In recent years, liberals have taken the lead in questioning the justice of this practice. With this in mind, Stuart Taylor, Jr., seeks to persuade moderates and conservatives that liberals may be right on this point. His argument was originally published in a 1999 issue of National Journal, *a periodical read primarily by conservatives—hence its provocative title. As you read, look for ways in which Taylor seeks to identify with a conservative audience as part of a strategy designed to persuade them to support a position that would strike them as liberal.*

A graduate of Princeton University and Harvard Law School, Stuart Taylor, Jr., was a Supreme Court reporter for the New York Times *before becoming a contributing editor at* Newsweek. *He has also written feature articles and essays for* The American Lawyer. *In addition, he frequently provides legal commentary on National Public Radio as well as on television networks such as ABC, CBS, NBC, and CNN.*

While fueled by demagogic rhetoric and political opportunism, the current uproar over allegedly racist police practices in New York City and elsewhere has spotlighted one clearly abusive practice that moderates, conservatives, and, indeed, police chiefs should join liberals in assailing: racial profiling. That is the apparently widespread police habit of using skin color or ethnicity as a factor in deciding whom to stop and search for evidence of crime.

Just this week, New Jersey Gov. Christine Todd Whitman° admitted that a 111-page internal review had confirmed a 1996 judicial ruling that some state police officers had engaged in racial profiling in deciding which cars to search during traffic stops on the turnpike.

Around the country, thousands of minority-group members have been humiliated by police stops and searches, often for conduct no more suspicious than "driving while black" or walking the streets of their communities. This, in turn, has helped to breed a deeply corrosive mistrust of law enforcement.

The full extent and the perniciousness of racial profiling are difficult to grasp for those of us who have not been targeted. The practice is virtually invisible to whites, except in the minority of cases in which police find illegal drugs or guns and make arrests. Almost all police organizations deny that they

---

Christine Todd Whitman: Became administrator of the Environmental Protection Agency under President George W. Bush.

condone racial profiling. It is easily camouflaged by nonracial pretexts for searching cars and pedestrians; and it is sometimes confused with proper police work.

All this, plus the assumption that falling crime rates mean that the police must be doing something right, helps explain why moderate and conservative leaders have so far expressed relatively little concern about racial profiling. But the result has been to leave a void to be filled by race-card-carrying police-bashers such as Al Sharpton° (sponsor of the Tawana Brawley hoax)° and Jesse Jackson (who recently accused police in New York City of declaring "open season on blacks").

This issue is too important to be left to opportunists such as these. More law enforcement officials and politicians alike should recognize that whatever short-term benefits racial profiling may produce in catching a few criminals are far outweighed by the long-term costs. The biggest cost is the poisoning of police relations with minority-group communities, and thus with potential witnesses and jurors in the communities most in need of effective law enforcement.

While there have been few systematic studies of racial profiling, the scattered data collected so far are striking.

In New Jersey, the report released on April 20 showed that 77 percent of motorists searched on the turnpike were black or Hispanic, even though 60 percent of those stopped were white.

In Maryland, according to statistics compiled by state police as part of a 1995 court settlement, 70 percent of the drivers searched on a stretch of Interstate 95 from January 1995 through September 1996 were black—even though blacks made up only 17 percent of all drivers (and of all speeders) on that road, according to a related study by the American Civil Liberties Union.

Thus, an innocent black driver was four times as likely to be searched as an innocent white driver. And this was after the state police had (in the court settlement) issued a written policy barring race-based stops.

Studies of car stops in places ranging from Volusia County, Fla., to Eagle County, Colo., also reflect dramatic racial disparities. And in Louisiana, a state police training film a few years ago told officers to use traffic stops to do drug searches of "males of foreign nationalities, mainly Cubans, Colombians, Puerto Ricans, or other swarthy outlanders."

The most telling evidence of the extent and offensiveness of race-based stops and searches may be the personal accounts of the many black and Hispanic people who see such stops as emblematic of a discriminatory criminal justice system.

"You cannot talk to an African-American who has not either had this experience or had a relative go through it," says David A. Harris, a law professor

5

10

Al Sharpton: New York clergyman and political activist who draws media attention to racial conflict. *Tawana Brawley:* Teenager who, in 1987, falsely claimed she had been abducted and raped by six police officers.

at the University of Toledo, whose research on car stops and searches has included interviews with large numbers of middle-class blacks. "It's a humiliating and angering experience," Harris reports. "One man said it's like someone pulling your pants down around your ankles....And any African-American who has teenage kids, especially male kids, . . . they've had 'the talk' with them, about what to do when—not if, when—they are stopped. This is in the nature of instructions for survival."

Is there any justification for racial profiling? Defenders of the practice point out that certain crimes are disproportionately committed by young black and Hispanic men—or by members of particular ethnic groups, such as Jamaicans or Colombians—and that police logically look for evidence where the criminals live, in the inner cities.

Such rationales reflect the tendency of practitioners and critics alike to 15 confuse racial profiling with a different phenomenon: the policies of police in places like New York City to patrol (and stop, and search) most aggressively in high-crime neighborhoods. When done with respect and sensitivity, this can produce safer communities and better community relations. When it veers into wholesale intimidation, and indiscriminate frisking of young men on the street, it can become indistinguishable from racial profiling.

Even critics acknowledge that racial profiling is not entirely irrational in treating young black inner-city men as presumptively more worthy of attention than, say, grandmothers. Jesse Jackson himself implied this when he said in 1993: "There is nothing more painful to me at this stage in my life than to walk down the street and hear footsteps and start thinking about robbery—then look around and see somebody white and feel relieved."

A citizen such as Jackson might be justified in keeping a prudent distance from a group of black youths in certain settings. But a police officer would not be justified (absent some particularized basis for suspicion) in picking up a black youth, standing him against a wall, and frisking him.

While "it is rational to be more suspicious of a young black man than an elderly white woman," in the words of a trenchant new book by David Cole, *No Equal Justice: Race and Class in the American Criminal Justice System,* that "does not make it right. First, the correlation of race and crime remains a stereotype, and most blacks will not conform to the stereotype. . . . A police officer who relies on race in stopping and questioning individuals is therefore likely to stop many more innocent than guilty individuals. Second, our nation's historical reliance on race for invidious discrimination renders suspect such consideration of race today, even if it might be 'rational' in some sense."

And outside of the inner cities, it's unclear that such practices as race-based traffic stops on major highways—in which police are usually looking not for murderers, rapists, or robbers but for drugs—produce any significant law enforcement benefit at all.

Meanwhile, the costs mount, as innocent people who are searched come 20 away feeling mistreated. This takes an incalculable toll on the willingness of many black and Hispanic citizens to cooperate with police, to provide leads, to testify as witnesses, and, when they serve as jurors, to convict guilty people.

What can be done about racial profiling? The practice is too deeply ingrained in police culture, and too easily camouflaged, to be eradicated by legislation or lawsuits. The best remedy may be for police chiefs to train their officers to shun such profiling, and to recruit more black and Hispanic officers.

In the short run, we need more studies to expose the extent of racial profiling. San Diego and San Jose, Calif., are both doing studies of their own police forces. Political pressure, lawsuits, and enlightened self-interest should spur other cities and states to do the same.

Meanwhile, Congress should give careful consideration to a proposal by Rep. John Conyers Jr., D–Mich., to require the Justice Department to collect and study racial and ethnic data about the drivers stopped and searched by state and local police.

Racial statistics can, of course, be manipulated to draw misleading inferences of discrimination, such as the wrong-headed notion that elite colleges discriminate against minorities by giving weight to Scholastic Aptitude Test scores in admissions. But unlike the case of SAT scores, racial profiling involves real discrimination. And on this issue, sunlight may be the best disinfectant.

QUESTIONS FOR DISCUSSION

1. At what points in this argument is it clear that Taylor is writing for an audience of moderates and conservatives?
2. Consider Taylor's characterization in paragraph 5 of Al Sharpton and Jesse Jackson. Is this an ad hominem argument or a justifiable attempt to identify with his audience?
3. How do you respond to the statistics quoted in paragraphs 8 and 9?
4. Where does Taylor recognize and respond to views different from his own?
5. At the conclusion of his argument, Taylor offers a series of propositions. Was is it a good writing decision to hold these propositions back until the conclusion? Is it effective to offer more than one solution to the problem of racial profiling?
6. If Taylor had shared a draft of this argument with you before publishing it, what would you have told him about his final paragraph?

SUGGESTIONS FOR WRITING

1. Write an argument for or against a widely used police procedure.
2. Focusing on the war on terrorism, write an argument for or against using racial profiling at airports.
3. Write an argument designed to establish whether race should or should not be considered when making decisions about people in areas that do not involve law enforcement.

LINKS ■ ■ ■

■ WITHIN THE BOOK

For an argument for racial justice made from an African-American point of view, see "Letter from Birmingham Jail" by Martin Luther King, Jr. (pages 534–548).

■ ELSEWHERE IN PRINT

Cole, David. *No Equal Justice: Race and Class in the American Criminal Justice System.* New York: New, 1999.

Markowitz, Michael W., and Delores D. Jones-Brown, eds. *The System in Black and White: Exploring the Connections between Race, Crime, and Justice.* Westport, CT: Praeger, 2000.

Meeks, Kenneth. *Driving While Black: What to Do If You Are the Victim of Racial Profiling.* New York: Broadway, 2000.

Pallone, Nathaniel J., ed. *Race, Ethnicity, Sexual Orientation, Violent Crime: The Realities and the Myths.* New York: Haworth, 2000.

Russell, Katheryn K. *The Color of Crime: Racial Hoaxes, White Fear, Black Protectionism, Police Harassment, and Other Macroaggressions.* New York: New York UP, 1998.

■ ONLINE

- The Myth of Racial Profiling
  <http://www.city-journal.org/html/11_2_the_myth.html>

- Racial Profiling in America: Arrest the Racism
  <http://www.aclu.org/profiling>

- Traffic Stops Statistics Study
  <http://thomas.loc.gov/cgi-bin/query/z?c106:S.821:>

THE DECLARATION OF INDEPENDENCE

Thomas Jefferson

In addition to serving two terms as president of the United States, Thomas Jefferson (1743–1826) was also vice president of the United States, secretary of state, minister to France, and governor of Virginia. A man of many interests and deep learning, he was also president of the American Philosophical Society and founder of the University of Virginia. But when surveying his long and distinguished career toward the end of his life, he was especially proud of his work on The Declaration of Independence.

As you read it, look closely at the principles with which Jefferson begins, think about what they mean, and consider how they contribute to the argument that follows. Pay close attention as well to Jefferson's language throughout this argument. Although The Declaration of Independence has become part of our national heritage, it began as a writing assignment that went through a number of different drafts. Before approving this document on July 4, 1776, Congress made twenty-four changes and deleted more than three hundred words. As you read the final draft, ask yourself how you would respond if given the chance to edit Jefferson. Would you vote to adopt the Declaration exactly as it stands, or would you recommend any changes?

When in the course of human events, it becomes necessary for one people to dissolve the political bands which have connected them with another, and to assume among the powers of the earth, the separate and equal station to which the Laws of Nature and of Nature's God entitle them, a decent respect to the opinions of mankind requires that they should declare the causes which impel them to the separation.

We hold these truths to be self-evident, that all men are created equal, that they are endowed by their Creator with certain unalienable rights, that among these are life, liberty and the pursuit of happiness. That to secure these rights, governments are instituted among men, deriving their just powers from the consent of the governed. That whenever any form of government becomes destructive of these ends, it is the right of the people to alter or to abolish it, and to institute new government, laying its foundation on such principles and organizing its powers in such form, as to them shall seem most likely to effect their safety and happiness. Prudence, indeed, will dictate that governments long established should not be changed for light and transient causes; and accordingly all experience hath shown, that mankind are more disposed to suffer, while evils are sufferable, than to right themselves by abolishing the forms to which they are accustomed. But when a long train of abuses and usurpations, pursuing invariably the same object, evinces a design to reduce them under absolute despotism, it is their right, it is their duty, to throw off such government, and to provide new guards for their future security. Such has been the patient sufferance of these Colonies; and such is now the necessity which constrains them to alter their former systems of government. This history of the present King of Great Britain° is a history of repeated injuries and usurpations, all having in direct object the establishment of an absolute tyranny over these States. To prove this, let facts be submitted to a candid world.

He has refused his assent to laws, the most wholesome and necessary for the public good.

He has forbidden his Governors to pass laws of immediate and pressing importance, unless suspended in their operation till his assent should be obtained; and when so suspended, he has utterly neglected to attend to them.

He has refused to pass other laws for the accommodation of large districts   5
of people, unless those people would relinquish the right of representation in the legislature, a right inestimable to them and formidable to tyrants only.

He has called together legislative bodies at places unusual, uncomfortable, and distant from the depository of their public records, for the sole purpose of fatiguing them into compliance with his measures.

He has dissolved representative houses repeatedly, for opposing with manly firmness his invasions on the rights of the people.

He has refused for a long time, after such dissolutions, to cause others to be elected; whereby the legislative powers, incapable of annihilation, have returned to the people at large for their exercise; the State remaining in the meantime exposed to all the dangers of invasion from without and convulsions within.

He has endeavoured to prevent the population of these states; for that purpose obstructing the laws for naturalization of foreigners; refusing to pass others to encourage their migration hither, and raising the conditions of new appropriations of lands.

He has obstructed the administration of justice, by refusing his assent to   10
laws for establishing judiciary powers.

He has made judges dependent on his will alone, for the tenure of their offices, and the amount and payment of their salaries.

He has erected a multitude of new offices, and sent hither swarms of officers to harass our people, and eat out their substance.

He has kept among us, in times of peace, standing armies without the consent of our legislatures.

He has affected to render the military independent of and superior to the civil power.

He has combined with others to subject us to a jurisdiction foreign to   15
our constitution, and unacknowledged by our laws; giving his assent to their acts of pretended legislation:

For quartering large bodies of armed troops among us:

For protecting them, by a mock trial, from punishment for any murders which they should commit on the inhabitants of these States:

---

the present King of Great Britain: George III, who ruled from 1760 to 1820.

For cutting off our trade with all parts of the world:

For imposing taxes on us without our consent:

For depriving us in many cases of the benefits of trial by jury: *20*

For transporting us beyond seas to be tried for pretended offences:

For abolishing the free system of English laws in a neighbouring Province, establishing therein an arbitrary government, and enlarging its boundaries so as to render it at once an example and fit instrument for introducing the same absolute rule into these Colonies:

For taking away our Charters, abolishing our most valuable laws, and altering fundamentally the forms of our governments:

For suspending our own legislatures, and declaring themselves invested with power to legislate for us in all cases whatsoever.

He has abdicated government here, by declaring us out of his protection   *25* and waging war against us.

He has plundered our seas, ravaged our coasts, burnt our towns, and destroyed the lives of our people.

He is at this time transporting large armies of foreign mercenaries to complete the works of death, desolation and tyranny, already begun with circumstances of cruelty and perfidy scarcely paralleled in the most barbarous ages, and totally unworthy the head of a civilized nation.

He has constrained our fellow citizens taken captive on the high seas to bear arms against their country, to become the executioners of their friends and brethren, or to fall themselves by their hands.

He has excited domestic insurrections amongst us, and has endeavoured to bring on the inhabitants of our frontiers, the merciless Indian savages, whose known rule of welfare, is an undistinguished destruction of all ages, sexes, and conditions.

In every stage of these oppressions we have petitioned for redress in the   *30* most humble terms: our repeated petitions have been answered only by repeated injury. A prince whose character is thus marked by every act which may define a tyrant is unfit to be the ruler of a free people.

Nor have we been wanting in attention to our British brethren. We have warned them from time to time of attempts by their legislature to extend an unwarrantable jurisdiction over us. We have reminded them of the circumstances of our emigration and settlement here. We have appealed to their native justice and magnanimity, and we have conjured them by the ties of our common kindred to disavow these usurpations, which would inevitably interrupt our connections and correspondence. They too have been deaf to the voice of justice and consanguinity. We must, therefore, acquiesce in the necessity, which denounces our separation, and hold them, as we hold the rest of mankind, enemies in war, in peace friends.

We, therefore, the Representatives of the United States of America, in General Congress assembled, appealing to the Supreme Judge of the world for the rectitude of our intentions, do, in the name, and by authority of the good people of these Colonies, solemnly publish and declare, That these

United Colonies are, and of right ought to be, Free and Independent States; that they are absolved from all allegiance to the British Crown, and that all political connection between them and the state of Great Britain, is and ought to be totally dissolved; and that as Free and Independent States, they have full power to levy war, conclude peace, contract alliances, establish commerce, and to do all other acts and things which Independent States may of right do. And for the support of this declaration, with a firm reliance on the protection of Divine Providence, we mutually pledge to each other our lives, our fortunes, and our sacred honor.

QUESTIONS FOR DISCUSSION

1. What do you think Jefferson meant by "men" in paragraph 2? What does it mean to have "unalienable rights"? And what do you think "the pursuit of happiness" means?
2. Jefferson begins his argument with truths that he declares to be "self-evident." Do any of the statements in paragraph 2 strike you as open to dispute?
3. Of the various charges Jefferson makes against King George III, which do you think are the most serious?
4. How fairly has Jefferson treated Native Americans in this document?
5. Has Jefferson taken any steps to protect his fellow colonists from the charge that they were acting rashly in declaring independence?
6. Modern conventions governing capitalization differ from those that were observed in the eighteenth century. When first published, paragraph 32 began with a reference to the "Representatives of the united States of America." Is there a difference between "united States of America" and "United States of America"?

SUGGESTIONS FOR WRITING

1. Slavery was legal in this country for almost a hundred years after the Declaration of Independence, and women were not allowed to vote in national elections until 1920. Do you think there are people living in this country today who still do not enjoy the right to "life, liberty, and the pursuit of happiness"? If so, write a "declaration of independence" supporting their rights.
2. According to Jefferson, George III was a tyrant guilty of "cruelty and perfidy scarcely paralleled in the most barbarous ages." Do research on George III, and then write an argument on his behalf.
3. Canada remained part of the British empire when the United States became independent, and Canada continues to be part of the British Commonwealth. Research the British Commonwealth, and write an argument for or against this kind of international organization.

LINKS ▪ ▪ ▪

▪ WITHIN THE BOOK

After reading the Declaration of Independence, consider how it provides support for Martin Luther King, Jr.'s "Letters from Birmingham Jail" (pages 534–548).

▪ ELSEWHERE IN PRINT

Becker, Carl Lotus. *The Declaration of Independence: A Study in the History of Political Ideas.* 1922. New York: Random, 1958.

Boyd, Julian, P. *The Declaration of Independence: The Evolution of the Text.* Ed. Gerard W. Gawalt. Rev. ed. Charlottesville: Intl. Center for Jefferson Studies, 1999.

Eicholz, Hans. *Harmonizing Sentiments: The Declaration of Independence and the Jeffersonian Ideal of Self-Government.* New York: Lang, 2001.

Maier, Pauline. *American Scripture: Making the Declaration of Independence.* New York: Knopf, 1997.

▪ ONLINE

- Brief Biography
  <http://gi.grolier.com/presidents/ea/bios/03pjeff.html>

- Jefferson Digital Archive
  <http://etext.virginia.edu/jefferson>

- Jefferson Papers
  <http://memory.loc.gov/ammem/mtjhtml/mtjhome.html>

- King George III
  <http://www.pro.gov.uk/virtualmuseum/millennium/olive/george/default.htm>

LETTER FROM BIRMINGHAM JAIL IN RESPONSE TO PUBLIC STATEMENT BY EIGHT ALABAMA CLERGYMEN

Martin Luther King, Jr.

By 1963 the movement for civil rights for African Americans had become a national issue, and the United States was bitterly divided between people who perceived this movement as a threat to social order and others who recognized that social justice required serious changes in our country. In that year, Martin Luther King, Jr. (1929–1968) led a nonviolent campaign to end segregation in Birmingham, Alabama. As a result, he was jailed for eight days—one of fourteen times he was imprisoned because of his work for civil rights. While in jail, he read a published statement by eight prominent clergymen who condemned his work and supported the police. King began his response by writing in the margins of the newspaper in which he had been denounced, continued it on scraps of paper supplied by a prison trustee, and concluded on a pad that his attorneys were eventually allowed to give him. Here is the letter to which King responded, followed by his reply. As you read, be alert for how King defends himself from the charges brought against him.

April 12, 1963

We the undersigned clergymen are among those who, in January, issued "An Appeal for Law and Order and Common Sense," in dealing with racial problems in Alabama. We expressed understanding that honest convictions in racial matters could properly be pursued in the courts, but urged that decisions of those courts should in the meantime be peacefully obeyed.

Since that time there had been some evidence of increased forbearance and a willingness to face facts. Responsible citizens have undertaken to work on various problems which cause racial friction and unrest. In Birmingham, recent public events have given indication that we all have opportunity for a new constructive and realistic approach to racial problems.

However, we are now confronted by a series of demonstrations by some of our Negro citizens, directed and led in part by outsiders. We recognize the natural impatience of people who feel that their hopes are slow in being realized. But we are convinced that these demonstrations are unwise and untimely.

We agree rather with certain local Negro leadership which has called for honest and open negotiation of racial issues in our area. And we believe this kind of facing of issues can best be accomplished by citizens of our own metropolitan area, white and Negro, meeting with their knowledge and experience of the local situation. All of us need to face that responsibility and find proper channels for its accomplishment.

Just as we formerly pointed out that "hatred and violence have no sanc-   5
tion in our religious and political traditions," we also point out that such
actions as incite to hatred and violence, however technically peaceful those
actions may be, have not contributed to the resolution of our local problems.
We do not believe that these days of new hope are days when extreme measures are justified in Birmingham.

We commend the community as a whole, and the local news media and
law enforcement officials in particular, on the calm manner in which these
demonstrations have been handled. We urge the public to continue to show
restraint should the demonstrations continue, and the law enforcement officials to remain calm and continue to protect our city from violence.

We further strongly urge our own Negro community to withdraw support from these demonstrations, and to unite locally in working peacefully
for a better Birmingham. When rights are consistently denied, a cause should
be pressed in the courts and in negotiations among local leaders, and not in
the streets. We appeal to both our white and Negro citizenry to observe the
principles of law and order and common sense.

Signed by:
C. C. J. Carpenter, D.D., LL.D., *Bishop of Alabama*
Joseph A. Durick, D.D., *Auxiliary Bishop, Diocese of Mobile, Birmingham*
Rabbi Milton L. Grafman, *Temple Emanu-El, Birmingham, Alabama*
Bishop Paul Hardin, *Bishop of the Alabama-West Florida Conference of the
    Methodist Church*
Bishop Nolan B. Harmon, *Bishop of the North Alabama Conference of the
    Methodist Church*
George M. Murray, D.D., LL.D., *Bishop Coadjutor, Episcopal Diocese of Alabama*
Edward V. Ramage, *Moderator, Synod of the Alabama Presbyterian Church in the
    United States*
Earl Stallings, *Pastor, First Baptist Church, Birmingham, Alabama*

**Following is the letter Martin Luther King, Jr., wrote in response to the clergy-
men's public statement.**

April 16, 1963

My Dear Fellow Clergymen:
    While confined here in the Birmingham city jail, I came across your recent
statement calling my present activities "unwise and untimely." Seldom do I
pause to answer criticism of my work and ideas. If I sought to answer all the
criticisms that cross my desk, my secretaries would have little time for anything
other than such correspondence in the course of the day, and I would have no
time for constructive work. But since I feel that you are men of genuine good
will and that your criticisms are sincerely set forth, I want to try to answer
your statement in what I hope will be patient and reasonable terms.

I think I should indicate why I am here in Birmingham, since you have been influenced by the view which argues against "outsiders coming in." I have the honor of serving as president of the Southern Christian Leadership Conference, an organization operating in every southern state, with headquarters in Atlanta, Georgia. We have some eighty-five affiliated organizations across the South, and one of them is the Alabama Christian Movement for Human Rights. Frequently we share staff, educational and financial resources with our affiliates. Several months ago the affiliate here in Birmingham asked us to be on call to engage in a nonviolent direct-action program if such were deemed necessary. We readily consented, and when the hour came we lived up to our promise. So I, along with several members of my staff, am here because I was invited here. I am here because I have organizational ties here.

But more basically, I am in Birmingham because injustice is here. Just as   10
the prophets of the eighth century B.C. left their villages and carried their "thus saith the Lord" far beyond the boundaries of their home towns, and just as the Apostle Paul left his village of Tarsus and carried the gospel of Jesus Christ to the far corners of the Greco-Roman world, so am I compelled to carry the gospel of freedom beyond my own home town. Like Paul, I must constantly respond to the Macedonian call for aid.

Moreover, I am cognizant of the interrelatedness of all communities and states. I cannot sit idly by in Atlanta and not be concerned about what happens in Birmingham. Injustice anywhere is a threat to justice everywhere. We are caught in an inescapable network of mutuality, tied in a single garment of destiny. Whatever affects one directly, affects all indirectly. Never again can we afford to live with the narrow, provincial "outside agitator" idea. Anyone who lives inside the United States can never be considered an outsider anywhere within its bounds.

You deplore the demonstrations taking place in Birmingham. But your statement, I am sorry to say, fails to express a similar concern for the conditions that brought about the demonstrations. I am sure that none of you would want to rest content with the superficial kind of social analysis that deals merely with effects and does not grapple with underlying causes. It is unfortunate that demonstrations are taking place in Birmingham, but it is even more unfortunate that the city's white power structure left the Negro community with no alternative.

In any nonviolent campaign there are four basic steps: collection of the facts to determine whether injustices exist; negotiation; self-purification; and direct action. We have gone through all these steps in Birmingham. There can be no gainsaying the fact that racial injustice engulfs this community. Birmingham is probably the most thoroughly segregated city in the United States. Its ugly record of brutality is widely known. Negroes have experienced grossly unjust treatment in the courts. There have been more unsolved bombings of Negro homes and churches in Birmingham than in any other city in the nation. These are the hard, brutal facts of the case. On the basis of these conditions, Negro leaders sought to negotiate with the city fathers. But the latter consistently refused to engage in good-faith negotiation.

Then, last September, came the opportunity to talk with leaders of Birmingham's economic community. In the course of the negotiations, certain promises were made by the merchants—for example, to remove the stores' humiliating racial signs. On the basis of these promises, the Reverend Fred Shuttlesworth and the leaders of the Alabama Christian Movement for Human Rights agreed to a moratorium on all demonstrations. As the weeks and months went by, we realized that we were the victims of a broken promise. A few signs, briefly removed, returned; the others remained.

As in so many past experiences, our hopes had been blasted, and the   15 shadow of deep disappointment settled upon us. We had no alternative except to prepare for direct action, whereby we would present our very bodies as a means of laying our case before the conscience of the local and the national community. Mindful of the difficulties involved, we decided to undertake a process of self-purification. We began a series of workshops on nonviolence, and we repeatedly asked ourselves: "Are you able to accept blows without retaliating?" "Are you able to endure the ordeal of jail?" We decided to schedule our direct-action program for the Easter season, realizing that except for Christmas, this is the main shopping period of the year. Knowing that a strong economic-withdrawal program would be the by-product of direct action, we felt that this would be the best time to bring pressure to bear on the merchants for the needed change.

Then it occurred to us that Birmingham's mayoral election was coming up in March, and we speedily decided to postpone action until after election day. When we discovered that the Commissioner of Public Safety, Eugene "Bull" Connor,° had piled up enough votes to be in the run-off, we decided again to postpone action until the day after the run-off so that the demonstrations could not be used to cloud the issues. Like many others, we waited to see Mr. Connor defeated, and to this end we endured postponement after postponement. Having aided in this community need, we felt that our direct-action program could be delayed no longer.

You may well ask: "Why direct action? Why sit-ins, marches and so forth? Isn't negotiation a better path?" You are quite right in calling for negotiation. Indeed, this is the very purpose of direct action. Nonviolent direct action seeks to create such a crisis and foster such a tension that a community which has constantly refused to negotiate is forced to confront the issue. It seeks so to dramatize the issue that it can no longer be ignored. My citing the creation of tension as part of the work of the nonviolent resister may sound rather shocking. But I must confess that I am not afraid of the word "tension." I have earnestly opposed violent tension, but there is a type of constructive, nonviolent tension which is necessary for growth. Just as Socrates felt that it was necessary to create

---

Eugene "Bull" Connor: Commissioner of Public Safety in Birmingham during 1937–1953 and 1957–1963. One of three commissioners responsible for governing Birmingham, and the commissioner with the most seniority, Connor (1897–1973) was a powerful opponent of integration who used the police to make war on civil rights demonstrators.

a tension in the mind so that individuals could rise from the bondage of myths and half-truths to the unfettered realm of creative analysis and objective appraisal, so must we see the need for nonviolent gadflies to create the kind of tension in society that will help men rise from the dark depths of prejudice and racism to the majestic heights of understanding and brotherhood.

The purpose of our direct-action program is to create a situation so crisis-packed that it will inevitably open the door to negotiation. I therefore concur with you in your call for negotiation. Too long has our beloved Southland been bogged down in a tragic effort to live in monologue rather than dialogue.

One of the basic points in your statement is that the action that I and my associates have taken in Birmingham is untimely. Some have asked: "Why didn't you give the new city administration time to act?" The only answer that I can give to this query is that the new Birmingham administration must be prodded about as much as the outgoing one, before it will act. We are sadly mistaken if we feel that the election of Albert Boutwell as mayor will bring the millennium to Birmingham. While Mr. Boutwell is a much more gentle person than Mr. Connor, they are both segregationists, dedicated to maintenance of the status quo. I have hope that Mr. Boutwell will be reasonable enough to see the futility of massive resistance to desegregation. But he will not see this without pressure from devotees of civil rights. My friends, I must say to you that we have not made a single gain in civil rights without determined legal and nonviolent pressure. Lamentably, it is an historical fact that privileged groups seldom give up their privileges voluntarily. Individuals may see the moral light and voluntarily give up their unjust posture; but, as Reinhold Niebuhr has reminded us, groups tend to be more immoral than individuals.

We know through painful experience that freedom is never voluntarily given by the oppressor; it must be demanded by the oppressed. Frankly, I have yet to engage in a direct-action campaign that was "well timed" in the view of those who have not suffered unduly from the disease of segregation. For years now I have heard the word "Wait!" It rings in the ear of every Negro with piercing familiarity. This "Wait" has almost always meant "Never." We must come to see, with one of our distinguished jurists, that "justice too long delayed is justice denied."

We have waited for more than 340 years for our constitutional God-given rights. The nations of Asia and Africa are moving with jetlike speed toward gaining political independence, but we still creep at horse-and-buggy pace toward gaining a cup of coffee at a lunch counter. Perhaps it is easy for those who have never felt the stinging darts of segregation to say, "Wait." But when you have seen vicious mobs lynch your mothers and fathers at will and drown your sisters and brothers at whim; when you have seen hate-filled policemen curse, kick, and even kill your black brothers and sisters; when you see the vast majority of your twenty million Negro brothers smothering in an airtight cage of poverty in the midst of an affluent society; when you suddenly find your tongue twisted and your speech stammering as you seek to explain to your

20

six-year-old daughter why she can't go to the public amusement park that has just been advertised on television, and see tears welling up in her eyes when she is told that Funtown is closed to colored children, and see ominous clouds of inferiority beginning to form in her little mental sky, and see her beginning to distort her personality by developing an unconscious bitterness toward white people; when you have to concoct an answer for a five-year-old son who is asking: "Daddy, why do white people treat colored people so mean?"; when you take a cross-country drive and find it necessary to sleep night after night in the uncomfortable corners of your automobile because no motel will accept you; when you are humiliated day in and day out by nagging signs reading "white" and "colored"; when your first name becomes "nigger," your middle name becomes "boy" (however old you are) and your last name becomes "John," and your wife and mother are never given the respected title "Mrs."; when you are harried by day and haunted by night by the fact that you are a Negro, living constantly at tiptoe stance, never quite knowing what to expect next, and are plagued with inner fears and outer resentments; when you are forever fighting a degenerating sense of "nobodiness"—then you will understand why we find it difficult to wait. There comes a time when a cup of endurance runs over, and men are no longer willing to be plunged into the abyss of despair. I hope, sirs, you can understand our legitimate and unavoidable impatience.

You express a great deal of anxiety over our willingness to break laws. This is certainly a legitimate concern. Since we so diligently urge people to obey the Supreme Court's decision of 1954 outlawing segregation in the public schools, at first glance it may seem rather paradoxical for us consciously to break laws. One may well ask: "How can you advocate breaking some laws and obeying others?" The answer lies in the fact that there are two types of laws: just and unjust. I would be the first to advocate obeying just laws. One has not only a legal but a moral responsibility to obey just laws. Conversely, one has a moral responsibility to disobey unjust laws. I would agree with St. Augustine that "an unjust law is no law at all."

Now, what is the difference between the two? How does one determine whether a law is just or unjust? A just law is a man-made code that squares with the moral law or the law of God. An unjust law is a code that is out of harmony with the moral law. To put it in the terms of St. Thomas Aquinas: An unjust law is a human law that is not rooted in eternal law and natural law. Any law that uplifts human personality is just. Any law that degrades human personality is unjust. All segregation statutes are unjust because segregation distorts the soul and damages the personality. It gives the segregator a false sense of superiority and the segregated a false sense of inferiority. Segregation, to use the terminology of the Jewish philosopher Martin Buber, substitutes an "I–it" relationship for an "I–thou" relationship and ends up relegating persons to the status of things. Hence, segregation is not only politically, economically and sociologically unsound, it is morally wrong and sinful. Paul Tillich has said that sin is separation. Is not segregation an existential expression of man's tragic separation, his awful estrangement, his terrible sinfulness? Thus it is that I can urge men to obey the 1954 decision of the Supreme Court, for it is morally right; and I can urge them to disobey segregation ordinances, for they are morally wrong.

Let us consider a more concrete example of just and unjust laws. An unjust law is a code that a numerical or power majority group compels a minority group to obey but does not make binding on itself. This is *difference* made legal. By the same token, a just law is a code that a majority compels a minority to follow and that it is willing to follow itself. This is *sameness* made legal.

Let me give another explanation. A law is unjust if it is inflicted on a   25
minority that, as a result of being denied the right to vote, had no part in enacting or devising the law. Who can say that the legislature of Alabama which set up that state's segregation laws was democratically elected? Throughout Alabama all sorts of devious methods are used to prevent Negroes from becoming registered voters, and there are some counties in which, even though Negroes constitute a majority of the population, not a single Negro is registered. Can any law enacted under such circumstances be considered democratically structured?

Sometimes a law is just on its face and unjust in its application. For instance, I have been arrested on a charge of parading without a permit. Now, there is nothing wrong in having an ordinance which requires a permit for a parade. But such an ordinance becomes unjust when it is used to maintain segregation and to deny citizens the First-Amendment privilege of peaceful assembly and protest.

I hope you are able to see the distinction I am trying to point out. In no sense do I advocate evading or defying the law, as would the rabid segregationist. That would lead to anarchy. One who breaks an unjust law must do so openly, lovingly, and with a willingness to accept the penalty. I submit that an individual who breaks a law that conscience tells him is unjust, and who willingly accepts the penalty of imprisonment in order to arouse the conscience of the community over its injustice, is in reality expressing the highest respect for law.

Of course, there is nothing new about this kind of civil disobedience. It was evidenced sublimely in the refusal of Shadrach, Meshach and Abednego to obey the laws of Nebuchadnezzar, on the ground that a higher moral law was at stake. It was practiced superbly by the early Christians, who were willing to face hungry lions and the excruciating pain of chopping blocks rather than submit to certain unjust laws of the Roman Empire. To a degree, academic freedom is a reality today because Socrates practiced civil disobedience. In our own nation, the Boston Tea Party represented a massive act of civil disobedience.

We should never forget that everything Adolf Hitler did in Germany was "legal" and everything the Hungarian freedom fighters° did in Hungary was "illegal." It was "illegal" to aid and comfort a Jew in Hitler's Germany. Even

---

Hungarian freedom fighters: In 1956 Hungarian citizens rose up against the Communist dictatorship in their country. Their revolt was suppressed when the Soviet Union responded by sending tanks into Budapest.

so, I am sure that, had I lived in Germany at the time, I would have aided and comforted my Jewish brothers. If today I lived in a Communist country where certain principles dear to the Christian faith are suppressed, I would openly advocate disobeying that country's antireligious laws.

I must make two honest confessions to you, my Christian and Jewish brothers. First, I must confess that over the past few years I have been gravely disappointed with the white moderate. I have almost reached the regrettable conclusion that the Negro's great stumbling block in his stride toward freedom is not the White Citizen's Counciler or the Ku Klux Klanner, but the white moderate, who is more devoted to "order" than to justice; who prefers a negative peace which is the presence of tension to a positive peace which is the presence of justice; who constantly says: "I agree with you in the goal you seek, but I cannot agree with your methods of direct action"; who paternalistically believes he can set the timetable for another man's freedom; who lives by a mythical concept of time and who constantly advises the Negro to wait for a "more convenient season." Shallow understanding from people of good will is more frustrating than absolute misunderstanding from people of ill will. Lukewarm acceptance is much more bewildering than outright rejection.

I had hoped that the white moderate would understand that law and order exist for the purpose of establishing justice and that when they fail in this purpose they become the dangerously structured dams that block the flow of social progress. I had hoped that the white moderate would understand that the present tension in the South is a necessary phase of the transition from an obnoxious negative peace, in which the Negro passively accepted his unjust plight, to a substantive and positive peace, in which all men will respect the dignity and worth of human personality. Actually, we who engage in nonviolent direct action are not the creators of tension. We merely bring to the surface the hidden tension that is already alive. We bring it out in the open, where it can be seen and dealt with. Like a boil that can never be cured so long as it is covered up but must be opened with all its ugliness to the natural medicines of air and light, injustice must be exposed, with all the tension its exposure creates, to the light of human conscience and the air of national opinion before it can be cured.

In your statement you assert that our actions, even though peaceful, must be condemned because they precipitate violence. But is this a logical assertion? Isn't this like condemning a robbed man because his possession of money precipitated the evil act of robbery? Isn't this like condemning Socrates because his unswerving commitment to truth and his philosophical inquiries precipitated the act by the misguided populace in which they made him drink hemlock? Isn't this like condemning Jesus because his unique God-consciousness and never-ceasing devotion to God's will precipitated the evil act of crucifixion? We must come to see that, as the federal courts have consistently affirmed, it is wrong to urge an individual to cease his efforts to gain his basic constitutional rights because the quest may precipitate violence. Society must protect the robbed and punish the robber.

I had also hoped that the white moderate would reject the myth concerning time in relation to the struggle for freedom. I have just received a letter from a white brother in Texas. He writes: "All Christians know that the colored people will receive equal rights eventually, but it is possible that you are in too great a religious hurry. It has taken Christianity almost two thousand years to accomplish what it has. The teachings of Christ take time to come to earth." Such an attitude stems from a tragic misconception of time, from the strangely irrational notion that there is something in the very flow of time that will inevitably cure all ills. Actually, time itself is neutral; it can be used either destructively or constructively. More and more I feel that the people of ill will have used time much more effectively than have the people of good will. We will have to repent in this generation not merely for the hateful words and actions of the bad people but for the appalling silence of the good people. Human progress never rolls in on wheels of inevitability; it comes through the tireless efforts of men willing to be co-workers with God, and without this hard work, time itself becomes an ally of the forces of social stagnation. We must use time creatively, in the knowledge that the time is always ripe to do right. Now is the time to make real the promise of democracy and transform our pending national elegy into a creative psalm of brotherhood. Now is the time to lift our national policy from the quicksand of racial injustice to the solid rock of human dignity.

You speak of our activity in Birmingham as extreme. At first I was rather disappointed that fellow clergymen would see my nonviolent efforts as those of an extremist. I began thinking about the fact that I stand in the middle of two opposing forces in the Negro community. One is a force of complacency, made up in part of Negroes who, as a result of long years of oppression, are so drained of self-respect and a sense of "somebodiness" that they have adjusted to segregation; and in part of a few middle-class Negroes who, because of a degree of academic and economic security and because in some ways they profit by segregation, have become insensitive to the problems of the masses. The other force is one of bitterness and hatred, and it comes perilously close to advocating violence. It is expressed in the various black nationalists groups that are springing up across the nation, the largest and best-known being Elijah Muhammad's Muslim movement. Nourished by the Negro's frustration over the continued existence of racial discrimination, this movement is made up of people who have lost faith in America, who have absolutely repudiated Christianity, and who have concluded that the white man is an incorrigible "devil."

I have tried to stand between these two forces, saying that we need emulate neither the "do-nothingism" of the complacent nor the hatred and despair of the black nationalist. For there is the more excellent way of love and nonviolent protest. I am grateful to God that, through the influence of the Negro church, the way of nonviolence became an integral part of our struggle. 35

If this philosophy had not emerged, by now many streets of the South would, I am convinced, be flowing with blood. And I am further convinced that if our white brothers dismiss as "rabble-rousers" and "outside agitators" those of us who employ nonviolent direct action, and if they refuse to support our nonviolent efforts, millions of the Negroes will, out of frustration and despair, seek solace and security in black-nationalist ideologies—a development that would inevitably lead to a frightening racial nightmare.

Oppressed people cannot remain oppressed forever. The yearning for freedom eventually manifests itself, and that is what has happened to the American Negro. Something within has reminded him of his birthright of freedom, and something without has reminded him that it can be gained. Consciously or unconsciously, he has been caught up by the *Zeitgeist,*° and with his black brothers of Africa and his brown and yellow brothers of Asia, South America and the Caribbean, the United States Negro is moving with a sense of great urgency toward the promised land of racial justice. If one recognizes this vital urge that has engulfed the Negro community, one should readily understand why public demonstrations are taking place. The Negro has many pent-up resentments and latent frustrations, and he must release them. So let him march; let him make prayer pilgrimages to the city hall; let him go on freedom rides—and try to understand why he must do so. If his repressed emotions are not released in nonviolent ways, they will seek expression through violence; this is not a threat but a fact of history. So I have not said to my people: "Get rid of your discontent." Rather, I have tried to say that this normal and healthy discontent can be channeled into the creative outlet of nonviolent direct action. And now this approach is being termed extremist.

But though I was initially disappointed at being categorized as an extremist, as I continued to think about the matter I gradually gained a measure of satisfaction from the label. Was not Jesus an extremist for love: "Love your enemies, bless them that curse you, do good to them that hate you, and pray for them which despitefully use you, and persecute you." Was not Amos an extremist for justice: "Let justice roll down like waters and righteousness like an ever-flowing stream." Was not Paul an extremist for the Christian gospel: "I bear in my body the marks of the Lord Jesus." Was not Martin Luther an extremist: "Here I stand; I cannot do otherwise, so help me God." And John Bunyan: "I will stay in jail to the end of my days before I make a butchery of my conscience." And Abraham Lincoln: "This nation cannot survive half slave and half free." And Thomas Jefferson: "We hold these truths to be self-evident, that all men are created equal. . . ." So the question is not whether we will be extremists, but what kind of extremists we will be. Will we be extremists for hate or for love? Will we be extremists for the preservation of injustice or for the extension of justice? In that dramatic scene on Calvary's hill three men were crucified. We must never forget that all three were crucified for the same crime—the crime of extremism. Two were extremists for immorality, and thus fell below their environment. The other, Jesus Christ, was an extremist for love, truth and goodness, and thereby rose above his environment. Perhaps the South, the nation and the world are in dire need of creative extremists.

Zeitgeist: German for "spirit of the times."

I had hoped that the white moderate would see this need. Perhaps I was too optimistic; perhaps I expected too much. I suppose I should have realized that few members of the oppressor race can understand the deep groans and passionate yearnings of the oppressed race, and still fewer have the vision to see that injustice must be rooted out by strong, persistent and determined action. I am thankful, however, that some of our white brothers in the South have grasped the meaning of this social revolution and committed themselves to it. They are still all too few in quantity, but they are big in quality. Some— such as Ralph McGill, Lillian Smith, Harry Golden, James McBride Dabbs, Ann Braden and Sarah Patton Boyle—have written about our struggle in eloquent and prophetic terms. Others have marched with us down nameless streets of the South. They have languished in filthy, roach-infested jails, suffering the abuse and brutality of policemen who view them as "dirty niggerlovers." Unlike so many of their moderate brothers and sisters, they have recognized the urgency of the moment and sensed the need for powerful "action" antidotes to combat the disease of segregation.

Let me take note of my other major disappointment. I have been so greatly disappointed with the white church and its leadership. Of course, there are some notable exceptions. I am not unmindful of the fact that each of you has taken some significant stands on this issue. I commend you, Reverend Stallings, for your Christian stand on this past Sunday, in welcoming Negroes to your worship service on a nonsegregated basis. I commend the Catholic leaders of this state for integrating Spring Hill College several years ago. *40*

But despite these notable exceptions, I must honestly reiterate that I have been disappointed with the church. I do not say this as one of those negative critics who can always find something wrong with the church. I say this as a minister of the gospel, who loves the church; who was nurtured in its bosom; who has been sustained by its spiritual blessings and who will remain true to it as long as the cord of life shall lengthen.

When I was suddenly catapulted into the leadership of the bus protest in Montgomery, Alabama, a few years ago, I felt we would be supported by the white church. I felt that the white ministers, priests and rabbis of the South would be among our strongest allies. Instead, some have been outright opponents, refusing to understand the freedom movement and misrepresenting its leaders; all too many others have been more cautious than courageous and have remained silent behind the anesthetizing security of stained-glass windows.

In spite of my shattered dreams, I came to Birmingham with the hope that the white religious leadership of this community would see the justice of our cause and, with deep moral concern, would serve as the channel through which our just grievances could reach the power structure. I had hoped that each of you would understand. But again I have been disappointed.

I have heard numerous southern religious leaders admonish their worshipers to comply with a desegregation decision because it is the law, but I have longed to hear white ministers declare: "Follow this decree because integration is morally right and because the Negro is your brother." In the midst of blatant injustices inflicted upon the Negro, I have watched white churchmen stand on the sideline and mouth pious irrelevancies and sanctimonious trivialities. In the midst of a mighty struggle to rid our nation of racial and economic injustice, I have heard many ministers say: "Those are social issues, with which the gospel has no real concern." And I have watched many churches commit themselves to a completely otherworldly religion which makes a strange, un–Biblical distinction between body and soul, between the sacred and the secular.

I have traveled the length and breadth of Alabama, Mississippi and all the   45 other southern states. On sweltering summer days and crisp autumn mornings I have looked at the South's beautiful churches with their lofty spires pointing heavenward. I have beheld the impressive outlines of her massive religious-education buildings. Over and over I have found myself asking: "What kind of people worship here? Who is their God? Where were their voices when the lips of Governor Barnett dripped with words of interposition and nullification? Where were they when Governor Wallace gave a clarion call for defiance and hatred? Where were their voices of support when bruised and weary Negro men and women decided to rise from the dark dungeons of complacency to the bright hills of creative protest?"

Yes, these questions are still in my mind. In deep disappointment I have wept over the laxity of the church. But be assured that my tears have been tears of love. There can be no deep disappointment where there is not deep love. Yes, I love the church. How could I do otherwise? I am in the rather unique position of being the son, the grandson, and the great-grandson of preachers. Yes, I see the church as the body of Christ. But, oh! How we have blemished and scarred that body through social neglect and through fear of being nonconformists.

There was a time when the church was very powerful—in the time when the early Christians rejoiced at being deemed worthy to suffer for what they believed. In those days the church was not merely a thermometer that recorded the ideas and principles of popular opinion; it was a thermostat that transformed the mores of society. Whenever the early Christians entered a town, the people in power became disturbed and immediately sought to convict the Christians for being "disturbers of the peace" and "outside agitators." But the Christians pressed on, in the conviction that they were "a colony of heaven," called to obey God rather than man. Small in number, they were big in commitment. They were too God-intoxicated to be "astronomically intimidated." By their effort and example they brought an end to such ancient evils as infanticide and gladiatorial contests.

Things are different now. So often the contemporary church is a weak, ineffectual voice with an uncertain sound. So often it is an archdefender of the status quo. Far from being disturbed by the presence of the church, the power structure of the average community is consoled by the church's silent— and often even vocal—sanction of things as they are.

But the judgment of God is upon the church as never before. If today's church does not recapture the sacrificial spirit of the early church, it will lose its authenticity, forfeit the loyalty of millions, and be dismissed as an irrelevant social club with no meaning for the twentieth century. Every day I meet young people whose disappointment with the church has turned into outright disgust.

Perhaps I have once again been too optimistic. Is organized religion too 50 inextricably bound to the status quo to save our nation and the world? Perhaps I must turn my faith to the inner spiritual church, the church within the church, as the true *ekklesia*° and the hope of the world. But again I am thankful to God that some noble souls from the ranks of organized religion have broken loose from the paralyzing chains of conformity and joined us as active partners in the struggle for freedom. They have left their secure congregations and walked the streets of Albany, Georgia, with us. They have gone down the highways of the South on tortuous rides for freedom. Yes, they have gone to jail with us. Some have been dismissed from their churches, have lost the support of their bishops and fellow ministers. But they have acted in the faith that right defeated is stronger than evil triumphant. Their witness has been the spiritual salt that has preserved the true meaning of the gospel in these troubled times. They have carved a tunnel of hope through the dark mountain of disappointment.

I hope the church as a whole will meet the challenge of this decisive hour. But even if the church does not come to the aid of justice, I have no despair about the future. I have no fear about the outcome of our struggle in Birmingham, even if our motives are at present misunderstood. We will reach the goal of freedom in Birmingham and all over the nation, because the goal of America is freedom. Abused and scorned though we may be, our destiny is tied up with America's destiny. Before the pilgrims landed at Plymouth, we were here. Before the pen of Jefferson etched the majestic words of the Declaration of Independence across the pages of history, we were here. For more than two centuries our forebears labored in this country without wages; they made cotton king; they built the homes of their masters while suffering gross injustice and shameful humiliation—and yet out of a bottomless vitality they continued to thrive and develop. If the inexpressible cruelties of slavery could not stop us, the opposition we now face will surely fail. We will win our freedom because the sacred heritage of our nation and the eternal will of God are embodied in our echoing demands.

Before closing I feel impelled to mention one other point in your statement that has troubled me profoundly. You warmly commended the Birmingham police force for keeping "order" and "preventing violence." I doubt that you would have so warmly commended the police force if you had seen its dogs sinking their teeth into unarmed, nonviolent Negroes. I doubt that you would so quickly commend the policemen if you were to observe their ugly and inhumane treatment of Negroes here in the city jail; if you were to watch them push and curse old Negro women and young Negro girls; if you

---

ekklesia: Greek for "assembly" or "congregation."

were to see them slap and kick old Negro men and young boys; if you were to observe them, as they did on two occasions, refuse to give us food because we wanted to sing our grace together. I cannot join you in your praise of the Birmingham police department.

It is true that police have exercised a degree of discipline in handling the demonstrators. In this sense they have conducted themselves rather "nonviolently" in public. But for what purpose? To preserve the evil system of segregation. Over the past few years I have consistently preached that nonviolence demands that the means we use must be as pure as the ends we seek. I have tried to make clear that it is wrong to use immoral means to attain moral ends. But now I must affirm that it is just as wrong, or perhaps even more so, to use moral means to preserve immoral ends. Perhaps Mr. Connor and his policemen have been rather nonviolent in public, as was Chief Pritchett in Albany, Georgia, but they have used the moral means of nonviolence to maintain the immoral end of racial injustice. As T. S. Eliot has said: "The last temptation is the greatest treason: To do the right deed for the wrong reason."

I wish you had commended the Negro sit-inners and demonstrators of Birmingham for their sublime courage, their willingness to suffer and their amazing discipline in the midst of great provocation. One day the South will recognize its real heroes. They will be the James Merediths, with the noble sense of purpose that enables them to face jeering and hostile mobs, and with the agonizing loneliness that characterizes the life of the pioneer. They will be old, oppressed, battered Negro women, symbolized in a seventy-two-year-old woman in Montgomery, Alabama, who rose up with a sense of dignity and with her people decided not to ride segregated buses, and who responded with ungrammatical profundity to one who inquired about her weariness: "My feets is tired, but my soul is at rest." They will be the young high school and college students, the young ministers of the gospel and a host of their elders, courageously and nonviolently sitting in at lunch counters and willingly going to jail for conscience' sake. One day the South will know that when these disinherited children of God sat down at lunch counters, they were in reality standing up for what is best in the American dream and for the most sacred values in our Judaeo-Christian heritage, thereby bringing our nation back to those great wells of democracy which were dug deep by the founding fathers in their formulation of the Constitution and the Declaration of Independence.

Never before have I written so long a letter. I'm afraid it is much too long to take your precious time. I can assure you that it would have been much shorter if I had been writing from a comfortable desk, but what else can one do when he is alone in a narrow jail cell, other than write long letters, think long thoughts and pray long prayers?

If I have said anything in this letter that overstates the truth and indicates an unreasonable impatience, I beg you to forgive me. If I have said anything that understates the truth and indicates my having a patience that allows me to settle for anything less than brotherhood, I beg God to forgive me.

I hope this letter finds you strong in faith. I also hope that circumstances will soon make it possible for me to meet each of you, not as an integrationist or a civil-rights leader but as a fellow clergyman and a Christian brother. Let us all hope that the dark clouds of racial prejudice will soon pass away and the deep fog of misunderstanding will be lifted from our fear-drenched communities, and in some not too distant tomorrow the radiant stars of love and brotherhood will shine over our great nation with all their scintillating beauty.

Yours for the cause of Peace and Brotherhood
Martin Luther King, Jr.

QUESTIONS FOR DISCUSSION

1. How does King present himself in this letter? Is his own character a factor in the argument he makes?
2. Where does King show that he is writing for an audience of clergymen? Is there any evidence suggesting that he may also have had a larger audience in mind as he wrote?
3. Most of paragraph 21 consists of a single sentence. How is this sentence structured, and what is its effect? If you were to divide this sentence, where would you do it? What would be the effect of breaking this sentence down into several shorter ones?
4. Imagine that you are a white southerner in 1963 who has misgivings about the civil rights movement. Are there any points where you would feel that King was making an effort to reassure you?
5. According to King, how can we tell the difference between laws that we should obey and laws that we should break? Under what circumstances is it right to break a law?
6. How does King see the church? How does he think Christianity has changed? What does he believe the church should be like?
7. What does King's letter reveal about African American history?

SUGGESTIONS FOR WRITING

1. What elements of this letter make it persuasive? Write an essay explaining how King has structured his argument and identifying the rhetorical strategies that make it effective.
2. Are you concerned about social justice? Identify a social problem in the world today, and write a letter that would persuade your classmates to do something about it.
3. King was awarded the Nobel Peace Prize, a prize given since 1901. The world, however, is rarely at peace. Write a letter to the United Nations, the World Trade Organization, the government of a specific country, or an organized group operating outside the law in which you argue for a change that would make the world more peaceful.

LINKS ■ ■ ■

■ WITHIN THE BOOK

Itabari Njeri (pages 68–72), Gloria Naylor (pages 74–76), and Audre Lorde (pages 712–713) also discuss prejudice against African Americans. For another example of King's work, see "I Have a Dream" (pages 456–459).

■ ELSEWHERE IN PRINT

Bass, S., Jonathan. *Blessed Are the Peacemakers: Martin Luther King, Jr., Eight White Religious Leaders, and the "Letter from Birmingham Jail."* Baton Rouge: Louisiana State UP, 2001.

Buber, Martin. *Good and Evil: Two Interpretations.* Trans. Ronald G. Smith and Michael Bullock. 1953. Upper Saddle River: Prentice, 1990.

Calloway-Thomas, Carolyn, and John Louis Lucaites, eds. *Martin Luther King, Jr., and the Sermonic Power of Public Discourse.* Tuscaloosa: U of Alabama P, 1993.

Lesher, Stephan. *George Wallace: American Populist.* Reading: Addison, 1994.

McWhorter, Diane. *Carry Me Home: Birmingham, Alabama: The Climactic Battle of the Civil Rights Revolution.* New York. Simon, 2001.

Tillich, Paul. *The Courage to Be.* 1952. New Haven. Yale UP, 2000.

Ward, Brian, and Tony Badger, eds. *The Making of Martin Luther King and the Civil Rights Movement.* New York: New York UP, 1996.

■ ONLINE

- Martin Buber
  <http://www.buber.de/en/start.html>

- Martin Luther King: A Historical Examination
  <http://www.martinlutherking.org>

- Martin Luther King Papers Project
  <http://www.stanford.edu/group/king >

- Paul Tillich
  <http://www.theology.ie/theologians/tillich.htm>

- Thomas Aquinas
  <http://aquinasonline.com>

WHY YOU CAN HATE DRUGS AND STILL WANT TO LEGALIZE THEM

Joshua Wolf Shenk

Drug use has a long history in our country, and so do efforts to control it. Governmental agencies have tried a number of policies ranging from arresting users to pressuring other nations to cut back on crops used to manufacture drugs. Once in a while, a major drug dealer is captured or customs agents seize a huge shipment of narcotics. But despite a "war on drugs" that has now been fought for at least thirty years, illegal drugs continue to be easily available in most states, and drug-related crimes continue to touch many lives. Could the time have come for a radically different approach? As you read the following argument by Joshua Wolf Shenk, be alert to how he follows through on both the ideas conveyed by his title: opposing drug use and at the same time legalizing it.

Shenk is a former editor at The Washington Monthly, *where this argument was first published in 1995. Based in New York City, he continues to write frequently about drug policy and mental illness.*

There's no breeze, only bare, stifling heat, but Kevin can scarcely support his wispy frame. He bobs forward, his eyes slowly closing until he drifts asleep, in a 45-degree hunch. "Kevin?" I say softly. He jerks awake and slowly rubs a hand over his spindly chest. "It's so hot in here I can hardly think," he says.

Kevin is wearing an "Americorps" baseball cap, and I ask him where he got it. The lids close over his glassy eyes and then open again, showing a look of gentle but deep confusion. He removes the hat, revealing hair the tone of a red shirt that's been through the washer a thousand times. He blinks again and glances at the cap. He has no idea.

This July, I spent a long, hot day talking to junkies in New York City, in a run-down hotel near Columbia University. Some, like Kevin, were reticent. Others spoke freely about their lives and addictions. I sat with Melissa for 20 minutes as she patiently hunted her needle-scarred legs for a vein to take a spike. She had just fixed after a long dry spell. "I was sick," she told me. "I could hardly move. And Papo"—she gestures toward a friend sitting across from her—"he helped me out. He gave me something to make me better."

To most Americans, addicts like Kevin and Melissa and Papo are not people, but arguments. Some victims of drug use inspire sympathy, or irritation, or just plain worry. But it is the junkies—seemingly bereft of humanity, subsisting in what one former addict calls "soul-death"—who justify our national attitude toward certain drugs: that they should be illegal, unavailable, and totally suppressed.

But this country has another drug problem, one with its own tragic sto- 5
ries. In 1993, Launice Smith was killed in a shoot-out between rival drug
dealers at a football game at an elementary school in Washington, D.C. There
were four other murder victims in the same neighborhood that day. Launice
stood out, though, because she was only four years old.

Addicts suffer from illegal drugs. But each year hundreds of children like
Launice are killed *because* drugs are illegal. It's difficult, but crucial, to understand this distinction. By turning popular drugs into illegal contraband, prohibition sparks tremendous inflation. Small amounts of plant leaves and powder
that cost only pennies to grow and process sell for hundreds of dollars on the
street. All told, the black market in this country takes in $50 to $60 billion in
income each year. In lawful society, such a large industry would be regulated
by rules and enforcement mechanisms. But the intense competition of the
black market is regulated only by violence. Rival entrepreneurs don't go to
the courts with a dispute. They shoot it out in the street.

The black market now holds entire communities in its grip. In addition
to the violence—and crime driven by addicts supporting expensive habits—
the fast cash of dealing lures many young people away from school, into the
drug trade, and often onto a track toward jail or death.

We are caught, then, between the Kevins and the Launices, between the
horror of drug abuse and the horror of the illegal drug trade. Making drugs
legally available, with tight regulatory controls, would end the black market,
and with it much of the violence, crime, and social pathology we have come
to understand as "drug-related." And yet, history shows clearly that lifting
prohibition would allow for more drug use, and more abuse and addiction.

I spent that day in New York to face this excruciating dilemma. It's easy
to call for an end to prohibition from an office in Washington, D.C. What
about when looking into Kevin's dim eyes, or confronting the images of crack
babies, shriveled and wincing?

The choice between two intensely unpleasant options is never easy. But, 10
considering this problem in all its depth and complexity, it becomes clear that
drug prohibition does more harm than good. We can't discount the problem
of drug abuse (and that includes the abuse of legal drugs). But prohibition
didn't keep Kevin from becoming an addict in the first place, and it certainly
isn't helping him stop. High prices for drugs do discourage some would-be
users, though far fewer than the government would like. The fact is we have
done a very poor job discouraging drug use with the blunt force of law. The
hundreds of billions of dollars spent on drug control in the last several decades
have yielded only a moderate decline in the casual use of marijuana and
cocaine. But there has been no decrease in hard-core addiction. The total
amount of cocaine consumed per capita has actually risen. And even casual
use is now creeping up.

Government does have a responsibility to limit the individual and social
costs of drug use, but such efforts must be balanced against the harm they

cause. And ending the drug war needn't mean a surrender to addiction, or an affirmation of reckless drug use. President Clinton's stance on cigarette addiction—that cigarettes can be both legal and tightly regulated, particularly with respect to advertising aimed at children—points to a middle ground. Potentially, we could do a *better* job of fighting drug abuse, while avoiding the vicious side-effects of an outright ban.

Comparing the Costs

Unfortunately, this country's discussion of "the drug problem" is marked by little clear analysis and much misinformation. Politicians and bureaucrats minimize or entirely ignore the consequences of prohibition. At the other extreme, libertarians call for government to withdraw from regulating intoxicants entirely. The press, meanwhile, does little to illuminate the costs and benefits of the current prohibition or our many other policy options. "We don't cover drug policy, except episodically as a cops and robbers story," says Max Frankel, the recently retired executive editor of *The New York Times.* He calls his paper's coverage of the subject "one of my failures there as an editor, and a failure of newspapers generally."

It's not that the consequences of prohibition can't be seen in the newspapers. In the *Times* last December, for example, Isabel Wilkerson wrote a stirring profile of Jovan Rogers, a Chicago crack dealer who entered the trade when he was 14 and ended up crippled by gunshot wounds. But Wilkerson, as reporters usually do, conveyed the impression that the pathology of the black market is unfortunate, but inevitable—not the result of policies that we can change.

In fact, Rogers' story is a vivid display of the lethal drug trade that prohibition creates, the temptation of bright young men, and the cycle of destruction that soon follows.

For his first job, Rogers got $75 a day to watch out for the police. Soon, he was earning thousands a day. And though Rogers said he began dealing to support his family—"If there's nothing to eat at night," he asked, "who's going to go buy something to make sure something is there? I was the only man in the house"—the big bucks also seized him where, like most teenagers, he was most vulnerable. "If you sell drugs, you had anything you wanted," he said. "Any girl, any friend, money, status. If you didn't, you got no girlfriend, no friends, no money. You're a nothing."

This story is all too common. In communities where two-thirds of the youth lack the schooling or skills to get a decent job, drug dealing is both lucrative and glamorous. Rich dealers are role models and images of entrepreneurial success—the Bill Gateses of the inner city. Unlike straight jobs, though, dealing drugs means entering a world of gruesome violence. Like all initiates, Rogers was issued a gun, and learned quickly to shoot—to discipline other dealers in the gang or to battle rival gangs for control over a corner or neighborhood. Sometimes he would shoot blindly, out of raw fear. Newspa-

15

pers report stories of "drug-related" murder. But drug *war* murder is more like it. The illegal drug trade is the country's leading cause of death by homicide—and the illegal drug trade wouldn't exist without prohibition.

Although it is popular these days to blame welfare for undermining the work ethic, often overlooked is the role played by the black market's twisted incentives, which lure men away from school and legitimate work—and, often, away from their families. In a recent two-page spread, *The Washington Post* celebrated successful students at the city's Eastern High School. Of the 76 students pictured, 64 were women—only 12 were men. The school's principal, Ralph Neal, acknowledges the role of the drug trade with a sigh, calling it a "tremendous temptation."

Writ large, the black market eventually consumes entire neighborhoods. At one time, the area of Philadelphia now referred to as "Badlands" was peppered with factories, mom-and-pop grocery stores, taverns, and theaters. Now drug dealers are positioned on street corners and in flashy cars, poised to fire their guns at the slightest provocation. Crack vials and dirty needles line the streets. Often, customers drive through in BMWs with New Jersey plates, making their buys and then scurrying back to the suburbs.

Of course, impoverished communities like this one have more troubles than just drug prohibition. But it is the black market, residents will tell you, that is a noose around their neck. Drive-by shootings and deadly stray bullets are bad enough, but some of the most devastating casualties are indirect ones. This summer two children suffocated while playing in an abandoned car in Southeast Washington. The kids avoided local playgrounds, one child said, because they feared "bullies and drug dealers."

"Kids in the inner city are scared to go to school," says Philippe Bourgois, a scholar who recently spent three and a half years with drug dealers in East Harlem writing *In Search of Respect: Selling Crack in El Barrio.* "You're going to pass five or six dealers hawking vials of crack on your way there. You face getting mugged in the hallway. The dealers . . . they drop out, but they don't stop going to school—that's where the action is." 20

A D.C. public school teacher told me that 13-year-old dealers, already fully initiated into the drug culture, crawl through a hole in the fence around her school's playground to talk to fifth and sixth graders. Once, after she and a security guard chased them off, a group of young dealers found her in the school's parking lot. "There's that snitching bitch," one kid said. "That's the bitch that snitched. I'm going to kill you, you snitching bitch." The drug war's Dr. Seuss.

A Nation behind Bars

The high prices caused by prohibition drive crime in another way: Addicts need cash to feed their habits. The junkies I met in New York told me they would spend between $200 and $600 a week for drugs. Melissa, for example, once had a good job and made enough to pay her bills and to buy dope. Then she got laid off and turned to prostitution to support her habit. Others steal to pay for their drugs—from liquor stores, from their families, from dealers, or from other addicts. According to a study by the Bureau of Justice Statistics, one out of every three thefts is committed by [someone] seeking drug money.

This crime wave does not restrict itself to the inner cities. Addicts seeking money to get a fix are very fond of the fine appliances and cash-filled wallets found in wealthier neighborhoods. Suburban high schools may not have swarms of dealers crawling through the fences, but dealers are there too. In fact, the suburbs are increasingly popular for dealers looking to take up residence.

Quite apart from the costs of the black market—the crime, the neighborhoods and lives ruined—Americans also pay a heavy price for the drug war itself. For fiscal 1996, Clinton has requested $14.6 billion for drug control (up from only $1.3 billion in 1983). State and local governments spend about twice that each year.

But these budgets reflect only a small portion of the costs. In 1980, the 25 United States had 330,000 people in jail; today, it's well over a million, and drug offenders account for 46 percent of that increase. On top of the cost of building prisons, it takes more than $30,000 per year to keep someone in jail. Naturally, prison spending has exploded. The country now spends nearly $30 billion annually on corrections. Between 1970 and 1990, state and local governments hiked prison spending by 232 percent.

Even worse, thanks to mandatory minimum sentences, the system is overloaded with non-violent drug users and dealers, who now often receive harsher penalties than murderers, rapists, and serious white collar criminals. Solicited by an undercover DEA agent to find a cocaine supplier, Gary Fannon facilitated the deal and received a sentence of life without parole. Larry Singleton raped a teenager, hacked off her arms between the wrist and elbow, and left her for dead in the desert. He received the 14-year maximum sentence and served only eight years. This disparity is not the exception in modern law enforcement. It is the rule. Non-violent drug offenders receive an average 60 months in jail time, *five times* the average 12-month-sentence for manslaughter convicts.

Some people may say: Build more jails. In an era of tax cuts and fiscal freezes, though, every dollar spent on corrections comes from roads, or health care, or education. Even with the huge growth in prison spending, three-fourths of all state prisons were operating over their maximum capacity in 1992. Even conservatives like Michael Quinlan, director of the federal Bureau of Prisons under Reagan and Bush, have had enough of this insanity. "They're locking up a lot of people who are not serious or violent offenders," he says. "That . . . brings serious consequences in terms of our ability to incarcerate truly violent criminals."

If sticking a drug dealer in jail meant fewer dealers on the street, perhaps this wave of incarceration would eventually do some good. But it doesn't work like that: Lock up a murderer, and you have one less murderer on the street. Lock up a dealer, and you create a job opening. It's like jailing an IBM executive; the pay is good, the job is appealing, so someone will move into the office before long. Clearing dealers from one neighborhood only means they'll move to another. Busting a drug ring only makes room for a competitor. "We put millions of drug offenders through the courts—and we have more people in jail per capita than any country except Russia—but we're not affecting the drug trade, let alone drug use," says Robert Sweet, U.S. district judge in the Southern District of New York.

"It's perfectly obvious," Sweet says, "that if you took the money spent housing drug offenders and enforcing the drug laws, and apply it to straight law enforcement, the results would be very impressive." Indeed, what politicians ignore is all too clear to judges, prosecutors, and cops. "The drug war can't be won," says Joseph McNamara, the former chief of police in Kansas City and San Jose, who also spent 10 years on the New York City force. "Any cop will tell you that."

What makes it even tougher for law enforcement is the pervasiveness of 30 corruption spawned by the black market in drugs. In May 1992, New York City police uncovered the largest corruption scandal in the department's 146-year history, most of it, according to the commission that investigated it, involving "groups of officers . . . identifying drug sites; planning raids; forcibly entering and looting drug trafficking locations, and sharing proceeds." There have been similar stories recently in Philadelphia, Washington, D.C., New Orleans, and Atlanta. Sadly, in movies like *The Bad Lieutenant,* art is imitating life. Cops shake down dealers, steal their cash, and sometimes deal the drugs themselves. Or they take bribes to protect dealers from arrest.

Despite these drug war casualties—and the dismal progress in stemming drug use—each year the war intensifies. Politicians from Newt Gingrich to Bill Bradley° now push for expanding the death penalty for dealers. But experience shows that the deterrent effect will be negligible. "There is no evidence that increasing penalties for drug dealing deters people from doing it," says Quinlan. "It just doesn't work like that—not when your chances of getting caught are so low, and the profits are so high." As Quinlan points out, the D.E.A. and White House count it as a success if drug prices are driven up, but that only makes the problem worse. On the streets, meanwhile, we have the worst of both worlds: Drugs are expensive enough to fuel a deadly black market, but people still buy them.

Illegal drugs, left unregulated, are also much more dangerous than they need to be. Imagine drinking whisky with no idea of its potency. It could be 30 proof or 190 proof—or diluted with a dangerous chemical. One addict I met, Mary, had blood-red sores running up her arms—from cocaine cut with meat tenderizer. Virtually all "overdose" deaths from the use of illegal drugs

---

Newt Gingrich: Republican congressman who was Speaker of the House of Representatives when this argument was first published. *Bill Bradley:* Democratic senator from New Jersey who sought to be nominated for president in 2000.

are due to contaminants or the user's ignorance of the drug's potency. "Just deserts," one might say. But isn't the basis of our drug policy supposed to be concern for people's health and well-being?

Unfortunately, this country's leaders have lost sight of that principle. "Policies," Thomas Sowell has written, "are judged by their consequences, but crusades are judged by how good they make the crusaders feel." Drug prohibition is very much of a crusade, discussed in moral terms, supported on faith, not evidence. The DEA stages high-profile drug raids—covered dutifully in newspapers and magazines—but is never able to limit supply. The government sends troops to burn poppy in South America and stubbornly insists, despite overwhelming evidence to the contrary, that interdiction can make a real difference in keeping drugs out of the country.

Meanwhile, drug treatment—no panacea, but certainly more effective in limiting drug use than law enforcement or interdiction—is continually underfunded. Candidate Clinton promised "treatment on demand" in 1992, but President Clinton has not delivered. Like Reagan and Bush, he has spent about two-thirds of the anti-drug budget on law enforcement and interdiction.

For a real blood boiler, consider the case of pregnant women addicted to drugs. Lee Brown, White House director of drug policy control, often talks of visiting crack babies in the hospital to shame those who would liberalize drug laws. But, like many addicts, pregnant women often avoid treatment or health care because they fear arrest. [35]

Although it's hard to believe, those who do seek help—for themselves and their unborn children—are often turned away. David Condliffe, who was the director of drug policy for New York City in the late eighties, conducted a survey that found that 85 percent of poor, pregnant crack addicts looking for treatment were refused everywhere they tried. Nationwide, treatment is available for only 10 percent of the 300,000 pregnant women who abuse illegal drugs. This is perhaps the greatest moral horror of our current policy—and it should shame everyone from President Clinton on down.

Beyond the Crusade

Regardless of your stance on drug policy, there can be no disagreement that we must demand honesty from public officials on this subject. Forget for a moment reporters' nonfeasance in covering the nuances of drug policy. When it comes to the drug war, they're also failing to expose coverups and outright lies.

As just one example, consider the case of needle exchange. Forty percent of new AIDS cases reported in 1992 (24,000 in total) came from infection through use of dirty needles. But the federal government continues to ban the use of AIDS-prevention funds for programs that replace dirty needles with clean ones.

This despite the fact that in 1994 the Centers for Disease Control issued a report concluding that needle exchange *does not* encourage heroin use, but *does* dramatically reduce HIV transmission. The report explicitly recommends that the federal ban be lifted. The Clinton Administration suppressed the report, but a copy finally leaked. Now, officials deny its basic finding. "[The CDC] pointed out that the jury is still out on needle exchange," Lee Brown told me. Either he hasn't read the report, or he is lying.

Even more infuriating, supporters of the drug war insist on confusing the harms of drug use with the harms of prohibition. William Bennett, for example, cites "murder and mayhem being committed on our cities' streets" as justification to intensify the drug war, when, as Milton Friedman wrote in an open letter to Bennett, "the very measures you favor are a major source of the evils you deplore." Meanwhile, in the current political climate, the likes of Joycelyn Elders°—who merely suggested we *study* the link between prohibition and violence—are shouted down.

Facing Drug Abuse

Cocaine can cause heart attacks in people prone to irregular heartbeats, such as basketball star Len Bias, and seizures in people with mild epilepsy; it's even more dangerous mixed with alcohol and other drugs. Heroin can lead to intense physical dependence—withdrawal symptoms include nausea, convulsions, and loss of bowel control. Even marijuana can be psychologically addictive; smoking too much dope can lead to respiratory problems or even cancer.

Illegal drugs have social costs as well. Consistent intoxication—whether it's a gram-a-day coke fiend, or a regular pot smoker with a miserable memory—can mean lost productivity, increased accidents, and fractured relationships.

And addiction . . . well, it's not pretty. Coke addicts often suffer acute depression without a fix. Heroin is even worse. David Morrison, recalling his furious struggle with heroin addiction in *Washington City Paper,* describes the misery of waiting for his dealer: "If sweet oblivion is the initial carrot, savage withdrawal is the enduring stick. In time, the dope fiend is not so much chasing a high as fleeing a debacle."

Given the terrible consequences of drug abuse, any reasonable person is bound to object: How could we even consider making drugs generally available? But have you asked why alcohol and tobacco are kept generally available?

Tobacco products—linked to cancer of the lungs, throat, larynx, and ovaries—cause 30 percent of all cancer deaths. Even more tobacco-related deaths come from heart attacks and strokes. Every year 435,000 Americans die premature deaths because of cigarettes. And, of course, nicotine is extremely addictive: The Surgeon General has found that the "capture" rate—the percentage of people who become addicted after trying it—is higher with cigarettes than any other drug, legal or illegal. Most nicotine addicts are hooked before age 18.

Alcohol is even more destructive. Extensive drinking often results in bleeding ulcers, cirrhosis of the liver, stomach and intestinal inflammation,

40

45

Joycelyn Elders: Surgeon General of the United States (1993–1994).

and muscle damage as well as severe damage to the brain and nervous system, manifested by blackouts and psychotic episodes.

As for social costs, alcohol is the most likely of all mind-altering substances to induce criminal behavior, according to the National Institute of Justice. Close to 11 million Americans are alcoholics, and another 7 million are alcohol abusers—meaning they've screwed up at work, been in an accident, or been arrested because of drinking. Drunk driving is the cause of a third of all traffic fatalities. Alcohol-related problems affect one out of every four American homes, and alcoholism is involved in 60 percent of all murders and 38 percent of child abuse cases. These statistics only confirm our everyday experience. Who doesn't know of a family shattered by an alcoholic, or someone who has suffered with an alcoholic boss?

The reason that alcohol and tobacco are legal, despite the damage they do, is that prohibition would be even worse. In the case of alcohol, we know from experience. The prohibition from 1919 to 1933 is now synonymous with violence, organized crime, and corruption. Financed by huge profits from bootlegging, gangsters like Al Capone terrorized cities and eluded the best efforts of law enforcement. It soon became too much.

After prohibition's repeal, consumption rates for alcohol did in fact rise. But as anyone who was alive in 1933 could tell you, the increase was hardly an explosion. And it seems likely that the rise was fueled by advertising and the movies. Drunks were likeable (bit-player Jack Norton played the amiable falling-down drunk in scores of movies of that era) or even glamorous (like William Powell in *The Thin Man* films). It took years for government, the media, and entertainers to realize their responsibility to push temperance— and even now they're not doing all they can.

What we have had a hard time learning is that there is a plethora of 50 options between prohibition and laissez-faire. In 1933, after prohibition, the federal government withdrew entirely from regulating the market in spirits. No limits were placed on marketing or advertising, and the siege from Madison Avenue and Hollywood began immediately. For years, the government seemed unable to counter the excesses of legal drug pushers like Philip Morris and Seagrams. Ads for tobacco, beer and liquor dominated the worlds of art and entertainment.

The tide began to turn in 1964, when the Surgeon General issued the first of a series of reports on the dangers of smoking. In 1971 cigarette ads were banned from TV and radio. The media began to open its eyes as well. Meanwhile, there was an equally important change in attitudes. It was once respectable to drink two or three martinis at a business lunch. Today it is not. Nor do we wink at drunk driving or smoking by pregnant women. Cigarette use, in fact, has declined dramatically since the sixties.

But much has been left undone. The TV and radio ban, for example, left the bulk of cigarette marketing untouched. And ironically, tobacco companies didn't much mind the ban, because it also dealt a severe blow to a campaign of negative advertising. Under the "fairness doctrine," TV and radio stations in the late sixties gave free air time to anti-smoking spots, such as one that mocked the Marlboro man by showing him coughing and wheezing. These ads were extremely effective, more so, many believed, than the Surgeon General's warnings. Once the tobacco ads were banned, though, TV and radio stations were no longer required to run the negative spots.

It is high time to begin a massive campaign of negative advertising against both cigarettes and alcohol. And we can ban advertising for intoxicants entirely. President Clinton, who has moved to restrict advertising that encourages smoking *and* to require tobacco companies to pay for a campaign against smoking, has taken a step in the right direction. [. . .]

In a recent essay in *The New Republic,* Thomas Laqueur criticized Clinton's initiative on cigarette advertising as the product of "prohibitionist energies." But this is the simple-minded either/or attitude that got us into such a mess. Yes, cigarettes and alcohol ought to be legally available. But that doesn't mean we can't curb the pushers, educate people about the dangers, and generally try to reduce the harm.

The same approach should be employed with now-illegal drugs. An end   55
to prohibition need not mean official endorsement of crack or heroin, but instead could be an opportunity to redouble efforts to limit their use. Drug use would rise after prohibition—but it wouldn't be the catastrophic explosion that drug warriors predict. They count on both distortions of history (claiming an explosion of alcohol use in 1933) and exaggerations of the dangers of cocaine, heroin, and speed—not to mention marijuana and hallucinogens. Though all intoxicants should be taken seriously, these drugs are neither as powerful, addictive, or attractive as many imagine. Among the population of non-users, 97 percent of Americans say they would be "not very likely" or "not at all likely" to try cocaine if it were legal. And even those who would try it in a legal regime would not find themselves immediately in the grip of an insatiable habit. As with alcohol, heavy dependence on cocaine and heroin is acquired over time.

It is a reasonable concern that the disadvantaged would be most vulnerable in a system where drugs are cheap and legally available. But the poor are also the ones paying the heaviest price for prohibition. Most drug users are not poor minorities, but these groups are most affected by the illegal drug trade. "Each of our inner cities has become a bloody Bosnia," writes David Morrison, the journalist and former addict. "But who with the power to make a difference really gives a damn? Having decamped for the suburbs, the middle classes don't have to see the dreadful damage done."

Of course, lifting prohibition would not be a panacea for our most troubled communities. But imagine the benefits of cutting out the black market. Profit would be eliminated from the drug trade, which means kids wouldn't be drawn to dealing, addicts wouldn't be pushed to thieving, and the sea of violence and crime would ebb. Innocent kids like Launice Smith wouldn't be caught in the crossfire. Students like Jovan Rogers, who survived the drug trade and returned to school, would be less likely to drop out in the first place.

And the intense marketing efforts of drug dealers in schoolyards and hallways would stop. (As it stands, dealers encourage users however they can—the more addicts, the more profits for them.)

Meanwhile, police could focus on real crime—and they'd have the prison space to lock up violent or repeat offenders. Businesses, now scared off by inner-city crime, might be drawn back into these communities, and a cycle of recovery could begin. For drug addicts, the federal government could spend the billions now wasted on law enforcement and interdiction to provide effective treatment.

At the same time, the government could clamp down on the alcohol and cigarette corporate behemoths, and make sure that they never get their hands on now-illegal drugs by controlling distribution through package stores—displaying warnings in the stores and on containers themselves. Advertising and marketing, clearly, would be prohibited and government would also have to fund an intensive campaign of public education to prevent misuse, abuse, and addiction.

Beyond government, we must recognize as a culture the damage done by drugs—even if we accept the rights of individuals to use them. The entertainment industry should take this responsibility very seriously. As it is, the scare tactics used by the government give even greater currency to Hollywood's images of the hip, outlaw drug user. 60

After so many years of prohibition—and a vociferous government effort to distort the truth—it's not hard to imagine why people would fear an epidemic of new drug addicts after prohibition. But such fears are exaggerated. The increase in use could be kept to a minimum by smart public policy. Meanwhile, we would be undoing the horror of present policy—which fractures communities, leaves kids scared to go to the playground, and pushes young men toward death or jail.

With reforms, we could stop this great damage. The good, almost certainly, would far overshadow the new problems created. Isn't it a moral imperative that we at least try? If legalization proves to be a failure—though the best evidence indicates it would not—we could return to present policy, or find a third way.

Many may be tempted to split the difference—maintain prohibition, but ease some of the penalties. Or legalize the mildest of the illegal drugs, such as marijuana. Or make drugs available to addicts by prescription. There's nothing to prevent experimenting with different strategies. But remember, the tighter the restrictions, the more fuel to the fire of the black market. Undermining the black market has to be the principle of any reform.

The other temptation is to justify the costs of prohibition in moral terms—"drugs are evil." But pining for a "drug-free America" doesn't change the reality that we'll never have one. Even Lee Brown concedes that the best he can do—with a budget approaching $15 billion dollars—is reduce drug use by 5 percent annually. Is dissuading a few hundred thousand marijuana users worth the terror of the black market?

Ultimately drug policy does come down to tradeoffs. The simple truth is   *65*
that humans are tempted by intoxicants. And, in a free society like ours, the
rights of life and liberty will always be accompanied by people pursuing stiff
drinks, or lines of cocaine, or marijuana cigarettes. Inflating the price of drugs
through prohibition and jailing sellers and users of drugs sprang from a noble
sentiment—that we could eliminate the scourge of addiction, or limit it significantly. Now we know that the enormous efforts in law enforcement have
yielded few benefits in curbing drug abuse—and are a paltry disincentive for
many drug users and would-be users. The prohibition experiment has failed.
The time has come to recognize the great harm it has done. The United States
is now akin to a person with poison ivy, scratching furiously at the rashes, and
holding fast in denial when they do not go away: Soon, the blood begins to
flow. These wounds show themselves every day, in brutal murders and bleak
urban landscapes.

We will always have a "drug problem" of some sort. The question is: What
kind of drug problem? Ultimately, choosing between regulation and prohibition turns on a simple question: Is it better to allow some individuals to make
a bad choice, or to subject many, many innocent people to drive-by shootings, rampant crime, and dangerous schools? The moral policy is to protect
the innocent—and then do our best to help the others as well.

QUESTIONS FOR DISCUSSION

1. What does Shenk achieve by opening his argument with examples of the
   drug addicts he interviewed as he was preparing this article? How does he
   hope readers will respond to these examples? In your opinion, which of
   them is the most effective?
2. According to Shenk, what are the negative consequences of prohibiting
   drugs?
3. Do you think that the government has a responsibility to limit drug use?
   Why not simply legalize drugs and let market factors determine who uses
   drugs and when?
4. According to Shenk, why can't we solve the drug crisis by simply putting
   more people in jail?
5. Does Shenk make any concessions designed to appeal to people who
   oppose the idea of legalizing drugs?
6. Do references to President Clinton make this piece seem dated? Or do
   you think Shenk's argument is still relevant despite references that are no
   longer current?

SUGGESTIONS FOR WRITING

1. Research drug laws in another country, and write an argument for or
   against enacting similar laws in the United States.

2. How has drug enforcement changed in the years since this argument was first published? Research current laws and procedures, and write an argument focused on whether or not the nation is making progress in the war on drugs.

3. What role, if any, should government play in providing treatment for drug addicts? Research programs in your state, and then write an argument for continuing, discontinuing, or changing current programs.

LINKS ■ ■ ■

■ WITHIN THE BOOK

For other arguments that call for a change in the law or in law enforcement, see those by John B. Anderson (pages 518–521) and Stuart Taylor, Jr. (pages 524–527).

■ ELSEWHERE IN PRINT

Baum, Dan. *Smoke and Mirrors: The War on Drugs and the Politics of Failure.* Boston: Little, 1996.

Bertram, Eva, Morris Blachman, Kenneth Sharpe, and Peter Andreas. *Drug War Politics: The Price of Denial.* Berkeley: U of California P, 1996.

Jonnes, Jill. *Hep-Cats, Narcs, and Pipe Dreams: A History of America's Romance with Illegal Drugs.* New York: Scribner's 1996.

Massing, Michael. *The Fix.* New York: Simon, 1998.

Miller, Richard L. *Drug Warriors and Their Prey: From Police Power to Police State.* Westport: Praeger, 1996.

Musto, David F. *The American Disease: Origins of Narcotic Control.* New Haven: Yale UP, 1973.

■ ONLINE

- Brief Biography
  <http://www.shenk.net>

- Bureau of Justice Statistics: Drug and Crime Facts
  <http://www.ojp.usdoj.gov/bjs/dcf/contents.htm>

- Drug Law Reform
  <http://www.drcnet.org>

- Drug War Facts
  <http://www.drugwarfacts.org>

PRIVACY, THE WORKPLACE, AND THE INTERNET°

Seumas Miller and John Weckert

Would you like your employer to read your e-mails and check the Web sites you visit? Do employers have the right to do so because they own the equipment you are using and want you to use your time efficiently and profitably? Is there a "right to privacy" that limits the extent to which employers (and others) can investigate where you have been and what you have been doing? These are some of the questions addressed by Seumas Miller and John Weckert in the following argument, which was first published by the Journal of Business Ethics *in 2000. As you read, consider how the argument is organized and at what points the authors respond to the arguments on behalf of the kind of surveillance they oppose.*

Seumas Miller and John Weckert both teach at Charles Stuart University in Australia. Miller is Foundation Professor of Social Philosophy, head of the School of Humanities and Social Sciences, and director of the Centre for Professional and Applied Ethics. Weckert is a senior lecturer in information technology, specializing in artificial intelligence and knowledge based systems.

ABSTRACT. This paper examines workplace surveillance and monitoring. It is argued that privacy is a moral right, and while such surveillance and monitoring can be justified in some circumstances, there is a presumption against the infringement of privacy. An account of privacy precedes consideration of various arguments frequently given for the surveillance and monitoring of employees, arguments which look at the benefits, or supposed benefits, to employees as well as to employers. The paper examines the general monitoring of work, and the monitoring of e-mail, listservers, and the World Wide Web. It is argued that many of the common justifications given for this surveillance and monitoring do not stand up to close scrutiny.

The coming into being of new communication and computer technologies has generated a host of ethical problems, and some of the more pressing concern the moral notion of privacy. Some of these problems arise from new possibilities of data collections and software for computer monitoring. For example, computers can now combine and integrate data bases provided by polling and other means to enable highly personalized and detailed voter profiles. Another cluster of problems revolves around the threat to privacy posed

---

This argument provides an example of APA-style documentation, a way of citing the use of sources. For a discussion of APA-style documentation, see pages 43–46.

by the new possibilities of monitoring and surveillance. For example, telephone tapping, interception of electronic mail messages, minute cameras, and virtually undetectable listening and recording devices give unprecedented access to private conversations and other private communications and interactions. Possibly the greatest threat to privacy is posed by the possibility of combining these new technologies and specifically combining the use of monitoring and surveillance devices with certain computer software and computer networks, including the Internet.

Concerns about the use of computer technology to monitor the performance and activity of employees in the workplace are not new (see Garson, 1988; Zuboff, 1988) and are widely discussed from a variety of perspectives, frequently in computer ethics texts. Johnson (1995) and Forester and Morrison (1991) raise questions regarding the monitoring of work, while Langford (1995) and Severson (1997) both discuss the monitoring of employees' e-mail. The works just cited mention arguments from the point of view of both employers and employees. Parker, Swope, and Baker (1990) take a different approach. Their discussion is based on a survey taken of attitudes towards monitoring both employees' e-mail and computer usage. Similar surveys have also been reported recently by Loch, Conger, and Oz (1998) and Hawk (1994). There are also a number of sociological examinations, including those by Perrolle (1996) and Rule (1996). An argument from the employees' point of view, highlighting employees' problems and concerns, is given by Nussbaum (1989). A number of other important discussions are considered later in this paper.

These discussions are useful, but their purposes are different from the current one in this paper. Applied ethics is interdisciplinary by nature, so questions must be examined from a variety of perspectives. Some of the works just cited highlight the problems or perceived problems, some report on what people actually believe, and some give a sociological analysis. The concern in this paper is to examine the question of employee monitoring from a philosophical point of view. Hence the emphasis is on analysis and argument, not on original empirical research.

Provision of an adequate philosophical account of the notion of privacy is a necessary precursor to setting the proper limits of intrusion by the various new technologies. Such an account of privacy would assist in defining the limits to be placed on unacceptably intrusive applications of new technologies. Moreover it would do so in such a way as to be sensitive to the forms of public space created by these technologies and not unreasonably impede those new possibilities of communication and information acquisition which are in fact desirable. As always, it is important to balance the rights of individuals against the needs of the community. On the one hand there is a fundamental moral obligation to respect the individual's right to privacy; on the other hand there are the legitimate requirements of, for example, employers to monitor the performances of their employees, and law enforcement agencies to monitor the communications and financial transactions of organized crime. Moreover the working out of these ethical problems is relativized to a particular institutional and technological context. The question as to whether e-mail, for example, ought to be assimilated to ordinary mail depends in part on the nature of the technology in question and the institutional framework in which it is deployed. Perhaps e-mail messages sent on a company owned computer network ought to be regarded as public communications within the organization however personal their content. These e-mail messages, unlike ordinary mail, are always stored somewhere in the backup system owned by the company and are therefore accessible to the dedicated company cybersleuth (Magney, 1996). In this paper the discussion will be restricted to the notion of privacy with reference to computer monitoring in the workplace. First, an outline of the general notion of privacy.

The notion of privacy has proven to be a difficult one to adequately explicate. One account which has been influential is that by Parent (1992):

> Privacy is the condition of not having undocumented personal knowledge about one possessed by others. . . . Personal knowledge . . . consists of facts about a person which most individuals in a given society at a given time do not want widely known about themselves (p. 92).

A problem with this definition is that personal knowledge and, therefore, privacy, is completely relativized to what people in a particular society at a particular time are prepared to disclose about themselves. Accordingly, if in some society everyone is prepared to disclose everything about themselves to everyone else, then they are still, on this account, in a condition of privacy. But they are surely not in a condition of privacy. Rather, they have chosen to abandon such a condition.

Presenting an alternative account is not easy; however, there are a number of general points that can be made (Miller, 1997; Benn, 1988; Warren & Brandeis, 1890). First, the notion of privacy has both a descriptive and a normative dimension. On the one hand privacy consists of not being interfered with, or having some power to exclude, and on the other privacy is held to be a moral right, or at least an important good. Most accounts of privacy acknowledge this much. For example, Warren and Brandeis gave an early and famous definition in terms of the right to be let alone. Naturally the normative and the descriptive dimensions interconnect. What ought to be must be something that realistically could be. The normative dimension of privacy is not a fanciful thing. The proposition must be rejected that the extent and nature of the enjoyment of rights to individual privacy is something to be determined by the most powerful forces of the day, be they market or bureaucratic forces. But it is equally important to avoid utopian sentimentality; it is mere self-indulgence to pine after what cannot possibly be.

Second, privacy is a desirable condition, power or moral right that a person has in relation to other persons and with respect to the possession of information by other persons about him/herself or the observation/perceiving of him/herself by other persons. The kind of "interference" in question is cognitive or perceptual (including perhaps tactile) interference.

Third, the range of matters regarded as private embraces much of what 10
could be referred to as a person's inner self. A demand—as opposed to a
request—by one person to know all about another person's thoughts, beliefs,
emotions, and bodily sensations and states would be regarded as unacceptable.
Naturally there are conditions under which knowledge concerning another
person's inner self are appropriate. A doctor, counselor, psychoanalyst or psychiatrist may need to know about a patient's bodily sensations and states, insofar as this was necessary for successful treatment and insofar as the patient had
consented to be treated. Nevertheless such information, while no longer
unavailable to the doctor or other care worker, would still be unavailable to
others, and for the care worker to disclose this information would constitute
a breach of confidentiality, except perhaps to another who may be required to
assist in the treatment.

Fourth, a person's intimate personal relations with other people are
regarded as private. So while a lover might be entitled to know his/her lover's
feelings toward him/her, others would not be so entitled. Indeed there would
typically be an expectation that such information would not be disclosed by a
lover to all and sundry.

Fifth, certain facts pertaining to objects I own, or monies I earn, are held
to be private, at least in most Western societies, simply in virtue of my ownership of them. Ownership appears to confer the right not to disclose information concerning the thing owned. Or at least there is a presumption in favour
of nondisclosure; a presumption that can be overridden by, for example, the
public interest in tax gathering.

Sixth, certain facts pertaining to a person's various public roles and practices, including one's voting decisions, are regarded as private. These kinds of
facts are apparently regarded as private in part by virtue of the potential,
should they be disclosed, of undermining the capacity of the person to function in these public roles or to compete fairly in these practices. If others
know how I vote, my right to freely support a particular candidate might be
undermined. If business competitors have access to my business plans they
will gain an unfair advantage over me. If a would-be employer knows my sexual preferences, he or she may unfairly discriminate against me.

Seventh, and more generally, a measure of privacy is necessary simply in
order for a person to pursue his or her projects, whatever those projects might
be. For one thing, reflection is necessary for planning, and reflection requires
privacy. For another, knowledge of someone else's plans can enable those plans
to be thwarted. Autonomy requires a measure of privacy.

Equipped with this working account of privacy, including a basic taxon- 15
omy of the kinds of information regarded as private, let us now consider a
number of ethical issues posed by computer monitoring and surveillance in
the workplace.

Employers clearly have some rights in seeing that their employees are
working satisfactorily. It is not only in the employer's interests that the
required tasks are performed efficiently and well. It is also in the interests of

other employees and in the interests of the general public. Employees do not want to have to work harder to support lazy or incompetent colleagues. Consumers do not want to buy substandard or overpriced products. But it does not follow from this that employees have no right to privacy when at work. Unfortunately, although some may say fortunately, the widespread use of computers has made workplace surveillance very easy.

Does this monitoring and surveillance matter? It is often defended by employers, who argue that it is in the interests of all. Employees who are not performing well are weeded out. Those doing their jobs well can be rewarded on objective criteria. In addition, and probably most importantly, it leads to more efficient and profitable businesses. But there are other important things in life besides efficiency and profitability. In particular, there is the right to privacy. As was indicated above, privacy considerations take a number of forms. All of these are conceivably relevant to employees in their place of work.

The existence of the right to privacy, and related rights such as confidentiality and autonomy, are sufficient to undermine extreme views such as the view that employees ought to be under surveillance every minute of the working day, or that they should be in a situation where every minute of the working day they suspect that they might be under surveillance, or that there should there be surveillance of a nature or extent in respect of which the employees are ignorant. These extreme situations involve unjustified invasions of privacy. Employers have certain rights in respect of their employees, but there is no general and absolute right to monitor and control employees. This is obvious from the fact that employers are restricted in a whole range of ways by the rights of employees. Employers cannot imprison or rob their employees, and flogging, in order to improve productivity, is not generally condoned. The reason, obviously, why employers cannot imprison or rob (or flog), is that these activities are violations of a human's rights, and the fact that someone is your employee does not confer the right to violate those rights. Even in cases where explicit contracts have been agreed to, there are limits to which either party can go in order to ensure that the other party adheres to that contract.

So much is obvious. What is less obvious is the extent to which an employer can justifiably infringe an employee's right to privacy. It has already been argued that there is a right to privacy, and, other things being equal, employees have this right. The violation of the employee's right to privacy of concern in this paper is that posed by the electronic surveillance and monitoring of an employee's activities made easy by current computer technology, particularly networking. Keystrokes can be monitored for speed and accuracy, and the work on your screen may be brought up on the screen of another without your knowledge. Common software for accessing the Internet logs all activity, so that a record is kept of all visits to all sites, and e-mail, listservers and so on can monitored. A supervisor can fairly easily find who did what on the Internet. Notwithstanding these technical possibilities of infringing privacy, protection of privacy is high on the list of principles supported by many professional computing association codes of ethics (Barroso, 1997). A good example is found in the Association for Computing Machinery (ACM) code (1992):

> Computing and communication technology enables the collection and exchange of personal information on a scale unprecedented in the history of civilization. Thus there is increased potential for violating the privacy of individuals and groups. It is the responsibility of professionals to maintain the privacy and integrity of data describing individuals . . .
>
> This imperative implies that only the *necessary amount of personal information* [emphasis added] be collected in a system, that retention and disposal periods for that information be clearly defined and enforced, and that personal information gathered for a specific purpose not be used for other purposes without consent of the individual(s). These principles apply to electronic communications, including electronic mail, and prohibit procedures that capture or monitor electronic user data, including messages, without the permission of users or bona fide authorization related to system operation and maintenance. (Section 1.7)

(This code, it should be noted, is the code of a professional computing body, and hence is aimed at computer professionals who often have access to private information stored electronically, in their daily work of creating, managing and maintaining computer systems and networks. There is no implication that *only* computer professionals have responsibilities with respect to individual privacy.)

The quotation above makes it appear that employee monitoring by computer technology is frowned upon by the ACM, and that computer professionals should have no part of it, either in developing necessary software or involvement in the monitoring itself. It could be argued, however, that this surveillance of employees falls within the class of a "necessary amount of personal information"; necessary to the well-functioning of a business. In order to assess the justifiability of computer monitoring, first some arguments for it will be considered, followed by a consideration of a number of criticisms.

Employees, as well as having at least a *prima facie* right to privacy, are also accountable to their employers because their employers have a right to a reasonable extent and quality of work output for the wages and salaries that they pay, and it is in the employees' interests (as well as the interests of employers) that their employers make a profit. Given potential conflict between these rights, perhaps an employee's right to privacy, *qua* employee, can, in a range of circumstances, be overridden. Three related types of justification are given, in terms of employers, customers, and employees. The most obvious is that with better-monitored employees, profitability is greater, although this is sometimes couched in terms of better quality customer service. For example, "quality of service telemarketing monitoring" is the way that the Telemarketing Association portrays employee monitoring (as cited in Levy, 1995). The Computer Business and Equipment Manufacturers' Association (as cited in Lund, 1992, p. 54) puts it like this:

20

> . . . the measurement of work by computer is a legitimate manage-
> ment tool that should be used wisely. Used appropriately, monitoring
> and related techniques, such as incentive pay or promotion based on
> productivity, can increase both an organization's effectiveness and the
> employee's ability to advance.

Here the emphasis is not just on the employer, it is particularly on the benefit
to the employee.

An interesting approach to computer monitoring is presented by
De Tienne (1993). She argues that this monitoring can be not only quite
benign but useful to employees:

> Not only will these computers keep closer tabs on employees, but
> based on this added information, the computer will be able to help
> employees do their jobs more effectively. . . .
>
> Information gathered via computer monitoring will increasingly be
> used to coach employees. Currently, many organizations use the infor-
> mation gathered as a basis for criticism. Companies will begin to real-
> ize that it is more motivating for employees to be coached rather than
> reproached.

So the claim is that computer monitoring of employees has multiple benefits, at least potentially. It improves the quality of goods and services, and so
is good for customers; it makes businesses more efficient, so profits rise, which
benefits employers; and it helps employees get higher pay and promotion, and
assists them in doing their jobs better. Given all these benefits, why is it questioned? There are two types of reasons, one type based on the unacceptable
consequences to the organization of monitoring and surveillance. Such consequences include ill health, stress and lowering of morale. The other type of
reason concerns the harm to employees, including, as a harm, infringement of
employees' rights to privacy. Other harms relate to employees' well-being.
There is evidence that computer monitored employees suffer health, stress
and morale problems to a higher degree than other employees (Bewayo, 1996;
Aiello & Kolb, 1996). If it does indeed generate these sorts of problems, then
these problems must be weighed against the benefits. It might be countered
that if the problems are too great, then monitoring will not make organizations more efficient, and so the practice will stop. Alternatively, the organizations which practice it will not be able to attract good employees, and so will
be forced to discontinue it. One weakness of this counter is that workers are
not always free to pick and choose their employers, particularly in times and
places of high unemployment. Many will almost certainly prefer to work
under conditions which they do not like than to not work at all. Another
flaw in the argument is that it is not necessarily true that practices which are
detrimental to health and morale will lead to less efficiency, at least not in the
short term. For example, forcing workers to work for long hours without rest
over extended periods could increase productivity in the short term but lead

to longer-term health problems. Raising the levels of stress through continual monitoring could have the same effect. If the work requires a relatively low level of skill, and if there is unemployment, workers are easily replaceable. Treating workers in this fashion may not be good for a business's long-term viability or profitability, but many businesses are not around for long. If the motive is short-term profitability, long-term effects are irrelevant. More importantly, treating workers in this fashion may be good for the profitability, long and short term, of that particular business. The problem may be the long-term ill effects on the business sector in general or on the specific industry sector in question.

The moral objection to computer monitoring is based on the principle 25 that a right cannot be infringed without very good reason. It would be rare that greater efficiency or profitability would constitute such a good reason. There clearly are times when a person's privacy rights can be overridden. An unconscious and unconsenting hospital patient, for example, may need constant monitoring, but that is for the patient's own good. A prison inmate might also need constant monitoring, but that might be for the protection of the community. Monitoring of employees, however, does not, in most circumstances, secure these fundamental rights to life and protection.

A defender of computer monitoring might argue that the moral problem only arises if employees have no input into the establishing of the monitoring system, or if they are not fully aware of its scope and implications. If these conditions are satisfied, there is no moral problem, because the employee has, in effect, consented to the system's use by accepting employment under those conditions.

While this has some initial attraction, on closer examination it is not so plausible. One reason is the same as that discussed in connection with health and morale. When unemployment is high, or if the person badly needs a job, there is not much force in consent. It is rather a case of economic coercion. A second problem is that, even if people do consent to some sort of treatment, it does not follow that it is moral to treat them in that manner. Slavery cannot be justified on the grounds that some slaves may not have minded their condition too much if they knew nothing better, and if they had always been taught that slavery was the natural order of things. Likewise, violation of privacy cannot be condoned simply because some employees are willing to accept it.

What can be made of the argument that employee monitoring can be to the benefit of the employees themselves? Their privacy is violated, but it is in a good cause. Three benefits to the employee have been suggested. One is that it can, if used properly, help them to improve their work practices. This might be true, but it would at best only justify short-term monitoring, and only with the employee's consent. Perhaps the techniques and satisfaction of clumsy lovers could be improved by information gained from spying on their activities, but that hardly seems to justify spying. A second benefit is said to be that employees can be assessed on purely objective criteria, say, number and accuracy of keystrokes. While objectivity is good, assessment of an employee's worth will usually have a substantial subjective element as well. A highly responsible or experienced person who types slowly may well improve the productivity of others. So at best this is a weak justification for infringement of privacy. Finally, it is argued that this monitoring will help get rid of "dead wood," workers who are not doing their fair share of the work. This will be good not only for the employer, but also for the other employees. However, while none of us wants to support lazy and incompetent colleagues, it is not clear that this will not have countervailing effects, namely, on the hardworking and competent workers also thus monitored. There could, of course, be limited and targeted monitoring where there was good reason to believe that particular employees were not meeting reasonable standards. This would seem to be a far more reasonable policy. However, this is clearly not *general* monitoring and surveillance of the kind being discussed here. Supporting such colleagues is not good, but violation of privacy would, to many, seem even worse. (For discussion of these three points see De Tienne, 1993; Lund, 1992; Fenner & Lerch, 1993.)

A stronger argument for employing surveillance is the control of crime in the workplace, especially theft and financial fraud. Law enforcement agencies can have rights which override those of individuals in certain circumstances when it is in the public interest. Theft and fraud in the workplace are still theft and fraud, so some surveillance can be justified in order to apprehend culprits.

Another form of monitoring, perhaps less worrying, but often discussed, is that of monitoring employees' e-mail. While this might be thought to be akin to opening private mail or listening in to private conversations, the argument is that, because the system on which the e-mail operates is owned by the employers, they have a right to read any messages (see Loch et al. 1998 for a discussion of a survey on this issue). But do they? The fact that two people are conversing in my house does not give me an automatic right to listen to what they are saying. But what if the two people are my employees? Does this make a difference? One argument that it does not might go as follows: All I am paying for is my employees' labor. What they say to customers might be my business, but what they say to each other is not if it does not obviously and directly harm the business. Perhaps the cases are not analogous, because in the e-mail case they are using my equipment, while in the other they are not. But what they say is still none of my business even if the consequences of what they say might be. The fact that they are continually having conversations might be overloading the equipment or hindering the work of others or themselves. Accordingly, banning or limiting private conversations might be justified. But this would not justify *monitoring* conversations. Perhaps this still misses the point. How will I know if the e-mail is being used for private discussions unless I monitor it? I will not know unless I am told. But if no problems are being caused by overuse and so on, then there is no need to worry. If no harm is being caused by personal e-mail, either to the computing equipment or to productivity, then monitoring what is said can have no purpose, except perhaps to satisfy curiosity. This is hardly a justification for violating a right. If there are problems such as the overloading of the system or inadequate work levels, then some steps may need to be taken, but even here actually reading messages would rarely be necessary. There could be a limit put on the length or number of messages, or the productivity of employees in question could be investigated. Employing people does not confer the right to monitor their private conversations, whether those conversations be in person or via e-mail.

It might still be argued that what one employee says to a second employee might be my business as employer, if their conversation is work related. But even this cannot in general be correct. Consider the following three situations. First, if the two employees are, say, doctors in a private hospital, then their work-related conversation might need to be protected by confidentiality. Second, what an employee is saying to a "customer" might be protected by confidentiality, for example, in the case of a lawyer working for a large corporation. In these circumstances a professional employee, that is, one who is a member of what is commonly thought of as a profession, for example, a medical doctor, lawyer or accountant, will need to be treated differently from a nonprofessional. Third, even nonprofessional employees need a measure of autonomy—conferred by privacy in the sense of noninterference and nonintrusion—in respect of one another and the public, if they are to take responsibility for their jobs and their performance in those jobs. Taking responsibility in this sense involves "being left alone" to do, or fail to do, the tasks at hand. Far from having the effect of ensuring that people do not make mistakes, intrusive and ongoing monitoring and surveillance might have the effect of causing employees to underperform because they are never allowed to take responsibility for outcomes and therefore become lazy or engage in corrupt practices. Consider in this connection a salesman trying to convince a customer to buy a house, or a mechanic trying to figure out what is wrong with a car, or a supervisor trying to instruct a new clerk. The conception of employees that those who favor monitoring or surveillance tend to have in mind seem to be those doing menial, repetitive jobs that do not require any autonomy or individual initiative or judgment in order to be performed.

The discussion so far in relation to the Internet has concerned only e-mail, but of course Internet access involves much more than just e-mail. Some employees have, on their employer's computing equipment, almost unlimited access to material, particularly through the World Wide Web (WWW). Is it an unjustified invasion of privacy for employers to monitor their employees' activity on the WWW, to check on the sites visited? Given costs, particularly in processing time, associated with activity on the WWW, some restrictions [l] be difficult to condemn an employer who [wo]rk-related tasks. Given general knowledge of [ch]ecks of the sites accessed by employees is not [problems arise in situations where employees [fo]r to do their jobs properly, for example, many [ ] Universities typically allow their staff com-[acc]ess. Does the university then have a right to [u]sing this access? In general it would seem not.

Loving both of u is breakin all the Rules...

From a privacy perspective, there is no problem with restricting access to certain sites by the use of software. Monitoring sites visited, however, is not such an acceptable way of restricting access. Monitoring someone's use of the Internet in this way is a bit like monitoring library use, and it is instructive to look at how the library profession views the privacy issue.

Librarians have long been concerned about maintaining the privacy of library users' reading habits. The American Library Association (1996) puts its concern this way:

> The ethical responsibilities of librarians . . . protect the privacy of library users. Confidentiality extends to "information sought or received, and materials consulted, borrowed, acquired," and includes database search records, reference interviews, circulation records, interlibrary loan records, and other personally identifiable uses of library materials, facilities, or services. (Section 2, 52.4)

Why have librarians traditionally been so concerned about privacy? The reading habits of library users are the business of nobody except the user, but that in itself is not too important. My preference for unsugared, black tea rather than the sweet, white variety is also the business of nobody but me and the person making it for me, but worrying about the privacy of this information seems a bit extravagant. While much information about users which is stored in library databases might not be much more important than my preference in tea, in general, reading habits do reveal a little more about a person. It can been argued that what someone reads is very close to what he or she thinks, and therefore the ability to discover what is read is, in effect, the ability to find out what is thought.

It is not difficult to imagine situations where governments, advertising agencies, or other groups could make use of this information for purposes which were not beneficial to the individual. For example, according to Million and Fisher (1986), in the United States the Moral Majority attempted to obtain the names of school districts and individuals who had borrowed a film on sexual maturity from the Washington State Library. Sometimes, of course, it might be beneficial to the community, for example when law enforcement agencies need information for criminal investigations. Borrowers, however, can be harmed if their records are not kept private. The burden of proof should be on those who want records made public or at least available. The privacy of the individual can be overridden, but only to protect more important individual rights or for the sake of very significant public goods (for further discussion see Weckert & Adeney, 1997). 35

Given that university librarians are part of the library profession, according to their own code of ethics, they are bound to keep library records private, including the borrowing records of university staff. From a professional librarian's point of view, then, it would be an invasion of privacy for the university to check on an employee's borrowing record, even though the library is university owned and operated. It is difficult to see where the relevant difference lies between the library and the Internet in this instance. Both are sources of information.

One complicating factor which rears its head in the context of e-mail and Internet monitoring is vicarious liability, that is, the liability an employer might have for the actions of his or her employees. *Black's Law Dictionary* defines it thus:

> The imposition of liability on one person for the actionable conduct of another, based solely on a relationship between the two persons. Indirect or imputed legal responsibility for acts of another; for example, the liability of an employer for the acts of an employee. . . . (1990, p. 1566)

Given this, it seems irresponsible of an employer not to monitor the e-mail of employees or their use of the Internet in general. If this does not happen, the employer could be liable for breaches of the law with respect to, for example, defamation, copyright infringement, and obscene material (Cutler, 1998). It does not follow from this, however, that an employer has the right to monitor employee activity on the Internet which the employee could reasonably expect to be private. It does, though, strengthen an employer's right to insist that his or her computing equipment is not to be used for anything apart from legitimate work related purposes. This policy must, of course, be made clear. It also might call into question the appropriateness of maintaining vicarious liability in some of these contexts. At any rate, the general point to be made here is that where an employer allows private e-mail and other Internet activity, his vicarious liability does not necessarily legitimize monitoring of that activity.

Finally, should employers be able to monitor listservers which are on their computer systems? For employers in general, this will probably be a rare situation, but not for universities. Suppose that a university runs courses by distance education, something which is becoming increasingly common. The lecturer and students decide to establish a listserver to facilitate discussion and to help overcome the isolation often felt by distance education students. Does the university have a right to monitor activity on that listserver without notifying the participants? It might be argued that they do, because the listserver is public in the same sense that a university lecture theatre is, and so any authorized university person has access. The analogy, however, is not good. If someone enters a lecture theatre, he or she is there for all to see. There is no question of secrecy. Suppose now that the university monitors lectures, not by having staff attend, but rather by secretly installing cameras and microphones. The analogy here is closer, but the monitoring does not seem so benign. It might be objected that in the listserver case there is nothing secret. The university monitor enrolls, so it is not too difficult to discover the monitoring. Just look to see who is enrolled. But that is not the point. If there is to be monitoring, the onus for making it public should not be on those monitored but on those monitoring.

Drawing an analogy between listservers and lecture theaters is misleading   *40*
in any case. While it is true that authorised university staff can attend lectures
in university-owned buildings without violating anyone's right to privacy,
nothing follows from this about secret listserver monitoring. Normally university lectures are not private. Anyone can come and listen. The situation
changes a little with tutorials, where there is more interaction, and at private
discussion between a lecturer and a student. It is not so clear that the university would be justified in authorising someone to monitor tutorials without
the tutors' and students' knowledge, or to monitor private student-lecturer
discussions. The claim that this is justified simply because these activities are
taking place on university property is dubious at best. Listservers seem more
like tutorials than lectures. There is some privacy. One cannot just look and
see what is happening, as is possible with a newsgroup. One must enroll. Secret
monitoring of class listservers, then, can be seen as a violation of privacy
rights, just as secret monitoring of tutorials would be.

Workplace monitoring is a practice which requires much more examination. Employers need an efficient and competent workforce in order to survive in a competitive environment, and customers demand and deserve high
quality goods and services. The employees who produce these goods and services have a responsibility to work to the best of their ability for the financial
reward that they receive, but they do not forfeit their rights to privacy by virtue
of being employees. Although workplace monitoring can be justified in some
circumstances, privacy is a moral right, and as such there is a presumption
against its infringement. This paper has argued that some of the common justifications given for this monitoring do not withstand close scrutiny.

A number of questions remain to be researched, both empirical and analytical. One of these questions is the relationship between monitoring and trust in
the workplace. It would appear that monitoring is a sign of distrust, and perhaps
employees who know that they are being monitored, and hence not trusted,
will become less trustworthy, in which case they will require more monitoring.
Superficially, at least, it appears that monitoring could precipitate a breakdown
in trust, which in the longer term would probably lead to a less efficient workforce. But this requires investigation. Another issue is the role of vicarious liability in the violation of individual employee privacy. It seems that the current law
(in countries which have it), or its interpretation, encourages or even necessi-
tates employee monitoring which is morally questionable. Perhaps the law
requires modification in the light of contemporary computer technology. Privacy is perhaps the topic most discussed by those concerned about the social
and ethical implications of computer technology. It deserves to be.

REFERENCES

Association for Computing Machinery. (1992). *ACM code of ethics and professional conduct.* Retrieved July 25, 1998, from http://www.acm.org/
constitution/code.html

Aiello, J. R., & Kolb, K. J. (1996). Electronic performance monitoring: A risk factor for workplace monitoring. In S. L. Sauter & L. R. Murphy (Eds.), *Organisational risk factors for job stress* (pp. 163–179). Washington, DC: American Psychological Association.

American Library Association. (1996). *ALA policy manual*. Retrieved July 25, 1998, from http://www.ala.org/alaorg/policymanual/libserve.html

Barroso Asenjo, P. (1997). Key ethical concepts for the Internet and for ethical codes of computer professionals. *Australian Computer Journal, 29,* 2–5.

Benn, S. A. (1988). *Theory of freedom*. Cambridge: Cambridge University Press.

Bewayo, E. (1996). Electronic management: Its downside especially in small business. In J. Kizza (Ed.), *Social and ethical effects of the computer revolution* (pp. 186–199). Jefferson, NC: McFarland.

Black, H. C. (1990). *Black's law dictionary* (6th ed.). St. Paul, MN: West.

Cutler, P. G. (1998, March 1). E-mail: Employees and liability. *Chemistry in Australia,* 30–31.

DeTienne, K. B. (1993). Big brother or friendly coach. *Futurist, 27,* 33–37.

Fenner, D. B., & Lerch, F. J. (1993). The impact of computerized performance monitoring and prior performance knowledge on performance evaluation. *Journal of Applied Social Psychology, 23,* 573–601.

Forester, T., & Morrison, P. (1991). *Computer ethics: Cautionary tales and ethical dilemmas in computing*. Cambridge, MA: MIT Press.

Garson, B. (1988). *The electronic sweatshop*. New York: Simon & Schuster.

Hawk, S. R. (1994). The effects of computerized performance monitoring: An ethical perspective. *Journal of Business Ethics, 13*(12) 949–957.

Johnson, D. G. (1994). *Computer ethics* (2nd ed.). Upper Saddle River, NJ: Prentice.

Langford, D. (1995). *Practical computer ethics*. Maidenhead, Berkshire, UK: McGraw-Hill.

Levy, M. (1995). The electronic monitoring of workers: Privacy in the age of the electronic sweatshop. *Legal References Services Quarterly, 14*(3).

Loch, K. D., Conger, S., & Oz, E. (1998). Ownership, privacy and monitoring in the workplace: A debate on technology and ethics. *Journal of Business Ethics, 17,* 653–663.

Lund, J. (1992). Electronic performance monitoring: A review of the research issues. *Applied Ergonomics, 23,* 54–58.

Magney, J. (1996). Computing and ethics: Control and surveillance versus cooperation and empowerment. In J. Kizza (Ed.), *Social and ethical effects of the computer revolution* (pp. 200–209). Jefferson, NC: McFarland.

Miller, S. (1997). Privacy and the Internet. *Australian Computer Journal, 29,* 12–15.

Million, A. C., & Fisher, K. N. (1986). Library records: A review of confidentiality laws and policies. Journal of Academic Librarianship, 11, 346–349.

Nussbaum, K. (1991). Computer monitoring: A threat to the right to privacy? In R. Dejoie, G. Fowler, & D. Paradice (Eds.), *Ethical issues in information systems.*

Parent, P. (1992). Privacy. In E. E. Cohen (Ed.), *Philosophical issues in journalism* (pp. 90–99). Boston: Boyd.

Parker, D. B., Swope, S., & Baker, B. N. (1990). *Ethical conflicts in information and computer science, technology, and business.* Wellesley, MA: QED Information Sciences.

Perrolle, J. A. (1996). Privacy and surveillance in computer-supported cooperative work. In D. Lyon & E. Zureik (Eds.), *Computers, surveillance, and privacy* (pp. 47–65). Minneapolis: University of Minnesota Press.

Rule, J. B. (1996). High-tech workplace surveillance: What's really new? In D. Lyon & E. Zureik (Eds.), *Computers, surveillance, and privacy* (pp. 66–76). Minneapolis: University of Minnesota Press.

Severson, R. J. (1997). *The principles of information ethics.* Armonk, NY: M. E. Sharp.

Warren, S., & Brandeis, L. (1890). The right to privacy. *Harvard Law Review, 4,* 193–220.

Weckert, J., & Adeney, D. (1997). *Computer and information ethics.* Westport, CT: Greenwood.

Zuboff, S. (1988). *In the age of the smart machine: The future of work and power.* New York: Basic.

QUESTIONS FOR DISCUSSION

1. What is the problem that these authors hope to resolve? Where and how do they establish their purpose for writing?
2. What do the authors mean when, in paragraph 6, they write that "the notion of privacy has both a descriptive and a normative dimension"?
3. Why is privacy desirable?
4. Under what circumstances can privacy be violated ethically or legally?
5. Where do the authors respond to views different from their own? How effective are their responses to these views?
6. What concessions do the authors make?
7. This is a long argument backed by extensive research. Yet at the end, the authors write that additional research is necessary. What questions remain to be resolved? After reading this argument, what would you most like to know about your own "right" to privacy?

SUGGESTIONS FOR WRITING

1. Write an argument defending the rights of employers to monitor the activities of their employees while employees are in the workplace.
2. Write an argument on behalf of what you see as your right to privacy at home, at school, in the workplace, or in your community.
3. Research current laws regulating privacy on the Internet, and write an argument defending the status quo or calling for a specific reform.

LINKS ■ ■ ■

■ WIT... ...HE B...

Fo... ..."The New Gold
...Why McDonald's Fries

...hers Are Sell-
...9.

... M. Workp... ...nd *Practical Solutions*.
...ngton: Thompso...

Sc...an, Ferdinand. *Privacy* ...*dom*. New York: Cambridge
UP, 1992.

Schroeder, Keith A., ed. *Life and Dea...* *on the Internet: How to Protect Your*
...*World Wide Web*. Menasha: Supple, 1998.

...*Guide to Protecting*
...ville: PMI, 2001.

...e.html>

...s Clearing House
...privacyrights.org>

■ Workplace Surveillance Project
<http://www.privacyf...

Handwritten notes (overlaid):

you were the first real love I ever had...

There are times when a women has to say whats on her mind...

...even ...she kn ...ts gonna hurt...

What About Love...

Don't you want someone to care about you?

I can't see you ...t you ...t want ...uy...

What about me?

No one else can have the part of me I gave to you...

...can't ...eak free...

8

Writing to Amuse Others

Writing to amuse, like writing to move or to persuade, requires that you focus on readers other than yourself. You may enjoy the experience and take pride in what you accomplish, but you cannot settle for amusing yourself alone. Writing to amuse gives you an opportunity for bringing pleasure to others. Seize the opportunity, and make the most of it.

THINKING ABOUT AUDIENCE

If you find pleasure in writing to amuse, it will come from knowing that you succeeded in bringing pleasure to others. Consider what happens when you tell a joke. If people laugh, you feel pleased that you told the joke—and told it well. However, if no one laughs, you'll probably feel disappointed or embarrassed but not pleased. An egotist might be so self-absorbed that he doesn't notice that others are not amused by his efforts at humor, but that may explain why he is not funny: He is focusing on himself rather than his audience.

Of course, an audience that is not laughing might still be amused—although this is unlikely in the case of a good joke. In telling some stories and writing some essays, you could be hoping to inspire only a wry smile that seems to say "I know what you mean; something like that happened to me, too." It is a rare and wonderful piece of writing that can make us laugh out loud. More common, but not necessarily less valuable, is writing that makes us smile at aspects of life about which we have mixed feelings—things that we can enjoy making fun of but would hesitate to abandon altogether. Patricia Volk's essay on technology can make us laugh without deciding to eliminate technology from our lives. Similarly, David Sedaris can make us laugh at an incompetent teacher with disgruntled students without making us feel that teaching and learning are worthless pursuits.

From this observation we can understand a basic principle about writing to amuse: Whether designed to produce belly laughs or merely to bring a twinkle of recognition to someone's eye, humor has an element of tension in it. Despite the great range of material that can be considered "comic," one constant feature is that humor always sends a double message: "Take me seriously, but don't take me seriously." People often laugh because of a sudden, surprising shift between the two parts of this message.

Laughter, however, is not always a sign of amusement, any more than amusement is always indicated by laughter. To release an excess of good spirits, you might laugh when you are having fun, even when no one has said or done anything funny. Strictly speaking, laughter is physiological—a motor and intellectual response that can be produced by many situations. And these situations are not necessarily amusing. Laughter can be inspired in ways that are essentially mean-spirited attempts to deprive other people of their humanity—as, for example, in the once common practice of laughing at dwarves. It can also signal anxiety, as in a nervous laugh, or hysteria, as when someone is emotionally overwrought and cannot stop laughing.

When writing to amuse, your primary object is to make readers enjoy themselves. You can be funny, but you should also be good-humored. This means having a sympathetic understanding of human frailty rather than a contempt for anyone or anything that seems different from what you are accustomed to. Ridicule is not genuinely amusing, and it lends itself easily to abuse. You should try to laugh *with* rather than *at,* since your purpose is to give pleasure through reconciliation. By helping readers laugh about their failures, you may help them fail less frequently. But by reminding people that failure is not unique, you can make them feel part of a larger community. Humor thus reconciles people to human imperfection.

THINKING ABOUT SUBJECTS

You are probably wondering by now what types of material are appropriate for humor. Answering this question is like trying to explain why a joke is funny. Part of the problem is that different people laugh at different things, and circumstances can determine whether or not something seems amusing to the same person on ⸱ ⸱⸱ ⸱n day. What seems funny in the morning could be annoying ⸱ Another problem is that much humor is topical ⸱⸱⸱ ⸱ltural context, so that what amused people in ⸱⸱⸱ ⸱eories about the comic) can provide only a ⸱⸱⸱ amuse people today. The humor of "Break- ⸱⸱⸱ le, depends on readers' being familiar with ⸱⸱⸱ t are a feature of contemporary American ⸱⸱⸱ ⸱ or culture could be altogether baffled by it ⸱⸱⸱ ⸱nd it funny.

Yet John R. Alden's work reflects one of the oldest theories of humor. Aristotle wrote in his *Poetics* that comedy—like poetry—springs from the pleasure people find in imitation. He argued that this pleasure is instinctive. Whether or not his argument is true, we can observe young children already delighting in imitation when they see someone mimic another person or when they mimic someone themselves. One way to approach "Breakfast at the FDA Café" is to consider how Alden mimics the language of consumer warnings. In a broader sense the other selections in this chapter also involve imitation in that their humor depends on the portrayal of experience readers can recognize. In "It's Nice Work, If You Can Avoid It," for example, Jeff Foxworthy imitates common excuses for staying home from work. And in "Eleventh-Hour Bride," Sandra Tsing Loh imitates the form that advice columns often take in popular magazines.

THE WRITER'S PERSONA

David Sedaris demonstrates another feature frequently found in writing to amuse. He establishes a nonthreatening *persona,* a first-person narrator who conveys a particular voice and point of view that may or may not be the author's own. *Persona* (derived from the Latin word for the masks used in the classical theater) is usually associated today with fiction, but the creation of a literary self is also useful when you are writing to amuse. One way to create a persona is to make yourself seem like an average but nevertheless engaging person who is faintly bewildered by whatever you want readers to be amused by. During the 1930s Will Rogers achieved great fame by cultivating this kind of voice. More recently, Garrison Keillor and Andy Rooney have succeeded with similar voices. Professional writers, like professional comics, choose how they want to present themselves to their audience, and they often choose to make themselves seem nonthreatening. Although Jeff Foxworthy, Henry Alford, and David Sedaris present themselves as semicompetent, they are by no means as inept as they pretend to be.

In presenting themselves as flawed somehow—dishonest, lazy, or bewildered by the situations in which they find themselves—writers like Foxworthy, Alford, and Sedaris also draw on another Aristotelian principle: that comedy concerns characters who have a "defect." According to Aristotle, "Comedy is [. . .] an imitation of persons inferior—not in the full sense of the word bad. [. . .] It consists of some defect or ugliness which is not painful or destructive." Like the characters in a comedy, comic writers often seem to have a flaw we ourselves may have. But they do not truly suffer from it, and this is one reason we can afford to laugh. The dishonesty Jeff Foxworthy attributes to himself is somehow reassuring: Anyone who has ever been tempted to fib to stay home from work or school is likely to understand what Foxworthy is doing. And his lies are so improbable that it's hard to believe that they would truly deceive anyone. We believe that he isn't "in the full sense of the word bad" and suspect that he's able to make a living despite his exaggerated defect.

By creating an engaging persona, writers can make readers laugh with them rather than at them. We may smile at the way writers like Foxworthy and Sedaris present themselves, but the principal source of amusement is some problem outside themselves that we—like them—can find irritating: getting up in the morning, completing a tedious job, or being told what to do by others. This leads to another important aspect of writing to amuse: Although such writing is not didactic, it is often designed as corrective. The assumption behind much comic writing is that if you can make people laugh, they will change their behavior. Patricia Volk implies that we would be wise to avoid buying unnecessary gadgets and appliances. In "How I'm Doing," David Owen suggests that we could benefit from reconsidering how we judge ourselves and our families, as well as the kind of language we use in the workplace. And readers who enjoy Henry Alford's "The Young Man and the Sea" may later find themselves thinking more critically about the rituals through which young men and women seek to affirm status in their gender.

THINKING ABOUT PURPOSE

Writing to amuse can, at times, take less friendly forms. In *satire,* for example, the corrective aspect of writing to amuse is readily apparent. The writer of a satire usually assumes a persona that is more likely to seem aloof than affable and may not use the first person at all. The satirist usually directs attention to the flaws of other people rather than to his or her own. The result can be very funny, but it can also be cruel. A basic bond between writer and audience exists even in satire, however. The satirist assumes that someone or some group has departed from behavior that is recognized as acceptable; this presumes that recognized standards exist and that the audience of a satire (if not its butt) believes in the standards that have been violated.

In keeping with its role as a social corrective, writing to amuse often reinforces traditional standards (such as marriage, which provides the happy ending that resolves so many comedies written for the stage). Beneath much humor is the message that people should grow up and stop acting silly, a conservative, responsible message made palatable through laughter.

But humor can also be subversive. As Mikhail Bakhtin, a Russian critic, has argued, comedy records "the defeat [. . .] of all that oppresses and restricts." For example, the Marx brothers often amused people by disrupting a very proper, pompous socialite. Or to take an example close at hand: Alden challenges government regulations even as he uses them as a source of humor. Although "Breakfast at the FDA Café" pokes fun at health advisories about popular kinds of food and drink, the essay as a whole invites the reader to think critically about the role of government agencies in regulating our lives. Similarly, Sandra Tsing Loh pokes fun at the stressful activities Americans frequently undertake when preparing to marry, implying that brides and grooms should plan simple weddings. And David Sedaris presents himself as an agent for change by providing an exaggerated version of the kind of incompetent teaching that should not be tolerated in our schools.

The disruptive potential of humor may be one reason why some people are suspicious of it. Convinced that comedy inspires social rebellion, Plato proposed banning comedians from his ideal republic, and Aristotle argued that comedy is like strong wine and, as such, is unsuitable for the young. Once people have begun to laugh at authority, the credibility of that authority is undermined. Dictators do not take kindly to jokes at their expense.

It would seem, then, that humor involves a certain amount of tension, because it encourages people to laugh at what, on some level, they think is no laughing matter. Hence, humor can seem to work simultaneously toward both reconciliation and rebellion. The rebellion is against rigid and artificial authority, rules, or behavior, while the reconciliation is aimed at restoring a natural sense of community. Alden assumes that regulations governing the way people are expected to eat have become too rigid. He is rebelling against authorities that insist he eat sensibly. But he is also attempting to reconcile people to what, in fact, many people want to do—enjoy themselves and not worry so much about maintaining a healthy diet.

THINKING ABOUT PATTERNS

The humor of Alden's piece depends on people's recognizing a frequently repeated pattern. The essay would not seem funny if the author were the only person who, when reading a menu, felt torn between eating wisely and dining well. In other cases comic writers exploit the idea of a repeated pattern much more directly. According to Henri Bergson, a French theorist who wrote what critics agree is an important work on laughter, one of the principal sources of humor is a situation in which people behave mechanically, repeating the same motion or saying the same thing. Once we begin to notice this repetition, it becomes predictable—and we are inclined to laugh when our expectations are fulfilled. For example, students may laugh after noticing that their professor always says "One last thing" at least twice in every class. Cartoons often depend heavily on this principle of predictable repetition: We know that the Roadrunner will always outmaneuver the Coyote, and the Coyote will always be back no matter how many times he falls off the cliff.

In an essay of your own, you could amuse readers by identifying a predictable form of behavior that you have observed in yourself or in others and then showing that pattern in action. Someone who is always ready to party, nap, or shop—or offer unsolicited advice, avoid paying bills, or turn all conversations to memories of his ex-girlfriend—could provide the inspiration for humor once you see the comic potential of behavior that seems unvaried and automatic.

WRITING TIPS

How can you go about writing an amusing essay? Although there is no formula guaranteed to succeed, the following guidelines may help you get started.

- *Choose your topic.* Your own experience, or the readings that follow, may
  suggest a variety of topics. But if you're stuck for an idea, try to identify a flaw in the behavior of people you know. The flaw you choose
  should be easy to observe so that you can count on its being
  recognized by your audience.

- *Cultivate an appropriate voice.* Address your readers as members of a
  community who share the same values and have suffered the same
  problems. Be careful not to make yourself sound superior to your
  readers or sound as if you would do anyone a real injury.

- *Experiment with wordplay.* One of the great sources of humor is the
  pleasure people derive from unexpected combinations of words. Surprise readers with a pun or a playful variation of a cliché. (An actress of
  questionable virtue once described herself as being "pure as the fresh-
  driven slush.") Or you can invent words that are delightful simply
  because of the way they sound.

- *Use repetition.* Although deliberate repetition can serve many rhetorical
  ends, it can be especially useful when you are trying to amuse. The
  repetition may take the form of someone's always saying the same
  thing or always reacting in a predictable way—such as Homer Simpson, who routinely makes foolish choices.

- *Test your choice.* A good way to measure your success in writing to
  amuse is to read a draft of your paper aloud to friends. But you should
  also ask yourself if there is anyone in whose presence you would be
  embarrassed to read it. A good-humored paper should be suitable for
  many audiences. It should produce a smile rather than a sneer. If you
  feel worried that your paper might give offense, you may be writing to
  ridicule rather than to amuse.

TECHNOLOGY MAKES ME MAD

Patricia Volk

> *If you've ever had trouble programming a VCR or found yourself wondering why your computer can't read the disk on which you carefully saved a paper that's due in twenty minutes, you're likely to understand the kind of frustration that Patricia Volk expresses in "Technology Makes Me Mad," which was first published by* The New York Times Magazine *in 1997.*
>
> *Formerly an art director at* Seventeen *magazine and at* Harper's Bazaar, *Volk has also worked as a senior vice president in the advertising industry. Her essays and short stories have appeared in* The Atlantic Monthly, Playboy, The New Yorker, Family Circle, *and* Cosmopolitan, *among other publications. With this background in mind, consider whether Volk may be creating a comic version of herself as you read the following selection.*

First there was breast-feeding. Then there was formula. Now there's patent No. 5,571,084, a microprocessor-controlled breast-pump vest with a programming chip that vacuums out milk for your baby without human contact. Why? So you can answer more E-mail?

Call me a technophobe. Technology drives me nuts. It even makes me lie. I hold for the operator, faking a rotary dial. When you call Metro North for a train from 125th Street to Dover Plains, you get the info in 16 seconds from a person. Take the touch-tone route and it's 5 minutes, 49 seconds.

"Please stay on the line. The next available representative will assist you." Ahhhhhhhh.

True, the electric coffee maker has changed my life. It brews eight perfect cups in five minutes flat and keeps the coffee hot all day. I'll never go back to perk or drip. But the front panel says "2:11 A.M." no matter what time it is. The thing has no buttons. Just a pressure-sensitive panel pressure-insensitive to me. "2:11 A.M. . . . 2:11 A.M." it flashes urgent-green round the clock. I'm thinking of covering it with the millennial cure for everything: duct tape.

In the early 19th century, English workers destroyed two improved stocking frames to thwart labor-saving technology. I'm no Luddite. I love pantyhose. The wheel is O.K., too. So are heated car seats, fetal monitors and ice makers. And what would I do without the phone? See people?   5

The best part of being a technophobe is that you get to blame everything bad on technology, whether it's technology's fault or not—the disappearance of the photobooth, peanut butter and jelly in the same jar, the horrible, unforgivable change in the taste of Hellmann's Real (hah!) Mayonnaise.

But I feel betrayed when my state-of-the-art fridge breaks down. State-of-the-art actually means no one's really sure it works right yet. Regardless of

585

what the accompanying literature says, there's no way you can slice a tomato in my new, improved Cuisinart.

Here's the worst. When I tried removing hair from my legs with a high-tech electronic device, it bit my knee. It wouldn't let go. A machine was whirring on my leg, a mechanical pit bull. Bleeding, I dialed the 800 number. A guy named Bruce talked me down.

"Oh, is it grabbing your knee?" he yawned.

"Uhhhhhhhh. . . ." I tried not to cry.   10

"O.K., now I want you to start by pulling out the plug. . . ."

Bruce offered to pick up all dermatology bills. He sounded as if he'd been talking down bit women all day.

The technology-impaired get a systolic surge when confronting any machine. We cover our reproductive organs when the microwave lights up. The eighth wonder of the world is what prevents electricity from spilling out all over the floor when the sockets are empty. Given the choice, we patronize drugstores that carry six brands of hairnets even though we don't use hairnets. We want to support hairnet availability in a world that's turned to ozone-eating hair spray. Why does Saran Wrap have a longer life expectancy than I do?

We know for a fact that things are made with too many parts. Why else would the dishwasher still work when there are three rubber items on the kitchen floor that never went back in? The Web is where the spider waits. Windows are what you look out. We like our phones black.

Everything good in life, what makes you feel something, has nothing to   15
do with technology—family, a peach, the beach. Pastrami on rye. A deep who-pulled-away-first? kiss.

A Short List of Technology I Could Easily Live Without: TV zappers, the VCR, running shoes that look as if they have pool floats for soles, artificial intelligence, morphing, olestra, miracle-fiber shoelaces that come undone *even when you double-knot.* Recently, every historic place I went in Vienna a man was lurking in the doorway shouting into his cell phone. If these babies are such technological wonders, why do people have to scream into them? The $2 billion Stealth bomber couldn't tell the difference between a mountain and a cloud? The last time I checked, a pilot could.

Past cyberspace, into outer space, I stare at the Sturgeon Moon. It's a full moon, a gorgeous moon. Then I remember—we've left junk up there. Aluminum flagpoles, parachute cloth, lunar rovers. Yup, junk on the moon. Or do I mean technology? "Get wood," an architect once told me. "Plastic only goes downhill."

It's 2:11, coffee time.

QUESTIONS FOR DISCUSSION

1. In her opening paragraph, Volk jokes that a new kind of breast pump will make it easier for nursing mothers to answer more e-mail. Why is this joke funny? What assumption about technology is being challenged here?

2. Paragraphs 2 and 3 and 8 through 12 involve getting "help" over the telephone. In using these examples, what has Volk assumed about her audience?
3. Consider the concessions that Volk makes to technology. Is there any pattern to the goods she admits enjoying?
4. What is Volk implying when she asks, "Why does Saran Wrap have a longer life expectancy than I do?"
5. What aspects of technology are essential to your own comfort? What would be on your own "Short List of Technology I Could Easily Live Without"?

SUGGESTIONS FOR WRITING

1. Consider occasions when technology has somehow let you down, whether it be your alarm clock failing to go off or your car refusing to start. Choose one specific experience and—however frustrating it may have been at the time—tell the story of what happened to you, making it as funny as you can.
2. Imagine yourself in a school from which technology has suddenly disappeared. Write a humorous essay describing the unexpected difficulties you would encounter.
3. Drawing on your experience with e-mail or online discussion groups, write an essay showing the humorous side of life on the Internet.

LINKS ■ ■ ■

■ WITHIN THE BOOK

In "Privacy, the Workplace, and the Internet" (pages 563–577), Seumas Miller and John Weckert discuss another problematic aspect of technology.

■ ELSEWHERE IN PRINT

Anuff, Joey, and Ana Marie Cox, eds. *Suck: Worst-Case Scenarios in Media, Culture, Advertising, and the Internet.* San Francisco: Wired, 1997.
Barry, Dave. *Dave Barry in Cyberspace.* New York: Crown, 1996.
Heim, Judy. *I Lost My Baby, My Pickup, and My Guitar on the Information Highway: A Humorous Trip Down the Highways, Byways, and Backroads of Information Technology.* San Francisco: Starch, 1995.
Levine, Rachel. *Cyberyenta's Old-Fashioned Wisdom for Newfangled Times.* Lincoln: Writers, 2000.
Volk, Patricia. *All It Takes: Stories.* New York: Atheneum, 1990.
——. *White Light.* New York: Atheneum, 1987.

(continues)

LINKS ■ ■ ■ *(continued)*

■ **ONLINE**

■ Institute for Women and Technology
  <http://www.iwt.org/home.html>

■ Luddism
  <http://carbon.cudenver.edu/~mryder/itc_data/luddite.html>

■ Technophobia and Technostress
  <http://www.kdinc.com/stress.htm>

IT'S NICE WORK, IF YOU CAN AVOID IT

Jeff Foxworthy

Most people have had days when they didn't feel like going to school or to work, and many people have been tempted to lie about why they decided to stay home. Recognizing this common failing, Jeff Foxworthy uses it as a subject for humor in the following excerpt from his book No Shirt. No Shoes. . . . NO PROBLEM! *(1996). Foxworthy is a stand-up comedian from the South where, according to the* Birmingham News, *he is "more popular than a pig at a barbecue." With several books in print, Foxworthy has also recorded three popular CDs, one of which was nominated for a Grammy. In addition, he can be seen on television through his specials for Showtime as well as through guest appearances on such programs as* The Tonight Show *and* Late Night with David Letterman. *Like many comedians, he frequently draws upon his family for material—including his father, "Big Jim" in the following piece.*

Finally, the day your folks warned, promised, and usually threatened would come has arrived. For better or for worse, your whole life changes.

I'm not talking about holy matrimony. This is worse.

No more allowance.

Out of gas and oil for the old Plymouth Duster? Need cash for dates? Want shells for the .22 and tobacco to chew? Bowling ball need repair? Forced to pay your own bail on a drunk and disorderly warrant?

What's a twenty-one-year-old to do?   5

Time to get a job. Time to see if Vern down at the garage thinks your talent for hot-wiring luxury vehicles can be bent to fixing them as well. There's lots of good jobs available. Besides, things could be worse. Just remember that somewhere, someone else is doing something with hot tar for five dollars an hour.

Thanks to Big Jim, I have a strong work ethic. I've always wanted to pay my own way and support my family. I like the freedom money in my pocket affords. Yet the conventional wisdom is that when the subject is work, Rednecks want to change the subject. People think we're lazy. The truth is that we're salt-of-the-earth working men and working women, even if the salt gets a little soggy in the humidity.

Then to what may we assign the blame for our slothful reputation? Once again: our accents. It's understandable. When it takes someone three times as long to make an excuse about why he's late for work—for the fifteenth time—it just *sounds* shiftless. But is that really fair? I don't think so.

It's hard work to come up with a believable lie.

By the way, I'll be a bit late coming in for this chapter. I slept in, but if   10
anyone asks, I'm saying my pet goat got ahold of my alarm clock and ate it.

I don't want to waste your time, so while you're waiting for me to shower, dress, have coffee and breakfast, read the paper, run a few errands, and maybe catch a matinee, I'll be happy to pass along some wisdom I've gathered about the art of lying to get out of work. I know I'm getting ahead of myself. I should probably talk about *working* before I get to the *lying,* but a good lie is like a good joke, and I can't resist a good joke. Both require forethought, timing, and a surprise ending.

Let's say you hit the snooze button fourteen times and you're running fifteen minutes late for the job. First, if you actually *show up* only fifteen minutes late, you're going to look like you kept hitting the snooze button. So relax. Sit, read the paper, drink a couple of cups of coffee.

I'm sorry. I can't go anywhere without my day-of-the-week undershorts, and I can't find Monday. (Musta been a great weekend.)

Now, for the lie. Don't use the standard, "I got stuck in traffic." They'll know you're lying. Think of something that is so bizarre that your boss will honestly feel sorry for you.

I don't recommend the dead relative lie for two reasons. First, it's hard to keep up with whom you've killed off and who's still living. Grandma can only pass away so often, although in some families like mine—remember, between Big Jim and Carole, they've been married nine times—there can be plenty of Grandmas to go around. But then up crops the second problem: guilt. If you're like me, saying, "Uncle Fred got hit by a train," will make you worry that Uncle Fred *will* get plowed by a locomotive. Then you'll be up on a murder rap for knowing way too much. So if you use a relative, don't kill them. A serious illness is just fine, and it could keep you out of prison.

I'll be out of the bathroom in a minute. I've still got to brush my tooth. 15

You can always claim that you're sick, but be sure to name an illness about which no one would dare ask questions. Projectile vomiting is acceptable, but explosive diarrhea is my personal favorite. That should end all discussion on the matter. If pushed, mumble something about "bad sausage," then say, "Oh-oh, here it comes aga . . ."

If you decide to feign personal injury, I recommend wearing an Ace bandage. Stuff an old T-shirt under it to simulate swelling, and moan constantly for effect. Make sure it's a believable injury. Falling in a corn reaper is too much if you only plan on being out for a day or two. Plus, strapping your arm to your side so your empty shirt sleeve can flap in the breeze will eventually become a big pain in the ass, possibly tear a rotator cuff, and ruin your fly-fishing cast.

I swear, I think the dog ran off again with my car keys.

What you really need is a story that will not only excuse tardiness but encourage your boss to give you the *entire* day off. With pay. How about this: "The sewer backed up into my house, the furniture is floating, and I can't find the kids." Who would expect you to work while your couch is drifting away? It's just bizarre enough to possibly be true. That's all you're shooting for anyway: possibility. Once you create a reasonable doubt for yourself, you are home free. So to speak.

Should anyone give you the third degree on your return to work, don't   20
hesitate to become indignant and stomp out of the room. Crying is also
extremely effective. Especially if you are a man.

*All right. Got my excuse, got my handkerchief, and am heading for the door.
Wait . . . I think I forgot something. . . .*

QUESTIONS FOR DISCUSSION

1. What kind of audience is most likely to enjoy this piece?
2. Do you think anyone could be offended by Foxworthy's humor? What
   kind of reader is least likely to be amused by this piece?
3. To what extent does Foxworthy's humor involve issues of social class? In
   your opinion, under what circumstances is it acceptable to joke about someone's class?
4. According to Foxworthy, "a good lie is like a good joke, and I can't resist a
   good joke." What is the relationship between joking and lying?
5. Foxworthy has focused on excuses for staying home from work. In your
   experience (strictly, of course, in terms of what you've *overheard*), what are
   the most common excuses for failing to attend class?

SUGGESTIONS FOR WRITING

1. Write an essay that focuses on some aspect of life in your part of the country, or within your social class, that could be amusing to readers who share
   your background.
2. Write a humorous dialogue between a college student who is trying to
   get an extension for a paper and a professor who is not sure how seriously
   to take him or her.
3. Write an essay that humorously shows a day in the life of someone who is
   working too hard.

LINKS ■ ■ ■

■ WITHIN THE BOOK

For an essay focused on a specific job that someone should not have
taken, see "The Learning Curve" (pages 611–617) by David Sedaris.

■ ELSEWHERE IN PRINT

Bellenger, Seale. *Hell's Belles: A Tribute to the Spitfires, Bad Seeds, and Steel
   Magnolias of the New and Old South.* Berkeley: Conari, 1997.

(continues)

LINKS ■ ■ ■ *(continued)*

■ ELSEWHERE IN PRINT

Bennett, Barbara. *Comic Visions, Female Voices: Contemporary Women Novelists and Southern Humor.* Baton Rouge: Louisiana State UP, 1998.
Foxworthy, Jeff. *The Final Helping of* You Might Be a Redneck If. . . . Atlanta: Longstreet, 1999.
——. *Hick Is Chic: A Guide to Etiquette for the Grossly Unsophisticated.* Atlanta: Longstreet, 1990.
——. *Redneck Classic: The Best of Jeff Foxworthy.* Atlanta: Longstreet, 1990.
——. *You Might Be a Redneck If. . . .* Atlanta: Longstreet, 1989.

■ ONLINE

- Creating Livable Alternatives to Wage Slavery
  <http://www.whywork.org>

- Nineteenth Century Protestant Work Ethic
  <http://65.107.211.206/history/dora/dora23.html>

- The Official Web Site of Jeff Foxworthy
  <http://www.jefffoxworthy.com>

- Procrastination Research Group
  <http://www.carleton.ca/~tpychyl>

BREAKFAST AT THE FDA CAFÉ

John R. Alden

"Everything that's any fun," the old joke used to run, "is illegal, immoral, or fattening." In this article from a 1991 issue of The Wall Street Journal, *John R. Alden postulates that today we need to add one or two new categories. As you read "Breakfast at the FDA Café," notice how Alden makes a common act—ordering breakfast in a restaurant—a source of humor as well as a social critique.*

An anthropologist at the University of Michigan, Alden reviews books on diverse topics for Smithsonian *and* Natural History *magazines.*

"I'll have two eggs over easy, home fries, a blueberry muffin, decaf coffee and the fresh-squeezed orange juice," I told my waiter.

"Very good, sir," he said, and hurried away.

I had just unfolded my paper as he came back with the coffee.

"Here you are," he said. "But before you can have this, our corporate legal department insists that we warn you that recent studies indicate that consumption of three or more cups of coffee a day may increase your risk of stroke and bladder cancer. This is decaffeinated, so I don't need to say that caffeine is addictive and can cause temporary but significant increases in your blood pressure and heartbeat. However, FDA regulations do require me to notify you that the decaffeination process may leave minute traces of carcinogenic solvents in the coffee beans." He poured.

I had nearly finished the front page when he returned with my breakfast. 5

"Your eggs," he said as he put my plate in front of me, "are fried in a polyunsaturated oil high in fat and calories. Eggs that are only lightly cooked may contain salmonella, an organism causing food poisoning, and the National Society for the Alleviation of Allergies warns that many Americans exhibit a mild allergic response to the ova of domestic fowl. Egg yolks contain large quantities of cholesterol, and the American Association of Cardiological Surgeons recommends that people over 40, particularly those who smoke or are more than 10 pounds overweight, limit their consumption to four eggs per week."

I sucked in my stomach.

"Potatoes," he continued, "are a member of the nightshade family, and any greenish patches on their skin may contain traces of an alkaloid poison called solanine. *The Physician's Reference Manual* says solanine can cause vomiting, diarrhea, and acute nausea. However, your potatoes have been carefully peeled, and our supplier has agreed to assume any liability that may arise from their consumption.

"The blueberry muffin contains enriched flour, cane sugar, eggs, butter, blueberries and low-sodium baking powder. The Institute of Alimentary Studies warns that a diet high in processed flour may add to your risk of stomach and intestinal cancer. The Center for Dietary Purity warns that processed wheat flour may be contaminated with up to two tenths of a part per billion of fungicides and rodenticides. It has been bleached and brominated and in cool wet years might also contain minute traces of ergot. Ingested in sufficient quantities, ergot can cause hallucinations and convulsions, arterial spasms, and induce abortions in pregnant women.

"Citizens Against Empty Calories, an independent research organization 10 funded in part by the American Beet Sugar Producers Association, warns that cane sugar is high in calories, low in nutritional value, and one of the principal dietary factors associated with dental cavities.

"Butter, like eggs, is high in cholesterol, a material that studies have identified as playing a potentially significant role in the development of arteriosclerosis and heart disease, particularly in genetically susceptible individuals. If any of your close relatives ever had a heart attack, the Department of Health and Human Services warns that your personal physician might advise you to limit your intake of butter, cream and other dairy products.

"Our blueberries are from Maine. They have not been fertilized or treated with pesticides. However, the U.S. Geological Survey has reported that many Maine blueberry barrens are located on granite, and granitic rock frequently contains measurable amounts of radioactive uranium, radium and radon gas.

"Finally, the baking powder used in these muffins contains sodium aluminum sulfate. Aluminum, some researchers suggest, may be a contributing factor in the development of Alzheimer's disease. The National Institute of Mental Health has not stated a position on this, but it *has* asked us to inform our customers that it will be funding a seven-year, $47 million study examining the association between aluminum consumption and senility syndromes."

He picked up a pitcher. "I have to inform you that our 'fresh-squeezed' orange juice was actually prepared before 6 this morning. It is now 8:30. The FDA and the Justice Department recently sued a restaurant in Georgia (*U.S. v. Mom's Home-baked Café*) for describing three-hour-old juice as 'fresh-squeezed.' Until that case is decided, our legal advisers have required us to get a waiver from any customer ordering a similar product."

I signed the form he handed me, and he stapled a copy to my bill. But as 15 I reached for the glass, he stopped me.

"Excuse me, please. Our salt and pepper shakers are clearly labeled, but corporate policy requires that I repeat the warnings to you verbally. On the salt it says, 'If consumed in large quantities, sodium chloride can be highly toxic, and habitual ingestion of this compound has been shown to cause life-threatening hypertension.' The other shaker says: 'Pepper. Use with extreme caution! The Center for Communicable Disease warns that sneezing associated with careless use of this powder may contribute to the transmission of rhinoviral and influenza-type diseases.' Finally, the Department of Consumer

Safety has determined that the tines of your fork are sharp, and new regulations require me to caution customers to use that utensil with extreme care."

He turned, and with a cheery "Enjoy your breakfast, sir," headed off to the next table. I picked at my meal but couldn't finish it. The food had gotten cold, and somehow I had lost my appetite.

QUESTIONS FOR DISCUSSION

1. What do you think prompted Alden to write this essay? Is he making fun of the FDA's warnings, or is he making fun of something else?
2. Describe the setting Alden chose for this piece. Would he be able to make his point in a different setting?
3. How does Alden use repetition for humorous effect? How does he use exaggeration?
4. Who is likely to enjoy this essay more, an audience of people who take pleasure from dining out frequently or people who are often on a diet? Why?
5. Alden treats the waiter much as a short story writer or a dramatist might. Describe this character and how he sounds.

SUGGESTIONS FOR WRITING

1. Have you ever been annoyed by what seems to be an endless bombardment of health messages, such as fitness requirements, ridiculous warnings on appliances, signs on pillows or plastic bags? Write an essay showing how you respond to these warnings.
2. Do any of the people you know have a strict sense of what they will or won't eat? Is it ever a challenge to cook for them or to eat out with them in a restaurant? If so, write an essay showing how these people are what they eat—or won't eat, as the case may be.
3. If you have worked in a restaurant, write an essay showing the humorous side of your experience there.

LINKS ■ ■ ■

■ WITHIN THE BOOK

If, like Alden, you enjoy eating food that is not nutritionally correct, you might enjoy "Grub" (pages 62–65) by Scott Russell Sanders.

■ ELSEWHERE IN PRINT

Cabiniss, Michell. *sourGRIPES™ Restaurant*. Belmont: Dragon, 2000.

(continues)

LINKS ■ ■ ■ *(continued)*

■ ELSEWHERE IN PRINT

Downey, Jim, and Tom Connor. *Zeguts Ridiculous Restaurants.* New York: Kensington, 1997.

Hoffman, Ken. *You Want Fries with That? A Collection.* Houston: Winedale, 1999.

Kraus, Scott. *Stuff and Other Junk: FDA Certified Generic Humor.* Valley City: Dutch, 1998.

Spitznagel, Eric. *The Junk Food Companion: The Complete Guide to Eating Badly.* New York: Penguin, 1999.

■ ONLINE

- Food and Drug Administration
  <http://www.fda.gov>

- Internet Satirical Newspaper Association
  <http://www.bandersnatch.com/isna.htm>

- Carni-Food
  <http://halfbakery.com/idea/Carni-Food>

HOW I'M DOING

David Owen

*In addition to frequent polls and marketing surveys that solicit information on Ameri-
can tastes and values, job evaluations have become increasingly common. Students are
asked to evaluate their teachers, and managers are asked to evaluate the employees
they supervise. So why not evaluations for parents? And why not let parents—and other
subjects for evaluation—have a say in determining the criteria by which they are judged?
Bearing these questions in mind may help you to understand David Owen's humor in
"How I'm Doing."*

Owen is a staff writer for The New Yorker, *which published the following selection
in 2000. A contributing editor of* Golf Digest, *he has also edited* Lure of the Links
*(1997), a well-received collection of golf writing. He is also the author of two books
about golf, one of which—*My Usual Game *(1995)—chronicles his own misadventures
on the golf course.*

In the hope of establishing a more equitable framework by which the
public can evaluate my effectiveness as a father, husband, friend, and worker, I
am pleased to announce that the methodology heretofore used in measuring
my performance is being revised. Beginning tomorrow, my reputation and
compensation will no longer be based on year-long, cumulative assessments
of my attainments but will instead be derived from periodic samplings of
defined duration, or "sweeps."

From now on, ratings of my success as a parent will be based solely on
perceptions of my conduct during the two weeks beginning March 7th (a.k.a.
"spring vacation"), the two weeks beginning August 1st (a.k.a. "summer vacation"), the seven days ending December 25th, and my birthday. No longer
will my ranking be affected by unsolicited anecdotal reports from minors
concerning my alleged "cheapness," "strictness," and "loser" qualities, or by
the contents of viewing diaries maintained by my dependents. Page views,
click-throughs, and People Meter data concerning me will also be disre-
garded, except during the aforementioned periods. The opinions of my children will no longer be counted in evaluations of my sense of humor.

Public appraisals of my behavior at parties will henceforth not be drawn
from overnight ratings provided by my wife; instead, my annual ranking will
be based on a random sampling of my level of intoxication during the week
following January 2nd. My official weight for the year will be my median
weight during the four weeks beginning July 1st. All measures of my geniality, thoughtfulness, romantic disposition, and willingness to compromise will
henceforth be calculated just three times per year: on September 15th (my

wife's birthday), August 26th (our anniversary), and February 14th. My high-school grades, S.A.T. scores, college grades, and income history will no longer be available for inclusion in any of my ratings, and in fact they will be expunged from my personal database. Evaluations of my success as a stock-market investor will no longer include the performance of my portfolio during the month of October.°

Beginning in 2001, my annual compensation will cease to consist of my total income over the twelve months of the fiscal year; instead, my yearly pay will be adjusted to equal not less than thirteen times my nominal gross earnings during the four weeks beginning February 1st, when the holiday season is over, my children are back in school, and my local golf course has not yet reopened for the spring. My critics may object that my output during February is not representative of my output during the rest of the year, especially when I am at the beach. However, I believe (and my auditors concur) that the work I do during periods of cold, miserable weather provides the best available indication of my actual abilities as a worker and therefore constitutes the only fair and objective basis for calculating my true contribution to the economy. Conversely, my federal income-tax liability will henceforth be based on an annualized computation of my total earnings between Memorial Day and Labor Day.

These changes are being made as a part of my ongoing effort to ensure   5
that public data concerning me and my personality are the very best available. This new protocol may be further modified by me at any time without advance notice, and, in any case, is not legally binding. In addition, all assessments of my performance are subject to later revision, as improved information becomes available. Specifically, my lifetime ratings in all categories may be posthumously adjusted, within thirty days of my death, to reflect the content of newspaper obituaries regarding me, should any such be published, and the things that people say about me at my funeral.

QUESTIONS FOR DISCUSSION

1. Consider Owen's use of the passive voice in this essay, as in "the methodology heretofore used in measuring my performance is being revised." How does the passive voice contribute to the humor of this piece?
2. Why would Owen want to restrict measurements of "geniality, thoughtfulness, romantic disposition, and willingness to compromise" to the three dates he chooses?
3. To what extent is the humor of this piece dependent upon Owen and his audience sharing a similar class background?
4. What is the object of Owen's humor? Is he making fun of the American interest in ratings, the status of fathers, or the language of job evaluations?

October: Often a bad month for the stock market, as in 1929 and 1987.

SUGGESTIONS FOR WRITING

1. Write a humorous evaluation of a family member's performance during the past year.
2. Write a year-end report in which you humorously narrate all that you failed to accomplish during the past year.
3. Choose an example of business writing, and write a parody of it.

LINKS ■ ■ ■

■ WITHIN THE BOOK

For another view of fatherhood, see Itabara Njeri's "Life with Father" (pages 68–72).

■ ELSEWHERE IN PRINT

Allen, Tim. *I'm Not Really Here.* New York: Hyperion, 1996.
Barry, Dave. *Dave Barry's Complete Guide to Guys: A Fairly Short Book.* New York: Random, 1995.
Gill, Brenden. *Here at the New Yorker.* New York: Random, 1975.
Owen, David. *My Usual Game: Adventures in Golf.* New York: Main St., 1996.
Ross, Lillian. *Takes: Stories from the Talk of the Town.* New York: Congdon, 1983.
Seinfeld, Jerry. *SeinLanguage.* New York: Bantam, 1993.

■ ONLINE

- A Humorous Look at Marriage
  <http://www.youmarriedhim.com>

- A Humorous Look at Parenting
  <http://pregnancytoday.com/reference/articles/malebonding.htm>

- Nap Time Notes
  <http://homeparents.about.com/gi/dynamic/
  offsite.htm?site=http%3A%2F%2Fwww.ddc.com%2Fnapnotes%2F>

ELEVENTH-HOUR BRIDE

Sandra Tsing Loh

In addition to writing humor, Sandra Tsing Loh composes music, writes short stories, and has performed in well-received, one-woman off Broadway shows such as Aliens in America *and* Bad Sex with Bud Kemp. *She is also a regular commentator for* Morning Edition *on National Public Radio. When discussing her diverse interests in an interview with Douglas Eby, she declared: "I think of myself as a humorist, and that's been really important; in everything I've done there's been comedy." She also notes that comics "come from an outsider place, and can take whatever enrages them or makes them cry or whatever, and transform that into something hysterically funny. I think that is the tool, that's what comics do; they are very much outsiders, they are not in power, they're the underdog, and that's what makes them funny."*

"Eleventh-Hour Bride" originally appeared in Buzz *magazine, for which Loh wrote a column in the 1990s. Several of these columns can be found in her collection* Depth Takes a Holiday: Essays from Lesser Los Angeles *(1996). She has also published in the* New York Times, Vogue, Elle, *and* Harper's Bazaar. *As you prepare to read the following example of Loh's work, consider how people you know have behaved when planning their weddings. Think also about the weddings you have attended and how wedding planning is promoted in various magazines aimed at young women.*

Enough months have passed; the wounds have healed; I can finally talk about my wedding. My wedding, since you ask, was like the great sinking of the *Titanic.* Then again, I knew it would be. That's why I was engaged for, oh, seven years.

Note how I keep referring to "my" wedding as opposed to "our" wedding—as if this were some auto-inflicted act. It is. Indeed, as the well-over-thirty (read "old") bride (for which there should be some special niche publication: *Old Bride Magazine*) plans her Special Day, the groom becomes but an extraneous character, a rubber mascot head, a blank screen upon which the ensuing drama of the bridal breakdown is to be shakily projected.

Sound ugly? Never mind. Postfeminist women still deserve that nuptial ballgown and tiara, even if it comes ten years late and we're feeling bloated. To this end, I offer these "11th-Hour Wedding Tips." That's right. While you should throw a big wedding, yes, I don't think you should spend more than two weeks planning it. Learn from my example. Two weeks is just long enough to complete the Hysteria Cycle without killing you both.

1. *Have the Wedding at Someone's House, Preferably Not Your Own.* For the years 1990–1994 inclusive, my dream was to get married on the cliffs of Big Sur—string quartet, sunset, strawberries, champagne. We'd put

up our fifty closest friends at the picturesque Big Sur Inn for one magical, unforgettable weekend. I made one phone call, got a grasp on general price and feasibility, and fell into a depression for four years.

2. *Marry Lutheran.* Unless you're religious—in that case, of course, go with the home team. And I envy you: Jews, Hindus, Catholics— come weddin' time agnostics have far less leg to stand on. When my brother got married, his Christian service posited marriage as a three-fold braid: "Husband, Wife, and Jesus." Discussing this, my sister and I began to snicker—then sobered up upon pondering the alternatives. What would our three-fold braid be? "You, Me, and My Therapist?" "You, Me and VISA?"

   I say, this is for life, so get all the help you can get. Anyway, bottom line: Make a big deal about going secular, and soon you'll find yourself lighting an aromatherapy candle, mumbling about some Great Spirit's circle of love, and being much more ashamed than if you had shut up and flown coach. Lutherans, which by coincidence Mike and I were raised as, give a short, decent service that soothes parents and stuns cynical, fortyish L.A. peers into a bemused and yet oddly respectful silence. *5*

3. *Don't Sweat the Guest List: You'll Screw It Up Anyway.* a) Are they friends from college? b) Have they had you over for dinner in the last year? c) Would they invite you to their wedding? If the answer is no, said L.A. couple is sure to be the most pissed at your not inviting them. "But when do we ever hear from them?" you ask the air. And then at 3 A.M., two months too late, the lovely gift basket they recently sent will rise in the dark like a ghost. You scream. And so you are doomed to wander in rumpled wedding gown, botched guest list trailing, forever lost in the Palace of Guilt with its many alcoves and cupolas.

4. *Two Weeks Before, Let Slip to a Few Female Acquaintances That You Have Made No Calls Re: Caterer, Flowers, Decor, Etc.* Why? Because it's fun. "And what have you chosen for your wedding colors?" a distant (twice-married) female relative asked me mellifluously on Sunday night, thirteen days before Ground Zero. A howl of laughter, while a satisfying conversation stopper, was not enough to fully articulate my position. I pressed on:

   "Wedding *colors?* I'm a person who can barely dress myself in the morning. Mike and I are getting married because we love each other. We've got the paperwork, our friends are coming, we'll have a big meal. That's it. It will be simple. This is a formal commitment between two adults, not a prom. We're too old to care about stuff like flowers and decorations and tuxedos."

   To which she repeated, with a kind of eerie calm: "Sandra? What have you chosen for your wedding colors?"

5. *Immediately Take 60 percent of All Hysterical Female Advice Given.* And now, of course, the descent into madness begins. Wedding colors? Who gives a flying fig about wedding colors! Not you. But should you? Are you missing out if you bypass the wedding colors? Will that make you less than female? Less than bridal? Less than married? Just generally . . . less?

   Suddenly a girlish pang of hurt wells up, a forgotten bolus of   10
   need from adolescence. You sense, vaguely, your Adult Head denying your Bride Head something princesslike, magical. What: There's a multimillion-dollar bridal industry in this country and you are not included? Who do they think you are? Gertrude Stein a-wielding gardening trowel?° So what if you're in your mid-thirties! That's just five years older than twenty-nine! You're far from washed up. You want to live! It's your last chance!

6. *Bridal Salons: No.* Your huge plastic Bride Head, all circuits sparking like in the Disney Electrical Parade, will now pull you into a bridal salon, eleven days before D-Day. Suddenly the Kate Hepburnesque white silk pantsuit that seemed so perfect is less than bridal, less than married, just generally . . . less.

   You need the bridal white satin, tulle veil, rhinestone crust. Thousand-dollar dresses hang accusingly before you in plastic body bags, glinting bluish under the fluorescents. You shrug one on. You immediately see that these are duchess of Czechoslovakia dresses. And you're of sallow half-Asian descent: The vision you see swathed in beads before you suggests the cheery title "Communion Day in Little Tijuana!" You burst into tears.

7. *Rather Than Being Mere Food Service Workers, Caterers Are Sensitive, Misunderstood Artists Who Are Continually Being Oppressed by an Ugly, Boorish World. Fifty Dollars a Person for Papaya Brie Quesadillas Is a Fabulous Deal.* No. Put that phone down. You are hysterical. Have a smart, sensible friend discipline these people. Not the Wedding Colors one.

8. *No Matter What They Say, It Takes Stylists Eight and a Half Hours to Do Hair. "My Wedding Starts in Twenty-five Minutes and It's in the Valley," Has No Impact on the La Cienega Salon Person.* Trust me.

9. *Don't Kill Anyone at Your Wedding.* "Can Mike turn on the Nintendo?"   15
   one hapless eight-year-old asked after I'd spent twenty minutes, hair and gown increasingly bedraggled, marshalling the crowd—which, thanks to the Palace of Guilt, had swollen to two hundred—for toasts. I'm told my lips pulled back into a Hellraiser mask: The child in question let out a scream of terror. (Note that I did not follow tip number one: Do not get married at your own house.)

Gertrude Stein a-wielding gardening trowel: An imitation of the kind of language sometimes used by Gertrude Stein (1874–1946), an experimental writer who favored simple clothing and was partnered to another woman.

10. *It Will End*. The day after my wedding was the happiest of my whole life. "Oh my God," I thought, "I never have to get married again." Mike thought so too. And so on that first day as husband and wife, we were in bliss.

QUESTIONS FOR DISCUSSION

1. Note the distinction Loh draws in paragraph 2 between speaking of "my wedding" as opposed to "our wedding." What does this distinction suggest about the way weddings are planned in the United States?
2. What do you think Loh means by "postfeminist"? How would a "post-feminist" differ from a "feminist"?
3. Consider the joke with which Loh ends the first paragraph in her second piece of advice, "Marry Lutheran." What assumptions is she making about her audience?
4. Loh claims that it is impossible not to make mistakes when choosing the guest list for a wedding. Under what kinds of pressure do engaged couples often operate when planning their list?
5. Is Loh making fun of weddings or of her own response to getting married?

SUGGESTIONS FOR WRITING

1. Write an advice column humorously describing how to plan for going away to college or preparing for a job interview.
2. Pick up an issue of *Modern Bride,* and write a parody of one of its articles.
3. Write a humorous account of the behavior you witnessed at a wedding that you attended.

LINKS ■ ■ ■

■ WITHIN THE BOOK

For a woman's view of another social ritual, see "The Sad Comedy of Really Bad Food" by Dara Moskowitz (pages 293–295).

■ ELSEWHERE IN PRINT

Lebowitz, Fran. *The Fran Lebowitz Reader.* New York: Vintage, 1994.

Loh, Sandra Tsing. *Depth Takes a Holiday: Essays from Lesser Los Angeles.* New York: Riverhead, 1996.

———. *If You Lived Here, You'd Be Home by Now.* New York: Riverhead, 1997.

Martin, Judith. *Miss Manners on Weddings.* New York: Crown, 1999.

Ross-Macdonald, Jane. *Alternative Weddings: An Essential Guide for Creating Your Own Ceremonies.* Dallas: Taylor, 1997.

(continues)

LINKS ■ ■ ■ *(continued)*

■ **ONLINE**

- Brief Biography
  <http://www.k2b2.com/Sandra.html>

- Marriage and Feminism
  <http://www.salon.com/mwt/feature/2001/08/15/i_do>

- Modern Bride
  <http://www.modernbride.com>

- Wedding Humor
  <http://www.weddinghumor.com>

THE YOUNG MAN AND THE SEA

Henry Alford

To understand the humor of the following selection, you need to understand that there is a tradition, in English-language literature, that involves narrating the history of young men who mature by going to sea. In American literature, many of these narratives—such as Moby Dick—*involve men in pursuit of a fish (as if by catching a big fish they could prove that their lives have value). As the title of the following selection reveals, "The Young Man and the Sea" evokes Hemingway's* The Old Man and the Sea *in particular. "The Young Man and the Sea" was first published in* New York Magazine, *a magazine read primarily by college-educated men and women who see themselves as urban sophisticates. The author of* Municipal Bondage (1995) *and* The Big Kiss (2000), *Henry Alford writes for* The New York Times Magazine, Spy, GQ, *and* Vanity Fair, *among other publications.*

It is the duty of the introspective, literary, male writer, in the course of his career as an introspective literary male, to write a story in which he unbosoms universal truths while engaged in the act of fishing. Bobbing upon the watery depths, alert to the sudden presence of thorny verities, or of haddock, he must descend deep into the pit of his humanity and then mine that rich ore of his profession: awful splendor. So when, earlier this summer, I went to the Hamptons° for three days of fishing, I knew that this was more than an opportunity to savor the blandishments of one of the Eastern seaboard's loveliest settings; this was an opportunity to practice eliciting stunned awe from the *Esquire* subscriber base and, perhaps, to make a dazzling literary metaphor of my dead father.

I started with sportfishing. At eight o'clock on a sunshiny Wednesday morning in Montauk harbor, I boarded *Lazybones,* a fifty-five-foot "party boat" that can accommodate forty-five. I told the ruggedly handsome mate who collected my $25 half-day fare, "I'm hoping to encounter awful splendor today." His expression betrayed bafflement. I explained, "You know how in fishing stories, the fisherman looks deep into the beast's eye and has a harrowing moment of self-realization?" The mate matter-of-factly responded, "That's not going to happen today." What was going to happen was fluke, or summer flounder. Each fisherman was given a rod as well as bait resembling indelicately prepared sushi. As we chugged out to the fog-saddled sea, I fell into conversation with a courtly, seventy-three-year-old, ponytailed gentleman. "My dear boy, you've never eaten fluke?" he said to me spiritedly, laying

---

The Hamptons: A few ocean-front towns on eastern Long Island, known for attracting the rich and fashionable during the summer.

his hand on my shoulder. "The most delicious thing in the world." My brain flashed: possible father surrogate?

I would like to be able to tell you that I now understand the wisdom of this man's statement, and that fluke is at present my daily bread. But over the course of the next four hours, I caught only one fish, and it was wee, well under the fifteen-inch minimum length. This would have been less damaging to my confidence were fluke fishing not so easy (you simply let your hook drop to the bottom then wait) or were the woman fishing adjacent to me—a first-timer who had confessed to mild seasickness—not so spectacularly successful. "Attaboy, lady!" the mate who'd collected my fare yelled at this woman after she had reeled in five fluke and one striped bass in the first two hours: "She's throwin' 'em over the rails!" When I asked this woman, "What's your secret?" she told me, "It's called 'I-don't-know-what-the-hell-I'm-doing.' " I smiled bleakly. At one point her line got tangled with another person's on the other side of the boat; moments later, the mate who untangled the lines appeared with an eighteen-inch fluke and said to the woman, "Here, this was on your line."

Fluke—or, as I came to think of it, Bizarre Coincidence—was apparently not my fish, and my inability to apprehend any of regulation size was keeping me from having important literary thoughts. At the conclusion of our voyage, I skulked back to my rental car with not a little embarrassment, neatly dodging the man who had called me "my dear boy," only to find that I had left my headlights on and my battery was dead. Six phone calls produced an intense, burly mechanic from B&B Auto Service in Montauk, who jumped my car. I explained that I was on business, writing "my big fishing story," and needed a receipt. As I sheepishly closed the car's hood, I was filled with the strange delusion that my fellow *Lazybones* fishermen—now wandering around the parking lot lugging plastic baggies filled with the fluke they had caught and had had filleted by the mates—would ritually mock me by smearing their fillets on my face and genitals. This did not happen. However, as I pulled out of the parking lot two minutes later, the mechanic roared his tow truck perpendicularly in front of me, cutting me off: I had failed to close my hood all the way. He jumped out of his truck and slammed it shut, yelling, "This way, they won't have to buy you a new windshield, too!" From inside my car, I gave him a meek wave, as if to plead, *Release me from this festival of inadequacy.*

You will nod empathically, I think, when I tell you that on my next out- 5 ing I gravitated to the soothing and picturesque. Indeed, I have seldom undertaken a more heart-stirring and visually glorious activity than that in which I found myself engaged the following morning: fly-fishing from a kayak, just offshore from the Shinnecock Indian Reservation in Shinnecock Bay, Southampton, at 7:30 A.M.—the earliest I have ever been awake east of Mastic-Shirley. I had engaged the services of North Sea Kayaking instructor Steve Lancia ($145 for three hours). Our first fifty-five minutes were spent standing onshore, practicing, without a fly on my line, the graceful art of casting; I slowly transformed my semaphore of intent into a surgical strike of aggression. Once we were out on the water, each in our own Old Town kayak, the combination of location and activity engendered in me a golden, International Coffees–type glow. Birds twittered, clammers clammed. I felt ready— ready to remark upon the noble proportions of a dying tuna, ready to behold a bluefish and then gravely announce, "We are all our fathers' sons."

But where were the fish? Finally, two hours into the outing, I had a strike. Steve, boyishly excitable, screamed, "Yes!" I reeled in hurriedly. Steve was genuinely enthusiastic: "I am so happy for you. I'm gonna get my camera. This is it, man. This is everything." I kept reeling in. Steve thought it might be "a blue." I was hoping for striped bass but would not sniff at a blue. When my quarry flashed in the water, Steve announced, "I think it's a skate"; we were sliding precipitately down the scale of fish desirability. The fish burst from the water. Steve exclaimed, "A sea robin! Very nice." He tried to put a spin on it, saying, "It's a beautiful fish—see the wings on it?" to which I murmured, "The showgirl of the fish community." Now, I don't mean to cast aspersions on showgirls, but for those of you who have never looked at a sea robin with the startling proximity that a kayak can afford you, here is the gist—think of a demented Genghis Khan. Add cancer-pocked flagella. Dip in polymer. In short, an entity to keep as far away as possible from the word *bisque*. An entity unlikely to elicit philosophical insight. We returned the fish to the water; I thanked Steve for his company and guidance, then headed on my way.

Bad luck runs in streaks. And so, although it should have surprised me when, upon returning to my lodgings at the Sea Breeze Inn in Amagansett, I discovered fourteen members of the Anglers Club, all on an Anglers Club fishing trip, it did not. I simply thought, "Of course. And then the innkeeper will turn out to be Mrs. Paul." Six minutes later, hearing the phrase *creel limit* being flung across the porch, I hustled into my car and sped off.

Heavy drinking commenced. Heavy drinking (so essential to manly contemplation) continued. As I remember it—it is almost dawn as I write this, and I am well into a bottle of Seagram's—it was at this juncture that I had my first epiphany. Namely, I was in the wrong Hampton. If you're looking for penetrating writerly aperçus, you don't go to Southampton, the tatty, spinsterish aunt of the Hamptons; nor to Montauk, the Hamptons' jovial, beer-gutted cousin. And you certainly don't go to East Hampton, that whorish geographical bauble. No, you must hie yourself to Beard-Tugging Central: Bridgehampton.

Down on Bridgehampton's Mecox Beach, notepad at my side, I watched a gorgeous sunset and found myself scribbling the notation *flutelike cry of the loon*. I thought: Yes. Yes. Perhaps I'm making my search for awful splendor too difficult, I thought. Maybe the equation Scenery + Boat + Pursuit of Fish was excessively ambitious, and should be divested of its third and most time-consuming component.

And so I headed off the next day to boat around Georgica Pond, the site of homes owned by Steven Spielberg, Martha Stewart, and Ron Perelman. Renting a kayak from Main Beach Surf & Sport in Wainscott for $65 for a

10

half-day, I told a friendly employee named Lars that I was "a journalist in recovery" and that I was "hoping to reconnect with my troubled childhood." He applauded this pursuit. It took me two hours to trace the perimeter of the beautiful, sun-dappled pond, a period marked by two renditions of the *Hawaii Five-O* theme song, a flirtation with a truculent swan, and a vague desire to present myself at the Spielberg compound as a sea-weary Schindler Wasp. Near, but not at, Martha Stewart's house, I saw a blonde, forties-ish woman in a white sweatshirt. Thinking that maybe my journey would lead me to The Mother, not The Father, I yelled across the pond, "Martha! I've brought the swan's-head gondola lawn chairs with the matching jabot drapery!" The woman squinted and walked away.

Perhaps speed would provide the antidote, I thought. So I drove up to the northern coast of East Hampton, to the lovely Cedar Point Park, where, at a Main Beach outpost, I rented a trimaran ($50 a half-day). The wind, coming from the northwest, was fierce, whitecaps dotted the water like tainted meringue. Indeed, so awesome was the wind that, although I am a mature salt, if not an old salt, I prevailed upon Tom, the twenty-three-year-old Main Beach employee manning the outpost, to sail with me. I sat in the one-man cockpit and worked the foot rudders while Tom worked the sail. The pontoons slapped against the water, exploding in a miasma of salty spray: Neptune's facial. We rocketed forth with startling speed; lightning would be faster, except it zags. Mirth abounded. I started laughing, and was unable to stop. There are moments in life that require precise words, and so I will try, through the dampening fog of the Seagram's, to summon up the proper ones. *Cowabunga* is one. Also, *tubular hellcraft.*

But still no awful splendor. So galvanized was I by sailing, however, that I decided to try fishing again. But when I arrived at Montauk harbor without a boat reservation the next day at noon, I discovered that the only option available to me was the Viking line's casino cruise, at a mere $3 (off-season) for a four-hour ride. I joined the fifteen other passenger-gamblers. As we cruised out to international waters, I went to the upper deck and lay in the sun without my shirt on; a mustachioed senior in a denim cap remarked, "I guess you lost your shirt!" to which I responded, "Good one." The slot machines broke down with some regularity during the voyage, prompting the mates to fix them, and to encourage us to buy drinks. At one point I almost tripped over the guts of a slot machine that cluttered up an aisle: Issuing from its viscera were what must have been 700 sweat-soaked slugs and quarters. Awful splendor.

I returned my car the following morning to the National Car Rental office at La Guardia. I explained to a soft-spoken National clerk that while I was writing "my big fishing story" out in the Hamptons, my car's battery had died and I had hired a mechanic. The woman apologized and offered me a $25 rebate. "But as it turned out," I told her, "it worked well for the story." To the limited extent that she was interested in this statement, her interest was marked by confusion. "That mechanic," I announced, "was the spitting image of my late father."

QUESTIONS FOR DISCUSSION

1. Consider Alford's use of language. What phrases indicate that he is writing a parody?
2. How does Alford present himself in this piece, and how does this self-presentation contribute to the humor of this piece?
3. What is the role of the "seventy-three-year-old, ponytailed gentleman" mentioned in paragraphs 2 and 4?
4. To what extent does the humor of this piece involve a contrast between different models of masculinity? Is there anything inherently funny about the gender expectations that prevail today?
5. Alford makes several references to what things cost. How do you respond to these references?

SUGGESTIONS FOR WRITING

1. Alford writes a parody of a ritual associated with male coming-of-age stories. Think of an activity engaged in by women when they seek to bond with other women, and write a humorous essay about that activity.
2. Write a humorous essay focused on how either men or women behave when playing a sport in high school or college.
3. Write an essay showing the comic aspects of a vacation that did not go as planned.

LINKS ■ ■ ■

■ WITHIN THE BOOK

In "Monologue to the Maestro" (pages 626–631), Ernest Hemingway describes a young man who goes to sea with an older man in pursuit of wisdom.

■ ELSEWHERE IN PRINT

Alford, Henry. *Big Kiss: One Actor's Desperate Attempt to Claw His Way to the Top.* New York: Villard, 2000.
——— *Municipal Bondage: One Man's Anxiety-Producing Adventures in the Big City.* New York: Random, 1993.
Conrad, Joseph. *Lord Jim.* 1900. New York: Oxford UP, 2000.
Hemingway, Ernest. *The Old Man and the Sea.* 1952. New York: Scribner's, 1999.

(continues)

LINKS ■ ■ ■ *(continued)*

■ **ELSEWHERE IN PRINT**

Maclean, Norman. *A River Runs Through It*. 1976. Chicago: U of
 Chicago P, 1989.
Melville, Herman. *Moby Dick; Or, The Whale*. 1851. New York: Penguin,
 1992.

■ **ONLINE**

- *Billy Budd, Sailor* (Annotated)
 <http://www.shsu.edu/~eng_wpf/authors/Melville/
 Billy-Budd.html>
- Fishing Humor
 <http://fishing.about.com/cs/fishinghumor>
- Herman Melville
 <http://www.melville.org>
- *The Old Man and the Sea* Synopsis
 <http://www.ernest.hemingway.com/oldman.htm>

THE LEARNING CURVE

David Sedaris

Have you ever taken a class from an incompetent teacher or been supervised by someone who did not understand how to do his or her job? Have you ever felt that you have somehow gotten yourself into a position that was too much responsibility for you? Have any of the activities in a college course ever seemed a little odd? If you can answer "yes" to any of these questions, you should enjoy the following essay by David Sedaris, in which he presents himself as an ill-prepared writing teacher who is desperate to fill up class time.

A former house cleaner who now lives in Paris, Sedaris is a regular contributor to National Public Radio and the author of many humorous essays. "The Learning Curve" is from his 2000 collection, Me Talk Pretty Someday. *Reviewing this collection for the* New York Times Book Review, *Craig Seligman advises, "Not one of the seventeen autobiographical essays in this new collection failed to make me crack up; frequently I was helpless. [. . .] Even the bleakest of them contain stuff you shouldn't read with your mouth full."*

A year after my graduation from the School of the Art Institute of Chicago, a terrible mistake was made and I was offered a position teaching a writing workshop. I had never gone to graduate school, and although several of my stories had been Xeroxed and stapled, none of them had ever been published in the traditional sense of the word.

Like branding steers or embalming the dead, teaching was a profession I had never seriously considered. I was clearly unqualified, yet I accepted the job without hesitation, as it would allow me to wear a tie and go by the name of Mr. Sedaris. My father went by the same name, and though he lived a thousand miles away, I liked to imagine someone getting the two of us confused. "Wait a minute," this someone might say, "are you talking about Mr. Sedaris the retired man living in North Carolina, or Mr. Sedaris the distinguished academic?"

The position was offered at the last minute, when the scheduled professor found a better-paying job delivering pizza. I was given two weeks to prepare, a period I spent searching for a briefcase and standing before my full-length mirror, repeating the words, "Hello, class, my name is Mr. Sedaris." Sometimes I'd give myself an aggressive voice and firm, athletic timbre. This was the masculine Mr. Sedaris, who wrote knowingly of flesh wounds and tractor pulls. Then there was the ragged bark of the newspaper editor, a tone that coupled wisdom with an unlimited capacity for cruelty. I tried sounding businesslike and world-weary, but when the day eventually came, my nerves kicked in and the true Mr. Sedaris revealed himself. In a voice reflecting doubt, fear, and an unmistakable desire to be loved, I sounded not like a thoughtful college professor but, rather, like a high-strung twelve-year-old girl; someone named Brittany.

My first semester I had only nine students. Hoping they might view me as professional and well prepared, I arrived bearing name tags fashioned in the shape of maple leaves. I'd cut them myself out of orange construction paper and handed them out along with a box of straight pins. My fourth-grade teacher had done the same thing, explaining that we were to take only one pin per person. This being college rather than elementary school, I encouraged my students to take as many pins as they liked. They wrote their names upon their leaves, fastened them to their breast pockets, and bellied up to the long oak table that served as our communal desk.

"All right, then," I said. "Okay, here we go." I opened my briefcase and realized that I'd never thought beyond this moment. The orange leaves were the extent of my lesson plan, but still I searched the empty briefcase, mindful that I had stupidly armed my audience with straight pins. I guess I'd been thinking that, without provocation, my students would talk, offering their thoughts and opinions on the issues of the day. I'd imagined myself sitting on the edge of the desk, overlooking a forest of raised hands. The students would simultaneously shout to be heard, and I'd pound on something in order to silence them. "Whoa, people," I'd yell. "Calm down, you'll all get your turn. One at a time, one at a time."

The error of my thinking yawned before me. A terrible silence overtook the room, and seeing no other option, I instructed my students to pull out their notebooks and write a brief essay related to the theme of profound disappointment.

I'd always hated it when a teacher forced us to invent something on the spot. Aside from the obvious pressure, it seemed that everyone had his or her own little way of doing things, especially when it came to writing. Maybe someone needed a particular kind of lamp or pen or typewriter. In my experience, it was hard to write without your preferred tools, but impossible to write without a cigarette.

I made a note to bring in some ashtrays, and then I rooted through the wastepaper basket for a few empty cans. Standing beneath the prominently displayed NO SMOKING sign, I distributed the cans and cast my cigarettes upon the table, encouraging my students to go at it. This, to me, was the very essence of teaching, and I thought I'd made a real breakthrough until the class asthmatic raised his hand, saying that, to the best of his knowledge, Aristophanes had never smoked a cigarette in his life. "Neither did Jane Austen," he said. "Or the Brontës."

I jotted these names into my notebook alongside the word *Troublemaker,* and said I'd look into it. Because I was the writing teacher, it was automatically assumed that I had read every leather-bound volume in the Library of Classics. The truth was that I had read none of those books, nor did I intend to. I bluffed my way through most challenges with dim memories of the movie or miniseries based upon the book in question, but it was an exhausting exercise, and eventually I learned it was easier to simply reply with a question, saying, "I know what Flaubert means to *me,* but what do *you* think of her?"

As Mr. Sedaris, I lived in constant fear. There was the perfectly under- 10 standable fear of being exposed as a fraud, and then there was the deeper fear that my students might hate me. I imagined them calling their friends on the phone. "Guess who *I* got stuck with," they'd say. Most dull teachers at least had a few credentials to back them up. They had a philosophy and a lesson plan and didn't need to hide behind a clip-on tie and an empty briefcase.

Whenever I felt in danger of losing my authority, I would cross the room and either open or close the door. A student needed to ask permission before regulating the temperature or noise level, but I could do so whenever I liked. It was the only activity sure to remind me that I was in charge, and I took full advantage of it.

"There he goes again," my students would whisper. "What's up with him and that door?"

The asthmatic transferred to another class, leaving me with only eight students. Of these, four were seasoned smokers who took long, contemplative drags and occasionally demonstrated their proficiency by blowing ghostly concentric rings that hovered like halos above their bowed heads. The others tried as best they could, but it wasn't pretty. By the end of the second session, my students had produced nothing but ashes. Their hacking coughs and complete lack of output suggested that, for certain writers, smoking was obviously not enough.

Thinking that a clever assignment might help loosen them up, I instructed my students to write a letter to their mothers in prison. They were free to determine both the crime and the sentence, and references to cellmates were strongly encouraged.

The group set to work with genuine purpose and enthusiasm, and I felt 15 proud of myself, until the quietest member of the class handed in her paper, whispering that both her father and her uncle were currently serving time on federal racketeering charges.

"I just never thought of my mom going off as well," she said. "This was just a really . . . depressing assignment."

I'd never known what an actual child-to-parent prison letter might be like, but now I had a pretty clear idea. I envisioned two convicts sharing a cell. One man stood at the sink while the other lay on a bunk, reading his mail.

"Anything interesting?" the standing man asked.

"Oh, it's from my daughter," the other man said. "She's just started college, and apparently her writing teacher is a real asshole."

That was the last time I asked my students to write in class. From that 20 point on, all their stories were to be written at home on the subject of their choice. If I'd had my way, we would have all stayed home and conducted the class through smoke signals. As it was, I had to find some way to pass the time and trick my students into believing that they were getting an education. The class met twice a week for two hours a day. Filling an entire session with one activity was out of the question, so I began breaking each session into a series of brief, regularly scheduled discussion periods. We began each day with Celebrity Corner. This was an opportunity for the students to share interesting bits of information provided by friends in New York or Los Angeles who were forever claiming firsthand knowledge of a rock band's impending breakup or movie star's dark sexual secret. Luckily everyone seemed to have such a friend, and we were never short of material.

Celebrity Corner was followed by the Feedbag Forum, my shameless call for easy, one-pot dinner recipes, the type favored by elderly aunts and grandmothers whose dental status demanded that all meat fall from the bone without provocation. When asked what Boiled Beef Arkansas had to do with the craft of writing, I did not mention my recent purchase of a Crock-Pot; rather, I lied through my rotten teeth, explaining that it wasn't the recipe itself but the pacing that was of interest to the writer.

After the Feedbag Forum it was time for Pillow Talk, which was defined as "an opportunity for you to discuss your private sex lives in a safe, intellectual environment." The majority of my students were reluctant to share their experiences, so arrangements were made with the audiovisual department. I then took to wheeling in a big color television so that we might spend an hour watching *One Life to Live.* This was back when Victoria Buchanan passed out at her twentieth high-school reunion and came to remembering that, rather than graduating with the rest of her class, she had instead hitchhiked to New York City, where she'd coupled with a hippie and given birth to a long-lost daughter. It sounds farfetched, but like a roast forsaken in the oven or a rescheduled dental appointment, childbirth is one of those minor details that tends to slip the minds of most soap opera characters. It's a personality trait you've just got to accept.

On *General Hospital* or *Guiding Light,* a similar story might come off as trite or even laughable. This, though, was *One Life to Live,* and no one could suddenly recall the birth of a child quite like Erika Slezak, who played both Victoria Buchanan and her alternate personality, Nicole Smith. I'd been in the habit of taping the show and watching it every night while eating dinner. Now that I was an academic, I could watch it in class and use the dinner hour to catch up on *All My Children.* A few students grumbled, but again I assured them that this was all part of my master plan.

Word came from the front office that there had been some complaints regarding my use of class time. This meant I'd have to justify my daily screenings with a homework assignment. Now the students were to watch an episode and write what I referred to as a "guessay," a brief prediction of what might take place the following day.

"Remember that this is not Port Charles or Pine Valley," I said. "This is 25 Llanview, Pennsylvania, and we're talking about the Buchanan family."

It actually wasn't a bad little assignment. While the dialogue occasionally falters, you have to admire daytime dramas for their remarkable attention to plot. Yes, there were always the predictable kidnappings and summer love triangles, but a good show could always surprise you with something as simple as the discovery of an underground city. I'd coached my students through half a dozen episodes, giving them background information and explaining that missing children do not just march through the door ten minutes after the critical delivery flashback. The inevitable reunion must unfold delicately and involve at least two-thirds of the cast.

I thought I'd effectively conveyed the seriousness of the assignment. I thought that in my own way I had actually taught them something, so I was angry when their papers included such predictions as "the long-lost daughter turns out to be a vampire" and "the next day Vicki chokes to death while eating a submarine sandwich." The vampire business smacked of *Dark Shadows* reruns, and I refused to take it seriously. But choking to death on a sandwich, that was an insult. Victoria was a Buchanan and would never duck into a sub shop, much less choke to death in a single episode. Especially on a Wednesday. Nobody dies on a Wednesday—hadn't these people learned anything?

In the past I had tried my hardest to be understanding, going so far as to allow the conjugation of nouns and the use of such questionable words as *whateverishly*. This, though, was going too far. I'd taught the Buchanans' Llanview just as my colleagues had taught Joyce's Dublin or Faulkner's Mississippi, but that was over now. Obviously certain people didn't deserve to watch TV in the middle of the afternoon. If my students wanted to stare at the walls for two hours a day, then fine, from here on out we'd just stick to the basics.

I don't know who invented the template for the standard writing workshop, but whoever it was seems to have struck the perfect balance between sadism and masochism. Here is a system designed to eliminate pleasure for everyone involved. The idea is that a student turns in a story, which is then read and thoughtfully critiqued by everyone in the class. In my experience the process worked, in that the stories were occasionally submitted, Xeroxed, and distributed hand to hand. They were folded into purses and knapsacks, but here the system tended to break down. Come critique time, most students behaved as if the assignment had been to confine the stories in a dark, enclosed area and test their reaction to sensory deprivation. Even if the papers were read out loud in class, the discussions were usually brief, as the combination of good manners and complete lack of interest kept most workshop participants from expressing their honest opinions.

With a few notable exceptions, most of the stories were thinly veiled accounts of the author's life as he or she attempted to complete the assignment. Roommates were forever stepping out of showers, and waitresses appeared out of nowhere to deliver the onion rings and breakfast burritos that stained the pages of the manuscripts. The sloppiness occasionally bothered me, but I had no room to complain. This was an art school, and the writing workshop was commonly known as the easiest way to fulfill one's mandatory English credits. My students had been admitted because they could admirably paint or sculpt or videotape their bodies in exhausting detail, and wasn't that enough? They told funny, compelling stories about their lives, but committing the details to paper was, for them, a chore rather than an aspiration. The way I saw it, if my students were willing to pretend I was a teacher, the least I could do was return the favor and pretend that they were writers. Even if someone

30

had used his real name and recounted, say, a recent appointment with an oral surgeon, I would accept the story as pure fiction, saying, "So tell us, Dean, how did you come up with this person?"

The student might mumble, pointing to the bloodied cotton wad packed against his swollen gum, and I'd ask, "When did you decide that your character should seek treatment for his impacted molar?" This line of questioning allowed the authors to feel creative and protected anyone who held an unpopular political opinion.

"Let me get this straight," one student said. "You're telling me that if I say something out loud, it's me saying it, but if I write the exact same thing on paper, it's somebody else, right?"

"Yes," I said. "And we're calling that fiction."

The student pulled out his notebook, wrote something down, and handed me a sheet of paper that read, "That's the stupidest fucking thing I ever heard in my life."

They were a smart group.   35

As Mr. Sedaris I made it a point to type up a poorly spelled evaluation of each submitted story. I'd usually begin with the high points and end, a page or two later, by dispensing such sage professional advice as, "Punctuation never hurt anyone" or "Think verbs!" I tended to lose patience with some of the longer dream sequences, but for the most part we all got along, and the students either accepted or politely ignored my advice.

Trouble arose only when authors used their stories to vindicate themselves against a great hurt or perceived injustice. This was the case with a woman whom the admissions office would have labeled a "returning student," meaning that her social life did not revolve around the cafeteria. The woman was a good fifteen years older than me and clearly disapproved of my teaching methods. She never contributed to Pillow Talk or the Feedbag Forum, and I had good reason to suspect it was she who had complained about the *One Life to Live* episodes. With the teenage freshmen, I stood a chance, but there was nothing I could do to please someone who regularly complained that she'd wasted enough time already. The class was divided into two distinct groups, with her on one side and everyone else on the other. I'd tried everything except leg irons, but nothing could bring the two sides together. It was a real problem.

The returning student had recently come through a difficult divorce, and because her pain was significant, she wrongly insisted that her writing was significant as well. Titled something along the lines of "I Deserve Another Chance," her story was not well received by the class. Following the brief group discussion, I handed her my written evaluation, which she quietly skimmed over before raising her hand.

"Yes," she said. "If you don't mind, I have a little question." She lit a cigarette and spent a moment identifying with the smoldering match. "Who are *you*," she asked. "I mean, just who in the hell are you to tell *me* that *my* story has no ending?"

It was a worthwhile question that was bound to be raised sooner or later.   40
I'd noticed that her story had ended in midsentence, but that aside, who was I to

offer criticism to anyone, especially in regard to writing? I'd meant to give the issue some serious thought, but there had been shirts to iron and name tags to make and, between one thing and another, I managed to put it out of my mind.

The woman repeated the question, her voice breaking. "Just who . . . in the stinking hell do you think . . . you are?"

"Can I give you an answer tomorrow?" I asked.

"No," she barked. "I want to know now. Who do you think you are?"

Judging from their expressions, I could see that the other side of the class was entertaining the same question. Doubt was spreading through the room like the cold germs seen in one of those slow-motion close-ups of a sneeze. I envisioned myself burning on a pyre of dream sequences, and then the answer came to me.

"Who am I?" I asked. "I am the only one who is paid to be in this room."   45
This was nothing I'd necessarily want to embroider on a pillow, but still, once the answer left my mouth, I embraced it as a perfectly acceptable teaching philosophy. My previous doubts and fears evaporated, as now I knew that I could excuse anything. The new Mr. Sedaris would never again back down or apologize. From here on out, I'd order my *students* to open and close the door and let *that* remind me that I was in charge. We could do whatever I wanted because I was a certified professional—it practically said so right there on my paycheck. My voice deepened as I stood to straighten my tie. "All right then," I said. "Does anyone else have a stupid question for Mr. Sedaris?"

The returning student once again raised her hand. "It's a personal question, I know, but exactly how much is the school paying you to be in this room?"

I answered honestly, and then, for the first time since the beginning of the school year, my students came together as one. I can't recall which side started it, I remember only that the laughter was so loud, so violent and prolonged that Mr. Sedaris had to run and close the door so that the real teachers could conduct their business in peace.

QUESTIONS FOR DISCUSSION

1. Early in this essay, the author jokes about being mistaken for his father when he is addressed as "Mr. Sedaris." How do you feel when addressed as "Mr.," "Ms.," "Miss," or "Mrs."? Do your feelings change depending upon the age of the person who is addressing you—or the site where the conversation takes place?

2. Most college students would be surprised if one of their teachers asked them to wear orange name tags shaped like maple leaves on the first day of class. Are there any activities or methods from your grade-school education that you think could be successfully adapted for the college classroom?

3. If unqualified teachers are sometimes hired at the last minute, why do you think that happens?

4. Of the activities "Mr. Sedaris" eventually organizes for his students, which would you least like to do?

5. In the courses that you have taken, have any been as ridiculous as the one described here? Have any been a waste of time? If so, why?
6. This essay ends with teacher and students coming together in harmony. Is this conclusion appropriate? What does Sedaris achieve by ending this way?

SUGGESTIONS FOR WRITING

1. If you have ever been in a class taught by a teacher who seemed incompetent, write a humorous description of that teacher's performance from a student's point of view.
2. Sedaris offers a bleak view of how peer review operates in a writing class. If you have ever been disappointed by how other readers have responded to your work, or by the effort put forth by someone with whom you are collaborating in some other field, write about that experience in a way that makes it seem amusing.
3. Imagine that you are teaching an introductory class in your weakest subject. Write an essay describing your first day in class.

LINKS ■ ■ ■

■ WITHIN THE BOOK

For another piece focused on the teaching of writing, see Ernest Hemingway's "Monologue to the Maestro" (pages 626–631).

■ ELSEWHERE IN PRINT

Ford, Michael Thomas. *It's Not Mean If It's True.* Los Angeles: Alyson, 2000.
Nagan, Greg. *The Five-Minute Iliad and Other Instant Classics.* New York: Simon, 2000.
Sedaris, David. *Barrel Fever: Stories and Essays.* Boston: Little, 1995.
––– *Holiday on Ice.* Boston: Little, 1998.
––– *Me Talk Pretty Someday.* Boston: Little, 2000.
––– *Naked.* Boston: Little, 1998.

■ ONLINE

- Humor in the Classroom
  <http://www.ntlf.com/html/lib/suppmat/v7n6bib.htm>

- Interviews with David Sedaris
  <http://www.barclayagency.com/sedaris.html>

- Unofficial David Sedaris Pages
  <http://free.freespeech.org/ari/sedaris>

9

Writing to Experiment with Form

Schools across the country have for many years offered courses in "creative writing," which is commonly understood to mean writing fiction, poetry, or drama. The problem with this designation is that, as useful as it has been as an easy reference, it implies that any writing but "fiction," "poetry," or "drama" is *not* creative. Thinking along these lines does serious injustice to the imagination, intelligence, and courage that inform other kinds of writing. Ironically, when we look for a convenient term for writing other than fiction, poetry, or drama, we often fall back on *nonfiction*—defining something in terms of what it is not and, in so doing, using a term that is so broad that it includes writing as diverse as memoir, exposition, and argument. But if we call a work *non*fiction for lack of a better term, it does not necessarily follow that the work in question lacks creativity. Anything written and revised by human beings is creative to some extent, since an individual intelligence—working alone or in collaboration with others—has made choices about what ideas to include, how to express them, and how to arrange them.

Nevertheless, a user's manual for a software program is very different from an essay by a writer like Annie Dillard—although both are, strictly speaking, nonfiction. When writers test the boundaries between different genres and take chances on what they say and how they present it, they are engaging in a kind of creative writing that is drawing increasing attention from literary theorists. Such writing is sometimes called "experimental writing" as a way of distinguishing it from creative writing as the term is commonly understood. A writer who is especially interested in creating new patterns can be said to be "writing to experiment with form."

Like any of the other motives discussed in this book, writing to experiment with form does not exist in a vacuum. When writing to understand experience, move readers, or amuse them, writers may experiment with the form their work takes as they seek to capture and convey meaning. All the writers included in this chapter have more than one motive, and you can find evidence of experimentation in chapters focused on other motives. (See, for example, the essays by Mark Doty, Peter Stark, and Alice Walker in Chapters 1, 2, and 6, respectively.) Moreover, if a work is to have any real value, form cannot be divorced from substance. A serious writer will not try to create a new form and then pour anything at hand into this vessel. Ideally, the form any work takes should be the form it needs; the form gives shape to content that benefits from being shaped in this way.

Of course, new forms are not invented every day of the week. Inventing something both new and useful is a great challenge. Because experimental writing is such a challenge, the writers who undertake it are likely to have both discipline and commitment. There is, after all, a great difference between designing a new form and carelessly scattering thoughts across the page in a way that may look creative but is actually formless. And it is important to understand that you can successfully experiment with form without feeling that it is your responsibility to invent a structure that has never been seen before. Whenever you try something that is new to you, you are experimenting, even if what you are attempting is not necessarily new to your readers. Moreover, the form you experiment with can have a long history. In this chapter, for example, Ernest Hemingway experiments by writing an essay in the form of a **dialogue**—a form that can be traced back to the philosophical dialogues of ancient Greece. But because dialogue is now usually associated with fiction and drama, an essay built around it can seem original, even though dialogue has been used in other ways for thousands of years.

If you are interested in experimenting with form, a dialogue can be a good place to begin, because its form is so clear. A good part of your challenge, in this case, would be to make sure that different speakers sound like different people. When writing dialogue, it is all too easy to write lines for several people that sound very much like the writer's own voice. But if you do not want to write an essay consisting entirely of dialogue, you can still experiment with form by introducing dialogue into an essay that is designed to fulfill another motive for writing.

Flexibility is thus one of the keys to experimenting successfully with form. While you can benefit from trying a ready-made form like dialogue, you should not hesitate to alter it if you find that it doesn't fit comfortably or suit your presentation. Instead of following a predetermined form (like the five-paragraph theme) that dictates what must happen in any given paragraph, you can adopt strategies that work for you and combine them in different ways. In this respect, writing to experiment with form honors a motive especially associated with essays.° The word *essay* comes from *essayer,* which means "to try" in French. By providing an opportunity to try and test ideas—instead of proving points and employing patterns that are already known—experimental essays follow a distinguished tradition that can be traced back to such writers as Michel de Montaigne and Francis Bacon.

---

essays: For a discussion of essays, see pages 313–318.

MONTAGE AND COLLAGE

Of the various essays in this chapter, you may find the form of George Orwell's "Marrakech" the most unusual. Orwell is writing what is called a **montage**—from the photographic term used to describe a rapid sequence of related short scenes or the process of making one picture out of many closely arranged pictures. When experimenting with this form, a writer composes a series of separate scenes and arranges them in a meaningful pattern with no transitions between them. These scenes are like a series of pictures arranged on the wall of an art gallery. The audience is expected to fill in the gaps between these scenes by reflecting on how each contributes to the meaning of the whole. By experimenting with this form, writers have ample opportunity to play with ideas, but they are also responsible for helping readers understand the nature and meaning of that play. If you study Orwell's essay closely, you will find that his arrangement follows a clear pattern and that certain images reappear in different pictures, helping to unify a work that—at first glance—may seem to be nothing more than a series of unrelated fragments.

The narrative fragments in Geeta Kothari's "If You Are What You Eat, then What Am I?" may seem to be more closely linked than the scenes in Orwell's essay, but Kothari is also working with montage—in this case to convey how she felt as a child when encountering significantly different kinds of food, the traditional cuisine of her Indian family and American dishes such as hot dogs, tuna salad, and brownies. Familiarity with montage can also help you understand an essay like Luc Sante's "I Was Born." You will find that this essay consists of seven short autobiographical sketches offering very different versions of the author's childhood—versions so different that they cannot all be true. It is impossible to read this essay without noticing that the author is contradicting himself. Further, the contradictions are so bold that readers can reasonably assume that the author is aware of contradicting himself and that these contradictory versions of his life must be intended to convey a kind of truth that is independent of factual accuracy—a philosophical truth about the nature of experience and the way in which memories are created.

One way to read Sante's essay is to view it as a montage in which every photograph is of the author and his family in a different kind of costume and acting out a different drama. The costumes and scripts may disguise who these people are or reveal truths about what they are like on the inside. Readers are invited to interpret Sante's childhood by comparing startling but different pictures. The form he uses challenges common assumptions about how readers can tell the difference between fiction and nonfiction. It also creates a confrontation between writer and reader: Because it is impossible to read this piece without noticing the major contradictions within it, readers are forced to decide whether to make the intellectual effort necessary for understanding. Some readers are likely to dismiss such work as "weird" and move on to something else. Others will be engaged by it. When you decide to experiment with form, you should consider that experimentation involves risks. And the more radical the experiment, the greater the risk.

Writers who enjoy experimenting with form also use **collage** rather than montage. Collage is an art form in which materials not usually associated with each other are pasted together—thus encouraging viewers to see each piece anew and to consider how different pieces play off one another. Whereas montage gives us a series of separate scenes, collage gives us a single surface and invites us to consider the work as a whole. If you see a collage in a museum or read an essay presented as a collage, you can, of course, analyze it by studying its specific components. But its structure indicates that the whole is more important than any of its parts.

The clearest example of collage in this chapter is "Oranges and Sweet Sister Boy" by Judy Ruiz. When you read it, you will find that a main narrative runs chronologically from the beginning of the essay to the end. But pasted on (or woven into) this narrative are pictures and pieces of writing that have—so to speak—been cut out of other cloth.

If you are interested in experimenting with collage, you can decide for yourself how many pieces to paste together and how different those pieces should be. But in making that decision, you should be mindful of the audience for whom you are writing and the context in which you are going to offer this work.

AUDIENCE

When you experiment with form, you often will be asking readers to invest more time in your work than they would have to spend if you followed a conventional, predictable plan. With this in mind, you should submit a work of experimental writing only when you are confident that your audience is willing to take this trouble. How can you tell? There's no foolproof way for determining in advance how readers will respond to your work; even readers you know well may surprise you at times with responses that, although elicited by the work you shared with them, were influenced by other issues in their lives. Few readers read with the same degree of attention and patience every time they sit down to read. But there are some clues that can help you decide if an audience is likely to be receptive to an experimental essay.

Readers who seem to welcome originality and who seem interested in what *you* think (as opposed to getting you to write what *they* think) may enjoy original form and expression as much as they enjoy original thought. Readers who have already responded to your work with thoughtful comments have demonstrated that they are willing to pay close attention to your work (as opposed to hurrying over it to pursue some other activity). Such readers also may be ready to take up the challenge of encountering an unexpected form. And if you see yourself writing primarily for a specific teacher, you can be guided not only by your assignment but also by the amount of emphasis the instructor has placed on organization. A teacher who has stressed the importance of outlining papers in advance is less likely to welcome an experimental essay than is a teacher who has encouraged you to draft and then see what kind of organization emerges from what you have written.

You should also remember that intelligent, imaginative readers simply may not have the time to study at length a paper that seems interesting but unconventional. Further, it would be a mistake to assume that instructors who insist on fixed patterns of arrangement are incapable of enjoying originality of form. These instructors might welcome experimental writing if they are not overwhelmed by the need to read large quantities of material under pressure. A heavy workload often explains why teachers and other readers insist that you follow a standard form; when they know how your essay is supposed to be organized, they can appraise its content more quickly. However, readers who have a large, steady diet that seems monotonous could be pleased to be served an unexpected dish. When writing for readers with whom you are already familiar, you should be able to make a fairly accurate guess about how creative you can be. And if you are in doubt, you can easily ask.

You can also imagine yourself writing for readers you have not actually met. For an experimental essay, you might benefit from envisioning an audience of well-educated, open-minded adults like those for whom essays in periodicals like *The New Yorker* and *Atlantic Monthly* seem intended. When you write for an audience of this sort, your actual readers may be willing to assume the role your work implies for them even if they usually see themselves as less sophisticated.

In terms of audience, you should remember as well that writers can be their own audience. Although writing is usually a transaction between different people, it can also be pursued for the writer's own benefit—as is the case, for example, if you freewrite or keep a personal journal. If you are interested in growing as a writer but suspect that the readers you actually know are unlikely to welcome experimental writing, you can do it on your own simply as an exercise or for the sheer joy of it. As you grow, your world will also grow, and the readers you will know next year may be very different from those currently in your life.

CONTEXT

According to a time-honored tradition, artists should learn the rules before earning the freedom to break them. In art school, this means mastering perspective and learning how to draw from life according to the principles that governed the old masters before painting like an abstract expressionist in bold strokes on a large canvas. This school of thought is well illustrated in *Strictly Ballroom,* an Australian comedy about ballroom dancing. The movie focuses on a young man whose parents were competitive ballroom dancers and who have raised him since early childhood to become a champion dancer. Now in his early twenties, the young man knows all the steps by heart and can dance them perfectly, but he's bored by them and wants to invent dances of his own.

The problem is that the world of competitive ballroom dancing is highly structured; all dancers are expected to execute the same steps and to express themselves only in minor variations on these steps, through the music they choose to dance to, and in their costumes. Anyone who invents steps—no matter how good they are—threatens this rigid system. You'll have to rent the video to see how this conflict is resolved. What's relevant at the moment, however, is this: The young man becomes a superb dancer in part because he *knows* all the steps; this knowledge enables him to improvise and combine moves that would not normally be expected in the same dance routine. He's learned the rules, and now he's ready to break them.

This school of thought has much to recommend it. When you are grounded in tradition and can do what others do, you are well positioned to identify what has not yet been done and then do it. Someone who lacks this kind of knowledge and experience can spend a lot of energy reinventing the wheel—a wheel that's weaker than those already on the road. But does this mean that only the most experienced writers can enjoy experimenting with form? Certainly not. You can experiment whenever the impulse moves you, but you may benefit from honoring the following principles:

- As noted earlier, you should share experimental writing with readers only when you have some reason to believe they'll be receptive to it. When making this decision, it is important to consider *when* you are asking them to read such work. Readers may be more receptive after they have had the chance to become acquainted with you and when they are not especially hurried. Remember that it usually takes longer to read an experimental essay than one that follows a standard form. As a general rule, make this request for readers' time after you have won their confidence or feel confident in your relationship with them. A specific writing assignment may provide a ready-made context for an experiment, but you can also create your own context by looking for a time that works for both you and your readers. Just as you need time to experiment with form, your readers need time to study the results of your experiment. An especially busy part of the semester, for example, may not be the best time for this kind of work.

- A college writing course, however, can provide an ideal context for experimenting with form—especially if your instructor encourages revision. As noted earlier, experimenting involves taking risks. Risks become less threatening when you know that you don't have to get everything right in your first draft. Whenever you have the chance to submit more than one draft of an essay for review, you would be wise to seize the opportunity to grow by attempting something you haven't already mastered. Experimenting with form is one way to grow as a writer. And if such an experiment seems overly ambitious for a specific context, you can still experiment with writing by trying out elements of style (such as parallelism and anaphora, discussed on pages 445–446) that would be new for your work.

Because experimenting with form happens most productively when writers feel at ease, the writing that results from this activity often has a personal dimension. All of the works included in this chapter employ the first person, the *I* that helps convey the sense of an individual mind at play. Using the first person also suggests that these writers have given readers their trust and expect trust in return. Annie Dillard invites readers into the privacy of her bedroom at the end of her essay, and Geeta Kothari invites readers into her family's kitchen as well as into other rooms that are important for her. The most personal essay in this chapter may well be "Oranges and Sweet Sister Boy," a work that focuses on the author's history with mental illness and her response to the news that her brother is planning to have a sex-change operation. Because her material is unconventional, Judy Ruiz chose to present it in an unconventional way. Naturally, you can write in the first person without sharing experience as intimate as Ruiz's, or, conversely, you yourself may feel most at ease when writing in other than first person. (See page 49.) Whether you use the first person or draw directly on personal experience matters less than your willingness to operate in a spirit of trust—trusting yourself by believing that you can grow by trying something new and trusting your readers by believing that they will welcome this kind of growth.

When you experiment with form, you venture into unfamiliar territory and thus take some risks. But if there are risks, there are also rewards: originality of expression and a heightened awareness of what can be achieved through language. Remember, however, that when you write an essay of this sort, you are venturing into the unknown and hope your readers will follow. It is your responsibility to glance back once in a while to make sure that they are still with you. By studying the essays included in this chapter, you will be able to see how other writers have undertaken this kind of adventure without abandoning readers in the middle of a literary wilderness.

MONOLOGUE TO THE MAESTRO

Ernest Hemingway

Ernest Hemingway (1899–1961), one of the most famous American writers of the twentieth century, won the respect of many readers with finely written short stories and novels such as The Sun Also Rises *and* A Farewell to Arms. *He also wrote nonfiction— including essays, reviews, and newspaper articles. In the following essay, first published in 1935 when he was at the height of his career, Hemingway experiments with form by presenting his ideas in a dialogue between a fictionalized version of himself (called "Your Correspondent") and a young man (called "Mice") who wants to be a writer. The dialogue has a long history in Western discourse; it is, after all, the form Plato used for conveying the ideas of Socrates. How well can it serve the needs of modern writers and readers? As you read "Monologue to the Maestro," consider the way the form influences how you respond to this piece.*

About a year and a half ago a young man came to the front door of the house in Key West and said that he had hitch-hiked down from upper Minnesota to ask your correspondent a few questions about writing. Arrived that day from Cuba, having to see some good friends off on the train in an hour, and to write some letters in the meantime, your correspondent, both flattered and appalled at the prospect of the questioning, told the young man to come around the next afternoon. He was a tall, very serious young man with very big feet and hands and a porcupine hair-cut.

It seemed that all his life he had wanted to be a writer. Brought up on a farm he had gone through high school and the University of Minnesota, had worked as a newspaper man, a rough carpenter, a harvest hand, a day laborer, and had bummed his way across America twice. He wanted to be a writer and he had good stories to write. He told them very badly but you could see that there was something there if he could get it out. He was so entirely serious about writing that it seemed that seriousness would overcome all obstacles. He had lived by himself for a year in a cabin he had built in North Dakota and written all that year. He did not show me anything that he had written then. It was all bad, he said.

I thought, perhaps, that this was modesty until he showed me a piece he had published in one of the Minneapolis papers. It was abominably written. Still, I thought, many other people write badly at the start and this boy is so extremely serious that he must have something; real seriousness in regard to writing being one of the two absolute necessities. The other, unfortunately, is talent.

Beside writing this young man had one other obsession. He had always wanted to go to sea. So, to shorten this account, we gave him a job as night watchman on the boat which furnished him a place to sleep and work and gave him two or three hours work each day at cleaning up and a half of each day free to do his writing. To fulfill his desire to go to sea, we promised to take him to Cuba when we went across.

He was an excellent night watchman and worked hard on the boat and at 5 his writing but at sea he was a calamity; slow where he should be agile, seeming sometimes to have four feet instead of two feet and two hands, nervous under excitement, and with an incurable tendency toward seasickness and a peasant reluctance to take orders. Yet he was always willing and hard working if given plenty of time to work in.

We called him the Maestro because he played the violin; this name was eventually shortened to the Mice, and a big breeze would so effectually slow up his co-ordination that your correspondent once remarked to him, "Mice, you certainly must be going to be a hell of a good writer because you certainly aren't worth a damn at anything else."

On the other hand his writing improved steadily. He may yet be a writer. But your correspondent, who sometimes has an evil temper, is never going to ship another hand who is an aspirant writer; nor go through another summer off the Cuban or any other coast accompanied by questions and answers on the practice of letters. If any more aspirant writers come on board the Pilar let them be females, let them be very beautiful, and let them bring champagne.

Your correspondent takes the practice of letters, as distinct from the writing of these monthly letters, very seriously; but dislikes intensely talking about it with almost anyone alive. Having had to mouth about many aspects of it during a period of one hundred and ten days with the good old Maestro, during much of which time your correspondent had to conquer an urge to throw a bottle at the Mice whenever he would open his mouth and pronounce the word writing, he hereby presents some of these mouthings written down.

If they can deter anyone from writing he should be deterred. If they can be of use to anyone your correspondent is pleased. If they bore you there are plenty of pictures in the magazine that you may turn to.

Your correspondent's excuse for presenting them is that some of the 10 information contained would have been worth fifty cents to him when he was twenty-one.

Mice: What do you mean by good writing as opposed to bad writing?

Your correspondent: Good writing is true writing. If a man is making a story up it will be true in proportion to the amount of knowledge of life that he has and how conscientious he is; so that when he makes something up it is as it would truly be. If he doesn't know how many people work in their minds and actions his luck may save him for a while, or he may write fantasy. But if he continues to write about what he does not know about he will find himself faking. After he fakes a few times he cannot write honestly any more.

Mice: Then what about imagination?

Y.C.: Nobody knows a damned thing about it except that it is what we get for nothing. It may be racial experience. I think that is quite possible. It is the one thing beside honesty that a good writer must have. The more he learns from experience the more truly he can imagine. If he gets so he can imagine truly enough people will think that the things he relates all really happened and that he is just reporting.

Mice: Where will it differ from reporting? 15

Y.C.: If it was reporting they would not remember it. When you describe something that has happened that day the timeliness makes people see it in their own imaginations. A month later that element of time is gone and your account would be flat and they would not see it in their minds nor remember it. But if you make it up instead of describe it you can make it round and whole and solid and give it life. You create it, for good or bad. It is made; not described. It is just as true as the extent of your ability to make it and the knowledge you put into it. Do you follow me?

Mice: Not always.

Y.C. (crabbily): Well for chrisake let's talk about something else then.

Mice (undeterred): Tell me some more about the mechanics of writing.

Y.C.: What do you mean? Like pencil or typewriter? For chrisake. 20

Mice: Yes.

Y.C.: Listen. When you start to write you get all the kick and the reader gets none. So you might as well use a typewriter because it is that much easier and you enjoy it that much more. After you learn to write your whole object is to convey everything, every sensation, sight, feeling, place and emotion to the reader. To do this you have to work over what you write. If you write with a pencil you get three different sights at it to see if the reader is getting what you want him to. First when you read it over; then when it is typed you get another chance to improve it, and again in the proof. Writing it first in pencil gives you one-third more chance to improve it. That is .333 which is a damned good average for a hitter. It also keeps it fluid longer so that you can better it easier.

Mice: How much should you write a day?

Y.C.: The best way is always to stop when you are going good and when you know what will happen next. If you do that every day when you are writing a novel you will never be stuck. That is the most valuable thing I can tell you so try to remember it.

Mice: All right. 25

Y.C.: Always stop while you are going good and don't think about it or worry about it until you start to write the next day. That way your subconscious will work on it all the time. But if you think about it consciously or worry about it you will kill it and your brain will be tired before you start. Once you are into the novel it is as cowardly to worry about whether you can go on the next day as to worry about having to go into inevitable action. You *have* to go on. So there is no sense to worry. You have to learn that to write a novel. The hard part about a novel is to finish it.

Mice: How can you learn not to worry?

Y.C.: By not thinking about it. As soon as you start to think about it stop it. Think about something else. You have to learn that.

Mice: How much do you read over every day before you start to write?

Y.C.: The best way is to read it all every day from the start, correcting as *30*
you go along, then go on from where you stopped the day before. When it
gets so long that you can't do this every day read back two or three chapters each day; then each week read it all from the start. That's how you make
it all of one piece. And remember to stop while you are still going good. That
keeps it moving instead of having it die whenever you go on and write yourself out. When you do that you find that the next day you are pooped and
can't go on.

Mice: Do you do the same on a story?

Y.C.: Yes, only sometimes you can write a story in a day.

Mice: Do you know what is going to happen when you write a story?

Y.C.: Almost never. I start to make it up and have happen what would
have to happen as it goes along.

Mice: That isn't the way they teach you to write in college. *35*

Y.C.: I don't know about that. I never went to college. If any sonofabitch
could write he wouldn't have to teach writing in college.

Mice: You're teaching me.

Y.C.: I'm crazy. Besides this is a boat, not a college.

Mice: What books should a writer have to read?

Y.C.: He should have read everything so he knows what he has to beat. *40*

Mice: He can't have read everything.

Y.C.: I don't say what he can. I say what he should. Of course he can't.

Mice: Well what books are necessary?

Y.C.: He should have read *War and Peace* and *Anna Karenina* by Tolstoi,
Midshipman Easy, Frank Mildmay and *Peter Simple* by Captain Marryat, *Madame
Bovary* and *L'Education Sentimentale* by Flaubert, *Buddenbrooks* by Thomas
Mann, Joyce's *Dubliners, Portrait of the Artist* and *Ulysses, Tom Jones* and *Joseph
Andrews* by Fielding, *Le Rouge et le Noir* and *La Chartreuse de Parme* by Stend-
hal, *The Brothers Karamazoff* and any two other Dostoevskis, *Huckleberry Finn*
by Mark Twain, *The Open Boat* and *The Blue Hotel* by Stephen Crane, *Hail
and Farewell* by George Moore, *Yeat's Autobiographies,* all the good De Maupas-
sant, all the good Kipling, all of Turgenieff, *Far Away and Long Ago* by W. H.
Hudson, Henry James' short stories, especially *Madame de Mauvers* and *The
Turn of the Screw, The Portrait of a Lady, The American*—

Mice: I can't write them down that fast. How many more are there? *45*

Y. C.: I'll give you the rest another day. There are about three times that
many.

Mice: Should a writer have read all of those?

Y. C.: All of those and plenty more. Otherwise he doesn't know what he
has to beat.

Mice: What do you mean 'has to beat'?

Y. C.: Listen. There is no use writing anything that has been written bet- *50*
ter before unless you can beat it. What a writer in our time has to do is write
what hasn't been written before or beat dead men at what they have done.

The only way he can tell how he is going is to compete with dead men. Most live writers do not exist. Their fame is created by critics who always need a genius of the season, someone they understand completely and feel safe in praising, but when these fabricated geniuses are dead they will not exist. The only people for a serious writer to compete with are the dead that he knows are good. It is like a miler running against the clock rather than simply trying to beat whoever is in the race with him. Unless he runs against time he will never know what he is capable of attaining.

Mice: But reading all the good writers might discourage you.

Y. C.: Then you ought to be discouraged.

Mice: What is the best early training for a writer?

Y. C.: An unhappy childhood.

Mice: Do you think Thomas Mann is a great writer?   55

Y. C.: He would be a great writer if he had never written another thing than *Buddenbrooks.*

Mice: How can a writer train himself?

Y. C.: Watch what happens today. If we get into a fish see exactly what it is that everyone does. If you get a kick out of it while he is jumping remember back until you see exactly what the action was that gave you the emotion. Whether it was the rising of the line from the water and the way it tightened like a fiddle string until drops started from it, or the way he smashed and threw water when he jumped. Remember what the noises were and what was said. Find what gave you the emotion; what the action was that gave you the excitement. Then write it down making it clear so the reader will see it too and have the same feeling that you had. That's a five finger exercise.

Mice: All right.

Y. C.: Then get in somebody else's head for a change. If I bawl you out   60 try to figure what I'm thinking about as well as how you feel about it. If Carlos curses Juan think what both their sides of it are. Don't just think who is right. As a man things are as they should or shouldn't be. As a man you know who is right and who is wrong. You have to make decisions and enforce them. As a writer you should not judge. You should understand.

Mice: All right.

Y. C.: Listen *now.* When people talk listen completely. Don't be thinking what you're going to say. Most people never listen. Nor do they observe. You should be able to go into a room and when you come out know everything that you saw there and not only that. If that room gave you any feeling you should know exactly what it was that gave you that feeling. Try that for practice. When you're in town stand outside the theatre and see how the people differ in the way they get out of taxis or motor cars. There are a thousand ways to practice. And always think of other people.

Mice: Do you think I will be a writer?

Y. C.: How the hell should I know? Maybe you have no talent. Maybe you can't feel for other people. You've got some good stories if you can write them.

Mice: How can I tell?   65

Y. C.: Write. If you work at it five years and you find you're no good you can just as well shoot yourself then as now.

Mice: I wouldn't shoot myself.

Y. C.: Come around then and I'll shoot you.

Mice: Thanks.

Y. C.: Perfectly welcome, Mice. Now should we talk about something else?   70

Mice: What else?

Y. C.: Anything else, Mice old timer, anything else at all.

Mice: All right. But—

Y. C.: No but. Finish. Talk about writing finish. No more. All gone for today. Store all close up. Boss he go home.

Mice: All right then. But tomorrow I've got some things to ask you.   75

Y. C.: I'll bet you'll have fun writing after you know just how it's done.

Mice: What do you mean?

Y. C.: You know. Fun. Good times. Jolly. Dashing off an old masterpiece.

Mice: Tell me

Y. C.: Stop it.   80

Mice: All right. But tomorrow—

Y. C.: Yes. All right. Sure. But tomorrow.

QUESTIONS FOR DISCUSSION

1. According to Hemingway, there are two "absolute necessities" for success in writing: "real seriousness in regard to writing" and "talent." Do you agree?
2. How does "writing" differ from "reporting"?
3. Consider the advice Hemingway gives young writers. Are there any ideas you find helpful? Is there anything confusing about it?
4. Consider the list of books Hemingway recommends as necessary reading. Have you read any of them? Has Hemingway made you want to read them? Do these books have anything in common?
5. Reading, according to Hemingway, enables a writer to know "what he has to beat." Do you think writing is a kind of competition? Do some writers win and others lose? Is there a limit to how many "winners" there can be?
6. How does Hemingway portray himself in this piece? How would you feel if offered the opportunity to study writing with a man like this?

SUGGESTIONS FOR WRITING

1. Write a letter to Hemingway in which you respond to his views on writing.
2. Hemingway calls this essay a "monologue" even though it is structured as a dialogue indicating that his own voice is dominant. Trying to retain the main points of this essay, revise "Monologue to the Maestro" so that "a young man from your own state" is the principal speaker.
3. Choose an activity that you feel competent in doing, and then write a dialogue in which you explain this activity to an interested student.

LINKS ■ ■ ■

■ WITHIN THE BOOK

In "The Learning Curve" (pages 611–617), David Sedaris offers a comic view of writing instruction.

■ ELSEWHERE IN PRINT

Bruccoli, Matthew J., ed. *Conversations with Ernest Hemingway.* Jackson: UP of Mississippi, 1986.

Hemingway, Ernest. *By-Line, Ernest Hemingway: Selected Articles and Dispatches of Four Decades.* Ed. William White. New York: Scribner's, 1967.

----. *The Complete Short Stories of Ernest Hemingway.* 1987. New York: Simon, 1998.

----. *Ernest Hemingway on Writing.* Ed. Larry Phillips. New York: Scribner's, 1984.

----. *The Old Man and the Sea.* 1952. New York: Scribner's, 1999.

----. *The Sun Also Rises.* 1926. New York: Scribner's, 1996.

■ ONLINE

- The Ernest Hemingway Foundation of Oak Park
  <http://www.hemingway.org>

- Ernest Hemingway Home and Museum in Key West
  <http://www.hemingwayhome.com>

- Hemingway in Cuba
  <http://www.theatlantic.com/issues/65aug/6508manning.htm>

- Virtual Hemingway
  <http://www.hemingwaysociety.org/virthem.htm>

THE DEER AT PROVIDENCIA

Annie Dillard

Drawn from the same collection as "Living Like Weasels," (pages 84–87), "The Deer at Providencia" focuses on an encounter with wildlife in the Amazon. Dillard traveled there as a tourist, and her response to what she witnessed strikes the other tourists in her group as inappropriate. As you read, try to understand why Dillard cannot offer the conventional response expected of her. And be prepared for what may seem like a sudden shift in direction once she returns home from her trip.

Dillard has been praised for having "a mystic's wonder at the physical world." As you read the following essay, you will find that she pays close attention to the physical world but does not pretend to understand everything she observes. And as you work on your own writing, you might benefit from advice that Dillard offers writers in another of her essays, "Write Till You Drop": "One of the few things I know about writing is this: Spend it all, shoot it, play it, lose it, all, right away, every time. Do not hoard what seems good for a later place in the book, or for another book; give it, give it now. The impulse to save something good for a better place is the signal to spend it now. Something more will arise for later, something better. These things fill from beneath, like well water. Similarly, the impulse to keep to yourself what you have learned is not only shameful, it is destructive. Anything you do not give freely and abundantly becomes lost to you. You open your safe and find ashes."

There were four of us North Americans in the jungle, in the Ecuadorian jungle on the banks of the Napo River in the Amazon watershed. The other three North Americans were metropolitan men. We stayed in tents in one riverside village, and visited others. At the village called Providencia we saw a sight which moved us, and which shocked the men.

The first thing we saw when we climbed the riverbank to the village of Providencia was the deer. It was roped to a tree on the grass clearing near the thatch shelter where we would eat lunch.

The deer was small, about the size of a whitetail fawn, but apparently full-grown. It had a rope around its neck and three feet caught in the rope. Someone said that the dogs had caught it that morning and the villagers were going to cook and eat it that night.

This clearing lay at the edge of the little thatched-hut village. We could see the villagers going about their business, scattering feed corn for hens about their houses, and wandering down paths to the river to bathe. The village headman was our host; he stood beside us as we watched the deer struggle. Several village boys were interested in the deer; they formed part of the circle we made around it in the clearing. So also did four businessmen from Quito who were attempting to guide us around the jungle. Few of the very different people standing in this circle had a common language. We watched the deer, and no one said much.

The deer lay on its side at the rope's very end, so the rope lacked slack to 5
let it rest its head in the dust. It was "pretty," delicate of bone like all deer, and thin-skinned for the tropics. Its skin looked virtually hairless, in fact, and almost translucent, like a membrane. Its neck was no thicker than my wrist; it was rubbed open on the rope, and gashed. Trying to paw itself free of the rope, the deer had scratched its own neck with its hooves. The raw underside of its neck showed red stripes and some bruises bleeding inside the muscles. Now three of its feet were hooked in the rope under its jaw. It could not stand, of course, on one leg, so it could not move to slacken the rope and ease the pull on its throat and enable it to rest its head.

Repeatedly the deer paused, motionless, its eyes veiled, with only its rib cage in motion, and its breaths the only sound. Then, after I would think, "It has given up; now it will die," it would heave. The rope twanged; the tree leaves clattered; the deer's free foot beat the ground. We stepped back and held our breaths. It thrashed, kicking, but only one leg moved; the other three legs tightened inside the rope's loop. Its hip jerked; its spine shook. Its eyes rolled; its tongue, thick with spittle, pushed in and out. Then it would rest again. We watched this for fifteen minutes.

Once three young native boys charged in, released its trapped legs, and jumped back to the circle of people. But instantly the deer scratched up its neck with its hooves and snared its forelegs in the rope again. It was easy to imagine a third and then a fourth leg soon stuck, like Brer Rabbit and the Tar Baby.

We watched the deer from the circle, and then we drifted on to lunch. Our palm-roofed shelter stood on a grassy promontory from which we could see the deer tied to the tree, pigs and hens walking under village houses, and black-and-white cattle standing in the river. There was even a breeze.

Lunch, which was the second and better lunch we had that day, was hot and fried. There was a big fish called *doncella*, a kind of catfish, dipped whole in corn flour and beaten egg, then deep fried. With our fingers we pulled soft fragments of it from its sides to our plates, and ate; it was delicate fish-flesh, fresh and mild. Someone found the roe, and I ate of that too—it was fat and stronger, like egg yolk, naturally enough, and warm.

There was also a stew of meat in shreds with rice and pale brown gravy. I 10
had asked what kind of deer it was tied to the tree; Pepe had answered in Spanish, "*Gama.*" Now they told us this was *gama* too, stewed. I suspect the word means merely game or venison. At any rate, I heard that the village dogs had cornered another deer just yesterday, and it was this deer which we were now eating in full sight of the whole article. It was good. I was surprised at its tenderness. But it is a fact that high levels of lactic acid, which builds up in muscle tissues during exertion, tenderizes.

After the fish and meat we ate bananas fried in chunks and served on a tray; they were sweet and full of flavor. I felt terrific. My shirt was wet and cool from swimming; I had had a night's sleep, two decent walks, three meals, and a swim—everything tasted good. From time to time each one of us, separately, would look beyond our shaded roof to the sunny spot where the deer was still convulsing in the dust. Our meal completed, we walked around the deer and back to the boats.

That night I learned that while we were watching the deer, the others were watching me.

We four North Americans grew close in the jungle in a way that was not the usual artificial intimacy of travelers. We liked each other. We stayed up all that night talking, murmuring, as though we rocked on hammocks slung above time. The others were from big cities: New York, Washington, Boston. They all said that I had no expression on my face when I was watching the deer—or at any rate, not the expression they expected.

They had looked to see how I, the only woman, and the youngest, was taking the sight of the deer's struggles. I looked detached, apparently, or hard, or calm, or focused, still. I don't know. I was thinking. I remember feeling very old and energetic. I could say like Thoreau that I have traveled widely in Roanoke, Virginia. I have thought a great deal about carnivorousness; I eat meat. These things are not issues; they are mysteries.

Gentlemen of the city, what surprises you? That there is suffering here, or that I know it?   *15*

We lay in the tent and talked. "If it had been my wife," one man said with special vigor, amazed, "she wouldn't have cared *what* was going on; she would have dropped *everything* right at that moment and gone in the village from here to there to there, she would not have *stopped* until that animal was out of its suffering one way or another. She couldn't *bear* to see a creature in agony like that."

I nodded.

Now I am home. When I wake I comb my hair before the mirror above my dresser. Every morning for the past two years I have seen in that mirror, beside my sleep-softened face, the blackened face of a burnt man. It is a wire-service photograph clipped from a newspaper and taped to my mirror. The caption reads: "Alan McDonald in Miami hospital bed." All you can see in the photograph is a smudged triangle of face from his eyelids to his lower lip; the rest is bandages. You cannot see the expression in his eyes; the bandages shade them.

The story, headed MAN BURNED FOR SECOND TIME, begins:

"Why does God hate me?" Alan McDonald asked from his hospital bed.

"When the gunpowder went off, I couldn't believe it," he said. "I just couldn't believe it. I said, 'No, God couldn't do this to me again.'"

He was in a burn ward in Miami, in serious condition. I do not even know if he lived. I wrote him a letter at the time, cringing.

He had been burned before, thirteen years previously, by flaming gaso-   20
line. For years he had been having his body restored and his face remade in dozens of operations. He had been a boy, and then a burnt boy. He had already been stunned by what could happen, by how life could veer.

Once I read that people who survive bad burns tend to go crazy; they have a very high suicide rate. Medicine cannot ease their pain; drugs just leak away, soaking the sheets, because there is no skin to hold them in. The people just lie there and weep. Later they kill themselves. They had not known, before they were burned, that the world included such suffering, that life could permit them personally such pain.

This time a bowl of gunpowder had exploded on McDonald.

> "I didn't realize what had happened at first," he recounted. "And then I heard that sound from 13 years ago. I was burning. I rolled to put the fire out and I thought, 'Oh God, not again.'
>
> "If my friend hadn't been there, I would have jumped into a canal with a rock around my neck."

His wife concludes the piece, "Man, it just isn't fair."

I read the whole clipping again every morning. This is the Big Time here, every minute of it. Will someone please explain to Alan McDonald in his dignity, to the deer at Providencia in his dignity, what is going on? And mail me the carbon.

When we walked by the deer at Providencia for the last time, I said to Pepe, with a pitying glance at the deer, "*Pobrecito*"—"poor little thing." But I was trying out Spanish. I knew at the time it was a ridiculous thing to say.

QUESTIONS FOR DISCUSSION

1. What details inspire sympathy for the deer tied up in the village? Why does Dillard inspire sympathy for a deer that she did not attempt to rescue?
2. Dillard makes a point of describing the lunch she enjoyed the day she saw the deer. How do you respond to knowing that she enjoyed eating warm fish roe as well as a stew of what seems to be deer meat—and that after lunch she "felt terrific"?
3. Why do the men in her group disapprove of her response to the deer? What are they failing to understand about her?
4. Why do you think Dillard keeps a picture of a burn victim on her mirror at home?
5. What relation does the story of Alan McDonald have to the story of the deer at Providencia? What has Dillard achieved by placing these two stories together?
6. Why is it significant that most of this essay is set in a village called "Providencia"?

SUGGESTIONS FOR WRITING

1. Imagine that you are one of the villagers who witnesses four North Americans having lunch in Providencia when their tour pauses there. Write an account for people in a neighboring village in which you describe the behavior of these visitors.
2. Consider behavior and activities practiced in your family or community. Choose one type of conduct that might seem confusing or disturbing to visitors from another country. Then write an essay in which you describe that conduct—conveying how you feel about it without making explicit judgments.
3. Think of things that either bother or please you. Choose two that apparently have nothing in common and then try writing about them both. Without comparing them directly or explaining why you feel they are somehow connected, try to help readers see how understanding one element makes understanding the second easier.

LINKS ▪ ▪ ▪

▪ WITHIN THE BOOK

Dillard's essay raises questions about the nature of suffering. "Am I Blue?" (pages 467–471) by Alice Walker also encourages readers to reflect on how people make animals suffer.

▪ ELSEWHERE IN PRINT

Dillard, Annie. *For the Time Being*. New York: Knopf, 1999.
———. *The Living*. New York: Harper, 1992.
———. *Tickets for a Prayer Wheel: Poems*. Columbia: U of Missouri P, 1974.
———. *The Writing Life*. New York: Harper, 1989.
MacDonald, Theodore, Jr. *Ethnicity and Culture amidst New "Neighbors":
The Runa of Ecuador's Amazon Region*. Boston: Allyn, 1999.

▪ ONLINE

- Burn Survivor Resources
  <http://www.burnsurvivor.com>
- Center for Global Environmental Education
  <http://cgee.hamline.edu/rivers/Resources/river_profiles/
  Amazon.html>
- Greenpeace: Amazon Documents
  <http://www.greenpeace.org/~forests/forests_new/html/content/
  docs.html>

MARRAKECH

George Orwell

Like "A Hanging" (pages 461–464), "Marrakech" shows how George Orwell (1903–1950) was concerned about the consequences of colonialism. In his essay "Why I Write," he identifies "political purpose" as one of the "four great motives for writing," the others being "sheer egotism," "aesthetic enthusiasm," and "historical purpose." By "political purpose," he explains that he means, "Desire to push the world in a certain direction, to alter other peoples' idea of the kind of society they should strive after." And he goes on to note, "The opinion that art should have nothing to do with politics is itself a political attitude."

A city in North Africa, Marrakech was a popular destination for American and European tourists when Morocco was ruled by the French; it still attracts many travelers. The following essay, first published in 1939, the year the Second World War began, provides a series of scenes of how the city looked during the colonial era. Orwell provides no transitions between these scenes, expecting his readers to see for themselves how each "snapshot" relates to another. As you read, consider what the scenes have in common.

As the corpse went past, the flies left the restaurant table in a cloud and rushed after it, but they came back a few minutes later.

The little crowd of mourners—all men and boys, no women—threaded their way across the market-place between the piles of pomegranates and the taxis and the camels, wailing a short chant over and over again. What really appeals to the flies is that the corpses here are never put into coffins, they are merely wrapped in a piece of rag and carried on a rough wooden bier on the shoulders of four friends. When the friends get to the burying-ground they hack an oblong hole a foot or two deep, dump the body in it and fling over it a little of the dried-up, lumpy earth, which is like broken brick. No gravestone, no name, no identifying mark of any kind. The burying-ground is merely a huge waste of hummocky earth, like a derelict building-lot. After a month or two no one can even be certain where his own relatives are buried.

When you walk through a town like this—two hundred thousand inhabitants, of whom at least twenty thousand own literally nothing except the rags they stand up in—when you see how the people live, and still more how easily they die, it is always difficult to believe that you are walking among human beings. All colonial empires are in reality founded upon that fact. The people have brown faces—besides, there are so many of them! Are they really the same flesh as yourself? Do they even have names? Or are they merely a kind of undifferentiated brown stuff, about as individual as bees or coral insects? They rise out of the earth, they sweat and starve for a few years, and then they sink back into the nameless mounds of the graveyard and nobody notices that they are gone. And even the graves themselves soon fade back into the soil. Sometimes, out for a walk, as you break your way through the prickly pear, you notice that it is rather bumpy underfoot, and only a certain regularity in the bumps tells you that you are walking over skeletons.

I was feeding one of the gazelles in the public gardens.

Gazelles are almost the only animals that look good to eat when they are still alive, in fact, one can hardly look at their hindquarters without thinking of mint sauce. The gazelle I was feeding seemed to know that this thought was in my mind, for though it took the piece of bread I was holding out it obviously did not like me. It nibbled rapidly at the bread, then lowered its head and tried to butt me, then took another nibble and then butted again. Probably its idea was that if it could drive me away the bread would somehow remain hanging in mid-air.

An Arab navvy° working on the path nearby lowered his heavy hoe and sidled slowly towards us. He looked from the gazelle to the bread and from the bread to the gazelle, with a sort of quiet amazement, as though he had never seen anything quite like this before. Finally he said shyly in French:

"I could eat some of that bread."

I tore off a piece and he stowed it gratefully in some secret place under his rags. This man is an employee of the Municipality.

When you go through the Jewish quarters you gather some idea of what the medieval ghettoes were probably like. Under their Moorish rulers the Jews were only allowed to own land in certain restricted areas, and after centuries of this kind of treatment they have ceased to bother about overcrowding. Many of the streets are a good deal less than six feet wide, the houses are completely windowless, and sore-eyed children cluster everywhere in unbelievable numbers, like clouds of flies. Down the centre of the street there is generally running a little river of urine.

In the bazaar huge families of Jews, all dressed in the long black robe and little black skull-cap, are working in dark fly-infested booths that look like caves. A carpenter sits cross-legged at a prehistoric lathe, turning chair-legs at lightning speed. He works the lathe with a bow in his right hand and guides the chisel with his left foot, and thanks to a lifetime of sitting in this position his left leg is warped out of shape. At his side his grandson, aged six, is already starting on the simpler parts of the job.

I was just passing the coppersmiths' booths when somebody noticed that I was lighting a cigarette. Instantly, from the dark holes all round, there was a frenzied rush of Jews, many of them old grandfathers with flowing grey beards, all clamouring for a cigarette. Even a blind man somewhere at the back of one

navvy: A workman employed in excavation.

of the booths heard a rumour of cigarettes and came crawling out, groping in the air with his hand. In about a minute I had used up the whole packet. None of these people, I suppose, works less than twelve hours a day, and every one of them looks on a cigarette as a more or less impossible luxury.

As the Jews live in self-contained communities they follow the same trades as the Arabs, except for agriculture. Fruit-sellers, potters, silversmiths, blacksmiths, butchers, leatherworkers, tailors, water-carriers, beggars, porters—whichever way you look you see nothing but Jews. As a matter of fact there are thirteen thousand of them, all living in the space of a few acres. A good job Hitler isn't here. Perhaps he is on his way, however. You hear the usual dark rumours about the Jews, not only from the Arabs but from the poorer Europeans.

"Yes, mon vieux, they took my job away from me and gave it to a Jew. The Jews! They're the real rulers of this country, you know. They've got all the money. They control the banks, finance—everything."

"But," I said, "isn't it a fact that the average Jew is a labourer working for about a penny an hour?"

"Ah, that's only for show! They're all moneylenders really. They're cun-   15
ning, the Jews."

In just the same way, a couple of hundred years ago, poor old women used to be burned for witchcraft when they could not even work enough magic to get themselves a square meal.

All people who work with their hands are partly invisible, and the more important the work they do, the less visible they are. Still, a white skin is always fairly conspicuous. In northern Europe, when you see a labourer ploughing a field, you probably give him a second glance. In a hot country, anywhere south of Gibraltar or east of Suez, the chances are that you don't even see him. I have noticed this again and again. In a tropical landscape one's eye takes in everything except the human beings. It takes in the dried-up soil, the prickly pear, the palm tree and the distant mountain, but it always misses the peasant hoeing at his patch. He is the same colour as the earth, and a great deal less interesting to look at.

It is only because of this that the starved countries of Asia and Africa are accepted as tourist resorts. No one would think of running cheap trips to the Distressed Areas.° But where the human beings have brown skins their poverty is simply not noticed. What does Morocco mean to a Frenchman? An orange-grove or a job in Government service. Or to an Englishman? Camels, castles, palm trees, Foreign Legionnaires, brass trays, and bandits. One could probably live there for years without noticing that for nine-tenths of the people the reality of life is an endless, back-breaking struggle to wring a little food out of an eroded soil.

Distressed Areas: Parts of Britain especially hard hit by economic depression.

Most of Morocco is so desolate that no wild animal bigger than a hare can live on it. Huge areas which were once covered with forest have turned into a treeless waste where the soil is exactly like broken-up brick. Nevertheless a good deal of it is cultivated, with frightful labour. Everything is done by hand. Long lines of women, bent double like inverted capital L's, work their way slowly across the fields, tearing up the prickly weeds with their hands, and the peasant gathering lucerne for fodder pulls it up stalk by stalk instead of reaping it, thus saving an inch or two on each stalk. The plough is a wretched wooden thing, so frail that one can easily carry it on one's shoulder, and fitted underneath with a rough iron spike which stirs the soil to a depth of about four inches. This is as much as the strength of the animals is equal to. It is usual to plough with a cow and a donkey yoked together. Two donkeys would not be quite strong enough, but on the other hand two cows would cost a little more to feed. The peasants possess no harrows, they merely plough the soil several times over in different directions, finally leaving it in rough furrows, after which the whole field has to be shaped with hoes into small oblong patches to conserve water. Except for a day or two after the rare rain-storms there is never enough water. Along the edges of the fields channels are hacked out to a depth of thirty or forty feet to get at the tiny trickles which run through the subsoil.

Every afternoon a file of very old women passes down the road outside 20 my house, each carrying a load of firewood. All of them are mummified with age and the sun, and all of them are tiny. It seems to be generally the case in primitive communities that the women, when they get beyond a certain age, shrink to the size of children. One day a poor old creature who could not have been more than four feet tall crept past me under a vast load of wood. I stopped her and put a five-sou piece (a little more than a farthing)° into her hand. She answered with a shrill wail, almost a scream, which was partly gratitude but mainly surprise. I suppose that from her point of view, by taking any notice of her, I seemed almost to be violating a law of nature. She accepted her status as an old woman, that is to say as a beast of burden. When a family is travelling it is quite usual to see a father and a grown-up son riding ahead on donkeys, and an old woman following on foot, carrying the baggage.

But what is strange about these people is their invisibility. For several weeks, always at about the same time of day, the file of old women had hobbled past the house with their firewood, and though they had registered themselves on my eyeballs I cannot truly say that I had seen them. Firewood was passing—that was how I saw it. It was only that one day I happened to be walking behind them, and the curious up-and-down motion of a load of wood drew my attention to the human being beneath it. Then for the first time I noticed the poor old earth-coloured bodies, bodies reduced to bones

---

five sou . . . farthing: A sou is a former French coin; five sou equaled a centime, or a hundredth of a franc. A farthing is a former British coin worth a quarter of a penny.

and leathery skin, bent double under the crushing weight. Yet I suppose I had not been five minutes on Moroccan soil before I noticed the overloading of the donkeys and was infuriated by it. There is no question that the donkeys are damnably treated. The Moroccan donkey is hardly bigger than a St. Bernard dog, it carries a load which in the British Army would be considered too much for a fifteen-hands mule, and very often its pack-saddle is not taken off its back for weeks together. But what is peculiarly pitiful is that it is the most willing creature on earth, it follows its master like a dog and does not need either bridle or halter. After a dozen years of devoted work it suddenly drops dead, whereupon its master tips it into the ditch and the village dogs have torn its guts out before it is cold.

This kind of thing makes one's blood boil, whereas—on the whole—the plight of the human beings does not. I am not commenting, merely pointing to a fact. People with brown skins are next door to invisible. Anyone can be sorry for the donkey with its galled back, but it is generally owing to some kind of accident if one even notices the old woman under her load of sticks.

As the storks flew northward the Negroes were marching southward—a long, dusty column, infantry, screw-gun batteries, and then more infantry, four or five thousand men in all, winding up the road with a clumping of boots and a clatter of iron wheels.

They were Senegalese, the blackest Negroes in Africa, so black that sometimes it is difficult to see whereabouts on their necks the hair begins. Their splendid bodies were hidden in reach-me-down khaki uniforms, their feet squashed into boots that looked like blocks of wood, and every tin hat seemed to be a couple of sizes too small. It was very hot and the men had marched a long way. They slumped under the weight of their packs and the curiously sensitive black faces were glistening with sweat.

As they went past, a tall, very young Negro turned and caught my eye.   25 But the look he gave me was not in the least the kind of look you might expect. Not hostile, not contemptuous, not sullen, not even inquisitive. It was the shy, wide-eyed Negro look, which actually is a look of profound respect. I saw how it was. This wretched boy, who is a French citizen and has therefore been dragged from the forest to scrub floors and catch syphilis in garrison towns, actually has feelings of reverence before a white skin. He has been taught that the white race are his masters, and he still believes it.

But there is one thought which every white man (and in this connection it doesn't matter twopence if he calls himself a socialist) thinks when he sees a black army marching past. "How much longer can we go on kidding these people? How long before they turn their guns in the other direction?"

It was curious, really. Every white man there had this thought stowed somewhere or other in his mind. I had it, so had the other onlookers, so had the officers on their sweating chargers and the white N.C.O.'s marching in the ranks. It was a kind of secret which we all knew and were too clever to tell; only the Negroes didn't know it. And really it was like watching a flock of cattle to see the long column, a mile or two miles of armed men, flowing peacefully up the road, while the great white birds drifted over them in the opposite direction, glittering like scraps of paper.

QUESTIONS FOR DISCUSSION

1. What is Orwell implying when he writes, in paragraph 8, "This man is an employee of the Municipality"?
2. What does Orwell accomplish by exploring aspects of Marrakech overlooked by the average tourist?
3. In paragraph 17 Orwell writes, "All people who work with their hands are partly invisible." Why are the laborers in Marrakech "partly invisible"? Are they seen by some people but overlooked by others? Are there "partly invisible" people in the United States today?
4. Orwell is well known for political novels such as *1984* and *Animal Farm*. Is there a political message in "Marrakech"?
5. Why do you think Orwell draws attention to storks and "great white birds" in paragraphs 23 and 27? How do you respond to this final scene?
6. Although the essay is divided into five sections, do the sections come together to make a whole? Is there a pattern to the arrangement of scenes Orwell describes? Are there any images that help tie the scenes together?

SUGGESTIONS FOR WRITING

1. Choose a place you know well, and write an essay composed of a series of scenes showing what that place is like. Without stating a specific thesis, arrange your scenes in a pattern that will help readers understand the vision you are sharing with them.
2. If you share Orwell's concern about social injustice, write a series of scenes that convey different aspects of a specific problem.
3. Write an essay exploring what a writer can accomplish by using the form Orwell has used in "Marrakech." What possibilities does it open? Does it pose any risks?

LINKS ■ ■ ■

■ WITHIN THE BOOK

The harmful effects of colonialism motivated "A Modest Proposal" (pages 488–494) by Jonathan Swift and the "Declaration of Independence" (pages 529–532) by Thomas Jefferson.

(continues)

LINKS ■ ■ ■ *(continued)*

■ ELSEWHERE IN PRINT

Fernea, Elizabeth Warnock. *A Street in Marrakech*. Garden City: Doubleday, 1975.

Orwell, George. *Animal Farm: A Fairy Story*. 1945. New York: Signet, 1996.

---. *Down and Out in Paris and London*. 1933. New York: Harcourt, 1983.

---. *Homage to Catalonia*. 1938. New York: Harcourt, 1987.

---. *1984*. 1949. New York: NAL, 1989.

---. *The Orwell Reader: Fiction, Essays, and Reportage*. Ed. Richard H. Rovere. New York: Harcourt, 1956.

Porch, Douglas. *The Conquest of Morocco*. New York: Knopf, 1983.

■ ONLINE

- African Colonialism
  <http://africanhistory.about.com/cs/eracolonialism>

- George Orwell Archive
  <http://codoh.com/thoughtcrimes/tcportorw.html>

- Marrakech
  <http://lexicorient.com/morocco/marrakech.htm>

- Political Writings of George Orwell
  <http://www.resort.com/~prime8/Orwell>

IF YOU ARE WHAT YOU EAT, THEN WHAT AM I?

Geeta Kothari

A member of the English Department at the University of Pittsburgh, Geeta Kothari writes both fiction and nonfiction. When discussing her anthology Did My Mama Like to Dance? *and why she writes about her own mother, Kothari offers a comment about her motive for writing that may help you to understand the organization and purpose of the following essay: "I feel an urgency to record the pieces of our life together, while understanding that no matter how hard I try, there will be things left unspoken or unasked."*

"If You Are What You Eat, Then What Am I?" was first published in 1999 by The Kenyon Review, *one of our county's most prestigious literary magazines. As its title suggests, the essay explores the role of food in shaping identity. In the case of Geeta Kothari, who is an Asian American, the foods that shaped her childhood were either Indian or American. As an adult, she now reflects on what she valued and what she took for granted as she ate at her family's table. As you read this essay, consider what Kothari achieves by dividing it into sections and how these sections relate to one another.*

> To belong is to understand the tacit codes of the people you live with.
> — MICHAEL IGNATIEFF, *Blood and Belonging*

I

The first time my mother and I open a can of tuna, I am nine years old. We stand in the doorway of the kitchen, in semidarkness, the can tilted toward daylight. I want to eat what the kids at school eat: bologna, hot dogs, salami— foods my parents find repugnant because they contain pork and meat byproducts, crushed bone and hair glued together by chemicals and fat. Although she has never been able to tolerate the smell of fish, my mother buys the tuna, hoping to satisfy my longing for American food.

Indians, of course, do not eat such things.

The tuna smells fishy, which surprises me because I can't remember anyone's tuna sandwich actually smelling like fish. And the tuna in those sandwiches doesn't look like this, pink and shiny, like an internal organ. In fact, this looks similar to the bad foods my mother doesn't want me to eat. She is silent, holding her face away from the can while peering into it like a half-blind bird.

"What's wrong with it?" I ask.

She has no idea. My mother does not know that the tuna everyone else's 5 mothers made for them was tuna *salad*.

"Do you think it's botulism?"

I have never seen botulism, but I have read about it, just as I have read about but never eaten steak and kidney pie.

645

There is so much my parents don't know. They are not like other parents, and they disappoint me and my sister. They are supposed to help us negotiate the world outside, teach us the signs, the clues to proper behavior: what to eat and how to eat it.

We have expectations, and my parents fail to meet them, especially my mother, who works full-time. I don't understand what it means, to have a mother who works outside and inside the home; I notice only the ways in which she disappoints me. She doesn't show up for school plays. She doesn't make chocolate-frosted cupcakes for my class. At night, if I want her attention, I have to sit in the kitchen and talk to her while she cooks the evening meal, attentive to every third or fourth word I say.

We throw the tuna away. This time my mother is disappointed. I go to   10
school with tuna eaters. I see their sandwiches, yet cannot explain the discrepancy between them and the stinking, oily fish in my mother's hand. We do not understand so many things, my mother and I.

II

On weekends, we eat fried chicken from Woolworth's on the back steps of my father's first-floor office in Murray Hill. The back steps face a small patch of garden—hedges, a couple of skinny trees, and gravel instead of grass. We can see the back window of the apartment my parents and I lived in until my sister was born. There, the doorman watched my mother, several months pregnant and wearing a sari, slip on the ice in front of the building.

My sister and I pretend we are in the country, where our American friends all have houses. We eat glazed doughnuts, also from Woolworth's, and french fries with ketchup.

III

My mother takes a catering class and learns that Miracle Whip and mustard are healthier than mayonnaise. She learns to make egg salad with chopped celery, deviled eggs dusted with paprika, a cream cheese spread with bits of fresh ginger and watercress, chicken liver pâté, and little brown-and-white checkerboard sandwiches that we have only once. She makes chicken *à la king* in puff pastry shells and eggplant Parmesan. She acquires smooth wooden paddles, whose purpose is never clear, two different egg slicers, several wooden spoons, icing tubes, cookie cutters, and an electric mixer.

IV

I learn to make tuna salad by watching a friend. My sister never acquires a taste for it. Instead, she craves

bologna
hot dogs
bacon
sausages

and a range of unidentifiable meat products forbidden by my parents. Their restrictions are not about sacred cows, as everyone around us assumes; in a pinch, we are allowed hamburgers, though lamb burgers are preferable. A "pinch" means choosing not to draw attention to ourselves as outsiders, impolite visitors who won't eat what their host serves. But bologna is still taboo.

V

Things my sister refuses to eat: butter, veal, anything with jeera. The baby-   15
sitter tries to feed her butter sandwiches, threatens her with them, makes her cry in fear and disgust. My mother does not disappoint her; she does not believe in forcing us to eat, in using food as a weapon. In addition to pbj,° my sister likes pasta and marinara sauce, bologna and Wonder Bread (when she can get it), and fried egg sandwiches with turkey, cheese, and horseradish. Her tastes, once established, are predictable.

VI

When we visit our relatives in India, food prepared outside the house is carefully monitored. In the hot, sticky monsoon months in New Delhi and Bombay, we cannot eat ice cream, salad, cold food, or any fruit that can't be peeled. Definitely no meat. People die from amoebic dysentery, unexplained fevers, strange boils on their bodies. We drink boiled water only, no ice. No sweets except for jalebi, thin fried twists of dough in dripping hot sugar syrup. If we're caught outside with nothing to drink, Fanta, Limca, Thums Up (after Coca-Cola is thrown out by Mrs. Gandhi)° will do. Hot tea sweetened with sugar, served with thick creamy buffalo milk, is preferable. It should be boiled, to kill the germs on the cup.

My mother talks about "back home" as a safe place, a silk cocoon frozen in time where we are sheltered by family and friends. Back home, my sister and I do not argue about food with my parents. Home is where they know all the rules. We trust them to guide us safely through the maze of city streets for which they have no map, and we trust them to feed and take care of us, the way parents should.

Mrs. Gandhi: Indira Gandhi (1917–1984), prime minister of India 1966–1977 and 1980–1984.

Finally, though, one of us will get sick, hungry for the food we see our cousins and friends eating, too thirsty to ask for a straw, too polite to insist on properly boiled water.

At my uncle's diner in New Delhi, someone hands me a plate of aloo tikki, fried potato patties filled with mashed channa dal and served with a sweet and a sour chutney. The channa, mixed with hot chilies and spices, burns my tongue and throat. I reach for my Fanta, discard the paper straw, and gulp the sweet orange soda down, huge drafts that sting rather than soothe.

When I throw up later that day (or is it the next morning, when a stom- 20 achache wakes me from deep sleep?), I cry over the frustration of being sin- gled out, not from the pain my mother assumes I'm feeling as she holds my hair back from my face. The taste of orange lingers in my mouth, and I remember my lips touching the cold glass of the Fanta bottle.

At that moment, more than anything, I want to be like my cousins.

VII

In New York, at the first Indian restaurant in our neighborhood, my father orders with confidence, and my sister and I play with the silverware until the steaming plates of lamb biryani arrive.

What is Indian food? my friends ask, their noses crinkling up.

Later, this restaurant is run out of business by the new Indo-Pak- Bangladeshi combinations up and down the street, which serve similar food. They use plastic cutlery and Styrofoam cups. They do not distinguish between North and South Indian cooking, or between Indian, Pakistani, and Bangladeshi cooking, and their customers do not care. The food is fast, cheap, and tasty. Dosa, a rice flour crepe stuffed with masala potato, appears on the same trays as chicken makhani.

Now my friends want to know, Do you eat curry at home? 25

One time my mother makes lamb vindaloo for guests. Like dosa, this is a South Indian dish, one that my Punjabi mother has to learn from a cook- book. For us, she cooks everyday food—yellow dal, rice, chapati, bhaji. Lentils, rice, bread, and vegetables. She has never referred to anything on our table as "curry" or "curried," but I know she has made chicken curry for guests. Vin- daloo, she explains, is a curry too. I understand then that curry is a dish cre- ated for guests, outsiders, a food for people who eat in restaurants.

VIII

I have inherited brown eyes, black hair, a long nose with a crooked bridge, and soft teeth with thin enamel. I am in my twenties, moving to a city far from my parents, before it occurs to me that jeera, the spice my sister avoids, must have an English name. I have to learn that haldi = turmeric, methi =

fenugreek. What to make with fenugreek, I do not know. My grandmother used to make methi roti for our breakfast, cornbread with fresh fenugreek leaves served with a lump of homemade butter. No one makes it now that she's gone, though once in a while my mother will get a craving for it and produce a facsimile ("The cornmeal here is wrong") that only highlights what she's really missing: the smells and tastes of her mother's house.

I will never make my grandmother's methi roti or even my mother's unsatisfactory imitation of it. I attempt chapati; it takes six hours, three phone calls home, and leaves me with an aching back. I have to write translations down: jeera = cumin. My memory is unreliable. But I have always known garam = hot.

IX

My mother learns how to make brownies and apple pie. My father makes only Indian food, except for loaves of heavy, sweet brown bread that I eat with thin slices of American cheese and lettuce. The recipe is a secret, passed on to him by a woman at work. Years later, when he finally gives it to me, when I finally ask for it, I end up with three bricks of gluten that even the birds and my husband won't eat.

X

My parents send me to boarding school, outside of London. They imag- 30
ine that I will overcome my shyness and find a place for myself in this all-girls' school. They have never lived in England, but as former subjects of the British Empire, they find London familiar, comfortable in a way New York— my mother's home for over twenty years by now—is not. Americans still don't know what to call us; their Indians live on reservations, not in Manhattan. Because they understand the English, my parents believe the English understand us.

I poke at my first school lunch—thin, overworked pastry in a puddle of lumpy gravy. The lumps are chewy mushrooms, maybe, or overcooked shrimp.

"What is this?" I don't want to ask, but I can't go on eating without knowing.

"Steak and kidney pie."

The girl next to me, red-haired, freckled, watches me take a bite from my plate. She has been put in charge of me, the new girl, and I follow her around all day, a foreigner at the mercy of a reluctant and angry tour guide. She is not used to explaining what is perfectly and utterly natural.

"What, you've never had steak and kidney pie? Bloody hell." 35

My classmates scoff, then marvel, then laugh at my ignorance. After a year, I understand what is on my plate: sausage rolls, blood pudding, Spam, roast beef in a thin, greasy gravy, all the bacon and sausage I could possibly want. My parents do not expect me to starve.

The girls at school expect conformity; it has been bred into them, through years of uniforms and strict rules about proper behavior. I am thirteen and contrary, even as I yearn for acceptance. I declare myself a vegetarian and doom myself to a diet of cauliflower cheese and baked beans on toast. The administration does not question my decision; they assume it's for vague, undefined religious reasons, although my father, the doctor, tells them it's for my health. My reasons, from this distance of many years, remain murky to me.

Perhaps I am my parents' daughter after all.

XI

When she is three, sitting on my cousin's lap in Bombay, my sister reaches for his plate and puts a chili in her mouth. She wants to be like the grownups, who dip green chilies in coarse salt and eat them like any other vegetable. She howls inconsolable animal pain for what must be hours. She doesn't have the vocabulary for the oily heat that stings her mouth and tongue, burns a trail through her small tender body. Only hot, sticky tears on my father's shoulder.

As an adult, she eats red chili paste, mango pickle, kimchee, foods that   40
make my eyes water and my stomach gurgle. My tastes are milder. I order raita at Indian restaurants and ask for food that won't sear the roof of my mouth and scar the insides of my cheeks. The waiters nod, and their eyes shift—a slight once-over that indicates they don't believe me. I am Indian, aren't I? My father seems to agree with them. He tells me I'm asking for the impossible, as if he believes the recipes are immutable, written in stone during the passage from India to America.

XII

I look around my boyfriend's freezer one day and find meat: pork chops, ground beef, chicken pieces, Italian sausage. Ham in the refrigerator, next to the homemade bolognese sauce. Tupperware filled with chili made from ground beef and pork.

He smells different from me. Foreign. Strange.

I marry him anyway.

He has inherited blue eyes that turn gray in bad weather, light brown hair, a sharp pointy nose, and excellent teeth. He learns to make chili with ground turkey and tofu, tomato sauce with red wine and portobello mushrooms, roast chicken with rosemary and slivers of garlic under the skin.

He eats steak when we are in separate cities, roast beef at his mother's   45
house, hamburgers at work. Sometimes I smell them on his skin. I hope he doesn't notice me turning my face, a cheek instead of my lips, my nose wrinkled at the unfamiliar, musky smell.

XIII

And then I realize I don't want to be a person who can find Indian food only in restaurants. One day my parents will be gone and I will long for the foods of my childhood, the way they long for theirs. I prepare for this day the way people on TV prepare for the end of the world. They gather canned goods they will never eat while I stockpile recipes I cannot replicate. I am frantic, disorganized, grabbing what I can, filing scribbled notes haphazardly. I regret the tastes I've forgotten, the meals I have inhaled without a thought. I worry that I've come to this realization too late.

XIV

Who told my mother about Brie? One day we were eating Velveeta, the next day Brie, Gouda, Camembert, Port Salut, Havarti with caraway, Danish fontina, string cheese made with sheep's milk. Who opened the door to these foreigners that sit on the refrigerator shelf next to last night's dal?

Back home, there is one cheese only, which comes in a tin, looks like Bakelite, and tastes best when melted.

And how do we go from Chef Boyardee to fresh pasta and homemade sauce, made with Redpack tomatoes, crushed garlic, and dried oregano? Macaroni and cheese, made with fresh cheddar and whole milk, sprinkled with bread crumbs and paprika. Fresh eggplant and ricotta ravioli, baked with marinara sauce and fresh mozzarella.

My mother will never cook beef or pork in her kitchen, and the foods she knew in her childhood are unavailable. Because the only alternative to the supermarket, with its TV dinners and canned foods, is the gourmet Italian deli across the street, by default our meals become socially acceptable.

XV

If I really want to make myself sick, I worry that my husband will one day leave me for a meat-eater, for someone familiar who doesn't sniff him suspiciously for signs of alimentary infidelity.

XVI

Indians eat lentils. I understand this as absolute, a decree from an unidentifiable authority that watches and judges me.

So what does it mean that I cannot replicate my mother's dal? She and my father show me repeatedly, in their kitchen, in my kitchen. They coach me over the phone, buy me the best cookbooks, and finally write down their secrets. Things I'm supposed to know but don't. Recipes that should be, by now, engraved on my heart.

Living far from the comfort of people who require no explanation for what I do and who I am, I crave the foods we have shared. My mother convinces me that moong is the easiest dal to prepare, and yet it fails me every time: bland, watery, a sickly greenish yellow mush. These imperfect imitations remind me only of what I'm missing.

But I have never been fond of moong dal. At my mother's table it is the   *55* last thing I reach for. Now I worry that this antipathy toward dal signals something deeper, that somehow I am not my parents' daughter, not Indian, and because I cannot bear the touch and smell of raw meat, though I can eat it cooked (charred, dry, and overdone), I am not American either.

I worry about a lifetime purgatory in Indian restaurants where I will complain that all the food looks and tastes the same because they've used the same masala.

XVII

About the tuna and her attempts to feed us, my mother laughs. She says, "You were never fussy. You ate everything I made and never complained."

My mother is at the stove, wearing only her blouse and petticoat, her sari carefully folded and hung in the closet. She does not believe a girl's place is in the kitchen, but she expects me to know that too much hing can ruin a meal, to know without being told, without having to ask or write it down. Hing = asafetida.

She remembers the catering class. "Oh, that class. You know, I had to give it up when we got to lobster. I just couldn't stand the way it looked."

She says this apologetically, as if she has deprived us, as if she suspects that   *60* having a mother who could feed us lobster would have changed the course of our lives.

Intellectually, she understands that only certain people regularly eat lobster, people with money or those who live in Maine, or both. In her catering class there were people without jobs for whom preparing lobster was a part of their professional training as caterers. Like us, they wouldn't be eating lobster at home. For my mother, however, lobster was just another American food, like tuna—different, strange, not natural yet somehow essential to belonging.

I learned how to prepare and eat lobster from the same girl who taught me tuna salad. I ate bacon at her house too. And one day this girl, with her houses in the country and Martha's Vineyard, asked me how my uncle was going to pick me up from the airport in Bombay. In 1973, she was surprised to hear that he used a car, not an elephant. At home, my parents and I laughed, and though I never knew for sure if she was making fun of me, I still wanted her friendship.

My parents were afraid my sister and I would learn to despise the foods they loved, replace them with bologna and bacon and lose our taste for masala. For my mother, giving up her disgust of lobster, with its hard exterior and foreign smell, would mean renouncing some essential difference. It would mean becoming, decidedly, definitely, American—unafraid of meat in all its forms, able to consume large quantities of protein at any given meal. My willingness to toss a living being into boiling water and then get past its ugly appearance to the rich meat inside must mean to my mother that I am somehow someone she is not.

But I haven't eaten lobster in years. In my kitchen cupboards, there is a thirteen-pound bag of basmati rice, jars of lime pickle, mango pickle, and ghee, cans of tuna and anchovies, canned soups, coconut milk, and tomatoes, rice noodles, several kinds of pasta, dried mushrooms, and unlabeled bottles of spices: haldi, jeera, hing. When my husband tries to help me cook, he cannot identify all the spices. He gets confused when I forget their English names and remarks that my expectations of him are unreasonable.

I am my parents' daughter. Like them, I expect knowledge to pass from me to my husband without one word of explanation or translation. I want him to know what I know, see what I see, without having to tell him exactly what it is. I want to believe that recipes never change. 65

QUESTIONS FOR DISCUSSION

1. Why, as a child, was Kothari disappointed with her parents?
2. Consider the last sentence in paragraph 11: "There, the doorman watched my mother, several months pregnant and wearing a sari, slip on the ice in front of the building." Why is the sari significant? What is Kothari implying about the doorman?
3. According to Kothari, her mother would not use "food as a weapon." What does it mean to use "food as a weapon"? Can you give an example from your own experience?
4. If you are what you eat, what kind of person is Kothari?
5. In what sense has Kothari become her "parents' daughter"?
6. Why does Kothari "want to believe that recipes never change"?
7. What does Kothari accomplish by dividing her essay into separate, numbered sections?

SUGGESTIONS FOR WRITING

1. According to the quotation from Michael Ignatieff with which Kothari prefaces her essay, "To belong is to understand the tacit codes of the people you live with." Without defining or explaining the codes of the people you live with (or have lived with), write an experimental essay showing these people behaving in ways that you were encouraged to emulate.
2. Write a series of scenes in which you show yourself eating foods you like or are expected to eat. Arrange these scenes in a pattern that will help readers to understand how your tastes have evolved.
3. Visit a restaurant serving a kind of food you have never had before. Order a variety of dishes and then explore what you have learned from this experience.

LINKS ■ ■ ■

■ WITHIN THE BOOK

For another essay about the relationship between food and identity, see "Grub" by Scott Russell Sanders (pages 62–65).

■ ELSEWHERE IN PRINT

Ignatieff, Michael. *Blood and Belonging: Journeys into the New Nationalism.* New York: Farrar, 1994.

–––. *The Warrior's Honor: Ethnic War and the Modern Conscience.* New York: Metropolitan, 1998.

Jaffrey, Madhur. *An Invitation to Indian Cooking.* Hopewell: Ecco, 1999.

Jhabvala, Ruth Prawer. *Heat and Dust.* New York: Harper, 1975.

Mukherjee, Bharati. *Jasmine.* New York: Grove, 1989.

Seth, Vikram. *A Suitable Boy.* New York: Harper, 1993.

■ ONLINE

- Adjusting to Life in the U.S.A.
  <http://www.new2usa.com/showpage.jsp?PageID=adjusting>

- Eating in America
  <http://www.eatinginamerica.de>

- History of Indian Food
  <http://www.indiafoodandfun.com/food/history.htm>

- History of Miracle Whip
  <http://www.kraftfoods.com/miraclewhip/zip/hist1.html>

I WAS BORN

Luc Sante

*As a child, Luc Sante moved four times between Belgium and the United States
before his family settled in New York. Reflecting on this experience, he told an interviewer for the* New York Times, *"For me, going back and forth between Belgium
and the United States when I was a kid, I had the feeling not only of traveling in space
but also traveling in time." Elsewhere, he describes himself as an "outsider" because he
grew up "being both an immigrant and having no ethnic community to belong to as a
Belgian—there aren't many of us Belgians running around." In addition to writing about
his search for identity, Sante also writes social history and popular culture, and his awards
include a Grammy for best album notes. He is currently Visiting Professor of Writing and
Photography at Bard College.*

In the following selection from The Factory of Facts *(1998), Sante experiments with
autobiography by trying out different versions of his past—thus testing the boundaries
between fiction and nonfiction. When you read "I Was Born," you will find that these
different versions cannot all be true if truth is determined by factual accuracy. Consider
what information seems likely to be accurate and what other kinds of truth are
conveyed by this experiment with form.*

I was born on May 25, 1954, in Verviers, Belgium, the only child of
Lucien Mathieu Amélie Sante and Denise Lambertine Alberte Marie Ghis-
laine Nandrin. Following the bankruptcy of my father's employer, an iron
foundry that manufactured wool-carding machinery, and at the suggestion of
friends who had emigrated earlier, my parents decided to move to the United
States in search of work. We arrived at Idlewild Airport in February 1959 and
moved in with my parents' friends in Summit, New Jersey. Prospects were
not as bright as they had been depicted, and that November we sailed back
to Belgium, but the situation there was no better, and early in 1960 we re-
emigrated. Several more such trips occurred over the next few years, spurred
by momentary hopes, by the Cuban Missile Crisis, by the illnesses and deaths
of my maternal grandparents. At length my parents decided to remain in
America, at least until the time came when they could retire to Belgium.

I was born in 1954 in Verviers, Belgium, the only child of Lucien and
Denise Sante. Following the bankruptcy of my father's employer, an iron
foundry that manufactured wool-carding machinery, and at the suggestion of
my mother's brother, René Nandrin, my parents decided to move to the Belgian Congo, where my father was to take up a position as local field director
for a palm-oil concern. In February 1959, we arrived in Coquilhatville, on

the banks of the Congo River, and moved into a company-owned villa in the European district. Suddenly we had servants and a chauffeured car. On the other hand, I came down with a succession of ailments aggravated by the climate and spent most of my time in bed. Barely a year later the Belgian government announced that the Congo would be granted its independence that June, and my parents' friends and colleagues began to show signs of alarm, sending prized possessions, for example, back to their families in Belgium. Emotions had risen to a point of panic by late May, when the first general elections were held. My parents and their friends dismissed their servants, fearing treachery. My father barricaded my mother and me inside the house and would himself not leave without a loaded revolver on his hip. Violent incidents began occurring, most of them in the south of the country, but some close enough that my father, over my mother's protests, sent us home. He followed a little over a month later, when fighting had become widespread; his employer turned over local control to native African managers. Connections made in the Congo led my father to a job with the Ministry of Commerce, and we moved to Berchem-Ste.-Agathe, a suburb of Brussels, where I recovered and later found I had a surprising aptitude for competitive cycling.

I was born in 1954 in Verviers, Belgium, the only child of Lucien and Denise Sante. Following the bankruptcy of his employer, an iron foundry that manufactured wool-carding machinery, my father tried to find another job, but without success. After depleting their savings and selling our house in Pepinster, as well as most of the major household possessions, my parents moved into a succession of progressively smaller and dingier apartments, finally winding up in a single room in Seraing, an industrial suburb of Liège, where my father got a barely remunerative stint as nightwatchman in a warehouse. We endured two years of this as a family. My mother became chronically ill, probably due to stress as much as to bad food and lack of heat, and consequently I was taken in by my cousins in the country. They, too, were feeling the pinch of the economy, however, and palmed me off on other relatives, who in turn passed me along after a while. I spent three years being thus shunted around, until the Christian Brothers admitted me as a hardship case at their boarding school in Liège in the winter of 1964. By then my mother had been hospitalized full-time and my father had retreated into a vigilant and apparently unbreakable silence. At the school I was constantly victimized by the other pupils, most of them offspring of well-to-do families. Finally, at thirteen, I snapped. I set a fire that consumed the dormitory and took the lives of five boys.

I was born in 1954 in Verviers, Belgium, the only child of Lucien and Denise Sante. My father's employer, an iron foundry that manufactured wool-carding machinery, miraculously escaped the effects of the recession of 1958 and the collapse of Verviers's textile industry by a rapid and timely change to the manufacture of radiators. My father, who had worked his way up to junior management from the labor ranks, devised a streamlined method of cooling molds that earned him a succession of promotions, ultimately to the top seat. By 1964 we had sold our row house in Pepinster and moved into a villa in a parklike setting on the heights of the "boulevard" district of Verviers. I grew up fast and was quickly bored by the provincial life around me. I barely maintained passing grades at St. François-Xavier, the local Jesuit *collège,* and would surely have failed and been expelled had it not been for my parents' social and political prominence. As it was, I was taking clandestine excursions—longer and longer ones—out into the world: to Amsterdam, to Paris, to London, to Majorca. I took every drug I could get my hands on, and I was possibly a father several times over; I was adept at vanishing when matters came to a head. My parents' threats to cut off my allowance became steadily more credible until, in the spring of 1971, I bribed the manager of the Place Verte branch of the Générale de Banque and withdrew my entire trust fund in cash—or nearly entire; I left a token five hundred francs. I flew to Marrakech, where I lived for eight months in a hotel frequented by members of British rock groups; until a run-in with one of the Berber chieftains who controlled the hashish traffic from the Rif caused me to fear for my life. I snared a series of van rides that took me to Goa, on the Indian Ocean, where I dwelt in a permanent cloud of dope in a waterfront flat. When my money ran out, I relocated to the beach. I contracted scabies and syphilis, but I didn't care.

I was born in 1954 in Verviers, Belgium, the only child of Lucien and 5 Denise Sante. Following the bankruptcy of my father's employer, an iron foundry that manufactured wool-carding machinery, my parents decided to emigrate to the United States, on no more firm a basis than a visit to the U.S. pavilion at the 1958 Brussels World's Fair. We arrived at Idlewild Airport in February 1959 with eight suitcases, my father's prewar memories of high-school English, and the name of someone's cousin who apparently lived in Long Island, New York, which my parents thought was a town. A taxi driver who knew some French took us to a hotel in Manhattan, which turned out to be a clip joint. We lost three of our suitcases before fleeing to another hotel, respectable enough but commensurately expensive. My parents combed telephone books in search of the cousin, but to no avail. They applied for help from the Belgian consulate and were turned away with frosty finality. They spent days on complex and indeterminate errands, looking for chimeric friends of relatives of friends, my father trying to look for jobs in his field without much idea of where to start. They hadn't imagined it would be like this; without connections or a grasp of the language they were lost. The money was rapidly dwindling, too; already there was not enough left for passage back to Europe, and soon they would no longer be able to foot the hotel bill. On the advice of the chambermaid, a kind woman from Puerto Rico—communication between her and my parents, conducted around a tongue none of them possessed, was comically histrionic—my parents relocated to a dank hostelry near Herald Square where the rooms were lit by fluorescent tubes. We lived on rolls and hot dogs. My mother made me sleep wrapped in a chiffon scarf to protect me from the cockroaches. My father took his watch, of a decent but undistinguished Swiss make, to a pawnshop, where he was given five dollars in return. Our suitcases, minus their contents, followed, and soon my parents' overcoats and their extra pairs of shoes went as well. They were beginning to consider applying to a church for assistance but were hindered by their pride. One day, when it seemed no other option remained, a man who lived down the hall from us offered my father a job. He was to deliver a manila envelope to an address in Newark; he would be paid fifty dollars. He accepted with alacrity and set off. That night, after I had fallen asleep, while my mother wept with fear at having heard nothing from him, two men in dark suits came to our room and took us away. They were FBI agents. My father had been arraigned for interstate traffic in narcotics; the house to which he made his delivery had been under surveillance for several weeks. My mother was held as a material witness in the Essex County Women's Correctional Facility. I was kept in a wing of Juvenile Hall for four days, in the course of which I repeatedly wet my bed and was punished by being deprived of food. Then I was sent to a foster home, with a large and strict Irish-American family in Irvington. My inability to speak English enraged the father, who would take me into the vest-pocket back yard and beat me with a razor strop. I was moved to another foster home, and then another and another—I lost count. I had no news from my parents. After a while I couldn't remember their faces.

I was born in 1954 in Verviers, Belgium, the only child of Lucien and Denise Sante. Following the bankruptcy of my father's employer, an iron foundry that manufactured wool-carding machinery, and with the knowledge that there were no other jobs to be had, a combined result of the collapse of the centuries-old Verviers textile industry and of the recession of 1958, my parents decided to go for broke. They sold our row house in Pepinster and the bulk of its contents, and we set off by train for Biarritz, the beautiful city in France fronting on the Bay of Biscay and backed against the Pyrenees. The trip was glorious; we laughed and sang songs and pointed out the window at the spectacular scenery. When we got there my parents checked into a modest hotel, left me with sandwiches and a pile of comics, and went to the casino. My father's plan was to parlay the stake amassed from selling off their possessions into a small fortune at the baccarat table. It didn't work.

I was born in 1954 in Verviers, Belgium, the only child of Lucien and Denise Sante. Following the bankruptcy of my father's employer, an iron foundry that manufactured wool-carding machinery, my parents sat on the floor. Dust accumulated. Things fell and were not picked up. Mold grew on the potatoes in the cellar. The milk solidified. The electricity was cut off. Neighboring boys threw stones that broke the windows, and cold air blew in. First insects, then rodents, and eventually birds arrived to make their homes with us. Soon snow covered the dust, and then soot covered the snow. We grew increasingly warm as we slept.

QUESTIONS FOR DISCUSSION

1. When you compare the different versions of Sante's past, are there any elements that seem consistent?
2. In your opinion, which version seems the most probable and which the least?
3. Of the versions in this piece, the longest is easily the fifth. Why do you think this one is so detailed?
4. Can you detect any pattern to the sequence in which Sante has arranged these seven versions of his early life?
5. Consider the final version of Sante's childhood. How well does it serve as the conclusion for this work as a whole?

SUGGESTIONS FOR WRITING

1. Write a fictional account of your childhood in which you imagine what your life would have been like if something quite different from what actually transpired had occurred.
2. Imagine several different versions of your life ten years from now. Write a series of scenes, arranged from least desirable to most desirable, in which you describe future possibilities for yourself.
3. Write a series of short narratives, each beginning with the same information but then taking a different direction. Then arrange these narratives in a pattern that will help readers make sense of them.

LINKS ■ ■ ■

■ WITHIN THE BOOK

For a more straightforward example of autobiography, see Itabari Njeri's "Life with Father" (pages 68–72).

■ ELSEWHERE IN PRINT

Hochschild, Adam. *King Leopold's Ghost: A Story of Greed, Terror, and Heroism in Colonial Africa.* Boston: Houghton, 1998.

Muniz, Vik, Luc Sante, and William J. Mitchell. *Making It Real.* New York: Independent Curators, 1997.

Sante, Luc. *Evidence.* New York: Farrar, 1992.

———. *The Factory of Facts.* New York: Pantheon, 1998.

———. *Low Life: Lures and Snares of Old New York.* New York: Farrar, 1991.

(continues)

LINKS ■ ■ ■ *(continued)*

■ **ONLINE**

- Belgian History
  <http://www.expatriate-online.com/moving/Belgium/general/History/insight_history.cfm>

- Luc Sante's Web Site
  <http://www.previewport.com/Home/sante.html>

- Resources on the Belgian Congo
  <http://www.Hartford-hwp.com/archives/35/index-efa.html>

ORANGES AND SWEET SISTER BOY

Judy Ruiz

Judy Ruiz, a poet, essayist, and writing teacher, begins the following essay by announcing that her brother has become her sister—that he has, in other words, become a transsexual. This is hardly the kind of news most people expect to receive when a relative calls them on the phone, and Judy Ruiz decided to write about this unusual experience in an unusual way. As you read, you will find that she has included blocks of text printed in a font different from the one used for most of the essay. Pay close attention to them and see if you can determine how they help Ruiz convey her response to her brother's news.

When asked about what can be achieved by writing essays like "Oranges and Sweet Sister Boy," Ruiz told an interviewer for Creative Nonfiction: *"Most ideally, creative nonfiction ends up saving the people of the world, those of us who have forgotten who we are, those of us who are on fire, those of us who must have stories. Stories are something that people like. Except for the really long, boring ones that leave the reader saying huh or duh after the first sentence; but you have to read them too—if they come to you—because there might be a perfect blue pearl hidden in the middle or near the end, some little sentence that will save you as you scramble around for your own salvation. That scrambling around is pretty much a full-time job."*

I am sleeping, hard, when the telephone rings. It's my brother, and he's calling to say that he is now my sister. I feel something fry a little, deep behind my eyes. Knowing how sometimes dreams get mixed up with not-dreams, I decide to do a reality test at once. "Let me get a cigarette," I say, knowing that if I reach for a Marlboro and it turns into a trombone or a snake or anything else on the way to my lips that I'm still out in the large world of dreams.

The cigarette stays a cigarette. I light it. I ask my brother to run that stuff by me again.

It is the Texas Zephyr° at midnight—the woman in a white suit, the man in a blue uniform; she carries flowers—I know they are flowers. The petals spill and spill into the aisle, and a child goes past this couple who have just come from their own wedding—goes past them and past them, going always to the toilet but really just going past them; and the child could be a horse or she could be the police and they'd not notice her any more than they do, which is not at all—the man's hands high up on the woman's legs, her skirt up, her stockings and garters, the petals and finally all the flowers

---

Texas Zephyr: A long-distance passenger train.

spilling out into the aisle and his mouth open on her. My mother. My father. I am conceived near Dallas in the dark while a child passes, a young girl who knows and doesn't know, who witnesses, in glimpses, the creation of the universe, who feels an odd hurt as her own mother, fat and empty, snores with her mouth open, her false teeth slipping down, snores and snores just two seats behind the Creators.

News can make a person stupid. It can make you think you can do something. So I ask The Blade question, thinking that if he hasn't had the operation yet that I can fly to him, rent a cabin out on Puget Sound. That we can talk. That I can get him to touch base with reality.

"Begin with an orange," I would tell him. "Because oranges are mildly intrusive by nature, put the orange somewhere so that it will not bother you—in the cupboard, in a drawer, even a pocket or a handbag will do. The orange, being a patient fruit, will wait for you much longer than say a banana or a peach."

I would hold an orange out to him. I would say, "This is the one that will   5 save your life." And I would tell him about the woman I saw in a bus station who bit right into her orange like it was an apple. She was wild looking, as if she'd been outside for too long in a wind that blew the same way all the time. One of the dregs of humanity, our mother would have called her, the same mother who never brought fruit into the house except in cans. My children used to ask me to "start" their oranges for them. That meant to make a hole in the orange so they could peel the rind away, and their small hands weren't equipped with fingernails that were long enough or strong enough to do the job. Sometimes they would suck the juice out of the hole my thumbnail had made, leaving the orange flat and sad.

The earrings are as big as dessert plates, filigree gold-plated with thin dangles hanging down that touch her bare shoulders. She stands in front of the Alamo while a bald man takes her picture. The sun is absorbed by the earrings so quickly that by the time she feels the heat, it is too late. The hanging dangles make small blisters on her shoulders, as if a centipede had traveled there. She takes the famous river walk in spiked heels, rides in a boat, eats some Italian noodles, returns to the motel room, soaks her feet, and applies small Band-Aids to her toes. She is briefly concerned about the gun on the nightstand. The toilet flushes. She pretends to be sleeping. The gun is just large and heavy. A .45? A .357 magnum? She's never been good with names. She hopes he doesn't try to. Or that if he does, that it's not loaded. But he'll say it's loaded just for fun. Or he'll pull the trigger and the bullet will lodge in her medulla oblongata, ripping through her womb first, taking everything else vital on the way.

In the magazine articles, you don't see this: "Well, yes. The testicles have to come out. And yes. The penis is cut off." What you get is tonsils. So-and-so has had a "sex change" operation. A sex change operation. How precious. How benign. Doctor, just what do you people do with those penises?

News can make a person a little crazy also. News like, "We regret to inform you that you have failed your sanity hearing."

The bracelet on my wrist bears the necessary information about me, but there is one small error. The receptionist typing the information asked me my religious preference. I said, "None." She typed, "Neon."

> Pearl doesn't have any teeth and her tongue looks weird. She says "Pumpkin pie." That's all she says. Sometimes she runs her hands over my bed sheets and says pumpkin pie. Sometimes I am under the sheets. Marsha got stabbed in the chest, but she tells everyone she fell on a knife. Elizabeth—she's the one who thinks her shoe is a baby—hit me in the back with a tray right after one of the cooks gave me extra toast. There's a note on the bulletin board about a class for the nurses: "How Putting A Towel On Someone's Face Makes Them Stop Banging Their Spoon/OR Reduction of Disruptive Mealtime Behavior By Facial Screening—7 P.M.—Conference Room." Another note announces the topic for remotivation class: "COWS." All the paranoid schizophrenics will be there.
>
> Here, in the place for the permanently bewildered, I fit right in. Not because I stood at the window that first night and listened to the trains. Not because I imagined those trains were bracelets, the jewelry of earth. Not even because I imagined that one of those bracelets was on my own arm and was the Texas Zephyr where a young couple made love and conceived me. I am eighteen and beautiful and committed to the state hospital by a district court judge for a period of one day to life. Because I am a paranoid schizophrenic.
>
> I will learn about cows.

So I'm being very quiet in the back of the classroom, and I'm peeling an orange. It's the smell that makes the others begin to turn around, that mildly intrusive nature. The course is called "Women and Modern Literature," and the diaries of Virginia Woolf are up for discussion except nobody has anything to say. I, of course, am making a mess with the orange; and I'm wanting to say that my brother is now my sister.

Later, with my hands still orangey, I wander in to leave something on a desk in a professor's office, and he's reading so I'm being very quiet, and then he says, sort of out of nowhere, "Emily Dickinson up there in her room making poems while her brother was making love to her best friend right downstairs on the dining room table. A regular thing. Think of it. And Walt Whitman out sniffing around the boys. Our two great American poets." And I want to

10

grab this professor's arm and say, "Listen. My brother called me and now he's my sister, and I'm having trouble making sense out of my life right now, so would you mind not telling me any more stuff about sex." And I want my knuckles to turn white while the pressure of my fingers leaves imprints right through his jacket, little indentations he can interpret as urgent. But I don't say anything. And I don't grab his arm. I go read a magazine. I find this:

> "I've never found an explanation for why the human race has so many languages. When the brain became a language brain, it obviously needed to develop an intense degree of plasticity. Such plasticity allows languages to be logical, coherent systems and yet be extremely variable. The same brain that thinks in words and symbols is also a brain that has to be freed up with regard to sexual turn-on and partnering. God knows why sex attitudes have not been subject to the corresponding degrees of modification and variety as language. I suspect there's a close parallel between the two. The brain doesn't seem incredibly efficient with regard to sex."

John Money said that. The same John Money who, with surgeon Howard W. Jones, performed the first sex change operation in the United States in 1965 at Johns Hopkins University and Hospital in Baltimore.

Money also tells about the *hijra*° of India who disgrace their families because they are too effeminate: "The ultimate stage of the *hijra* is to get up the courage to go through the amputation of penis and testicles. They had no anesthetic." Money also answers anyone who might think that "heartless members of the medical profession are forcing these poor darlings to go and get themselves cut up and mutilated," or who think the medical profession should leave them alone. "You'd have lots of patients willing to get a gun and blow off their own genitals if you don't do it. I've had several who got knives and cut themselves trying to get rid of their sex organs. That's their obsession!"

Perhaps better than all else, I understand obsession. It is of the mind. And it is language-bound. Sex is of the body. It has no words. I am stunned to learn that someone with an obsession of the mind can have parts of the body surgically removed. This is my brother I speak of. This is not some lunatic named Carl who becomes Carlene. This is my brother.

So while we're out in that cabin on Puget Sound, I'll tell him about LuAnn. She is the sort of woman who orders the in-season fruit and a little cottage cheese. I am the sort of woman who orders a double cheeseburger and fries. LuAnn and I are sitting in her car. She has a huge orange, and she peels it so the peel falls off in one neat strip. I have a sack of oranges, the small ones. The peel of my orange comes off in hunks about the size of a baby's

---

hijra: Males of indeterminate gender because of the nature of their bodies or the way in which they live.

nail. "Oh, you bought the *juice* oranges," LuAnn says to me. Her emphasis on the word "juice" makes me want to die or something. I lack the courage to admit my ignorance, so I smile and breathe "yes," as if I know some secret, when I'm wanting to scream at her about how my mother didn't teach me about fruit and my own blood pounds in my head wanting out, out.

> There is a pattern to this thought as there is a pattern for a jump-suit. Sew the sleeve to the leg, sew the leg to the collar. Put the gar-ment on. Sew the mouth shut. This is how I tell about being quiet because I am bad, and because I cannot stand it when he beats me or my brother.

"The first time I got caught in your clothes was when I was four years old and you were over at Sarah what's–her–name's babysitting. Dad beat me so hard I thought I was going to die. I really thought I was going to die. That was the day I made up my mind I would *never* get caught again. And I never got caught again." My brother goes on to say he continued to go through my things until I was hospitalized. A mystery is solved.

He wore my clothes. He played in my makeup. I kept saying, back then, that someone was going through my stuff. I kept saying it and saying it. I told the counselor at school. "Someone goes in my room when I'm not there, and I *know* it—goes in there and wears my clothes and goes through my stuff." I was assured by the counselor that this was not so. I was assured by my mother that this was not so. I thought my mother was doing it, snooping around for clues like mothers do. It made me a little crazy, so I started deliberately leav-ing things in a certain order so that I would be able to prove to myself that someone, indeed, was going through my belongings. No one, not one person, ever believed that my room was being ransacked; I was accused of just mak-ing it up. A paranoid fixation.

And all the time it was old Goldilocks.

So I tell my brother to promise me he'll see someone who counsels adult children from dysfunctional families. I tell him he needs to deal with the fact that he was physically abused on a daily basis. He tells me he doesn't remem-ber being beaten except on three occasions. He wants me to get into a sup-port group for families of people who are having a sex change. Support groups are people who are in the same boat. Except no one has any oars in the water.

I tell him I know how it feels to think you are in the wrong body. I tell him how I wanted my boyfriend to put a gun up inside me and blow the woman out, how I thought wearing spiked heels and low–cut dresses would somehow help my crisis, that putting on an ultrafeminine outside would mask the maleness I felt needed hiding. I tell him it's the rule, rather than the excep-tion, that people from families like ours have very spooky sexual identity problems. He tells me that his sexuality is a birth defect. I recognize the lingo. It's support-group-for-transsexuals lingo. He tells me he sits down to pee. He told his therapist that he used to wet all over the floor. His therapist said, "You

can't aim the bullets if you don't touch the gun." Lingo. My brother is hell-
bent for castration, the castration that started before he had language: the castration of abuse. He will simply finish what was set in motion long ago.

I will tell my brother about the time I took ten sacks of oranges into a
school so that I could teach metaphor. The school was for special students—
those who were socially or intellectually impaired. I had planned to have them
peel the oranges as I spoke about how much the world is like the orange. I
handed out the oranges. The students refused to peel them, not because they
wanted to make life difficult for me—they were enchanted with the gift. One
child asked if he could have an orange to take home to his little brother.
Another said he would bring me ten dollars the next day if I would give him
a sack of oranges. And I knew I was at home, that these children and I shared
something that *makes* the leap of mind the metaphor attempts. And something in me healed.

A neighbor of mine takes pantyhose and cuts them up and sews them up   20
after stuffing them. Then she puts these things into Mason jars and sells them,
you know, to put out on the mantel for conversation. They are little penises
and little scrotums, complete with hair. She calls them "Pickled Peters."
A friend of mine had a sister who had a sex change operation. This young
woman had her breasts removed and ran around the house with no shirt on
before the stitches were taken out. She answered the door one evening. A
young man had come to call on my friend. The sex-changed sister invited
him in and offered him some black bean soup as if she were perfectly normal
with her red surgical wounds and her black stitches. The young man left and
never went back. A couple years later, my friend's sister/brother died when
s/he ran a car into a concrete bridge railing. I hope for a happier ending. For
my brother, for myself, for all of us.

My brother calls. He's done his toenails: Shimmering Cinnamon. And
he's left his wife and children and purchased some nightgowns at a yard sale.
His hair is getting longer. He wears a special bra. Most of the people he works
with know about the changes in his life. His voice is not the same voice I've
heard for years; he sounds happy.
My brother calls. He's always envied me, my woman's body. The same body
I live in and have cursed for its softness. He asks me how I feel about myself.
He says, "You know, you are really our father's first-born son." He tells me he
used to want to be me because I was the only person our father almost loved.
The drama of life. After I saw that woman in the bus station eat an orange
as if it were an apple, I went out into the street and smoked a joint with some
guy I'd met on the bus. Then I hailed a cab and went to a tattoo parlor. The tattoo artist tried to talk me into getting a nice bird or butterfly design; I had chosen a design on his wall that appealed to me—a symbol I didn't know the
meaning of. It is the Yin-Yang, and it's tattooed above my right ankle bone. I

supposed my drugged, crazed consciousness knew more than I knew: that yin combines with yang to produce all that comes to be. I am drawn to androgyny.

Of course there is the nagging possibility that my brother's dilemma is genetic. Our father used to dress in drag on Halloween, and he made a beautiful woman. One year, the year my mother cut my brother's blond curls off, my father taped those curls to his own head and tied a silk scarf over the tape. Even his close friends didn't know it was him. And my youngest daughter was a body builder for a while, her lean body as muscular as a man's. And my sons are beautiful, not handsome: they look androgynous.

Then there's my grandson. I saw him when he was less than an hour old. He was naked and had hiccups. I watched as he had his first bath, and I heard him cry. He had not been named yet, but his little crib had a blue card affixed to it with tape. And on the card were the words "Baby Boy." There was no doubt in me that the words were true.

When my brother was born, my father was off flying jets in Korea. I went to the hospital with my grandfather to get my mother and this new brother. I remember how I wanted a sister, and I remember looking at him as my mother held him in the front seat of the car. I was certain he was a sister, certain that my mother was joking. She removed his diaper to show me that he was a boy. I still didn't believe her. Considering what has happened lately, I wonder if my child-skewed consciousness knew more than the anatomical proof suggested.

I try to make peace with myself. I try to understand his decision to alter himself. I try to think of him as her. I write his woman name, and I feel like I'm betraying myself. I try to be open-minded, but something in me shuts down. I think we humans are in big trouble, that many of us don't really have a clue as to what acceptable human behavior is. Something in me says no to all this, that this surgery business is the ultimate betrayal of the self. And yet, I want my brother to be happy.

It was in the city of San Antonio that my father had his surgery. I rode the bus from Kansas to Texas, and arrived at the hospital two days after the operation to find my father sitting in the solarium playing solitaire. He had a type of cancer that particularly thrived on testosterone. And so he was castrated in order to ease his pain and to stop the growth of tumors. He died six months later.

Back in the sleep of the large world of dreams, I have done surgeries under water in which I float my father's testicles back into him, and he—the brutal man he was—emerges from the pool a tan and smiling man, parting the surface of the water with his perfect head. He loves all the grief away.

I will tell my brother all I know of oranges, that if you squeeze the orange peel into a flame, small fires happen because of the volatile oil in the peel. Also, if you squeeze the peel and it gets into your cat's eyes, the cat will blink and blink. I will tell him there is no perfect rhyme for the word "orange," and that if we can just make up a good word we can be immortal. We will become obsessed with finding the right word, and I will be joyous at our legitimate pursuit.

I have purchased a black camisole with lace to send to my new sister. And a card. On the outside of the card there's a drawing of a woman sitting by a pond and a zebra is off to the left. Inside are these words: "The past is ended. Be happy." And I have asked my companions to hold me and I have cried. My self is wet and small. But it is not dark. Sometimes, if no one touches me, I will die.

Sister, you are the best craziness of the family. Brother, love what you love.

QUESTIONS FOR DISCUSSION

1. What is the purpose of the blocks of text included in paragraphs 2, 5, 8, 10, and 13?
2. In paragraphs 4, 5, and 19, Ruiz imagines how an orange could help her brother. Why would anyone consider the orange to be "a patient fruit"? What does eating an orange have to do with her brother's situation?
3. What does Ruiz reveal about her own experience in the process of responding to her brother's call? Why is she comforted to discover that her brother used to wear her clothes?
4. Ruiz tells her brother that people from dysfunctional families have "very spooky sexual identity problems"? Is this a fair response to her brother? Is it reasonable to assume that someone who has undergone a sex change did so as the result of a sexual identity "problem"?
5. Although she reports making a serious effort to empathize with her brother, Ruiz also writes, "I try to be open-minded, but something in me shuts down. I think we humans are in big trouble, that many of us don't really have a clue as to what acceptable human behavior is." Do you have a clue? How would you respond if someone close to you chose to have a sex-change operation?

SUGGESTIONS FOR WRITING

1. Think of someone who is relatively close to you and yet very different from you. Write an essay in which you explore what draws you together and what keeps you apart.
2. Consider occasions in your life when you have received important news. Write an essay conveying how this news inspired diverse feelings and memories. Like Ruiz, experiment with including blocks of memories and other responses in your principal narrative.
3. Write an essay in which you discuss an aspect of popular culture from the perspective of a gender other than your own.

LINKS ■ ■ ■

■ WITHIN THE BOOK

In "Levi's" (pages 57–59), Marilyn Schiel also writes about the relationship beween siblings of different gender.

■ ELSEWHERE IN PRINT

Brown, Mildred, C., and Chloe A. Rounsley. *True Selves: Understanding Transsexualism*. San Francisco: Jossey-Bass, 1996.

Califia, Pat. *Sex Changes: The Politics of Transgenderism*. San Francisco: Cleis, 1997.

Colapinto, John. *As Nature Made Him: The Boy Who Was Raised as a Girl*. New York: Harper, 2000.

Fausto-Sterling, Anne. *Sexing the Body: Gender Politics and the Construction of Sexuality*. New York: Basic, 2000.

Ruiz, Judy. *Talking Razzmatazz: Poems*. Columbia: U of Missouri P, 1991.

■ ONLINE

- Medicine and Transgender Politics
  <http://www.bcholmes.org/tg/tgmedicine.html>
- Sexual Identity
  <http://www.umkc.edu/sites/hsw/gendid/sexident.html>
- Transgender Family Resources
  <http://www.hrc.org/familynet/subsection.asp?subsection=28>
- Transgender Forum
  <http://www.tgforum.com>

Writing to Understand Reading

Everyone has had the experience of trying to read something that is difficult to understand. But another type of reading experience is even more common: thinking that we understand what we have read when there are actually dozens of points we have passed right over. Although much is still unknown about reading, we do know that people read in different ways and that a dozen people reading the same text are likely to see and remember a dozen different versions. With so many words printed on a page, the eye is unlikely to give equal attention to every line. Readers may agree about what a text seems to say overall, or they may disagree strongly. But whether they agree or disagree, they will have reached their conclusions by different routes.

When reading, many people skip over words or allusions they do not understand, and they do it so routinely they sometimes don't realize they are doing it. They are also likely to pause at different points—to answer the phone, take a sip of coffee, or simply rest their eyes. These pauses can influence which parts of a text are remembered most clearly. Moreover, reading triggers specific associations for each reader derived from his or her own personal experience. We all bring our own unique experiences, personality, and knowledge of the world to any text we read. To a significant degree, we *create* the meaning we derive from reading.

Most critics now agree that there is no single correct way to interpret a text. This principle can yield results that are both liberating and enriching, since freeing readers to explore individual responses can add to the overall understanding of what a text can mean. Twelve people reading the same text can offer twelve different responses, all of them valuable. However, if more time and care have been invested in them, some responses will be more illuminating than others.

One of the best ways of testing your understanding of a text—and improving on that understanding—is to write about what you read. Whether you are summarizing the information a work includes, evaluating the author's achievement, or exploring the ideas that have been raised, writing about reading requires you to think about the text. This usually means returning to it and studying it carefully. To illustrate how writing can lead to a better understanding of reading, this chapter focuses on writing about literature as it has been traditionally defined: fiction, drama, and poetry. Some critics define literature more broadly to include everything available in print. Whatever your definition, you can apply most of the techniques discussed here to almost anything you read.

RECOGNIZING WAYS TO APPROACH A TEXT

Like most types of writing, writing about literature can take a variety of different forms.

- You can *summarize* a work by briefly stating its key points.
- You can *evaluate* a work by identifying its strengths and weaknesses.
- You can *explicate* a work by providing a line-by-line explanation of what it means and how it achieves that meaning.
- You can *analyze* a work by discussing one or more of its parts.

The approach you take should be determined by your rhetorical situation. Your instructor may assign a specific approach, or you may need to decide for yourself which one best suits your audience and the material you will be writing about.

    Summarizing is useful when a work is long, tells a story, offers information, or makes an argument. When writing about literature, you may frequently find yourself needing to summarize a novel, story, play, or occasionally even a poem. A summary of a literary work can stand alone as a separate assignment, but more often it is part of a paper that then goes on to either evaluate or analyze the summarized work. As a general rule, you should write a summary only if you have been specifically asked to do so or if you believe that your audience may not be familiar with the work you want to discuss. An audience that has read the work recently might ask, "Why are you telling me this? I know it already." However, an audience unfamiliar with the work may have trouble following your discussion without benefit of a brief summary. For this reason, a writer reviewing a new book in a newspaper will usually include some summary along with evaluation. You, too, may have occasion to summarize a work that you want to examine critically. But be cautious: Some writers drift into writing a summary because they find it easier to retell a story than to interpret it. When choosing to write a summary, make sure that your choice is deliberate, that your summary serves a clear purpose, that it covers the main points, and that it is as short as you can make it. (For additional information on summarizing, see pages 101–102.)

    Evaluating, like summarizing (which it often includes), makes the most sense when the work is unfamiliar to your audience. Both summaries and reviews attempt to provide a sense of the work as a whole, but whereas summaries are neutral and focus exclusively on context, reviews also include opinions. In addition to providing a brief summary of the work, a reviewer usually identifies its theme and sometimes compares it with other works by the author that the audience might already know. (This is especially likely in reviews of a newly published book by a well-known author.)

At the heart of any review, however, is the reviewer's evaluation of the work's merit. Is the work original or predictable, thorough or superficial? These are among the questions a reviewer might address as he or she offers at least one piece of evidence (such as a short quotation) that will support each opinion. Readers expect these opinions, since one of their reasons for reading a review is to decide whether they want to read the work in question. The extent to which readers are influenced by a review often depends on the degree to which they trust the reviewer's judgment—either because they are already familiar with the reviewer or simply because the reviewer writes so well that he or she seems to be credible. The review itself is unlikely to make an extensive argument, since it attempts to accomplish several goals quickly. Most reviews average no more than a thousand words. That might sound like a long assignment if you are staring at a blank sheet of paper or computer screen with no idea what to write about, but it's very little when you consider all that a reviewer is expected to cover. (For additional information about evaluation, see Chapter 4.)

An *explication* also attempts to cover an entire work, but in this case the emphasis is on interpreting the work rather than summarizing it or appraising its quality. If you choose to explicate a work, you are responsible for explaining the function and meaning of everything in it. Consequently, explication is usually reserved for short works, especially poems (or excerpts, such as an important speech within a longer work). A line-by-line explication of a long novel such as *War and Peace* would require many years of work and interest a relatively small audience. Explicating a poem like "If This Is Paradise," however, may well be the best way to help other readers understand its meaning, and it can be done within a reasonable amount of time and space.

When you are looking for topics for writing about literature, *analysis* offers the greatest range of possibilities, for it opens up room for multiple interpretations of different parts of a work. Analyzing a work requires you to recognize its parts, and many works have ready-made divisions in them. A novel, for instance, is usually divided into chapters (and sometimes groups of chapters); a play, into acts and scenes. A short story might consist of two or three separate scenes, and a poem might be divided into stanzas. You can choose to write about one of these divisions—limiting yourself, for example, to the chapter in which Huckleberry Finn pretends to be a girl or to the suicide scene in *Romeo and Juliet*. But there are many other ways of dividing a work of literature. Analytical papers can be written on the following features:

- The role of a story within the story
- The significance of specific dialogue
- The portrayal of one of the characters

- The setting and why it is appropriate
- The theme or central idea that the work conveys to you
- The use of figurative language or symbolism to convey more than one meaning
- A pattern of imagery that evokes specific pictures, sounds, or smells
- The organization of the work and why it is structured as it is

Each of these possibilities can be modified depending on your interests, the needs of your readers, and the nature of the text. You may decide to broaden or narrow your focus. For example, you may decide to contrast two characters if you have the space and if doing so will be more illuminating than analyzing a single character. Or you could focus on one of several symbols that you have identified if you have a lot to say about it and relatively little to say about the others. But whatever part of the whole you select, you should try to make your analysis of that part contribute to your readers' understanding of the work as a whole.

PREPARING TO WRITE

On some occasions you may feel motivated to write about something immediately after you have read it. In fact, a good way to improve both your reading and your writing is to keep a journal devoted specifically to recording responses to what you read. The entries in a reading journal typically include brief summaries that can help you review for exams, comments evaluating the strengths and weaknesses of the material, questions that you'd like to raise during class discussion of the assignment, and reflections of your own that were inspired along the way.

Even if you do not regularly keep a reading journal, you should try to honor any impulse to write about what you read. If you sometimes wish that you had more to say when people discuss their reading, you are especially likely to benefit from getting something down on paper whenever you feel stimulated by a particular assignment. Imagine yourself having the chance to talk with the author of the material you've read. What would you praise? What would you ask about? And what, if anything, would you complain about? Sometimes, it's hard to find the words to get such a conversation started; but once you've started, you've increased the likelihood of touching on something that can lead to a better understanding of the work.

When you are assigned an out-of-class paper about literature, there are a number of things you can do to make sure you'll have something to say when you begin to write.

- **Note your preliminary response.** The first step in writing to understand reading is defining your preliminary response. If you have the option of choosing to write about one of several works, ask yourself which inspired the strongest reaction. Which did you like best or least? If you are required to write about a specific work, you can modify this question by asking yourself which aspects of the work appealed to you and which did not. Discovering a text (or part of one) that you enjoyed can help you write a good paper, since you will be writing about material that you are willing to spend time with. However, good papers can also result from writing about readings that you did *not* like: Consider how much fun Mark Twain must have had demolishing *The Deerslayer* in "Fenimore Cooper's Literary Offenses" (see pages 330–339). In either case, you are writing about material to which you have a clear response, and this is usually easier than starting with material about which you have no particular feelings one way or the other.

- **Reread the work about which you have chosen to write.** Once you know what work you will be writing about, the next step is to reexamine it. Although you may not be able to reread an entire novel (or other long work), you should always be able to reread a story, poem, or play before writing an out-of-class paper about it. As you read, annotate the work by marking key passages and making marginal notations as questions and ideas occur to you. You may already have annotated the text during your initial reading, but you are almost certain to notice new dimensions as you reread. Be sure to look up any words or allusions that you passed over on your initial reading, and be alert for the repetition of words or ideas. Deliberate repetition often signals a way to better understand a text. You might ask yourself, for example, why "Abalone, Abalone, Abalone" is not simply titled "Abalone," or you might note the repeated references to Mrs. Wright's isolation in *Trifles*. You should also note any pattern of related references, such as a number of different references to the weather or to clothing. Most important, you should reconsider your initial response to the work. If you enjoyed reading it at first, how well does it hold up under another reading? Can you identify specific parts that gave you pleasure? If you are writing about a text that you initially disliked, are you coming to like it better as you spend more time with it? Or are you coming to a clearer understanding of why you find it objectionable?

- **Ask yourself questions about the work.** You should not feel as if you must understand every dimension of the text as you are reading it. If you continue to think about it after you have reread it, ideas will continue to occur to you. Asking yourself questions is a good way to keep these thoughts coming. For example, you can use the pentad (pages 12–14) to ask yourself such questions as "How does the setting of this work relate to what happens?" Or "What act is most central, and who is responsible for it?" Moving beyond the pentad, you might ask, "Why has this work been arranged in the order in which it appears? Why does it begin and end where it does?" Or "Are there any inconsistencies? Are there changes that are not accounted for or any departures from what seems to be the main idea?" You can ask yourself questions like these whenever you have a few minutes to devote to your own thoughts. Some of the best ideas in your paper may result from answering a question you are thinking about as you walk across campus, wash some dishes, or stand in line at the post office. Preparing to write a paper about literature means engaging yourself imaginatively and intellectually in the work you are going to write about. Make your mind receptive to ideas by frequently turning your thoughts to the work during the period between receiving the assignment and writing your first draft.

■ **Test your choice.** If you think actively about a work that inspired a strong response, you will probably generate more than one possible topic for writing. At this point you should evaluate these topics for their appropriateness. For instance, if you have been asked to write a paper of a specified length, some topics may be too narrow and others too broad. You should also think about your audience's potential interest in the topic. Even if you write best when imagining a broader audience, ask yourself what you know about your instructor. How would he or she respond to a paper that seemed to do nothing more than restate points that had already been made in class? Conversely, how receptive would your instructor be to a paper that challenged the views set forth in a class lecture? These are questions that have to be answered on an individual basis. But as a general rule, good writers are willing to take chances, and most instructors welcome a paper with fresh ideas as long as they have been well thought out and are well supported.

■ **Define your thesis.** Once you have decided on the topic for your paper, you will know what parts of the literary work require additional study and which parts you will not need to discuss. But having a topic is not the same as having a thesis. Your topic identifies the aspect of the text that you will be writing about; your thesis is the central idea you intend to convey about that topic. Although your thesis may occur to you immediately after your initial reading, you will often know your topic before you feel certain about your thesis. If you are writing a paper about "Winners," for example, you may decide to write about the relationship between the two central characters in that story, but then you need to decide whether that relationship changes or remains stable. Your thesis may be clear to you before you begin to write, or—as is often the case—the thesis may emerge as you draft.

■ **Gather your evidence.** A thesis requires support. When interpreting or evaluating literature, think of yourself as writing a type of argument requiring evidence for whatever you claim. Although knowing something of the historical context in which a work was written can often add to your understanding of it, the data supporting your claim should usually come from the text itself. (An exception is a research paper in which evidence comes from a number of sources. But, even in this case, much of the evidence will come normally from the text that generated the topic.) Think critically about the evidence you discover, and be prepared to search for additional support, if necessary. Be careful at this stage not to ignore anything that seems to conflict with what you hope to prove. Considering apparent contradictions can prompt you to anticipate objections from your reader and thus help you strengthen your argument. Or you may decide that you need to revise your thesis so that it more accurately reflects your evidence.

WRITING THE PAPER

If you have considered your audience, chosen your topic, defined your thesis, and gathered evidence to support it, your next challenge is to decide how to organize your material.

Some papers are organized on the basis of the work that is being written about. If you are explicating a poem, for example, you can go through it in order line by line. If you are writing a character analysis, you can trace the character's development throughout the work. And if you are discussing a theme or the use of a specific literary device, you can present your evidence in the order in which it appeared in the text. At times, however, you may wish to have more flexibility, moving around in the work from point to point. Instead of tracing a character's development from the beginning to the end, you can organize your analysis in paragraphs or sections devoted to the character's various personality traits and arrange your material in whatever order best suits your purpose. Or instead of writing a line-by-line explication of a poem, you can organize your paper to focus in turn on various dimensions such as imagery, metaphor, and rhyme.

But whatever your preliminary plan, you should be prepared to modify it if drafting generates good ideas that you didn't realize you had until you started to write. When writing about literature, you may very well find yourself arguing a position different from the one you had originally planned—or you may find that you have much to say about what you expected to be a minor point in your paper, in which case you need to reconsider your focus. Discoveries like these are a normal part of the writing process, and they can be both illuminating and fun. Remember that you are writing to understand reading, not writing to honor an outline.

Because you cannot understand fully and exactly what you want to say until you have finished drafting a paper, revision is essential. Although there is nothing wrong with drafting a paper that ends up arguing something different from the thesis with which it begins, there *is* something wrong with handing it in that way. When revising a paper about literature, be sure to ask yourself if you wrote what you intended. You may need to revise your thesis, make serious cuts, or introduce evidence to support your claims. (For additional information about revision, see pages 26–30.)

Here are a few additional points to keep in mind when revising a paper about literature.

- **Think about how well you have responded to the needs of your audience.** Have you summarized material that didn't need to be summarized or failed to summarize material your audience may not have read? Have you explained any unusual words or references that readers may not understand? Conversely, have you insulted the intelligence of your readers by identifying a reference they would certainly know?

- **Consider how you sound.** When writing a paper about literature, you are assuming the role of a teacher trying to help others to better understand the work. Try not to sound apologetic by overusing phrases like "in my opinion," for they diminish your authority as a writer. But be careful not to go to the other extreme and sound contemptuous of anyone who might disagree with you. Strive for a thoughtful, confident, and reasonable tone. You should sound as if you believe what you are writing and want others to believe it too, but you should not sound as if you believe that you alone are right.

- **Reexamine the number and length of any quotations within the paper.** Quotations are often necessary to support claims, but some quotations may be longer than they have to be, and too many of them can keep your own voice from reaching readers. Remember that you are the writer of your paper; quotations should be subordinate to what you have to say. If your own words seem to do little more than link quotations together, you will need to become more actively involved in the paper. Keep quotations as short as possible, and be sure to weave them smoothly into what you are saying and make their significance clear by discussing what you quote. As a general rule, the longer the quote, the more you need to say about it. But even short quotations sometimes call for extensive discussion.

Also, be sure to observe the conventions appropriate for writing about literature when you revise your paper:

- **Use the present tense** (sometimes called "the literary present") for writing about what happens in a work of fiction, drama, or poetry.

    Tom Sawyer persuades other boys to paint his fence.

- **Identify writers initially by their full name**—William Shakespeare, Joyce Carol Oates—and subsequently by their last name, regardless of gender: Shakespeare and Oates, not William or Ms. Oates.

- **Follow MLA guidelines for documentation** unless you are given other instructions. (See pages 38–43.)

  When quoting from a play that is divided into acts, scenes, and line numbers, identify quotations with these three numbers (separated by periods) rather than with a page reference.

  > Iago warns Othello that jealousy is a "green-eyed monster" (3.3.167).

  When quoting from a poem, provide references to line numbers (without an abbreviation for line). Use a slash to indicate line divisions when quoting two or three lines. Leave a blank space before and after the slash. (As with a prose quotation, set off longer quotations by indenting ten spaces from the left margin.)

  > One of the most difficult questions this poem raises is what the speaker means by saying, "I live between the heron and the wren, / Beasts of the hill and serpents of the den" (5–6).

After you have revised your paper, of course, you will still need to edit it—refining your style and making any necessary changes in grammar, punctuation, and spelling. (For a discussion of editing, see pages 30–31.) But as you make these final changes, you can feel confident about what you have written if you know that you have looked closely at a work, chosen a clearly defined approach for writing about it, and supported any claims you have made. Such a paper will reveal a serious effort to understand what another writer has created.

ABALONE, ABALONE, ABALONE

Toshio Mori

Born in Oakland, California, Toshio Mori (1910–1980) grew up working in his family's nursery business. Influenced by such writers as Sherwood Anderson and William Saroyan, he eventually published numerous stories focused on life within Japanese-American communities. Although these stories have come to be widely admired, success did not come easily to Mori. The publication of his first collection of stories, Yokohama, California, *was pushed back from 1942 to 1949 because of the Second World War. Like many Japanese Americans on the West Coast, Mori was held in an internment camp from 1941 to 1944 even though he was an American citizen.*

The following story, which is very short, has only two characters and a very simple plot. But like many longer stories, it has what is often called a "turning point"—a moment in the story when a character changes as the result of something that has happened. Be alert for the turning point as you read this story, and decide whether the change is beneficial. It may help you to know that an abalone is a type of large mollusk found in warm seas. Its flesh is eaten, and its ornamental shell is a source of mother-of-pearl.

Before Mr. Abe went away I used to see him quite often at his nursery. He was a carnation grower just as I am one today. At noontime I used to go to his front porch and look at his collection of abalone shells.

They were lined up side by side against the side of his house on the front porch. I was curious as to why he bothered to collect them. It was a lot of bother polishing them. I had often seen him sit for hours on Sundays and noon hours polishing each one of the shells with the greatest of care. Of course I knew these abalone shells were pretty. When the sun strikes the insides of these shells it is something beautiful to behold. But I could not understand why he continued collecting them when the front porch was practically full.

He used to watch for me every noon hour. When I appeared he would look out of his room and bellow, "Hello, young man!"

"Hello, Abe-*san,*" I said. "I came to see the abalone shells."

Then he came out of the house and we sat on the front porch. But he did not tell me why he collected these shells. I think I have asked him dozens of times but each time he closed his mouth and refused to answer.

"Are you going to pass this collection of abalone shells on to your children?" I said.

"No," he said. "I want my children to collect for themselves. I wouldn't give it to them."

"Why?" I said. "When you die?"

Mr. Abe shook his head. "No. Not even when I die," he said. "I couldn't give the children what I see in these shells. The children must go out for themselves and find their own shells."

"Why, I thought this collecting hobby of abalone shells was a simple affair," I said.

"It is simple. Very simple," he said. But he would not tell me further.

For several years I went steadily to his front porch and looked at the beautiful shells. His collection was getting larger and larger. Mr. Abe sat and talked to me and on each occasion his hands were busy polishing shells.

"So you are still curious?" he said.

"Yes," I said.

One day while I was hauling the old soil from the benches and replacing it with new soil I found an abalone shell half buried in the dust between the benches. So I stopped working. I dropped my wheelbarrow and went to the faucet and washed the abalone shell with soap and water. I had a hard time taking the grime off the surface.

After forty minutes of cleaning and polishing the old shell it became interesting. I began polishing both the outside and the inside of the shell. I found after many minutes of polishing I could not do very much with the exterior side. It had scabs of the sea which would not come off by scrubbing and the surface itself was rough and hard. And in the crevices the grime stuck so that even with a needle it did not become clean.

But on the other side, the inside of the shell, the more I polished the more lustre I found. It had me going. There were colors which I had not seen in the abalone shells before or anywhere else. The different hues, running berserk in all directions, coming together in harmony. I guess I could say they were not unlike a rainbow which men once symbolized. As soon as I thought of this I thought of Mr. Abe.

I remember running to his place, looking for him. "Abe-*san*!" I said when I found him. "I know why you are collecting the abalone shells!"

He was watering the carnation plants in the greenhouse. He stopped watering and came over to where I stood. He looked me over closely for awhile and then his face beamed.

"All right," he said. "Do not say anything. Nothing, mind you. When you have found the reason why you must collect and preserve them, you do not have to say anything more."

"I want you to see it, Abe-*san*," I said.

"All right. Tonight," he said. "Where did you find it?"

"In my old greenhouse, half buried in the dust," I said.

He chuckled. "That is pretty far from the ocean," he said, "but pretty close to you."

At each noon hour I carried my abalone shell and went over to Mr. Abe's front porch. While I waited for his appearance I kept myself busy polishing the inside of the shell with a rag.

One day I said, "Abe-*san,* now I have three shells."

"Good!" he said. "Keep it up!"

"I have to keep them all," I said. "They are very much alike and very much different."

"Well! Well!" he said and smiled.

That was the last I saw of Abe-*san.* Before the month was over he sold his   30
nursery and went back to Japan. He brought his collection along and thereafter I had no one to talk to at the noon hour. This was before I discovered the fourth abalone shell, and I should like to see Abe-*san* someday and watch his eyes roll as he studies me whose face is now akin to the collectors of shells or otherwise.

QUESTIONS FOR DISCUSSION

1. How do you picture the narrator of this story? How old is he? What is he like at the beginning of the story? Is he the same at the end? If not, how does he change, and where does this change begin?
2. Why does Mr. Abe refuse to discuss his collection? Why doesn't he plan to leave it to his children?
3. The act of polishing an abalone shell would seem to be very simple. But is it as simple as it seems? Why is it worth doing?
4. This story begins and ends with references to Mr. Abe going away, and paragraphs 8 and 9 mention his eventual death. What does this sense of passing away contribute to the story?
5. How do you interpret the title? Could someone understand the title without reading the story?

SUGGESTIONS FOR WRITING

1. Describe the setting of "Abalone, Abalone, Abalone," and explain why it is appropriate for what happens.
2. Write an essay focused on Mr. Abe, conveying your sense of his character and what details in the story led you to this view of him.
3. A symbol is something that means both what it is and something more than it is. The rainbow (mentioned in paragraph 17) has been used as a symbol for new beginnings. If you think the abalone shell is a symbol, write an essay explaining what it symbolizes and how you came to this conclusion.

LINKS ■ ■ ■

■ **WITHIN THE BOOK**

In "Monologue to the Maestro" (pages 626–631), Ernest Hemingway also shows a mentor trying to convey the importance of observation.

■ **ELSEWHERE IN PRINT**

Mori, Toshio. *The Chauvinist and Other Stories.* Los Angeles: UCLA, 1979.
---. *Unfinished Message: Selected Works of Toshio Mori.* Berkeley: Heyday,
    2000.
---. *Yokohama, California.* Caldwell: Caxton, 1949.
Nagai, Kafu. *American Stories.* Trans. Mitsuko Iriye. New York: Columbia
    UP, 2000.

■ **ONLINE**

- Abalone
  <http://www.taosnet.com/platinum/data/light/species/
  abalone.html>

- Japanese-American Literature
  <http://www.ku.edu/!~rmelton/literature/asianlit/japanlit.htm>

- Selected Works of Toshio Mori
  <http://www.ralphmag.org/AL/toshio-mori.html>

WINNERS

Lon Otto

Imagine finding a way to win a contest you do not deserve to win. You know you shouldn't cheat but are tempted by the prospect of an attractive prize. You are also being encouraged to cheat by your best friend—someone a little older and more aggressive than you are. What happens then? As you read the following story by Lon Otto about two boys trying to win a fishing contest, be alert for ways they manage to justify their behavior and eventually come to see themselves as victims.

"Winners" was first published in Cover Me *(1988), Otto's second collection of stories. In her review of this collection for the* New York Times Book Review, *Joyce Reiser Kornblatt writes, "Lon Otto's talents are formidable and the best stories in* Cover Me *demonstrate them impressively. Playful, contemplative, outrageous and comforting, this is a writer whose gifts continue to develop. At his best, he is an adventurous stylist whose wise vision shines through the fires of language he can set burning quite beautifully on the page."*

At first we thought it was a floating plastic bleach bottle, maybe somebody's illegal minnow-trap marker tangled in the lilies. It might have been a clump of the lily pads themselves, flipped over by the wind, their pale undersides glaring in the late-morning sun. We didn't recognize what it was until we were almost on top of it, our boat nosed into the weeds that were keeping it from washing ashore. Keith and I looked at each other.

This was the summer after my parents got divorced. My father had taken me and my best friend on a fishing trip to Rhinelander, Wisconsin, where there was a contest in progress at Schramm's Sporting Goods. While Dad was paying for our licenses, Keith and I had checked out the refrigerated glass case in front of the store, with the leading bass, northern, muskie, walleye, crappie, lake trout, and sunfish lying frozen on a bed of chipped ice. The prizes for each category were displayed in the front window, from a stiff muskie rod and heavy reel with star drag and oversize handle down to a delicate fly rod and tiny reel, which some sportsmen evidently used to catch sunnies.

"What was the prize for walleye?" Keith asked now, peering over the side of the boat.

"I don't know. That Penn Silver Eagle and a Stratoflex, I think. Christ, this would have won easy."

It was the biggest walleye we'd ever seen, eight or nine pounds, we guessed, floating belly up, white, and a little bloated, so it rode high in the water. The turtles hadn't gotten to it yet, as far as we could tell, but who knew what we'd find on the dorsal side. The turtles usually start on the tail, though, and that seemed still intact.

5

"If we'd caught this baby, we'd be set. We'd've been winners for sure."

Keith said, "Let's do. Let's catch it." And he reached for the landing net.

"We can't," I said. "We'd never get away with it. It's already dead."

"You see any live fish in Schramm's display case? That crummy little wall-eye in there—was it alive?"

"You got to *catch* them, man. They write up what lure you used and everything." 10

"Okay." He lifted his rod, cast the jitterbug toward open water, and slowly retrieved it, the lure wobbling and bubbling across the surface in that fat, juicy action that is always so satisfying, even when nothing is biting. He paused, teasing it every once in a while, and led it slowly up to the walleye's mouth. He jiggled the lure against the closed bony plates and yanked hard, setting the hooks.

"Got it!" he screamed. The hooks were on the outside, but it sometimes ends up that way even with living fish. "Net him, man, before he gets away! God, what a fighter!" As Keith hauled the big stiff fish this way and that, churning the water, I reached for the net and scooped it underneath the walleye's tail. Dad had taught me always to net a fish headfirst, especially one as big as this, so that when it jumps, it just gets in deeper, but this guy wasn't going anywhere. I lifted it with effort, half the fish sticking out awkwardly, and hoisted it over the gunwale. Keith helped by pulling up on the line. We lowered it between us.

"I thought it might just fall apart," I said. "But it's still pretty good."

"Damn right," Keith said. "It's almost perfect." The dorsal fin was splayed up like a sail, chewed here and there, but nothing worse than a long and strenuous life might have done. The huge eyes were a beautiful milky color, and the scales were about five shades lighter than they should have been, except where some little black things were growing. The mouth, I saw, wasn't really closed but gaped open a little, exposing the tiger's teeth that are always a surprise in such a studious-looking fish as a walleye.

I was beginning to think it might work, we'd get away with it, we'd be winners. Then Keith gave that sickening laugh that was one of the reasons why most people at school didn't like him too much. "I was just thinking," he said. "What if the mouth opened up some more, sort of real slow, and then an enormous leech or something crawled out?" 15

I was used to Keith, and his sense of humor didn't bother me, except that I started worrying again. "How long do you think it's going to last?" I asked. "Maybe we should get it back in the water, so it'll stay cool." We pried out the hooks, which hadn't sunk in past the barbs, and jammed the point of my stringer through the soft part just behind the hard lips. Then we heaved it over the side and tied the other end of the stringer to an oarlock. I cranked up the outboard (this was the first summer that Dad let me handle a motor by myself) and took us in slowly, the high-riding walleye plowing across the wake like a battleship.

Nobody was around the dock when we tied up, so we lugged the walleye up to the cabin, laid it in the shade, and went inside to get something to drink. Dad had taken the ski boat up a chain of little lakes to the Tomahawk Flowage, where he was going to cast for muskies. Fortunately Keith was thirteen, almost a year older than me, and knew how to drive a stick. We would be able to get to town and back before my father came in.

The dinky freezer compartment of the cabin's refrigerator held only a metal tray of ice, a heavily frosted box of frozen vegetables, and a couple packages of bass fillets. We emptied everything in the freezer into a garbage bag, drank some Cokes, and tossed in the rest of the soft drinks and beers from the refrigerator. It would be enough, we thought, to keep the fish cool.

When we heard some furious barking, we rushed outside and found the resort owner's German shepherd rolling around on top of our walleye. We drove him off by throwing beer cans at him and were relieved to find only minor damage. The scales were torn up along one side, but the commotion had actually squashed down some of the bloated quality, so things were about even.

We loaded the walleye into the garbage sack, arranged the ice cubes and   20
cans and frozen food around it, and carried it up to where the car was parked. I was going to put it in the trunk, but Keith pointed out that it would be hot as an oven in there from standing in the sun all morning. The fish would explode. So we placed it on the back seat, opened all the windows, and headed for Rhinelander, about twenty miles away.

Keith was not really such a good driver, tending to go off onto the shoulder when he laughed and taking turns a little too generously. We were making good time, however, when he slammed on the brakes to avoid hitting a squirrel. You could never tell about Keith: sometimes he would go out of his way to kill something, but at other times he was very considerate. I banged my head on the windshield, and it wasn't until we heard cans rolling around that we noticed the stuff on the back seat had been flung onto the floor and scattered. The walleye's tail was sticking out of the garbage bag, and the smell started to get to us. Keith stopped laughing and drove as fast as he dared, faster than the old Audi had ever been driven, trying to outdistance the odor or blow it out the windows.

When we got to the outskirts of town, a complication occurred to me. "How are we going to share the prize?" I asked.

"What do you mean, 'share'? *I* caught it."

I knew he was kidding, but still it was going to be awkward. "No, really," I said, "what are we going to do? There's only one rod and reel. We could match for it, I guess, or maybe they would give us two of something not so expensive. We don't need anything that fancy."

"I did catch it," Keith said again.   25

"I netted it," I said, unable to believe he would betray me that way. "That was most of the work."

"You tried to talk me out of it. You said we couldn't enter a found fish in the contest. I don't want any cheap shit. I want that Penn Silver Eagle and I want that Stratoflex." He stomped on the accelerator for emphasis, and we screamed around some old farmer's truck.

"This is *my* trip!" I shouted over the roar of wind. "*My* dad paid for everything. This is *my* car. *I'm* the broken-home kid, and if anyone deserves that prize, it's me! You're just my goddamn *guest,* man."

We were passing the strip of motels, roadhouses, and fast-food joints, and Keith slowed down a little as a concession to the increased traffic, though we were still overtaking everything in sight. He started to laugh, and I hit him as hard as I could on the muscle of his arm. The car bounced up on a divider strip, then swerved back and came to a stop at the entrance of an A&W.

"Okay," Keith said, "lighten up. I was just kidding."   30

"I knew that," I said. "So what are we going to do?"

Somebody started honking at us to get out of the way. Keith gave him the finger and drove slowly toward town, half on the road and half on the shoulder, thinking. Finally he said, "Okay, here's what we do. You get the Stratoflex, I get the Silver Eagle." I started to protest, but he slapped his hand over my mouth. "Wait. We keep them together, though. We take turns using them—me on odd days, you on even days. When we get enough money saved up, you buy a new reel and I buy a new rod." He slammed the steering wheel decisively.

I had to admit that it was a good plan. "But I want the Silver Eagle. You take the Stratoflex."

"Done."

"You take even days, and I'll take odd."   35

He shook his head. "No way, man. I got to have odd."

"Why?"

"I just have to, is all."

I agreed to take even days, and we drove the rest of the way into town and parked right in front of Schramm's. We dumped out the cans and frozen foods that were still in the garbage sack, pushed the fish back in, and carried it into the store. When we passed the display case out front, Keith gave a thumbs-down sign to the five-pound walleye lying there on ice.

It was almost noon, and the store was pretty crowded, but people gave us   40
plenty of room. An old guy came up then—Schramm, I guessed—and asked what was going on. He was one of these really big guys who are always a little bent over, like bears. Keith dropped the sack onto the floor, pulled out the walleye, and laid it on the sack. Schramm backed off a step and swore into his hand.

"We're entering it in the contest," Keith said.

"Are you crazy? Get that damn thing out of here." The fish really didn't look as good as it had an hour or so before, but you could still tell it was a walleye.

"I know it took us a little too long to get this baby in," Keith said, "but it's got four pounds on that walleye out there, easy. Nothing's going to beat this fish."

"I can't put that piece of carrion in my display case. It looks like it's been dead in the water for a week. Where are your parents, boys?"

I said, "My dad's over at the courthouse, filing some sort of brief. He said   45
that since we caught the fish, we should collect our prize."

Schramm stared down at the fish, keeping his hand over his mouth and nose. While we were standing there, three or four people came in, sniffed, and backed out. A couple of men were looking at what was going on, but they were keeping their distance.

"God almighty," Schramm gasped at last. "Look, I'll give you five bucks for the effort. But get that thing out of here."

"Like hell!" I said. "That Silver Eagle alone is worth fifty. We want the whole deal. We're winners, man. So pay up."

Schramm looked up and saw a little group of customers and clerks gathering at the far end of the aisle, where they kept water-skis and coils of bright yellow tow rope. "Look, son," he said to me, "maybe you better leave and come back with your father."

"He said we should take care of it ourselves. He's real busy."   50

"Even if the fish was fresh," Schramm said, "the contest isn't over for another three days. Something bigger could come in."

"So we'll wait," Keith said. "Put this monster in the case, and then we'll see if anything can beat it. Nothing's going to beat it—you know that."

One of the customers gagged suddenly and ran for the back door. A couple of the men laughed, in a low, choked fashion. Schramm cursed painstakingly under his breath. He went behind the cash register, rang it open, and took out some bills. He came back and said, "I'll give you each ten dollars. That's twenty dollars for a stinking sack of garbage. Take it and get the hell out of here, or I'll throw you out."

Keith and I looked at each other and shrugged. Schramm shouted, "Eddie!" One of the clerks who had been watching from the water-ski aisle came forward, holding a handkerchief over his nose.

"Need some help, Mr. Crane?" he mumbled into the rag.   55

"Take this out back and bury it."

"Where?"

"Deep! Now!"

While Eddie, breathless, gathered up the huge fish in the garbage bag as best he could and headed for the back of the store, scattering the onlookers, the big man handed us each a ten-dollar bill. "Don't try this again," he warned us. "Now get out of here. Spend that somewhere else."

When we got out to the car, Keith started laughing. "We did it, man!   60
Twenty bucks!"

"Shit," I said. "That bastard cheated us."

"Come on."

"It wasn't even Schramm," I said. "It was 'Mr. Crane.' We *won* that contest. It's like he stole that rod and reel from us. We were winners, and that son of a bitch cheated us. And we let him do it."

Keith looked down at the ten-dollar bill in his hand as if it were dirt. We climbed into the car in silence, and while Keith drove, I twisted around and retrieved a couple cans of Coke from the mess in back. Keith steered one-handed and took a long pull of the pop. Suddenly he laughed his worst laugh, spurting Coke out of his nostrils, and yanked the car onto a side street.

"I got the perfect plan," he said when he was able to talk again. "We go   65
back right away and see where that guy buries our walleye. Then after dark we go dig it up, break open the display case, and put it in where it belongs. That fat jerk will piss in his pants."

"Forget it," I said bitterly, "just drive," knowing that we were helpless against adult treachery and betrayal. I hurled the half-empty can out the window and watched it tumble, streaming pop like smoke from a crashing jet. "Come on, Keith," I said, "floor this sucker!" The town fled from us in confusion.

QUESTIONS FOR DISCUSSION

1. The boys in this story are young adolescents; one is thirteen, the other nearly a year younger. How does Otto convey a sense of their age? How does he differentiate between the two?
2. When he first sees the dead walleye, the narrator says, "If we'd caught this baby, we'd be set. We'd've been winners for sure." At the end of the story he tells the clerk in the sporting goods store, "We're winners, man. So pay up." What accounts for his change in perspective?
3. What does it mean to be a winner? In what sense are these boys "winners"?
4. Is it significant that the narrator's parents had divorced before this story takes place?
5. How do you interpret the closing line of this story, "The town fled from us in confusion"?

SUGGESTIONS FOR WRITING

1. The boys in this story are left feeling "helpless against adult treachery and betrayal." Write an essay exploring why they feel this way. Focus on information about the boys and how they are treated that you find in the story itself.
2. Consider the setting of this story, when it is set as well as where. Write an essay explaining how this setting helps account for the boys' behavior.
3. Write an essay focused on the relationship between the two boys in this story. Does it change, or does it remain the same?

LINKS ■ ■ ■

■ **WITHIN THE BOOK**

For a sense of how children in another culture compete, see Nicholas D. Kristof's "In Japan, Nice Guys (and Girls) Finish Together" (pages 207–210).

■ **ELSEWHERE IN PRINT**

Agee, Jonis. *A .38 Special and a Broken Heart: Short Stories.* Minneapolis: Coffeehouse, 1995.

(continues)

LINKS ■ ■ ■ *(continued)*

■ **ELSEWHERE IN PRINT**

Carver, Raymond. *Cathedral*. New York: Vintage, 1983.
Dybek, Stuart. *The Coast of Chicago*. New York: Knopf, 1990
Otto, Lon. *Cover Me: Short Stories*. Minneapolis: Coffeehouse, 1988.
——. *A Nest of Hooks*. Iowa City: U of Iowa P, 1978.

■ **ONLINE**

- Fishing Guides
  <http://www.1fghp.com/contents.html>

- *On the Decay of the Art of Lying* by Mark Twain
  <http://www.boondocksnet.com/twaintexts/art_of_lying.html>

- Rhinelander, Wisconsin
  <http://www.rhinelanderchamber.com>

DAYSTAR

Rita Dove

Rita Dove is a Pulitzer Prize–winning poet who became the first African-American woman to be named Poet Laureate of the United States. She is the author of many volumes of poetry—including Museum and Mother Love. In "Daystar," one of the poems in Thomas and Beulah (1986), she pictures a busy mother who finds a few moments of peace by sitting outside while her children are napping. As you read, be alert for what the poem reveals about this woman and her relationship with her husband.

A graduate of Miami University in Ohio, Dove earned her M.F.A. at the University of Iowa. She now holds eighteen honorary doctorates and serves as Commonwealth Professor of English at the University of Virginia. She also contributes a weekly column on poetry for the Washington Post and can be heard on numerous television and radio broadcasts. In 1996 she received the Charles Frankel Prize, the federal government's highest honor for writers and scholars.

She wanted a little room for thinking:
but she saw diapers steaming on the line,
a doll slumped behind the door.

So she lugged a chair behind the garage
to sit out the children's naps.   5

Sometimes there were things to watch—
the pinched armor of a vanished cricket,
a floating maple leaf. Other days
she stared until she was assured
when she closed her eyes   10
she'd see only her own vivid blood.

She had an hour, at best, before Liza appeared
pouting from the top of the stairs.
And just *what* was mother doing
out back with the field mice? Why,   15

building a palace. Later
that night when Thomas rolled over and
lurched into her, she would open her eyes
and think of the place that was hers
for an hour—where   20

691

she was nothing,
pure nothing, in the middle of the day.

QUESTIONS FOR DISCUSSION

1. Why does the woman portrayed in this poem place her chair behind the garage? Why doesn't she stay closer to the house?
2. Among the things this woman has watched outdoors are "the pinched armor of a vanished cricket" and a "floating maple leaf." What do these details reveal about her?
3. In what sense is this woman "building a palace" when she sits outside?
4. Lines 2, 6, 9, 11, and 18 all involve vision. What is it that this woman sees?
5. Why would anyone enjoy being "pure nothing, in the middle of the day"?

SUGGESTIONS FOR WRITING

1. Write an essay in which you explain what "Daystar" reveals about the woman who is the mother of Liza and the wife of Thomas.
2. Consider how Dove breaks lines in this poem and where she leaves space between lines. Then write an essay in which you discuss what you learned from the poem's form.
3. Read other poems in *Thomas and Beulah*. Choose one that helps you to understand "Daystar"; then write an essay establishing how the two poems intersect.

LINKS ■ ■ ■

■ WITHIN THE BOOK

Peter J. Gomes, in "What *Does* the Bible Say about Women?" (pages 218–228), and Susan Glaspell, in *Trifles* (pages 732–742), convey reasons why a woman might need to take a break.

■ ELSEWHERE IN PRINT

Dove, Rita. *Darker Face of the Earth: A Play.* 3rd ed. Ashland: Story Line, 2000.
———. *Grace Notes: Poems.* New York: Norton, 1989.
———. *Mother Love: Poems.* New York: Norton, 1995.
———. *Museum: Poems.* Pittsburgh: Carnegie-Mellon UP, 1983.
———. *Thomas and Beulah: Poems.* Pittsburgh: Carnegie-Mellon UP, 1986.

■ **ONLINE**

- An Explication of Rita Dove's *Daystar*
  <http://members.aol.com/wwyldleap/daystar.html>
- Rita Dove Home Page
  <http://www.people.virginia.edu/~rfd4b/>
- Rita Dove Information Site
  <http://voices.cla.umn.edu/authors/RitaDove.html>
- U.S. Poet Laureates
  <http://usgovinfo.about.com/library/weekly/bllaureate.htm>

THE DRIVING RANGE

Leslie Adrienne Miller

Leslie Miller earned her M.F.A. in creative writing at the University of Iowa and her Ph.D. at the University of Houston, where she studied with Edward Hirsch (an example of whose work can be found on pages 719–720). In a review of Miller's most recent volume of poetry, Yesterday Had a Man in It, *Hirsch describes Miller as "a poet of rich abandon, of sensuous longing and headlong desire for the Other turned back against the self, with regret, with fury. I am moved by these poems of independence infused with a dark self-knowledge, with a wry wisdom and tough vulnerability, with a hopefulness she cannot forget, will not forgo."*

Be alert for these qualities as you read "The Driving Range," which comes from an earlier volume by Miller: Ungodliness (1994). *This poem is set on a late summer night on a stretch of suburban highway lined with shopping centers. Searching for "things [. . .] you can't get anywhere else," the woman who speaks this poem encounters a vision that reminds her of her past and the distance she has traveled from it. As you read, note what the speaker finds attractive about this vision and why she ultimately rejects it.*

Even though I have something against them
I must admit they are a beautiful
spectacle, spotlit men as far as the eye
can go along this darkening reach of road.
Miniature with distance, their faces blur   5
and their tailored trousers turn in a clean
line with the body's arc, extending
and returning to itself without appearing
to have moved at all. I've come alone
out to the gleaming stretches of suburban   10
shopping centers, a thrill in the late
summer night, in the stoplights drifting
farther and farther apart, the rose glow
of the city blooming in my rearview mirror.
There are things out here you can't get   15
anywhere else: saris, leather, gold, tents,
bulk boxes of trinkets, and visions like this
embroidered with light, but it's a long way
from where I live, and there are stories
about how the clean, spacious road lures you   20
into rolling down your window, and men
who know this and run across dark intersections
to hold a gun on you. But I roll down

my window anyway to cut the blind glare
of the stadium lights along the driving range.   25
Benign air whispers in, and the row of men
in their cage of light are as curiously
lovely as glassed insects, intricate,
designed for flight; their silver clubs
describe glinting circles around well-made   30
shoulders as they swoop toward the tiny balls.
I was expected to marry a man like that,
but something went wrong, and I have never
been near enough to one, though I might
have brushed their custom-shirted arms   35
in theaters or waiting rooms, might have
taken up their papers left on airport chairs
laced with the scent of something well-preserved.
I look at them now from a distance, dark
between us, eight lanes of highway,   40
and there is only a moment to consider
the vision, to wonder why I never came
any closer: a lawyer, a doctor,
even an insurance agent, any man
given a set of silver clubs and lessons   45
from the father in this necessary art.
Even if I chose to now, I couldn't
make it back to the country club's chintz
powder room where my mother urged me
to repair my face because a suitable boy   50
had just come into the dining room
with his suitable parents.
What I have against them is not exactly
their neatly filled, black appointment books,
their clean genitals lying in nests   55
of sweetened hair, or their pressed trousers
filed in closets by season and occasion,
but the perfection of their remoteness,
their absence, and that radiance,
always promised me, that was never   60
quite close enough to touch.

QUESTIONS FOR DISCUSSION

1. In what sense are the men at the driving range "a beautiful spectacle"?
   What language in the poem conveys a sense of their beauty?
2. What does the speaker have against the men she is watching? In what sense
   are they "miniature with distance"?

3. Where is the driving range? What has drawn the speaker to its vicinity? What is she looking for?
4. What divides the speaker from the men she is watching? Would she like to overcome this division, or is she content to be alone?
5. What could the speaker mean when she describes golf as "this necessary art"? Is she being ironic? Or is golf truly a necessary art in some way?

SUGGESTIONS FOR WRITING

1. Drawing on what the poem reveals of her past and her present, write an essay describing the speaker of this poem.
2. Have you traveled a long distance from where you once lived? Do you ever feel separated from your past by "eight lanes of highway"? Write an essay exploring what you have in common with the speaker of this poem—or how you differ.
3. Write an essay focused on what "The Driving Range" says about men.

LINKS ■ ■ ■

■ WITHIN THE BOOK

In "Execution" (pages 719–720), Edward Hirsch also uses a sport to convey ideas through poetry.

■ ELSEWHERE IN PRINT

Miller, Leslie Adrienne. *Staying Up for Love.* Pittsburgh: Carnegie-Mellon UP, 1990.
———. *Ungodliness.* Pittsburgh: Carnegie-Mellon UP, 1994.
———. *Yesterday Had a Man in It.* Pittsburgh: Carnegie-Mellon UP, 1998.

■ ONLINE

- Brief Biography
  <http://www.stthomas.edu/engl/Facultybios/leslie_adrienne_miller.htm>
- Poems by Miller
  <http://www.pshares.org/Authors/authorDetails.cfm?prmAuthorID=1058>
- A Reading by Miller
  <http://www.startribune.com/bookmark/authors/miller.html>

IF THIS IS PARADISE

Dorianne Laux

A former gas station manager who also worked as a cook and a maid, Dorianne Laux began writing poetry when she was raising two children and taking classes at a junior college. She then completed her education at Mills College and, two years later, published her first book of poems, Awake *(1990). Awarded a fellowship from the National Endowment for the Arts, she continued to write. "If This Is Paradise" is from her second volume of poetry,* What We Carry *(1994). You will find that it is composed of questions. As you first read the poem, try to enjoy its language. Then, when you reread, think about how the poem suggests answers to the questions it raises.*

Laux teaches at the University of Oregon, where she also directs the school's creative writing program. Her poetry has been published in such distinguished journals as The Harvard Review, The Southern Review, The Kenyon Review, *and* Ploughshares. *It has also been broadcast by National Public Radio.*

The true mystery of the world is the visible . . .
—OSCAR WILDE

If this is paradise: trees, beehives,
boulders. And this: bald moon, shooting
stars, a little sun. If in your hands
this is paradise: sensate flesh,
hidden bone, your own eyes   5
opening, then why should we speak?
Why not lift into each day like the animals
that we are and go silently
about our true business: the hunt
for water, fat berries, the mushroom's   10
pale meat, tumble through waist–high grasses
without reason, find shade and rest there,
our limbs spread beneath the meaningless sky,
find the scent of the lover
and mate wildly. If this is paradise   15
and all we have to do is be born and live
and die, why pick up the stick at all?
Why see the wheel in the rock?
Why bring back from the burning fields
a bowl full of fire and pretend that it's magic?   20

QUESTIONS FOR DISCUSSION

1. How does the poem answer the first question it raises, "why should we speak?"

2. What images in this poem make an animal-like life seem appealing?
3. Consider the words with which each line ends. Why are these words significant?
4. Why would a stick be worth picking up? What would follow from picking up a stick? Why does the speaker say "the stick" rather than "a stick"?
5. According to your reading of this poem, what *is* "paradise"?
6. How does the quotation from Oscar Wilde contribute to the poem's meaning?

SUGGESTIONS FOR WRITING

1. Write an essay explaining why "If This Is Paradise" follows from the idea, "The true mystery of the world is the visible . . ."
2. Consider all the references to nature that you find in this poem, and write an essay explaining how they contribute to the poem's meaning.
3. Read *What We Carry* or *Smoke,* and then write an essay explicating a Laux poem of your own choice.

LINKS ■ ■ ■

■ WITHIN THE BOOK

For a work in a different genre that explores the intensity of "sensate flesh" and "eyes opening," see Annie Dillard's "Living Like Weasels" (pages 84–87).

■ ELSEWHERE IN PRINT

Addonizio, Kim, and Dorianne Laux. *The Poet's Companion: A Guide to the Pleasures of Writing Poetry.* New York: Norton, 1997.
Laux, Dorianne. *Awake: Poems.* Brockport: BOA, 1990.
---. *Smoke: Poems.* Rochester: BOA, 2000.
---. *What We Carry: Poems.* Brockport: BOA, 1994.
Olds, Sharon. *The Dead and the Living.* New York: Knopf, 1984.

■ ONLINE

- Academy of American Poets: Dorianne Laux
  <http://www.poets.org/poets/poets.cfm?prmID=803>
- Brief Biography
  <http://www.webdelsol.com/LITARTS/laux>
- Oscar Wilde
  <http://www.showgate.com/tots/wildeweb.html>
- Perspectives on Paradise
  <http://www.humanityquest.com/topic/Index.asp?theme1=paradise>

BIG BLACK CAR

Lynn Emanuel

Born in New York City, Lynn Emanuel believes that her motive for writing developed in her childhood. Her mother was a successful public relations executive who frequently read poetry aloud to her, and her father was an artist, sculptor, and actor who helped her to see the value of being unconventional. Emanuel's books include Hotel Fiesta, The Dig *(1992)—in which "Big Black Car" first appeared—and* Then, Suddenly. *In 1994,* Hotel Fiesta *and* The Dig *were reprinted in a single volume by the University of Illinois Press. Reviewing that volume for the* Boston Review *in 1996, a critic describes Emanuel as "a master of [. . .] double-edged, hard-boiled delivery [who] often assumes a customized toughness to clip a wildly emotional character." As you read "Big Black Car," think about what seems "double-edged" and "hard-boiled" about the words used by the speaker, and be alert for what might be "wildly emotional" about that person.*

A graduate of Bennington College, the City College of New York, and the University of Iowa, Emanuel teaches at the University of Pittsburgh, where she also serves as director of the writing program.

> . . . anything with wheels
> is a hearse in the making.
> —RICHARD MILLER

I thought, You'll never get me
anywhere near that motor's flattened
skull, the hoses' damp guts, the oil
pan with its tubes and fluids; I thought,
I'll never ride the black bargello°   5
of the treads or be locked up
behind its locks and keys,
or stare at the empty sockets
of those headlights, the chrome
grill so glazed with light it blurs—   10
oily, edible, about to melt.
You'll never get me into that back seat,
the ruptured upholstery hemorrhaging
batting is not for me, nor the spooky
odometer, nor the gas-gauge letters   15
spilled behind the cracked,
milky glass. The horn, like Saturn,
is suspended in its ring of steering wheel;

---

bargello: A type of needlework that produces a zig-zag pattern.

and below it the black tongue of the gas pedal,
the bulge of the brake, the stalk   *20*
of the stick shift, and I thought, You'll never . . .
But here I am, and there in the window
the tight black street comes unzipped
and opens to the snowy underthings,
the little white stitches and thorns   *25*
of a starry sky, and there, beyond
the world's open gate, eternity
hits me like a heart attack.

QUESTIONS FOR DISCUSSION

1. Consider the number of images in this poem that evoke the human body. How do these images affect you?
2. Why would the speaker be reluctant to get into the big black car described in this poem? How do you account for the speaker's decision to climb in?
3. What gender is the speaker? What elements in the poem support your answer?
4. What is the purpose of the ellipsis at the end of line 21?
5. At the end of the poem, how does the speaker feel what opens up after driving in the car?
6. What is the relationship between wheels and death, as suggested by the quotation from Richard Miller?

SUGGESTIONS FOR WRITING

1. Working closely with the language in this poem, write an essay explaining why a big black car can be both dangerous and sexy.
2. Read two other poems by Lynn Emanuel, and write an essay in which you try to explain what her work is like to someone who does not usually read poetry.
3. Chose a material object other than a car, and write about its potential as a subject for poetry.

LINKS ■ ■ ■

■ WITHIN THE BOOK

If you are drawn to the tension between fear and desire conveyed in this poem, you might also enjoy "Oranges and Sweet Sister Boy" by Judy Ruiz (pages 661–668).

■ **ELSEWHERE IN PRINT**

Emanuel, Lynn. *The Dig: Poems.* Urbana: U of Illinois P, 1992.
---. *Hotel Fiesta: Poems.* Athens: U of Georgia P, 1984.
---. *Then, Suddenly.* Pittsburgh: U of Pittsburgh P, 1999.
Levine, Philip. *Selected Poems.* New York: Atheneum, 1984.

■ **ONLINE**

- Academy of American Poets: Lynn Emanuel
  <http://www.poets.org/poets/poets.cfm?prmID=82>

- Articles on Lynn Emanuel at Ploughshares
  <http://www.pshares.org/Authors/
  authorDetails.cfm?prmAuthorID=444>

- Brief Biography
  <http://www.english.pitt.edu/homepages/lynnbio.html>

- Poetry in Review: Lynn Emanuel
  <http://www.webdelsol.com/InPosse/zawinski9.htm>

WEARING INDIAN JEWELRY

Heid Erdrich

The daughter of a German-American father and a Metis/Ojibway mother, Heid Erdrich grew up in North Dakota, where her parents taught at the Bureau of Indian Affairs Indian School. Educated at Dartmouth College and Johns Hopkins University, Erdrich has been writing and publishing poetry since she was in high school. Understanding her family background may help you to understand how and why "Wearing Indian Jewelry" explores issues of cultural identity. This poem is taken from her first book, Fishing for Myth *(1997). Upon its publication, Erdrich was praised for having a voice "as genuine as a meadowlark" and for being able to reveal the mythic significance beneath everyday experience. Commenting on the process of writing* Fishing for Myth, *Erdrich states, "When events or memories seem impossible or inexplicable, I listen for the voice that tells how they came to be—the story voice, the myth-teller. These poems are the result of that listening."*

Erdrich teaches at the University of St. Thomas in St. Paul, Minnesota. She is currently completing her second collection of poems, the working title of which is Honey.

I was wondering why that guy
wore the blanket coat, bone choker, rock
watch, woven buckle, quilled Stetson—
I was wondering why he wore
that beaded vest, like a ledger drawing   5
or a Winter Count, its skinny figure
forever sneaking after two bison
around belly to back,
around back to belly—
I was wondering why, when he said,   10
I wear these getups every day—
Every day, because these things
are sacred, these things are prayer.

Then I knew I could live this life
if I had blue horses   15
painted around and around me,
shells and beads like rain in my ear
praying *Prairie open in me*
at stoplight, hard city, last call, bank line,
coffee break, shopping cart, keycode,   20

702

Prairie open in me
Prairie open in me
every day every day every day.

QUESTIONS FOR DISCUSSION

1. In what sense does Erdrich use the word *jewelry* in this poem?
2. Which of the items mentioned in the first stanza can you picture? If there are any that you cannot picture, how can you find out what they mean?
3. Consider lines 11–13, which are italicized to indicate that they are spoken by the "guy" mentioned in line 1. Do you think someone who uses a word like "getups" can truly understand that objects of clothing are "sacred"?
4. What kind of life does the speaker have in mind when referring to "this life" in line 14?
5. How do you interpret the phrase, "Prairie open in me"? Why would the speaker need this prayer on the occasions mentioned in lines 19–20?

SUGGESTIONS FOR WRITING

1. Write an essay describing the speaker of this poem.
2. Write an essay explaining what you think it would mean to be protected by "blue horses / around and around" you.
3. Research the American prairie, and then write an essay defining what is sacred about the prairie and the difference between the prairie being open *for* you and *in* you.

LINKS ■ ■ ■

■ WITHIN THE BOOK

Writing in another genre, Rebecca Solnit offers information about Native-American values in "The New Gold Rush" (pages 115–120).

■ ELSEWHERE IN PRINT

Blaeser, Kimberly. *Absentee Indians.* East Lansing: Michigan State UP, 2002.
---. *Trailing You: Poems.* Greenfield Center: Greenfield Review, 1994.
Erdrich, Heid E. *Fishing for Myth: Poems.* Minneapolis: Rivers, 1997.
Harjo, Joy. *In Mad Love and War.* Middletown: Wesleyan UP, 1990.
---, and Gloria Bird, eds. *Reinventing the Enemy's Language: Contemporary Native American Women's Writing of North America.* New York: W. W. Norton, 1998.

(continues)

LINKS ■ ■ ■ *(continued)*

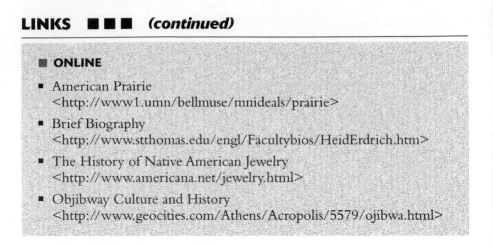

■ **ONLINE**

- American Prairie
  <http://www1.umn/bellmuse/mnideals/prairie>
- Brief Biography
  <http://www.stthomas.edu/engl/Facultybios/HeidErdrich.htm>
- The History of Native American Jewelry
  <http://www.americana.net/jewelry.html>
- Objibway Culture and History
  <http://www.geocities.com/Athens/Acropolis/5579/ojibwa.html>

DEFINING US

Rafael Campo

A Cuban-American poet who is also a physician teaching at Harvard Medical School, Rafael Campo is the author of What the Body Told *(1996), the award-winning collection from which "Defining Us" is drawn. The speaker of this poem is a gay man. As you read, try to understand what Campo is saying about what it means to be gay. But be alert also to what the poem says about love—whatever form it may take.*

In addition to publishing his own poems and essays in periodicals such as The Lancet, The New York Times Magazine, Out, *and* The Progressive, *Campo translates the Spanish poet Federico García Lorca. For writing about gay, lesbian, and bisexual issues, he has won two Lambda Awards, one for poetry and one for memoir. He has also won the National Poetry Series award and a grant from the Guggenheim Foundation. In his medical practice, he takes special interest in Latino health and HIV/AIDS medicine.*

No knowledge is more powerful
Than knowing love, than knowing how
To love despite a world so full

Of the intent to hate. I know
Of others who are like me now.   5
I've seen us on *Arsenio*°;

I've seen us march on Washington,
The love I felt so deep I feared
It was a dream. But one in ten

Of us, supposedly, got stunned   10
In utero with something queer,
A sort of poison laser gun

(A hormone gone berserk, some say,
While others tout a faulty gene).
All that I know is this: I'm gay,   15

And knowledge is less powerful
Than love, and that whatever dream
I have, in him it is fulfilled.

Arsenio: A television talk show.

QUESTIONS FOR DISCUSSION

1. According to the speaker of this poem, the world is filled with "the intent to hate." What is the difference between a world filled with hate and a world filled with the intent to hate?
2. What is the difference between experiencing love and "knowing" love? Why do you think the speaker attaches so much importance to the "knowledge" of love?
3. Consider lines 10 through 14. What is the speaker saying about sexual orientation? How important to him is the question of what makes some people straight and others gay?
4. How does the speaker of this poem feel about being gay?
5. After initially claiming that knowledge of love is more important than any other kind of knowledge, the speaker concludes by stating that "knowledge is less powerful / Than love, . . ." How do you interpret the last three lines of this poem?

SUGGESTIONS FOR WRITING

1. Consider the title "Defining Us." Write an essay in which you identify the "us" in question, and explain what this poem says about how people get defined.
2. Write an essay in which you discuss Campo's use of rhyme in "Defining Us."
3. Choose another poem by Campo that focuses on the nature of sexual orientation. Write an essay explaining what that poem says about the experience of being gay, lesbian, bisexual, or transsexual.

LINKS ■ ■ ■

■ WITHIN THE BOOK

For another work by a poet addressing how gay men are defined, see Mark Doty's "Sweet Chariot" (pages 89–94).

■ ELSEWHERE IN PRINT

Campo, Rafael. *Diva.* Durham: Duke UP, 1999.
———. *The Other Man Was Me: A Voyage to the New World.* Houston: Público, 1994.
———. *The Poetry of Healing: A Doctor's Education in Empathy, Identity, and Desire.* New York: Norton, 1997.
———. *What the Body Told.* Durham: Duke UP, 1996.
Dent, Tory. *What Silence Equals.* New York: Persea, 1993.

■ **ONLINE**

- The Academy of American Poets: Rafael Campo
  <http://www.poets.org/poets/
  poets.cfm?prmID=186&CFID=3714437&CFTOKEN=59232937>

- The Cuban Cultural Center of New York
  <http://www.sonsublime.com/cultural_links.htm>

- Interview with Rafael Campo
  <http://arts.endow.gov/artforms/Lit/Campo.html

SHERBET

Cornelius Eady

Born in Rochester, New York, and now living in New York City, Cornelius Eady teaches at the State University of New York at Stony Brook, where he also directs the Poetry Center. His work has won awards from the Academy of American of Poets, the Guggenheim Foundation, The National Endowment for the Arts, and the Rockefeller Foundation. His six volumes of poetry include The Gathering of My Name *(1991)—in which "Sherbet" is a selection.*

The setting of the poem is a hotel restaurant in Virginia, a state in which interracial marriage was illegal as recently as 1967. This background may help you to understand what happens in the poem. As you read, be alert for words that signal racial tension. Then, as you reread, consider how "Sherbet" also addresses the limits and possibilities of poetry.

The problem here is that
This isn't pretty, the
Sort of thing which

Can easily be dealt with
With words. After   5
All it's

A horror story to sit,
A black man with
A white wife in

The middle of a hot   10
Sunday afternoon at
The Jefferson Hotel in

Richmond, VA, and wait
Like a criminal for service
From a young white waitress   15

Who has decided that
This looks like something
She doesn't want

To be a part of. What poetry
Could describe the   20
perfect angle of

This woman's back as
She walks, just so,
Mapping the room off

Like the end of a   *25*
Border dispute, which
Metaphor could turn

The room more perfectly
Into a group of
Islands? And when   *30*

The manager finally
Arrives, what language
Do I use

To translate the nervous
Eye motions, the yawning   *35*
Afternoon silence, the

Prayer beneath
His simple inquiries,
The sherbet which

He then brings to the table personally,   *40*
Just to be certain
The doubt

Stays on our side
Of the fence? What do
We call the rich,   *45*

Sweet taste of
Frozen oranges in
This context? What do

We call a weight that
Doesn't fingerprint,   *50*
Won't shift

And can't explode?

QUESTIONS FOR DISCUSSION

1. What does this poem say about the nature of poetry and the expectations
   many people have for it? How is the speaker trying to move beyond those
   expectations?

2. Why is the experience described in this poem a "horror story"?
3. Why would the speaker of this poem feel that he is being treated like a "criminal"?
4. Consider Eady's use of "mapping" and "border dispute." What do these words evoke for you?
5. Why does the manager serve the couple in this poem? How does the speaker interpret this service?
6. How would you answer the last two questions raised by this poem?

SUGGESTIONS FOR WRITING

1. This poem is composed of short lines and sentences that run for several stanzas. Write an essay explaining how this structure contributes to poem.
2. The setting of this poem is specific: The Jefferson Hotel in Richmond, Virginia. Research miscegenation law in Virginia, and write an essay that would help other readers of this poem to understand the tension it conveys.
3. Write a paper explaining the significance of the hotel being named "The Jefferson Hotel."

LINKS ■ ■ ■

■ WITHIN THE BOOK

See Martin Luther King's "I Have a Dream" (pages 456–459) for a vision of a nation in which race should not keep people apart.

■ ELSEWHERE IN PRINT

Eady, Cornelius. *Autobiography of a Juke Box.* Pittsburgh: Carnegie-Mellon UP, 1997.
---. *Brutal Imagination: Poems.* New York: Putnam, 2001.
---. *The Gathering of My Name.* Pittsburgh: Carnegie-Mellon UP, 1991.
---. *Victims of the Latest Dance Craze: Poems.* Chicago: Ommation, 1985.
---. *You Don't Miss Your Water.* New York: Holt, 1995.
Hughes, Langston. *The Collected Poems of Langston Hughes.* Ed. Arnold Rampersad. New York: Knopf, 1994.

■ ONLINE

- Academy of American Poets: Cornelius Eady
  <http://www.poets.org/poets/Poets.cfm?prmID=57>
- Cornelius Eady: "Nature Poem"
  <http://www.english.upenn.edu/~afilreis/88/eady-nature.html>

■ **ONLINE** *(continued)*

- Cornelius Eady: "Thelonius Monk"
  <http://home.achilles.net/~howardm/eady.shtml>
- Miscegenation Laws
  <http://www.eugenics-watch.com/roots/chap07.html>

POWER

Audre Lorde

Audre Lorde (1934–1992) is widely considered one of the most important American poets of the late twentieth century. Much of her work, which includes fiction and memoir as well as poetry, focuses on the need to fight racial and sexual injustice. In addition to being the poet laureate of New York state, Lorde was also a social activist who lectured nationally and helped other women of color publish their work. A few years before her early death from breast cancer—a struggle about which she wrote in The Cancer Journals*—Lorde noted, "As a forty-nine-year-old Black lesbian feminist socialist mother of two, including one boy, and a member of an interracial couple, I usually find myself a part of some group defined as other, deviant, inferior, or just plain wrong." Bearing this statement in mind may help you to understand the following example of her work.*

Lorde published her first poem when she was still in high school—a poem that her teachers didn't like but that nevertheless appealed to the editors of a national magazine. She once said that she began to write poetry "when I couldn't find the poems to express the things I was feeling." As you read "Power," ask yourself what kind of feeling it expresses.

The difference between poetry and rhetoric
is being
ready to kill
yourself
instead of your children.   5

I am trapped on a desert of raw gunshot wounds
and a dead child dragging his shattered black
face off the edge of my sleep
blood from his punctured cheeks and shoulders
is the only liquid for miles and my stomach   10
churns at the imagined taste while
my mouth splits into dry lips
without loyalty or reason
thirsting for the wetness of his blood
as it sinks into the whiteness   15
of the desert where I am lost
without imagery or magic
trying to make power out of hatred and destruction
trying to heal my dying son with kisses
only the sun will bleach his bones quicker.   20

The policeman who shot down a 10-year-old in Queens
stood over the boy with his cop shoes in childish blood
and a voice said "Die you little motherfucker" and
there are tapes to prove that. At his trial
this policeman said in his own defense   25
"I didn't notice the size or nothing else
only the color," and
there are tapes to prove that, too.

Today that 37-year-old white man with 13 years of police forcing
has been set free   30
by 11 white men who said they were satisfied
justice had been done
and one black woman who said
"They convinced me" meaning
they had dragged her 4′10″ black woman's frame   35
over the hot coals of four centuries of white male approval
until she let go the first real power she ever had
and lined her own womb with cement
to make a graveyard for our children.

I have not been able to touch the destruction within me.   40
But unless I learn to use
the difference between poetry and rhetoric
my power too will run corrupt as poisonous mold
or lie limp and useless as an unconnected wire
and one day I will take my teenaged plug   45
and connect it to the nearest socket
raping an 85-year-old white woman
who is somebody's mother
and as I beat her senseless and set a torch to her bed
a greek chorus will be singing in 3/4 time   50
"Poor thing. She never hurt a soul. What beasts they are."

QUESTIONS FOR DISCUSSION

1. This poem opens with a startling statement about the difference between
   poetry and rhetoric, and it returns to this difference in lines 41 through
   44. How could poetry lead to killing oneself, and how could rhetoric lead
   to killing children?
2. Lines 6 through 20 describe a disturbing dream that becomes easier to
   understand after we read the events described in lines 21 through 39. Why
   is there a dead child in the dream? How would the poem change if the
   dream came after the two stanzas about the policeman?

3. What do the words quoted in the third stanza reveal? Why does the speaker twice mention that there are tapes to prove what the policeman said?
4. According to the speaker, why did a black woman serving on the jury agree to set the policeman free?
5. What lines in the poem relate to the title?
6. Does the speaker intend to rape an 85-year-old white woman? If not, how could this ever happen? Do you see any irony in line 51?

SUGGESTIONS FOR WRITING

1. How would you describe the tone of "Power"? Write an essay in which you define the emotion conveyed by the speaker and show the language that supports your view.
2. Define in your own words the difference between poetry and rhetoric. According to your definition, is "Power" poetry or rhetoric?
3. Write an essay focused on what you think this poem says about race or gender.

LINKS ■ ■ ■

■ WITHIN THE BOOK

The relationship between language and racism is also explored by Gloria Naylor in "Mommy, What Does 'Nigger' Mean?" (pages 74–76).

■ ELSEWHERE IN PRINT

Lorde, Audre. *The Black Unicorn.* New York: Norton, 1978.
———. *Coal.* New York: Norton, 1976.
———. *The Marvelous Arithmetics of Distance: Poems, 1987–1992.* New York: Norton, 1993.
———. *Sister Outsider: Essays and Speeches.* Trumansburg: Crossing, 1984.
———. *Zami: A New Spelling of My Name.* Watertown: Persephone, 1982.

■ ONLINE

- Brief Biography
  <http://www.lambda.net/~maximum/lorde.html>
- Police Brutality
  <http://www.wwnorton.com/catalog/spring01/policeex.htm>
- Tribute to Audre Lorde, Scholarship and, Related Resources
  <http://www.colorado.edu/journals/standards/V5N1/Lorde/lorde_toc.html>

OFF FROM SWING SHIFT

Garrett Hongo

*A common misconception about poetry, especially among people who do not read
it, is that poetry is supposed to be about a limited number of subjects—like love and
nature—that are somehow "poetic." Another common misconception is that poetry must
be beautiful and inspirational. Experienced readers recognize that poetry, like fiction and
drama, is about life in all its fullness and complexity. As you read the following poem, try
to understand what the speaker is saying about his father's life.*

*Born in Hawaii and raised in a racially diverse, working-class neighborhood in Los
Angeles, Garrett Hongo often writes about issues of class and race, including his own
experience as a Japanese American. When discussing his work with an interviewer from
Contemporary Authors, Hongo stated, "I write to be a voice that I can listen to, one
that makes sense and raises my own consciousness. And I write for all people who might
want the same thing, no matter what race, class, or nationality. Finally, I write for my
father in a very personal way. He was a great example to me of a man who refused to
hate, or, being different himself, to be afraid of difference, who accepted the friendship
of the strange and underprivileged people ostracized by the rest of society. I want my
poems to be equal to his heart."*

Late, just past midnight,
freeway noise from the Harbor
and San Diego° leaking in
from the vent over the stove,
and he's off from swing shift at Lear's.   5
Eight hours of twisting circuitry,
charting ohms and maximum gains
while transformers hum
and helicopters swirl
on the roofs above the small factory.   10
He hails me with a head-fake,
then the bob and weave
of a weekend middleweight
learned at the Y on Kapiolani
ten years before I was born.   15

The shoes and gold London Fogger
come off first, then the easy grin

The Harbor and San Diego: Freeways in Los Angeles.

saying he's lucky as they come.
He gets into the slippers
my brother gives him every Christmas,   20
carries his Thermos over to the sink,
and slides into the one chair at the table
that's made of wood and not yellow plastic.
He pushes aside stacks
of *Sporting News* and *Outdoor Life,*   25
big round tins of Holland butter cookies,
and clears a space for his elbows, his pens,
and the *Racing Form's* Late Evening Final.

His left hand reaches out,
flicks on the Sony transistor   30
we bought for his birthday
when I was fifteen.
The right ferries in the earphone,
a small, flesh-colored star,
like a tiny miracle of hearing,   35
and fits it into place.
I see him plot black constellations
of figures and calculations
on the magazine's margins,
alternately squint and frown   40
as he fingers the knob of the tuner
searching for the one band
that will call out today's results.

There are whole cosmologies
in a single handicap,   45
a lifetime of two-dollar losing
in one pick of the Daily Double.

Maybe tonight is his night
for winning, his night
for beating the odds   50
of going deaf from a shell
at Anzio° still echoing
in the cave of his inner ear,
his night for cashing in
the blue chips of shrapnel still grinding   55
at the thickening joints of his legs.

———————

Anzio: A site where the Allies invaded Italy during World War II.

But no one calls
the horse's name, no one
says Shackles, Rebate, or Pouring Rain.
No one speaks a word.   *60*

QUESTIONS FOR DISCUSSION

1. What is a "swing shift"? In what sense is the man in the poem "off" from
   swing shift?
2. The first word in this poem is "Late." What does this suggest to you? Does
   it have a double meaning?
3. What contrast provides the focus for the opening stanza?
4. Consider lines 44 and 45. What does "handicap" mean in this context?
   How can there be "whole cosmologies / in a single handicap"? Does line
   44 relate to any other lines in the poem?
5. What is the effect of repeating "no one" in lines 57 through 60?
6. Why are the horses named "Shackles," "Rebate," and "Pouring Rain"?

SUGGESTIONS FOR WRITING

1. Describe the man who is the focus of this poem. What is his life like?
2. Write an essay focused on what this poem says about gambling.
3. An *image* is a detail that appeals to one of our senses; it is usually something we can visualize (such as "big round tins of Holland butter cookies"), but it can also be something we can hear, taste, or smell. Identify the
   images used in this poem, and explain what they suggest.

LINKS ■ ■ ■

■ WITHIN THE BOOK

Itabari Njeri, in "Life with Father" (pages 68–72), also writes about a
father who had hopes that remained unfulfilled.

■ ELSEWHERE IN PRINT

Hongo, Garrett, ed. *The Open Boat: Poems from Asian America.* New York:
  Anchor, 1993.
———. *The River of Heaven: Poems.* New York: Knopf, 1988.
———, ed. *Under Western Eyes: Personal Essays from Asian America.* New York:
  Anchor, 1995.
———. *Volcano: A Memoir of Hawa'i.* New York: Knopf, 1995.
Mitsui, James Masao. *From a Three-Cornered World: New and Selected
  Poems.* Seattle: U of Washington P, 1997.

(continues)

LINKS ■ ■ ■ *(continued)*

■ **ONLINE**

- Brief Biography
  <http://www.poets.org/poets/Poets.cfm?prmID=167>

- Garret Hongo: Poetry and Related Resources
  <http://www.english.uiuc.edu/maps/poets/g_l/hongo/hongo.htm>

- Garret Hongo: Related Articles in Ploughshares
  <http://www.pshares.org/Authors/
  authorDetails.cfm?prmAuthorID=711>

EXECUTION

Edward Hirsch

Edward Hirsch publishes his poetry in widely circulated magazines such as The New Yorker *and* The New Republic *as well as journals such as* American Poetry Review *and* Paris Review. *He is the author several volumes of poetry, including* For the Sleepwalkers, Wild Gratitude, *and* The Night Parade. *"Execution" was first published in the Atlantic Monthly and then included in* The Night Parade *(1989). Winner of the Rome Prize from the American Academy and Institute of Arts and Letters as well as the National Book Critics Circle Award, Hirsch has also received awards from the National Endowment for the Arts and the Guggenheim Foundation in addition to a $295,000 "Genius Grant" from the John D. and Catherine T. MacArthur Foundation. He teaches poetry at the University of Houston, where one of his students was Leslie Adrienne Miller, author of "The Driving Range" (pages 694–695).*

When discussing poetry with an interviewer for Contemporary Authors, *Hirsch declared, "I would like to speak in my poems with what the Romantic poets called `the true voice of feeling,'" adding "I believe, as Ezra Pound once said, that when it comes to poetry only emotion endures." As you read the following example of his work, consider what kind of emotion it conveys.*

The last time I saw my high school football coach
He had cancer stenciled into his face
Like pencil marks from the sun, like intricate
Drawings on the chalkboard, small *x*'s and *o*'s
That he copied down in a neat numerical hand   5
Before practice in the morning. By day's end
The board was a spiderweb of options and counters,
Blasts and sweeps, a constellation of players
Shining under his favorite word, *Execution,*
Underlined in the upper right-hand corner of things.   10
He believed in football like a new religion
And had perfect, unquestioning faith in the fundamentals
Of blocking and tackling, the idea of warfare
Without suffering or death, the concept of teammates
Moving in harmony like the planets—and yet   15
Our awkward adolescent bodies were always canceling
The flawless beauty of Saturday afternoons in September,
Falling away from the particular grace of autumn,
The clear weather, the ideal game he imagined.
And so he drove us through punishing drills   20

On weekday afternoons, and doubled our practice time,
And challenged us to hammer him with forearms,
And devised elaborate, last-second plays—a flea-
Flicker, a triple reverse—to save us from defeat.
Almost always they worked. He despised losing   25
And loved winning more than his own body, maybe even
More than himself. But the last time I saw him
He looked wobbly and stunned by illness,
And I remembered the game in my senior year
When we met a downstate team who loved hitting   30
More than we did, who battered us all afternoon
With a vengeance, who destroyed us with timing
And power, with deadly, impersonal authority,
Machine-like fury, perfect execution.

QUESTIONS FOR DISCUSSION

1. In addition to titling this poem "Execution," Hirsch italicizes this word in line 9 and then uses it for the last word in the poem. Why is this word significant?
2. How does the speaker in this poem feel about his former football coach? What do you think of the coach?
3. According to this poem, why might men or women enjoy playing football?
4. Can a game of football ever live up to "the ideal game" that can exist in the imagination?
5. Consider the "downstate team" described at the end of the poem. How does this team contribute to the poem's meaning?

SUGGESTIONS FOR WRITING

1. Write an essay explaining what Hirsch is saying about how people use football as "a new religion."
2. Write an essay explaining what the poem is saying about winning and losing.
3. Consider other sports that you enjoy. Choose one, and then write an essay describing those elements of the sport that have poetic potential.

LINKS ■ ■ ■

■ WITHIN THE BOOK

For another poem about loss, see "Visitation" (pages 728–730) by Mark Doty, one of Hirsch's colleagues at the University of Houston.

■ **ELSEWHERE IN PRINT**

Hirsch, Edward. *Earthly Measures: Poems.* New York: Knopf, 1994.
——. *For the Sleepwalkers: Poems.* New York: Knopf, 1981.
——. *How to Read a Poem and Fall in Love with Poetry.* New York: Harcourt, 1999.
——. *The Night Parade: Poems.* New York: Knopf, 1989.
——. *On Love: Poems.* New York: Knopf, 1998.

■ **ONLINE**

- Academy of American Poets: Edward Hirsch
  <http://www.poets.org/poets/poets.cfm?prmID=158>
- Edward Hirsch: "How to Read these Poems"
  <http://www.duke.edu/doubletake/issues/06/hirsch.html>
- Edward Hirsch at Previewport
  <http://www.previewport.com/Home/hirsch.html>

40 DAYS AND 40 NIGHTS

Henri Cole

Educated at the College of William and Mary, the University of Wisconsin-Milwaukee, and Columbia University, Henri Cole was executive director of the Academy of American Poets from 1982 to 1988. Currently the Fannie Hurst Professor of Poetry at Brandeis University, he is also Briggs-Copeland Lecturer in Poetry at Harvard University. The citation he received when awarded the Rome Fellowship in Literature from the American Academy of Arts and Letters reads: "In poetry nervously alive to the maladies of the contemporary, yet suffused by a rare apprehension of the delight of the senses, Henri Cole has relished the world while being unafraid to satirize it. In poems that are both decorative and plain-spoken he permits his readers to share a keen and unsentimental view of the oddities, horrors, and solaces surrounding them at the end of the twentieth century." As you read the following example of his work early in the twenty-first century, consider whether it shows evidence of the qualities for which his work has been praised.

In this poem—from The Look of Things *(1994)—Cole presents a speaker who is being tested for a disease that is never named in the poem but can be inferred. As you read, be alert for images that suggest what kind of disease is in question here and how the speaker feels.*

Opening a vein he called my radial,
the phlebotomist introduced himself as Angel.
Since the counseling it had been ten days
of deep inversion—self-recrimination weighed
against regret, those useless emotions.   5
Now there would be thirty more enduring the notion
of some self-made doom foretold in the palm.

Waiting for blood work with aristocratic calm,
big expectant mothers from Spanish Harlem
appeared cut-out, as if Matisse had conceived them.   10
Their bright smocks ruffling like plumage before the fan,
they might themselves have been angels, come by land.

Consent and disclosure signed away, liquid gold
of urine glimmering in a plastic cup, threshold
of last doubt crossed, the red fluid was drawn   15
in a steady hematic ooze from my arm.
"Now, darling, the body doesn't lie," Angel said.
DNA and enzymes and antigens in his head

true as lines in the face in the mirror
on his desk.   *20*

      I smiled, pretending to be cheered.
In the way that some become aware of God
when they cease becoming overawed
with themselves, no less than the artist concealed
behind the surface of whatever object or felt   *25*
words he builds, so I in my first week
of waiting let the self be displaced by each
day's simplest events, letting them speak
with emblematic voices that might teach me.
They did . . . until I happened on the card   *30*
from the clinic, black-framed as a graveyard.
Could the code 12/22/90 have represented
some near time, December 22, 1990, for repentance?
The second week I believed it. The fourth I
rejected it and much else loved, until the eyes   *35*
teared those last days and the lab phoned.

Back at the clinic—someone's cheap cologne,
Sunday lamb yet on the tongue, the mind cool as a pitcher
of milk, a woman's knitting needles aflutter,
Angel's hand in mind—I watched the verdict-lips move,   *40*
rubbed my arm, which, once pricked, had tingled then bruised.

QUESTIONS FOR DISCUSSION

1. How do you interpret the title of this poem? What associations does it
   bring to mind?
2. A technician named Angel draws the speaker's blood. In what sense, if any,
   is this person an angel?
3. What does the poem reveal about the speaker's education, gender, and
   social class?
4. What kind of changes does the speaker undergo during the course of this
   poem?
5. Consider the last five lines: What significance do words like *lamb, tongue,
   milk, needles, pricked,* and *bruised* have in this poem?

SUGGESTIONS FOR WRITING

1. On the basis of your interpretation of specific details in the poem, write a
   description of the speaker in "40 Days and 40 Nights."
2. Write an essay in which you discuss what this poem reveals about the
   nature of religious experience.

3. What does this poem convey about the experience of being an outpatient in a medical clinic? Write an essay focused on the setting of "40 Days and 40 Nights."

LINKS   ■ ■ ■

■ WITHIN THE BOOK

After studying this poem, try returning to it after reading or rereading Mark Doty's "Sweet Chariot" (pages 89–94).

■ ELSEWHERE IN PRINT

Cole, Henri. *The Look of Things.* New York: Knopf, 1995.
———. *The Visible Man.* New York: Knopf, 1998.
———. *The Zoo Wheel of Knowledge.* New York: Knopf, 1989.
Phillips, Carl. *Cortege.* St. Paul: Graywolf, 1995.
———. *From the Devotions: Poems.* St. Paul: Graywolf, 1998.

■ ONLINE

- Brief Biography
  <http://www.americanacademy.org/fellows/Alumni/Spring00/cole_/body_cole_.html>
- Henri Cole: "The Blue Grotto"
  <http://www.randomhouse.com/boldtype/0400/cole/poem.html>
- Henri Cole: What's American about American Poetry?
  <http://www.poetrysociety.org/cole.html>

RECLAIMING THE WALK

John F. O'Brien

Born in Vermont and now living in St. Paul, Minnesota (where he gets plenty of opportunities to shovel snow), John O'Brien writes frequently about his search for meaning through close observation of the natural world. As you read "Reclaiming the Walk," be alert for details that convey why the speaker is determined to clear his sidewalk even if that work hurts—and consider whether the poem is about something more than snow.

The following poem is from O'Brien's first collection of poetry, Marked by Water—*the high quality of which earned the poet a McKnight Fellowship for Writers in 1999. He is currently working on a second volume,* The Asking Year, *which focuses on the experience of being a father. When discussing what he enjoys about writing poetry, O'Brien emphasizes "the surprise of disappearing into something I did not expect."*

Order lost months ago,
the neat, shovel-lifting edge
a scraggly bed now, unmade

the pocked, smooth, rumpled
white sheet—stained, slick,   5
formidably ugly, full of spite.

An improper tool—
half-moon sod cutter—
descends again and again.

The force of anger   10
a sizable slab,
the force of fear
a clean break,
the force of order
a hundred fragments   15
to be swept away.

Tender hands bleed
handle grain raised,
the blade rises
a killing motion,
measured impotent thrust   20

a cold trickle of sweat
skin torn, arms numbed
the repeated motion
jarring meeting   25
of ice and blade.

Impotent, fearful,
wishing the blade
pierce deep,
the reluctant give   30
of life-filled flesh torn
by the heat of violence,
a joyous yielding
feel the dying blood run
from winter's cold shroud.   35

QUESTIONS FOR DISCUSSION

1. Why is the speaker determined to clear the walk, and why is it such a struggle?
2. What significance is there in such images as bleeding hands, torn skin, and a blade that pierces deeply?
3. Consider lines 19 and 20, in which "the blade rises / a killing motion." In your opinion, what is the speaker trying to kill?
4. In lines 21 and 27, the thrusting blade is perceived as "impotent." What does this word suggest to you, and how does it relate to other words in the poem?
5. Where does this poem leave the speaker? Is this person in better shape or worse?

SUGGESTIONS FOR WRITING

1. Write an essay in which you establish the gender of the speaker in "Reclaiming the Walk."
2. What does this poem say about "the force of order"? Write an essay focused on why the speaker is willing to work so hard at clearing a sidewalk.
3. Drawing on the poem and your own experience, write an essay in which you explain the psychological or spiritual satisfaction that comes through completing a specific domestic task.

LINKS ■ ■ ■

■ WITHIN THE BOOK

In "As Freezing Persons Recollect the Snow" (pages 105–113), Peter Stark describes another person struggling with ice and snow.

■ ELSEWHERE IN PRINT

Atwood, Margaret. *Selected Poems, 1965–1975.* Boston: Houghton, 1987.

Huddle, David. *The Nature of Yearning.* Layton: Peregrine, 1992.

Kinnell, Galway. *Mortal Acts, Mortal Words.* Boston: Houghton, 1980.

Stafford, William. *Stories That Could Be True: New and Collected Poems.* New York: Harper, 1977.

Warren, Robert Penn. *The Collected Poems of Robert Penn Warren.* Ed. John Burt. Baton Rouge: Louisiana State UP, 1998.

■ ONLINE

- Conceptual Metaphor Home Page
  <http://www.cogsci.berkeley.edu>

- McKnight Fellowships
  <http://www.loft.org/conmckm.htm>

- Snow Shoveling in St. Paul
  <http://www.stpaul.gov/depts/citynews/snowshovel.htm>

VISITATION

Mark Doty

Although the speaker of a poem is more like a character invented by the poet rather than the actual poet, this poem draws on the personal experience with grief that Mark Doty discusses in his memoir Heaven's Coast, *an excerpt from which appears in "Writing to Understand Experience." The setting is probably Provincetown, Massachusetts, where Doty lives during the summer. When he won the Witter Bynner Prize for Poetry, awarded by the American Academy of Arts and Letters, Doty was praised for "writing elegies so full of life we find our hopes restored." As you read "Visitation," from* Sweet Machine *(1998), consider how it is both a tribute to the dead and a celebration of life— or a poem in which hope is restored. You might also find it useful to know that Doty has been praised for paying close attention to nature and exploring how nature can be inspirational. With this in mind, you may discover what can be learned from the whale described in "Visitation."*

When I heard he had entered the harbor,
and circled the wharf for days,
I expected the worst: shallow water,

confusion, some accident to bring   5
the young humpback to grief.
Don't they depend on a compass

lodged in the salt-flooded folds
of the brain, some delicate
musical mechanism to navigate

their true course? How many ways,   10
in our century's late iron hours,
might we have led him to disaster?

That, in those days, was how
I'd come to see the world:
dark upon dark, any sense   15

of spirit an embattled flame
sparked against wind-driven rain
till pain snuffed it out. I thought,

This is what experience gives us,
and I moved carefully through my life   20
while I waited. . . . Enough,

it wasn't that way at all. The whale
—exuberant, proud maybe, playful,
like the early music of Beethoven—

cruised the footings for smelts   25
clustered near the pylons
in mercury flocks. He

(do I have the gender right?)
would negotiate the rusty hulls
of the Portuguese fishing boats   30

––Holy Infant, Little Marie––
with what could only be read
as pleasure, coming close

then diving, trailing on the surface
big spreading circles   35
until he'd breach, thrilling us

with the release of pressured breath,
and the bulk of his sleek young head
—a wet black leather sofa

already barnacled with ghostly lice—   40
and his elegant and unlikely mouth,
and the marvelous afterthought of the flukes,

and the way his broad flippers
resembled a pair of clownish gloves
or puppet hands, looming greenish white   45

beneath the bay's clouded sheen.
When he had consumed his pleasure
of the shimmering swarm, his pleasure, perhaps,

in his own admired performance,
he swam out the harbor mouth,   50
into the Atlantic. And though grief

has seemed to me itself a dim,
salt suspension in which I've moved,
blind thing, day by day,

through the wreckage, barely aware   55
of what I stumbled toward, even I
couldn't help but look

at the way this immense figure
graces the dark medium,
and shines so: heaviness   60

which is no burden to itself.
What did you think, that joy
was some slight thing?

QUESTIONS FOR DISCUSSION

1. Why would someone assume that a whale in a harbor must be in trouble of some kind?
2. How do you interpret the phrase "our century's late iron hours"?
3. What is the function of the ellipsis in stanza 7?
4. Why does the speaker speculate about the whale's gender?
5. How do the names of the fishing boats contribute to the poem?
6. What does this poem reveal about the speaker?
7. How does seeing a playful whale affect the speaker?

SUGGESTIONS FOR WRITING

1. Identify religious references in this poem. Then, working closely with the text, write an essay explaining the spiritual dimension of "Visitation."
2. Study the description of the whale in this poem. Then write an essay explaining why the speaker is drawn to this creature.
3. Listen to some of the early music of Beethoven, and then write an essay about how this music makes you feel and what it makes you picture as you reread "Visitation."

LINKS ■ ■ ■

■ WITHIN THE BOOK

For background on Doty's experience that could help you to understand "Visitation," see "Sweet Chariot" (pages 89–94).

▪ ELSEWHERE IN PRINT

Dobyns, Stephen. *Body Traffic: Poems.* New York: Viking, 1990.

Doty, Mark. *Atlantis: Poems.* New York: Harper, 1995.

——. *Heaven's Coast: A Memoir.* New York: Harper, 1996.

——. *My Alexandria: Poems.* Urbana: U of Illinois P, 1993.

——. *Sweet Machine: Poems.* New York: Harper, 1998.

Mitchell, Stephen, trans. and introd. *The Book of Job.* Rev. ed. San Francisco: North, 1987.

▪ ONLINE

▪ Brief Biography
  <http://www.poets.org/
  poets.cfm?prmID=92&CFID=3714437&CFTOKEN=59232937>

▪ Mark Doty: Poetry, Scholarship, and Related Resources
  <http://www.english.uiuc.edu/maps/poets/a_f/doty/doty.htm>

▪ Mark Doty: "Shelter"
  <http://www.salon.com/weekly/doty.html>

▪ Whales
  <http://www.keele.ac.uk/depts/as/Literature/MobyDick/
  amlit.whale-pages.html>

TRIFLES

Susan Glaspell

If you have ever read a story called "A Jury of Her Peers," you will recognize the plot of Trifles. *Susan Glaspell (1882–1948) based that story on the following play, which she wrote in 1916. According to Glaspell, both the play and the story were inspired by an experience she had while working for a newspaper in Des Moines, Iowa. As you read the play, try to imagine how lonely and isolated a midwestern farm could be before the introduction of electricity, radio, and television. Consider how the men in the play treat the women. Be sure to read the stage instructions, and note how the women change when the men are offstage.*

In addition to writing fourteen plays, Glaspell helped found the Provincetown Players—a Massachusetts-based group that encouraged experimental theater and facilitated the work of several important playwrights, most notably Eugene O'Neill. The winner of a Pulitzer Prize in drama, she also wrote fifty short stories and nine novels.

Scene: *The kitchen in the now abandoned farmhouse of* JOHN WRIGHT, *a gloomy kitchen, and left without having been put in order—unwashed pans under the sink, a loaf of bread outside the bread-box, a dish-towel on the table—other signs of incomplete work. At the rear the outer door opens and the* SHERIFF *comes in followed by the* COUNTY ATTORNEY *and* HALE. *The* SHERIFF *and* HALE *are men in middle life, the* COUNTY ATTORNEY *is a young man; all are much bundled up and go at once to the stove. They are followed by the two women—the* SHERIFF'S *wife first; she is a slight wiry woman, a thin nervous face.* MRS. HALE *is larger and would ordinarily be called more comfortable looking, but she is disturbed now and looks fearfully about as she enters. The women have come in slowly and stand close together near the door.*

COUNTY ATTORNEY: *(rubbing his hands)* This feels good. Come up to the fire, ladies.

MRS. PETERS: *(after taking a step forward)* I'm not—cold.

SHERIFF: *(unbuttoning his overcoat and stepping away from the stove as if to mark the beginning of official business)* Now, Mr. Hale, before we move things about, you explain to Mr. Henderson just what you saw when you came here yesterday morning.

COUNTY ATTORNEY: By the way, has anything been moved? Are things just as you left them yesterday?

SHERIFF: *(looking about)* It's just the same. When it dropped below zero last night I thought I'd better send Frank out this morning to make a fire for us—no use getting pneumonia with a big case on, but I told him not to touch anything except the stove—and you know Frank.

COUNTY ATTORNEY: Somebody should have been left here yesterday.

SHERIFF: Oh—yesterday. When I had to send Frank to Morris Center for that man who went crazy—I want you to know I had my hands full yesterday. I knew you could get back from Omaha by today and as long as I went over everything here myself—

COUNTY ATTORNEY: Well, Mr. Hale, tell just what happened when you came here yesterday morning.

HALE: Harry and I had started to town with a load of potatoes. We came along the road from my place and as I got here I said, "I'm going to see if I can't get John Wright to go in with me on a party telephone." I spoke to Wright about it once before and he put me off, saying folks talked too much anyway, and all he asked was peace and quiet—I guess you know about how much he talked himself; but I thought maybe if I went to the house and talked about it before his wife, though I said to Harry that I didn't know as what his wife wanted made much difference to John—

COUNTY ATTORNEY: Let's talk about that later, Mr. Hale. I do want to talk about that, but tell now just what happened when you got to the house.

HALE: I didn't hear or see anything; I knocked at the door, and still it was all quiet inside. I knew they must be up, it was past eight o'clock. So I knocked again, and I thought I heard somebody say, "Come in." I wasn't sure, I'm not sure yet, but I opened the door—this door *(indicating the door by which the two women are still standing)* and there in that rocker—*(pointing to it)* sat Mrs. Wright.

(They all look at the rocker.)

COUNTY ATTORNEY: What—was she doing?

HALE: She was rockin' back and forth. She had her apron in her hand and was kind of—pleating it.

COUNTY ATTORNEY: And how did she—look?

HALE: Well, she looked queer.

COUNTY ATTORNEY: How do you mean—queer?

HALE: Well, as if she didn't know what she was going to do next. And kind of done up.

COUNTY ATTORNEY: How did she seem to feel about your coming?

HALE: Why, I don't think she minded—one way or other. She didn't pay much attention. I said, "How do, Mrs. Wright it's cold, ain't it?" And she said, "Is it?"—and went on kind of pleating at her apron. Well, I was surprised; she didn't ask me to come up to the stove, or to set down, but just sat there, not even looking at me, so I said, "I want to see John." And then she—laughed. I guess you would call it a laugh. I thought of Harry and the team outside, so I said a little sharp: "Can't I see John?" "No," she says, kind o' dull like. "Ain't he home?" says I. "Yes," says she, "he's home." "Then why can't I see him?" I asked her, out of patience. "Cause he's dead," says she. "*Dead?*" says I. She just nodded her head, not getting a bit excited, but rockin' back and forth. "Why—where is he?" says I, not knowing what to say. She just pointed upstairs—like that *(himself pointing to the room above)*. I got up, with the idea of going up there. I walked from there to here—then I says, "Why, what did he die of?" "He died of a rope round his neck," says she, and just went on pleatin' at her apron. Well, I went out and called Harry. I thought I might—need help. We went upstairs and there he was lyin'—

COUNTY ATTORNEY: I think I'd rather have you go into that upstairs, where you can point it all out. Just go on now with the rest of the story.

HALE: Well, my first thought was to get that rope off. It looked . . . *(stops, his face twitches)* . . . but Harry, he went up to him, and he said, "No, he's dead all right, and we'd better not touch anything." So we went back downstairs. She was still sitting that same way. "Has anybody been notified?" I asked. "No," says she unconcerned. "Who did this, Mrs. Wright?" said Harry. He said it business-like—and she stopped pleatin' of her apron. "I don't know," she says. "You don't *know*?" says Harry. "No," says she. "Weren't you sleepin' in the bed with him?" says Harry. "Yes," says she, "but I was on the inside." "Somebody slipped a rope round his neck and strangled him and you didn't wake up?" says Harry. "I didn't wake up," she said after him. We must 'a looked as if we didn't see how that could be, for after a minute she said, "I sleep sound." Harry was going to ask her more questions but I said maybe we ought to let her tell her story first to the coroner, or the sheriff, so Harry went fast as he could to Rivers' place, where there's a telephone.

COUNTY ATTORNEY: And what did Mrs. Wright do when she knew that you had gone for the coroner?

HALE: She moved from that chair to this one over here *(pointing to a small chair in the corner)* and just sat there with her hands held together and looking down. I got a feeling that I ought to make some conversation, so I said I had come in to see if John wanted to put in a telephone, and at that she started to laugh, and then she stopped and looked at me—scared. *(the COUNTY ATTORNEY, who has had his notebook out, makes a note)* I dunno, maybe it wasn't scared. I wouldn't like to say it was. Soon Harry got back, and then Dr. Lloyd came, and you, Mr. Peters, and so I guess that's all I know that you don't.

COUNTY ATTORNEY: *(looking around)* I guess we'll go upstairs first—and then out to the barn and around there. *(to the SHERIFF)* You're convinced that there was nothing important here—nothing that would point to any motive.

SHERIFF: Nothing here but kitchen things.

(The COUNTY ATTORNEY, after again looking around the kitchen, opens the door of a cupboard closet. He gets up on a chair and looks on a shelf. Pulls his hand away, sticky.)

COUNTY ATTORNEY: Here's a nice mess.

(The women draw nearer.)

MRS. PETERS: *(to the other woman)* Oh, her fruit; it did freeze. *(to the LAWYER)* She worried about that when it turned so cold. She said the fire'd go out and her jars would break.

SHERIFF: Well, can you beat the women! Held for murder and worryin' about her preserves.

COUNTY ATTORNEY: I guess before we're through she may have something more serious than preserves to worry about.

HALE: Well, women are used to worrying over trifles.

(The two women move a little closer together.)

COUNTY ATTORNEY: *(with the gallantry of a young politician)* And yet, for all their worries, what would we do without the ladies? *(the women do not unbend. He goes to the sink, takes a dipperful of water from the pail and pouring it into a basin, washes his hands. Starts to wipe them on the roller-towel, turns it for a cleaner place)* Dirty towels! *(kicks his foot against the pans under the sink)* Not much of a housekeeper, would you say, ladies?

MRS. HALE: *(stiffly)* There's a great deal of work to be done on a farm.

COUNTY ATTORNEY: To be sure. And yet *(with a little bow to her)* I know there are some Dickson county farmhouses which do not have such roller towels.

(He gives it a pull to expose its length again.)

MRS. HALE: Those towels get dirty awful quick. Men's hands aren't always as clean as they might be.

COUNTY ATTORNEY: Ah, loyal to your sex, I see. But you and Mrs. Wright were neighbors. I suppose you were friends, too.

MRS. HALE: *(shaking her head)* I've not seen much of her of late years. I've not been in this house—it's more than a year.

COUNTY ATTORNEY: And why was that? You didn't like her?

MRS. HALE: I liked her all well enough. Farmers' wives have their hands full, Mr. Henderson. And then—

COUNTY ATTORNEY: Yes—?

MRS. HALE: *(looking about)* It never seemed a very cheerful place.

COUNTY ATTORNEY: No—it's not cheerful. I shouldn't say she had the homemaking instinct.

MRS. HALE: Well, I don't know as Wright had, either.

COUNTY ATTORNEY: You mean that they didn't get on very well?

MRS. HALE: No, I don't mean anything. But I don't think a place'd be any cheerfuller for John Wright's being in it.

COUNTY ATTORNEY: I'd like to talk more of that a little later. I want to get the lay of things upstairs now.

(He goes to the left, where three steps lead to a stair door.)

SHERIFF: I suppose anything Mrs. Peters does'll be all right. She was to take in some clothes for her, you know, and a few little things. We left in such a hurry yesterday.

COUNTY ATTORNEY: Yes, but I would like to see what you take, Mrs. Peters, and keep an eye out for anything that might be of use to us.

MRS. PETERS: Yes, Mr. Henderson.

(The women listen to the men's steps on the stairs, then look about the kitchen.)

MRS. HALE: I'd hate to have men coming into my kitchen, snooping around and criticising.

(She arranges the pans under sink which the LAWYER *had shoved out of place.)*

MRS. PETERS: Of course it's no more than their duty.

MRS. HALE: Duty's all right, but I guess that deputy sheriff that came out to make the fire might have got a little of this on. *(gives the roller towel a pull)* Wish I'd thought of that sooner. Seems mean to talk about her for not having things slicked up when she had to come away in such a hurry.

MRS. PETERS: *(who has gone to a small table in the left rear corner of the room, and lifted one end of a towel that covers a pan)* She had bread set.

(Stands still.)

MRS. HALE: *(eyes fixed on a loaf of bread beside the bread-box, which is on a low shelf at the other side of the room. Moves slowly toward it)* She was going to put this in there. *(picks up loaf, then abruptly drops it. In a manner of returning to familiar things)* It's a shame about her fruit. I wonder if it's all gone. *(gets up on the chair and looks)* I think there's some here that's all right, Mrs. Peters. Yes— here; *(holding it toward the window)* this is cherries, too. *(looking again)* I declare I believe that's the only one. *(gets down, bottle in her hand. Goes to the sink and wipes it off on the outside)* She'll feel awful bad after all her hard work in the hot weather. I remember the afternoon I put up my cherries last summer.

(She puts the bottle on the big kitchen table, center of the room. With a sigh, is about to sit down in the rocking-chair. Before she is seated realizes what chair it is; with a slow look at it, steps back. The chair which she has touched rocks back and forth.)

MRS. PETERS: Well, I must get those things from the front room closet. *(she goes to the door at the right, but after looking into the other room, steps back)* You coming with me, Mrs. Hale? You could help me carry them.

(They go in the other room; reappear, MRS. PETERS *carrying a dress and skirt,* MRS. HALE *following with a pair of shoes.)*

MRS. PETERS: My, it's cold in here.

(She puts the clothes on the big table, and hurries to the stove.)

MRS. HALE: *(examining the skirt)* Wright was close. I think maybe that's why she kept so much to herself. She didn't even belong to the Ladies Aid. I suppose she felt she couldn't do her part, and then you don't enjoy things when you feel shabby. She used to wear pretty clothes and be lively, when she was Minnie Foster, one of the town girls singing in the choir. But that—oh, that was thirty years ago. This all you was to take in?

MRS. PETERS: She said she wanted an apron. Funny thing to want, for there isn't much to get you dirty in jail, goodness knows. But I suppose just to make her feel more natural. She said they was in the top drawer in this cupboard. Yes, here. And then her little shawl that always hung behind the door. *(opens stair door and looks)* Yes, here it is.

(Quickly shuts door leading upstairs.)

MRS. HALE: *(abruptly moving toward her)* Mrs. Peters?

MRS. PETERS: Yes, Mrs. Hale?

MRS. HALE: Do you think she did it?

MRS. PETERS: *(in a frightened voice)* Oh, I don't know.

MRS. HALE: Well, I don't think she did. Asking for an apron and her little shawl. Worrying about her fruit.

MRS. PETERS: *(starts to speak, glances up, where footsteps are heard in the room above. In a low voice)* Mr. Peters says it looks bad for her. Mr. Henderson is awful sarcastic in a speech and he'll make fun of her sayin' she didn't wake up.

MRS. HALE: Well, I guess John Wright didn't wake when they was slipping that rope under his neck.

MRS. PETERS: No, it's strange. It must have been done awful crafty and still. They say it was such a—funny way to kill a man, rigging it all up like that.

MRS. HALE: That's just what Mr. Hale said. There was a gun in the house. He says that's what he can't understand.

MRS. PETERS: Mr. Henderson said coming out that what was needed for the case was a motive; something to show anger, or—sudden feeling.

MRS. HALE: *(who is standing by the table)* Well, I don't see any signs of anger around here. *(she puts her hand on the dish towel which lies on the table, stands looking down at the table, one half of which is clean, the other half messy)* It's wiped to here. *(makes a move as if to finish work, then turns and looks at loaf of bread outside the breadbox. Drops towel. In that voice of coming back to familiar things.)* Wonder how they are finding things upstairs. I hope she had it a little more red-up° up there. You know, it seems kind of *sneaking*. Locking her up in town and then coming out here and trying to get her own house to turn against her!

MRS. PETERS: But Mrs. Hale, the law is the law.

MRS. HALE: I s'pose 'tis. *(unbuttoning her coat)* Better loosen up your things, Mrs. Peters. You won't feel them when you go out.

(MRS. PETERS *takes off her fur tippet,° goes to hang it on hook at back of room, stands looking at the under part of the small corner table.)*

MRS. PETERS: She was piecing a quilt.

(She brings the large sewing basket and they look at the bright pieces.)

---

red-up: Readied up; orderly.
tippet: A scarf for covering the neck and sometimes the shoulders.

MRS. HALE: It's log cabin pattern. Pretty, isn't it? I wonder if she was goin' to quilt it or just knot it?

(Footsteps have been heard coming down the stairs. The SHERIFF *enters followed by* HALE *and the* COUNTY ATTORNEY.)

SHERIFF: They wonder if she was going to quilt it or just knot it!

(The men laugh, the women look abashed.)

COUNTY ATTORNEY: (rubbing his hands over the stove) Frank's fire didn't do much up there, did it? Well, let's go out to the barn and get that cleared up.

(The men go outside.)

MRS. HALE: (resentfully) I don't know as there's anything so strange, our takin' up our time with little things while we're waiting for them to get the evidence. *(She sits down at the big table smoothing out a block with decision)* I don't see as it's anything to laugh about.
MRS. PETERS: (apologetically) Of course they've got awful important things on their minds.

(Pulls up a chair and joins MRS. HALE *at the table.)*

MRS. HALE: (examining another block) Mrs. Peters, look at this one. Here, this is the one she was working on, and look at the sewing! All the rest of it has been so nice and even. And look at this! It's all over the place! Why, it looks as if she didn't know what she was about!

(After she has said this they look at each other, then start to glance back at the door. After an instant MRS. HALE *has pulled at a knot and ripped the sewing.)*

MRS. PETERS: Oh, what are you doing, Mrs. Hale?
MRS. HALE: (mildly) Just pulling out a stitch or two that's not sewed very good. *(threading a needle)* Bad sewing always made me fidgety.
MRS. PETERS: (nervously) I don't think we ought to touch things.
MRS. HALE: I'll just finish up this end. *(suddenly stopping and leaning forward)* Mrs. Peters?
MRS. PETERS: Yes, Mrs. Hale?
MRS. HALE: What do you suppose she was so nervous about?
MRS. PETERS: Oh—I don't know. I don't know as she was nervous. I sometimes sew awful queer when I'm just tired. *(*MRS. HALE *starts to say something, looks at* MRS. PETERS, *then goes on sewing)* Well I must get these things wrapped up. They may be through sooner than we think. *(putting apron and other things together)* I wonder where I can find a piece of paper, and string.
MRS. HALE: In that cupboard, maybe.
MRS. PETERS: (looking in cupboard) Why, here's a bird-cage. *(holds it up)* Did she have a bird, Mrs. Hale?
MRS. HALE: Why, I don't know whether she did or not—I've not been here for so long. There was a man around last year selling canaries cheap, but I

don't know as she took one; maybe she did. She used to sing real pretty herself.

MRS. PETERS: *(glancing around)* Seems funny to think of a bird here. But she must have had one, or why would she have a cage? I wonder what happened to it.

MRS. HALE: I s'pose maybe the cat got it.

MRS. PETERS: No, she didn't have a cat. She's got that feeling some people have about cats—being afraid of them. My cat got in her room and she was real upset and asked me to take it out.

MRS. HALE: My sister Bessie was like that. Queer, ain't it?

MRS. PETERS: *(examining the cage)* Why, look at this door. It's broke. One hinge is pulled apart.

MRS. HALE: *(looking too)* Looks as if someone must have been rough with it.

MRS. PETERS: Why, yes.

(She brings the cage forward and puts it on the table.)

MRS. HALE: I wish if they're going to find any evidence they'd be about it. I don't like this place.

MRS. PETERS: But I'm awful glad you came with me, Mrs. Hale. It would be lonesome for me sitting here alone.

MRS. HALE: It would, wouldn't it? *(dropping her sewing)* But I tell you what I do wish, Mrs. Peters. I wish I had come over sometimes when *she* was here. I—*(looking around the room)*— wish I had.

MRS. PETERS: But of course you were awful busy, Mrs. Hale—your house and your children.

MRS. HALE: I could've come. I stayed away because it weren't cheerful—and that's why I ought to have come. I—I've never liked this place. Maybe because it's down in a hollow and you don't see the road. I dunno what it is, but it's a lonesome place and always was. I wish I had come over to see Minnie Foster sometimes. I can see now—*(shakes her head)*

MRS. PETERS: Well, you mustn't reproach yourself, Mrs. Hale. Somehow we just don't see how it is with other folks until—something comes up.

MRS. HALE: Not having children makes less work—but it makes a quiet house, and Wright out to work all day, and no company when he did come in. Did you know John Wright, Mrs. Peters?

MRS. PETERS: Not to know him; I've seen him in town. They say he was a good man.

MRS. HALE: Yes—good; he didn't drink, and kept his word as well as most, I guess, and paid his debts. But he was a hard man, Mrs. Peters. Just to pass the time of day with him—*(shivers)* Like a raw wind that gets to the bone. *(pauses, her eye falling on the cage)* I should think she would 'a wanted a bird. But what do you suppose went with it?

MRS. PETERS: I don't know, unless it got sick and died.

(She reaches over and swings the broken door, swings it again, both women watch it.)

MRS. HALE: You weren't raised round here, were you? *(MRS. PETERS shakes her head)* You didn't know—her?

MRS. PETERS: Not till they brought her yesterday.

MRS. HALE: She—come to think of it, she was kind of like a bird herself—real sweet and pretty, but kind of timid and—fluttery. How—she—did—change. *(silence; then as if struck by a happy thought and relieved to get back to everyday things)* Tell you what, Mrs. Peters, why don't you take the quilt in with you? It might take up her mind.

MRS. PETERS: Why, I think that's a real nice idea, Mrs. Hale. There couldn't possibly be any objection to it, could there? Now, just what would I take? I wonder if her patches are in here—and her things.

(They look in the sewing basket.)

MRS. HALE: Here's some red. I expect this has got sewing things in it. *(brings out a fancy box)* What a pretty box. Looks like something somebody would give you. Maybe her scissors are in here. *(Opens box. Suddenly puts her hand to her nose)* Why—*(MRS. PETERS bends nearer, then turns her face away)* There's something wrapped up in this piece of silk.

MRS. PETERS: Why, this isn't her scissors.

MRS. HALE: *(lifting the silk)* Oh, Mrs. Peters—it's—

(MRS. PETERS bends closer.)

MRS. PETERS: It's the bird.

MRS. HALE: *(jumping up)* But, Mrs. Peters—look at it! Its neck! Look at its neck! It's all—other side *to*.

MRS. PETERS: Somebody—wrung—its—neck.

(Their eyes meet. A look of growing comprehension, of horror. Steps are heard outside. MRS. HALE slips box under quilt pieces, and sinks into her chair. Enter SHERIFF and COUNTY ATTORNEY. MRS. PETERS rises.)

COUNTY ATTORNEY: *(as one turning from serious things to little pleasantries)* Well ladies, have you decided whether she was going to quilt it or knot it?

MRS. PETERS: We think she was going to—knot it.

COUNTY ATTORNEY: Well, that's interesting, I'm sure. *(seeing the bird-cage)* Has the bird flown?

MRS. HALE: *(putting more quilt pieces over the box)* We think the—cat got it.

COUNTY ATTORNEY: *(preoccupied)* Is there a cat?

(MRS. HALE glances in a quick covert way at MRS. PETERS.)

MRS. PETERS: Well, not *now*. They're superstitious, you know. They leave.

COUNTY ATTORNEY: *(to SHERIFF PETERS, continuing an interrupted conversation)* No sign at all of anyone having come from the outside. Their own rope. Now let's go up again and go over it piece by piece. *(they start upstairs)* It would have to have been someone who knew just the—

(MRS. PETERS sits down. The two women sit there not looking at one another, but as if peering into something and at the same time holding back. When they talk

now it is in the manner of feeling their way over strange ground, as if afraid of what they are saying, but as if they cannot help saying it.)

MRS. HALE: She liked the bird. She was going to bury it in that pretty box.

MRS. PETERS: *(in a whisper)* When I was a girl—my kitten—there was a boy took a hatchet, and before my eyes—and before I could get there—*(covers her face an instant)* If they hadn't held me back I would have—*(catches herself, looks upstairs where steps are heard, falters weakly)*—hurt him.

MRS. HALE: *(with a slow look around her)* I wonder how it would seem never to have had any children around. *(pause)* No, Wright wouldn't like the bird—a thing that sang. She used to sing. He killed that, too.

MRS. PETERS: *(moving uneasily)* We don't know who killed the bird.

MRS. HALE: I knew John Wright.

MRS. PETERS: It was an awful thing was done in this house that night, Mrs. Hale. Killing a man while he slept, slipping a rope around his neck that choked the life out of him.

MRS. HALE: His neck. Choked the life out of him.

(Her hand goes out and rests on the bird-cage.)

MRS. PETERS: *(with rising voice)* We don't know who killed him. We don't know.

MRS. HALE: *(her own feeling not interrupted)* If there'd been years and years of nothing, then a bird to sing to you, it would be awful—still, after the bird was still.

MRS. PETERS: *(something within her speaking)* I know what stillness is. When we homesteaded in Dakota, and my first baby died—after he was two years old, and me with no other then—

MRS. HALE: *(moving)* How soon do you suppose they'll be through, looking for the evidence?

MRS. PETERS: I know what stillness is. *(pulling herself back)*. The law has got to punish crime, Mrs. Hale.

MRS. HALE: *(not as if answering that)* I wish you'd seen Minnie Foster when she wore a white dress with blue ribbons and stood up there in the choir and sang. *(a look around the room)* Oh, I *wish* I'd come over here once in a while! That was a crime! That was a crime! Who's going to punish that?

MRS. PETERS: *(looking upstairs)* We mustn't—take on.

MRS. HALE: I might have known she needed help! I know how things can be—for women. I tell you, it's queer, Mrs. Peters. We live close together and we live far apart. We all go through the same things—it's all just a different kind of the same thing. *(brushes her eyes, noticing the bottle of fruit, reaches out for it)* If I was you, I wouldn't tell her her fruit was gone. Tell her it *ain't*. Tell her it's all right. Take this in to prove it to her. She—she may never know whether it was broke or not.

MRS. PETERS: *(takes the bottle, looks about for something to wrap it in; takes petticoat from the clothes brought from the other room, very nervously begins winding this around the bottle. In a false voice)* My, it's a good thing the men couldn't hear us. Wouldn't they just laugh! Getting all stirred up over a little thing like a—dead canary. As if that could have anything to do with—with— wouldn't they *laugh*!

(The men are heard coming down stairs.)

MRS. HALE: *(under her breath)* Maybe they would—maybe they wouldn't.

COUNTY ATTORNEY: No, Peters, it's all perfectly clear except a reason for doing it. But you know juries when it comes to women. If there was some definite thing. Something to show—something to make a story about—a thing that would connect up with this strange way of doing it—

(The women's eyes meet for an instant. Enter HALE *from outer door.)*

HALE: Well, I've got the team around. Pretty cold out there.

COUNTY ATTORNEY: I'm going to stay here a while by myself. *(to the* SHER-IFF*)* You can send Frank out for me, can't you? I want to go over everything. I'm not satisfied that we can't do better.

SHERIFF: Do you want to see what Mrs. Peters is going to take in?

(The LAWYER *goes to the table, picks up the apron, laughs.)*

COUNTY ATTORNEY: Oh, I guess they're not very dangerous things the ladies have picked out. *(Moves a few things about, disturbing the quilt pieces which cover the box. Steps back)* No, Mrs. Peters doesn't need supervising. For that matter, a sheriff's wife is married to the law. Ever think of it that way, Mrs. Peters?

MRS. PETERS: Not—just that way.

SHERIFF: *(chuckling)* Married to the law. *(moves toward the other room)* I just want you to come in here a minute, George. We ought to take a look at these windows.

COUNTY ATTORNEY: *(scoffingly)* Oh, windows!

SHERIFF: We'll be right out, Mr. Hale.

*(*HALE *goes outside. The* SHERIFF *follows the* COUNTY ATTORNEY *into the other room. Then* MRS. HALE *rises, hands tight together, looking intensely at* MRS. PETERS, *whose eyes make a slow turn, finally meeting* MRS. HALE'S. *A moment* MRS. HALE *holds her, then her own eyes point the way to where the box is concealed. Suddenly* MRS. PETERS *throws back quilt pieces and tries to put the box in the bag she is wearing. It is too big. She opens box, starts to take bird out, cannot touch it, goes to pieces, stands there helpless. Sound of a knob turning in the other room.* MRS. HALE *snatches the box and puts it in the pocket of her big coat. Enter* COUNTY ATTORNEY *and* SHERIFF.*)*

COUNTY ATTORNEY: *(facetiously)* Well, Henry, at least we found out that she was not going to quilt it. She was going to—what is it you call it, ladies?

MRS. HALE: *(her hand against her pocket)* We call it—knot it, Mr. Henderson.

(CURTAIN)

QUESTIONS FOR DISCUSSION

1. Consider the kitchen in which *Trifles* takes place. How does it function as the setting for the play?
2. What is the most important act that takes place on stage? What important acts have taken place before the play begins?
3. Describe the marriage between the Wrights. What lines lead you to this impression?
4. What does the Sheriff reveal about himself when he says, "Nothing here but kitchen things"? And "Well, can you beat the women! Held for murder and worryin' about her preserves"?
5. According to Mrs. Hale, "women are used to worrying over trifles." Does your response to this line change as the play unfolds?
6. Why do Mrs. Hale and Mrs. Peters conceal the dead canary? What motivates them to sympathize with Mrs. Wright?
7. How do you read the final line of this play? Does it have a meaning the men do not understand?

SUGGESTIONS FOR WRITING

1. Compare and contrast Mrs. Hale and Mrs. Peters.
2. What does *Trifles* say about women and the way they are treated by men? Look not only at what the men say and do in this play but also at how the women act.
3. Consider all aspects of the time and place where the action in this play occurs. Then write an essay explaining the role of time and place in *Trifles*.

LINKS ▪ ▪ ▪

▪ WITHIN THE BOOK

In "What Happened to the Anasazi?" (pages 237–243), Catherine Dold also shows how close observations of scene can solve a mystery.

▪ ELSEWHERE IN PRINT

Glaspell, Susan. *Fidelity: A Novel*. Boston: Small, 1915.
———. *Lifted Masks and Other Works*. Ed. Eric S. Rabkin. Ann Arbor: U of Michigan P, 1993.
———. *Plays by Susan Glaspell*. Ed. and introd. C. W. E. Bigsby. New York: Cambridge UP, 1987.
Halpern, Daniel, ed. *Plays in One Act*. Hopewell: Ecco, 1991.
Lane, Eric, ed. *Telling Tales: New One-Act Plays*. New York: Penguin, 1993.

(continues)

LINKS ■ ■ ■ *(continued)*

■ ONLINE

- Brief Biography
  <http://www.scribblingwomen.org/sbbio.html>

- Provincetown Playhouse
  <http://home.nyu.edu/~jqk2598/provincetown.html>

- Susan Glaspell: Research
  <http://www.csustan.edu/english/reuben/pal/chap8/glaspell.html>

- Susan Glaspell, *Trifles:* Teaching Suggestions and Related Resources
  <http://www.webenglishteacher.com/glaspell.html>

Glossary

academic discourse Written or spoken language that honors the formal conventions prevailing in the disciplines taught at a college or university

act In Kenneth Burke's **pentad,** the event; what the **agent** does; what happened; also, one of the main divisions of a drama

agency In Kenneth Burke's **pentad,** how the **act** was performed; the means by which the event happened

agent In Kenneth Burke's **pentad,** the one who performs the **act;** the actor; usually a person but occasionally an inanimate or abstract entity

alliteration The repetition of initial consonant sounds

allusion An unexplained reference to something or someone outside the work, usually a literary or historical character, place, or event

analogy An extended comparison of two similar but unrelated things that uses the familiar to explain the unfamiliar, the simple to explain the complex

analysis Division of a whole into its parts

anaphora A word or phrase repeated for rhetorical effect at the beginning of consecutive sentences or clauses

annotate: To mark a text by writing comments in its margins, in addition to noting key passages

assonance Repetition of vowel sounds, especially of initial vowels

audience The reader(s) envisioned by a writer when composing a specific text

backing Additional information that can be brought forward, if necessary, to support the evidence (or data) in an argument

brainstorming A technique for generating ideas by recording thoughts for a specific period of time

causal chain Interlinked causes and effects in which what happens causes something else to happen, which in turn becomes the cause generating another effect, and so on

cause and effect A rhetorical strategy in which a writer explains why something happened or what its results were

ceremonial speech Speech to move an audience generally sympathetic to the speaker's position, usually to mark an occasion such as a funeral or political gathering

claim Any point that a writer is trying to prove, especially a thesis or proposition

classical topics Ways of thinking about a subject to discover what to say about it, ways to explore an idea

classification Sorting things into categories on the basis of some specific similarity

cliché An expression that has become worn out through excessive use

climate The social, economic, and political factors that influence a writer's world

coherence A pattern of organization in which each sentence leads to the sentence that follows

comparison and contrast Noting similarities and/or differences between ideas or objects

concession The recognition, within an argument, that an opposing view has merit or that a proposition may be imperfect

context The circumstances and conditions in which an act of writing occurs—especially time, place, and climate

couplet A stanza containing two lines that usually rhyme

criterion A standard for judgment (plural is *criteria*)
external: a standard on which a number of people would agree
internal: a personal, nonverifiable standard of judgment

dangling modifier A word or phrase that does not logically refer to the word(s) linked to it

data Random pieces of fact, opinion, and inference from which information is constructed; in argument, the evidence used to support a claim

deduction A kind of reasoning that begins with a generalization, includes a specific related fact, and leads to a conclusion that fits both

definition A rhetorical strategy in which the essential nature or meaning of a thing is explained

description A rhetorical strategy that focuses on conveying a writer's sensory experience of a subject

discovery draft A written exploration of a subject in an effort to develop a thesis

division A rhetorical strategy that examines a subject by breaking it down into its parts

drafting Composing a preliminary version of any written text

dramatism Kenneth Burke's theory that features the dynamic interactions of the elements of a text; see also **pentad**

editing A stage in the writing process, devoted primarily to eliminating unnecessary words, improving clarity, and correcting errors

enthymeme A deductive argument in which the major premise is unstated; see also **deduction**

ethos The quality in writing that impresses the reader with the authority and integrity of the writer

example A rhetorical strategy that makes its point by using facts or anecdotes to illustrate an idea

explication An explanation of the function and meaning of everything in a particular literary work or part of a work

fact A kind of data that can be verified as true through more than one means and on numerous occasions

figurative language The use of words in an imaginative sense
imagery: words or phrases conveying sensory experiences such as sight, sound, and smell
metaphor: a comparison of two dissimilar things without using a connective such as *like* or *as*
simile: a comparison, using *like* or *as,* of two dissimilar things

foot In poetry, a single unit of meter containing a particular arrangement of accented and unaccented syllables

freewriting A way of developing ideas by writing down thoughts (usually on a particular subject) as they occur

genre A recognized form of literature—such as an essay, poem, or novel—that can be clearly distinguished from other forms

identification Kenneth Burke's term for the means by which people overcome their differences by discovering what they have in common

imagery See **figurative language**

induction Reasoning to reach a conclusion based on the significance of a series of examples or other evidence

inference A tentative conclusion based on limited knowledge and assumptions about what seems likely to be true

jargon Technical language used by experts in a specific field and usually not readily understood by others

journalists' questions Questions answered in the lead of an effective newspaper story: who, what, when, where, why, and how

logical fallacies Flaws in reasoning that can weaken an argument

logic, substantive A method of reasoning that uses **claims, data, warrants,** and **qualifiers** to come to a conclusion

logos The thought and language in an argument appealing to the rational abilities of an audience

mapping A graphical way to discover ideas for writing by distributing topics over a sheet of paper and linking them to show relationships

memoir An account of remembered events

metaphor See **figurative language**

motive A need or desire that generates writing; a purpose, an intention, a rationale for writing

narration A rhetorical strategy recounting events, usually in a chronological sequence; telling a story

opinion A judgment based on an individual's values, principles, or tastes

parallel construction A means for expressing similar ideas in similar words, phrases, clauses, or sentences

paraphrase Restating a passage in different words that convey the same meaning

pathos The writer's appeal to the reader's emotions, beliefs, attitudes, and values

pentad Kenneth Burke's analysis of the dramatic component of writing; see also **act, agency, agent, purpose, scene**

persona The social, literary, psychological, or cultural personality a writer constructs when presenting himself or herself in writing

personal response The reaction of an individual reader to a specific text

premise The underlying value or belief that one assumes as a given truth at the beginning of an argument

process The steps necessary to accomplish something, as, for instance, the *writing process;* also, a rhetorical strategy for explaining how to do something

proofreading The final stage in the writing process; checking a text to make sure it is free of errors

proposition A specific proposal that an argument is designed to support

purpose A motive, or what a writer hopes to achieve; also an element of the **pentad** (why the **agent** performed the **act**)

qualifiers Terms such as *probably* or *unless* that recognize exceptions to a claim

ratio In Kenneth Burke's **pentad,** the dynamic interaction of elements of a text—e.g., **act** and **scene, agent** and **scene**—that enriches the reader's understanding

refutation Evidence or reasons used to explain why an argument is unconvincing

review An evaluation of an unfamiliar text that offers both a sense of the text and a judgment of its quality

revision Reworking a draft of one's writing, with attention to matters of audience, purpose, completeness, coherence, and unity

rhetoric The study of principles leading toward the skillful and effective use of language; the analysis of the interaction among idea, text, and language

rhetorical situation The elements that determine how writers can compose meaningful texts for readers; **author, audience, purpose, topic, and context**

rhyme A correspondence in the final sounds of two (or more) words

Rogerian argument A kind of persuasion emphasizing reconciliation of opposing views

satire Writing that focuses on the lapses of judgment by others and seeks to correct these lapses by exposing them to public ridicule

scene An element of the **pentad;** *where* and *when* the **agent** performed the **act**

simile See **figurative language**

sonnet A poem containing fourteen lines, each of which contains five units called *feet*. Each foot consists of an unaccented syllable followed by an accented syllable; the lines are rhymed in three 4-line segments and a couplet, or two 4-line segments and a 6-line sestet. The rhyme scheme reflects the development of the thought

stanza In poetry, a number of lines that are grouped together and separated from other lines—especially when the lines in question follow a regular pattern

subject What the writing is about; the general area addressed

substantive logic See **logic, substantive**

summary A condensation of a work, presenting only the major point or points

syllogism The standard form of deductive argument in which a major premise and a minor premise combine to form a conclusion

symbol The use of one thing to represent something else

synthesis A condensation of major points from more than one text

thesis The point to be made about the **topic**, a specific idea that an essay or article is designed to support

topic The specific part of the **subject** to be developed

topoi A Greek word for the strategies useful for presenting convincing arguments; see also **classical topics**

unity A pattern of organization achieved by keeping related ideas together, especially in paragraphs, sections, or chapters

valid Follows the necessary sequence of ideas in deductive reasoning

warrant An explanation, based on evidence (*backing*), that shows why a **claim** follows from the **data**

Acknowledgments

Text Credits

JOHN R. ALDEN, "Breakfast at the FDA Café," originally in *The Wall Street Journal*, 1991. Reprinted by permission of the author.

HENRY ALFORD, "The Young Man and the Sea," *New York Magazine*, June 29, 1998. Reprinted with permission from the author.

JOHN B. ANDERSON, "Flunk the Electoral College, Pass Instant Runoffs," *The Progressive*, January, 2001. Reprinted with permission from The Progressive, 409 E. Main Street, Madison, WI 53703, www.progressive.org.

LOUIS BARBASH, "Clean Up or Pay Up" from *The Washington Monthly*, July/August 1990. Copyright © 1990 The Washington Monthly. Reprinted with permission from the publisher.

JOHN BERGER, "Images of Women in European Art" from John Berger, *Ways of Seeing*, Viking Penguin, 1972, pp. 45–64. Copyright © 1972 by John Berger. Used by permission of Viking Penguin, a division of Penguin Putnam, Inc.

SUSAN BORDO, "Beauty (Re)discovers the Male Body" from Susan Bordo, *The Male Body*, Farrar, Straus & Giroux, 1999. Copyright ©1999 by Susan Bordo. Reprinted by permission of Farrar, Straus and Giroux, LLC.

IAN BURUMA, "The Joys and Perils of Victimhood," *The New York Review of Books*, April 8, 1999, Vol. 46. Copyright © 1999 NYREV, Inc. Reprinted with permission from The New York Review of Books.

RAFAEL CAMPO, "Defining Us" from *What the Body Told*. Copyright © 1996 by Rafael Campo. Reprinted by permission of Georges Borchardt, Inc.

LARRY CARLAT, "You Are Me" originally in *Esquire*, March 1998. Reprinted by permission of the author.

IRIS CHANG, "The Nanking Safety Zone," from Iris Chang, *The Rape of Nanking: The Forgotten Holocaust of World War II,* Basic Books, 1997. Copyright © 1997 by Iris Chang. Reprinted by permission of Basic Books, a member of Perseus Books, L.L.C.

HENRI COLE, "40 Days and 40 Nights" from *The Look of Things*. Copyright © 1994 by Henri Cole. Reprinted by permission of Alfred A. Knopf, Inc.

CONSUMER REPORTS, "It's Only Water, Right?" *Consumer Reports*, August 2000. Copyright © 2000 by Consumers Union of U.S., Inc. Yonkers, NY 10703-1057, a nonprofit organization. Reprinted with permission for educational purposes only. No commercial use or photocopying permitted. To learn more about Consumers Union, log onto www.ConsumerReports.org.

ALAN M. DERSHOWITZ, "Shouting 'Fire!'" Originally in *The Atlantic Monthly*, January 1989. Reprinted by permission of the author.

SEUMAS MILLER and JOHN WECKERT, "Privacy, the Workplace and the Internet," *Journal of Business Ethics*, Vol. 28, 2000, pp. 255–265. With kind permission from Kluwer Academic Publishers.

TOSHIO MORI, "Abalone, Abalone, Abalone," from *The Chauvinist and Other Stories*. Reprinted by permission of the Estate of Toshio Mori and Asian American Studies Center, UCLA.

DARA MOSKOWITZ, "The Sad Comedy of Really Bad Food." Reprinted by permission of the author.

GLORIA NAYLOR, "Mommy, What Does 'Nigger' Mean? A Question of Language." Originally appeared in *The New York Times Magazine,* 1986. Copyright © 1986 Gloria Naylor. Reprinted by permission of Sterling Lord Literistic, Inc.

ITABARI NJERI, "Life with Father." Originally appeared in *Harper's Magazine,* January 1990. Copyright © 1990 by Itabari Njeri. Reprinted by permission of Miriam Altschuler on behalf of the author.

JOHN F. O'BRIEN, "Reclaiming the Walk." Reprinted by permission of the author.

GEORGE ORWELL, "A Hanging" from *Shooting An Elephant and Other Essays* by George Orwell. Copyright © 1950 by Sonia Brownell Orwell and renewed 1978 by Sonia Pitt-Rivers. Reprinted by permission of Harcourt, Inc.; "Marrakech," from *Such, Such Were the Joys.* Copyright © 1953 by the Estate of Sonia Brownell Orwell and renewed 1981 by Mrs. George K. Perutz, Mrs. Miriam Gross, and Dr. Michael Dickson, Executors of the Estate of Sonia Brownell Orwell. Reprinted by permission of Harcourt, Inc.

LON OTTO, "Winners," from *Cover Me* by Lon Otto, Coffee House Press, 1988. Copyright © 1988 by Lon Otto. Reprinted by permission of the publisher.

DAVID OWEN, "How I'm Doing." First published in *The New Yorker,* July 3, 2000, p. 33. Copyright © 2000 David Owen. Reprinted by permission of the author.

CYNTHIA OZICK, "She: Portrait of the Essay as a Warm Body," from *Quarrel & Quandary* by Cynthia Ozick. Copyright © 2000 by Cynthia Ozick. Used by permission of Alfred A. Knopf, a division of Random House, Inc.

TIM ROGERS, "Tough Break." Originally appeared in *American Way Magazine*, March 15, 1994. Reprinted by permission of the author.

JONATHAN ROWE, "Reach Out and Annoy Someone," *The Washington Monthly*, November 2000, pp. 35–37. Copyright © 2000 by Washington Monthly Publishing, LLC, 733 15th Street, N.W., Washington, DC 20005. (202) 393-5155. Web site: www.washingtonmonthly.com. Reprinted with permission from the publisher.

JUDY RUIZ, "Oranges and Sweet Sister Boy." Originally appeared in *Iowa Woman,* Summer 1988. Reprinted by permission of the author.

SCOTT RUSSELL SANDERS, "Grub," from *Wigwag,* June 1990. Reprinted by permission.

LUC SANTE, "I Was Born," from *The Factory of Facts* by Luc Sante. Copyright © 1998 by Luc Sante. Reprinted by permission of Pantheon Books, a Division of Random House, Inc.

MARILYN SCHIEL, "Levi's." Copyright © 1991 by Marilyn Schiel. Reprinted by permission of the author.

ERIC SCHLOSSER, "Why McDonald's Fries Taste So Good," from *Fast-Food Nation: The Dark Side of the All-American Meal*, Houghton-Mifflin, 2001. Copyright © 2001 by Eric Schlosser. Reprinted with permission from Houghton-Mifflin Company. All rights reserved. First published in *Atlantic Monthly*.

DAVID SEDARIS, "The Learning Curve," from David Sedaris, *Me Talk Pretty One Day*, Little, Brown, 2000. Copyright © 2000 by David Sedaris. By permission of Little, Brown and Company.

JOSHUA WOLF SHENK, "Why You Can Hate Drugs and Still Want to Legalize Them," from *The Washington Monthly*, October 1995. Copyright © 1995 by Washington Monthly Publishing, LLC, 733 15th Street, N.W., Washington, D. C. 20005. (202) 393-5155. Web site: www.washingtonmonthly.com.

RAYMOND SICKINGER, "Hitler and the Occult: The Magical Thinking of Adolf Hitler," *Journal of Popular Culture*, v. 34.2, Fall 2000. Reprinted with permission from Popular Press.

REBECCA SOLNIT, "The New Gold Rush," *Sierra*, July/August 2000. Reprinted with permission from Sierra Magazine; permission conveyed through Copyright Clearance Center, Inc.

PETER STARK, "As Freezing Persons Recollect the Snow: First Chill, Then Stupor, Then Letting Go," from *Outside*, January 1997. Copyright ©1997 by Peter Stark. Reprinted by permission of the author.

STUART TAYLOR, JR., "Racial Profiling: The Liberals are Right," *National Journal*, April 24, 1999. Copyright © 1999 by National Journal Group, Inc. All rights reserved. Reprinted by permission.

PATRICIA VOLK, "Technology Makes Me Mad," originally from *The New York Times*, September 28, 1997. Reprinted with permission from the author.

ALICE WALKER, "Am I Blue?" from *Living by the Word: Selected Writings 1973–1987*. Copyright © 1986 by Alice Walker. Reprinted by permission of Harcourt, Inc.

BARBIE ZELIZER, "Conveying Atrocity in Image," *Remembering to Forget* by Barbie Zelizer, University of Chicago Press, 1998. Reprinted with permission from The University of Chicago Press.

Photo Credits

Page 170 Special Collections, Yale Divinity School Library **Page 179** Special Collections, Yale Divinity School Library **Page 185** Associated Press, The Journal Star **Page 241** Courtesy of Mesa Verde National Park, CO, neg. no. CO-MV45-001 **Page 303** © Bettmann/CORBIS **Page 351** The NeXT block logo is a registered trademark of NeXT Software, Inc., registered in the U.S. and other countries and used with permission. The use of the NeXT block logo does not necessarily reflect NeXT's approval or disapproval of viewpoints represented by the author. McGraw-Hill's pub-

Index to the Readings by Rhetorical Strategy (Mode)

Comparison and Contrast

Cause and Effect

Definition

Analysis

Argument

Index of Authors, Titles, and Subjects

(handwritten note)
- mail Boxes
- Holiday Greeting
- uniforms
- Laundry Pickup
- Abe Lincoln Essay
- Crim. Assignment
- Buy Black Tub 4 clothes.
- Gather stuff to Mail home